Roget's
THESAURUS

Roget's
THESAURUS

BASED ON
*ROGET'S International Thesaurus
of English Words and Phrases*

Edited by C.O. Sylvester Mawson
Assisted by Katharine Aldrich Whiting

HarperPaperbacks
A Division of HarperCollinsPublishers

HarperPaperbacks   *A Division of* HarperCollins*Publishers*
10 East 53rd Street, New York, N.Y. 10022

First HarperPaperbacks printing: August 1991

Printed in the United States of America

HarperPaperbacks and colophon are trademarks of HarperCollins*Publishers*

10 9 8 7 6 5 4 3 2

INTRODUCTION

A *Thesaurus*, says the dictionary, is "a treasury or storehouse; hence a repository, especially of words, as a dictionary." But, in a sense, this book is the opposite of a dictionary. You turn to a dictionary when you have a word but are not sure enough what it means—how it has been used and what it may be expected to do. You turn to the *Thesaurus* when you have your meaning already but don't yet have the word. It may be on the tip of your tongue, or in the back of your mind or the hollow of your thought, but what it is you don't yet know. It is like the missing piece of a puzzle. You know well enough that the other words you try out won't do. They are not the right shape. They say too much or too little. They haven't the punch or have too much. They are too flat or too showy, too kind or too cruel. But the word which just fills the bill won't come, so you reach for the *Thesaurus*.

Like the dictionary, it is a dangerous book in all sorts of ways. Sometimes you wake up—after half an hour—and realize that the problem of the missing word is still where it was. You have just been wandering happily about in the treasure house looking its riches over, forgetting what you came in for. It has worse dangers. Sometimes the words you find start new streams of thought which wash everything out.

Then not the word only but the idea too will be missing. In this "Lost Chord" situation, the best thing to conclude is that so evanescent an idea was hardly worth keeping. Sometimes, worse still, Temptation assails you. Instead of the right word—the word your thought was yearning for as its mysterious predestined mate—some

v

brazen hussy or wastrel of a vocable, never met and never thought of before, seizes your regard.

> *O these encounterers*
> *That give a coasting welcome ere it comes*

Beware! As Confucius' pupil said, "For one word a man is often deemed to be wise and for one word he is often deemed to be foolish. We ought to be careful indeed what we say."

A big vocabulary is a grand thing when well understood and resourcefully used. But all grandeurs have their penalties. It is the business of a *Thesaurus* to take us into all verbal company—to introduce us to every sort and condition of word, with no guarantee, expressed or implied, as to what they may not do to us if we trust them without proper inquiry.

> *Who hath given man speech*
> *Or who hath set therein*
> *A thorn for peril and a snare for sin*

cries the Chorus in *Atalanta in Calydon*.

The great Railway strike in England turned upon the phrase "definitive terms." One side took it to mean "unchangeable"; the other explained too late that they only meant "full and detailed." Well does Peter Mark Roget observe, "A misapplied or misapprehended term is sufficient to give rise to fierce and interminable disputes; a misnomer has turned the tide of popular opinion; a verbal sophism has decided a party question; an artful watchword, thrown among combustible materials has kindled the flame of deadly warfare and changed the destiny of an empire."

That is the tragic side. The comic possibilities more concern us here. People who swagger about in borrowed words may, like Porthos in *The Three Musketeers*, impress the inexperienced. They bring the wrong sorts of smiles to the lips of the discerning.

To know the words without the things is perilous indeed. "How often," said the lecturer, "have I dallied by the shores of Lac Leman or strolled on the delightful slopes overlooking Lake Geneva." "Pardon me," said a member of the audience, "but are they not synonymous?" "You may think so, Sir," replied the speaker, "but for my part I consider Lac Leman by far the more synonymous of the two." Awful warnings of this sort abound. "I always tell my children to look it up in the dictionary or the encyclopedia," said the Sea Captain. "That is what they are there for. Always be exact . . . No, I don't wear my ribbons in public places. Seems to me they are a bit promiscuous."

But when is a word our own? What is a mastery of language? How in fact do we acquire a vocabulary worthy of the name?

The answer of course is: By experience with words, by living with great books and good talkers, by watching their words at work and at play—in brief, by becoming *familiar* with words. Mere acquaintanceship with them is not profitable here. An acquaintance is one whose name and face you know, without more than a rough idea of his being and business. A familiar is one about whom you know as much as possible. Words are astonishingly like people. They have characters, they almost have personalities—are honest, useful, obliging . . . or treacherous, vain, stubborn . . . They shift, as people do, their conduct with their company. They are an endless study in which we are studying nature and ourselves at that meeting point where our minds are trying to give form to or take it from the world.

Peter Mark Roget a century ago had high hopes of the help his arrangement of words might be to thought and to the construction of a common second language such as Basic English may become. There is nothing fantastic about such hopes. In drawing up his scheme of divisions his model was biological classification. He was a physician and Secretary of the Royal Society. But we need not take Roget's actual categories too seriously. To criticize them would be to bring up all the hardest problems there are. They serve their purpose—which is to remind us systematically of all that we know about words. "It is not sufficiently considered," said Dr. Johnson, "that men require more often to be reminded than to be informed." For information about words we go to the dictionary— the bigger it is the better. We go to the *Thesaurus* in the hope that something we really know already will come back to us in our need. How vast is the realm of our current oblivion. "I know," said Benjamin Paul Blood, "as having known, the secret of existence." Nothing will better make us realize how nearly true this is than an hour spent in the treasury. How incredibly much we understand if only we can mobilize our understanding. Roget's *Thesaurus* is one of the greatest of all *memoria technica.* It is an astonishing thought that we can carry it in the pocket.

I. A. RICHARDS

CONTENTS

ABBREVIATIONS USED IN THIS BOOK

abbr. abbreviated, abbreviation
adj. adjective, adjectival expression
adv. adverb, adverbial expression
Am. *or* Amer. America, American
Am. hist. American history
Am. Ind. American Indian
anat. anatomy
anon. anonymous
Ar. Arabic
arch. architecture
archæol. archæology
arith. arithmetic
astrol. astrology
astron. astronomy
Bib. Biblical
biol. biology
bot. botany
Brit. British
Can. Canada, Canadian
chem. chemistry
Chin. Chinese
class. classical
colloq. colloquial
com. commerce, commercial
conj. conjunction
Du. Dutch
Dan. Danish
dial. dialect, dialectal
dim. diminutive
E. East
eccl. ecclesiastical
Eng. English, England
erron. erroneous, -ly
esp. especially
exc. except
F. French
fem. feminine
fig. figurative, -ly
G. *or* Ger. German
Gr. Greek
Gr. Brit. Great Britain
her. heraldry
Hind. Hindustani
hist. history, historical
Icel. Icelandic
Ind. Indian
Ir. Irish, Ireland
int. interjection
It. Italian

Jap. Japanese
joc. jocular
L. Latin
l.c. lower case
masc. masculine
math. mathematics
mil. military
Moham. Mohammedan
myth. mythology
n. noun
naut. nautical
neut. neuter
Norw. Norwegian
obs. obsolete
opp. opposed
orig. original, -ly
parl. parliamentary
path. pathology
Pg. Portuguese
pharm. pharmacy
philos. philosophy
physiol. physiology
pl. plural
pol. *or* polit. political
pop. popular, -ly
prep. preposition
prov. proverb, provincial
psychol. psychology
R. C. Ch. Roman Catholic Church
relig. religion
rhet. rhetoric, rhetorical
Russ. Russian
S. Am. South American
Scand. Scandinavian
Scot. Scottish, Scotland
sing. singular
Skr. Sanskrit
Sp. Spanish
surg. surgery
Sw. Swedish
tech. technical
theat. theatrical
theol. theology
typog. typography
Univ. University
U. S. United States
v. verb
zool. zoology

HOW TO USE THE BOOK

. To find a synonym or antonym for any given WORD:

Turn to the Index* and find the particular word or any term of kindred meaning; then refer to the category indicated (the numbers printed in bold face at the top outer corner of each page). There in its proper grouping, the indexed word will be found, together with a wide selection of related terms. Synonyms and antonyms are placed in adjoining positions. For example, suppose a synonym is wanted for the word "cold" in the sense of "indifferent." Turn to the Index, where the following references will be found:

> cold, *adj.*
>   *frigid* **383**
>   *insensible* **823**
>   *indifferent* **866**

The italicized words give the general sense of the synonyms in the respective categories. The bold-faced figures denote that the indexed word is itself the heading or keyword of a distinct group. Thus, in this example, under **383** we find a list of adjectives grouped under the word "cold" in the literal sense of the term.

Turning to No. 866 (the sense required), we read through the varied list of synonyms ("indifferent, frigid, lukewarm," etc.) and select the most appropriate expression. To widen the selection, suggested references are given to allied lists; while in the adjoining category (No. 865) are grouped the corresponding antonyms "eager, keen, burning, ardent," etc.). The groups are arranged, not merely to apply synonyms for some special word, but also to suggest new lines of thought and to stimulate the imagination.

. To find suitable words to express a given IDEA:

Find in the Index some word relating to the idea, and the categories referred to will supply the need.

For example, suppose a writer wishes to convey the idea of "rest." Turning to No. 265, he will find *nouns* giving such associated senses as "quiet," "pause," "resting place," or *verbs* with the sense of "be still," "remain," "quell," or *adjectives* such as "quiescent," "still," "silent," and the like. The mere reading of the entire list will help to crystallize the idea and give it utterance.

II. To find appropriate words or new ideas on any given SUBJECT:

Turn up the subject or any branch of it. The Index itself will frequently suggest various lines of thought, while reference to the indicated groups will provide many words and phrases that should prove helpful.

Thus, suppose "poetry" is the theme, No. 597 will be found most suggestive. Or again, the subject may be "the drama" (599), "music" (415), "the vegetable kingdom" (367), "national legislatures" (696), "psychical research" (992a), or

(page 311)

xi

"mythology" (979). The writer may perhaps be hazy about the titles of th
ruling chiefs of India. Reference to 875 will prevent his applying a Hindu tit
to a Mohammedan prince. He may wish to know the term for a "plain" in di
ferent parts of the world; No. 344 will tell him exactly. The subject may be suc
an everyday one as "food" (298), "automobiles" (272), "aviation" (267 and 269a
or various kinds of "amusements" (840); whatever it is, the search will not prov
altogether unprofitable.

N.B.—To grasp the underlying principle of the classificatio
study the *Tabular Synopsis of Categories* (pp. xiv-xxviii).

The guide numbers always refer to the *section* numbers in th
text, and *not* to pages.

PLAN OF CLASSIFICATION

TABULAR SYNOPSIS OF CATEGORIES

Class I. ABSTRACT RELATIONS

I. EXISTENCE

1. Existence	2. Nonexistence
3. Substantiality	4. Unsubstantiality
5. Subjectiveness	6. Objectiveness
7. State	8. Circumstance

II. RELATION

9. Relation	10. Irrelation
11. Consanguinity	
12. Correlation	
13. Identity	14. Contrariety
	15. Difference
16. Uniformity	16a. Want of Uniformity
17. Similarity	18. Dissimilarity
19. Imitation	20. Nonimitation
	20a. Variation
21. Copy	22. Prototype
23. Agreement	24. Disagreement

III. QUANTITY

25. Quantity	26. Degree
27. Equality	28. Inequality
	29. Mean
	30. Compensation
31. Greatness	32. Smallness
33. Superiority	34. Inferiority
35. Increase	36. Decrease
37. Addition	38. Deduction
39. Adjunct	40. Remainder
	40a. Decrement
41. Mixture	42. Simpleness
43. Junction	44. Disjunction
45. Vinculum	
46. Coherence	47. Incoherence
48. Combination	49. Decomposition
50. Whole	51. Part
52. Completeness	53. Incompleteness
54. Composition	55. Exclusion (from a compound)
56. Component	57. Extraneousness

IV. ORDER

58. Order	59. Disorder
60. Arrangement	61. Derangement
62. Precedence	63. Sequence
64. Precursor	65. Sequel

Class III. MATTER

I. MATTER IN GENERAL

II. INORGANIC MATTER

(1) Solids

(2) Fluids

350. Conduit
352. Semiliquidity
354. Pulpiness

351. Air Pipe
353. Bubble. Cloud
355. Unctuousness
356. Oil
356a. Resin

III. ORGANIC MATTER

(1) VITALITY

357. Organization
359. Life

358. Inorganization
360. Death
361. Killing
362. Corpse
363. Interment

364. Animal Life
366. Animal
368. Zoology
370. Management of Animals
372. Mankind
373. Man

365. Vegetation
367. Vegetable
369. Botany
371. Management of Plants

374. Woman

(2) SENSATION

375. Physical Sensibility
377. Physical Pleasure

376. Physical Insensibility
378. Physical Pain

(1) Touch

379. Touch
380. Sensations of Touch

381. Numbness

(2) Heat

382. Heat
384. Calefaction
386. Furnace
388. Fuel
389. Thermometer

383. Cold
385. Refrigeration
387. Refrigerator

(3) Taste

390. Taste
392. Pungency
393. Condiment
394. Savoriness
396. Sweetness

391. Insipidity

395. Unsavoriness
397. Sourness

(4) Odor

398. Odor
400. Fragrance

399. Inodorousness
401. Fetor

Class V. VOLITION

I. INDIVIDUAL VOLITION

600. Will
602. Willingness
604. Resolution
604a. Perseverance
606. Obstinacy

609. Choice

611. Predetermination
613. Habit
615. Motive
617. Plea
618. Good
620. Intention
622. Pursuit

625. Business
626. Plan
627. Method
628. Mid-course
630. Requirement
631. Instrumentality
632. Means
633. Instrument
634. Substitute
635. Materials
636. Store
637. Provision
639. Sufficiency
641. Redundance
642. Importance
644. Utility
646. Expedience
648. Goodness
650. Perfection
652. Cleanness
654. Health
656. Healthiness
658. Improvement
660. Restoration
662. Remedy
664. Safety
666. Refuge
668. Warning
669. Alarm
670. Preservation

601. Necessity
603. Unwillingness
605. Irresolution

607. Apostasy
608. Caprice
609a. Absence of Choice
610. Rejection
612. Impulse
614. Desuetude
615a. Absence of Motive
616. Dissuasion
619. Evil
621. Chance
623. Avoidance
624. Relinquishment

629. Circuit

638. Waste
640. Insufficiency

643. Unimportance
645. Inutility
647. Inexpedience
649. Badness
651. Imperfection
653. Uncleanness
655. Disease
657. Unhealthiness
659. Deterioration
661. Relapse
663. Bane
665. Danger
667. Pitfall

935. Flatterer
937. Vindication
939. Probity

942. Disinterestedness
944. Virtue
946. Innocence
948. Good Man. Good Woman
950. Penitence
952. Atonement
953. Temperance

955. Asceticism
956. Fasting
958. Sobriety
960. Purity

963. Legality
965. Jurisprudence
966. Tribunal
967. Judge
968. Lawyer
969. Lawsuit
970. Acquittal
973. Reward

936. Detractor
938. Accusation
940. Improbity
941. Knave
943. Selfishness
945. Vice
947. Guilt
949. Bad Man. Bad Woman
951. Impenitence

954. Intemperance
954a. Sensualist

957. Gluttony
959. Drunkenness
961. Impurity
962. Libertine
964. Illegality

971. Condemnation
972. Punishment
974. Penalty
975. Scourge

V. RELIGIOUS AFFECTIONS

976. Deity
977. Angel
979. Mythic and Pagan Deities
          980a. Specter
981. Heaven
983. Theology
983a. Orthodoxy
985. Revelation (Biblical)

987. Piety

990. Worship

978. Satan
980. Evil Spirits

982. Hell

984. Heterodoxy
986. Sacred Writings (Non-
          Biblical)

988. Impiety
989. Irreligion
991. Idolatry
992. Sorcery
992a. Psychical Research
993. Spell
994. Sorcerer

995. Churchdom
996. Clergy
998. Rite
999. Canonicals
1000. Temple

997. Laity

ROGET'S POCKET THESAURUS
AND WORD FINDER

CLASS I

WORDS EXPRESSING ABSTRACT RELATIONS

I. EXISTENCE

1. EXISTENCE. — *N.* **existence,** being, entity, subsistence, presence, omnipresence, ubiquity.

reality, actuality, fact, matter of fact, truth, verity.

essence, inner reality, vital principle.

Science of existence: ontology.

V. **exist,** be, subsist, live, breathe; vegetate; happen, take place; occur, prevail.

consist in, lie in; be comprised in.

abide, continue, endure, last, remain.

Adj. **existent,** subsistent, extant; afloat, on foot, current, prevalent.

real, actual, positive, absolute; veritable, true; substantial, essential.

well founded, well grounded, authentic.

Adv. **actually,** in fact, in reality; indeed.

2. NONEXISTENCE. — *N.* **nonexistence,** inexistence; nonentity; nullity; nihilism; blank; absence, emptiness, void, vacuum; nothingness.

annihilation, extinction, destruction, abolition, extirpation, nirvana, obliteration.

V. **not exist,** be null and void; cease to exist; pass away, perish, be *or* become extinct; die out; disappear, vanish, fade, melt away, dissolve, be no more; die, etc., 360.

annihilate, nullify; abrogate, etc., 756; destroy, etc., 162; remove, displace, vacate; obliterate, extirpate.

Adj. **inexistent,** nonexistent; negative, blank; null, missing, absent, etc., 187.

unreal, baseless, unsubstantial, shadowy, spectral, visionary.

unborn, uncreated, unbegotten.

1

extinct, gone, lost, departed; defunct, etc. (*dead*), 360.

fabulous, ideal, etc. (*imaginary*), 515.

3. SUBSTANTIALITY.—*N.* substantiality; person, thing, object, article; something, a being, creature, body, substance, matter, etc., 316; groundwork, materiality.

Adj. substantial, essential; personal, bodily, corporeal, tangible, etc. (*material*), 316.

4. UNSUBSTANTIALITY.—*N.* unsubstantiality, nothingness, nihility; bubble, etc., 353.

nothing, naught, *nil* [L.], nullity, zero, cipher; blank, void, hollowness.

thing of naught, man of straw, lay figure; nonentity.

phantom, apparition, specter, shadow, dream, vision, will-o'-the-wisp, *ignis fatuus* [L.].

V. **vanish,** evaporate, fade, sink, fly, dissolve, melt away; die away, die out; disappear, etc., 449.

Adj. **unsubstantial;** baseless, groundless; ungrounded; without foundation.

visionary, imaginary, immaterial, spectral, etc., 980*a*; dreamy; shadowy; ethereal, airy, gaseous, imponderable, tenuous, vague, vaporous, dreamlike, illusory, unreal.

vacant, vacuous; empty, void, blank, hollow.

5. SUBJECTIVENESS.—*N.* subjectiveness, intrinsicality, inherence, immanence, indwelling; ego; essence, quintessence, elixir; gist, pith, core, kernel, marrow, backbone, heart, soul, life, substance.

principle, nature, constitution.

temper, temperament; spirit, humor, quality, disposition.

aspect, mood, feature, peculiarity, idiosyncrasy.

Adj. **intrinsic,** subjective; fundamental, implanted, inherent, essential, natural; innate, inborn, inbred, ingrained, indwelling, immanent, inwrought; radical, incarnate, hereditary, inherited, congenital, indigenous, native; in the grain, bred in the bone, instinctive; characteristic, ineradicable, fixed.

Adv. practically, virtually, substantially, in effect.

6. OBJECTIVENESS.—*N.* objectiveness, extraneousness, extrinsicality.

Adj. **extrinsic,** objective; extraneous, external, incidental, accidental, nonessential, unessential, accessory; contingent, fortuitous, casual.

implanted, ingrafted; inculcated, infused.

7. STATE.—*N.* state, condition, category; estate, lot, mood, temper.

dilemma, pass, predicament, quandary, corner, fix [*colloq.*], plight.

frame, fabric, stamp, mold; constitution.

form, shape; tone, tenor, trim, guise, fashion, mode, style, character.

8. CIRCUMSTANCE.—*N.* circumstance, situation, phase, position; footing, standing, status.

occasion, juncture, contingency.

predicament, emergency; exigency, crisis, pinch, pass, plight.

Adj. circumstantial, conditional, provisional; contingent, incidental; adventitious.

Adv. thus, in such wise; in *or* under the circumstances (*or* conditions).

accordingly, that being the case; since, seeing that.

conditionally, provided, if, in case; if so, unless, in the event of; provisionally.

II. RELATION

9. RELATION.—*N.* relation, bearing, relativity, reference, connection, concern; analogy; similarity; homogeneity, affinity, alliance, nearness, association; consanguinity, etc., 11; relationship, relevancy.

ratio, proportion; comparison.

link, tie, bond.

V. relate to, refer to; bear upon, regard, concern, touch, affect, pertain to, belong to; correlate.

associate, connect; link, bind.

Adj. relative, relating to, referable to; belonging to.

related, connected, associated, affiliated; allied, collateral, cognate, affinitive.

relevant, applicable, in the same category.

Adv. as regards, concerning, with relation to, with regard to; by the way, in the matter of.

10. [Want or absence of relation] IRRELATION.—*N.* irrelation, dissociation; inapplicability; disconnection, disjunction; inconsequence, disagreement, heterogeneity; irrelevancy.

V. have no relation to, have no bearing upon, have nothing to do with.

Adj. unrelated, irrespective, unallied, disconnected, unconnected, heterogeneous; isolated.

extraneous, strange, alien, foreign, outlandish, exotic.

irrelevant, inapplicable, not pertinent, unessential, inapposite, beside the mark.

remote, farfetched, out-of-the-way, forced, detached, apart, incidental, parenthetical, episodic.

Adv. parenthetically, by the way, by the by; incidentally, without regard to.

11. [Relations of kindred] CONSANGUINITY.—*N.* consanguinity, relationship, kindred, blood; parentage, paternity; lineage, connection, alliance; people [as, *my people*], family, ties of blood, blood relation.

kinsman, kinsfolk; kith and kin; relative, relation; connection, next of kin; near relation, distant relation.

family, fraternity; brotherhood, sisterhood.

race, stock, generation; clan, tribe; strain, breed.

V. be related to, claim kinship with.

Adj. related, akin, consanguineous, allied, affiliated; kindred.

12. [Double or reciprocal relation] CORRELATION.—*N.* correlation, interdependence, reciprocity, mutuality, correspondence, interchange, exchange, barter.

alternation, seesaw, to-and-fro.

V. reciprocate, alternate, interact; interchange, exchange; correlate.

Adj. reciprocal, mutual, correlative; correspondent, corresponding; alternate; interchangeable; equivalent, complementary.

13. IDENTITY.—*N.* identity, sameness, unity, convertibility, equality, etc., 27; homogeneity; self, oneself.

monotony, repetition, etc., 104.

facsimile, etc. *(copy)*, 21; similarity, etc., 17; exactness, fidelity, same, selfsame, counterpart.

V. coincide, coalesce.

treat as identical (*or* the same), render identical; identify.

Adj. identical, self, selfsame, ditto.

coincident, coinciding, coalescent, indistinguishable; one; equivalent, convertible, equal.

14. CONTRARIETY.—*N.* contrariety, contrast, foil, antithesis, counterpart, complement; oppositeness; antagonism, opposition, clashing, repugnance, antipathy.

inversion, subversion, reversal, the opposite, the reverse, the inverse, the converse, antipodes.

V. be contrary, contrast with, oppose, differ from.

invert, reverse, turn topsy-turvy, turn upside down, transpose.

contradict, contravene; antagonize, etc., 708.

Adj. contrary, opposite, counter, adverse, averse, converse, reverse; opposed, antithetical, contrasted, antipodean, diametrically opposite; antagonistic, conflicting, inconsistent, contradictory; hostile, inimical.

**15. DIFFERENCE.—*N*. difference, dissimilarity, variance, variation, variety; diversity, divergence, heterogeneity, contrast, antithesis; disagreement, disparity, inequality, distinction, contradiction, contrariety.

nice (*or* fine, subtle) distinction, discrimination; modification.

V. differ, vary; mismatch, contrast; diverge from, depart from, deviate from; modify, change, alter.

discriminate, distinguish, etc., 465.

Adj. different, diverse, heterogeneous; varied, variant, divergent, incongruous, modified; diversified, various.

other, another, not the same; unequal, etc., 28; unmatched, widely apart.

distinctive, characteristic, discriminative, distinguishing; diagnostic.

**16. UNIFORMITY.—*N*. uniformity; homogeneity, stability, continuity, permanence, consistency, accordance, conformity; agreement, etc., 23; consonance.

regularity, constancy, evenness, sameness, unity, even tenor, routine.

V. accord with, etc., 23; conform to; assimilate; level, smooth.

Adj. uniform, homogeneous, of a piece, consistent; even, equable, constant, level; invariable, regular, unvaried, undiversified, unvarying, singsong, dreary, monotonous.

Adv. always, ever, evermore, perpetually, forever, everlastingly, invariably.

**16a. WANT OF UNIFORMITY.—*N*. diversity, irregularity, unevenness; uncomformity, dissimilarity, dissimilitude, divergence, heterogeneity.

Adj. diversified, varied, irregular, checkered, uneven; multifarious, of various kinds.

**17. SIMILARITY.—*N*. similarity, resemblance, likeness, semblance, affinity, approximation, parallelism; agreement, etc., 23; analogy, correspondence; brotherhood, family likeness.

repetition, etc., 104; sameness, etc. (*identity*), 13; uniformity, etc., 16.

the like; match, fellow, companion, pair, mate, twin, double, counterpart, brother, sister; one's second self, *alter ego* [L.]; chip of the old block, birds of a feather.

simile, parallel, type, image, etc. (*representation*), 554.

V. resemble, look like, favor [*colloq.*], follow, echo, reproduce, bear resemblance; savor of, smack of; approximate; parallel, match, rhyme with; take after; imitate, etc., 19.

Adj. similar, resembling, like, alike; twin.

analogous, parallel, of a piece; such as.

akin to, etc. (*consanguineous*), 11; correlative, corresponding, cognate, allied to.

approximate, near, close, something like, near [as, *near* silk, *colloq.*], mock, pseudo, simulating, representing.

exact, etc. (*true*), 494; lifelike, faithful, true to life; the very image of, cast in the same mold.

Adv. as if, so to speak; as it were, as if it were; *quasi* [L.], just as.

18. DISSIMILARITY.—*N.* dissimilarity, dissimilitude; unlikeness, diversity, disparity, divergence, variation; difference, etc., 15; novelty, originality.

V. **vary,** etc. (*differ*), 15; differ from; diversify.

Adj. **dissimilar,** unlike, disparate; divergent, nonidentical, unique, new, novel, unprecedented, original; diversified, etc., 16*a*.

Adv. **otherwise,** alias.

19. IMITATION.—*N.* imitation, copying; repetition, duplication; quotation; reproduction.

mockery, aping, mimicry.

simulation, impersonation; parrotism, parrotry; representation, etc., 554; semblance, pretense; copy, etc., 21.

paraphrase; parody, etc., 21.

plagiarism; forgery, etc., 544.

imitator, echo, cuckoo, parrot, ape, monkey, mimic; copyist.

V. **imitate,** copy, mirror, reflect, reproduce, repeat; do like, echo, re-echo, catch; match, parallel; forge, counterfeit.

mimic, ape, simulate, impersonate, act, etc. (*drama*), 599; represent, etc., 554; parody, travesty, caricature, burlesque, take off, mock; borrow.

follow in the steps (*or* wake) of, take pattern by, follow suit [*colloq.*], follow the example of, walk in the shoes of, take after, model after; emulate.

Adj. **imitative,** modeled after; molded on, borrowed, counterfeit, imitation, false, pseudo, near [as, *near* silk, *colloq.*]; mock, mimic.

Adv. **literally,** verbatim, word for word, exactly, precisely.

20. NONIMITATION.—*N.* nonimitation, originality, creativeness.

Adj. **unimitated,** uncopied; unmatched, unparalleled; inimitable, etc., 33; unique, original, primordial, creative; exceptional, rare, uncommon, unexampled, out-of-the-way, unwonted.

20a. VARIATION.—*N.* variation, alteration, change, imitation; modification; discrepancy.

divergency, deviation, deflection; aberration; innovation.

V. **vary,** etc. (*change*), 140; deviate, etc., 279; diverge; alternate.

Adj. **varied,** modified; diversified, etc., 16*a*; dissimilar, etc., 18.

21. [Result of imitation] COPY.—*N.* copy, facsimile, counterpart, effigy, form, likeness, similitude, semblance, cast, tracing; imitation, etc., 19; model, representation, study; portrait, etc., 554; duplicate, transcript, transcription; reflection, shadow, echo; reprint, replica, transfer, reproduction, repetition.

servile copy, counterfeit, forgery.

parody, caricature, burlesque, travesty, paraphrase; cartoon.
Adj. **faithful,** lifelike, similar, close, exact.

22. [Thing copied] PROTOTYPE.—*N.* prototype, original, model, pattern, precedent, standard; type; archetype, exemplar, example.

copy, text, design; keynote.

die, mold; matrix, last, mint, seal, punch, stamp, intaglio, negative.

V. be an example, set an example.

23. AGREEMENT.—*N.* agreement, accord, accordance, unison, harmony, concord, union, unity, unanimity; understanding, *entente cordiale* [F.], concert [as, the *concert* of Europe].

conformity, uniformity, consistency; correspondence, parallelism, apposition.

fitness, aptness, relevancy; pertinence, aptitude, propriety, applicability, admissibility, compatibility.

adaptation, adjustment, accommodation; assimilation.

consent, etc. (*assent*), 488; concurrence, consensus; co-operation.

V. **agree,** accord, harmonize; correspond, tally, consent, etc. (*assent*), 488; suit, fit, befit; square with, dovetail, match, resemble, parallel.

adapt, accommodate, graduate; adjust, etc. (*render equal*), 27; regulate, reconcile.

Adj. **agreeing,** accordant, correspondent, congenial; coherent; harmonious, reconcilable, conformable; consistent, compatible; in accordance with, in harmony with, in keeping with.

apt, apposite, pertinent, pat; to the point; happy, felicitous, germane, applicable, relevant, admissible.

fit, adapted, appropriate, suitable; meet, etc. (*expedient*), 646.

24. DISAGREEMENT.—*N.* disagreement, discord, dissonance, disunion, discrepancy, unconformity, incongruity, dissension, conflict, opposition, antagonism, difference, misunderstanding.

disparity, disproportion; inequality, variance, divergence.

unfitness, inaptitude, impropriety, inapplicability, irrelevancy.

V. **disagree,** clash, conflict, dispute, quarrel, jar, interfere.

Adj. **disagreeing,** discordant, inharmonious; hostile, antagonistic, repugnant, clashing, jarring, factious, dissentient, incompatible, irreconcilable, inconsistent with; incongruous; repugnant to.

inapt, inept, inappropriate, improper, unsuited, unsuitable, inapplicable; unfit, unbefitting, unbecoming; ill-timed, unseasonable, ill-adapted, infelicitous, irrelevant.

uncongenial, unsympathetic, ill-assorted, mismatched.

Adv. in defiance of, in contempt of, in spite of.

III. QUANTITY

25. [Absolute quantity] QUANTITY.—*N.* quantity, magnitude; size, bulk, volume, mass, amount, measure, measurement, substance, strength.

[Science of quantity] mathematics.

[Definite quantity] armful, handful, mouthful, spoonful, stock, batch, lot, dose; quota, pittance, driblet.

Adj. quantitative, some, any, more or less.

26. [Relative quantity] DEGREE.—*N.* degree, grade, step, extent, measure, amount, ratio, standard, height, pitch; reach, mark, stage, rate, range, scope, caliber; gradation, shade; tenor, compass; sphere, station, rank, standing; interval, space [*music*]; intensity, strength.

V. graduate, calibrate, measure.

Adj. comparative, gradual, shading off.

Adv. by degrees, gradually, step by step, little by little, inch by inch, drop by drop; to some extent.

27. [Sameness of quantity or degree] EQUALITY.—*N.* equality, parity, symmetry, balance, poise; evenness, monotony, level; equivalence, equipoise, equilibrium; par, quits; distinction without a difference, identity, similarity.

tie, dead heat; drawn game, drawn battle; neck-and-neck race.

match, peer, compeer, equal, mate, fellow, brother; equivalent.

V. equal, match, keep pace with, run abreast; come up to; balance.

equalize, level, dress [*mil.*], balance, handicap, trim, adjust, poise; strike a balance; restore equilibrium.

Adj. equal, even, level, monotonous, symmetrical, co-ordinate; on a par with, on a level with, up to the mark.

equivalent, tantamount; quits; synonymous; convertible; all one, all the same; drawn [as, *a game*].

Adv. equally, to all intents and purposes.

28. [Difference of quantity or degree] INEQUALITY.—*N.* inequality, disparity, odds; difference, etc., 15; unevenness, shortcoming; superiority, etc., 33; inferiority, deficiency, inadequacy.

V. **be unequal,** have the advantage, turn the scale; overmatch, etc., 33; fall short of.

Adj. **unequal,** uneven, partial, inadequate, deficient; overbalanced, unbalanced, top-heavy, lopsided.

unequaled, unparalleled, unrivaled, unique, matchless, inimitable, peerless.

29. MEAN.—*N.* **mean,** medium, average, balance, rule, run, golden mean, middle; compromise, neutrality.

V. **average,** split the difference, strike a balance, pair off.

Adj. **mean,** intermediate; middle, etc., 68; average, normal, standard; neutral.

mediocre, middle class, bourgeois, commonplace.

Adv. **on an average,** in the long run; in round numbers.

30. COMPENSATION.—*N.* **compensation,** equation; indemnification; compromise, measure for measure, retaliation, equalization.

setoff, offset; makeweight, counterpoise, ballast; indemnity, equivalent, *quid pro quo* [L.]; amends, counterbalance, counterclaim.

pay, payment, reward, etc., 973.

V. **compensate,** indemnify; counterpoise, balance, counterbalance, offset, set off; square, make up for, equalize, etc., 27; recoup, redeem; pay, reward, etc., 973.

Adj. **compensating,** compensatory, equivalent, equal.

Adv. **notwithstanding,** but, however, yet, still, nevertheless, although, though; howbeit, albeit; at all events, in spite of, despite, on the other hand, at the same time.

31. GREATNESS.—*N.* **greatness,** vastness, magnitude; size, etc., 192; multitude; immensity, enormity, might, strength, intensity, fullness.

great quantity, quantity, deal [*colloq.*], volume, bulk, mass, heap; stock, store, load, shipload; abundance, sufficiency.

fame, distinction, grandeur, dignity; importance, etc., 642.

V. **be great,** soar, tower, loom, rise above, transcend; bulk, bulk large.

enlarge, etc. (*increase*), 35; wax, magnify, grow, expand, swell, dilate.

Adj. **great,** large, considerable, big, bulky, huge, etc., 192; titanic; voluminous, ample, abundant; many, etc., 102; full, intense; signal.

goodly, noble, precious, mighty; extraordinary; important, etc., 642; supreme, etc., 33; complete, etc., 52; arrant, downright; uttermost; profound, intense, consummate; rank, unmitigated, glaring, flagrant.

world-wide, widespread, far-famed, extensive.

august, grand, dignified, sublime, majestic.

vast, immense, enormous, extreme; inordinate, excessive, extravagant, monstrous, crass, gross; towering, stupendous, prodigious.

unlimited, etc. (*infinite*), 105; unutterable, indescribable, ineffable, unspeakable, inexpressible, fabulous.

absolute, positive, stark, decided, unequivocal, essential, perfect.

remarkable, notable, noticeable, noteworthy, renowned.

Adv. in a great or high degree: greatly, much, indeed, very, very much, most; pretty, enough, in a great measure, passing, richly; on a large scale; by wholesale; mightily, powerfully; extremely, exceedingly, intensely, indefinitely, immeasurably, incalculably, infinitely.

in a positive degree: truly, etc. (*truth*), 494; decidedly, unequivocally, absolutely, essentially, fundamentally, radically, downright, in all conscience.

in a complete degree: entirely, completely, wholly; abundantly, amply, fully, widely.

in a supreme degree: pre-eminently, superlatively, supremely, incomparably.

in a too great degree: immoderately, monstrously, preposterously, exorbitantly, excessively, enormously, out of all proportion.

in a marked degree: particularly, remarkably, singularly, curiously, uncommonly, unusually, peculiarly, notably, signally, strikingly, pointedly, chiefly; famously, egregiously, prominently, glaringly, emphatically, incredibly.

in a violent degree: furiously, violently, severely, desperately, tremendously, extravagantly.

in a painful degree: painfully, sadly, sorely, bitterly, piteously, grievously, miserably, cruelly, woefully, lamentably, shockingly, frightfully, dreadfully, fearfully, terribly, horribly, distressingly, balefully.

32. SMALLNESS.—*N.* smallness, littleness, paucity; fewness, sparseness, scarcity, insignificance, unimportance.

small quantity, modicum, minimum; atom, particle, trifle, electron, molecule, corpuscle, point, speck, dot, mote, jot, iota; minutiæ, details; tittle, spark; grain, scruple, minim; drop, sprinkling, dab, dash, tinge, dole, mite, bit, morsel, crumb, scrap, shred, tag, splinter, rag; snip, sliver, paring, shaving, hair; thimbleful, handful, capful, mouthful; fragment, fraction.

V. be small, lie in a nutshell.

diminish, etc. (*decrease*), 36; contract, shrink, dwindle, wane.

Adj. small, little, stunted; diminutive, etc. (*small in size*), 193; minute, miniature, inconsiderable, paltry, etc. (*unimportant*), 643; scanty, scant, limited, meager, sparing; few, etc., 103; moderate, modest.

inappreciable, infinitesimal, atomic, microscopic, molecular.

mere, simple, sheer, stark, bare.

Adv. in a small degree: to a small extent, on a small scale; a little, slightly, imperceptibly; miserably, wretchedly; insufficiently, imperfectly, faintly, feebly, passably.

in a certain or limited degree: partially, in part, in a certain degree, to a certain degree *or* extent; comparatively, rather, in some degree *or* measure; somewhat; simply, only, purely, merely; at least, at most, ever so little, thus far, after a fashion.

almost, nearly, well-nigh, not quite, all but, near upon, close upon, near the mark; within an ace (*or* inch) of, on the brink of; scarcely, hardly, barely, only just, no more than.

in an uncertain degree: about, thereabouts, somewhere about, nearly.

in no degree: noway, nowise, not at all, not in the least, not a bit, not a jot, in no wise, in no respect, by no means, on no account.

33. SUPERIORITY.—*N.* superiority, majority, plurality; advantage; preponderance, prevalence.

nobility, etc. (*rank*), 875; superman, overman.

supremacy, supremeness, primacy, pre-eminence, lead; maximum, record; crest, climax, culmination, summit, peak, transcendence; lion's share, excess, surplus, overweight, redundance.

V. exceed, excel, transcend, outdo, outbalance, overbalance, outweigh, outrank, outrival, out-Herod Herod; pass, surpass, overtop, overmatch; cap, culminate, beat, cut out [*colloq.*]; beat hollow [*colloq.*], outstrip, eclipse, throw into the shade; predominate, prevail; precede, take precedence, come first, bear the palm, break the record.

Adj. superior, greater, major, higher, exceeding; distinguished, ultra.

supreme, greatest, maximum, utmost, paramount, pre-eminent, foremost, crowning, excellent, peerless, matchless; unrivaled, unparalleled, unequaled, unapproached, unsurpassed; superlative, incomparable, transcendent.

Adv. beyond, more, over; over and above; at its height.

in a superior or supreme degree: eminently, pre-eminently, surpassingly, superlatively, supremely, principally, especially, particularly, peculiarly.

34. INFERIORITY.—*N.* inferiority, shortcoming, deficiency; minimum; imperfection; meanness, poorness, baseness, shabbiness.

Personal inferiority: the people, etc., 876; subordination.

V. be inferior, fall short of, come short of, not come up to; become smaller, decrease, yield the palm, play second fiddle.

Adj. inferior, smaller; less, lesser, deficient, reduced, lower, subordinate, secondary, junior, minor, humble; second rate; unimportant, etc., 643.

Adv. less, short of, under.

35. INCREASE.—*N.* increase, augmentation, addition, enlargement, extension, expansion, growth, increment, accretion, development, accumulation, inflation, enhancement, aggravation, exaggeration.

gain, produce, product, profit, advantage, booty, plunder.

V. increase, augment, add to, enlarge, etc., 31; advance, rise, mount, ascend.

aggrandize, raise, exalt; deepen, heighten, lengthen, thicken; inflate, intensify, enhance, magnify, redouble, double; aggravate, exaggerate.

Adj. increasing, growing, crescent, multiplying, intensifying, intensive.

Adv. crescendo, increasingly.

36. DECREASE.—*N.* decrease, diminution, lessening, subtraction, reduction, abatement, declension; shrinkage, contraction, curtailment, abridgment.

subsidence, wane, ebb, decline; ebb tide, neap tide, ebbing.

V. decrease, diminish, lessen; abridge, shorten, shrink, contract; dwindle, fall away, waste, wear; wane, ebb, decline, subside, languish, decay, crumble.

discount, belittle, minimize, depreciate, extenuate, lower, weaken, attenuate; dwarf, reduce, shorten, subtract; mitigate, ease, moderate.

Adv. decrescendo, decreasingly.

37. ADDITION.—*N.* addition, annexation, accession, re-enforcement; increase, etc., 35; increment.

affix, codicil, tag, appendage, postscript, adjunct, supplement; accompaniment, insertion.

V. add, annex, affix, subjoin, tack to, append, tag, attach; interpose, introduce, insert.

compute, total, cast (*or* sum, count) up.

re-enforce, strengthen, augment.

Adj. additional, supplemental, supplementary; extra, spare, further, fresh, more, other, auxiliary, contributory, accessory.

Adv. in addition, more; and, also, likewise, too, furthermore, further; besides, to boot; over and above, moreover; as well as, together with, along with, in conjunction with.

38. DEDUCTION.—*N.* deduction, subtraction, retrenchment; abstraction, mutilation, amputation, curtailment, abbreviation.

rebate, etc. (*decrement*), 40a; minuend, subtrahend; decrease, etc., 36.

V. **deduct**, subtract, retrench; withdraw; take from, take away; detract, reduce, eliminate, diminish, curtail, shorten; deprive of, etc. (*take*), 789; weaken.

mutilate, amputate, cut off, cut away, excise.

pare, thin, prune, scrape, file.

Adv. **less**; short of; minus, without, except, excepting, with the exception of, save, exclusive of.

39. [Thing added] ADJUNCT.—*N.* **adjunct**, addition, affix, suffix, appendage, annex, augmentation, increment, re-enforcement, accessory, accompaniment, etc., 88; addendum (*pl.* addenda); complement, supplement, sequel.

rider, offshoot, episode, side issue, corollary, codicil, etc. (*addition*), 37.

V. **add**, annex, etc., 37.

Adj. **additional**, etc., 37.

40. [Thing remaining] REMAINDER.—*N.* **remainder**, residue, remains, remnant, rest, relic; leavings, odds and ends, residuum, dregs, refuse, stubble, ruins, wreck, skeleton, fossil, stump, rump.

surplus, excess; balance [*commercial slang*]; result; superfluity, redundance; survival.

V. **remain**, survive, be left; exceed.

Adj. **remaining**, left, residual, residuary; over, odd; surviving; net; superfluous, etc. (*redundant*), 641.

40a. [Thing deducted] DECREMENT.—*N.* **decrement**, discount, rebate, defect, loss, deduction; waste.

41. MIXTURE.—*N.* **mixture**, admixture, junction, etc., 43; amalgamation, combination, etc., 48; infusion, transfusion; infiltration; interlarding, interpolation, etc., 228; adulteration.

Thing mixed: tinge, tincture, touch, dash, smack, spice, seasoning, infusion.

Compounds: alloy, amalgam; brass, pewter; miscellany, medley, mess, hash, hodgepodge, patchwork, jumble; potpourri, mosaic.

half-blood, half-breed, half-caste, crossbreed; mulatto, quadroon, octoroon, Eurasian; mule, cross, hybrid, mongrel.

V. **mix**, join, etc., 43; combine, etc., 48; mingle, commingle, intermingle, interlard, interpolate, intertwine, interweave; associate with.

imbue, infuse, diffuse, suffuse, transfuse, instill, infiltrate, dash, tinge, tincture, season, blend, cross; alloy, amalgamate, compound, adulterate.

Adj. mixed, composite, half-and-half, hybrid, mongrel, heterogeneous; motley, variegated, miscellaneous, promiscuous, indiscriminate.

Adv. among, amid, with; in the midst of.

42. [Freedom from mixture] SIMPLENESS.—*N.* simpleness, purity, homogeneity.

elimination, sifting, purification, etc. (*cleanness*), 652.

V. render simple, simplify.

sift, winnow, bolt, eliminate; exclude, get rid of; clear, purify, etc. (*clean*), 652.

Adj. simple, uniform, homogeneous, single, pure, clear; elemental, elementary.

43. JUNCTION.—*N.* junction, joining, union; connection, conjunction, annexation, attachment; marriage, wedlock; confluence, communication, meeting, reunion; assemblage, etc., 72; coherence, etc., 46; combination, etc., 48.

joint, joining, juncture, pivot, hinge, articulation; seam, gore, gusset, link, bond.

contingency, emergency, predicament, crisis, concurrence.

V. join, unite, connect; associate; put together, piece together, embody.

attach, fix, fasten, bind, secure, tighten, clinch, tie, strap, sew, lace, stitch, knit, button, buckle, hitch, lash, splice, gird, tether, moor, picket, chain; fetter, hook, link, yoke, bracket; marry; bridge over, span.

pin, nail, screw, bolt, hasp, clasp, clamp, rivet; solder, cement, etc., 46.

entwine, interlace, intertwine, interweave; entangle.

Adj. joined, joint; corporate, compact.

firm, fast, close, tight, taut, secure, inseparable. indissoluble.

Adv. jointly, in conjunction with, etc. (*in addition to*), 37; fast, firmly.

44. DISJUNCTION.—*N.* disjunction, disconnection, disunion, disengagement, dissociation, discontinuity, etc., 70; isolation, insularity, insulation, separateness; dispersion.

separation, parting; detachment, segregation; divorce; cæsura, division, subdivision, break, fracture, rupture; dismemberment, dissection, disintegration, severance, disruption, cleavage.

fissure, breach, rent, rift, crack, slit, cut, incision.

V. disjoin, disconnect, disengage, disunite, dissociate, divorce, part, detach, unfasten, separate, disentangle, cut off, segregate set apart, keep apart; insulate, isolate; cut adrift, loose, set free. liberate.

divide, sunder, subdivide, sever, dissever, cut, chop, saw, snip,
nip, cleave, rive, rend, slit, rip, split, splinter, chip, crack, snap,
break, tear, burst; wrench, rupture, hack, hew, slash, slice, carve,
quarter, dissect, anatomize; partition, parcel.

disintegrate, dismember, disband; disperse, etc., 73; dislocate,
break up.

part, part company; separate, leave; alienate, estrange.

Adj. disjoined, discontinuous, disjunctive; isolated, insular;
separate, apart, asunder, loose, free, adrift.

Adv. separately, one by one, severally, apart, asunder.

45. [Connecting medium] VINCULUM.—*N.* vinculum, link;
connective, connection; junction, etc., 43; hyphen; bracket;
bridge, steppingstone; bond, cord; rope, line, cable, hawser,
painter; chain; string, etc. (*filament*), 205.

fastening, tie; ligament, ligature; strap; tackle, rigging; yoke,
band, headband, fillet, snood, brace, thong, girdle, noose, lariat,
lasso, knot, girth, cinch.

cement, glue, gum, paste, size, solder, mortar, plaster, putty.

shackle, rein, etc. (*means of restraint*), 752.

V. bridge over, span; connect, etc., 43.

46. COHERENCE.—*N.* coherence, cohesion, cohesiveness,
adherence, adhesion, adhesiveness; conglomeration, aggregation,
consolidation, soldering, connection; relativity.

tenacity, toughness; stickiness; inseparability.

conglomerate, concrete, etc., 321.

V. cohere, adhere, coagulate, stick, cling, cleave, hold, close
with, clasp, hug.

glue, agglutinate, cement, paste, gum; solder, weld; cake, consolidate, solidify, agglomerate.

Adj. adhesive, cohesive, adhering, tenacious, tough; sticky,
etc., 352.

47. INCOHERENCE.—*N.* incoherence, nonadhesion; looseness, laxity, relaxation; loosening, disjunction, etc., 44.

V. loosen, make loose, slacken, relax; unglue, etc., 46; detach,
etc., 44.

Adj. nonadhesive, noncohesive, incoherent, detached, loose,
baggy, slack, lax, relaxed, segregated, unconsolidated; uncom-
bined, etc., 48.

48. COMBINATION.—*N.* combination, mixture, etc., 41;
junction, etc., 43; union, unification, synthesis, incorporation,
amalgamation, coalescence, fusion, brew, blend, blending; centralization.

alloy, compound, amalgam, composition, resultant.

V. **combine,** unite, incorporate, alloy, intermix, interfuse, interlard, amalgamate, embody, absorb, blend, merge, fuse, consolidate, coalesce, solidify, impregnate, centralize.

league, federate, confederate, fraternize, club, associate, amalgamate, couple, pair, ally.

Adj. **combined,** conjoint; ingrained, imbued.

allied, amalgamated, federate, confederate, corporate, leagued.

49. DECOMPOSITION.—*N.* **decomposition,** analysis, dissection, dissolution, breakup; disjunction, etc., 44; disintegration.

decay, rot, putrefaction, putrescence, putridity, caries, corruption.

V. **decompose,** analyze, dissolve; resolve into its elements, dissect, disintegrate, disperse; crumble into dust.

rot, decay, consume, putrefy.

50. [Principal part] WHOLE.—*N.* **whole,** totality, integrity, entirety, completeness; integer, integral.

all, the whole, total, aggregate, sum, sum total.

bulk, mass, lump, tissue, staple, body, greater part, main part; lion's share.

V. **form a whole,** embody, amass; aggregate, assemble; amount to.

Adj. **whole,** total, gross, entire; complete, etc., 52; wholesale, sweeping; comprehensive.

indivisible, indissoluble, indissolvable.

Adv. **wholly,** altogether; as a whole, totally, completely, entirely, all, all in all, wholesale, in a body, collectively, in the aggregate, in the main, on the whole, bodily, substantially.

51. PART.—*N.* **part,** portion; item, particular; aught, any; division; sector, segment; fraction, fragment; detachment, subdivision.

section, chapter, verse; article, clause.

piece, lump, bit, cut, cutting; chip, chunk, slice, scrap, crumb, morsel, moiety, particle; installment, dividend; share.

member, limb, arm, wing, scion, branch, bough, joint, link, offshoot, ramification, twig, spray, spring; runner, tendril; leaf, leaflet; stump.

V. **part,** divide, disjoin, etc., 44; partition, etc. (*apportion*), 786.

Adj. **fractional,** fragmentary, sectional; incomplete, partial, divided, broken, cut, cropped, shorn.

divisible, dissoluble, dissolvable.

Adv. **partly,** in part, partially; piecemeal, by installments, in detail.

52. COMPLETENESS.—*N.* **completeness,** intactness, completion, etc., 729; fill, saturation, entirety; totality, integrity; perfection, etc., 650; solidarity, unity, all, high tide, flood tide, spring tide.

V. complete, etc. (*accomplish*), 729; fill, charge, load, replenish; make up, eke out, supply deficiencies; fill up, fill in, satiate; saturate.

Adj. complete, entire, whole, intact, perfect, full, absolute, thorough; solid, undivided.

brimful, brimming, chock-full; saturated, crammed; replete, etc. (*redundant*), 641; fraught, laden.

exhaustive, radical, sweeping, thoroughgoing.

regular, unmitigated, sheer, unqualified, unconditional, free, abundant, etc. (*sufficient*), 639.

completing, supplemental, supplementary.

Adv. completely, altogether, outright, wholly, totally, utterly, quite; effectually, fully, in all respects, in every respect; out and out; throughout, from first to last, from head to foot, from top to toe, every whit, every inch.

53. INCOMPLETENESS.—*N.* incompleteness, deficiency, shortcoming, want, lack, insufficiency, imperfection, etc., 651; immaturity.

Part wanting: defect, deficit, omission; shortage; break, etc. (*discontinuity*), 70; missing link.

V. be incomplete, fall short of, lack, etc. (*be insufficient*), 640.

Adj. incomplete, uncompleted, imperfect, unfinished; defective, deficient, wanting, failing, in arrear, short, short of; perfunctory, sketchy, crude, immature.

mutilated, garbled, hashed, mangled, butchered, docked, truncated.

in progress, in hand; going on, proceeding.

54. COMPOSITION.—*N.* composition, constitution; make-up; combination, etc., 48; embodiment; formation.

authorship, compilation, composition, production, invention; writing.

painting, etching, design, etc. (*painting*), 556; relief, etc. (*sculpture*), 557.

typesetting, typography, etc., 591.

V. be composed of, consist of.

include, etc., 76; contain, hold, comprehend, admit, embrace, embody.

compose, constitute, form, make; fabricate, weave, construct; compile, scribble, draw, write.

55. EXCLUSION.—*N.* exclusion, omission, exception, rejection, repudiation; exile, seclusion, lockout, ostracism, prohibition.

separation, segregation, elimination, expulsion.

V. **exclude,** bar; leave out, shut out; reject, repudiate, blackball, ostracize; lay aside, put aside, set apart; relegate, segregate; strike off, strike out; neglect, banish, etc. (*seclude*), 893; separate, etc. (*disjoin*), 44.

pass over, omit; eliminate, weed out.

Adj. **exclusive,** inadmissible, preclusive, preventive, prohibitive.

Adv. **except,** exclusive of, save.

56. COMPONENT.—*N.* **component,** integral part, element, constituent, ingredient, contents; feature; member, etc. (*part*), 51; personnel.

V. **enter into,** be *or* form part of, etc., 51; merge in, share in, participate; belong to, appertain to; combine, unite.

form, make, constitute, compose, fabricate, etc., 54.

Adj. **inherent,** intrinsic, essential.

inclusive, all-embracing, comprehensive.

57. EXTRANEOUSNESS.—*N.* **extraneousness,** extrinsicality, exclusion; alienism.

foreign body (substance *or* element).

alien, stranger, intruder, interloper, foreigner, newcomer; immigrant, emigrant; outsider, barbarian, tenderfoot [*slang*].

Adj. **extraneous,** foreign, alien, exterior, external; outlandish, barbaric, barbarian.

excluded, inadmissible; exceptional.

Adv. **abroad,** in foreign parts, in foreign lands; oversea, overseas.

IV. ORDER

58. ORDER.—*N.* **order,** regularity, uniformity, symmetry, harmony; course, routine; method, disposition, arrangement, array, system, economy, discipline, orderliness, subordination.

gradation, progression; series, etc. (*continuity*), 69.

rank, place, etc. (*term*), 71.

V. **adjust,** regulate, systematize, standardize; time.

Adj. **orderly,** regular; in order, in trim, neat, tidy, methodical, uniform, symmetrical, shipshape, businesslike, systematic, normal, habitual.

Adv. **in order,** methodically, in turn, in its turn; step by step, systematically, by clockwork.

59. DISORDER.—*N.* **disorder,** derangement; irregularity, untidiness; anomaly, etc. (*unconformity*), 83; anarchy, anarchism, disunion; discord.

confusion, disarray, jumble, botch, litter, farrago, mess, muddle, hodgepodge, imbroglio, chaos, clutter, medley.

complexity, complication, entanglement, intricacy; perplexity; network, maze, labyrinth; wilderness, jungle; tangled skein.

turmoil, ferment, etc. (*agitation*), 315; trouble, disturbance, convulsion, tumult, uproar, riot, rumpus [*colloq*.], fracas, pandemonium, Babel, saturnalia.

V. disorder, botch, disturb, derange, etc., 61; entangle, ravel, ruffle, rumple.

Adj. disorderly, out of order, out of place, irregular, desultory; anomalous, etc. (*unconformable*), 83; disorganized; straggling; unmethodical, unsystematic; untidy, slovenly, messy [*colloq*.], indiscriminate, chaotic, confused; deranged, etc., 61; topsy-turvy, disjointed, out of joint.

complex, intricate, complicated, perplexed, involved, entangled, knotted, tangled, inextricable.

troublous, tumultuous, turbulent; riotous, etc. (*violent*), 173.

60. [Reduction to Order] **ARRANGEMENT.**—*N.* arrangement, plan, etc., 626; preparation, provision; disposal, disposition; distribution, sorting, assortment, allotment, apportionment, graduation, organization, groupings; analysis, classification, division, systematization, codification.

Result of arrangement: orderliness, form, array, digest; synopsis, etc. (*compendium*), 596; table; register, etc. (*record*), 551; organism; stipulation, settlement.

V. arrange, dispose, fix, place; form; set in order, set out; compose, space, range, graduate, marshal, array, rank, group, parcel out, allot, apportion, distribute, assign the parts; dispose of, assort, sort; tidy [*colloq*.].

classify, class, file, list; register, etc. (*record*), 551; catalogue, tabulate, index, alphabetize, grade, codify.

methodize, regulate, systematize, co-ordinate, organize; unravel, disentangle.

Adj. arranged, embattled, in battle array; cut and dried; methodical, orderly, regular, systematic, on file; tabular.

61. [Bringing into disorder] **DERANGEMENT.**—*N.* derangement, muss [*colloq.* U. S.], mess; disorder, etc., 59; discomposure, disturbance; disorganization, dislocation; inversion, etc., 218; insanity, etc., 503.

V. derange, disarrange, discompose, displace, misplace; mislay, disorder; disorganize; embroil, convulse, unsettle, disturb, confuse, trouble, perturb, disconcert, jumble; muddle; unhinge, dislocate, put out of joint, throw out of gear.

turn topsy-turvy, etc. (*invert*), 218; bedevil; complicate, involve, perplex, confound; tangle, entangle; tousle [*colloq*.], dishevel, ruffle; rumple, etc. (*fold*), 258; become insane, etc., 503.

litter, scatter; mix; etc., 41.

62. [Consecutive Order] PRECEDENCE.—*N.* precedence, the lead, superiority, etc., 33; importance, consequence; premise; antecedence, precursor, etc., 64; priority, preference.

prefix, affix; preamble; prelude, overture, voluntary.

V. precede, forerun, come before, come first; head, lead, lead the way; introduce, usher in; rank, outrank; take precedence.

prefix; premise, prelude, preface; affix.

Adj. preceding, precedent, antecedent; anterior; prior, etc., 116; before; former, foregoing, aforesaid, said; introductory, etc., 64.

Adv. before; in advance, etc. (*precession*), 280.

63. SEQUENCE.—*N.* sequence, train; following, succession; afterclap, afterglow, aftermath, afterpiece, aftertaste.

continuation, prolongation; order of succession.

V. succeed, come after, ensue, come next.

follow, tag [*colloq.*], heel, dog, shadow, hound, hunt; trace, retrace.

append, place after, subjoin.

Adj. succeeding, sequent; subsequent; proximate, next; consecutive, etc. (*continuity*), 69.

latter, posterior, etc., 117.

Adv. after, subsequently; behind, etc. (*rear*), 235.

64. PRECURSOR.—*N.* precursor, antecedent, precedent, predecessor; forerunner, pioneer; outrider; leader, bellwether; herald, harbinger.

prelude, preamble, preface, prologue, foreword, proem, exordium, introduction; heading, frontispiece, groundwork; preparation, etc., 673; overture, voluntary; premises.

prefigurement, etc., 511; omen, etc., 512.

Adj. introductory, preludial, prefatory, precursory, inaugural, preliminary.

65. SEQUEL.—*N.* sequel, suffix, tail, queue, train, wake, trail, rear; retinue, suite; appendix, postscript, postlude, conclusion, epilogue; peroration; codicil; continuation; appendage, tag, aftergrowth, afterpiece, afterthought, second thoughts; outgrowth.

follower, successor, pursuer, adherent, partisan, disciple, client; sycophant, parasite.

66. BEGINNING.—*N.* beginning, commencement, opening, outset, incipience, inception; introduction, etc. (*prelude*), 64; initial; inauguration, embarkation, rising of the curtain; curtain raiser, maiden speech; exordium; outbreak, onset, brunt; initiative, first move; start, starting point; dawn, etc. (*morning*), 125.

origin, etc. (*cause*), 153; source, rise; bud, germ, egg, embryo, rudiment; genesis, birth, nativity, cradle, infancy.

head, heading; title page; van, etc. (*front*), 234.

entrance, entry; inlet, orifice, mouth, porch, portal, portico, door; gate, gateway; postern, wicket, threshold, vestibule; border, frontier.

rudiments, elements, outlines, grammar, alphabet, ABC.

V. begin, commence; rise, arise; originate, initiate, open, start; dawn, set in, take its rise, enter upon; set out, etc. (*depart*), 293; embark in; make one's debut; institute; set about, set to work; make a start; break ground, cross the Rubicon; undertake, etc., 676.

usher in, lead the way, take the lead *or* initiative; inaugurate, head; lay the foundations, etc. (*prepare*), 673; found, etc. (*cause*), 153; set up, set on foot, launch, broach; open up, open the door to.

come into existence, take birth; burst forth, break out; spring up, crop up.

recommence; begin at the beginning, begin again, start afresh.

Adj. initial, prime, introductory, incipient; inaugural; embryonic, rudimentary; primal, primary, primeval, etc. (*old*), 124; aboriginal; natal.

first, maiden, foremost, front, head, leading.

Adv. first, in the first place, in the bud, in embryo, from the beginning, formerly.

67. END.—*N.* end, close, termination, conclusion, finish, completion, finis, finale, period, term, terminus, last, extreme, extremity; fag end, tip, nib, point, tail, tag, peroration, appendix, epilogue; consummation, denouement, fall of the curtain; goal, destination, terminal, limit, stoppage; expiration; dissolution, death, etc., 360; doomsday.

last stage, evening (*of life*); coup de grâce [F.], deathblow; knockout.

V. end, close, finish, terminate, conclude; expire, die, etc., 360; come to a close, perorate; run out, pass away.

bring to an end, put an end to, make an end of; achieve, etc. (*complete*), 729; stop, etc., 142.

Adj. final, terminal; conclusive; crowning, etc. (*completing*), 729; last, ultimate; hindermost; rear, etc., 235.

ended, settled, decided, over.

Adv. finally, in fine; at the last; once for all.

68. MIDDLE.—*N.* middle, midst, thick, midmost; mean, etc., 29; medium, middle term; center, core, kernel, nucleus, hub, heart, bull's-eye; mid-course, neutrality, compromise.

equidistance, bisection; equator, diaphragm, midriff.

Adj. **middle,** medial, mid, midmost; intermediate, equidistant, central, pivotal, mediterranean, equatorial.

Adv. **midway,** halfway, in the middle; amidships.

69. [Uninterrupted sequence] CONTINUITY.—continuity, continuousness, succession, round, suite, progression, series, train, chain; scale; gradation, course; perpetuity.

procession, cavalcade, parade; column; retinue, cortege, funeral, ovation.

pedigree, genealogy, lineage, history, family tree, race; ancestry, descent, family, house; line, line of ancestors; strain.

rank, file, line, row, range, tier.

V. **arrange in a series,** string together, file, list, thread, tabulate.

Adj. **continuous,** continued; consecutive, progressive, gradual, serial, successive; uninterrupted, unbroken, entire; linear; perennial, constant.

Adv. **continuously,** in a line, in succession, in turn; running, gradually, in file, in single file, in Indian file.

70. [Interrupted sequence] DISCONTINUITY.—*N.* discontinuity, disconnectedness; disconnection, etc., 44; interruption, break, fracture, flaw, fault, crack, cut; gap, etc. (*interval*), 198, intermission, alternation.

V. **alternate,** interchange, intermit.

discontinue, pause, interrupt, intervene; break, break off, interpose, etc., 228; disconnect, etc. (*disjoin*), 44; dissever.

Adj. **discontinuous,** disconnected, broken, interrupted, fitful, irregular, spasmodic, desultory; intermittent, alternate, recurrent, periodic.

Adv. **at intervals,** by snatches, by jerks, by fits and starts.

71. TERM.—*N.* term, rank, station, stage, step; degree, etc., 26; scale, grade, status, state, position, standing, footing, place, mark, period, range.

72. [Collective Order] ASSEMBLAGE.—*N.* assemblage, collection, levy, gathering, ingathering, mobilization, meet, forgathering, muster, team; concourse, conflux, congregation.

meeting, levee, reunion, drawing room, at home; social gathering, 892; assembly, congress, house, senate, legislature, etc., 696, convocation, caucus, convention.

company, platoon, faction, caravan, posse, watch, squad, corps, troop, troupe; army, regiment.

miscellany, miscellanea, compilation; symposium; library, etc (*store*), 636.

crowd, throng; flood, rush, deluge; rabble, mob, host, etc (*multitude*), 102; rout, press, crush, horde, body, tribe; crew, gang, knot, squad, force, band, party; bunch, drive, roundup.

clan, brotherhood, association, etc. (*party*), 712.

group, cluster, clump, set, batch, lot, pack; budget, assortment, bunch; parcel, packet, bundle, package, bale, fagot, wisp, truss, tuft, shock, clump; grove, thicket; rick, stack, sheaf, swath; volley, shower, storm, cloud.

accumulation, etc. (*store*), 636; heap, lump, pile, mass, pyramid; drift, snowball, snowdrift; amassment; conglomeration, aggregation, concentration, convergence, congestion, quantity, etc. (*greatness*), 31.

V. be *or* come together, assemble, collect, muster; meet, unite, join, rejoin; cluster, flock, swarm, surge, stream, herd, crowd, huddle, throng, associate; congregate, concentrate, resort, forgather.

bring together, assemble, muster, collect, gather; hold a meeting, convene, convoke; rake up, dredge, heap, mass, pile; pack, cram, lump together; compile, group, concentrate, unite, amass, accumulate, hoard, store.

Adj. dense, serried, teeming, swarming, populous.

73. DISPERSION.—*N.* dispersion, disjunct on, etc., 44; divergence, radiation, broadcast, spread, dissemination, diffusion, dissipation, distribution; apportionment, allotment.

V. disperse, scatter, sow, disseminate, sow broadcast, diffuse, radiate, broadcast, shed, spread, bestrew, dispense, disband, dismember, distribute; apportion, etc., 786; dispel, cast forth, draft off; strew, cast, sprinkle; issue, deal out, retail, utter.

Adj. scattered, disseminated, strown, strewn, dispersed, diffuse, diffusive, sparse, broadcast, sporadic, widespread; epidemic, etc. (*general*), 78; adrift, stray; disheveled.

74. [Place of meeting] FOCUS.—*N.* focus, center, gathering place, rendezvous, rallying point, headquarters, resort, haunt, retreat, club; tryst, trysting place, place of meeting.

V. focus, bring to a point, bring to a focus; rally, meet.

75. [Distributive Order] CLASS.—*N.* class, division, subdivision, category, head, order, section; department, province, domain, sphere.

kind, sort, type, estate, genus, species, variety, family, race, tribe, caste, clan, breed, kin; clique, coterie, set; sect, gender, sex.

description, denomination, persuasion, connection, designation, character, stamp; selection, specification.

76. INCLUSION.—*N.* inclusion, admission, incorporation, comprisal, reception.

composition, embodiment, formation.

V. include, comprise, comprehend, contain, admit, embrace, receive, inclose, etc. (*circumscribe*), 229; incorporate, cover, embody, encircle; reckon among, number among; refer to; place under, arrange under, take into account.

Adj. inclusive, included, including; comprehensive, sweeping, all-embracing.

77. EXCLUSION [from a class].—*N.* exclusion, rejection; *see* exclusion (*from a compound*), 55.

78. GENERALITY.—*N.* generality, universality, catholicity, miscellany, miscellaneousness; common run, prevalence, rifeness.

everyone, everybody, all hands [*colloq.*], all the world and his wife [*humorous*], anybody.

V. be general, prevail.

render general, spread, broaden, universalize, generalize.

Adj. general, generic, collective; current, wide, broad, comprehensive, sweeping; encyclopedic, panoramic; widespread, etc. (*dispersed*), 73; common, prevalent, prevailing, rife, epidemic.

universal, catholic, world-wide.

every, all, unspecified, miscellaneous, indefinite.

Adv. generally, always, in general, generally speaking; for the most part.

79. SPECIALTY.—*N.* specialty, speciality, individuality, peculiarity; personality, characteristic, mannerism, idiosyncrasy, singularity, originality; trait, distinctive feature.

particulars, details, items, counts; minutiæ.

V. specify, particularize; individualize, specialize; designate, determine; denote, indicate, point out, select, differentiate; itemize, enter into detail.

Adj. special, especial, particular, individual, specific, proper, personal, original, private, respective, definite, minute, certain, peculiar, marked, appropriate, characteristic, exclusive, restricted; singular, exceptional; typical, representative.

Adv. each, apiece, one by one, severally, respectively, in detail. namely, that is to say, viz.; to wit.

80. RULE.—*N.* regularity, uniformity, constancy, clockwork precision; punctuality, etc. (*exactness*), 494; even tenor, rut; system; routine, custom; formula; canon, convention, maxim, rule, regulation; standard, model, precedent; conformity, etc., 82.

law, order of things; normality, normalcy, normal state, ordinary condition, standing order; hard and fast rule.

Adj. regular, uniform, symmetrical, constant, steady; according to rule, etc., 82; normal, habitual, customary, etc., 613; methodical, orderly, systematic.

81. MULTIFORMITY.—*N.* multiformity, variety, diversity.

Adj. multiform, multifold, multifarious, multiplex; manifold, many-sided; protean, heterogeneous, motley, mosaic.

indiscriminate, irregular, diversified, diverse; of every description.

82. CONFORMITY.—*N.* conformity, observance; conventionality, etc. (*custom*), 613; agreement, accord.

example, instance, exemplification, illustration, specimen, sample.

conventionalist, formalist, bromide [*slang*], Philistine.

V. conform to, adapt oneself to.

be regular, travel in a rut; obey rules; agree with, comply with, fall in with; be guided by, harmonize, conventionalize, follow the fashion; do at Rome as the Romans do; swim with the stream.

exemplify, illustrate, cite, quote.

Adj. conformable to rule, adaptable, consistent, agreeable, compliant; regular, etc., 80; according to rule, well regulated, orderly, uniform, symmetric.

conventional, etc. (*customary*), 613; ordinary, common, habitual, usual; strict, rigid, uncompromising.

typical, normal, formal; canonical, orthodox, exemplary, illustrative, in point.

Adv. conformably, by rule; in accordance with, in keeping with; according to; as usual, as a matter of course.

invariably, etc. (*uniformly*), 16.

83. UNCONFORMITY.—*N.* nonconformity, unconformity, nonobservance, unconventionality, informality; anomaly, anomalousness, exception, peculiarity; breach *or* violation of custom; eccentricity, oddity, rarity.

individuality, singularity, originality, idiosyncrasy, mannerism.

aberration, irregularity; singularity; exemption; qualification, proviso.

nonconformist, Bohemian, nondescript character, original, freak, prodigy, wonder, miracle, curiosity.

mongrel, half-caste, etc., 41.

outcast, outlaw, Ishmael, pariah.

V. be uncomformable, leave the beaten path; break (*or* violate) a law *or* custom; stretch a point.

Adj. uncomfortable, exceptional, eccentric; abnormal, unnatural, anomalous, misplaced, out of order, irregular, arbitrary, lawless; informal, stray, eccentric, peculiar, exclusive, egregious.

unusual, unaccustomed, unwonted, uncommon; rare, singular, unique, curious, odd, extraordinary, strange, monstrous; wonderful, etc., 870; remarkable, noteworthy, queer, quaint, nondescript, original, unorthodox, unconventional, Bohemian, unprecedented, unparalleled, unexampled, unheard of; fantastic, newfangled, eccentric, grotesque, bizarre; unfamiliar, outlandish.

heterogeneous, amorphous, mongrel, hybrid; unsymmetric, etc., 243.

Adv. unconformably; except, unless, save.

V. NUMBER

84. NUMBER.—*N.* number, symbol, numeral, figure, cipher, digit, integer, round number; series.

sum, product, total, aggregate, difference.

ratio, proportion, percentage; progression; arithmetical progression.

power, root, exponent, index, logarithm.

85. NUMERATION.—*N.* numeration, numbering; tale, tally, enumeration, reckoning, computation, calculation, calculus; measurement, etc., 466; statistics.

arithmetic, algebra, differential calculus, calculus of differences.

muster, poll, census, roll call; account, etc. (*list*), 86.

Instruments: abacus, calculating machine, adding machine, cash register.

arithmetician, calculator, algebraist, geometrician, trigonometrician, mathematician, actuary, statistician.

V. number, count, enumerate; call over, run over; take an account of, call the roll, muster, poll; sum up, cast up; tell off, cipher, reckon, reckon up, estimate, compute, calculate.

check, prove, demonstrate, balance, audit, overhaul, take stock. total, amount to, come to.

Adj. numeral, numerical; arithmetical, analytic, algebraic, statistical, computable, calculable, commensurable, commensurate.

86. LIST.—*N.* list, catalogue, card index; inventory, schedule; register, etc. (*record*), 551; account; bill, bill of costs; tally, file, index, table, contents; book, ledger; synopsis, syllabus; scroll, screed, invoice, manifest, bill of lading; prospectus, program; bill of fare, menu; score, bulletin, census, statistics, returns; directory, atlas, gazetteer; calendar, almanac.

dictionary, lexicon, glossary, vocabulary, wordbook, thesaurus. roll; muster roll; roll of honor; roster, slate, poll, panel.

V. list, enroll, schedule, inventory, register, catalogue, invoice, bill, book, slate, post, docket; empanel, tally, file, index, tabulate, enter, census.

87. UNITY.—*N.* unity, oneness; individuality; unification, etc., 48; completeness, completion.

one, unit; individual.

V. isolate, insulate.

render one; unite, etc. (*join*), 43, (*combine*), 48.

Adj. **one**, sole, lone, single, solitary; individual, apart, alone; unaccompanied, unattended, singlehanded; singular, odd, unique, isolated; insular.

88. ACCOMPANIMENT.—*N.* accompaniment, adjunct, accessory; context; appendage, appurtenance; attribute.

company, association, partnership; companionship.

attendant, companion, associate, colleague, partner; consort, spouse; satellite, hanger-on, shadow; escort, suite, train, retinue, convoy, follower, etc., 65.

V. **accompany**, attend, convoy, chaperon; associate with, couple with.

Adj. **accompanying**, fellow, twin, joint; associated with, coupled with; accessory, attendant.

Adv. **with**, withal; together with, along with, in company with; therewith, herewith; and, etc. (*addition*), 37.

together, in a body, collectively, in conjunction.

89. DUALITY.—*N.* duality, dualism; duplicity; polarity.

two, deuce, couple, couplet, both, twain, brace, pair, twins, Castor and Pollux, gemini, fellows; yoke, span; distich.

V. **pair**, mate, couple, bracket, yoke.

Adj. **two**, twain, both; dual, twin; duplex, etc., 90; tête-à-tête.

90. DUPLICATION.—*N.* duplication, doubling, reduplication; iteration, etc. (*repetition*), 104; renewal.

duplicate, facsimile, copy, replica, counterpart, etc. (*copy*), 21.

V. **double**; redouble, reduplicate; repeat, etc., 104; renew, renovate.

Adj. **double**; doubled; twofold, two-sided, duplex; double-faced, double-headed; twin, duplicate, second; dual.

Adv. **twice**, once more; over again, etc. (*repeatedly*), 104.

91. [Division into two parts] BISECTION.—*N.* bisection, halving, bifurcation, forking, branching, ramification, dichotomy.

half, moiety.

V. **bisect**, halve, divide, separate, split, cut in two, cleave.

fork, bifurcate, branch off *or* out, ramify.

Adj. **bisected**, cloven, cleft; bifurcated; semi-, demi-, hemi-.

92. TRIALITY.—*N.* triality [*rare*], trinity,[1] triunity.

three, triad, triplet, trio; triangle, trident, tripod, trireme, triumvirate.

third power, cube.

Adj. **three**; triform, tertiary.

93. TRIPLICATION.—*N.* triplication, triplicity; trilogy.

V. **treble**, triple; cube.

Adj. **treble**, triple; threefold; third.

[1] *Trinity* is hardly ever used except in a theological sense; *see* Deity, 976.

Adv. **three times,** thrice; in the third place, thirdly; threefold, triply, trebly.

94. [Division into three parts] **TRISECTION.**—*N.* trisection, tripartition, third, third part.

V. trisect, divide into three parts, third.

95. **QUATERNITY.**—*N.* quaternity [*rare*], four, quartet, quadruplet; square, quadrilateral; quadrangle.

V. square, biquadrate, reduce to a square.

Adj. four; quadratic; quadrangular, quadrilateral.

96. **QUADRUPLICATION.**—*N.* quadruplication.

V. quadruplicate, multiply by four.

Adj. fourfold, quadruple; fourth.

Adv. four times, in the fourth place, fourthly.

97. [Division into four parts] **QUADRISECTION.**—*N.* quadrisection, quadripartition; quartering; fourth; quart, quarter; farthing; quarto.

V. quarter, divide into four parts, quadrisect.

98. **FIVE, ETC.**—*N.* five, quintet, pentagon, pentameter.

six, half a dozen; hexagon, hexameter, sextet.

seven, heptagon, heptameter, heptarchy.

eight, octave, octagon, octameter, octavo, octet.

nine, nonagon.

ten, decade, decagon, decasyllable, decemvir, decemvirate, decennium.

twelve, dozen; **thirteen,** long dozen, baker's dozen; **twenty,** score; **fifty,** half a hundred; **sixty,** threescore; **seventy,** threescore and ten; **eighty,** fourscore; **ninety,** fourscore and ten.

hundred, centenary, century; bicentenary, tercentenary.

thousand, millennium; myriad.

V. quintuplicate, sextuple; centuplicate.

Adj. **five,** fifth, quintuple; pentangular, pentagonal. **sixth,** sextuple, hexagonal, hexangular. **seventh,** septuple, heptagonal, heptangular. **eight,** octuple, octagonal, octangular. **tenth,** tenfold, decimal, decagonal, decasyllabic. **eleventh,** undecennial, undecennary. **twelfth,** duodenary, duodenal. **sixtieth,** sexagesimal. **seventieth,** septuagesimal.

centuple, centuplicate, centennial, centenary; hundredth; thousandth, millenary, millennial, etc.

99. **QUINQUESECTION, ETC.**—*N.* quinquesection, division by five, etc., 98; decimation; tithe; fifth, etc.

Adj. decimal, tenth; duodecimal, twelfth; sexagesimal, sexagenary; hundredth, centesimal; millesimal, etc.

100. [More than one] **PLURALITY.**—*N.* plurality, one or two, two or three, etc.; a few, several; multitude, etc., 102; majority.

Adj. plural, more than one, upwards of, some, certain.

100a. [Less than one] **FRACTION.**—*N.* fraction, fractional part; part, portion, fragment, etc., 51.

Adj. fractional, fragmentary, inconsiderable, partial.

101. ZERO.—*N.* zero, nothing; naught, nought; cipher; none, nobody.

102. MULTITUDE.—*N.* multitude, multitudinousness, multiplicity; profusion, etc. (*plenty*), 639; legion, host, array, army, galaxy; numbers; scores; heap, power, sight, lot, lots [*all five colloq.*], swarm, bevy, cloud, flock, herd, drove, shoal, school, flight, covey, hive, brood, litter, farrow, fry, nest; mob, crowd, etc. (*assemblage*), 72.

V. be numerous, swarm with, teem with, be alive with, crowd, swarm, outnumber, multiply; people.

Adj. many, several, sundry, various, alive with; numerous; profuse, manifold, multitudinous, teeming, populous, outnumbering, crowded, thick, galore [*colloq.*]; thick-coming, endless, etc. (*infinite*), 105.

103. FEWNESS.—*N.* fewness, paucity, scarcity, sparseness, sparsity; handful; small quantity, etc., 32; rarity, infrequency; minority.

Diminution of number: reduction, weeding, elimination; decimation; eradication.

V. render few, reduce, diminish, weed out, eliminate, thin, decimate.

Adj. few, scant, scanty; thin, rare, scarce, sparse, few and far between; exiguous; infrequent.

104. REPETITION.—*N.* repetition, iteration, recapitulation, reiteration; monotone; duplication, reduplication, monotony, harping, recurrence; reappearance, reproduction; periodicity, etc., 138; succession, run; alliteration; rhythm, tautology; diffuseness, redundancy.

echo, encore, burden of a song, refrain, undersong.

cuckoo, etc. (*imitation*), 19; reverberation, vibration, resonance; drumming, etc. (*roll*), 407; renewal, etc. (*restoration*), 660.

V. repeat, iterate, reiterate, redouble, reproduce, echo, re-echo, drum, harp upon, hammer; rehearse; resume, return to, recapitulate.

recur, revert, return, reappear; renew, etc. (*restore*), 660.

duplicate, reduplicate.

Adj. repeated, repetitious, recurrent, recurring; frequent, incessant; redundant, tautological; another.

monotonous, harping, iterative, unvaried; habitual, etc., 613.

aforesaid, aforenamed; said.

Adv. repeatedly, often, again, anew, afresh, once more; ditto encore, again and again; over and over, frequently, etc., 136.

105. INFINITY.—*N.* infinity, infinitude, infiniteness; perpetuity, immortality; inexhaustibility, immensity, boundlessness.

V. be infinite, have no limits (*or* bounds), go on forever.

Adj. infinite, immense; numberless, countless, measureless, innumerable, immeasurable, incalculable, illimitable, interminable, unfathomable; without limit, without end, limitless, endless, boundless; untold, unnumbered, unmeasured, unbounded, unlimited; perpetual, etc., 112.

VI. TIME

106. TIME.—*N.* time, duration; period, term, stage, space, span, spell, snap, season; course.

intermediate time, while, interim, interval; intermission, interregnum, interlude; respite.

era, epoch, eon, cycle, age, reign, dynasty, administration.

V. continue, last, endure, stay, go on, remain, persist, abide, stand, stick [*colloq.*], hold out; intervene; elapse, etc., 109.

pass time, spend *or* while away time, tide over; employ time, seize an opportunity; linger on, drag on; tarry, etc., 110; wast time, etc. (*be inactive*), 683; procrastinate, etc., 133.

Adj. permanent, etc. (*durable*), 110; timely, opportune, seasonable.

Adv. while, whilst, during; in the course of; in the time when; meantime, meanwhile, in the meantime, in the interim, from day to day; for a time, for a season; till, until, up to, yet; th whole time, all the time; throughout; for good, permanently, always.

then, hereupon, thereupon, whereupon.

107. Absence of time.—*N.* no time.

Adv. never, ne'er; at no time, at no period; on no occasion, nevermore.

108. [Definite duration or portion of time] PERIOD.—*N.* period; octave, semester, quarter, moon, year, decennial, decennium; decade, lifetime, generation; epoch, era, century, age, millennium.

109. [Indefinite duration] COURSE.—*N.* corridors (*or* sweep, vista, halls, progress, process, lapse, flow, tide, march, flight) of time; duration, etc., 106.

Indefinite time: eon, age.

V. elapse, lapse, flow, run, proceed, advance, pass; fly, slip, slide, glide; crawl, drag; expire, go by, pass by, be past.

Adv. **in time,** in due time (*or* season, course); in course of time, in the fullness of time.

110. [Long duration] **DURABILITY.**—*N.* durability, durableness, permanence, continuance, persistence, lastingness, standing; immutability, stability; survival; longevity, etc. (*age*), 128; delay, etc. (*lateness*), 133; slowness.

an age, a long time, eon, century, an eternity; perpetuity, etc., 112.

V. last, endure, stand, remain, abide, continue, etc., 106.

tarry, etc., 133; drag on, protract, prolong; spin out, eke out, draw out; temporize, gain time.

outlast, outlive, survive.

Adj. permanent, durable, lasting; chronic, long-standing; persistent; lifelong, livelong; endless, fixed, long-lived, perennial; perpetual, etc., 112.

prolonged, protracted, spun out; lingering, long-winded; slow, etc., 275.

Adv. long, for a long time; long ago, etc. (*in a past time*), 122; all the day long, the livelong day; all the year round; permanently.

111. [Short duration] **TRANSIENCE.**—*N.* transience, transiency, evanescence, impermanence; changeableness, etc., 149; mortality; span; nine days' wonder, bubble; interregnum, interim.

velocity, etc., 274; suddenness, abruptness.

V. be transient, flit, pass away, fly, gallop, vanish, sink, melt, fade, evaporate.

Adj. transient, transitory, passing, evanescent, fleeting, fugitive; temporal, temporary, provisional, provisory; cursory; short-lived, ephemeral; deciduous; perishable, mortal; precarious; impermanent.

brief, quick, brisk, fleet; meteoric, volatile, summary; pressed for time, etc. (*haste*), 684; sudden, momentary, spasmodic, instantaneous.

Adv. temporarily, for the moment, for a time; awhile, soon, etc. (*early*), 132; briefly.

112. [Endless duration] **PERPETUITY.**—*N.* perpetuity, eternity, aye; immortality, perpetuation.

V. eternalize, immortalize, eternize, perpetuate.

Adj. perpetual, eternal, everlasting, continual, endless, unending; ceaseless, incessant, uninterrupted, unceasing; interminable; unfading, never-ending, deathless, immortal, undying, imperishable.

Adv. perpetually, always, ever, evermore, aye; forever, in all ages, without end, to the end of time; till doomsday; constantly, etc. (*very frequently*), 136.

113. [Point of time] INSTANTANEITY.—*N.* **instantaneity**, in stantaneousness; suddenness, abruptness.

moment, instant, second, twinkling, flash, breath.

V. **be instantaneous;** flash.

Adj. **instantaneous,** momentary, extempore, sudden, abrup

Adv. **instantaneously,** in no time; presto, instanter, in a tric in a jiffy [*colloq.*], suddenly, in the same breath; at once, plump immediately, etc. (*early*), 132; extempore, on the spur of th moment; slapdash, etc. (*haste*), 684.

114. [Estimation, measurement, and record of time] CHRO NOMETRY.—*N.* **chronometry,** chronology, horology.

almanac, calendar; register, registry; chronicle, annals, journa diary.

timekeeper, clock, watch, repeater; chronometer, timepiec dial, sundial, hourglass.

V. **register,** date, chronicle; measure time, beat time, mar time.

Adj. **chronologic** *or* chronological, temporal.

115. [False estimate of time] ANACHRONISM.—*N.* **anac** ronism, error in time, error in chronology, misdate; anticipatio disregard (*or* neglect, oblivion) of time.

V. **misdate;** antedate, postdate, anticipate; take no note of tim

Adj. **misdated;** undated; overdue; out of date, anachronisti behind time, ahead of time.

116. PRIORITY.—*N.* **priority,** predecessor, precedence, pr existence; precursor, antecedent, forerunner; the past, etc., 12

V. **precede,** come before; pre-exist, forerun; go before, lea head; presage, herald, usher in, introduce, announce.

be beforehand. etc. (*be early*), 132; anticipate, forestall.

Adj. **prior,** previous, preceding, anterior, antecedent; pr existent; former, aforementioned, foregoing, before-mentione aforesaid, said; introductory, etc. (*precursory*), 64.

Adv. **before,** prior to; earlier; previously, ere, already, ye beforehand; on the eve of.

117. POSTERIORITY.—*N.* **posteriority;** succession, sequenc following, continuance, prolongation; futurity, future; successo sequel, etc., 65; remainder.

V. **follow after,** pursue, come after, go after; succeed, supe vene; ensue, result.

Adj. **subsequent,** posterior, following, after, later, succeedin successive, ensuing, posthumous; future, etc., 121; after-dinne

Adv. **subsequently,** after, afterward, since, later; next, clo upon, thereafter, thereupon.

118. PRESENT TIME.—*N.* the present time, the present juncture *or* occasion; the times, time being; twentieth century.

Adj. present, actual, instant, current, latest, existing.

Adv. at this time, at this moment, etc., 113; now, at present; today, nowadays; already; even now, but now, just now; for the time being.

119. DIFFERENT TIME.—*N.* different time, other time.

Adv. then, at that time (*or* moment, instant); on that occasion.

when; whenever, whensoever; whereupon, upon which; at various times.

once, formerly, once upon a time.

120. SIMULTANEOUSNESS.—*N.* simultaneousness, synchronism, coexistence, coincidence, concurrence.

contemporary, coeval.

V. coexist, concur, accompany, keep pace with; synchronize.

Adj. simultaneous, coexisting, coincident, synchronous, concomitant, concurrent; coeval; contemporary, contemporaneous.

Adv. simultaneously, together, in concert; in the same breath.

121. THE FUTURE.—*N.* future, futurity, hereafter, time to come; morrow, tomorrow, by and by, doomsday, day of judgment, crack of doom.

approach of time, advent; destiny, etc., 152.

heritage, heirs, posterity, descendants.

prospect, anticipation, expectation; foresight, etc., 510.

V. anticipate, expect, await, foresee; forestall, etc. (*be early*), 132.

approach, await, threaten; impend, etc. (*be destined*), 152; come on, draw near.

Adj. future, to come; coming, impending, overhanging, imminent; next, near, close at hand; eventual, ulterior; prospective, in prospect.

Adv. prospectively, hereafter, in future; in course of time, eventually, ultimately, sooner or later.

soon, early; on the eve of, on the point of, about to.

122. THE PAST.—*N.* the past, past time, days of yore, days of old, times past, former times, yesterday, the olden time; retrospection, memory, priority.

antiquity, antiqueness, time immemorial, history, remote time; remote past; paleontology, archeology, antiquarianism.

antiquary, antiquarian, archeologist.

ancestry, lineage, forefathers.

V. pass, lapse, blow over.

Adj. past, gone, gone by, over, passed away, bygone, elapsed,

lapsed, expired, extinct, exploded, forgotten, irrecoverable; obsolete, antiquated, outworn.

former, pristine, quondam, late; ancestral.

foregoing, last, latter; recent.

looking back, retrospective, retroactive; archeological.

Adv. formerly, of old, of yore, time was, ago; anciently, long ago; lately, latterly, of late; ere now, before now, hitherto, heretofore; already, yet, up to this time.

123. NEWNESS.—*N.* newness, novelty; youth, juvenility, immaturity.

innovation; renovation, restoration.

upstart, *nouveau riche* [F.], parvenu.

modernism, modernness, modernity; modernization; latest fashion.

V. renew, renovate; rejuvenate; modernize.

Adj. new, novel, recent, fresh, green; young, etc., 127; raw, immature; virgin, untried; modern, late; newborn, new-fashioned, newfangled, newfledged; just out [*colloq.*], unhandled; brand-new, up-to-date [*colloq.*], renovated, spick-and-span.

Adv. newly, afresh, anew, lately, just now, latterly, of late.

124. OLDNESS.—*N.* oldness, age, antiquity.

maturity, matureness, ripeness.

decline, decay; senility, superannuation, dotage.

archaism, antiquarianism; thing of the past, relic of the past.

tradition, custom, immemorial usage, common law; folklore.

V. be old, have had its day, have seen its day.

become old, age, fade.

Adj. old, ancient, antique; time-honored, venerable, hoary; elder, eldest; firstborn; senile, etc., 128.

primitive, prime, primeval, aboriginal; antediluvian, prehistoric, dateless, patriarchal, archaic, classic, medieval; ancestral.

immemorial, traditional, unwritten, inveterate, rooted.

antiquated, of other times, of the old school, old world; obsolete, out-of-date, out-of-fashion, gone by, stale, old-fashioned, exploded, extinct, timeworn, crumbling, secondhand.

125. MORNING. [Noon]—*N.* morning, morn, forenoon, antemeridian, A.M., prime, dawn, daybreak; dayspring, peep of day, break of day, aurora, sunrise, daylight, cockcrow.

noon, midday, noonday, noontide, meridian, prime; nooning, noontime.

spring, springtide, springtime, seedtime; vernal equinox.

summer, summertide, summertime, midsummer.

Adj. matin, matutinal.

noon, noonday, midday.

spring, vernal.

summer, estival.

126. EVENING. [Midnight]—*N.* evening, eve, decline of day, close of day, eventide, vespers, nightfall, curfew, dusk, gloaming, twilight, sunset, sundown, bedtime.

afternoon, post meridiem [L.], P.M.

midnight; dead of night, witching time.

autumn, fall; harvesttime; autumnal equinox; Indian summer.

winter.

Adj. vesper, nightly, nocturnal; autumnal.

wintry, winterly.

127. YOUTH.—*N.* youth; juvenility; infancy, babyhood; childhood; boyhood, girlhood; rising generation; minority, immaturity, teens, tender age, bloom.

cradle, nursery.

flower of life, springtide of life, seedtime of life, golden season of life; heyday of youth, school days.

Adj. young, youthful, juvenile, green, callow, sappy, beardless, underage, in one's teens; younger, junior; newfledged, unfledged, unripe.

128. AGE.—*N.* age; oldness, old age, advanced age, senility, years, gray hairs, declining years, decrepitude, superannuation, second childhood, dotage; vale of years, decline of life; green old age, ripe age; longevity.

seniority, eldership, primogeniture; elders, etc. (*veteran*), 130; dean, father.

V. age, grow old, decline, wane.

Adj. aged; old, etc., 124; elderly, senile; ripe, mellow, declining, waning, past one's prime; gray, gray-headed, hoar, hoary, venerable, patriarchal, timeworn, antiquated, effete, decrepit, superannuated; advanced in life (*or* years); stricken in years; doting, etc. (*imbecile*), 499.

older, elder, oldest, eldest; senior; firstborn.

129. INFANT.—*N.* infant, babe, baby; nursling, suckling.

child, tot, mite, chick, kid [*slang*], little one, brat, pickaninny [*colored child*], urchin, elf.

youth, boy, lad, laddie, slip, sprig, stripling, youngster, cub, whippersnapper [*colloq.*], schoolboy, hobbledehoy, young hopeful, cadet, minor.

girl, lass, lassie, wench, damsel; maid, maiden, virgin; nymph, colleen, flapper, minx, schoolgirl; hoyden, tomboy, romp.

Adj. infantile, infantine, puerile, boyish, girlish, childish, babyish, kittenish; boylike, girllike, newborn; young, etc., 127.

130. VETERAN.—*N.* veteran, old man, patriarch, graybeard;

grandfather, sexagenarian, octogenarian, nonagenarian, centenarian; Methuselah; elders, forefathers; dotard, etc., 501.

granny, crone, hag, beldam.

Adj. veteran; aged, etc., 128.

131. ADOLESCENCE.—*N.* adolescence, majority, adulthood, womanhood, manhood, virility; flower of age; full bloom; spring of life.

man, etc., 373; woman, etc., 374; adult.

middle age, maturity, full age, prime of life, meridian of life.

V. come of age, come to man's estate, come to years of discretion; attain majority; come out [*colloq.*].

Adj. adolescent, pubescent, of age, of full age, of ripe age; out of one's teens, grown up, full-grown, manly, manlike, virile, adult; womanly; marriageable.

middle-aged, mature, in one's prime; matronly.

132. EARLINESS.—*N.* earliness, punctuality, promptitude, readiness, expedition, quickness, haste, etc. (*velocity*), 274; suddenness.

prematurity, precocity, precipitation, anticipation.

V. be early, be beforehand.

anticipate, forestall, take time by the forelock, steal a march upon; bespeak, secure, engage, pre-engage.

accelerate, expedite, etc. (*quicken*), 274; make haste, etc. (*hurry*), 684.

Adj. early, timely, seasonable, punctual, forward; prompt, etc. (*active*), 682.

premature, precipitate, precocious, anticipatory.

sudden, instantaneous, immediate; unexpected, etc., 508.

imminent, impending, near.

Adv. early, soon, anon, betimes, ere long, before long; punctually, in time; on time, on the dot [*slang*].

beforehand; prematurely, too soon; precipitately, hastily; in anticipation; unexpectedly, unawares.

suddenly, etc. (*instantaneously*), 113; at short notice, extempore; on the spur of the moment, at once; on the spot, on the instant, at sight, offhand, straight, straightway; forthwith, immediately, quickly, speedily, apace; presently, by and by, directly.

133. LATENESS.—*N.* lateness; tardiness, etc. (*slowness*), 275.

delay, procrastination, postponement, adjournment, prorogation, retardation; protraction, prolongation; moratorium; after-time; respite, truce, reprieve, stop, stay, suspension, remand.

V. be late, tarry, wait, stay, bide, take time; dawdle, etc. (*be inactive*), 683; linger, loiter, gain time; hang fire; stand over, lie over; hang.

put off, defer, delay, lay over, suspend; stave off; retard, postpone, adjourn, prorogue, procrastinate; dally, prolong, protract, spin out, draw out, table, lay on the table, shelve; reserve, temporize, filibuster, stall [*slang*].

be kept waiting, dance attendance; cool one's heels [*colloq.*]; await, expect, wait for.

Adj. late, tardy, dilatory; slow, leisurely, behindhand, backward, unpunctual; overdue, belated, delayed; posthumous.

Adv. late; backward, at the eleventh hour, at length, at last; ultimately; behind time; too late.

slowly, deliberately, at one's leisure.

134. TIMELINESS.—*N.* timeliness, opportunity, opening, occasion, show [*colloq.*]; suitable time *or* season, high time; nick of time; golden opportunity, clear stage, fair field; spare time, leisure.

crisis, turn, emergency, juncture, conjuncture; turning point.

V. **improve the occasion**; seize an opportunity; use (*or* profit by) an opportunity; give (*or* grant) an opportunity; suit the occasion, etc. (*be expedient*), 646; strike the iron while it is hot, make hay while the sun shines.

Adj. timely, well timed, opportune, seasonable; appropriate, suitable.

lucky, providential, fortunate, happy, favorable, propitious, auspicious.

occasional, accidental, extemporaneous, extemporary; contingent, provisional.

Adv. opportunity, in due time; for the nonce; in the nick of time, just in time; at the eleventh hour, now or never.

by the way, by the by; while on this subject, speaking of; extempore; on the spur of the moment.

135. UNTIMELINESS.—*N.* untimeliness, unseasonableness, unsuitable time, improper time; evil hour; intrusion; anachronism.

V. **be ill-timed**, mistime, intrude, come amiss, break in upon; be busy, be occupied, be engaged.

lose an opportunity; neglect an opportunity; allow *or* suffer the opportunity to pass (*or* slip, go by, escape); waste time; let slip through the fingers.

Adj. ill-timed, mistimed, ill-fated, ill-omened, ill-starred; untimely, unseasonable, out of season; inopportune, inconvenient, untoward, unlucky, inauspicious, unpropitious, unfortunate, unfavorable, unsuited; inexpedient.

unpunctual, etc. (*late*), 133; premature, etc. (*early*), 132.

136. FREQUENCY.—*N.* frequency, repetition, iteration, reiteration.

V. **keep on**; reiterate, repeat, recur, etc., 104; do nothing but.

Adj. **frequent**, not rare, thick-coming, incessant, perpetual, continual, constant, habitual, etc., 613.

Adv. **often**, oft, ofttimes, frequently; repeatedly, in quick succession; daily, every day; habitually, commonly.

perpetually, continually, constantly, incessantly, at all times. sometimes, occasionally, at times, now and then, again and again.

137. INFREQUENCY.—*N.* **infrequency**, infrequence, rarity; uncommonness.

Adj. **infrequent**, uncommon, sporadic; rare, few, scant, scarce; unprecedented.

Adv. **seldom**, rarely, scarcely, hardly; not often, infrequently, uncommonly, sparsely, scarcely ever, hardly ever.

138. REGULARITY [of recurrence].—*N.* **periodicity**, intermittence; oscillation, vibration; beat, pulse, pulsation; rhythm, alternation; round, revolution, rotation, regularity, bout, turn; routine; cycle.

anniversary, biennial, triennial, quadrennial, quinquennial, sextennial, septennial, octennial, decennial; tricennial, jubilee, centennial, centenary, bicentennial, bicentenary, tercentenary; birthday, natal day, fete day, saint's day, feast, festival, fast, holiday.

Christmas, Yuletide, New Year's Day, Ash Wednesday, Maundy Thursday, Good Friday, Easter; Halloween, All Saints' Day; All Souls' Day; Candlemas; Memorial *or* Decoration Day, Independence Day, Labor Day, Thanksgiving, ground-hog day, woodchuck day, leap year, St. Swithin's Day, Midsummer Day; May Day.

V. **return**, revolve, recur, come round again; beat, pulsate; alternate; intermit.

Adj. **periodic**, periodical; serial, recurrent, cyclic, cyclical, rhythmic, recurring, intermittent; alternate, every other; every.

regular, steady, constant, methodical, punctual.

Adv. **by turns**, in turn, in rotation, alternately, off and on, round and round.

139. IRREGULARITY [of recurrence].—*N.* **irregularity**, uncertainty, unpunctuality; fitfulness, capriciousness.

Adj. **irregular**, uncertain, unpunctual, capricious, erratic, desultory, fitful, flickering; rambling, spasmodic; unmethodical, unsystematic, unequal, uneven, variable.

Adv. **by fits and starts.**

VII. CHANGE

140. CHANGE.—*N.* **change**, alteration, mutation, permutation, variation, modification, modulation, inflection, mood, qualification, innovation, deviation, shift, turn; diversion, variety, break.

conversion, etc. (*gradual change*), 144; revolution, etc., 146; inversion, reversal; displacement, transposition, removal, transference.

transformation, metamorphosis, transfiguration, transmutation; transubstantiation; transmigration, metempsychosis; avatar.

changeableness, etc., 149.

V. change, alter, vary, modulate, diversify, qualify, tamper with; turn, shift, veer, jibe, jib, tack, chop, warp, swerve, deviate, dodge; turn aside; take a turn, turn the corner.

modify, work a change, patch, piece, transform, transfigure, transmute, convert, revolutionize; metamorphose, ring the changes; innovate, introduce new blood, shuffle the cards; shift the scene, turn over a new leaf.

recast, remodel; reverse, etc., 218; convert into, etc., 144.

Adj. changed, newfangled; changeable, changeful, variable, devious, transitional.

141. PERMANENCE.—*N.* permanence, fixity, persistence, endurance; durability; standing, *status quo* [L.]; maintenance, preservation, conservation; conservatism; stability, constancy; quiescence, etc., 265; obstinacy, inflexibility.

V. endure, persist, remain, stay, tarry, rest, hold, last, bide, abide, dwell, maintain, keep; stand fast, subsist, live, outlive, survive; hold one's ground (*or* footing).

Adj. permanent, stable, fixed, settled, established, irremovable, durable; unchanged, intact, inviolate; persistent; conservative; unfailing, unfading.

Adv. for good, at a stand, at a standstill, as you were!

142. CESSATION.—*N.* cessation, discontinuance; intermission, remission; suspense, suspension; interruption; stop; hitch [*colloq.*]; stoppage, halt.

pause, rest, lull, respite, truce, armistice, stay; interregnum. In debate: closure, cloture.

deadlock, checkmate, dead center, dead stand, dead stop; end. punctuation: comma, semicolon, colon, period, full stop; cæsura.

V. cease, discontinue, desist, stay; break off, leave off; hold, stop, pull up, stop short; check, stick, hang fire; halt, pause, rest; come to a stand; arrive, etc., 292; go out, die away, wear away, pass away, lapse; be at an end.

have done with, give over; give up, etc. (*relinquish*), 624.

interrupt, suspend, intermit, remit; put an end to, bring to a stand (*or* standstill), stop, cut short, arrest.

143. CONTINUANCE [in action].—*N.* continuance, continuation; pursuance, maintenance, extension, perpetuation, prolongation; persistence, perseverance; repetition.

V. **continue**, persist, go on, keep on, hold on; abide, pursue; stick to; maintain its course; keep up, drag on, stick [*colloq.*], persevere, endure, carry on; keep the field, keep the ball rolling.

sustain, uphold, hold up, follow up, perpetuate, prolong, maintain; preserve.

Adj. **continuing**, uninterrupted, unvarying, persistent, unceasing, unvaried, sustained, chronic; undying, immortal, perpetual.

144. [Gradual change to something different] CONVERSION. —*N.* **conversion**, reduction, transmutation, assimilation; chemistry, alchemy; growth, progress; naturalization; transportation.

passage, transit, transition, transmigration; shifting, flux; phase.

convert, neophyte, proselyte; pervert, renegade, apostate, turncoat.

V. **be converted into**; become, turn to *or* into; turn out, lapse, shift; pass into, grow into, merge into; melt, grow, wax, mature, mellow.

convert into, resolve into; make, render; mold, form, remodel, reform, reorganize; bring to, reduce to.

145. REVERSION.—*N.* **reversion**, return; revulsion; turning point, turn of the tide; alternation, rotation; inversion, etc., 218; recoil, reaction; retrospection, retrogression; restoration, relapse, atavism, throwback.

V. **revert**, reverse, return, turn back; relapse; invert; recoil; retreat; restore; undo, unmake; turn the scale.

146. [Sudden or violent change] REVOLUTION.—*N.* **revolution**, revolt; breakup; destruction, etc., 162; clean sweep, debacle, overturn, overthrow, rebellion, rising, uprising, mutiny, counterrevolution, bolshevism.

spasm, convulsion, throe, revulsion; earthquake, eruption, upheaval, cataclysm, explosion.

V. **revolutionize**, revolt, rebel, rise; remodel, recast.

Adj. **revolutionary**, catastrophic, cataclysmic, cataclysmal, insurgent, Red, insurrectionary, mutinous, rebellious; bolshevistic *or* bolshevik.

147. [Change of one thing for another] SUBSTITUTION.—*N.* **substitution**, commutation, supplanting.

substitute, scapegoat; alternative; makeshift, temporary expedient, shift, apology, stopgap; alternate; dummy, double; changeling; representative, deputy.

price, purchase money, consideration, equivalent.

V. **substitute**, put in the place of, change for, give place to; take the place of, supplant, supersede, replace, cut out [*colloq.*]; commute, redeem, compound for.

Adj. substituted, vicarious.

Adv. instead; by proxy; in place of, in lieu of.

148. [Double or mutual change] INTERCHANGE.—*N.* interchange, exchange; commutation, permutation; transposition, shuffle; alternation, reciprocity; swap [*colloq.*], barter, exchange; retaliation, reprisal; retort, requital, cross fire.

V. interchange, exchange, bandy, barter, transpose, swap [*colloq.*], reciprocate, commute; give and take, retaliate; retort; requite.

Adj. reciprocal, mutual; interchangeable.

international, interstate, interurban, interdenominational; interscholastic, intercollegiate.

Adv. in exchange, vice versa, conversely, by turns, turn about.

149. CHANGEABLENESS.—*N.* changeableness, mutability, inconstancy; versatility, mobility; instability, vacillation, irresolution, indecision; fluctuation, vicissitude; alternation, oscillation.

Comparisons: moon, kaleidoscope, chameleon, quicksilver, shifting sands, weath-ercock, vane, weathervane, harlequin, turncoat; wheel of fortune.

restlessness, fidgets, disquiet; disquietude, unrest; agitation, etc., 315.

V. fluctuate, vary, waver, flicker, flutter, shift, shuffle, shake, totter, tremble, vacillate, shift to and fro; oscillate, pulsate, vibrate; alternate.

Adj. changeable, changeful; changing, mutable, variable, kaleidoscopic; protean, versatile, mobile.

inconstant, unsteady, unstable, unfixed, unsettled; fluctuating, wavering, vibratory, restless, tremulous; erratic, fickle; mercurial, irresolute, indecisive; capricious, fitful, spasmodic; vagrant, wayward; desultory, transient, etc., 111.

150. STABILITY.—*N.* stability, immutability, unchangeableness, constancy; immobility; soundness, vitality, stabilization; stiffness, solidity; permanence, etc., 141; obstinacy, obduracy.

fixture, establishment; leopard's spots.

standpatter [*politics*].

V. be firm, stick fast; stand firm, remain firm; stand pat [*colloq.*]. establish, settle, fix, set, stabilize; retain, keep hold; make good, make sure; fasten, etc. (*join*), 43; perpetuate.

settle down; strike root, take root.

Adj. unchangeable, immutable; unaltered, unalterable, constant; permanent, persistent, persistent, invariable, undeviating; stable, durable, perennial; irretrievable, irrevocable, indissoluble, indestructible, imperishable, indelible.

fixed, steadfast, firm, solid; deep-rooted, ineradicable; fast, steady, confirmed, inveterate; immovable, rooted; settled, stereotyped, established, vested; obstinate, etc., 606; incontrovertible, valid.

stuck fast, transfixed, aground, stranded.

151. PRESENT EVENTS.—*N.* eventuality, event, occurrence, incident, affair, transaction, proceeding, fact; phenomenon.

circumstance, particular; happening, adventure; crisis, pass, emergency, contingency; concern, business.

consequence, issue, result, termination, conclusion.

affairs, matters; the world, life, things, doings; the times.

V. happen, occur; take place, come to pass, take effect; present itself; fall out, turn out, befall, betide; turn up, crop up, arrive; ensue, result; arise, start; take its course, pass off.

experience; meet with; fall to the lot of; be one's lot; find, encounter; undergo, pass through, go through, endure, bear, suffer, abide, stand, brook.

Adj. eventful, stirring, full of incident; memorable, momentous, signal; current, on foot, at issue, in question; incidental.

Adv. eventually, ultimately, finally; in the event of, in case.

152. FUTURE EVENTS.—*N.* destiny, fatality, fate, lot, doom, fortune; future, future state; future existence, hereafter· next world, world to come; life to come; prospect.

V. impend, hang over, threaten, loom, await, approach; foreordain, preordain; destine, predestine, doom.

Adj. impending, destined; coming, in store, to come, instant, at hand, near, imminent; in the wind, in prospect.

Adv. in time, in the long run; all in good time; eventually.

VIII. CAUSATION

153. CAUSE.—*N.* cause, origin, source, principle, element; prime mover, ultimate cause; author, producer, creator, determinant; mainspring, agent; leaven; groundwork, foundation, support.

causality, causation; origination; production, etc., 161.

spring, fountain, well; fountainhead, reservoir, wellspring; genesis; derivation; remote cause; influence.

pivot, hinge, turning point; heart, hub, focus.

reason, reason why; ground, occasion; final cause; undercurrents.

rudiment, egg, germ, nucleus, seed.

nest, cradle, nursery, birthplace, hotbed.

V. cause, originate, give rise to, occasion, sow the seeds of; bring to pass, bring about; produce; create, develop; set on foot, entail; found, institute.

procure, induce. draw down, superinduce, evoke, elicit, provoke.

contribute, conduce to, have a hand in, influence; determine, decide, turn the scale.

Adj. **causal,** original; primary, originative, generative, productive, creative; formative; radical; in embryo, embryonic.

Adv. from the beginning, in the first place; because, etc., 155.

154. EFFECT.—*N.* **effect,** consequence; aftergrowth, afterclap, aftermath; derivative; derivation; result; resultant; upshot, issue, outcome, conclusion; catastrophe, end; development, outgrowth; fruit, crop, harvest, product.

production, work, handiwork, fabric, performance; creature, creation; offspring, offshoot; first fruits.

V. **be the effect of,** be due to, be owing to; originate in *or* from; rise from, spring from, emanate from, come from, issue from, flow from, result from; depend upon, hang upon, hinge upon, turn upon.

Adj. **owing to;** resulting from; due to; caused by; derived from, evolved from; derivative; hereditary.

Adv. **consequently,** it follows that, as a consequence, in consequence; necessarily, eventually.

155. [Assignment of cause] ATTRIBUTION—*N.* **attribution,** theory, assignment, reference to, accounting for; imputation; derivation.

explanation, interpretation, reason why.

V. **attribute to,** ascribe to, impute to, refer to, lay to, trace to; blame; saddle; account for, derive from; theorize.

Adj. **attributed;** attributable, referable; due to; owing to.

Adv. **hence,** thence, therefore, for, since, on account of, because, owing to; forasmuch as; whence.

why? wherefore? whence? how comes it? how is it? how so?

156. [Absence of assignable cause] CHANCE¹.—*N.* **chance,** accident, fortune, hazard, luck, fluke [*cant*], casualty, hit; fate, lottery, tossup [*colloq.*]; throw of the dice; heads or tails, wheel of fortune.

probability, possibility, contingency, odds, run of luck; main chance.

gamble, speculation, gaming, game of chance.

V. **chance,** turn up; fall to one's lot; be one's fate; stumble on, light upon; blunder upon, hit, hit upon.

Adj. **casual,** fortuitous, accidental, chance, haphazard, random, incidental, unintentional, unpremeditated.

¹The word *chance* has two distinct meanings: the first, the absence of assignable *cause*, as above; and the second, the absence of *design*—for the latter see 621.

Adv. **by chance,** by accident; at random, casually; perchance, etc. (*possibly*), 470.

157. POWER.—*N.* **power;** potency, efficacy, puissance, might, energy, vigor, force; ascendancy, sway, almightiness, omnipotence; authority, weight, control; influence, predominance.

ability, competence, efficiency, efficacy; validity, cogency; vantage ground.

capability, capacity: faculty, quality, attribute, endowment, virtue, gift, property, qualification.

V. **empower;** give *or* confer power; invest, endue; endow, arm; strengthen, etc., 159.

electrify, magnetize, energize, galvanize.

Adj. **powerful,** puissant, potent, capable, able; cogent, valid, effective, effectual, efficient, efficacious, adequate, competent; predominant; mighty, omnipotent, almighty.

forcible, energetic; influential; productive.

electric, magnetic, galvanic, dynamic, potential.

Adv. by virtue of, by dint of.

158. IMPOTENCE.—*N.* **impotence;** inability, disability, incapacity, incapability; ineptitude; inefficiency, incompetence, disqualification; inefficacy, etc. (*inutility*), 645; failure, etc., 732.

helplessness, prostration, paralysis, collapse, exhaustion, senility, superannuation, decrepitude, imbecility, inanition.

mollycoddle, old woman, milksop, sissy [*colloq.*], mother's darling.

collapse, faint, swoon, drop; go by the board; end in smoke, etc. (*fail*), 732.

render powerless, disable, disarm, incapacitate, disqualify, unfit, invalidate, undermine, deaden, cramp, tie the hands; prostrate, paralyze, muzzle, cripple, maim, lame, throttle, strangle, silence, spike the guns; unhinge, unfit; put out of gear.

unman, unnerve, devitalize, attenuate, enervate.

shatter, exhaust, weaken, enfeeble.

Adj. **powerless,** impotent, helpless; incapable, incompetent, inefficient, ineffective, unfit, unfitted, unqualified, disqualified; crippled, disabled; senile, decrepit, superannuated; paralytic, paralyzed, nerveless, out of joint, out of gear; unnerved, unhinged; done up [*colloq.*], done for [*colloq.*], dead-beat [*colloq.*], exhausted, shattered, prostrate, demoralized, harmless; unarmed, weaponless, defenseless.

nugatory, null and void, inoperative, good for nothing, ineffectual, inadequate, inefficacious, etc. (*useless*), 645.

159. STRENGTH.—*N.* **strength;** power, etc., 157; energy, vigor, force; main (*or* physical, brute) force; spring, elasticity.

vitality, virility, lustihood, stamina, nerve, muscle, sinews, physique; grit.

athletics, athleticism; gymnastics, calisthenics.

athlete, gymnast, acrobat; Atlas, Hercules.

strengthening, invigoration, refreshment.

Science of forces: dynamics, statics.

V. strengthen, invigorate, brace, nerve, fortify, buttress, sustain, harden, steel; gird, set up, gird up one's loins; recruit, set on one's legs [*colloq.*]; vivify; refresh, reinforce, restore.

Adj. strong, mighty, vigorous, forcible; hard, stout, robust, sound, sturdy, husky [*colloq.*], hardy, powerful, potent, puissant.

resistless, irresistible, invincible, impregnable, unconquerable, indomitable, incontestable, valid; overpowering, overwhelming, all-powerful.

able-bodied; athletic, Herculean, muscular, brawny, wiry, well knit, sinewy, strapping, stalwart, lusty.

manly, manful; masculine, male, virile, in the prime of manhood.

Adv. strongly, by force, by main force.

160. WEAKNESS.—*N.* weakness, debility, relaxation, languor, enervation; impotence, etc., 158; infirmity, effeminacy; fragility; inactivity, etc., 683.

anemia, bloodlessness, deficiency of blood, poverty of blood.

loss of strength, delicacy; decrepitude; invalidism.

V. be weak; drop, crumble, give way; totter, dodder; tremble, shake; halt, limp; fade, languish, decline, flag, fail.

weaken, enfeeble, debilitate, shake, relax, sap, enervate, unnerve; cripple, unman; cramp, reduce, sprain, strain, dilute, impoverish.

Adj. weak, faint, feeble, infirm; impotent; relaxed, unnerved, unstrung, limp, strengthless, powerless; weakly, sickly, flaccid.

soft, effeminate, womanish.

frail, fragile; flimsy, sleazy, papery, unsubstantial, gimcrack, rickety, jerry-built; broken, decrepit, lame, shattered, shaken, crazy, shaky, tumbledown.

unsound, spent, effete; decayed, rotten, worn, seedy, languishing, wasted, laid low, the worse for wear; on its last legs.

161. [Power in operation] PRODUCTION.—*N.* production, creation, construction, formation, fabrication, manufacture; building, architecture, erection; organization; establishment; workmanship, performance; achievement; flowering, efflorescence, fruition; genesis, birth; evolution, development, growth; breeding; propagation.

publication; works, opus (*pl.* opera) [L.]; authorship.

structure, building, edifice, fabric, erection, pile.

V. **produce,** perform, operate, do, make, form, construct, fabricate, frame, contrive, manufacture; build, raise, rear, erect; establish, constitute, compose, evolve, coin, organize, institute; achieve, accomplish.

flower, blossom, bear fruit, bear, bring forth, give birth to, usher into the world; generate, propagate, engender, create; breed, develop, bring up.

induce, superinduce; cause, etc., 153.

Adj. **productive;** prolific, etc., 168; creative, formative, constructive; generative; teeming.

162. [Nonproduction] DESTRUCTION.—*N.* **destruction;** waste, dissolution, breaking up, disruption; disorganization; demolition, overthrow, subversion, suppression; abolition, etc., 756; sacrifice; ravage, devastation, incendiarism; revolution, etc., 146; road to ruin; sabotage.

fall, downfall, ruin, perdition; breakdown, breakup; cave-in [*colloq.*]; wreck, shipwreck, cataclysm.

extinction, extermination, annihilation; doom, crack of doom.

V. **perish,** fall, fall to the ground, tumble, topple; fall to pieces, break up, crumble, go to wrack and ruin; go by the board, be all over with, go to pieces, totter to its fall.

destroy, do (*or* make) away with, waste; nullify, annul, sacrifice, demolish, overturn, overthrow, overwhelm; upset, subvert, put an end to; do for [*colloq.*], undo, break down, cut down, pull down, dismantle, mow down, blow down; suppress, quash, put down, crush, blot out, efface, obliterate, cancel, erase, strike out, expunge, delete; dispel, dissipate, dissolve; consume.

smash, crash, quell, squash [*colloq.*], shatter, shiver, batter; tear (*or* pull, crush) to pieces; ruin, fell; sink, swamp, scuttle, wreck, shipwreck, engulf, submerged; lay in ruins, raze, level; deal destruction, lay waste, ravage, gut; devour, desolate, devastate, blast, exterminate, eradicate, annihilate.

Adj. **destructive,** subversive, cataclysmic, ruinous, incendiary, suicidal, deadly, all-destroying, all-devouring.

163. REPRODUCTION.—*N.* **reproduction,** renovation; restoration, etc., 660; renewal, revival, regeneration, revivification; apotheosis; resuscitation, reanimation, resurrection, reappearance.

V. **reproduce,** restore, etc., 660; revive, renovate, renew, repeat, regenerate, revivify, resuscitate, reanimate, refashion, multiply.

Adj. **reproductive,** resurgent, reappearing; renascent; Hydra-headed.

164. PRODUCER.—*N.* **producer,** originator, inventor, author, founder, generator, mover, architect, grower, raiser, introducer, creator; maker, etc. (*agent*), 690; prime mover.

165. DESTROYER.—*N.* **destroyer**, wrecker, annihilator; cankerworm, etc. (*bane*), 663; assassin, etc. (*killer*), 361; executioner, etc. (*punish*), 975; iconoclast, vandal, nihilist.

166. PATERNITY.—*N.* **paternity**, fathership, fatherhood; parentage.

parent, father, sire, dad [*colloq.*], papa, pater [*colloq.*], daddy [*colloq.*], paterfamilias; ancestor.

motherhood, maternity, mother, dam, mamma, mammy, mam [*colloq.*], matriarch, materfamilias.

stem, trunk, tree, stock, pedigree, house, lineage, line, family, race, tribe, clan; genealogy, family tree, descent, extraction, birth, ancestry; forefathers, forebears.

Adj. **parental**; paternal; maternal; ancestral, linear, patriarchal; racial.

167. POSTERITY.—*N.* **posterity**, progeny, breed, issue, offspring, brood, family, children, heirs; rising generation.

descendant, scion, offshoot, chip of the old block, heir, heiress, heir apparent, heir presumptive.

child, son, daughter, baby, kid [*colloq.*], imp, brat, cherub, tot, innocent, urchin, chit [*colloq.*]; infant, etc., 129.

lineage, line, straight descent, heredity, sonship, primogeniture.

Adj. **hereditary**, lineal.

filial, sonlike, daughterly, dutiful.

168. PRODUCTIVENESS.—*N.* **productiveness**, fecundity, fertility, luxuriance; multiplication, propagation, fructification.

V. **fructify**; generate, impregnate; teem, spawn, multiply; produce, etc., 161; conceive.

Adj. **productive**, prolific, copious; teeming, fertile, fruitful, plenteous, luxuriant; generative, life-giving; originative.

169. UNPRODUCTIVENESS.—*N.* **unproductiveness**, infertility, sterility, barrenness, unfruitfulness; unprofitableness, etc. (*inutility*), 645.

waste, desert, Sahara, wild, wilderness.

V. **be unproductive**; hang fire, flash in the pan, come to nothing.

Adj. **unproductive**, barren, unfertile, arid, sterile, unfruitful, fruitless, useless, fallow; unprofitable, etc. (*useless*), 645.

170. AGENCY.—*N.* **agency**, operation, force, function, office, maintenance, exercise, work, swing, play.

causation, impelling force; mediation, intervention, instrumentality; influence, etc., 175; action, etc. (*voluntary*), 680; method, procedure.

V. **operate,** work; act, perform, play, support, sustain, maintain, take effect, quicken, strike; have play, have free play; bring to bear upon.

Adj. **operative,** efficient, efficacious, practical, effectual; at work, on foot; acting, in operation, in force, in action.

171. ENERGY.—*N.* **energy,** force; intensity, vigor, strength, backbone [*colloq.*], vim [*colloq.*], mettle, pep [*slang*], fire, go [*colloq.*], high pressure; human dynamo.

activity, agitation, effervescence, ferment, fermentation, ebullition, stir, bustle; voluntary, energy, etc., 682; mental energy, etc., 604; resolution, stimulation; exertion, etc. (*effort*), 686.

V. **give energy,** energize, stimulate, strengthen, invigorate, kindle, excite, inflame, exert; sharpen, intensify.

Adj. **energetic,** strong, forcible, active, strenuous, brisk, forceful, mettlesome, enterprising, go-ahead [*colloq.*]; potent, etc. (*powerful*), 157; intense, keen, sharp, acute, incisive, trenchant.

poignant, virulent, caustic, corrosive, mordant; harsh, stringent, drastic.

172. INERTNESS.—*N.* **inertness,** inertia, inactivity, torpor, languor, quiescence, inaction, passivity, stagnation.

mental inertness; sloth; inexcitability, etc., 826; irresolution, indecision, vacillation; obstinacy, etc., 606.

V. **be inert,** hang fire, be inactive; smolder.

Adj. **inert,** inactive, passive; torpid, etc., 683; sluggish, logy, stagnant, dull, heavy, slack, tame, slow, lifeless, dead.

latent, dormant, smoldering, unexerted.

Adv. in suspense, in abeyance.

173. VIOLENCE.—*N.* **violence,** vehemence, might, impetuosity, boisterousness, disorder, effervescence, ebullition; turbulence, bluster; uproar, riot, row [*colloq.*], rumpus [*colloq.*].

ferocity, rage, fury, exasperation; malignity; severity, etc., 739; force, brute force; outrage.

fit, paroxysm, spasm, convulsion, throe; hysterics, passion, etc., 825.

outbreak, outburst, discharge, volley, explosion, blast, detonation, eruption, volcano, earthquake, thunderstorm.

fury, berserk, dragon, demon, tiger, wild beast; fire-eater [*colloq.*], etc. (*blusterer*), 887.

V. **be violent;** ferment, effervesce; rampage; run wild, run amuck, rage, roar, riot, storm; boil, boil over; fume, foam, ride roughshod, out-Herod Herod.

explode, go off, detonate, fulminate, let off, let fly, discharge, thunder, blow up, flash, flare, burst.

render violent; stir up, quicken, excite, incite, urge, lash, stimulate; irritate, inflame, kindle, foment, exasperate, convulse, infuriate, madden, lash into fury.

Adj. violent, vehement, acute, sharp; rough, tough [*colloq.*], rude, bluff, brusque, abrupt, boisterous, wild, impetuous, rampant; savage, fierce, ferocious.

turbulent, tumultuous; disorderly, raging, troublous, riotous, obstreperous, uproarious; frenzied, mad, insane; desperate, rash; infuriate, furious, frantic, outrageous; stormy, etc. (*wind*), 349.

fiery, flaming, scorching, hot, red-hot.

unbridled, unruly; headstrong, ungovernable, uncontrollable, irrepressible.

spasmodic, convulsive, explosive; detonating; volcanic, meteoric.

Adv. violently, amain; by storm, by force, by main force, with might and main, at one fell swoop; in desperation, with a vengeance.

174. MODERATION.—*N.* moderation; lenity, etc., 740; temperateness, temperance, gentleness, mildness, quiet, sobriety; mental calmness, composure, etc. (*inexcitability*), 826.

alleviation, assuagement, mitigation, relaxation, tranquilization, pacification.

moderator; sedative, lenitive, palliative; opiate, balm.

V. moderate, slacken, soften, mitigate, palliate, alleviate, allay, assuage, appease, temper, mollify, lull, soothe, compose, still, calm, cool, quiet, tranquilize, hush, quell, sober, pacify, smooth, deaden, smother; blunt, subdue, chasten; weaken, etc., 160; lessen, decrease; check, tame, curb, restrain.

Adj. moderate, gentle, mild; cool, sober, temperate, reasonable, lenient, measured; calm, unruffled, quiet, tranquil, still, halcyon; peaceful, peaceable, pacific.

Adv. in moderation, within bounds.

175. [Indirect Power] INFLUENCE.—*N.* influence; importance, etc., 642; weight, pressure, pull [*colloq. or slang*]; interest; preponderance, prevalence, sway; predominance, upper hand, ascendancy; dominance, reign; control, domination, hold; authority, power, potency, capability, spell, magic, magnetism.

footing; purchase, support; play, leverage, vantage ground, advantage.

patronage, protection, auspices; patron, etc. (*auxiliary*), 711; tower of strength.

V. be influential, carry weight, sway, bias, actuate, weight, tell; magnetize, work upon; take root, take hold; pervade, run through; be rife.

dominate, subject; predominate, outweigh; override, overbear; have or gain the upper hand, prevail.

lead, control, rule, manage, master, get control of, make one's influence felt; take the lead, pull the strings; turn the scale; set the fashion.

Adj. influential, effective, potent; important, etc., 642; weighty; prevalent, rife, rampant; dominant, predominant, authoritative, recognized.

Adv. with telling effect, with authority.

176. TENDENCY.—*N.* tendency, aptness, aptitude, proneness, proclivity, bent, turn, tone, bias, set, warp, leaning (*with* to or toward), predisposition, inclination, liability, propensity, susceptibility; quality, nature, temperament; idiosyncrasy; cast, vein, grain, humor, mood, trend, drift.

V. tend, contribute, conduce, lead, influence, dispose, incline, verge, bend to, warp, turn, work toward, gravitate toward, trend; affect; carry, redound to, bid fair to; promote, etc. (*aid*), 707.

Adj. tending; conducive, working toward, in a fair way to, likely to, calculated to; liable, etc., 177; subservient, instrumental, useful; subsidiary, accessory.

177. LIABILITY.—*N.* liability, susceptibility; possibility, contingency.

V. be liable, incur, lay oneself open to, be subjected to, run the chance, stand a chance; lie under, expose oneself to, open a door to.

Adj. liable, subject, in danger, open to, exposed to; answerable, responsible, accountable, amenable; apt to; dependent on.

contingent, incidental, possible, on the cards, within range of, at the mercy of.

178. CONCURRENCE.—*N.* concurrence, co-operation, collaboration; conformity, agreement, accord; alliance; complicity, collusion, partnership, union.

V. concur, conduce, conspire, contribute; agree, unite, harmonize, combine; hang or pull together, co-operate; keep pace with, run parallel.

Adj. concurrent, conformable, joint, co-operative, concordant, harmonious, in alliance with, of one mind, at one with.

179. COUNTERACTION.—*N.* counteraction, opposition; contrariety, contradiction; antagonism, polarity; clashing, collision, interference, resistance, friction; reaction, recoil; counterblast, neutralization, check, hindrance; repression, restraint.

V. counteract, clash, cross, interfere with, conflict with; contravene; jostle; militate against, stultify, antagonize, frustrate, oppose, overcome, overpower, withstand, resist, impede, hinder, repress, restrain; recoil, react.

neutralize, offset, undo, cancel; counterpoise, counterbalance.
Adj. antagonistic, conflicting, reactionary; contrary, etc., 14.
Adv. although, notwithstanding; in spite of; against.

CLASS II

Words Relating To SPACE

I. SPACE IN GENERAL

180. [Indefinite space] SPACE.—*N.* space, extension, extent, proportions, expanse, stretch; room, accommodation, capacity; scope, compass, range, latitude, field; sweep, play, swing; spread, expansion.

elbowroom, leeway, seaway, headway; margin; sphere, arena.

open space, free space, void, waste, desert, wild, wilderness; moor, down, downs, upland, moorland; prairie, steppe, llano, campagna.

unlimited space; heavens, ether, infinity; world, wide world.

Adj. spacious, roomy, extensive, extended, expansive, capacious, ample; widespread, vast, world-wide, wide, far-flung, boundless, limitless, endless, infinite; shoreless, trackless, pathless.

Adv. extensively; by and large; everywhere, far and near (*or* wide), here, there, and everywhere; from pole to pole, from the four corners of the earth, from all points of the compass; to the four winds, to the uttermost parts of the earth.

181. [Definite space] REGION.—*N.* region, sphere, ground, soil, area, realm, hemisphere, quarter, orb, circuit, circle; pale, etc. (*limit*), 233; tract, clearing; domain.

county, shire, canton, province, department, parish, diocese, township, commune, ward, bailiwick; principality, duchy, palatinate, archduchy, dukedom, dominion, colony, commonwealth, territory, country; fatherland, motherland; kingdom, empire.

precinct, arena, district, beat; patch, plot, inclosure, close, enclave, field, paddock, etc. (*inclosure*), 232; street.

clime, climate, zone, meridian, latitude.

Adj. territorial, provincial, regional, insular; local, parochial.

182. [Limited space] PLACE.—*N.* place, spot, whereabouts, point; niche, nook, corner, hole, pigeonhole, etc. (*receptacle*), 191; compartment; premises, courtyard, square, place, piazza, plaza, forum; hamlet, village, etc. (*abode*), 189; pen, etc. (*inclosure*), 232; location, site, locality, situation.

Adv. somewhere, in some place, here and there, in various places.

183. SITUATION.—*N.* situation, position, locality, latitude and longitude; footing, status, standing; standpoint; stage; aspect, attitude, posture, pose.

place, site; station, post, seat, whereabouts; environment, ground; bearings, direction, spot, etc. (*limited space*), 182.

topography, geography; map, plan, chart.

V. be situated, be situate, be located; lie; have its seat in.

Adj. situate, situated; local, topical, topographical.

Adv. hereabouts, thereabouts, whereabouts; in place, here, there.

184. LOCATION.—*N.* location, situation; lodgment; stowage; packing, lading; establishment, settlement, installation; insertion, etc., 300.

anchorage, roadstead, mooring.

settlement, plantation, colony; habitation, etc. (*abode*), 189.

domestication; colonization; naturalization.

V. place, situate, locate, localize, put, lay, set, seat; station, park (as, *an automobile*), lodge, quarter, post, install; house, stow, pack; load, lade; establish, fix, root; graft; plant, etc. (*insert*), 300; deposit, store, store away.

billet on, quarter upon, saddle with.

settle, domesticate, colonize, found, people; take root, strike root; anchor, cast anchor, moor, tether, picket; settle down; take up one's abode, establish *or* locate oneself; keep house; squat, burrow, get a footing; bivouac, encamp, pitch one's tent; inhabit, etc., 186.

Adj. placed; situate, ensconced, imbedded, rooted; moored, at anchor.

185. DISPLACEMENT.—*N.* displacement, misplacement, dislocation, derangement, transposition.

ejection, expulsion, eviction; exile, banishment, ostracism.

removal, etc. (*transference*), 270; transshipment, moving, shift.

V. displace, dislodge, disestablish; misplace, unseat, disturb; set aside, remove, take away, cart away, draft off; exile, etc. (*seclude*), 893.

unload, empty, etc. (*eject*), 297; transfer, etc., 270; dispel.

vacate, depart, evacuate.

Adj. displaced; unplaced, unhoused, unsettled; houseless, homeless, out of place; out of a situation.

186. PRESENCE.—*N.* presence, attendance; occupancy, occupation; ubiquity, omnipresence.

permeation, pervasion; diffusion.

bystander, etc. (*spectator*), 444.

V. be present, make one of; look on, attend, remain; find *or* present oneself; lie, stand.

inhabit, occupy, dwell, reside; stay, sojourn; live, abide; lodge, tenant; people.

frequent, resort to, haunt; revisit.

pervade, permeate; overspread; fill, run through.

Adj. present; situate; moored, at anchor; resident, domiciled; ubiquitous, omnipresent.

peopled, inhabited, populous.

Adv. here, there, everywhere; aboard, on board, at home, afield; on the spot; in presence of, before.

187. ABSENCE.—*N.* absence, nonresidence, absenteeism; nonattendance, cut [*colloq.*]; alibi.

emptiness; void, vacuum, vacancy.

interval, hiatus, interruption; interregnum.

truant, absentee.

V. be absent; keep away, play truant, absent oneself, stay away, hold aloof.

withdraw, retreat, retire; go away.

Adj. absent, not present, away, nonresident, gone, from home; missing; lost; wanting; omitted.

empty, void; vacant, vacuous, blank; untenanted, unoccupied, uninhabited, tenantless; desert, deserted, uninhabitable.

Adv. without, minus, nowhere; elsewhere; in default of; sans.

188. INHABITANT.—*N.* inhabitant; resident, dweller, indweller, addressee, occupier, occupant, householder; inmate; tenant, incumbent; settler, squatter, backwoodsman, planter, habitant, colonist; islander; denizen, citizen; burgher, townsman, burgess; villager; cottager, cotter; boarder, lodger.

native, aborigine, aboriginal.

people, etc. (*mankind*), 372; population; colony, settlement; household.

V. inhabit, dwell, etc., 186.

Adj. indigenous, native, domestic; domiciled; naturalized; vernacular.

189. HABITATION.—*N.* habitation, abode, dwelling, lodging, domicile, residence, address, berth, housing, quarters, headquarters.

home, fatherland, motherland, country; homestead, hearth, chimney corner; roof, household, housing, native soil, native land.

county, parish, etc. (*region*), 181.

retreat, haunt, habitat, resort; nest, arbor, bower, grotto; lair, den, cave, hole, hiding place, cell, sanctum sanctorum, eyrie, rookery, hive; covert, perch, roost.

anchorage, roadstead, roads; dock, basin, wharf, quay, port, harbor.

camp, bivouac, encampment, cantonment, barracks, quarters; tent, wigwam, tepee; igloo.

farm, farmhouse, grange.

cot, cabin, hut, hovel; shanty, dugout, chalet, log cabin, log house; shack [*colloq*], shed, booth, stall, pen, fold; stable, barn; kennel, sty, cote, dovecote, coop, hutch; cowhouse, cowshed.

house, mansion, place, villa, cottage, lodge, hermitage, rotunda, tower, château, castle, pavilion, hotel, court, manor house, hall, palace; kiosk, bungalow, country seat; apartment (or brownstone, duplex, frame, shingle, flat, tenement) house; three-decker; building, buildings.

hamlet, village, dorp [Dutch], rancho [Sp. Amer.].

town, borough, city, capital, metropolis; suburb; province, country; county town, county seat.

street, place, terrace, parade, esplanade, boardwalk, embankment, road, row, lane, alley, court, quadrangle, close, yard, passage.

square, polygon, circus, crescent, block, arcade, colonnade, cloister; market place.

assembly room, auditorium, concert hall, armory, gymnasium; cathedral, church, chapel, meetinghouse, etc. (*temple*), 1000; parliament, etc. (*council*), 696.

inn, hotel, tavern, caravansary, alehouse, saloon, club, clubhouse; grill room, chophouse, coffeehouse, eating house; canteen, restaurant, buffet, café, cabaret.

sanatorium, health resort, sanitarium; spa, watering place.

V. inhabit, etc., 186; take up one's abode, etc. (*locate oneself*), 184.

Adj. urban, metropolitan; cosmopolitan; suburban.

provincial, rural, rustic, country, countrified.

190. [Things contained] CONTENTS.—*N.* contents; cargo, lading, freight, shipment, load, bale, burden; cartload, shipload; stuffing.

V. load, lade, ship, pile, fill, stuff.

191. RECEPTACLE.—*N.* receptacle, container; inclosure, etc., 232; recipient, receiver; compartment, cell; hole, corner, niche, recess, nook; crypt; stall; pigeonhole; mouth.

stomach, paunch, belly, crop, craw, maw.

bag, sack, wallet, pocket, pouch; purse; knapsack, haversack, satchel, reticule; saddlebags; portfolio; valise, grip [*colloq*.], suitcase, handbag, schoolbag, brief case, traveling bag, Gladstone bag.

case, chest, box, coffer, caddy, casket; reliquary, shrine; caisson; desk, bureau; trunk, portmanteau, bandbox.

vessel, utensil; vase, canister, jar; basket, pannier, hamper; crate; creel; cradle, bassinet.

For liquids: cistern, reservoir; vat, caldron, barrel, cask, keg, tun, butt, firkin, tub; bottle, jar, decanter, ewer, carafe, canteen, flagon; demijohn; flask, vial, phial; cruet, caster; urn, percolator, coffeepot, teapot, samovar; bucket, pail; pot, tankard, jug, pitcher, mug, porringer; receiver, retort, alembic, crucible; can, kettle; bowl, basin; punch bowl, cup, goblet, beaker, chalice, tumbler, glass.

plate, platter, dish, tray, waiter, salver.

ladle, dipper; shovel, trowel, spatula.

cupboard, closet; locker, bin; buffet, sideboard; drawer, chest of drawers, chiffonier; till, safe; bookcase, cabinet.

chamber, apartment, room, cabin; office, court, hall, suite of rooms, apartment, flat, tenement; parlor, living (or sitting, drawing, reception) room; best room [*colloq*.]; boudoir; sanctum; bedroom, dormitory; refectory, dining room; nursery, schoolroom; library, study; studio; smoking room, den.

attic, loft, garret; cellar, vault, hold, cockpit; cubbyhole; basement, kitchen, pantry, scullery; storeroom, lumber room; dairy, laundry; garage; hangar; outhouse, penthouse; lean-to, shed.

portico, porch, stoop, veranda, piazza.

bower, arbor, summerhouse; grotto; conservatory, greenhouse.

II. DIMENSIONS

192. SIZE.—*N.* size, dimensions, proportions; magnitude, bulk, volume; largeness, greatness; expanse, amplitude, mass; capacity; tonnage; cordage; caliber.

lump, block, mass; clod, mountain, mound; heap, etc. (*assemblage*), 72.

corpulence, obesity, plumpness.

immensity, hugeness, monstrosity, enormity.

giant, Titan, Hercules, Gargantua; monster, mammoth, whale, behemoth, leviathan, elephant, jumbo [*colloq.*]; colossus.

V. be large, become large, etc. (*expand*), 194.

Adj. large, big, great, considerable, bulky, voluminous, ample, massive; capacious, comprehensive, spacious; mighty, towering.

stout, corpulent, fat, plump, chubby; portly, burly, brawny, fleshy.

unwieldy, hulky, hulking, lumpish, overgrown; puffy, swollen, bloated.

huge, immense, enormous, titanic, mighty; vast; stupendous; monster, monstrous; gigantic; elephantine, mammoth; giant, colossal, cyclopean, Gargantuan.

193. LITTLENESS.—*N.* littleness, smallness; epitome; microcosm; vanishing point.

dwarf, pygmy, midget; Lilliputian, elf; doll, puppet, manikin; Tom Thumb.

mite, insect, arthropod, ephemerid, ephemera, bug [*pop.*], larva.
atom, monad, animalcule, animalculum (*pl.* animalcula), molecule, microbe, germ, micro-organism, bacterium (*pl.* bacteria), amoeba.

particle, speck, dot, mote; scrap; spark; scintilla; fragment, fraction; grain, powder, dust; minutiæ, etc. (*unimportance*), 643.

V. belittle, lie in a nutshell; become small, decrease; contract, etc., 195.

Adj. little, small, minute, diminutive, microscopic; inconsiderable, petty; limited, cramped; puny, runty, tiny, wee [*colloq.*], elfin, miniature, pocket; undersized, stunted, dwarf, dwarfed, dwarfish, pygmy; Lilliputian; invisible, infinitesimal, homeopathic.

Adv. in a small compass, in a nutshell; on a small scale.

194. EXPANSION.—*N.* expansion, dilation; growth, increase, enlargement, amplification; extension, augmentation, aggrandizement; spread, increment, development, swell, dilatation; obesity, corpulence; dropsy, swelling, distension, puffiness, inflation.

V. enlarge, expand, widen, extend, grow, increase, swell, fill out; dilate, stretch, spread; wax; bud, shoot, sprout, germinate, put forth, open, burst forth; outgrow; overrun.

spread, augment, aggrandize; distend, develop, amplify, spread out, widen, magnify; inflate, blow up; stuff, fatten, pad, cram, bloat; exaggerate.

Adj. **expanded,** larger; swollen, expansive, widespread, overgrown, exaggerated, bloated, fat, tumid, dropsical; corpulent, obese; puffy, distend, bulbous; full-blown, full-grown; big, etc., 192.

195. CONTRACTION.—*N.* **contraction,** reduction, diminution; decrease, etc., 36; lessening, shrinking; atrophy; emaciation, attenuation.

compression, condensation, constraint, compactness; compendium, abstract, epitome; strangulation; astringency.

V. **decrease,** lessen, grow less, dwindle, shrink, contract, narrow, shrivel, collapse, wither, fall away, waste, wane, ebb.

diminish, boil down; deflate, exhaust, empty; constrict, condense, compress, squeeze, crush; pinch, tighten, strangle; cramp; dwarf; shorten, etc., 201; circumscribe, limit, bound, confine.

pare, reduce; attenuate; rub down, scrape, file, grind, chip, shave, shear.

Adj. **contracting,** astringent; shrunk, shrunken, contracted; strangulated; wizened; stunted; waning; compact.

196. DISTANCE.—*N.* **distance,** remoteness; space, etc., 180; far cry to; elongation; drift, offing, background; remote region; reach, span.

outpost, outskirt; horizon, skyline; foreign parts, antipodes.

V. **be distant;** extend to, stretch to, reach to, spread to, stretch away to; range, outreach.

Adj. **distant,** far, far off, far away, remote; telescopic; yon, yonder; ulterior; transatlantic, transalpine; ultramundane, antipodean; inaccessible, out-of-the-way; unapproachable.

Adv. **far off,** far away, afar, afar off; away; beyond range, aloof; wide of, clear of; abroad, yonder, farther, further, beyond; far and wide, from pole to pole; out of range, out of hearing.

apart, asunder; at arm's length.

197. NEARNESS.—*N.* **nearness,** proximity, propinquity; vicinity, vicinage, neighborhood, contiguity, etc., 199.

short distance, short cut; earshot, close quarters, range, stone's throw; gunshot, hair's breadth, span.

purlieus, neighborhood, vicinage, environs, suburbs, confines.

bystander, spectator; neighbor.

approach, approximation, access; convergence, meeting.

V. **be near,** adjoin, abut, neighbor, trench on; border upon, verge upon; approximate; stand by, hang about; cling to, clasp, hug; huddle; hover over.

bring *or* draw near; converge, etc., 290; crowd, pack, huddle.

Adj. near, nigh, close (*or* near) at hand, close, neighboring, bordering upon, contiguous, adjacent, adjoining; proximate, approximate; at hand, handy; intimate.

Adv. near, nigh, hard by, close to, close upon; hard upon; at the point of; next door to; within reach (*or* call, hearing, earshot, range); on the verge of; in sight of; at close quarters; beside, alongside, side by side; in juxtaposition; at the heels of.

about; thereabouts; roughly, in round numbers; approximately, as good as, well-nigh.

198. INTERVAL.—*N.* interval, space; separation, division; hiatus, cæsura; interruption; interregnum; interstice.

parenthesis; void, vacuum; incompleteness, deficiency.

cleft, break, gap, opening; hole, puncture; chasm, mesh, crevice, chink, cranny, crack, slit, fissure, rift, fault, flaw, breach, fracture, rent, gash, cut.

gorge, defile, pass, ravine, canyon, crevasse; abyss, abysm; gulf; inlet, strait; furrow, etc., 259; gully, gulch, notch.

V. gape, yawn; separate, etc., 44.

199. CONTACT.—*N.* contact, contiguity, contiguousness, proximity, apposition, abuttal, abutment, juxtaposition, touching, meeting; conjunction, adhesion, etc., 46.

borderland; frontier, etc. (*limit*), 233.

V. adjoin, join, abut on, neighbor, border, march with; graze, touch, meet; coincide; coexist; adhere, etc., 46.

Adj. contiguous, touching, in contact, conterminous, end to end; close, etc. (*near*), 197.

200. [Linear Dimensions] LENGTH.—*N.* length, longitude, extent, span; mileage.

line, bar, rule, stripe, streak.

lengthening, prolongation, production, protraction; tension, extension.

Measures of length: line, nail, inch, hand, palm, foot, cubit, yard, ell, fathom, rood, pole, furlong, mile, knot, league; chain; meter, kilometer, centimeter, etc. pedometer, odometer, odograph, viameter, log [*naut.*], speedometer, telemeter, scale.

V. be long, stretch out, sprawl; extend to, reach to, stretch to.

lengthen, let out, extend, elongate; stretch; prolong, protract; draw out, spin out.

Adj. long, elongate, lengthy, outstretched, extended; lengthened, interminable.

linear, lineal; longitudinal.

lanky, lank, slab-sided [*slang*], rangy; tall; long-limbed.

Adv. lengthwise, at length, longitudinally, along; tandem; in a line; from end to end, from stem to stern, from head to foot, from top to toe; fore and aft; over all.

201. SHORTNESS.—*N.* **shortness,** brevity, littleness, etc., 193; a span.

abridgment, shortening, abbreviation, retrenchment, curtailment, epitomization, condensation; reduction, etc. (*contraction*), 195; epitome, etc. (*compendium*), 596.

elision, ellipsis; conciseness, brevity.

V. **shorten,** curtail, retrench, abridge, abbreviate; take in, reduce; compress, contract; epitomize, abstract, summarize, condense; cut, pare down, clip, dock, lop, prune, shear, shave, mow, crop, stunt; nip, check the growth of, foreshorten [*drawing*].

Adj. **short,** brief, curt; compendious, compact; stubby, pudgy, squatty; stumpy [*colloq.*], thickset, chunky, scrub, stocky, squat, dumpy; pug, turned up; little, etc., 193; concise, etc., 572; summary.

202. BREADTH, THICKNESS.—*N.* **breadth,** width, latitude, amplitude.

diameter, bore, caliber; radius.

thickness; corpulence, etc. (*size*), 192; expansion, dilatation.

V. **expand,** etc., 194; thicken, widen.

Adj. **broad,** wide, ample, extended, outspread, outstretched.

thick, dumpy, squat, thickset, stubby, etc., 201.

203. NARROWNESS, THINNESS.—*N.* **narrowness,** slenderness; closeness.

line; hair's breadth.

thinness, tenuity; leanness, lankiness, emaciation.

shaving; strip, etc. (*filament*), 205; thread, skeleton, shadow, scrag, mere skin and bone.

narrowing, tapering; contraction, etc., 195.

V. **narrow,** taper; contract, etc., 195.

Adj. **narrow,** close; slender, thin, fine, delicate, threadlike, finespun, taper, slim; scant, scanty, spare; contracted.

lean, emaciated, skinny, scrawny, meager, gaunt, rawboned, lank, lanky, weedy [*colloq.*]; starved, starveling; attenuated, shriveled, pinched, spindle-legged, spindle-shanked, spindling; worn to a shadow; hatchet-faced; lantern-jawed.

204. LAYER.—*N.* **layer,** stratum, course, bed, coping, substratum, floor, stage, story, tier.

leaf, sheet, flake, scale, coat, peel, membrane, film, slice, shaving, wafer.

stratification, lamination, foliation; scaliness.

V. **slice,** shave, pare, peel.

plate, coat, veneer; cover, etc., 223.

Adj. scaly, filmy, membranous, flaky, foliated, stratified.

205. FILAMENT.—*N.* filament, line; fiber, vein, hair, cobweb, capillary, strand, tendril, gossamer.

thread, yarn, packthread, cotton.

string, twine, twist, cord, rope, tape, ribbon, wire.

strip, shred, slip, band, fillet, lath, splinter.

Adj. fibrous, threadlike, wiry, stringy, ropy; capillary, wire-drawn; hairy, etc. (*rough*), 256.

206. HEIGHT.—*N.* height, altitude, elevation, eminence, pitch; loftiness, sublimity.

tallness, stature; prominence, etc., 250; apex, zenith, culmination.

colossus, etc. (*size*), 192; giant.

height, mount, mountain, hill; headland, foreland, promontory; ridge, dune, rising ground, down, uplands, highlands; knoll, hummock, hillock, mound; bluff, cliff, peak.

tower, pillar, column, obelisk, monument, belfry, steeple, spire, minaret, campanile, turret, dome, cupola; pyramid, pagoda.

pole, pikestaff, Maypole, flagstaff; mast, mainmast, topmast.

high water; high (*or* flood, spring) tide.

V. tower, soar, hover; cap, culminate; overhang, surmount, rise above, command, overtop, rise, ascend.

heighten, uprear, uplift, upraise, elevate.

Adj. high, elevated, eminent, exalted, lofty, sublime; tall, gigantic, big, colossal; towering, beetling, soaring, elevated; higher, superior, upper, supernal; highest, etc. (*topmost*), 210.

lanky, etc. (*thin*), 203.

upland, hilly, mountainous, alpine, heaven-kissing, cloud-capped.

overhanging, impending, incumbent, overlying; superimposed.

Adv. on high, high up, aloft, up, above, overhead; in the clouds.

207. LOWNESS.—*N.* lowness, levelness, flatness; debasement, prostration; depression, hollow; lowlands.

basement, cellar, vault, crypt, cavern; hold; base, etc., 211.

low water, low (*or* ebb, neap) tide.

V. be low, lie low, underlie; crouch, wallow, grovel; lower, etc. (*depress*), 308.

Adj. low, low-lying, level; flat; crouched, squat, prostrate, depressed, debased.

lower, inferior, under, nether.

lowest, nethermost, lowermost.

Adv. under, beneath, underneath, below, down, downward; underfoot, underground; downstairs, belowstairs; at a low ebb; below par.

208. DEPTH.—*N.* depth, profundity, depression, hollow.

pit, shaft, well, crater, chasm, crevasse, deep, abyss, bowels of the earth, bottomless pit.

soundings, draft, submersion, plunge, dive; plummet, lead.

V. deepen, sink, excavate, mine, sap, dig, burrow.

sound, heave the lead, take soundings.

Adj. deep, deep-seated, profound, buried; sunk, submerged, subaqueous, submarine, subterranean, underground.

bottomless, fathomless, unfathomed, unfathomable, abysmal, down-reaching, yawning.

Adv. out of one's depth, beyond one's depth; over head and ears.

209. SHALLOWNESS.—*N.* shallowness, superficiality; shoals.

Adj. shallow, slight, superficial; skin-deep, ankle-deep, knee-deep, shoal.

210. SUMMIT.—*N.* summit, top, vertex, apex, zenith, pinnacle, acme, crown; height, pitch, maximum; goal, consummation; climax, turning point; culmination; turn of the tide, fountainhead.

tip, tiptop; crest, crow's-nest, cap, peak; brow, head.

architrave, frieze, cornice, coping, coping stone, capital, headpiece, capstone, pediment, entablature; attic, loft, garret, housetop, upper story, roof (*covering*), 223.

V. crown, top, cap, crest, surmount, overtop; culminate.

Adj. highest (high, etc., 206), top, topmost, overmost, uppermost, tiptop; capital, head, polar; supreme, supernal.

211. Base.—*N.* base, basement; plinth, dado, wainscot; baseboard, mopboard; bedrock, hardpan; foundation, substructure, substratum, ground, earth, pavement, floor, paving; footing, groundwork, basis.

bottom, nadir, foot, sole, toe, hoof, root; keel.

Adj. bottom, undermost, nethermost; fundamental; founded on, based on.

212. VERTICALITY.—*N.* verticality, perpendicularity, erectness.

cliff, steep, crag, bluff, palisades; wall, precipice.

V. be vertical, stand erect *or* upright, stick up, cock up.

render vertical, set up, raise up, erect, rear, raise, pitch.

Adj. vertical; upright, erect, perpendicular, plumb, bolt upright.

Adv. on end; endwise; at right angles.

213. HORIZONTALITY.—*N.* horizontality; flatness; level, plane, stratum.

recumbency; lying down, reclination, proneness, supination, prostration.

V. be horizontal, lie, recline, lie flat; sprawl, loll.

render horizontal, lay, level, flatten, even, raze, smooth, align.

prostrate, knock down, floor, fell, ground, cut (*or* hew) down, mow down.

Adj. horizontal, level, even, plane, flush; flat, smooth.

recumbent, prone, supine, prostrate.

Adv. on one's back; on all fours; on its beam ends.

214. PENDENCY.—*N.* pendency, dependency; suspension, hanging.

pendant, drop, eardrop, tassel, lobe; tail, train, queue, pigtail; pendulum.

chandelier, gaselier.

V. be pendent; hang, depend, swing, dangle, lower, droop; flap, trail, beetle, jut, overhang.

suspend, hang, sling, hook up, hitch, fasten to, append.

Adj. pendent, pendulous, hanging; dependent; beetling, jutting over, overhanging; lowering; suspended.

215. SUPPORT.—*N.* support, ground, foundation, base, basis, fulcrum, purchase, footing, hold; stage, platform; rest, resting place; groundwork, substratum; floor.

supporter; aid, etc., 707; prop, truss, stand, stalk; bracket; ledge, shelf, table, trestle; rung; round; staff, stick, crook, crutch.

post, pillar, column, pediment, pedestal; caryatid; buttress, jamb, mullion, stile, abutment.

frame, framework; scaffold, skeleton, beam, rafter, girder, lintel, joist; keystone; arch; mainstay.

seat, throne, dais; divan, ottoman, sofa, davenport, couch, daybed; stall; chair, wing chair, armchair, easy chair, elbowchair, rocking chair, Morris chair; settee, form, bench; saddle, sidesaddle, pillion; packsaddle; pommel, horn.

stool, hassock, footstool.

bed, bedstead, four-poster; pallet; cot; hammock, shakedown; crib, trundle bed, cradle; litter, stretcher; bunk, berth; mat, rug, cushion; lap.

V. support, bear, carry, hold, sustain, shoulder; hold up, back up, bolster up, shore up, uphold, brace, truss, stay, prop; maintain; aid, etc., 707.

Adj. supporting, supported; fundamental.

216. PARALLELISM.—*N.* parallelism, equidistance, concentricity.

V. be parallel, parallel, equal.

Adj. parallel, coextensive, equidistant; collateral, concentric, concurrent; abreast, equal, even, alongside.

Adv. alongside, abreast, broadside on.

217. OBLIQUITY.—*N.* obliquity, inclination, incline, slope, slant; leaning, tilt; bias, diagonal, zigzag, list, twist, sag, cant, lurch; distortion, etc., 243; bend, curve.

acclivity, steepness; rise, ascent, pitch, grade, rising ground, hill, bank; cliff, precipice, etc. (*vertical*), 212; shelving beach; declivity, dip, fall.

V. be oblique; slope, slant, lean, cant, incline, shelve, decline, descend, bend; heel over, careen; sag, slouch, sidle, skid.

render oblique; sway, bias; slope, slant, tilt; incline, bend, crook; distort, etc., 243; zigzag, stagger [*mech.*].

Adj. oblique, inclined; sloping, tilted; askew, asquint, bias, aslant, diagonal, transverse, athwart; indirect, wry, awry, crooked; sinuous, zigzag; knock-kneed, etc. (*distorted*), 243.

uphill, rising, ascending; steep, abrupt, precipitous.

downhill, falling, descending; declining, shelving, declivitous.

Adv. obliquely; on one side, askew, askance, awry, edgewise, at an angle; sidelong, sidewise, slantwise.

218. INVERSION.—*N.* inversion, subversion, reversion; opposition, polarity; contrariety, contradiction, reversal, transposition, transposal; turn of the tide; overturn, revolution; somersault; revulsion.

V. be inverted, turn (*or* go, wheel) about, turn (*or* tilt, topple) over; capsize, turn turtle.

invert, subvert; reverse; upturn, overturn, upset, overset, turn topsy-turvy; transpose.

Adj. inverted, wrong side out (*or* up); inside out, upside down; on one's head, topsy-turvy.

inverse; reverse, etc. (*contrary*), 14; opposite.

Adv. inversely, conversely; heels over head, head over heels.

219. CROSSING.—*N.* crossing; intersection, grade crossing.

network, reticulation; net, web, mesh, netting, lace, plait; sieve, screen; wicker; mat, matting; trellis, lattice, grating, grille, gridiron, tracery, fretwork, filigree; entanglement.

crucifix, cross, rood, crisscross.

V. cross, intersect, interlace, intertwine, intertwist, interweave, interlink, crisscross; twine, entwine, weave, twist, wreathe; dovetail, mortise, splice, link.

plait, pleat, plat, braid; entangle, ravel; net, knot.

Adj. crossed, matted, transverse, intersected, cross; cross-shaped, cruciform; netlike, retiform, latticed, grated, barred, streaked.

Adv. cross, athwart, thwart, transversely; at grade; crosswise, across.

220. EXTERIORITY.—*N.* exteriority; outside, exterior; surface, superficies; skin, covering; face, facet.

V. be exterior, lie around, environ, encircle.

externalize, objectify, visualize, envisage, actualize.

Adj. exterior, external, extraneous; outer, outermost; outward, outlying, outside, outdoor.

outstanding; extrinsic, incidental: superficial, skin-deep.

Adv. externally, out, without, over, outwards, out of doors, in the open air.

221. INTERIORITY.—*N.* interiority; inside, interior; interspace, subsoil.

contents, etc., 190; substance, pith, marrow; heart, bosom, breast; recesses, innermost recesses; cave, etc. (*concavity*), 252.

inmate, intern, inhabitant, etc., 188.

V. inclose, etc. (*circumscribe*), 229; intern; embed, etc. (*insert*), 300; place within, keep within.

Adj. interior, internal; inner, intimate, inside, inward, inmost, innermost; deep-seated, inherent, ingrained, innate, inborn, inbred, intrinsic.

home, inland, domestic, family, indoor.

Adv. internally; inwards, within, indoors, withindoors; at home.

222. CENTRALITY.—*N.* centrality; centralization, concentration; center; middle, midst; focus; center of gravity.

core, kernel, nucleus; heart, pole, axis, bull's-eye, nave, hub; marrow, pith; metropolis.

V. centralize, concentrate; bring to a focus; converge, etc., 290.

Adj. central; middle, axial, pivotal, nuclear, focal, concentric; middlemost; metropolitan.

223. COVERING.—*N.* covering, cover; canopy, awning, tent, marquee, wigwam, tepee; umbrella, parasol, sunshade; veil; shield, etc. (*defense*), 717.

roof, ceiling, thatch, tiles, slates, leads, shingles; dome, cupola.
coverlet, counterpane, sheet, quilt, blanket, rug; eiderdown quilt, comforter; pillowcase, pillowslip; linoleum, oilcloth; tarpaulin.
integument: skin, pellicle, fleece, fur, leather, lambskin, sable, beaver, ermine, hide, coat, buff, pelt, peltry [*collective noun*]; cuticle, cutis, epidermis; clothing, etc., 225.
peel, rind, crust, bark, husk, shell.
sheath, sheathing, capsule, pod, casing, case, wrapping, wrapper; envelope; cornhusk, corn shuck.
veneer, facing; scale, layer; incrustation, coating, paint, stain, varnish, enamel, whitewash, plaster, stucco.

V. cover, superimpose, overlay, overspread; wrap, incase, face, case, veneer, paper; clapboard, shingle; conceal, etc., 528.

coat, paint, stain, varnish, incrust, crust, cement, stucco, plaster; smear, daub, besmear, bedaub; gild, plate, japan, lacquer, enamel, whitewash.

Adj. covered, hooded, cowled, armored, armor-plated; ironclad; scaly.

224. LINING.—*N.* lining, coating, inner coating; filling, stuffing, wadding, padding; facing, bushing; sheathing.

V. line, stuff, incrust, wad, pad, fill, face, ceil, bush, wainscot, sheathe.

225. CLOTHING.—*N.* clothing, dress; covering, etc., 223; raiment, costume, attire, toilet, habiliment; vesture, vestment;

garment, garb, wardrobe, apparel, wearing apparel, clothes, finery, etc. (*ornament*), 847.

outfit, equipment, trousseau; uniform, khaki; livery, gear, harness, turnout, accouterment, caparison, suit, trappings.

dishabille, undress, tea gown, wrapper, negligee, dressing gown, kimono; rags, tatters, old clothes.

robe, habit, gown, dress, frock; blouse, middy blouse, waist, shirtwaist; suit; coat; toga, tunic, smock.

dress suit, dress clothes, evening dress, dinner coat, dinner jacket; Tuxedo [*colloq.*]; glad rags [*slang*].

cloak, mantle, shawl, veil; cape, plaid [Scot.], muffler, overcoat, greatcoat; oilskins, slicker, mackintosh, waterproof, ulster; poncho; pea-jacket; sweater, blazer, cardigan, jersey; Mackinaw coat.

jacket, vest, waistcoat; gaberdine.

skirt, petticoat, kilt; bloomers.

trousers, breeches, pants [*colloq.*]; overalls; shorts; tights; drawers; knickers [*colloq.*].

headdress, headgear, coiffure [F.], crush hat, opera hat; tam-o'-shanter, topee [India], sombrero; cap, hat, bonnet, panama, leghorn; derby; nightcap, skullcap; hood, coif; wimple: snood; crown, etc., 247; wig, front, peruke, periwig; turban, fez, tarboosh, shako, busby, bearskin; kepi, helmet; mask, domino.

body clothes, underclothing, linen; shirt, undervest, undershirt; smock, shift, chemise; nightgown, nightshirt, pajamas; bedgown.

tie, neckerchief, neckcloth; ruff, collar, cravat, stock, handkerchief, scarf; bib, tucker; boa; girdle, cummerbund [India].

shoe, Oxford shoe, Oxford tie, pump, sneakers, boot, slipper, moccasin, sandal, galosh, arctic, overshoe, rubber; patten, clog; snowshoes, ski.

stocking, hose, sock; hosiery.

glove, gauntlet; mitten, mitt.

V. clothe, array, dress, accouter, rig, fit out, deck, drape, robe, enrobe, gown, attire, apparel, equip; harness, caparison; cover, wrap, shroud, swathe, swaddle.

wear; don; put on, slip on; mantle.

Adj. clothed, clad, invested, habited.

226. DIVESTMENT.—*N.* divestment; nudity, bareness, nakedness; dishabille, etc., 225.

baldness, hairlessness.

V. divest, uncover, expose, lay open, lay bare, denude, bare, strip; undress, disrobe, dismantle; put off, take off, doff.

peel, bare, slough, excoriate, skin, scalp, flay, bark, husk.

Adj. naked, nude, bare, stark-naked, exposed; undressed, undraped, unclad, ungarmented, unclothed.

bald, hairless, beardless; shaven, clean-shaven.

227. ENVIRONMENT.—*N.* environment, encompassment; surroundings, outskirts, suburbs, purlieus, precincts, environs, entourage, neighborhood, vicinage, vicinity.

V. environ, surround, beset, compass, encompass, inclose, encircle, circle, girdle, hedge, embrace, gird, belt, engird; skirt, hem in; circumscribe, etc., 229; beleaguer, invest, besiege, beset, blockade.

Adj. surrounding, begirt; suburban.

Adv. **around,** about: without; on every side, on all sides.

228. INTERLOCATION.—*N.* **interlocation,** interjacence, interpenetration; interjection, interpolation, interlineation, interspersion, intercalation.

intervention, interference, interposition, intrusion; insinuation; insertion.

intermediary, go-between, interagent, middleman, medium.

partition, diaphragm, midriff; wall, party wall; panel, bulkhead.

V. **intervene,** come between, get between, interpenetrate.

introduce, import; throw in, edge in, run in, work in; interpose, insinuate, interject, interpolate, insert, intersperse, interlard, dovetail, splice, mortise.

interfere, intrude, obtrude; thrust in, etc. (*insert*), 300.

Adj. **intervening,** parenthetical, episodic; intrusive; embosomed.

Adv. **between,** among; amid, amidst; in the thick of; betwixt and between [*colloq.*]; parenthetically.

229. CIRCUMSCRIPTION.—*N.* **circumscription,** limitation, inclosure; confinement, etc. (*restraint*), 751; envelope, case.

V. **circumscribe,** limit, bound, confine, inclose; surround, etc., 227; hedge in, rail in, fence round, hedge round; picket; corral; imprison, restrain.

enfold, bury, incase, enshrine, enclasp; clothe, 225; embosom.

Adj. **circumscribed,** begirt, girt; lapped; buried in, immersed in; embosomed, imbedded, mewed up; imprisoned, etc., 751; landlocked.

230. OUTLINE.—*N.* **outline,** circumference; perimeter, periphery; circuit, lines, contour, profile, silhouette, lineaments, relief, bounds; coast line, horizon.

zone, belt, girdle; girth; band; baldric, zodiac; tire, pale, etc. (*inclosure*), 232; circlet, etc., 247.

V. **outline,** delineate, silhouette, block, sketch, circumscribe, etc., 229.

231. EDGE.—*N.* **edge,** verge, brink, brow, brim, margin, border, confine, skirt, rim, side; lip.

threshold, door, porch; portal, etc. (*opening*), 260.

shore, coast, strand, bank; quay, wharf, dock, mole, landing.

fringe, flounce, frill, furbelow; valance; trimming, edging, skirting, hem, selvage, welt; frame.

V. **edge,** coast, border, skirt; fringe, flounce, hem.

232. INCLOSURE.—*N.* **inclosure,** envelope; case, etc. (*receptacle*), 191; wrapper; girdle, etc., 230.

pen, fold; sty, paddock, pasture; pound; corral, yard; net, seine.

fence, pale, paling, balustrade, rail, railing, wall; hedge, hedgerow.

barrier, barricade, cordon, stockade; gate, gateway; weir; door, hatch, prison, etc., 752.

dike, ditch, trench, drain, moat.

V. inclose, circumscribe, etc., 229.

233. LIMIT.—*N.* limit, boundary, bounds, pale, confine, term, bourn, verge; termination, terminus, terminal; stint; frontier, border, marches.

boundary line, landmark; turning point.

V. limit, bound, compass, confine, define, circumscribe.

Adj. definite; terminal; frontier, bordering, border, boundary.

Adv. thus far, thus far and no further.

234. FRONT.—*N.* front, foreground, forefront; face, frontage, façade, proscenium, frontispiece; priority; obverse (*of a medal*).

van, vanguard, advanced guard; front rank; outpost; first line; scout.

brow, forehead; visage, physiognomy, features, countenance; bow, stem, prow; jib; bowsprit.

pioneer, etc. (*precursor*), 64.

V. front, face, confront, brave, dare, defy, oppose; breast; come to the front *or* fore.

Adj. fore, foremost, headmost; forward, anterior, front, frontal.

Adv. before, in front, in the van, in advance; ahead; in the foreground.

235. REAR.—*N.* rear, back; rear rank, rearguard; background, hinterland.

tail, scut (*as of a hare*), brush (*of a fox*).

afterpart; stern, poop; postern door; tailpiece, crupper.

wake; train, retinue, suite, cortege.

reverse; other side of the shield.

V. be behind; fall astern; bring up the rear; heel, tag, shadow, follow, pursue.

Adj. back, rear, hindmost; posterior; after.

Adv. behind, in the rear *or* background; at the heels of; after, aft, abaft, astern, rearward, backward.

236. SIDE.—*N.* side, flank, quarter, lee; wing; profile; gable, gable end; broadside.

points of the compass; East, sunrise, Orient, Levant; West, Occident, sunset.

V. flank, skirt, outflank; sidle; border; be on one side.

Adj. lateral, sidelong; collateral; flanking, skirting.

eastern, eastward, east, Orient, Oriental, auroral, Levantine. western, west, westerly, westward, Occidental.

Adv. sidewise, sidelong, sideling, broadside on; abreast, alongside, beside; aside; by, by the side of; side by side; to windward, to leeward; laterally; right and left.

237. OPPOSITE.—*N.* **opposite,** opposite side, reverse, inverse; counterpart, antithesis; opposition, polarity; inversion, etc., 218.

antipodes, opposite poles; North and South.

Adj. **opposite,** reverse, converse; antipodal, diametrical, antithetic, counter; fronting, facing.

northern, north, northerly, northward, hyperborean, boreal, polar, arctic.

southern, south, southerly, southward, austral, antarctic.

Adv. **over,** over the way, over against; against; face to face, vis-à-vis [F.].

238. RIGHT.—*N.* **right,** right hand; offside, starboard.

Adj. **dextral,** dexterous, right-handed, dexter.

ambidexter, ambidextrous.

239. LEFT.—*N.* **left,** left hand, south paw [*slang*]; near side; larboard, port.

Adj. **left-handed,** sinistral.

III. FORM

240. FORM.—*N.* **form,** figure, shape, make, formation, frame, construction, cut, build, contour, outline, stamp, type, cast, mold, fashion; structure, etc., 329; sculpture, architecture.

feature, lineament, turn; phase, etc. (*aspect*), 448; posture, attitude, pose.

V. **form,** shape, figure, fashion, carve, cut, chisel, hew, cast; roughhew, sketch, block out; trim, model, knead, mold, sculpture; cast, stamp; build, etc. (*construct*), 161.

Adj. **structural;** plastic, formative, impressible; creative.

shapely, well proportioned, symmetrical, well made, well formed, trim, neat.

241. ABSENCE OF FORM.—*N.* **formlessness,** shapelessness, misproportion, uncouthness; rough diamond; disorder, etc., 59; deformity, etc., 243; disfigurement, defacement; mutilation.

V. **deface,** disfigure, deform, mutilate, derange, etc., 61; blemish, mar.

Adj. **formless,** shapeless, amorphous, unshapely, misshapen, unsymmetrical, malformed, unformed; anomalous.

rough, rude, barbarous, rugged, scraggy; in the rough.

242. [Regularity of form] SYMMETRY.—*N.* **symmetry,** shapeliness, finish; beauty, etc., 845; proportion, eurythmics, uniformity, parallelism; centrality; radiation; branching, ramification; regularity, evenness.

Adj. symmetrical, shapely, well set, finished; beautiful, etc., 845; classic, chaste, severe.

regular, uniform, balanced; equal, even, parallel.

243. [Irregularity of form] DISTORTION.—*N.* distortion, contortion; knot, warp, buckle, screw, twist; crookedness, obliquity; grimace, deformity, malformation; monstrosity, misproportion, ugliness, disfigurement.

V. distort, contort, twist, warp, buckle, screw, wrench, wrest, writhe, deform, misshape.

Adj. distorted, out of shape, irregular, unsymmetric, awry, wry, askew, crooked, gnarled; not true, not straight; deformed; misshapen, misproportioned, ill-proportioned; ill-made; humpbacked, hunchbacked; bandy-legged, bow-legged; knock-kneed.

244. ANGULARITY.—*N.* angularity, bifurcation; fold, etc., 258; notch, etc., 257; fork, crotch, angle, bend, elbow, knee, knuckle; zigzag; right angle, acute angle, obtuse angle; obliquity, etc., 217.

corner, nook, recess, niche.

triangle; rectangle, square; lozenge, diamond; rhomb, rhombus, rhomboid; quadrangle, quadrilateral; parallelogram; polygon, pentagon, hexagon, heptagon, octagon, oxygon, decagon; cube, prism, pyramid.

V. fork, branch, ramify, bifurcate, bend hook.

Adj. angular, bent, crooked, aquiline, jagged, serrated; forked, bifurcate, crotched, zigzag, hooked; akimbo; oblique, etc., 217.

245. CURVATURE.—*N.* curvature, curvedness, incurvature, bend; flexure, crook, hook, bending; deflection, turn; deviation, detour; sweep; curl; sinuosity, etc., 248.

curve, arc, arch, arcade, vault, bow, cresent, half-moon, horseshoe, loop, festoon; parabola, hyperbola; tracery.

V. be curved, sweep, sag; deviate, etc., 279; turn; re-enter. render curved, bend, curve, deflect, inflect; crook; turn, round, arch, arch over, bow, coil, curl, recurve.

Adj. curved, curvate, devious; recurved, arched, vaulted; oblique, etc., 217; circular, etc., 247; bell-shaped; bow-shaped, embowed; crescent, crescent-shaped, horned; heart-shaped, cordate; hook-shaped, hooked, hooklike; moon-shaped, lunar, sickleshaped.

246. STRAIGHTNESS.—*N.* straightness, directness; inflexibility; straight (*or* bee, right, direct) line; short cut.

V. be straight, have no turning, go straight, steer for.

render straight, straighten, rectify; set *or* put straight; unbend, unfold, uncurl, uncoil, unravel.

Adj. straight, rectilinear; direct, even, right, true, in a line; undeviating, unswerving, straight as an arrow; inflexible.

perpendicular, plumb, vertical, upright, erect.

247. [Simple circularity] CIRCULARITY.—*N.* circularity, roundness; rotundity, etc., 249.

circle, circlet, ring, hoop; bracelet, armlet; loop, wheel, cycle, orb, orbit, disk, circuit, zone, belt, cordon, band; hub, nave; sash, girdle, cestus, cincture, baldric, wreath, garland; crown, coronet, chaplet, snood, fillet; necklace, collar; noose, lasso.

ellipse, oval; ellipsoid, cycloid.

V. round; ring, encircle, etc., 227.

Adj. round, rounded, circular, oval, elliptic, elliptical, egg-shaped.

248. [Complex circularity] CONVOLUTION.—*N.* convolution, involution, winding, wave, undulation, sinuosity, sinuousness, meandering, twist, twirl; contortion.

coil, roll, curl, spiral, corkscrew, worm, tendril, scallop, kink; serpent, snake, eel; maze, labyrinth.

V. wind, twine, twirl, wreathe, entwine; wave, undulate, meander; twist, coil, roll; wrinkle; curl, friz, indent, scallop; wring, contort.

Adj. winding, twisted, convoluted; circling, snaky, serpentine, sinuous, undulating, undulated, wavy.

involved, intricate, mazy, tortuous, labyrinthine; circuitous, kinky, curly.

spiral, coiled, screw-shaped.

Adv. in and out, round and round.

249. ROTUNDITY.—*N.* rotundity, roundness, sphericity, globularity.

cylinder, barrel, drum; roll, roller, rolling pin, column.

sphere, globe, ball, spheroid, globule; bulb, bullet, pellet, pill, marble, pea, knob.

V. sphere, form into a sphere, roll into a ball, give rotundity, round.

Adj. rotund; round, etc. (*circular*), 247; cylindrical, conical, spherical, globular, bulbous; egg-shaped, ovoid, ovate; bell-shaped, etc., 245.

250. CONVEXITY.—*N.* convexity, prominence, projection, swelling, swell, bulge, protuberance, protrusion, excrescency.

excrescence, hump; bow; clump, bunch; bulb, bump, knob; knot; boss; tooth, peg; ridge, rib, snag; peak, etc. (*sharpness*), 253; growth, tumor; pimple, wart, wen; fungus, blister; nipple, teat, dug, breast.

proboscis, nose, beak, snout, nozzle.

belly, paunch; abdomen.

arch, cupola, dome, vault.

relief, cameo; low relief, bas-relief, high relief.

point of land, hill, mount, mountain; cape, promontory; foreland, headland; hummock, ledge, spur.

V. project, bulge, protrude; bag, belly, pout, bunch; jut out, stand out, stick out, stick up; hang over, beetle.

raise, etc., 307; emboss.

Adj. prominent, protuberant, projecting; bossed, bossy, convex, bunchy, hummocky, bulbous; bloated, swollen, distended; bowed, arched; bold; bellied; gibbous; club-shaped, knobby, gnarled; salient, in relief, raised.

251. FLATNESS.—*N.* flatness; smoothness.

plane; level, plain, tableland, plateau; stratum; plate, table, tablet, slab.

V. flatten; level, etc., 213; fell.

Adj. flat, plane, even, smooth; flush; level, horizontal; recumbent, supine, prostrate.

Adv. flat, flatwise. lengthwise, horizontally.

252. CONCAVITY.—*N.* concavity, depression, dip; hollow, hollowness; indentation, intaglio, cavity, dent, dint, dimple; honeycomb.

excavation, pit, sap, mine, shaft; caisson; trough, etc. (*furrow*), 259; bay, etc. (*of the sea*), 343.

cup, basin, crater; punch bowl; cell, etc.(*receptacle*), 191; socket.

valley, vale, dale, dell, dingle, glen.

cave, cavern, cove; grot, grotto; hole, burrow, kennel, tunnel; gully, etc., 198.

excavator, sapper, miner.

V. render concave; depress, hollow, gouge; stave in; scoop, scoop out; dig, delve, excavate, dent, dint, perforate; mine, sap, undermine, burrow, tunnel.

Adj. concave, hollow; funnel-shaped; retreating; cavernous; porous, perforated; honeycombed.

253. SHARPNESS.—*N.* sharpness, acuteness; saliency.

point, spike, spine, spit, needle, pin; prick, barb; spur; horn, antler; snag; tag; thorn, bristle; tooth, tusk; tine.

beard, porcupine, hedgehog, brier, bramble, thistle, bur; currycomb, comb.

peak, crag, crest, cone, sugar loaf; spire, pyramid, steeple.

cutting edge, knife edge, blade, edge tool, cutlery, knife, penknife, razor; scalpel, lancet; plowshare, colter; hatchet, ax, pick, cleaver, scythe, sickle, scissors, shears; sword, etc. (*arms*), 727; bodkin, etc. (*perforator*), 262.

sharpener; hone, strop; grindstone, whetstone, steel, emery, carborundum.

V. be sharp; taper to a point; bristle with; cut, etc., 44.

sharpen, whet, point, barb, set, strop, grind.

Adj. **sharp,** keen; acute, pointed; tapering; spiked, spiky, studded, peaked, salient; prickly, spiny, thorny, bristling, barbed, spurred, bearded, thistly, briery; craggy, jagged, snaggy; cone-shaped, conical.

keen-edged, cutting; sharp-edged, knife-edged; sharpened.

254. BLUNTNESS.—*N.* bluntness, dullness.

V. **be** *or* **render blunt,** dull; take off the point *or* edge; blunt, turn.

Adj. **blunt,** dull, dullish, obtuse, pointless, unpointed; unsharpened.

255. SMOOTHNESS.—*N.* smoothness; polish, gloss; lubrication.

smoother; roller, steam roller; sandpaper, emery paper; flat-iron, sadiron; burnisher.

V. **smooth;** plane; file; mow, shave; level, roll; macadamize; polish, burnish, sleek, iron, press, mangle; lubricate, oil, grease, wax, anoint.

Adj. **smooth;** polished; even; sleek, glossy, silken, silky; velvety; slippery, glassy, oi'y.

256. ROUGHNESS.—*N.* roughness, asperity; corrugation.

hair, mat, thatch, mop; scalp lock; tress, lock, curl, ringlet; shag; mane; eyelashes, lashes; beard, whiskers; mustache; imperial, goatee; fringe; hair shirt.

plumage; plume, crest; feather, tuft.

nap, pile, grain, texture.

V. **roughen,** rough, rough up, crinkle, ruffle, crumple, rumple; corrugate; stroke the wrong way, rub the fur the wrong way.

Adj. **rough,** uneven; rugged, jagged; cross-grained, gnarled, gnarly, knotted, scraggly, scraggy; craggy, cragged; unkempt, unpolished, roughhewn; prickly, etc. (*sharp*), 253.

hairy, bristly, hirsute, tufted, bushy; nappy, bearded, shaggy.

Adv. against the grain; in the rough; on edge.

257. NOTCH.—*N.* notch, dent, nick, cut, indent, indentation; embrasure, battlement.

saw, tooth, scallop; jag.

V. notch, nick, mill, score, cut, dent, indent, jag, scarify, scallop.

Adj. notched, dentate, toothed, serrate *or* serrated.

258. FOLD.—*N.* fold, crease, flexure, pleat, plait, tuck, gather; joint, elbow, double; wrinkle, pucker, crow's-feet; crinkle, crumple; dog's-ear; ruffle, flounce; corrugation.

V. fold, double, pleat, plait, crease, wrinkle, cocker, crinkle, curl, shrivel, rumple, corrugate, ruffle, crumple, pucker; dog's-ear, tuck, ruck, hem, gather.

259. FURROW.—*N.* **furrow,** groove, rut, scratch, streak, crack, score, incision, slit.

trench, ditch, dike, moat, trough, channel, gutter, ravine, etc., 198; depression.

V. **furrow,** flute, groove, carve, corrugate, cut, chisel, plow; incise, engrave, etch, grave.

Adj. **furrowed,** ribbed, striated, fluted, corduroy.

260. OPENING.—*N.* **opening,** aperture, yawning; chasm, etc., 198.

outlet, inlet; pore; vent, venthole, blowhole, airhole; orifice, mouth, sucker, muzzle, throat, gullet, nozzle.

window, casement, lattice; embrasure; light; skylight, fanlight; bay window, bow window, oriel, dormer.

portal, porch, gate, postern, wicket, trapdoor, hatch, door; cellarway, driveway, gateway, doorway, hatchway, gangway.

way, path, etc., 627; thoroughfare; channel, gully; passage, passageway.

alley, lane, mall, aisle, glade, vista.

tube, pipe, main; water pipe. etc., 350; air pipe, etc., 351; vessel, canal, gut, fistula; smokestack, chimney, flue; bore, caliber.

tunnel, mine, pit, shaft; gallery.

hole, puncture, perforation; pinhole, loophole, peephole, eye, eyelet; slot.

sieve, strainer, colander, riddle, screen.

opener, key, master key; open-sesame.

V. **open,** gape, yawn, fly open.

perforate, pierce, tap, bore, drill; transpierce, transfix; enfilade, impale, spike, spear, gore, spit, stab, pink, puncture, lance; stick, prick, riddle.

uncover, unclose; punch, stave in; mine, etc. (*scoop out*), 252.

Adj. **open;** perforated, wide-open, agape, ajar, unclosed; gaping, yawning; patent.

tubular; pervious, permeable; porous, honeycombed.

261. CLOSURE.—*N.* **closure,** blockade, shutting up, sealing, obstruction; contraction, constipation; impermeability; blind alley; cul-de-sac [F.].

V. **close,** plug, block up, stop up, fill up, cork up, button up, stuff up, dam up; blockade; obstruct, bar, bolt, stop, seal; choke, throttle; ram down, dam, cram; clinch; shut, slam, snap.

Adj. **closed,** shut, unopened; unpierced, impervious, impermeable; impenetrable; impassable, pathless, wayless; untrodden.

tight, unventilated, airtight, watertight, hermetically sealed; snug.

262. PERFORATOR.—*N.* **perforator,** piercer, borer, auger, chisel, gimlet, drill, awl, scoop, corkscrew, dibble, trepan, lancet, probe, bodkin, needle, stiletto; punch, gouge; spear, etc. (*weapon*), 727; puncher; punching machine, punching press.

263. STOPPER.—*N.* stopper, stopple; plug, cork, bung, spike, spill, stopcock, tap, faucet; valve, spigot; rammer; ram, ramrod; piston; stopgap; wadding, stuffing, padding, sponge [*surg.*], tourniquet.

doorkeeper, gatekeeper, janitor, concierge [F.], porter, warder, beadle, usher, guard, sentinel; watchdog.

IV. MOTION

264. MOTION.—*N.* motion, movement; move; mobility, movableness, motive power; mobilization.

stream, flow, flux, run, course, stir.

rate, pace, tread, footfall, step, stride, gait; velocity, clip [*colloq.*]; progress, locomotion.

journey, etc., 266; voyage, sail, cruise, passage; transit, etc., 270.

unrest, restlessness, etc., 149.

V. move, go, hie, budge, stir, pass, flit; hover around *or* about; shift, slide, glide, roll, flow, stream, run, drift, sweep along; wander, etc. (*deviate*), 279; walk, etc., 266.

put in motion, set in motion; impel, etc., 276; propel, etc., 284; mobilize.

Adj. moving, in motion, traveling; transitional, shifting, movable, mobile, motive, motor; mercurial; restless, etc. (*changeable*), 149; nomadic, etc., 266; erratic, etc., 279; evolutionary.

Adv. under way; on the move (*or* wing, fly, tramp, march).

265. REST.—*N.* rest; stillness, quiescence; stagnation, stagnancy, fixity, immobility, catalepsy; quietism.

quiet, tranquility, calm; repose, relaxation; dead calm; silence, peace, hush; sleep, etc. (*inactivity*), 683.

pause, lull, etc. (*cessation*), 142; stand, standstill; deadlock, dead stand; full stop; embargo.

resting place; bivouac; home, abode; bed, etc. (*support*), 215; haven, etc (*refuge*), 666; goal, destination, bourn.

V. be still, stand still, stand fast, stand firm, lie still, keep quiet, repose, rest; vegetate, stagnate.

remain, stay; stand, tarry, mark time; pull up, draw up; hold, halt, stop, discontinue, stop short, pause; bring to, heave to, lay to; anchor, cast anchor, come to anchor, ride at anchor, lie to; rest on one's laurels, take breath.

dwell, etc., 186; settle, settle down; alight, dismount, arrive.

quell, becalm, hush, calm, still, tranquilize, stay, lull to sleep, lay an embargo on.

Adj. quiescent, still; silent, hushed, quiet; motionless, moveless; fixed; stationary; at rest, at a stand, at a standstill, at anchor; stock-still; sedentary, untraveled, stay-at-home; becalmed, stagnant, quiet; unmoved, calm, restful; immovable, stable; sleeping, etc. (*inactive*), 683.

266. [Locomotion by land] JOURNEY.—*N.* travel, traveling, wayfaring; campaigning.

excursion, journey, expedition, tour, trip, circuit, pilgrimage, march, walk, promenade, constitutional [*colloq.*], stroll, saunter, ramble, hike [*colloq.*], tramp, turn, stalk, perambulation; outing, ride, drive, airing, jaunt.

riding, equitation, horsemanship.

roving, vagrancy, nomadism; vagabondism, hoboism; migration; emigration, immigration. *Wanderlust*, [Ger.].

itinerary, route, guide; handbook; roadbook; Baedeker.

procession, parade, cavalcade, caravan, file, cortege, column. vehicle, etc., 272.

traveler, etc., 268.

station, stop, stopping place, terminal, terminus, depot, railway station.

V. travel, journey, flit, take wing; migrate, emigrate, immigrate; trek; tour, peregrinate.

motor, bicycle, cycle [*colloq.*], spin, speed; trolley [*colloq.*]. motorize, electrify.

wander, roam, range, prowl, rove, jaunt, ramble, stroll, saunter, perambulate, meander, straggle; gad, gad about.

take horse, ride, drive, trot, amble, canter, gallop, prance, frisk, caracole.

walk, march, step, tread, pace; plod, trudge, wend; promenade; track; hike [*colloq.*], tramp; stalk, stride; strut, bowl along, toddle; paddle; peg on, jog on, shuffle on.

glide, slide, coast, skim, skate.

file off, march in procession, defile.

go to, repair to, resort to, hie to, betake oneself to.

Adj. traveling, journeying; itinerant, peripatetic, roving, rambling, vagrant, migratory, nomadic.

self-moving, automobile, automotive, locomotive.

wayfaring, wayworn; travel-stained.

267. [Locomotion by water or air] NAVIGATION.—*N.* voyage, cruise, sail, passage, aquatics; boating, yachting, cruising; ship, etc., 273.

headway, sternway, leeway; fairway.

oar, scull, sweep, pole; paddle, screw, propeller, turbine; sail, canvas.

aeronautics, aerial navigation, balloonery; balloon, etc., 273; ballooning; aviation, airmanship; flying, flight, volplaning, planing [*colloq.*], hydroplaning, volplane, glide, dive, nose-dive, spin, looping the loop; wing; pinion, aileron.

mariner, etc., 269; aviator, etc., 269*a.*

V. sail; embark, etc., 293; spread sail, gather way, make sail, carry sail; ride the waves, ride out the storm.

navigate, scud, boom, drift, course, cruise, steam; coast, hug the shore.

row, paddle, pull, scull, punt.

float, swim, skim, dive, wade.

Aeronautics: fly, soar, drift, hover, aviate; volplane, plane [*colloq.*], glide, dive, fly over, nose-dive, spin, loop the loop, land; take wing, take a flight.

Adj. nautical, maritime, naval; seafaring, seagoing; coasting; afloat; navigable.

aeronautic, aeronautical, aerial.

aquatic, natatory, natatorial.

Adv. under way (*or* sail, canvas, steam), in motion, in progress, on the wing; afloat.

268. TRAVELER.—*N.* traveler, wayfarer, voyager, passenger; commuter, straphanger [*colloq.*].

tourist, excursionist, globe-trotter [*colloq.*]; explorer, adventurer, mountaineer; wanderer, rover, straggler, rambler; landsman, landlubber, vagrant, loafer, tramp, hobo, vagabond, Bohemian, gypsy, nomad, Arab; pilgrim, palmer; immigrant; emigrant.

fugitive, refugee; runaway; renegade.

courier, messenger, runner; Mercury.

pedestrian, walker, foot passenger, hiker [*colloq.*], tramper.

rider, horseman, equestrian, cavalier; jockey, trainer, breaker, roughrider; huntsman, whip; postilion, postboy.

driver, coachman, charioteer, carter, wagoner, drayman, truckman; cabman, cab driver.

Railroad: engineer; fireman, stoker; conductor, motorman.

Automobile: driver, chauffeur, automobilist, motorist.

269. MARINER.—*N.* mariner, navigator; sailor, seaman, seafarer, seafaring man, sea dog [*colloq.*]; tar, bluejacket, gob [*slang*]; marine; midshipman, middy [*colloq.*]; able seaman, hand; crew; captain, commander, master mariner, skipper; mate, boatswain; boatman, ferryman, waterman, lighterman, longshoreman; gondolier; oar, oarsman, rower.

steersman, coxswain, cox [*colloq.*], helmsman, pilot.

269a. AERONAUT.—*N.* aeronaut, aviator, airman, flier, aviatress *or* aviatrix, pilot, observer, spotter [*mil. cant*], scout, bomber, ace; balloonist.

270. TRANSFERENCE.—*N.* transfer, transference; removal; deportation, extradition; conveyance, carriage; contagion, infection; transfusion; transfer, etc. (*of property*), 783.

transit, transition; passage, ferry; portage, carry; carting, cartage; shipment, freight; transmission, transport, transportation; translation; transposition, transposal.

deposit, moraine, drift, alluvium.

gift, bequest, legacy, deed, lease; quitclaim.

freight, cargo, mail, baggage, luggage, goods.

V. transfer, transmit, transport, transplant, transfuse; convey, carry, bear; hand, pass, forward; shift; bring, fetch, reach; conduct, convoy.

send, delegate, consign, relegate, deliver; ship, freight, embark; transpose; drag, etc., 285; mail, post.

Adj. transferable, assignable, negotiable, transmissible, movable, portable; contagious, infectious.

271. CARRIER.—*N.* carrier, porter, redcap, bearer, freighter, expressman; stevedore; coolie; conductor, chauffeur, truck driver; letter carrier, postman; pigeon post, carrier pigeon.

beast of burden, beast, cattle, horse, steed; charger, war horse; hunter; race horse, racer, courser, Arab, barb; blood horse, thoroughbred; palfrey, cob; nag, jade, hack; pack (*or* draft, cart, dray) horse; mare, filly, colt, foal.
pony, Shetland; broncho, cow pony, mustang.
ass, donkey, jackass, burro; mule.
reindeer; camel, dromedary, llama, elephant.

vehicle, etc., 272; ship, etc., 273.
Adj. equine, asinine; electric, motor, express.

272. VEHICLE.—*N.* vehicle, conveyance, carriage, caravan, car, van.

wagon, dray, cart, lorry, truck.

tumbrel, barrow, wheelbarrow, handbarrow; dump cart; baby carriage, gocart, perambulator; wheel chair; police van, patrol wagon, Black Maria [*colloq.*]; Conestoga wagon, prairie schooner; jinrikisha, ricksha [*colloq.*].
equipage, coach, chariot, phaeton, wagonette, break, drag, landau, barouche, victoria, brougham; sulky, runabout.
post chaise, mail stage, diligence, stage, stagecoach; horsecar, omnibus, bus [*colloq.*]; cab, hansom, four-wheeler, hack; dogcart, trap [*colloq.*], buggy, chaise. team, pair, span, tandem, four-in-hand.
litter, palanquin, sedan; stretcher, hurdle; ambulance.
sled, bob, bobsled; toboggan; sledge, sleigh; ski, snowshoes, skates, roller skates.

cycle, bicycle, tricycle, tandem; machine [*colloq.*], wheel [*colloq.*], motorcycle; velocipede, hobbyhorse.

automobile, motorcar, limousine, sedan, touring car, roadster, coupé, motor [*colloq.*], machine [*colloq.*], car, auto [*colloq.*], autocar, runabout; truck, tractor; taxicab, taxi [*colloq.*], motorbus; flivver [*slang*], jitney [*colloq.*].

Allied automobile terms: tonneau, chassis, hood, top, ignition, spark plug, generator, distributor, magneto, self-starter, gear, gear box, differential, cylinder, manifold, intake, exhaust, carburetor, ammeter, speedometer, oil gauge, primer, clutch, universal joint, crank shaft, transmission, tire, rim; gasoline; trailer; garage; chauffeur, etc., 268.

train; express, mail; car, coach; baggage car; rolling stock; trolley, electric car, electric [*colloq.*].

Adj. vehicular; traveling, etc., 266.

273. SHIP.—*N.* ship, vessel, boat, sail; craft, bottom.

navy, marine, fleet, flotilla.

shipping, man-of-war, etc., 726; merchant ship, merchantman; packet, liner; whaler; slaver; collier; coaster, freight steamer, freighter, lighter; trawler, fishing boat; pilot boat; yacht.

ship, sailing vessel, clipper ship, windjammer [*colloq.*], bark; brig, brigantine, schooner; fore-and-after [*colloq.*]; sloop, cutter, revenue cutter, yawl, ketch, smack, lugger, barge, scow, cat, catboat.
steamer, steamboat, steamship; tug.
boat, rowboat; shallop, skiff, pinnace; launch; lifeboat, longboat, jolly boat, gig, cockboat, tender, cockleshell, dory, canoe, dugout, dinghy, punt, outrigger; float, raft, iceboat.
coracle, gondola, galley, argosy, galleon; junk, sampan [both Chinese]; dhow [Arab.]; trireme; derelict.

Aeronautics: aircraft; balloon, airship, dirigible, zeppelin, airplane, monoplane, biplane, triplane; air cruiser, flying boat, hydroplane; kite, parachute.

Allied aeronautical terms: fuselage, gondola, wings, controls, aileron, lifting power, rudder; tail, hangar.

Adj. marine, maritime, naval, nautical, seafaring, ocean-going; seaworthy.

aeronautic, aerial; airworthy.

Adv. afloat, aboard; on board, on shipboard.

274. VELOCITY.—*N.* velocity, speed, celerity, swiftness, rapidity; expedition, etc. (*activity*), 682; acceleration; haste, etc., 684.

spurt, sprint, rush, dash, race, steeplechase; round pace; flight. pace, gallop, canter, trot, round trot, run, hand gallop.

V. speed, hie, hasten, spurt, sprint, scamper, scuttle, trip, post; scud, scurry, whiz; run, dart, swoop, fly, race, shoot, tear, whisk, sweep, skim, scorch [*colloq.*], rush, dash; bolt, run away; ride hard; hurry, hasten, haste; accelerate, quicken; carry sail, crowd sail.

Adj. fast, speedy, swift, rapid, quick, fleet; nimble, agile, expeditious; express; active, brisk, light-footed, nimble-footed; winged.

Adv. apace; at full speed, full gallop; posthaste; in double-quick time; whip and spur; by leaps and bounds; in high (gear *or* speed) [*automobiling*].

275. **SLOWNESS.**—*N.* slowness, tardiness; languor, etc. (*inactivity*), 683; drawl.

jog trot, dogtrot; amble, rack, pace, single-foot, walk; mincing steps; dead march, slow march.

retardation; slackening; delay, etc. (*lateness*), 133.

slow goer, slowpoke [*colloq.*]; loiterer, sluggard, dawdler; tortoise, snail.

V. move slowly; creep, crawl, lag, walk, linger, loiter, saunter; plod, trudge, lumber; trail, drag; dawdle, etc., 683; worm one's way, inch, inch along, jog on, toddle, waddle, slouch, shuffle, halt, hobble, limp, shamble; flag, falter, totter, stagger; mince, take one's time.

retard, relax, slacken, check, moderate, rein in, curb; reef, shorten *or* take in sail; brake, slacken speed, backwater, back pedal.

Adj. slow, slack; tardy; dilatory, etc. (*inactive*), 683; leisurely; deliberate, gradual; languid, sluggish, apathetic, phlegmatic, lymphatic; moderate.

dull, slow [*colloq.*], prosaic, boring, wearisome, uninteresting, humdrum.

Adv. at half speed, in slow time; with clipped wings; in low (gear *or* speed) [*automobiling*].

gradually, by degrees, step by step, bit by bit.

276. [Motion conjoined with force] **IMPULSE.**—*N.* impulse, impetus; momentum; push, thrust, shove, boom, boost, explosion, etc. (*violence*), 173; propulsion, etc., 284.

clash, collision, encounter, shock, brunt, crash, bump; impact; charge, onset; percussion, concussion.

blow, stroke, knock, tap, rap, slap, smack, pat, dab; fillip; bang; hit, whack, thwack, cuff, buffet, punch, thump, kick, cut, thrust, lunge; carom, cannon; jab.

Science of mechanical forces: mechanics, dynamics.

V. impel, push; start, set going; drive, urge; boom, boost; thrust, prod; elbow, shoulder, jostle, hurtle, shove, butt, jog, jolt; throw, etc. (*propel*), 284.

strike, knock, thump, beat, bang, slam, dash, punch, thwack, whack; batter, tamp, buffet, cudgel, belabor; lunge, jab, kick; hit, tap, rap, slap, pat.

collide, foul; telescope; bump, butt.

Adj. impulsive, propulsive, dynamic.

277. **RECOIL.**—*N.* recoil, rebound, ricochet, backlash, boom-

erang: kick; elasticity, etc., 325; reflex, reflux; reverberation, resonance, repulse; reaction, revulsion.

reactionary, recalcitrant.

V. recoil, react; balk, jib; rebound, reverberate, echo; ricochet.

Adj. refluent, recalcitrant, reactionary.

278. DIRECTION.—*N.* direction, bearing, course, set, trend, run, drift, tenor; tendency, etc., 176; dip, tack, aim.

points of the compass, cardinal points.

line, path, road, range, line of march, alignment; airline, beeline.

V. tend toward, conduct to, go to; point to, bend, verge, incline, dip; steer for, make for, aim at, level at; take aim; hold a course; be bound for; make a beeline for.

Adj. bound for; direct, straight; undeviating, unswerving.

directable, steerable, dirigible, guidable.

Adv. toward, on the road to; hither, thither, whither; directly; straight, point-blank; in a bee (*or* direct, straight) line to, as the crow flies; windward, in the wind's eye.

through, via, by way of.

279. DEVIATION.—*N.* deviation; warp, refraction; sweep; deflection, zigzag.

diversion, digression, aberration, drift, sheer, divergence, ramification, forking; detour.

Oblique motion: tack, yaw [*both naut.*]; echelon [*mil.*]; knight's move [*chess*].

V. deviate, alter one's course, turn, bend, curve, swerve, heel, bear off; jibe, yaw, wear, sheer, tack [*all naut.*]; sidle, edge, veer, diverge; wind, twist; turn aside, wheel, steer clear of; dodge, step aside, shy, jib; glance off.

deflect; divert, shift, switch, shunt; sidetrack.

stray, straggle; digress, wander, meander; go astray, ramble, rove, drift.

Adj. deviating, errant; excursive, discursive; devious, desultory, rambling; stray, vagrant, circuitous, roundabout, sidelong, indirect, crooked, zigzag; oblique.

280. PRECEDING.—*N.* preceding, leading, heading, precedence, priority, the lead, van, front; precursor, etc., 64.

V. precede, go before, forerun; introduce, herald; head, take the lead; lead, steal a march, get ahead, outstrip; take precedence.

Adv. in advance, before, ahead, in the van, in front.

281. FOLLOWING.—*N.* following, attendance; pursuant; sequence, sequel.

follower, attendant, satellite, pursuer, shadow, dangler, train.

V. follow; pursue, etc., 622; go after; attend, dance attendance on, dog; shadow; hang on the skirts of; camp on the trail.

lag, loiter, linger, fall behind.

Adv. behind; in the rear; after, etc. (*order*), 63 (*time*), 117.

282. [Motion forward] PROGRESSION.—*N.* progression, progress, progressiveness; advance, advancement, headway; march, etc., 266; rise, improvement, etc., 658.

V. advance; proceed, go, go on, progress, get on, gain ground, forge ahead, press onward, step forward, make progress (*or* head, headway); go ahead, shoot ahead; distance.

Adj. progressive, advanced, up-to-date; enterprising, go-ahead [*colloq.*].

Adv. forward, onward; forth, on, ahead, under way.

283. [Motion backward] REGRESSION.—*N.* regression, retrogression, retreat, retirement, recession, withdrawal.

reflux, refluence, backwater, ebb, return; reflexion, recoil.

countermotion, countermovement, countermarch; tergiversation, backsliding, fall; deterioration, relapse, reversion.

V. recede, return, revert, retreat, retire; retrograde, back, back out [*colloq.*], back down [*colloq.*], balk; withdraw; recoil, rebound; turn back, fall back, put back; lose ground, drop astern; backwater, put about [*naut.*], veer, shy, double, wheel, countermarch; ebb, regurgitate.

Adj. retrograde, retrogressive; regressive, refluent, reflex, contraclockwise, counterclockwise; balky, perverse, reactionary.

284. PROPULSION.—*N.* propulsion, projection; push, etc. (*impulse*), 276; ejection; throw, fling, toss, shot, discharge, shy.

Science of propulsion: gunnery, ballistics.

missile, projectile; gun, etc. (*arms*), 727.

marksman, rifleman, good shot, dead shot, crack shot; sharpshooter, etc. (*combatant*), 726; gunner; archer, bowman.

V. propel, project, throw, fling, cast, pitch, toss, jerk, heave, shy, hurl.

dart, lance, tilt; drive, sling, pelt, pitchfork.

send; let off, fire off, discharge, shoot; launch, send forth, let fly; dash.

start, put *or* set in motion, set going, trundle, bundle off; impel, etc., 276; expel, eject.

Adj. propulsive, projectile, ballistic.

285. TRACTION.—*N.* traction, draft, pull, haul.

V. draw, pull, haul, lug, rake, trawl, draggle, drag, tug, tow, trail, train; take in tow.

Adj. tractile, tractional, ductile.

286. [Motion toward] APPROACH.—*N.* approach, approximation; access; advent.

pursuit, chase, hunt.

V. **approach,** converge, near, get (*or* draw) near; move toward, drift; gain upon; pursue, etc., 622; make land.

Adj. approximate, convergent; impending, imminent.

287. [Motion from] RECESSION.—*N.* recession, retirement, withdrawal; retreat; regression, etc., 283; departure, etc., 293; flight.

V. **recede,** go, go back, move back, retire, withdraw, ebb, shrink; drift away; depart, etc., 293; retreat, retire, fall back; run away, fly, flee.

288. ATTRACTION.—*N.* attraction, attractiveness; pull, magnetism, gravity.

loadstone, lodestar, polestar, magnet.

lure, bait, charm, decoy.

V. **attract,** pull, drag, draw, magnetize, bait, trap, decoy, charm, lure, allure.

Adj. attractive, attracting, seductive.

289. REPULSION.—*N.* repulsion; antipathy; repulse, abduction.

V. **repel,** push *or* drive from, etc., 276; chase, dispel; abduct; send away; repulse; keep at arm's length, turn one's back upon.

Adj. repellent, repulsive.

290. [Motion nearer to] CONVERGENCE.—*N.* convergence, confluence, concourse, concurrence, concentration; meeting.

assemblage, etc., 72; resort, etc., 74.

V. **converge,** concur; come together, unite, meet, close in upon; center, concentrate.

Adj. convergent, confluent, concurrent; centripetal.

291. [Motion farther off] DIVERGENCE.—*N.* divergence, ramification, forking; separation, detachment, dispersion, deviation, etc., 279.

V. **diverge,** ramify, branch off, fly off; spread, scatter, disperse, etc., 73; part, sever, separate, sunder.

Adj. divergent, radial, centrifugal.

Adv. broadcast.

292. ARRIVAL.—*N.* arrival, advent; landing; debarkation, disembarkation.

destination, bourn, goal; harbor, haven, port; terminus, terminal; home, journey's end; anchorage, refuge.

meeting, joining, encounter, rejoining; return, re-entry.

V. **arrive,** get to, come to; come; reach, attain; overtake; make, fetch; join, rejoin; return; enter, appear, drop in, visit.

alight, light, dismount, detrain.

land, cast anchor, put in, debark, disembark.

meet, encounter, come across; come (*or* light) upon.

Adv. here, hither.

293. DEPARTURE.—*N.* departure, embarkation; outset, start; removal; exit, etc. (*egress*), 295; exodus, hegira, flight.

leave-taking, adieu, farewell, good-by, Godspeed; valediction, valedictory, valedictorian.

V. depart; go, go away, go off, set out, start, issue, march out, debouch, sally forth; sally, go forth; retire, withdraw, remove; cut [*colloq. or slang*], take flight, take wing; fly, flit; strike tents, decamp, break camp, take leave; disappear, etc., 449; entrain; saddle, bridle, harness up, hitch up [*colloq.*].

quit, vacate, evacuate, abandon.

embark, go abroad; set sail, put to sea, sail, take ship; get under way, weigh anchor.

Adv. hence, whence, thence.

294. [Motion into] INGRESS.—*N.* ingress; entrance, entry; influx, inroad, incursion, invasion, irruption; penetration, infiltration; insinuation, insertion, etc., 300.

immigration, incoming, foreign influx.

import [*used esp. in pl.*], importation.

immigrant, incomer, newcomer, colonist.

inlet; mouth, door, etc. (*opening*), 260; path, etc., 627; conduit, etc., 350.

V. enter; come in, pour in, flow in; set foot on; burst *or* break in upon, invade; penetrate, infiltrate.

Adj. incoming, inbound, inward.

295. [Motion out of] EGRESS.—*N.* egress, exit, issue; emergence; outbreak; outburst; eruption; emanation; evacuation; leakage, percolation, oozing, drain, drainage; gush, outpour, effluence, outflow, discharge.

export [*used esp. in pl.*], exportation; shipment.

emigration, exodus, departure.

emigrant, migrant, colonist.

outlet, vent, spout, faucet, tap, sluice, floodgate; mouth, opening, door; pathway; conduit.

V. emerge, emanate, issue; go (*or* come, pass, pour, flow) out of.

exude, discharge, leak; run through, percolate; strain, distill; perspire, sweat; drain, seep, ooze, filter, infiltrate, gush, spout, flow out; pour, trickle; find vent; escape, etc., 671.

Adj. eruptive, porous, pervious, leaky; outgoing, outbound, outward bound.

296. [Motion into, actively] RECEPTION.—*N.* reception; admission, admittance, entree; importation; initiation, introduction, absorption; suction, sucking; eating, drinking, etc. (*food*), 298; insertion, etc., 300.

V. give entrance to, introduce, usher, admit, initiate; receive, import, bring in; absorb, imbibe, instill, implant, induct, inhale; let in, take in.

swallow, gulp; eat, drink, etc., 298.

Adj. introductory, initiatory, preliminary.

297. [Motion out of, actively] EJECTION.—*N.* ejection, rejection, expulsion, eviction, dislodgment, banishment, exile, deportation, expedition; discharge, evacuation, eruption, eruptiveness; tapping, drainage; emetic; vomiting.

V. eject, reject; expel, discard; ostracize, boycott; banish, exile, fire [*slang*], throw away *or* aside, push out *or* off, send off *or* away; discharge, dismiss, turn *or* cast adrift; turn out, throw overboard.

evict, oust, dislodge; turn out of doors, deport, expatriate.

emit, send out, pour out, dispatch, shed, void, evacuate; give vent to; tap, draw off; pour forth; squirt, spurt, spill; breathe, blow, exhale.

empty; drain, sweep off; clear off, draw off; clean out, purge; tap, broach.

root out, root up, unearth, eradicate; weed out, get out; eliminate, get rid of, do away with, shake off.

vomit, spew; cast up, bring up; disgorge.

unpack, unlade, unload, unship; dump.

298. [Eating] FOOD.—*N.* eating, mastication, rumination; gastronomy, carnivorousness, vegetarianism, gluttony, etc., 957.

mouth, jaws, mandible [*esp. of birds*], chops.

drinking, potation, draft, libation; carousal, etc. (*amusement*), 840; drunkenness, etc., 959.

food, meat, nourishment, nutriment, sustenance, nurture, subsistence, provender, corn, feed, fodder, provision, ration, board; commissariat, etc. (*provisions*), 637; prey, forage, pasture, pasturage; fare, cheer; diet, dietary; regimen; staff of life, bread.

eatables, victuals, edibles, grub [*slang*], meat; bread, viands, delicacy, dainty, creature comforts, ambrosia; good cheer, good living.

table, cuisine [F.], bill of fare, menu, table d'hôte [F.], à la carte [F.].

meal, repast, feed [*colloq.*], spread [*colloq.*]; mess; refreshment, entertainment; refection, collation, picnic, feast, banquet, potluck.

mouthful, tidbit, morsel.

drink, beverage, liquor, potion, dram, draft.

restaurant, café, eating house.

V. eat, feed, fare, devour, swallow, take; gulp, bolt; fall to; dispatch; tuck in [*slang*], dine, banquet, gormandize, etc., 957; crunch, chew, masticate, nibble, gnaw, mumble.

live on; feed upon; browse, graze, crop; bite, champ, munch, ruminate.

drink, quaff, sip, sup; lap; tipple, guzzle, carouse.

cater, purvey, etc., 637.

Adj. eatable, edible, esculent; dietetic; culinary; nutritive, nutritious; succulent.

underdone, rare; well done; overdone; high [*of game*]; ripe [*of cheese*].

drinkable, potable; bibulous.

omnivorous, carnivorous, flesh-eating, herbivorous, graminivorous, piscivorous.

299. EXCRETION.—*N.* excretion, discharge, emanation, exhalation, secretion, effusion, perspiration, sweat.

hemorrhage, bleeding; outpouring, etc. (*egress*), 295; diarrhea.

saliva, spittle, sputum (*pl.* sputa), spit; catarrh; lava.

V. excrete, etc. (*eject*), 297; secrete; exhale, emanate, etc. (*come out*), 295.

300. [Forcible ingress] INSERTION.—*N.* insertion, implantation, introduction; interpolation, interlineation, insinuation, etc. (*intervention*), 228; injection, inoculation, infusion; ingress, etc., 294; immersion; submersion, dip, plunge.

V. insert, introduce, put in (*or* into), run into; inject; imbed, inlay, inweave; interject, etc., 228; infuse, instill, inoculate, impregnate, imbue.

graft, ingraft, bud, plant, implant.

obtrude; thrust in, stick in, ram in, stuff in, tuck in, press in, drive in; pierce, etc. (*make a hole*), 260.

immerse, merge; bathe, soak, etc. (*water*), 337; dip, plunge, etc., 310.

301. [Forcible egress] EXTRACTION.—*N.* extraction; removal, elimination, extrication, eradication, extirpation, extermination; ejection, etc., 297; export, etc. (*egress*), 295; wrench.

V. extract, draw; take out, draw out, pull out, tear out, pluck out, pick out, get out; wring from, wrench; extort; root up, weed out; eradicate, uproot, pull up, extirpate.

elicit, evolve, bring forth, draw forth; extricate.

eliminate, etc. (*eject*), 297; remove.

express, squeeze out, press out, distill.

302. [Motion through] PASSAGE.—*N.* passage, transmission; permeation, penetration; infiltration; ingress; egress, exit, issue; path, road, way; conduit, opening; journey, voyage, sail, cruise.

V. pass, pass through; perforate, penetrate, permeate, thread, cut across; ford, cross; make (*or* work, thread, worm, force) one's way; find a way (*or* vent); transmit, make way, traverse.

303. [Motion beyond] **OVERRUNNING.**—*N.* overrunning, overrun, inroad, advance, infraction, transgression, encroachment, infringement; transcendence; redundance, etc., 641.

V. overrun, pass, go beyond, go by, shoot ahead of; steal a march upon, gain upon.

outstrip, override, overshoot the mark; outrun, outride, outrival, outdo; beat; distance; throw into the shade; exceed, transcend, surmount; tower above, surpass.

encroach, overstep, transgress, trespass, infringe, intrude, invade.

Adv. ahead, beyond the mark.

304. [Motion short of] **SHORTCOMING.**—*N.* shortcoming, failure, falling short; default, defalcation; delinquency; fizzle [*colloq.*], slump [*colloq.*]; flash in the pan.

incompleteness, deficiency; defect, imperfection, fault; insufficiency, etc., 640; noncompletion, nonfulfillment; failure, etc., 732.

V. fall short, come short of, not reach; want; keep within bounds (*or* the mark, compass).

collapse, fail, break down, flat out [*colloq.*], come to nothing; fall down, slump, fizzle out [*all colloq.*]; fall through, fall to the ground; cave in [*colloq.*], end in smoke, miss the mark.

Adj. deficient; at fault; short, short of; out of depth; perfunctory, remiss.

305. [Motion upward] **ASCENT.**—*N.* ascent, ascension; rising, rise, upgrowth, upward flight; upgrade; leap, etc., 309; grade, ramp, acclivity, hill, etc., 217.

stairway, staircase, stairs; flight of steps *or* stairs; ladder, scaling ladder; companionway [*naut.*]; escalator, elevator.

V. ascend, rise, mount, arise, uprise; go up, get up, work one's way up, start up, spring up, shoot up; aspire, aim high.

climb, shin [*colloq.*], swarm [*colloq.*], clamber, scramble, escalade, surmount, wind upward, scale.

tower, soar, spire, go aloft, fly aloft; surge; leap, etc., 309.

Adj. rising; ascendant; upcast; buoyant.

Adv. up, upward, skyward, heavenward; upturned; uphill.

306. [Motion downward] **DESCENT.**—*N.* descent, inclination, declension, declination; drop; cadence; subsidence, lapse; downcome, comedown, setback, fall; slump [*colloq.*], downfall, tumble, stumble, slip, tilt, trip, lurch.

avalanche, landslide, slide, snowslide, glissade.

declivity, dip, decline, pitch, drop, downgrade.

V. descend, go (*or* drop, come) down, fall, gravitate, drop, slip, skid, slide, settle; decline, sink, subside, droop, slump [*colloq.*].

get down, dismount, alight, light; swoop; stoop, etc., 308; fall prostrate, precipitate oneself; let fall.

tumble, trip, stumble, lurch, pitch, topple; tilt, sprawl.

Adj. steep, sloping, declivitous; beetling, overhanging; bottomless, fathomless, abysmal.

descending; down, downcast, descendent; deciduous.

Adv. downward, downhill.

307. ELEVATION.—*N.* elevation; raising; erection, lift; upheaval; sublimation, exaltation; prominence, relief.

lever, crowbar, crane, derrick, windlass, capstan, winch; dredge, dredger.

elevator, dumbwaiter; escalator.

V. elevate, raise, heighten, lift, erect; set up, tilt up; rear, hoist, heave; uplift, upraise, uprear; buoy, mount, exalt; sublimate.

take up, drag up, fish up; dredge.

Adj. elevated, upturned, stilted, rampant.

308. DEPRESSION.—*N.* depression, lowering; dip, etc. (*concavity*), 252.

overthrow, overturn; upset; prostration, reduction, abasement, subversion.

bow, curtsy, dip [*colloq.*], bob, duck, genuflexion, kowtow, obeisance, salaam.

V. depress, lower, cast down, let drop, let fall; sink, debase, bring low, abase, reduce, precipitate.

overthrow, overturn, overset, upset, prostrate, level, fell; down [*colloq.*], cast (*or* throw, fling, dash, pull, knock, hew) down, raze.

sit, sit down, squat; recline, sprawl.

crouch, stoop, bend, cower.

bow, curtsy, genuflect, kowtow, duck, bob, dip, kneel; incline, make obeisance, salaam, prostrate oneself, bow down.

Adj. depressed; at a low ebb; prostrate, horizontal.

309. LEAP.—*N.* leap, jump, hop, spring, bound, vault.

caper, dance, gambol, frisk, prance, curvet, caracole, buck; hop, skip, and jump.

V. leap, jump, hop, spring, bound, vault, clear, ramp, skip.

prance, dance, caper; buck; curvet, caracole, bob, bounce, flounce; frisk, jump about, romp, frolic, gambol; cavort, cut capers [*colloq.*].

Adj. leaping, saltatorial; frisky, lively, frolicsome.

Adv. on the light fantastic toe.

310. PLUNGE.—*N.* plunge, dip, dive, nose-dive [*aviation*], header [*colloq.*]; submergence, submersion, immersion.

diver; diving bird.

V. plunge, dip, souse, duck; dive, plump; take a header [*colloq.*]; make a plunge; bathe; pitch.

submerge, submerse; immerse; douse, sink, engulf, send to the bottom.

founder, welter, wallow; get out of one's depth; go to the bottom.

Adj. submergible, submersible.

311. CIRCULAR MOTION.—*N.* circulation, turn, excursion, circumnavigation, circumflexion; wheel, compass, lap, circuit; turning, evolution; coil, spiral.

V. turn, bend, wheel; go about, put about [*both naut.*]; go (*or* turn) round, round, turn a corner; double a point [*naut.*]; make a detour.

circle, encircle, circumscribe, circuit, describe a circle, circumnavigate; go the round.

wind, circulate, meander; whisk, twirl, twist, coil.

wallow, welter, roll.

Adj. circuitous, roundabout, devious.

312. ROTATION—*N.* rotation, revolution, gyration, circulation, roll; pirouette, convolution.

eddy, vortex, whirlpool, maelstrom; swirl, surge; whir, whirl; cyclone, tornado; vertiginousness, vertigo.

V. rotate, roll, revolve, spin, turn, turn round, encircle, circulate, swirl, gyrate, wheel, whirl, twirl; roll up, furl; box the compass.

Adj. rotating, rotary; vertiginous.

313. UNFOLDMENT.—*N.* unfoldment, unfolding, development; evolvement, evolution; inversion.

V. evolve; unfold, unroll, unwind, uncoil, untwist, unfurl, untwine, unravel; disentangle; develop.

Adj. evolutional, evolutionary.

314. [Motion to and fro] OSCILLATION.—*N.* oscillation, vibration, undulation, pulsation; pulse, beat, throb.

alternation; coming and going; ebb and flow, flux and reflux, systole and diastole; ups and downs.

fluctuation; vacillation, irresolution, indecision.

swing, wave, beat, shake, wag, seesaw, teeter.

V. oscillate, vibrate, undulate, wave; rock, teeter, sway, swing, dangle; pulsate, beat; wag, waggle; nod, bob, curtsy; wobble.

fluctuate, reel, quake; quiver, quaver, shake, flicker; wriggle; roll, toss, pitch; flounder, stagger, totter.

alternate, pass and repass, shuttle, ebb and flow, come and go; vacillate.

Adj. oscillating; undulatory, vibratory; pendulous.

Adv. to and fro, up and down, back and forth, in and out, seesaw, zigzag, from side to side, shuttlewise.

315. [Irregular motion] AGITATION.—*N.* agitation, stir, tremor, shuffling, shake, ripple, jog, jolt, jar, jerk, shock, trepidation, quiver, quaver, dance; tarantella; twitter, flicker, flutter.

disquiet, perturbation, commotion, turmoil, turbulence; tumult, hubbub, rout, bustle, fuss, racket.

twitching, chorea, St. Vitus' dance; staggers, blind staggers; epilepsy, fits.

spasm, throe, throb, palpitation, convulsion, paroxysm, seizure, grip, cramp.

disturbance, disorder; restlessness, changeableness, instability.

ferment, fermentation, ebullition, effervescence, hurly-burly; tempest, storm, whirlpool, vortex, etc., 312; whirlwind, tornado, cyclone, typhoon.

V. **be agitated;** shake, tremble, flutter, flicker; quiver, quaver, quake; shiver, writhe, toss; shuffle, tumble, stagger, bob, reel, sway; wag, waggle, wriggle; stumble, shamble, flounder, totter, flounce, flop, dance, curvet, prance, cavort; squirm; twitch; bustle.

throb, pulsate, beat, palpitate, go pitapat.

ferment, effervesce, foam, boil, boil over, bubble, bubble up; simmer.

agitate, shake, convulse, toss, tumble, wield, brandish, flap, flourish, whisk, jerk, jolt, jog, joggle, disturb, stir, shake up, churn.

Adj. **agitated,** shaking, tremulous; convulsive, jerky; effervescent, unquiet, restless.

Adv. by fits and starts; in convulsions, in fits, in a flutter.

CLASS III

WORDS RELATING TO MATTER

I. MATTER IN GENERAL

316. MATERIALITY.—*N.* **materiality,** corporality; substantiality, material existence; incarnation, flesh and blood.

matter, body, substance, brute matter, protoplasm, stuff, element, principle, material, substratum.

object, article, thing, something; still life; materials, etc., 635. Science of matter: physics; natural philosophy; physical science. materialist, physicist.

V. **materialize,** substantiate, incorporate, embody, incarnate.

Adj. **material,** bodily, corporeal, corporal, physical, incarnate, materialized, embodied; sensible, tangible, ponderable, palpable, substantial; unspiritual, materialistic.

objective, impersonal, nonsubjective.

317. IMMATERIALITY.—*N.* immateriality, insubstantiality, incorporality, unsubstantiality, spirituality; astral plane.

personality; I, myself, me.

ego, spirit, etc. (*soul*), 450; astral body, etheric double, subliminal self, subconscious self, higher self.

spiritualism, spiritism; animism.

spiritualist, spiritist; animist.

V. dematerialize, disembody, spiritualize.

Adj. immaterial, incorporeal, incorporate, unsubstantial; spiritistic, animistic; discarnate, bodiless, disembodied; extramundane, unearthly; spiritual, etc. (*psychical*), 450.

subjective, personal, nonobjective.

318. WORLD.—*N.* world, creation, nature, universe; earth, globe, sphere, wide world; cosmos, macrocosm.

heavens, sky, empyrean, starry cope (*or* host); firmament.

heavenly bodies, luminaries, stars, asteroids; galaxy, Milky Way; constellations, planets, satellites; comet, meteor, falling (*or* shooting) star; solar system.

sun, orb of day, daystar [*poetic*], Helios, Apollo, Phoebus, etc. (*sun god*), 423.

moon, Diana, Luna, Phoebe, Cynthia, Selene, silver-footed queen.

Adj. cosmic, mundane, terrestrial, earthly, sublunary.

celestial, empyreal, heavenly, solar; lunar; starry, stellar, sidereal, astral; nebular.

Adv. in all creation, on the face of the globe, here below, under the sun.

319. GRAVITY.—*N.* gravity, gravitation; weight, heft, heaviness, ponderousness, specific gravity, pressure, load, burden, ballast, counterpoise; mass.

Weighing instrument: balance, scales, steelyard, beam, weighbridge.

Science of gravity: statics.

V. weigh, load, press; counterweigh, poise; gravitate.

Adj. weighty, heavy, ponderous, ponderable; cumbersome, burdensome, cumbrous, unwieldy, massive; static.

320. LEVITY.—*N.* levity, lightness, imponderability, buoyancy, volatility.

ferment, leaven, yeast, pepsin.

V. be light, float, swim.

render light, lighten.

ferment, work, raise, leaven.

Adj. light, subtle, imponderous, imponderable, ethereal, airy, feathery, gossamery; volatile, vaporous, buoyant, floating, foamy, frothy; portable.

fermenting, fermentative, yeasty.

II. INORGANIC MATTER

(1) Solids

321. DENSITY.—*N.* **density,** solidity, solidness; impenetrability, impermeability; costiveness, constipation.

condensation; solidification, consolidation, concretion, coagulation; cohesion, etc., 46; petrifaction, etc. (*hardening*), 323; thickening, crystallization, precipitation.

solid body, mass, block, lump; concretion, concrete, conglomerate; stone, rock, cake; card.

sediment, lees, dregs, settlings.

V. **be dense,** compress, squeeze, ram down; solidify; cement, set, consolidate, condense, congeal, coagulate, curd, curdle; fix, clot, thicken, cake, candy, precipitate, deposit, cohere, crystallize; petrify, harden, stiffen.

compress, squeeze, ram down.

Adj. **dense,** solid, solidified; coherent, cohesive, compact; close, serried, thickset; substantial, massive, impenetrable, concrete, hard; crystalline, thick, stodgy.

undissolved, unmelted, unliquefied, unthawed.

indivisible; indissoluble, insoluble.

322. RARITY.—*N.* **rarity,** tenuity; subtlety.

rarefaction, attenuation, expansion, inflation; ether, etc. (*gas*), 334.

V. **rarefy,** expand, dilate, attenuate, thin.

Adj. **rare,** subtle, thin, fine, tenuous, compressible, flimsy, slight, light, porous; rarefied, unsubstantial.

323. HARDNESS.—*N.* **hardness,** firmness, rigidity, inflexibility, temper, callosity; induration, petrifaction, ossification; crystallization.

V. **harden,** render hard, temper, stiffen, cement, indurate, petrify, ossify.

Adj. **hard,** rigid, stubborn, stiff, firm; stark, unbending, unyielding, inflexible, tense.

adamantine, stony, granitic, rocky, horny, callous, bony, cartilaginous.

324. SOFTNESS.—*N.* **softness,** pliableness, flexibility, pliancy, pliability, malleability, ductility, tractility, plasticity, flaccidity, laxity, flabbiness, mollification, softening.

V. **soften,** render soft, mollify, mellow; mash; knead, massage. **bend,** give, yield, relent, relax.

Adj. **soft,** tender; mollified; supple, pliant, pliable, flexible, lithe, lithesome, limber; plastic; ductile, malleable, tractable; yielding; flabby, flaccid, lax, limp, flimsy; mellow; spongy.

downy, woolly, fluffy, feathery.

325. ELASTICITY.—*N.* **elasticity,** springiness, spring, resilience *or* resiliency, buoyancy; recoil, rebound, reflex.

V. **be elastic;** spring back, recoil.

Adj. **elastic,** springy, resilient, buoyant.

326. INELASTICITY.—*N.* **inelasticity,** flaccidity, laxity; want of elasticity, etc., 325.

Adj. **inelastic,** flaccid, yielding; not elastic.

327. TENACITY.—*N.* **tenacity,** toughness, strength; cohesiveness, cohesion, adhesion; stubbornness, etc. (*obstinacy*), 606; gumminess, glutinousness, viscidity.

Adj. **tenacious,** cohesive, tough, strong, resisting; adhesive, stringy, viscid, gummy, glutinous, gristly, cartilaginous; stubborn, etc. (*obstinate*), 606.

328. BRITTLENESS.—*N.* **brittleness,** fragility; frailty; shortness.

V. **break,** crack, snap, split, shiver, splinter, crumble, crash, crush, burst, give way; fall to pieces; crumble to dust.

Adj. **brittle,** breakable, delicate, fragile, frail; splintery; crisp, short [*as of pastry*].

329. STRUCTURE.—*N.* **structure,** organization, constitution, organism, anatomy, frame, mold, fabric, construction; framework, architecture; stratification.

texture, contexture; tissue, grain, web, surface, nap; roughness; warp and woof (*or* weft); fineness (*or* coarseness) of grain.

Adj. **structural,** organic; anatomic *or* anatomical.

textile; fine-grained, coarse-grained, ingrained; ingrain; fine, delicate, subtile, subtle, gossamer, gossamery, filmy; coarse; homespun, linsey-woolsey.

330. POWDERINESS.—*N.* **powderiness,** grittiness, sandiness, friability.

powder, dust, sand, shingle; sawdust; grit; meal, bran, flour, rice, spore; crumb, seed, grain; particle.

Reduction to powder: pulverization, comminution, granulation, disintegration, abrasion, detrition; mill, grater, rasp, file, pestle and mortar, grindstone, quern, millstone.

V. **pulverize,** powder, comminute, granulate, reduce to powder; scrape, file, abrade, grind, grate, rasp, pound, bruise, beat, crush, craunch, crunch, crumble, disintegrate.

Adj. powdery, granular, mealy, floury, farinaceous, branny, dusty, sandy, gritty.

pulverable *or* pulverizable, friable, crumbly, shivery.

331. FRICTION.—*N.* friction, rubbing, abrasion, rub; massage; erasure; elbow grease [*colloq.*].

eraser, rubber, India rubber.

V. rub, abrade, scratch, scrape, scrub, fray, rasp, graze, curry, scour, polish, rub out, erase, file, grind, etc. (*pulverize*), 330; massage.

332. [Absence or prevention of friction] LUBRICATION.—*N.* lubrication, anointment, oiling.

smoothness, polish, gloss; unctuousness.

lubricant, lubricator; ointment, salve, balm, unguent.

V. lubricate, oil, grease; lather, soap; wax; anoint.

(2) Fluids

333. FLUIDITY.—*N.* fluidity, liquidity, liquidness; liquefaction; solubility; gaseity, etc., 334.

solution; fluid; liquid; juice, sap, lymph, serum.

Science of liquids at rest: hydrostatics, hydrodynamics, hydrokinetics.

V. be fluid; run; flow, etc. (*water in motion*), 348; liquefy, etc., 335.

Adj. liquid, fluid; juicy, succulent, sappy; rheumy; fluent, flowing; liquefied, uncongealed; soluble.

334. GASEITY.—*N.* gaseity, gaseousness, vaporousness; volatility; aeration; gasification; flatulence.

elastic fluid, gas, air, vapor, ether, steam, fume, effluvium; cloud, etc., 353.

Science of elastic fluids: pneumatics, aerostatics, aerodynamics, aerography, aeromechanics.

V. gasify, render gaseous; aerate; vaporize, etc., 336.

Adj. gaseous, ethereal, aery, aerial, airy, vaporous, volatile, flatulent.

335. LIQUEFACTION.—*N.* liquefaction, liquescence; deliquescence; melting, fusion; thaw; solubleness; solution.

mixture, decoction, infusion, solution.

V. dissolve, liquefy; run; melt, thaw, fuse; hold in solution; percolate.

Adj. liquefied; soluble, dissolvable; solvent, dissolvent.

336. VAPORIZATION.—*N.* vaporization, atomization; fumigation, steaming; distillation; gasification; evaporation.

vaporizer, atomizer, spray, evaporator, still, retort.

V. vaporize, gasify, atomize; spray; distill, sublimate, evaporate; exhale, emit vapor; fumigate; fume, smoke, reek, steam.

Adj. volatile, vapory, vaporous, gaseous; volatilized.

337. WATER.—*N.* water, lymph; aqua [L.], *eau* [F.]; fluid, etc., 333.

washing, bathing, bath, immersion; dilution; infiltration, irrigation, seepage.

deluge, etc. (*water in motion*), 348; high water, flood tide, spring-tide.

sprinkler, shower *or* shower bath; nozzle; atomizer, etc., 336.

water, dilute, add water; moisten, etc., 339; steep, soak, drench, wet, dip, immerse, submerge; duck; drown; wash, lave, bathe, sprinkle, dabble; inundate, deluge; irrigate; infiltrate, percolate, seep.

inject; gargle, syringe.

Adj. watery, aquatic, lymphatic; infiltrative, seepy; drenching; diluted, weak; wet, etc. (*moist*), 339.

338. AIR.—*N.* air, etc. (*gas*), 334; atmosphere; ventilation.

the open, open air; sky, blue sky.

weather, climate; rise and fall of the barometer (*or* mercury).

Science of air: aerology, aerometry, aerography; meteorology, climatology; pneumatics; aeronautics, etc., 267.

aeronaut, etc., 269a.

barometer, aneroid, weatherglass, weather gauge.

weather vane, weathercock, vane.

V. air, ventilate, fan, etc. (*wind*), 349.

fly, soar, drift, hover; aviate, etc. (*aeronautics*), 267.

Adj. containing air, flatulent, effervescent; windy, etc., 349.

atmospheric, airy; aerial, aeriform; aery, pneumatic.

meteorological, barometric, aerographic, weatherwise.

Adv. in the open air, in the open, under the stars, out of doors, outdoors; alfresco [It.].

339. MOISTURE.—*N.* moisture; moistness, humidity; dew; marsh, etc., 345.

V. moisten, wet, sponge, damp, bedew; infiltrate, saturate; soak, sodden, seethe, sop; drench, etc. (*water*), 337.

perspire, etc. (*exude*), 295.

Adj. moist, damp; watery, etc., 337; undried, humid, wet, dank, muggy; dewy; juicy.

sodden, soppy, soggy, dabbled; reeking, dripping, soaking, saturated, soft, sloppy, muddy: swampy, etc. (*marshy*), 345; irriguous.

340. DRYNESS.—*N.* dryness, aridness, aridity, drought.

desiccation, evaporation; drainage.

V. dry, dry up, soak up; sponge, swab, wipe, drain, parch, sear; desiccate, evaporate.

Adj. dry, rainless, fair, pleasant, fine; arid, sear, droughty, waterless, dried, desiccated; juiceless, sapless; corky; husky, parched; waterproof, watertight.

341. OCEAN—*N.* ocean, sea, main, high seas, deep, salt water; waters, waves, billows; tide, etc. (*water in motion*), 348; offing, watery waste, pond [*humorous for Atlantic*], the seven seas; ocean lane, steamer track.

Neptune, Poseidon, Oceanus, Thetis, Triton, naiad, Nereid; sea nymph, siren, mermaid, merman; trident, dolphin.

oceanography; oceanographer.

Adj. oceanic, marine, maritime; seaworthy, seagoing.

342. LAND.—*N.* land, earth, ground, soil, dry land, terra firma [L.].

continent; mainland, main; peninsula, chersonese; delta; neck of land, isthmus; oasis; promontory, etc. (*projection*), 250; highland, etc. (*height*), 206; plain, etc., 344.

realty, real estate, property, acres.

coast, shore, strand, beach; bank; seaboard, seaside, seacoast, seashore; reclamation, made land.

fatherland, home, country, native land; region, etc., 181.

soil, glebe, clay, loam, marl, gravel, mold, subsoil, clod.

rock, crag, cliff, boulder.

landsman, landlubber, tiller of the soil; agriculturist, etc., 371.

V. land, disembark, debark, come to land, come (*or* go) ashore.

Adj. earthy; continental, midland; earthly, terrestrial; littoral, alluvial; landed, territorial; geographic *or* geographical.

Adv. ashore, on shore, on land, on dry land, on terra firma.

343. GULF, LAKE.—*N.* gulf, bay, inlet, bight, estuary, bayou, fiord, frith *or* firth; mouth; lagoon, cove, creek; natural harbor; roads; sound, strait, narrows.

lake, loch [Scot.], mere, tarn, pond, pool; well, artesian well; ditch, dike, dam, race, millrace; tank, reservoir.

344. PLAIN.—*N.* plain, open country; basin, downs, waste, desert, wild, steppe [*Russia*], grassland; tundra [*Arctic*], pampas [*esp. in Argentina*], savanna [*as in Brazil; also, a treeless plain, as in Florida*], campo [*S. Amer.*], llano [*S. Amer.*], prairie, heath, common, moor, moorland; bush; plateau, tableland, mesa; uplands; reach, stretch, expanse; alkali flat.

meadow, mead, pasture, lea, pasturage, field.

lawn, green, plot, grassplot.

greensward, sward, turf, sod, grass; heather.

grounds; estate, park, common, campus.

345. MARSH.—*N.* marsh, swamp, morass, peat bog, fen, bog, quagmire, slough; mud, slush.

Adj. marsh, marshy, fenny, swampy, boggy, soft; muddy, squashy, spongy.

346. ISLAND.—*N.* island, isle, islet; reef, atoll; archipelago; islander.

V. insulate, island.

Adj. insular, seagirt; archipelagic.

347. [Fluid in motion] STREAM.—*N.* stream, etc. (*of water*), 348 (*of air*), 349.

V. flow, etc., 348; blow, etc., 349.

348. [Water in motion] RIVER.—*N.* running water, jet, squirt, spout, splash, rush, gush, sluice.

waterspout, waterfall; fall, cascade, Niagara; cataract, inundation, deluge; chute, washout.

rain, rainfall; drizzle, shower; downpour, cloudburst; rains, rainy season, monsoon.

stream, course, flux, flow, current, tide, race, millrace, tiderace.

spring; fount, fountain; rill, rivulet, streamlet, brooklet; branch; brook, river; reach; tributary.

body of water, torrent, rapids, flood; spring (*or* high, flood, full) tide; bore, eagre; ebb, reflux; undercurrent, undertow; eddy, vortex, whirlpool, maelstrom.

wave, billow, surge, swell, ripple; tidal wave; comber, rollers, ground swell, surf, breakers, white horses.

Science of fluids in motion: hydrodynamics; hydraulics, hydrostatics, hydrokinetics, hydromechanics.

V. flow, run; meander; gush, pour, spout, roll, jet, well, issue; drop, drip, dribble, plash, trickle, distill, percolate; stream, surge, swirl, overflow, inundate, deluge, flow over, splash, swash; murmur, babble, purl, gurgle, spurt, ooze, flow out, etc. (*egress*), 295.

flow into, fall into, open into, drain into; discharge itself, disembogue.

Cause a flow: pour; pour out, etc. (*emit*), 297; shower down; irrigate, drench, etc. (*wet*), 337; spill, splash.

Stop a flow: stanch; dam, plug, stop up, cork, dam up, obstruct, choke, cut off.

rain; pour; shower, sprinkle, drizzle; set in.

Adj. flowing, fluent, meandering, flexuous; choppy, rolling; tidal.

rainy, showery, drizzly, drizzling, wet.

349. [Air in motion] WIND.—*N.* wind, draft, air; breath, puff, whiff, zephyr, blow, stream, current.

gust, blast, breeze, squall, half a gale, gale.

trade wind, trades, monsoon.

storm, tempest, hurricane, whirlwind, tornado, cyclone, typhoon, simoom [*as in Asia Minor*], harmattan [*W. coast of Africa*], sirocco [*as in W. Africa, Texas, and Kansas*], khamsin [*Egypt*], mistral [*Mediterranean*]; blizzard, norther, northeaster, northeast gale.

wind gauge, anemometer, anemograph; weathercock, weather vane, vane.

breathing, respiration, inspiration, inhalation, expiration, exhalation; blowing, fanning, inflation; ventilation.

V. blow, waft; storm.

respire, breathe, inhale, exhale; inspire, expire; puff, gasp, wheeze· snuff, snuffle; sniff, sniffle; sneeze, cough, hiccup.

inflate, pump, blow up.

whistle, scream, roar, howl, sing, sing in the shrouds, growl.
Adj. windy, breezy, gusty, squally.

stormy, tempestuous, blustering, cyclonic, typhonic; boisterous, violent.

350. [Channel for the passage of water] CONDUIT.—N. conduit, channel, duct, watercourse, canyon, coulee, water gap, gorge, ravine, chasm; race; aqueduct, canal; flume, dike, main· arroyo, gully, gulch; moat, ditch; gutter, drain, sewer, culvert; scupper; funnel, trough, siphon, pump, hose; pipe, tube; artery; spout, gargoyle; weir, floodgate, water gate, sluice, lock, valve.

Anatomy: artery, vein, blood vessel, pore; aorta; intestines, bowels; esophagus, gullet; throat.

351. [Channel for the passage of air] AIR PIPE—N. air pipe, airhole, blowhole, breathing hole, touchhole, venthole, spilehole, bung, bunghole; shaft, air shaft, smoke shaft, flue, chimney, funnel, vent, ventilator.

nostril, nozzle, throat; windpipe, trachea.

352. SEMILIQUIDITY.—N. semiliquidity; stickiness, pastiness, adhesiveness; thickening, jellification.

mud, slush, slime, ooze; moisture, humidity; marsh, etc., 345.

V. thicken, coagulate, gelatinize; jellify, jelly, jell [*colloq.*]; emulsify; mash, squash [*collog*], churn, beat up.

Adj. semifluid, semiliquid; half-melted, half-frozen; milky, muddy, curdled; thick, gelatinous, mucilaginous, glutinous, sticky; ropy; clotted.

353. [Mixture of air and water] BUBBLE, CLOUD.—N. bubble; foam, froth, spray, surf; spume, scum; lather, suds, yeast.

effervescence, babbling, fermentation; evaporation.

cloud, vapor, fog, mist, haze, steam; scud, rack, cumulus; nebula, cirrus, curl cloud; thunderhead; stratus.

V. bubble, boil, foam, spume, froth; effervesce, ferment, fizz; aerate.

cloud, overcast, overcloud, befog, becloud, mist, fog, overshadow, shadow.

Adj. bubbling, frothy, effervescent, sparkling, fizzy, heady. cloudy, nebulous; vaporous; overcast.

354. PULPINESS.—*N.* pulpiness; fleshiness; pulp, paste, dough, sponge, batter, curd, pap, jam, poultice.

V. pulp, mash, squash [*colloq.*], macerate; coagulate, etc., 352.

Adj. pulpy; [*of fruit*] fleshy, succulent.

355. UNCTUOUSNESS.—*N.* unctuousness, oiliness; lubrication; unguent, salve, cerate; ointment, etc. (*oil*), 356; anointment; lubricant.

V. oil, anoint, lubricate, etc., 332; smear, salve, grease, lard.

Adj. unctuous, oily, oleaginous, fat, fatty, greasy; waxy, soapy, slippery.

356. OIL.—*N.* oil, fat, butter, cream, grease, tallow, suet, lard, dripping, blubber; glycerin; coconut butter; soap, soft soap; wax; paraffin, benzine, kerosene, naphtha, gasoline, petroleum; ointment, pomade, unguent, liniment.

356a. RESIN.—*N.* resin, rosin, gum; shellac, varnish, mastic, lacquer, sealing wax; amber, ambergris; bitumen, pitch, tar, asphalt.

V. varnish, etc. (*overlay*), 223; rosin, resin.

Adj. resinous, lacquered, tarred, tarry, pitched, pitchy, gummed, gummy, waxed; bituminous, asphaltic.

III. ORGANIC MATTER

(1) Vitality

357. ORGANIZATION.—*N.* organization, structure, organized nature, animated nature; living beings; organic remains; organism; animal and plant life, fauna and flora.

fossils; fossilization, petrifaction; paleontology; paleontologist.

Science of living beings: biology, natural history;[1] zoology, etc., 368, botany; physiology, anatomy, organic chemistry; evolution, Darwinism.

protoplasm, bioplasm; cell, proteid, protein, albumen, germinal matter, germ plasm, germ cell; amoeba, protozoan.

naturalist, biologist, zoologist, botanist, bacteriologist, embryologist.

---

[1]The term *natural history* is also used as relating to all the objects in nature whether organic or inorganic, and including, therefore, *mineralogy, geology, meteorology,* etc.

V. **organize,** systematize, form, arrange, construct.

fossilize, petrify, mummify.

Adj. **organic,** organized, structural; cellular, protoplasmic.

fossilized, petrified.

358. INORGANIZATION.—*N.* **mineral kingdom,** mineral world; unorganized (*or* inorganic) matter.

Science of the mineral kingdom: mineralogy, geology, metallurgy.

V. **mineralize;** pulverize, turn to dust.

Adj. **inorganic,** inanimate, unorganized, mineral.

359. LIFE.—*N.* **life;** vitality; existence, etc.; animation.

vital spark, vital flame, lifeblood; respiration, breath, breath of life.

vivification; oxygen; life force; vitalization; revival; revivification, etc., 163; life to come, etc. (*destiny*), 152.

Science of life: physiology, biology, embryology.

nourishment, nutriment, etc. (*food*), 298.

V. **live,** be alive, breathe, subsist, exist, walk the earth.

be born, see the light, come into the world; quicken; revive; come to life.

give birth to, etc. (*produce*), 161; bring to life, put life into, vitalize; vivify, reanimate, restore, resuscitate.

Adj. **living,** alive; in life, in the flesh, breathing, quick, animated; lively, etc. (*active*), 682; vital, vivifying.

360. DEATH.—*N.* **death,** decease, demise; mortality; dying, dissolution, departure, release, rest, eternal rest; loss, bereavement.

cessation (*or* loss, extinction) of life.

river of death; Jordan, Stygian shore; the great adventure.

angel of death, death's bright angel; death, doom, fate, destiny.

death song, dirge, requiem, elegy, threnody.

V. **die,** expire, perish; breathe one's last; lose *or* lay down one's life; die a violent death; give (*or* yield) up the ghost.

die for one's country, make the supreme sacrifice, go West [*First World War euphemism*].

Adj. **dead,** lifeless, inanimate; deceased, late; departed, defunct; gone, no more; bereft of life.

deadly, mortal, fatal.

dying, moribund, at the point of death, at death's door, at the last gasp.

361. [Destruction of life; violent death] **KILLING.—***N.* **killing,** homicide, manslaughter; murder, assassination; effusion of blood; bloodshed, slaughter, carnage, butchery, massacre.

war, warfare, organized murder; battle; war to the death, etc. (*warfare*), 722; Armageddon; deadly weapon, etc. (*arms*), 727.

deathblow, finishing stroke, *coup de grace* [F.], quietus; execution, etc. (*capital punishment*), 972; martyrdom.

suffocation, strangulation, garrote; hanging, etc., *v.*

slayer, butcher, murderer, Cain, assassin, cutthroat, garroter, thug, gallows, executioner, etc. (*punishment*), 975; apache, gunman [*colloq.*], bandit.

regicide, parricide, fratricide [*these words refer to both doer and deed*].

suicide, self-murder, self-destruction, hara-kiri [Jap.], suttee; immolation, holocaust.

fatal accident, violent death, casualty, disaster, calamity.

Destruction of animals: slaughtering; sport; the chase, venery; hunting, coursing, shooting, fishing; pigsticking.

sportsman, huntsman, hunter, Nimrod; fisherman, angler.

shambles, slaughterhouse.

V. **kill**, put to death, slay, shed blood; murder, assassinate, butcher, slaughter, immolate; massacre, decimate; put an end to; dispatch, do to death, do for [*colloq.*]; hunt, shoot, saber, stab, bayonet, put to the sword.

strangle, garrote, hang, throttle, choke, stifle, suffocate; smother, asphyxiate, drown.

execute; behead, guillotine; hang; electrocute.

die a violent death; commit suicide; kill (*or* make away with, put an end to) oneself.

Adj. **murderous**, slaughterous, sanguinary, bloody-minded, bloodthirsty; homicidal; red-handed, bloody, bloodstained, gory.

mortal, fatal, deadly, lethal; mutually destructive, internecine; suicidal.

362. CORPSE.—*N.* corpse, carcass, skeleton, relics, remains, dust, ashes, earth, clay; mummy; carrion.

ghost, shade, phantom, specter, apparition, spirit, revenant, spook [*colloq.*].

363. INTERMENT.—*N.* interment, burial, sepulture, entombment; obsequies, funeral, funeral rite, wake; knell, passing bell, death bell, tolling; dirge, etc. (*lamentation*), 839; dead march, muffled drum; pall, bier, litter, hearse, catafalque.

cremation, burning; pyre, funeral pile.

undertaker, funeral director.

mourner, mute; pallbearer, bearer.

graveclothes, shroud, winding sheet; cerecloth, cerements.

coffin, casket; urn; sarcophagus.

burial place, grave, pit, sepulcher, tomb, vault, crypt, catacomb, mausoleum; cemetery, burial ground, graveyard, churchyard; God's acre; potter's field; barrow, tumulus; charnel house, dead-house; morgue, mortuary; burning ghat [India]; crematorium, crematory.

gravedigger, sexton.

monument; gravestone, headstone, tombstone; hatchment, stone, marker, cross; epitaph, inscription.

autopsy, post-mortem examination *or* post mortem [L.].

disinterment, exhumation.

V. inter, bury, entomb; inurn; cremate.

disinter, exhume, unearth.

Adj. funereal, funeral, mortuary, sepulchral, cinerary; burial; elegiac.

364. ANIMAL LIFE.—*N.* animal life, animalism.

human system; breath; flesh, flesh and blood; physique, strength, power, vigor, force; spring, elasticity, tone.

V. incarnate, incorporate.

Adj. fleshly, carnal, human, corporeal.

365. VEGETATION.—*N.* vegetation, vegetable life, growth, herbage, flowerage.

V. vegetate, germinate, sprout, grow, shoot up, luxuriate, grow rank, flourish, flower, blossom; cultivate.

Adj. vegetative, vegetal, vegetable; leguminous, etc., 367.

luxuriant, rank, dense, lush, wild.

366. ANIMAL.—*N.* animal kingdom, fauna, brute creation.

animal, creature, created being, living thing; dumb animal, dumb friend, dumb creature; brute, beast.

mammal, quadruped, bird, reptile, fish, crustacean, shellfish, mollusk, worm, insect, zoophyte; animalcule, etc., 193.

beasts of the field, fowls of the air; flocks and herds, livestock, domestic animals, wild animals, game.

Domestic animals: horse, etc. (*beast of burden*), 271; cattle, ox; bull, bullock; cow, milch cow, Jersey, calf, heifer, shorthorn, yearling, steer; sheep; lamb, ewe, ram; pig, swine, boar, hog, sow; yak, zebu, buffalo.

dog, hound, canine; pup, puppy; whelp, cur [*contemptuous*], mongrel.

cat, feline, puss, pussy, tabby; tomcat *or* tom; mouser; Angora, Persian, Maltese, tortoise-shell; kitten, kitty.

Wild animals: deer, buck, doe, fawn, stag, hart, hind, roe, roebuck, caribou, elk, moose, reindeer, wapiti *or* American elk, fallow deer, red deer.

antelope, gazelle, American antelope *or* pronghorn, chamois.

ape, monkey, gorilla, marmoset, chimpanzee, lemur, baboon, orangutan.

fox, reynard, vixen (*fem.*); dingo, coyote; wildcat, lynx, bobcat; skunk.

lion, tiger, etc. (*wild beast*), 913.

rat, mouse.

lizard, saurian, iguana, newt, chameleon, Gila monster, dragon; crocodile, alligator.

whale, shark, porpoise, walrus, seal, octopus, devilfish; swordfish; pike; salmon, trout, etc.

Birds: feathered tribes, singing bird, warbler, dickybird [*colloq.*].

canary, vireo, linnet, finch, goldfinch, siskin, crossbill, chewink, peewee, titmouse *or* chickadee, nightingale, lark; magpie, cuckoo, mocking bird, catbird, starling; robin, sparrow, swallow, etc.

swan, cygnet, goose, gander, duck, drake, wild duck, mallard.

gull, sea gull, albatross, petrel, stormy petrel *or* Mother Carey's chicken; owl, bird of night; hawk, vulture, buzzard; eagle, bird of freedom.

game, ruffed grouse, grouse, blackcock, duck, plover, rail, snipe, pheasant.

poultry, fowl, cock, rooster, chanticleer, barndoor fowl, barnyard fowl, hen, chicken, chick; guinea fowl, guinea hen; peafowl, peacock, peahen.

Insects: bee, honeybee, queen bee, drone; ant, white ant, termite; wasp, locust, grasshopper, cicada, cicala, cricket; dragonfly; beetle; butterfly, moth; fly, mosquito; earwig; bug, buffalo bug, gypsy moth, weevil.

vermin, lice, cooties [*slang*], flies, fleas, cockroaches *or* roaches, water bugs, bugs, bedbugs, mosquitoes; rats, mice, weasels.

snake, serpent, viper; asp, adder, coral snake *or* harlequin snake, krait [India], cobra, cobra de capello, king cobra, rattlesnake *or* rattler, copperhead, constrictor, boa constrictor, boa, python.

Mythological: basilisk, cockatrice, salamander; griffin; chimera; Python, Hydra, Cerberus.

Adj. animal; zoological; equine; bovine; canine; feline; fishy, piscatorial; ophidian, reptilian, snakelike.

367. VEGETABLE.—*N.* vegetable, vegetable kingdom; flora.

organism, plant, tree, shrub, bush, creeper, vine; herb, seedling; exotic; annual, perennial; pulse, greens.

foliage, leafage, verdure; branch, bough, stem, trunk; leaf, spray, leaflet, frond, pad, flag, petal, needle, sepal; spray, runner, shoot, tendril.

flower, blossom, bud, floweret, flowering plant.

tree, sapling, seedling; oak, elm, beech, birch, timber tree, pine, palm, spruce, fir, hemlock, yew, larch, cedar, juniper, chestnut, maple, alder, ash, myrtle, magnolia, walnut, olive, poplar, willow, linden, lime; fruit tree; arboretum, etc., 371.

banyan, teak, acacia, deodar, fig tree, eucalyptus, gum tree.

woodlands, virgin forest, forest primeval, forest, wood, timberland, timber, wood lot; weald, park, greenwood, grove, copse, coppice, thicket, chaparral, jungle, bush.

undergrowth, underwood, brushwood, brake, scrub, heath, heather, fern, bracken, furze, gorse, broom, sedge, rush, bulrush, bamboo; weed, moss, lichen, turf, grass, herbage.

grassland, plain, etc., 344.

seaweed, alga (*pl.* algae), dulse, kelp, rockweed, sea lettuce, gulfweed, sargasso, sargassum; Sargasso Sea.

V. vegetate, grow, flourish, bloom, flower, blossom; bud, etc. (*expand*), 194; timber, retimber, plant, trim, graft, prune, cut.

Adj. vegetable, vegetative, vegetarian; leguminous, herbaceous, herbal, botanic *or* botanical; arboreous, arboreal, sylvan; grassy, verdant, verdurous; floral; ligneous, wooden, woody; bosky, copsy; mossy, turfy. deciduous, evergreen.

native, domestic, indigenous, native-grown, home-grown.

368. [Science of animals] **ZOOLOGY.**—*N.* zoology, zoography, morphology, anatomy, histology, embryology; comparative anatomy, animal physiology, comparative physiology, anthropology, ornithology, ichthyology, entomology, paleontology.

zoologist, zoographer, zoographist, anatomist, anthropologist, ornithologist, ichthyologist, entomologist, paleontologist.

Adj. zoological, zoologic; zoographical.

369. [Science of plants] BOTANY.—*N.* botany, phytology, phytobiology, vegetable chemistry; vegetable physiology, dendrology; flora; botanic garden, etc. (*garden*), 371.

botanist, phytologist, phytobiologist, dendrologist; horticulturist, etc., 371; herbalist, herbist, herbarian.

V. botanize, herborize.

Adj. botanic *or* botanical, dendroid, dendriform, herby, herbal; horticultural.

370. MANAGEMENT OF ANIMALS.—*N.* domestication, domesticity, manège, veterinary art; breeding, taming.

menagerie, zoological garden, zoo [*colloq.*]; bear pit; aviary; apiary, beehive, hive; aquarium, fishery, fish hatchery, fish pond; hennery, incubator.

Keeper: herder, cowherd, grazier, drover, cowkeeper; shepherd, shepherdess; gamekeeper; trainer, breeder; cowboy, cowpuncher; horse trainer, bronchobuster [*slang*]; beekeeper, apiarist, apiculturist.

veterinarian, veterinary surgeon, vet [*colloq.*], horse doctor, horseshoer.

inclosure, stable, barn; sheepfold, sty; cage, hencoop.

V. tame, domesticate; corral, round up; break in, gentle, break, bust [*slang*], break to harness, train; ride, drive; spur, prick, lash, goad, whip; yoke, harness, harness up [*colloq.*], hitch, hitch up [*colloq.*], cinch.

groom, tend, rub down, brush, currycomb; water, feed, fodder; bed down, litter.

tend stock, milk, shear; water, etc. (*groom*), *v.*; herd; raise, bring up.

hatch, incubate, sit, brood, cover.

Adj. tame, domestic, domesticated, housebroken, broken, gentle, docile.

371. MANAGEMENT OF PLANTS.—*N.* agriculture, cultivation, husbandry, farming; tillage, gardening, vintage; horticulture, arboriculture, forestry; floriculture; landscape gardening.

husbandman, horticulturist, gardener, florist; agriculturist, yeoman, farmer, granger, cultivator, tiller of the soil, plowman; logger, lumberman, lumberjack, forester, woodcutter, pioneer, backwoodsman.

garden; botanic (*or* flower, kitchen, market, truck) garden; nursery; greenhouse, hothouse, conservatory; grassplot, lawn; shrubbery, arboretum, orchard; vineyard, orangery.

field, meadow, mead, green, common.

V. cultivate, till, till the soil, farm, garden, sow, plant; reap, mow, cut; manure, dress the ground; dig, spade, delve, hoe, plow, harrow, rake, weed; force, seed, turf; transplant, thin out, bed, prune, graft.

Adj. arable, plowable, tillable.

rural, rustic, country, agrarian, pastoral, bucolic, Arcadian.

372. MANKIND.—*N.* mankind, man; human race (*or* species, kind, nature); humanity, mortality, generation.

Science of man: anthropology, ethnology, ethnography.

human being; person, personage; individual, creature, fellow creature, mortal, body, somebody, one, someone; soul, living soul; party [*slang or vulgar*].

people, persons, folk, public, society, world; community, general public; nation, state, realm, republic; commonweal, commonwealth; body politic; the masses, etc. (*commonalty*), 876; population; lords of creation; ourselves.

Adj. human, mortal, personal, individual; national, civic, public social.

373. MAN.—*N.* man, male; gentleman, sir, master; yeoman, chap [*colloq.*], swain, fellow, blade, beau; husband, etc. (*youth*), 129.

mister, Mr., *monsieur* (*abbr.* M., *pl.* Messrs.) [F.], *Herr* [Ger.], *signor* [It., *used before name*], *signore* [It.], *signorino* [It., *dim. of signore*], *señor* [Sp.], *senhor* [Pg.].

Male animal: cock, drake, gander, dog, boar, stag, hart, buck, horse, stallion, gelding; tom, tomcat; he-goat, billy goat [*colloq.*]; ram; bull, bullock; capon; ox, steer.

Adj. male, masculine, manly, virile; unwomanly, unfeminine.

374. WOMAN.—*N.* woman, female, petticoat.

womankind, womanhood; the sex, fair sex, softer sex.

dame [*archaic except as an elderly woman or as slang*], madam, lady, donna, belle, matron, dowager, good woman, squaw; wife.

spinster, old maid, bachelor girl, new woman, girl, etc. (*youth*), 129.

mistress, Mrs., *madame* (*pl. mesdames*) [F.], *Frau* [Ger.], *signora* [It.], *señora* [Sp.], *senhora* [Pg.]; miss, *mademoiselle* (*pl. mesdemoiselles*) [F.], *Fräulein* [Ger.], *signorina* [It.], *señorita* [Sp.], *senhorita* [Pg.].

Effeminacy: betty, molly, mollycoddle, old woman, tame cat [*all contemptuous*].

Female animal: hen; bitch, slut; sow, doe, roe, mare; she-goat, nanny goat [*colloq.*], nanny [*colloq.*]; ewe, cow; lioness, tigress; vixen.

harem, seraglio, purdah [India].

Adj. female, feminine, womanly, ladylike, matronly, girlish, maidenly; womanish, effeminate, unmanly.   *

(2) Sensation

375. PHYSICAL SENSIBILITY.—*N.* sensibility, sensitiveness, feeling, impressibility, susceptibility.

sensation, impression; consciousness.

V. **feel,** perceive, be sensitive to.

render sensitive, sharpen, refine, excite, stir, cultivate, tutor.

cause sensation, impress, excite (*or* produce) an impression.

Adj. **sensitive,** sensuous; perceptive, sentient, sensible; conscious, alive, alive to impressions, impressionable, responsive. acute, sharp, keen, vivid, lively.

Adv. **to the quick;** on the raw [*slang*].

376. PHYSICAL INSENSIBILITY.—*N.* insensibility, obtuseness, paralysis, anesthesia, hypnosis, stupor, coma, sleep.

anesthetic; opium, ether, chloroform, chloral; nitrous oxide, laughing gas; cocaine, novocain; refrigeration.

V. **render insensible,** blunt, cloy, satiate; benumb, numb, deaden, freeze, paralyze; anesthetize; put to sleep, hypnotize, stupefy, stun.

Adj. **insensible,** unfeeling, senseless, callous, hard, hardened, casehardened, proof, obtuse, dull; paralytic, palsied, numb, dead.

377. PHYSICAL PLEASURE.—*N.* **pleasure,** bodily enjoyment, animal gratification, gusto, relish, delight, sensual delight, sensuality; luxuriousness, dissipation, round of pleasure; comfort, ease, luxury, lap of luxury; creature comforts; purple and fine linen; bed of roses.

treat; diversion, entertainment, banquet, refreshment, feast.

happiness, felicity, bliss, beatitude, etc. (*mental enjoyment*), 827.

V. **enjoy,** relish; luxuriate in, revel in, bask in, wallow in; feast on, gloat over, smack the lips.

please, charm, delight, enchant, etc., 829.

Adj. **comfortable,** cosy, snug, luxurious, in comfort, at ease, in clover [*colloq.*].

agreeable, etc., 829; grateful, refreshing, comforting, cordial, genial; gratifying, sensuous; palatable, delicious, sweet; fragrant; melodious, harmonious; lovely, etc. (*beautiful*), 845.

Adv. **in comfort,** on a bed of roses, on flowery beds of ease.

378. PHYSICAL PAIN.—*N.* **pain,** suffering, dolor, ache, smart; shoot, shooting, twinge, pang, gripe, hurt, cut; sore, soreness; discomfort.

spasm, cramp; crick, stitch; convulsion, throe; throb, colic, gripes.

torment, torture, agony, anguish, rack, crucifixion, martyrdom.

V. **suffer,** feel (*or* suffer, undergo) pain; ache, smart, bleed, tingle, shoot, twinge; writhe, wince.

pain, give pain, inflict pain; lacerate; hurt, chafe, sting, bite, gnaw, stab, grate, gall, fret, prick, pierce, wring, convulse; torment, torture; rack, agonize; crucify; flog, etc. (*punish*), 972.

Adj. **painful,** aching, poignant, excruciating, biting; on the rack; sore, raw.

(1) *Touch*

379. [Sensation of pressure] TOUCH.—*N.* **touch,** contact, tangency, impact, feeling; graze, glance, brush, lick; manipulation, rubbing, kneading, massage.

V. **touch,** feel, handle, finger, thumb, paw, fumble, grope; stroke, massage, rub, knead, manipulate, wield; throw out a feeler.

Adj. **tactual,** tangible, palpable, tangent, lambent.

380. SENSATIONS OF TOUCH.—*N.* **itching,** tickling, titillation.

itch, scabies; mange.

V. **itch,** tingle, creep, thrill, sting; prick, prickle.

tickle, titillate.

Adj. **ticklish,** titillative.

itchy, mangy; creepy, crawly.

381. [Insensibility to touch] NUMBNESS.—*N.* **numbness;** physical insensibility, etc., 376; anesthesia.

V. **benumb,** etc., 376; stupefy, drug, deaden, paralyze.

Adj. **numb,** benumbed, insensible, unfeeling, deadened; intangible, impalpable; dazed, comatose, narcotic.

(2) *Heat*

382. HEAT.—*N.* **heat,** caloric; temperature, warmth, incandescence.

summer, dog days, heat wave, broiling sun; sun, etc. (*luminary*), 423.

flush, glow, blush, redness; fever.

fire, spark, scintillation, flash, flame, blaze; bonfire; wildfire; sheet of fire, lambent flame.

hot springs, geysers; thermae, hot baths, Turkish bath; steam.

V. **be hot,** glow, flush, sweat, swelter, bask, smoke, reck, stew, simmer, seethe, boil, burn, singe, scorch, scald, broil, blaze, flame; smolder, parch, pant.

heat, etc. (*make hot*), 384; incandesce.

thaw, fuse, melt, liquefy.

Adj. **warm,** mild, genial; tepid, lukewarm.

hot, heated, fervid, fervent, baking, ardent, sunny, sunshiny, torrid, tropical, thermal.

close, sultry, stifling, stuffy, suffocating, oppressive, sweltering.

fiery; incandescent, ebullient, glowing, aglow, reeking, smoking; live; on fire, blazing, in flames, in a blaze; alight, afire, ablaze, smoldering.

feverish, febrile, inflamed, burning; in a fever.

383. COLD.—*N.* **cold,** coldness, frigidity, inclemency.

winter; depth of winter; hard winter; arctic, antarctic.

ice; sleet; hail, hailstone; frost, rime, hoarfrost; icicle, thick-ribbed ice; iceberg, floe, berg, ice field, ice pack, glacier.

snow, snowflake, snowball, snowdrift, snowstorm, snowslip, snow avalanche.

chill, chilliness, shivering, goose flesh, chilblains, frostbite, chattering of teeth.

V. **be cold,** shiver, quake, shake, tremble, shudder, chill, freeze.

Adj. **cold,** cool, chill, chilly, frigid; fresh, keen, bleak, raw, inclement, bitter, biting, cutting, nipping, piercing, pinching; shivering, anguish; frostbitten.

icy, glacial, frosty, freezing, wintry, boreal, arctic, snowbound, icebound, frost-bound, frozen.

Adv. with chattering teeth.

384. CALEFACTION.—*N.* **calefaction,** tepefaction, heating, melting, fusion, liquefaction, combustion; cremation; calcination; incineration; carbonization; cauterization.

ignition, kindling, inflammation, conflagration; incendiarism, arson; auto-da-fé [Pg.], the stake, burning at the stake; suttee.

incendiary, arsonist, pyromaniac, fire bug.

boiling, ebullition, ebullience, decoction; hot spring, geyser.

crematory, crematorium, incinerator; furnace, etc., 386.

wrap, blanket, flannel, wool, fur; wadding, lining, interlining; clothing, etc., 225.

Products of combustion: cinder, ash, embers, slag, clinker; coke, carbon, charcoal.

V. **heat,** warm, chafe, foment; make hot; sun oneself, bask in the sun.

fire, set fire to, set on fire; kindle, enkindle, light, ignite; rekindle.

melt, thaw, fuse; liquefy, dissolve.

burn, scorch; inflame; roast, toast, fry, grill, singe, parch, bake; brand, cauterize, sear, burn in; corrode, char, carbonize, calcine, incinerate, smelt; reduce to ashes.

take *or* **catch fire;** blaze, etc. (*flame*), 382.

boil, stew, cook, seethe, scald, parboil, simmer.

Adj. heated, warmed; burnt, scorched; molten; volcanic. inflammable, inflammatory, combustible.

385. REFRIGERATION.—*N.* refrigeration, cooling, congelation, glaciation; solidification; ice; icebox, ice chest; refrigerator.

fire extinguisher, asbestos; fireman, fire brigade, fire department, fire engine.

V. cool, fan, refresh; ice, refrigerate, congeal, freeze, benumb, chill, petrify, pinch, nip, cut, pierce, bite.

extinguish, put out, stamp out; damp, slack, quench.

Adj. incombustible, asbestic, unflammable, uninflammable; fireproof.

386. FURNACE.—*N.* furnace, stove; cookstove, cooker, oven, brick oven, tin oven, Dutch oven, range, fireless cooker; forge, fiery furnace; volcano; kiln, brickkiln, limekiln.

brasier, tripod, salamander, heater, warming pan, footstove, foot warmer; radiator, register, coil; boiler, caldron, pot; urn, kettle; chafing dish; retort, crucible, alembic, still; flatiron, sadiron; toasting fork, toaster.

galley, caboose; hothouse, conservatory; bakehouse; washhouse, laundry.

fireplace, hearth, grate, firebox; andiron, firedog, fire irons; poker, tongs, shovel, hob, trivet; damper, crane, pothooks, chains, turnspit, spit, gridiron.

hot bath; thermae; Turkish (*or* Russian, vapor, electric, sitz, hip, shower) bath; bathroom, lavatory.

387. REFRIGERATOR.—*N.* refrigerator, icebox, ice chest; cold storage; refrigerating plant; icehouse; ice-cream freezer, freezer; ice bag, ice pack, cold pack; ice pail, cooler, wine cooler.

refrigerant, freezing, mixture, ice, ammonia.

388. FUEL.—*N.* fuel, firing, combustible, coal, anthracite, bituminous coal; carbon, slack, cannel coal *or* cannel, lignite, coke, charcoal; turf, peat; oil, gas, natural gas, electricity; ember, cinder, ash, slag, clinker; tinder, touchwood; punk.

log, backlog, yule log, firewood, fagot, kindling wood, kindlings, brushwood.

fumigator, incense, joss stick; smudge; disinfectant.

brand, firebrand, torch; fuse, wick; spill, match, light.

V. coal, stoke; feed, fire, etc., 384.

Adj. carbonaceous; combustible, inflammable; slow-burning, free-burning.

389. THERMOMETER.—*N.* thermometer, thermometrograph, thermostat, thermoscope; differential thermometer, telethermometer, pyrometer.

(3) *Taste*

390. TASTE.—*N.* taste, flavor, gusto, savor, relish; smack, tang; aftertaste.

palate; tongue; tooth; stomach.

V. taste, flavor, savor, smack; tickle the palate, etc. (*savory*), 394.

Adj. tasty, savory, flavored, spiced; palatable, etc., 394.

391. INSIPIDITY.—*N.* insipidity; tastelessness, unsavoriness.

Adj. insipid; tasteless, unsavory, unflavored, jejune, savorless; weak, stale, flat, vapid, wishy-washy [*colloq.*].

392. PUNGENCY.—*N.* pungency, piquancy, poignancy, tang, nip.

sharpness, acridity; sourness, unsavoriness.

dram, cordial, nip, bracer [*colloq.*], pick-me-up [*colloq.*], potion, liqueur.

tobacco, nicotine; smoke, cigar, cheroot, stogy; cigarette, fag [*slang*], Havana, Cuban tobacco; weed [*colloq.*]; snuff.

V. season, spice, bespice, salt, pepper, pickle, brine, devil, curry.

Adj. pungent, strong, high-flavored, full-flavored, high-seasoned; gamy, high; sharp, piquant, racy; biting, mordant; spicy; seasoned, spiced; hot, peppery; acrid, bitter; sour, acid, etc., 397; unsavory, etc., 395.

salt, saline, brackish, briny.

393. CONDIMENT.—*N.* condiment, flavoring, seasoning, sauce, spice, relish; pickle; chutney; appetizer.

V. season, etc. (*render pungent*), 392.

394. SAVORINESS.—*N.* savoriness, tastiness, palatability; delectability; relish, zest.

appetizer, hors d'oeuvre [F.].

delicacy, titbit, dainty, ambrosia, nectar.

V. be savory; tickle the palate (*or* appetite); tempt the appetite, taste good.

relish, like, smack the lips.

Adj. savory, tasty; good, palatable; pleasing, nice, dainty, exquisite, delicate; delectable, toothsome, appetizing, delicious; rich, luscious, ambrosial, nectareous; distinctive.

395. UNSAVORINESS.—*N.* unsavoriness; acridness, sourness, etc., 397; acerbity; gall and wormwood.

V. be unpalatable, sicken, disgust, nauseate, pall, turn the stomach.

Adj. unsavory, unpalatable, ill-flavored; bitter, acrid, acrimonious.

offensive, repulsive, nasty, sickening, nauseous; loathsome; unpleasant, etc., 830.

396. SWEETNESS.—*N.* sweetness, saccharinity.

sugar, saccharin; preserve, jam, sugar candy, sugarplum.

sweets, confectionery, caramel, lollipop, bonbon, jujube, comfit, sweetmeat, confection; honey, manna; glucose, sirup, treacle, molasses, maple sirup, maple sugar; taffy, butterscotch.

Sweet beverages: nectar; mead, liqueur, sweet wine.

pastry, cake, pie, tart, puff, pudding.

V. **sweeten,** sugar, sugar off [*local*]; candy.

Adj. **sweet,** sugary, saccharine, candied, honied, luscious, cloying, honey-sweet, nectareous; dulcet, mellifluous.

397. SOURNESS.—*N.* **sourness,** acerbity, acidity; acid.

V. **render sour,** acidify, acidulate, acetify; ferment.

Adj. **sour;** acid, acidulated; subacid; tart, crabbed; hard, unripe, green; astringent, styptic.

(4) *Odor*

398. ODOR.—*N.* **odor,** smell, scent; effluvium; emanation, exhalation; fume, trail, redolence.

V. **have an odor** (*or* **scent**); smell, exhale; give out a smell (*or* odor); scent.

smell, scent, snuff, sniff, inhale.

Adj. **odorous,** odoriferous; strong-scented, redolent, pungent.

Relating to the sense of smell: olfactory; quick-scented, keen-scented.

399. INODOROUSNESS.—*N.* **inodorousness,** absence (*or* want) of smell.

deodorization; deodorizer, deodorant.

V. **be inodorous** (*or* **scentless**); not smell.

Adj. **inodorous,** scentless; without smell (*or* odor).

400. FRAGRANCE.—*N.* **fragrance,** aroma, redolence, perfume, bouquet; sweet smell (*or* odor), scent.

perfumery; incense, frankincense; musk, myrrh, attar, bergamot, balm, civet, potpourri, tuberose, hyacinth, heliotrope, rose, jasmine, lily, lily of the valley, violet, pomander; toilet water; eau de cologne [F.], cologne, cologne water.

bouquet, nosegay, posy [*colloq.*], boutonniere [F.], buttonhole [*colloq.*].

spray; wreath, garland, chaplet.

Scent containers: smelling bottle, scent bottle, vinaigrette; scent bag, sachet; thurible, censer, incense burner, atomizer, spray.

V. **be fragrant** (*or* **scented**); have a perfume (*or* aroma); smell sweet, scent, perfume; embalm.

Adj. **fragrant,** aromatic, redolent, spicy, balmy, scented; sweet-smelling, sweet-scented; perfumed; incense-breathing, ambrosial.

401. FETOR—*N.* **fetor,** bad smell (*or* odor), stench, stink, fetidness, fustiness, mustiness; rancidity; foulness.

V. **have a bad smell,** smell, stink, smell strong, smell offensively.

Adj. **fetid;** strong-smelling; high, bad, strong, offensive, noisome, rank, rancid, moldy, tainted, musty; smelling, stinking; putrid, rotten, foul; suffocating.

(5) Sound

402. SOUND.—*N.* sound, noise; sonority, sonorousness; strain; accent, twang, intonation; tune, cadence; audibility; resonance, vibration; voice, etc., 580.

Science of sound: acoustics, phonetics, phonology, phonography; telephony, radiophony.

V. sound, make a noise; give out sound, emit sound; resound.

Adj. sounding, sonorous, resonant, audible, distinct; auditory, acoustic.

phonetic, phonic, sonant.

403. SILENCE.—*N.* silence, stillness, quiet, peace, hush, lull; rest [*music*]; muteness; silence of the tomb (*or* grave).

V. silence, still, hush, stifle, muffle, gag, stop; muzzle, put to silence.

Adj. silent; still, stilly; noiseless, quiet, calm, soundless, hushed; speechless; aphonic, surd, mute.

solemn, soft, awful, deathlike.

Adv. in dead silence.

404. LOUDNESS.—*N.* loudness, power, vociferation, uproariousness.

din, loud noise, clang, clangor, clatter, noise, roar, uproar, hubbub, racket, hullabaloo, pandemonium; fracas; outcry, etc., 411; explosion, detonation.

blare, trumpet blast, flourish of trumpets, fanfare, blast, peal, swell, alarum, boom; resonance, etc., 408.

V. be loud (*or* deafening); peal, swell, clang, boom, thunder, roar; deafen, stun, rend the air, awake the echoes; resound, etc., 408; speak up, shout, etc. (*vociferate*), 411; bellow, etc. (*cry as an animal*), 412.

Adj. loud, sonorous, deep, full, powerful; noisy, blatant; clangorous, thundering, deafening, earsplitting, piercing; shrill, etc., 410; obstreperous, uproarious; clamorous, vociferous, fullmouthed, stentorian.

Adv. loudly, noisily; aloud; at the top of one's lungs, lustily, in full cry.

405. FAINTNESS.—*N.* faintness, inaudibility; faint sound, whisper, breath; undertone; murmur, hum, buzz, purr, lap [*of waves*], plash; sough, moan, rustle; tinkle.

hoarseness, huskiness.

silencer, muffler; soft pedal, damper, mute, sordine [*all music*].

V. whisper, breathe; mutter, etc. (*speak imperfectly*), 583.

murmur, purl, hum, gurgle, ripple, babble, flow; rustle; tinkle.

muffle, deaden, mute, subdue.

Adj. **faint,** low, dull; stifled, muffled; inaudible; hoarse, husky; gentle, soft; floating; purling, flowing; muttered; whispered; liquid; soothing; dulcet, etc. (*melodious*), 413.

Adv. **in a whisper,** with bated breath, *sotto voce* [It.]; between the teeth; aside; piano, pianissimo [*both music*]; out of earshot; inaudibly, faintly.

406. [Sudden and violent sounds] **SNAP.**—*N.* **snap,** etc., *v.;* toot, shout, yell, yap [*dial.*], yelp, bark.

report, thump, knock, clap, thud; burst, thunderclap, thunderburst, eruption, blowout [*tire*], explosion, discharge, detonation, firing, salvo, volley.

V. **snap,** rap, tap, knock; click; clash; crack, crackle; crash; pop; slam, bang, clap; thump, toot, yelp, bark, fire, explode, rattle, burst on the ear.

407. [Repeated and protracted sounds] **ROLL.**—*N.* **roll,** etc., *v.;* drumming, rumbling, howl, dingdong; ratatat, rubadub, tattoo; pitapat; quaver, clutter, charivari, racket; peal of bells, devil's tattoo; drumfire, barrage; whir, rattle, drone; reverberation.

V. **roll,** drum, boom; whir, rustle, tootle, roar, drone, rumble, rattle, clatter, patter, clack.

hum, trill, shake; chime, peal, toll; tick, beat.

408. RESONANCE.—*N.* **resonance;** ring, chime, ringing, clangor, bell note, tintinnabulation, vibration, reverberation.

bass; basso [It.], basso profundo [It.]; baritone, contralto; pedal point, organ point; snoring, snore.

V. **resound,** reverberate, re-echo; ring, sound; chink, clink; jingle, tinkle; chime; gurgle, mutter, murmur; plash, echo, ring in the ear.

Adj. **resonant,** reverberant, resounding, reverberating; deeptoned, deep-mouthed; hollow, sepulchral; gruff, etc. (*harsh*), 410.

408a. NONRESONANCE.—*N.* **nonresonance,** dead sound; thud, thump, muffled drums, cracked bell; damper, sordine, mute; muffler, silencer.

V. **muffle,** deaden, mute; sound dead; stop (*or* deaden) the sound.

Adj. **nonresonant,** dead, mute; muffled, deadened.

409. [Hissing sounds] **SIBILATION.**—*N.* **sibilation,** hissing; zip; hiss, buzz; sneezing, sternutation.

V. **hiss,** buzz, whiz; rustle; fizz, fizzle; wheeze, whistle, sizzle, swish.

Adj. **sibilant;** hissing; rustling; wheezy.

410. [Harsh or high sounds] **STRIDENCY.**—*N.* **stridency;** stridor, harshness, raucousness; sharpness; creak, jar; creaking, grating; discord, dissonance.

high note, shrill note; soprano, treble, tenor, alto, falsetto; head voice, head tone; shriek, yell, cry, wail, pipe.

V. **grate,** creak, saw, snore, jar, burr, pipe, twang, jangle, clank; scream, etc. (*cry*), 411; set the teeth on edge, pierce (*or* split) the ears; yelp, etc. (*animal sound*), 412; buzz, etc. (*hiss*), 409.

Adj. **grating,** creaking, jangling, jarring, strident, harsh, coarse, hoarse, raucous; metallic; rough, rude; gruff, grum, sepulchral, hollow.

high, sharp, acute, shrill; piercing, high-pitched; cracked; discordant.

411. CRY.—*N.* **cry,** shout; shriek; hubbub; bark, etc. (*animal*), 412.

outcry, vociferation, ejaculation, hullabaloo, chorus, clamor, hue and cry, plaint; lungs; stentor.

V. **cry,** roar, shout, bawl; halloo, halloa, yo-ho, whoop; yell, bellow, hoot, boo; howl, scream, screech, shriek; shrill, squeak, squeal, squall; whine, pipe.

cheer, huzza, hurrah, yell.

moan, grumble, groan.

snort, snore; grunt, etc., 412.

vociferate, raise (*or* lift) the voice; yell out, call out, sing out, cry out; exclaim, give cry, clamor; rend the air; make the welkin ring; shout at the top of one's voice.

Adj. **clamorous,** clamant, vociferous; stentorian, etc. (*loud*), 404; open-mouthed; full-mouthed.

412. [Animal sounds] ULULATION.—*N.* **ululation,** howling, cry, roar; call, note, howl, bark, yelp, bowwow, belling; woodnote; insect cry; twittering, drone.

V. **ululate,** howl; cry, roar, bellow; bark, yelp; bay, bay the moon; yap, growl, snarl, howl; grunt, snort, squeak; neigh, bray; mew, purr, caterwaul; bleat, low, moo; crow, screech, croak, caw, coo, gobble, quack, cackle, cluck; chirp, cheep, chirrup, peep, sing, twitter; chatter, hoot, wail; hum, buzz; hiss; blat [*colloq.*].

413. MELODY. CONCORD.—*N.* **melody,** rhythm, measure; rhyme, etc. (*poetry*), 597; euphony.

Musical terms: pitch, timbre, intonation, tone, overtone.
orchestration, harmonization, modulation, phrasing.
staff *or* stave, line, space, brace; bar, rest; passage, phrase; trill *or* shake, turn, arpeggio [It.].
note, musical note, notes of a scale; sharp, flat, natural; high note, etc., 410; low note, etc., 408; interval; semitone.
breve, semibreve *or* whole note, minim *or* half note, crotchet *or* quarter note, quaver *or* eighth note, semiquaver *or* sixteenth note, demisemiquaver *or* thirty-second note; sustained note, drone.
scale, gamut; diapason; key, clef, chord.
harmony, concord; tonality; consonance; part; unison; chime.
Science of harmony: harmony, harmonics; thorough bass, counterpoint; composer.

opus (*pl. opera*) [L.], piece of music, etc., 415.

V. **harmonize,** chime, symphonize, transpose, orchestrate; blend, put in tune, tune, accord, string.

Adj. **harmonious,** harmonic, in concord, in tune, in concert, in unison.

melodious, musical, tuneful, tunable; sweet, dulcet, mellow, mellifluous; soft; clear, silvery; euphonious; enchanting, etc. (*pleasure-giving*), 829; fine-toned, silver-toned, full-toned, deep-toned.

414. DISCORD.—*N.* **discord,** dissonance, want of harmony; harshness, etc., 410; charivari, racket; Babel, pandemonium.

V. **be discordant** (*or* harsh); jar, etc. (*sound harshly*), 410.

Adj. **discordant,** dissonant, out of tune, tuneless; unmusical, untunable; unmelodious, inharmonious; singsong; harsh, etc., 410; jarring.

415. MUSIC.—*N.* **music;** minstrelsy; strain, tune, air, melody; piece of music; rondo, rondeau, pastoral; cavatina, fantasia, toccata [It.]; fugue, canon; potpourri, medley; incidental music; variations, roulade, cadenza, cadence, trill; serenade, nocturne.

instrumental music; orchestral score, full score; composition, opus (*pl. opera*) [L.]; concert piece; concerto [It.]; symphony, sonata, symphonic poem, tone poem; chamber music; movement; overture, prelude, voluntary; string quartet (*or* quintet).

lively music, polka, reel, etc. (*dance*), 848; ragtime, jazz; syncopation, martial music, march; allegro, presto.

slow music, Lydian measures; adagio, largo, andante; lullaby, cradle song, berceuse [F.]; dirge, etc. (*lament*), 839; dead march; minuet.

vocal music, vocalism; chant; psalm, psalmody, hymnology; hymn; canticle; oratorio; opera, operetta; cantata; song, lay, ballad, ditty, carol; recitative, aria.

solo, duet, trio, quartet, quintet, sestet, septet, double quartet, chorus; part song, descant, glee, madrigal, catch, round, chorale; antiphon; accompaniment; inside part, second, alto, tenor, bass; score, piano score, vocal score.

concert, musicale, recital, chamber concert, popular concert *or* pop [*colloq.*], open-air concert; serenade; community singing, singsong [*colloq.*].

method, solfeggio [It.], tonic sol-fa, sight singing, sight reading.

V. **compose,** write, etc., 416; attune, tune.
perform, execute, play, etc., 416.

Adj. **musical;** instrumental, vocal, choral, lyric, melodic; operatic; classic, modern, orchestral, symphonic, contrapuntal; program, imitative; harmonious, etc., 413.

416. MUSICIAN. [Performance of music]—*N.* **musician,** virtuoso, performer, player, minstrel; bard, etc. (*poet*), 597; accompanist, instrumentalist, organist, pianist, violinist, fiddler; flutist, harpist, fifer, trumpeter, cornetist, piper, drummer.

orchestra; strings, woodwind, brass; band, brass band, military band, German band, jazz band; street musicians.

vocalist, singer, warbler; songbird; songster, songstress; chorister; chorus singer; choir, chorus.

Orpheus, Apollo, the Muses, Polyhymnia, Erato, Euterpe, Terpsichore.

conductor, choirmaster, bandmaster, concertmaster, drum major, song leader, precentor.

performance, execution, touch, expression.

V. **play,** tune, tune up, pipe, pipe up, strike up, sweep the chords, fiddle, strike the lyre, beat the drum; blow (*or* wind) the horn; twang, pluck, pick; pound, thump; drum, thrum, strum, beat time; execute, perform; accompany.

compose, set to music, arrange, harmonize, orchestrate.

sing, troll, chant, intone, hum, warble, twitter, carol, chirp, chirrup, lilt, quaver, trill, shake.

Adj. **musical;** lyric, dramatic; bravura, florid, brilliant.

417. MUSICAL INSTRUMENTS.—*N.* musical instruments; orchestra (*including* strings, woodwind, brass, and percussive instruments); band; string band, military band, brass band.

418. [Sense of sound] **HEARING.**—*N.* hearing, audition; audibility; acoustics; ear for music.

ear; eardrum, tympanum.

Instruments: ear trumpet, audiphone, dentiphone, speaking trumpet; phonograph, gramophone, graphophone, microphone, victrola; stethoscope; telephone, radiophone, wireless telephone, radio.

hearer, auditor, audience, listener; eavesdropper.

V. **hear,** overhear; hark, hearken; list, listen; strain one's ears, attend to, give attention, prick up one's ears; give ear, give a hearing to.

Adj. **hearing,** auditory, acoustic, phonic; auricular; auditive.

419. DEAFNESS—*N.* deafness, hardness of hearing, inaudibility; deaf-mute; deaf-and-dumb alphabet.

V. **deafen,** render deaf, stun, split the ears (*or* eardrum).

Adj. **deaf,** hard (*or* dull) of hearing; stunned, deafened; stone-deaf; inattentive.

inaudible, out of earshot (*or* hearing).

(6) *Light*

420. LIGHT.—*N.* light, ray, beam, stream (*of light*), gleam, streak; sunbeam, moonbeam; aurora, dawn, daylight, day, sunshine; glint, glare, glow, afterglow; sun, etc., 423.

reflection, refraction, dispersion.

halo, glory, nimbus, aureole, aura.

spark, scintilla, scintillation, flash, blaze, coruscation; flame, glare, blaze; lightning; phosphorescence.

luster, sheen, shimmer, gloss, brightness, brilliancy, splendor, effulgence; illumination, radiance, radiation.

Science of light: optics, radiometry; photography; phototelegraphy, radiotelegraphy; actinic rays, radioactivity; Röntgen rays, X rays, ultraviolet rays.

illuminant, gas, etc., 423.

V. shine, glow, beam, glitter, glisten, gleam; flare, blaze, glare, shimmer, glimmer, flicker, sparkle, scintillate, coruscate, flash.

daze, dazzle, bedazzle.

lighten, enlighten, light, irradiate, illume, illumine, illuminate; kindle, etc., 384.

Adj. luminous, lucent; light, sunny, bright, vivid, splendid, resplendent, refulgent, lustrous, brilliant, radiant, lambent; aglow.

shiny, glossy, burnished, glassy.

clear, cloudless, unclouded.

421. DARKNESS.—*N.* darkness, duskiness; blackness, swarthiness; obscurity, gloom, murk, murkiness; dusk; dimness, etc., 422.

night; midnight; dead of night.

shadow, shade; obscuration, adumbration; eclipse; radiograph.

V. darken, obscure, shade, dim; lower, overcast, overshadow, cloud, becloud, bedim.

extinguish, put out, blow out, snuff out.

Adj. dark, darkling, obscure; black, etc. (*color*), 431; nocturnal.

somber, dusky; dingy, lurid, gloomy, murky; shady, umbrageous; overcast, etc. (*dim*), 422; cloudy, etc., 426.

422. DIMNESS.—*N.* dimness, paleness, dullness, duskiness, mistiness.

twilight, dusk, nightfall, gloaming; dawn, daybreak, break of day, Aurora; moonlight, moonshine [*poetic*], starlight.

V. cloud over, gloom, lower.

twinkle, glimmer, flicker.

pale, fade, grow dim.

dim, bedim, obscure, shade, shadow, darken, cloud, becloud.

Adj. dim, dull, dingy, dusky, lackluster; cloudy, misty, hazy.

leaden, lurid, dun; overcast, dirty.

423. [Source of light] LUMINARY.—*N.* luminary; light, ray, beam; flame, etc. (*fire*), 382; spark, scintilla; phosphorescence.

Heavenly bodies: sun, orb of day, daystar [*poetic*]; star; constellation; galaxy, Milky Way; polestar, Polaris; morning star, Lucifer; evening star, Venus; moon, etc., 318.

sun god, Helios, Phoebus, Apollo, Hyperion, Ra [*Egypt*].

phosphorus; *ignis fatuus* [L.]; jack-o'-lantern, will-o'-the-wisp.

polar lights, northern lights, aurora borealis [L.], aurora australis [L.]; aurora.

Artificial light: gas, gaslight, electric light, electric torch; headlight, searchlight; spotlight, flashlight, limelight, calcium light; lamplight, lamp, lantern, dark lantern, bull's-eye; candle, taper, rushlight; torch, flambeau, brand; gaselier, chandelier; candelabrum, sconce, luster, candlestick; fireworks, pyrotechnics.

signal light, rocket, balefire, beacon fire; lighthouse.

V. illuminate, etc. (*light*), 420.

Adj. self luminous; phosphorescent; radiant, etc. (*light*), 420.

424. SHADE.—*N.* shade; awning, etc. (*cover*), 223.

screen, curtain, portiere [F.]; shutter, blind.

veil, mantle, mask.

cloud, mist, shadow; smoke screen [*mil.*].

blinkers, blinders; smoked glasses, colored spectacles.

V. veil, draw a curtain; cast a shadow, etc. (*darken*), 421.

Adj. shady, umbrageous, shadowy.

425. TRANSPARENCY.—*N.* transparency, transparence, translucence, diaphanousness; lucidity, limpidity; fluorescence; translumination.

V. be transparent (*or* pellucid); transmit light.

Adj. transparent, pellucid, lucid, diaphanous; translucent, limpid, clear, serene, crystalline.

426. OPACITY.—*N.* opacity, opaqueness; cloudiness; film; cloud, etc., 353.

V. be opaque; obstruct the passage of light.

Adj. opaque, impervious to light; dim, etc., 422; turbid, thick, muddy, cloudy, foggy, vaporous; smoky, murky, smeared, dirty.

427. SEMITRANSPARENCY.—*N.* semitransparency, opalescence, milkiness, pearliness; mist, haze, steam.

V. cloud, frost, cloud over, frost over.

Adj. semitransparent, semidiaphanous, semiopaque; opalescent, opaline; pearly, milky; frosted, hazy, misty.

428. [Specific Light] COLOR.—*N.* color, hue, tint, tinge, dye, complexion, shade, tincture; coloration; glow, flush; tone, key.

primary color, complementary color; coloring, keeping, tone, value.

spectrum, spectrum analysis; prism, spectroscope, kaleidoscope.

pigment, coloring matter, paint, dye, wash, distemper, stain; medium.

V. color, dye, tinge, stain, tint, tone; paint, wash, distemper, ingrain, grain, illuminate, emblazon.

Adj. colored, dyed; chromatic, prismatic; double-dyed.

bright, vivid, intense, deep; fresh, rich, gorgeous; brightcolored, gay.

gaudy, florid; garish; showy, flaunting; flashy; many-colored, parti-colored, variegated; raw, crude; glaring, flaring.

mellow, harmonious, pearly, sweet, delicate, subtle, tender.

dull, sad, somber, sad-colored, grave, gray, dark.

429. ABSENCE OF COLOR.—*N.* decoloration, discoloration; pallor, paleness, sallowness.

neutral tint, monochrome, black and white.

V. lose color, fade, become colorless, turn pale; pale, fade out.

deprive of color, decolor, wash out, tone down; whiten, bleach, blanch.

Adj. colorless, uncolored, hueless, pale, pallid; pale-faced, anemic; faint, dull, cold, muddy, leaden, dun, wan, sallow, dingy, ashy, ashen, ghastly, cadaverous, glassy, lackluster; discolored.

light-colored, fair, blond, ash-blond; white, etc., 430; towheaded.

430. WHITENESS.—*N.* whiteness, showiness, hoariness.

whitewash, whiting, whitening, calcimine.

V. whiten, bleach, blanch, silver, frost.

whitewash, calcimine, white.

Adj. white, snow-white, snowy, frosted, hoar, hoary; silvery, silver, milk-white, milky.

whitish, creamy, pearly, ivory, fair, blond, ash-blond; blanched; light.

431. BLACKNESS.—*N.* blackness, darkness, obscurity; swarthiness, swartness; lividness.

Negro, Negress, blackamoor, man of color, colored man, colored woman, nigger [*colloq., usually contemptuous*], darky [*colloq.*], black, Ethiop, Ethiopian, Hottentot, Pygmy, Bushman, African.

V. black, blacken, blot, blotch, smut, smudge, smirch; darken, etc., 421.

Adj. black, sable, somber, livid, dark, inky, ebon, pitchy, sooty; swart, swarthy, dusky, dingy, murky; blotchy, smudgy; low-toned.

432. GRAY.—*N.* gray, etc., *adj.*; grayness; neutral tint, silver, dove color, pepper and salt, chiaroscuro [It.].

V. render gray, gray.

Adj. gray; iron-gray, dun, drab, dingy, leaden, pearly, dove-colored, silver, silvery, silvered; dapple-gray; ashen, ashy; grizzly, grizzled.

433. BROWN.—*N.* brown, etc., *adj.*; brownness.

V. render brown, brown, tan, embrown, bronze.

Adj. brown, nut-brown, seal-brown, mahogany, chocolate; fawn, ecru, tawny; tan, fawn-colored, snuff-colored, liver-colored.

reddish-brown, terra cotta, russet, foxy, bronze, coppery, copper-colored, maroon; bay, roan, sorrel; chestnut, henna, auburn, hazel.

sunburned; tanned, etc., *v.*

434. RED.—*N.* red, etc., *adj.*; flesh color, flesh tint, color, warmth; redness, ruddiness, blush.

V. **redden,** rouge, crimson, incarnadine; ruddle, rust.

blush, flush, color, color up, mantle, redden.

Adj. **red,** scarlet, cardinal, vermilion, carmine, crimson, pink, rose, cerise, cherry, salmon, maroon, carnation, magenta, solferino, damask.

reddish; sanguine, bloody, gory; coral, coralline, rosy, roseate; blood-red, wine-red, wine-colored, ruby, rufous, bricky, reddish-brown, etc., 433; rose (*or* ruby, cherry, claret, flame, flesh, peach, salmon, brick, rust) -colored.

red-complexioned, red-faced, florid, burned, rubicund, ruddy, red, high-colored, glowing, sanguine, blooming, rosy, hectic, flushed, inflamed.

Of hair: sandy, carroty, brick-red, Titian, auburn, chestnut.

435. GREEN.—*N.* green, etc., *adj.*; greenness, verdancy, verdure.

Adj. **green,** verdant, olive; verdurous; emerald (*or* pea, grass, apple, sea, leaf, bottle, Irish, Kelly) green; greenish, aquamarine, blue-green.

436. YELLOW.—*N.* yellow, etc., *adj.*; yellowness; jaundice.

V. **render yellow,** yellow, gild.

Adj. **yellow,** aureate, golden, gold, gilt, gilded, lemon, fallow; sallow, jaundiced; tawny, cream, creamy; flaxen, yellowish, buff; gold (*or* saffron, citron, lemon, amber, straw, primrose, cream) -colored.

437. PURPLE.—*N.* purple, etc., *adj.*; royal purple; gridelin, amethyst; damson, heliotrope.

V. **render purple,** purple, empurple.

Adj. **purple,** violet, plum-colored, lavender, lilac, puce, mauve, purplish, amethystine, magenta, solferino, heliotrope; livid; purplish.

438. BLUE.—*N.* **blue,** etc., *adj.*; azure [*her.*]; indigo; sapphire, blueness, bluishness; bloom.

Adj. **blue,** azure, cerulean, sky-blue, navy-blue, midnight-blue, cadet-blue, robin's-egg-blue, baby-blue, ultramarine, aquamarine, electric-blue, steel-blue; bluish; cold.

439. ORANGE.—*N.* **orange,** old gold; gold color, etc., *adj.*

Adj. **orange,** orange (*or* gold, brass, apricot) -colored; warm, hot, glowing, flame-colored.

440. VARIEGATION.—*N.* **variegation;** iridescence, play of colors, spottiness; tricolor.

check, plaid, tartan, patchwork; marquetry, parquet, parquetry, mosaic, checkerwork; chessboard, checkers; harlequin.

V. **variegate,** stripe, streak, checker, fleck, speckle, besprinkle,

sprinkle; stipple, dot, tattoo, inlay, tessellate; damascene; embroider, quilt.

Adj. variegated, many-colored, many-hued, divers-colored, parti-colored, polychromatic; kaleidoscopic.

iridescent, opaline, opalescent, prismatic, pearly, shot, tortoiseshell.

mottled, pied, piebald, skewbald; motley, marbled, pepper-and-salt, dappled.

checkered, checked, plaid, mosaic, tessellated.

spotted, spotty; powdered; speckled, freckled, flea-bitten, studded; flecked.

barred, veined, brindled, tabby, watered.

441. [Perception of light] VISION.—*N.* vision, sight, optics, eyesight.

view, look, glance, ken, glimpse, glint, peep, peek; gaze, stare, leer; contemplation, regard, survey; inspection, reconnaissance, watch, espionage, autopsy; sight-seeing, globe-trotting [*colloq.*].

viewpoint, standpoint, point of view; loophole, watchtower.

field of view; theater, amphitheater, arena, vista, horizon; bird's-eye view, panoramic view.

eye, visual organ, organ of vision, naked eye; clear (*or* sharp, quick, eagle) sight.

V. see, behold, discern, perceive, descry, sight, make out; discover, distinguish, recognize, spy, espy, command a view of; witness, contemplate, look on, see at a glance.

look, view, eye, survey, scan, inspect; reconnoiter, glance, cast a glance; observe, etc. (*attend to*), 457; watch, keep watch; watch for, etc. (*expect*), 507; peep, peek, peer, pry, take a peep.

look intently; strain one's eyes; rivet the eyes upon; stare, gaze; pore over, gloat on, gloat over; leer, ogle, glare; goggle; squint, gloat, look askance.

Adj. ocular, visual, optic *or* optical; ophthalmic; visible, etc., 446.

clear-sighted, clear-eyed, farsighted; eagle-eyed, hawk-eyed, lynx-eyed, keen-eyed, Argus-eyed.

Adv. at sight, at first sight, at a glance, at the first blush.

442. BLINDNESS.—*N.* blindness, sightlessness, benightedness, cataract; dim-sightedness, etc., 443; Braille.

V. be blind, not see; lose one's sight; grope in the dark.

blind; blindfold, hoodwink, dazzle; put one's eyes out; throw dust into one's eyes; screen, hide.

Adj. blind, eyeless, sightless, visionless; dark; stone-blind, stark-blind, undiscerning; dim-sighted, etc., 443.

Adv. blindly, blindfold; darkly.

443. DIM-SIGHTEDNESS.—*N.* **Imperfect vision:** dim (*or* short, near, long) -sightedness; purblindness, blearedness, myopia, astigmatism; color blindness, snow blindness; ophthalmia; cataract.

squint, cross-eye, cast in the eye, swivel eye, cockeye, goggle-eyes.

Limitation of vision: blinker, blinder; screen, curtain, veil.

Fallacies of vision: refraction, distortion, illusion, mirage, phantasm, phantom; vision; specter, apparition, ghost; will-o'-the-wisp, etc., 423.

V. be dim-sighted, see double; see through a glass darkly; wink, blink, squint, look askance, screw up the eyes, glare, glower.

dazzle, glare, swim, blur.

Adj. dim-sighted, myopic, nearsighted, shortsighted, astigmatic; blear-eyed, goggle-eyed, one-eyed; half-blind, purblind; cockeyed [*colloq.*], dim-eyed, mole-eyed.

444. SPECTATOR.—*N.* spectator, beholder, observer, looker-on, onlooker, witness, eyewitness, bystander, passer-by; sight-seer; rubberneck [*slang*].

spy, scout; sentinel, etc. (*warning*), 668.

grandstand [*fig.*], bleachers [*fig.*], gallery.

V. witness, behold, etc. (*see*), 441; look on, etc. (*be present*), 186.

445. OPTICAL INSTRUMENTS.—*N.* optical instruments; lens, magnifier, microscope; spectacles, glasses, goggles, eyeglass, pince-nez; periscope; telescope, glass, lorgnette, binocular; spyglass, opera glass, field glass; burning glass, convex lens; prism.

camera, hand camera, kodak [*trade name*]; moving-picture machine, magic lantern, stereopticon; stereoscope, kaleidoscope.

mirror, reflector, speculum; looking glass, pier glass, cheval glass.

optics, optician; photography, photographer; optometry, optometrist; microscopy, microscopist.

446. VISIBILITY.—*N.* visibility, perceptibility, conspicuousness, distinctness, appearance, etc., 448; exposure; manifestation, etc., 525; ocular demonstration; field of view, vista, horizon.

V. appear, open to the view; catch the eye; present (*or* show, manifest, reveal, expose, betray) itself; stand forth, stand out; materialize; show; arise; peep out, peer out; start up, spring up; gleam, glimmer; glitter, glow, loom; glare; burst forth; burst upon the view; heave in sight [*naut. or colloq.*]; come into view, come out, come forth, come forward; attract the attention, etc., 457.

expose to view, show, display.

Adj. visible, perceptible, discernible, apparent; in view, in full view, in sight; exposed to view.

distinct, plain, clear, definite; obvious, etc. (*manifest*), 525; recognizable; glaring, palpable, staring, conspicuous.

Adv. before one, under one's very eyes, in sight of.

447. INVISIBILITY.—*N.* invisibility, imperceptibility; indistinctness; mystery; latency, obscurity; concealment, mystification.

V. be invisible (*or* imperceptible); be hidden, etc. (*hide*), 528; escape notice.

render invisible; conceal, etc., 528; put out of sight.

Adj. invisible, imperceptible; out of sight, not in sight, unseen; viewless; inconspicuous; covert, latent.

indistinct; dim; mysterious, dark, obscure; confused, indistinguishable, shadowy, indefinite, undefined, ill-defined, blurred, out of focus; misty, veiled, concealed.

448. APPEARANCE.—*N.* appearance, phenomenon, sight, show, scene, view; lookout, outlook, prospect, vista, perspective, bird's-eye view, scenery, landscape, seascape, picture, tableau; display, exposure, rising of the curtain.

spectacle, pageant; peep show, magic lantern, biograph, cinematograph, cinema [*colloq.*], moving pictures, movies [*colloq.*], photoplay, photodrama; panorama.

aspect, angle, phase, shape, form, guise, look, complexion, color, image, mien, air, cast, carriage, port, demeanor; presence, expression, point of view, light.

lineament, feature, trait, lines; outline, outside; contour, silhouette, face, countenance, visage, profile; physiognomy.

V. appear, be visible, seem, look, show; cut a figure, figure; present to the view; show, etc. (*make manifest*), 525; look like, resemble.

Adj. apparent, seeming, ostensible; on view.

Adv. to all appearance, ostensibly, seemingly, on the face of it, at the first blush, at first sight, to the eye.

449. DISAPPEARANCE.—*N.* disappearance, evanescence, eclipse; departure, exit; vanishing point.

V. disappear, vanish, dissolve, fade, melt away, pass, go, depart, be gone, leave no trace; be lost to view (*or* sight), pass out of sight.

efface, etc., 552.

Adj. disappearing, evanescent; missing, lost; lost to sight.

CLASS IV

WORDS RELATING TO THE INTELLECTUAL FACULTIES

I. FORMATION OF IDEAS

450. INTELLECT.—*N.* **intellect,** mind, understanding, reason; rationality; intellectual faculties (*or* powers); senses, consciousness, observation, intellectuality, mentality, intelligence; conception, judgment, wits, brains, parts, capacity, genius; wit; ability; wisdom; ideality, idealism.

ego, soul, spirit; heart, breast, bosom; subconscious self, subliminal consciousness.

seat of thought, brain; head, headpiece; skull, cranium.

Science of mind: psychology, psychoanalysis; psychophysics; metaphysics; philosophy.

psychical research; telepathy, thought transference, thought reading; clairaudience; clairvoyance, mediumship; spiritualism, etc., 992*a.*

V. **reason,** understand, think, reflect, cogitate, conceive, judge, contemplate, meditate; ruminate, etc. (*think*), 451.

note, notice, mark; take notice of; be aware of, realize; appreciate.

Adj. **intellectual,** mental, rational; psychological; conscious, percipient, brainy [*colloq.*].

hyperphysical, subconscious, subliminal; telepathic, clairvoyant; psychic *or* psychical, spiritual, metaphysical, transcendental.

450a. ABSENCE OF INTELLECT.—*N.* **want of intellect** (*or* mind, understanding); unintellectuality; imbecility, etc., 490.

Adj. **unendowed with** (*or* void of) reason; unintelligent, etc. (*imbecile*), 499.

451. THOUGHT.—*N.* **thought;** reflection, cogitation, consideration, meditation, study, speculation, deliberation, brainwork, cerebration; close study, application.

mature thought; afterthought, reconsideration, second thoughts; retrospection, examination.

abstraction, abstract thought, contemplation, musing; reverie, etc., 458; depth of thought.

V. **think,** reflect, cogitate, consider, reason, deliberate: contemplate, meditate, ponder, muse, dream, ruminate, speculate; brood over, con over, study; bend (*or* apply) the mind; digest, discuss, hammer at, hammer out; weigh, realize, appreciate; fancy.

harbor, cherish, entertain, nurture (*as an idea*), imagine; bear in mind; reconsider.

suggest itself, present itself, occur to; come into one's head; strike one, come uppermost; enter (or cross, flash across, occupy) the mind.

Adj. thoughtful, pensive, meditative, reflective, cogitative, contemplative, speculative, deliberative, studious, introspective, philosophical.

absorbed, rapt; lost in thought; engrossed in, intent.

Adv. all things considered, taking everything into consideration (or account).

452. ABSENCE OF THOUGHT.—*N.* vacancy of mind, poverty of intellect; thoughtlessness, etc. (*inattention*), 458; inanity, fatuity, vacuity.

V. put away thought; relax (or divert) the mind; make the mind a blank, let the mind lie fallow; indulge in reverie, etc. (*be inattentive*), 458.

Adj. vacant, inane, unintellectual, unoccupied, unthinking, irrational, unreasoning, thoughtless, inattentive; diverted; bigoted, narrow-minded.

453. [Object of thought] IDEA.—*N.* idea, notion, conception, thought; apprehension, impression, perception; sentiment, reflection, observation, consideration; abstract idea.

view, opinion, theory; conceit, fancy; fantasy, etc., 515.

viewpoint, point of view; aspect, angle; field of view.

454. [Subject of thought] TOPIC.—*N.* subject, subject matter; matter, motif, theme, topic, thesis, text, business, affair, matter in hand, argument; motion, resolution, case, point, proposition, theorem; field of inquiry; moot point, point at issue; problem, etc. (*question*), 461.

V. enter the mind, etc., 451.

Adv. under consideration, under advisement; in question, in the mind; at issue, before the house, on foot, on the carpet.

455. [Desire of knowledge] CURIOSITY.—*N.* curiosity; inquisitiveness; interest, thirst for knowledge, mental acquisitiveness; inquiring mind.

investigator, inquirer, etc., 461.

busybody, newsmonger; Peeping Tom, Paul Pry, eavesdropper; gossip.

V. be curious; take an interest in, investigate; stare, gape; see the sights.

pry, nose, search, ferret out.

Adj. curious, inquiring, etc., 461; inquisitive, burning with curiosity, overcurious, prying; inquisitorial; agape, expectant.

456. [Absence of curiosity] INCURIOSITY.—*N.* incuriosity; incuriousness; apathy, unconcern, indifference.

V. **be incurious** (*or* indifferent); have no curiosity, etc., 455; be bored by, take no interest in.

Adj. **incurious**, uninquisitive, indifferent; impassive, etc., 823; uninterested, bored.

457. ATTENTION.—*N.* attention; intentness, alertness; thought, etc., 451; observance, observation; consideration, reflection; heed; heedfulness; notice, regard; circumspection, etc. (*care*), 459; study, scrutiny; inspection, revision, revisal.

minuteness, circumstantiality, attention to detail.

V. **attend**, watch, observe, look, see, view, notice, regard, take notice, mark; pay attention to, give heed to; occupy oneself with; contemplate, etc. (*think of*), 451, look to, see to; heed, mind, take cognizance of, entertain, recognize; make (*or* take) note of; note.

examine, scan, scrutinize, consider; overhaul, revise, pore over; inspect, review.

revert to, hark back to; come to the point.

meet with attention; attract notice, fall under one's notice; be under consideration.

call attention to, bring under one's notice; point out (*or* to, at), indicate; direct attention to; show; bring forward.

Adj. **attentive**, mindful, heedful, observant, regardful; alive to, awake to, on the job [*colloq.*], alert; taken up with, occupied with; engrossed in, wrapped in, absorbed, rapt; watchful; intent on, open-eyed; on the watch.

458. INATTENTION.—*N.* inattention, inconsideration, want of consideration, inconsiderateness; oversight; inadvertence, disregard; want of thought; heedlessness, etc. (*neglect*), 460; unconcern.

abstraction; absence of mind, absorption, preoccupation, distraction, reverie, brown study [*colloq.*], woolgathering.

V. **be inattentive** (*or* unobservant); overlook, disregard; pass by, neglect; think little of; pay no attention to; dismiss from one's mind; drop the subject, think no more of; turn a deaf ear to.

confuse, disconcert, discompose, perplex, bewilder, fluster, flurry; call off *or* distract the attention (thoughts, mind); put out of one's head.

Adj. **inattentive**, unobservant, undiscerning, unmindful, unheeding, regardless; listless, apathetic; blind, deaf; volatile, scatter-brained, flighty, giddy; unreflecting; inconsiderate, thoughtless; wild, harum-scarum [*colloq.*], heedless, careless, neglectful.

abstracted, absent, distrait [F.], woolgathering, dreamy; dazed, absent-minded; lost in thought; rapt, in the clouds, daydreaming; preoccupied, engrossed; in a reverie; off one's guard; caught napping.

459. CARE. [Vigilance]—*N.* care, solicitude, anxiety; heed, concern, heedfulness; scruple.

vigilance; watchfulness, surveillance, watch, vigil, lookout, watch and ward; espionage, reconnoitering; watching.

alertness, attention, prudence, forethought, circumspection, precaution, caution; accuracy, exactness; minuteness, attention to detail.

watcher, watchman, watchdog.

V. be careful, take care, be cautious; take precautions; pay attention to, etc., 457; take care of; look *or* see to, look after, keep an eye upon; chaperon, matronize, keep watch, mount guard, watch.

Adj. careful, regardful, heedful; prudent, discreet, cautious; considerate, thoughtful; provident; alert; sure-footed.

guarded, on one's guard; on the alert (*or* watch, lookout); awake, vigilant; watchful, wakeful, Argus-eyed, lynx-eyed.

scrupulous, punctilious, conscientious; tidy, orderly; clean; accurate, exact.

Adv. carefully, with care, gingerly.

460. NEGLECT.—*N.* neglect; carelessness; negligence; omission, procrastination; supineness, apathy; inattention, etc., 458; imprudence, improvidence, recklessness; slovenliness, untidiness; dirt; inexactness, inaccuracy.

trifler, waiter on providence; Micawber; slacker.

V. neglect, take no care of, let slip, let go; lose sight of.

delay, defer, procrastinate, postpone, adjourn, pigeonhole, shelve, table, lay on the table.

overlook, disregard; pass over, pass by; let pass; wink at, connive at.

scamp; trifle, slight, slur; skim, skip, take a cursory view of, run over, dip into; slur *or* slip over; push aside, throw into the background, sink; ignore; forget.

Adj. neglectful, negligent, remiss; heedless, careless; thoughtless, inconsiderate; perfunctory, offhand.

unwary, unwatchful, unguarded, off one's guard.

supine, apathetic; inattentive, etc., 458; nonchalant, indifferent; imprudent, reckless; slovenly, disorderly; dirty; inexact, inaccurate; improvident, unthrifty.

neglected, unheeded, uncared for, unattended to; abandoned, shunted, shelved.

461. INQUIRY. [Subject of inquiry. QUESTION.]—*N.* inquiry; request, etc., 765; search, research, quest; pursuit, prosecution.

examination, review, scrutiny, investigation; inquest, inquisition; trial; exploration; exploitation, ventilation; sifting; calculation, analysis, dissection; study, consideration.

reconnoitering, reconnaissance, espionage.

questioning, interrogation, interrogatory; challenge, examination, third degree [*colloq*.], cross-examination; discussion; catechism.

question, query, problem, poser, desideratum, point (*or* matter) in dispute; moot point; issue, question at issue; bone of contention, enigma, etc. (*secret*), 533; knotty point.

inquirer, investigator, inquisitor, inspector, querist, examiner, catechist; scrutator, scrutinizer; analyst.

V. inquire, seek, search, make inquiry, look for, scan, reconnoiter, explore, sound, rummage, ransack, pry, peer, look round; overhaul; look behind the scenes; nose, nose out, trace up; hunt out, fish out, ferret out; unearth.

track, seek a clue; hunt, trail, shadow, mouse, dodge, trace, pursue, experiment, etc., 463.

examine, study, consider, calculate; dip *or* dive into, probe, sound, fathom, scrutinize, analyze, anatomize, dissect, parse, resolve, sift, winnow, thresh out; investigate, look into, discuss, canvass, subject to examination, quiz, pose; audit, tax, pass in review.

question, ask, demand; interrogate, catechize, pump; cross-question, cross-examine; grill [*colloq*], put through the third degree [*colloq*.].

Adj. inquiring, inquisitive, catechetical, inquisitorial, analytic; interrogative.

undetermined, undecided, tentative; in question, in dispute, in issue, under consideration; moot, proposed; doubtful, etc. (*uncertain*), 475.

462. ANSWER.—*N.* answer, response, reply, rejoinder; retort, repartee; antiphon, acknowledgment; password; echo; counterstatement, countercharge, contradiction.

[Law] defense, plea, reply, rejoinder, rebutter, surrebutter, surrejoinder.

solution, explanation; discovery, disclosure; cause; clue.

oracle, etc., 513.

V. answer, respond, reply, rebut, retort, rejoin; give answer; acknowledge, echo.

[Law] defend, reply, surrejoin, surrebut, plead, rebut.

explain, interpret; solve, etc. (*unriddle*), 522; discover, fathom, hunt out, inquire; satisfy, set at rest, determine.

Adj. responsive, respondent, antiphonal; oracular; conclusive.

463. EXPERIMENT.—*N.* experiment, essay, trial, attempt;

analysis, investigation; verification, probation, proof, criterion, diagnosis, test, crucial test; assay, ordeal.

　　speculation, random shot, leap in the dark; feeler, pilot balloon.

　　experimenter, experimentalist, assayer, analyst; prospector, adventurer; speculator, gambler, stock gambler, plunger [*slang*].

　　V. **experiment**, essay, try, venture, make an experiment, make trial of; rehearse; put to the test, prove, verify, test.

　　grope, grope for, feel one's way, fumble, throw out a feeler; send up a pilot balloon; see how the land lies (*or* wind blows); feel the pulse; fish for, angle, trawl, cast one's net.

　　Adj. **experimental**, probationary; analytic, speculative, tentative, empirical.

　　on trial, on examination, on *or* under probation, under suspicion; on one's trial.

　　464. COMPARISON.—*N.* comparison, contrast, parallelism, balance; identification; simile, similitude, allegory, etc. (*metaphor*), 521.

　　V. **compare**, collate, confront, contrast, balance; parallel.

　　Adj. **comparative**, relative, contrastive; metaphorical, etc., 521.

　　Adv. relatively; as compared with.

　　465. DISCRIMINATION.—*N.* discrimination, distinction, differentiation, diagnosis, nice perception; estimation; nicety, refinement, taste, judgment; tact, discernment, acuteness, penetration.

　　V. **discriminate**, distinguish, separate; draw the line, sift; estimate, etc. (*measure*), 466; sum up, criticize; take into account, weigh carefully.

　　Adj. **discriminating**, critical, diagnostic, perceptive, discriminative, distinctive; nice, acute.

　　465a. INDISCRIMINATION.—*N.* indiscrimination, indistinction; want of discernment; uncertainty, etc. (*doubt*), 475.

　　V. **confound**, confuse, jumble, heap indiscriminately; swallow whole.

　　Adj. **indiscriminate**, indistinguishable, lacking distinction, undistinguished, undistinguishable; promiscuous, undiscriminating.

　　466. MEASUREMENT.—*N.* measurement, mensuration, survey, valuation, appraisement, assessment, estimate, estimation; dead reckoning [*naut.*]; reckoning, gauging; horsepower, candle power.

　　measure, gauge; yard measure, standard, rule, foot rule, spirit level, plumb line; square, T-square, steel square, compass, dividers, calipers; log, log line, patent log [*naut.*]; meter, line, rod, check.

　　flood mark, high-water mark, load-line mark.

　　scale; graduation, graduated scale; vernier, quadrant, theodolite; beam, steelyard, weighing machine, balance.

　　latitude and longitude, altitude and azimuth.

　　geometry; topography, cartography; surveying, land surveying.

　　surveyor, land surveyor, topographer, cartographer.

V. **measure,** meter; value, assess, rate, appraise, estimate, form an estimate; standardize; span, pace, step, inch, divide, gauge, balance, poise, weigh; plumb, probe, sound, fathom; survey, plot, block in, block out, rule, draw to scale.

Adj. **metrical,** metric; measurable; topographic *or* topographical, cartographic *or* cartographical.

467. [Materials for reasoning] EVIDENCE.—*N.* **evidence;** facts, premises, data, grounds, proof; confirmation, corroboration, ratification, authentication.

testimony, attestation; affirmation, declaration; deposition.

authority, warrant, credential, diploma, voucher, certificate, document, deed, warranty; autograph, handwriting, signature, seal, countersign; exhibit; citation, reference, quotation; admission, etc. (*assent*), 488.

witness, eyewitness, deponent [*law*]; sponsor.

writ, summons, etc. (*lawsuit*), 696.

V. **evince,** show, betoken, indicate, denote, imply, involve, argue, bespeak.

have weight, carry weight; tell, speak volumes, speak for itself.

testify, bear witness, give evidence, depose, witness, vouch for; certify, attest, acknowledge.

confirm, ratify, corroborate, indorse, support, bear out, vindicate, uphold, warrant.

adduce, evidence, cite, quote; refer to, call, call to witness; bring forward, bring into court; allege, plead.

establish, make out a case; authenticate, substantiate, verify, make good.

Adj. **evidential,** indicative, deducible, inferential, firsthand, authentic, documentary; cumulative, corroborative, confirmatory; significant, weighty, overwhelming, conclusive.

oral, hearsay, circumstantial, presumptive.

Adv. **by inference;** according to, in corroboration of.

468. COUNTEREVIDENCE.—*N.* **counterevidence,** rejoinder, disproof, refutation, negation, denial; plea, etc., 617; vindication.

V. **refute,** rebut, oppose; confute, etc. (*refute*), 479; subvert; destroy, check, weaken; contravene; contradict, deny, alter the case; turn the tables; prove a negative.

Adj. **contradictory,** conflicting; unattested, unauthenticated, unsupported, supposititious, trumped up.

Adv. **on the other hand** (*or* side), in opposition; in rebuttal.

469. QUALIFICATION.—*N.* **qualification,** limitation, modification, coloring; allowance, consideration, extenuating circumstances; mitigation.

condition, proviso, exception; exemption; saving clause.

V. qualify, limit, modify, affect, give a color to, narrow, temper; allow for, take into account.

Adj. qualifying, extenuating, palliative; conditional; exceptional; hypothetical, contingent.

Adv. provided, if, unless, but, yet; according as; conditionally, admitting, supposing; even, although, though.

470. POSSIBILITY.—*N.* possibility, potentiality, practicability, feasibility, workableness; potency; compatibility, etc. (*agreement*), 23.

contingency, chance, etc., 156.

V. be possible, stand a chance; admit of, bear.

render possible, put in the way of, bring to bear, bring together.

Adj. possible, conceivable, imaginable, credible; compatible, etc., 23; likely.

practicable, feasible, workable, achievable; within reach, accessible, surmountable; attainable, obtainable.

Adv. possibly, perhaps, perchance, peradventure, haply.

471. IMPOSSIBILITY.—*N.* impossibility, impracticability, incredibility, hopelessness, infeasibility; discrepancy.

V. attempt impossibilities; square the circle, find the elixir of life, discover the philosopher's stone, discover the grand panacea, find the fountain of youth, discover the secret of perpetual motion; make bricks without straw; weave a rope of sand; be in two places at once; gather grapes from thorns.

Adj. impossible, not possible, absurd, contrary to reason, unlikely, unreasonable, incredible, visionary, impractical, inconceivable, improbable, unimaginable, unthinkable.

impracticable, unachievable, infeasible; insuperable, insurmountable, inaccessible, unattainable, unobtainable; out of the question; incompatible, etc., 24; impassable, impervious, self-contradictory.

472. PROBABILITY.—*N.* probability, likelihood, likeness, verisimilitude, plausibility; color, semblance, show of; presumption; credibility; prospect; chance, etc., 156.

V. be probable, lend color to; point to; imply, bid fair, promise, stand (*or* run) a good chance.

presume, infer, venture, suppose, take for granted, flatter oneself; expect, etc., 507; count upon, etc. (*believe*), 484.

Adj. probable, likely, hopeful, presumable, presumptive, apparent.

plausible, specious, ostensible, colorable, reasonable, credible.

Adv. in all probability, most likely, apparently, seemingly, to all appearance.

473. IMPROBABILITY.—*N.* improbability, unlikelihood; bare possibility; long odds; incredibility.

V. **be improbable,** go beyond reason, strain one's credulity; have a small chance.

Adj. **improbable,** unlikely, rare, unheard of, inconceivable; unimaginable, incredible.

474. CERTAINTY.—*N.* **certainty;** necessity, etc., 601; certitude, sureness, surety, assurance; infallibility, reliability, inevitableness; fact; positive fact, matter of fact.

bigotry, positiveness, dogmatism, dogmatization; fanaticism. dogmatist, doctrinaire, bigot; zealot, fanatic.

V. **render certain,** insure, assure; clinch, make sure; determine, decide; know, etc. (*believe*), 484.

Adj. **certain,** sure, inevitable, assured, solid, well founded.

unqualified, absolute, positive, definite, clear, unequivocal, categorical, unmistakable, decisive.

conclusive, undeniable, unquestionable; indisputable, incontestable, indubitable; irrefutable; final; undoubted, unquestioned, undisputed; questionless.

authoritative, authentic, official.

evident, manifest; self-evident, axiomatic.

infallible, unerring; unchangeable, etc., 150; trustworthy, reliable.

dogmatic, opinionated, dictatorial, doctrinaire; fanatical, bigoted.

Adv. **certainly,** undoubtedly, indubitably; for certain, surely, no doubt, doubtless, to be sure, of course, as a matter of course, in truth, truly, without fail.

475. UNCERTAINTY.—*N.* **uncertainty,** incertitude, doubt, doubtfulness, dubiousness.

hesitation, suspense, perplexity, embarrassment, dilemma, bewilderment; puzzle, quandary; timidity, etc. (*fear*), 860; vacillation, wavering, indetermination.

vagueness, haze, fog, obscurity, ambiguity, open question, blind bargain, pig in a poke, leap in the dark.

fallibility, unreliability, untrustworthiness; precariousness.

V. **hesitate,** flounder, miss one's way, wander aimlessly, beat about; lose oneself, lose one's head.

perplex, pose, puzzle, confuse, confound, bewilder, nonplus. doubt, etc. (*disbelieve*), 485.

Adj. **uncertain,** unsure; casual, random, aimless, doubtful, dubious; insecure, unstable, indecisive, irresolute; unsettled, undecided, undetermined, in question; experimental, tentative.

vague, indefinite, ambiguous, equivocal, undefined, confused; mysterious, cryptic, veiled, obscure, undefinable; oracular.

perplexing, enigmatic, paradoxical, apocryphal, problematical.

fallible, questionable, debatable, untrustworthy, unreliable.

puzzled, perplexed; lost, astray, adrift, at sea, at fault, at a loss, at one's wit's end, distracted, distraught.

476. REASONING.—*N.* reasoning, ratiocination; inference, induction, generalization.

logic, art of reasoning, dialectics; deduction, induction; synthesis, analysis; syllogism.

discussion, comment; ventilation; inquiry, etc., 461.

argumentation, controversy, debate; polemics, wrangling, contention.

argument, case, plea, proposition, terms, premises, data, principle.

arguments, reasons, pros and cons.

reasoner, logician, dialectician, casuist; disputant, controversialist; wrangler, arguer, debater.

V. **reason,** argue, discuss, debate, dispute, contend, wrangle; chop logic; controvert, deny; canvass; consider, examine.

Adj. **reasoning,** rational; argumentative, controversial, dialectic, polemical; disputatious.

logical, syllogistic, inductive, deductive, synthetic *or* synthetical, analytic *or* analytical; relevant, germane.

Adv. **for,** because, hence, whence, seeing that, since, then, thence, so; whereas, considering, therefore, wherefore; consequently, *ergo* [L.], thus, accordingly.

finally, in conclusion, in fine, after all, on the whole.

477. [Absence of reasoning] **INTUITION.** [Specious reasoning] **SOPHISTRY.**—*N.* intuition; instinct, association of ideas; rule of thumb; presentiment.

sophistry, casuistry, equivocation, evasion, mental reservation, chicanery; perversion, mystification; speciousness; nonsense, etc., 497; hairsplitting, quibbling; begging of the question.

sophism, quibble, quirk, fallacy, subterfuge, shift, subtlety; inconsistency; claptrap.

V. **pervert,** quibble, equivocate, mystify, evade, elude; gloss over, varnish; misteach, etc., 538; mislead, etc. (*error*), 495; misrepresent, etc. (*lie*), 544; cavil, refine, split hairs; misjudge, etc., 481; beg the question, reason in a circle.

Adj. **intuitive,** instinctive, impulsive.

illogical, unreasonable, false, unsound, invalid; unwarranted, gratuitous; incongruous, inconsequent, inconsequential; unconnected; inconsistent; unscientific; untenable, inconclusive, incorrect, fallacious, groundless, unproved.

specious, sophistic *or* sophistical, casuistic; deceptive, illusive, illusory, hollow, plausible; evasive; irrelevant, inapplicable.

weak, feeble, poor, flimsy, loose, vague, irrational; nonsensical, absurd, foolish, etc. (*imbecile*), 499; frivolous; pettifogging, quibbling.

478. DEMONSTRATION.—*N.* demonstration, proof; conclusiveness; evidence, etc., 467; verification, etc., 462.

V. demonstrate, prove, establish, make good; show, evince, verify, etc., 467; settle the question.

follow; stand to reason; hold good, hold water [*colloq.*].

Adj. demonstrative; demonstrable; unanswerable, conclusive, decisive, convincing; irresistible, irrefutable, undeniable.

demonstrated, proved; unconfuted, unanswered, unrefuted; evident, self-evident, axiomatic.

deducible, inferential, following.

Adv. of course, in consequence, consequently, as a matter of course.

479. CONFUTATION.—*N.* confutation, refutation; answer, disproof, conviction, invalidation; exposure, exposé [F.], retort.

V. confute, refute, parry, negative, disprove, expose, show up; rebut, defeat, demolish, upset, subvert, overthrow, overturn, confound; invalidate; convince, silence; clinch an argument.

Adj. confutable, refutable; capable of refutation.

480. [Results of reasoning] JUDGMENT.—*N.* judgment, decision, determination, finding, verdict, sentence, decree; opinion, etc. (*belief*), 484; good judgment.

result, conclusion, upshot; deduction, inference, corollary.

estimation, valuation, appreciation; arbitrament, arbitration; assessment.

estimate, award; review, criticism, critique, notice, report.

plebiscite, voice, casting vote; vote, suffrage, election.

arbiter, arbitrator; judge, umpire; assessor, referee; inspector; censor.

reviewer, critic; connoisseur; commentator, annotator.

V. judge, conclude, opine; come to (*or* arrive at) a conclusion; ascertain, determine.

deduce, derive, gather, collect, infer.

estimate, form an estimate, appreciate, value, count, assess, rate, rank, account; regard, consider, think of; size up [*colloq.*].

decide, settle; try, pronounce, rule; find, pass judgment, sentence, doom, decree; give (*or* deliver) judgment; adjudge, adjudicate; arbitrate, award; confirm.

review, comment, criticize; examine, etc., 457; investigate, etc., 461.

Adj. judicious, judicial; determinate, conclusive, confirmatory.

critical, hypercritical, hairsplitting, censorious.

Adv. **on the whole,** all things considered, therefore, wherefore.

480a. [Result of search or inquiry] DISCOVERY.—*N.* **discovery,** detection, disclosure, find, revelation.

V. **discover,** find, determine, evolve; fix upon; find (*or* trace, make, root) out; spot [*colloq.*], fathom, bring out, draw out, educe, elicit, bring to light, dig up, unearth, disinter.

solve, resolve; unriddle, unravel, find a clue to; interpret; disclose; see through, detect; catch; scent, smell out.

recognize, realize, verify, make certain of, identify.

481. MISJUDGMENT.—*N.* **misjudgment,** obliquity of judgment, warped judgment; miscalculation, misconception, misinterpretation, etc., 523; hasty conclusion.

preconception, prejudgment, foregone conclusion; presumption, preconceived idea; prejudice, predilection, prepossession; presentiment, foreboding; fixed idea, obsession.

partisanship, clannishness; *esprit de corps* [F.], prestige, party spirit, class prejudice, class consciousness, race prejudice, provincialism.

quirk, shift, quibble, equivocation, evasion, subterfuge.

bias, warp, twist; hobby, whim, craze, cult, fad, crotchet, partiality.

V. **misjudge,** misconjecture, misconceive, misunderstand; miscalculate, misreckon; overestimate, etc., 482; underestimate, etc., 483.

prejudge, dogmatize; have a bias, run away with the notion; jump to a conclusion; blunder, etc., 699.

bias, warp, twist; prejudice, prepossess.

Adj. **misjudging,** ill-judging, wrong-headed; superficial; prejudiced, prepossessed; shortsighted, purblind; partial, one-sided; warped.

narrow, narrow-minded, provincial, parochial, insular; mean-spirited, confined, illiberal, intolerant, infatuated, fanatical, positive, dogmatic, dictatorial, pragmatic; egotistical, conceited, opinionated; bigoted, etc. (*obstinate*), 606; unreasonable, stupid, etc., 499; credulous, gullible.

482. OVERESTIMATION.—*N.* **overestimation,** exaggeration, hyperbole; optimism, much ado about nothing; tempest in a teacup; fine writing, rodomontade, gush [*colloq.*], hot air [*slang*].

egoism, egotism, bombast, conceit; vanity; megalomania.

egoist, egotist, megalomaniac; optimist; braggart, boaster, braggadocio, swaggerer.

V. **overestimate,** overrate, overpraise; strain, magnify; exaggerate, etc., 549.

eulogize, gush over [*colloq.*], boost; puff [*colloq.*]; extol.

Adj. **inflated,** puffed up; grandiose, stilted, pompous, pretentious, bombastic.

483. UNDERESTIMATION.—*N.* **underestimation,** undervaluation; depreciation, etc. (*detraction*), 934; pessimism; self-detraction, self-depreciation; modesty, etc., 881.

pessimist, depreciator, knocker [*slang*], crapehanger [*slang*].

V. **underrate,** underestimate, undervalue; depreciate; disparage, detract, decry, ridicule, deride; slight, etc. (*despise*), 930; neglect; slur over.

make light (*or* little) **of,** belittle, run down [*colloq.*], minimize, set no store by, set at naught, disregard.

Adj. **depreciating,** depreciative, depreciatory; pessimistic.

depreciated, unappreciated, unvalued, unprized.

484. BELIEF.—*N.* **belief,** credence; credit; assurance; faith, trust, confidence, presumption; hope.

conviction, principle; persuasion, certainty, opinion, view, conception, impression, surmise; conclusion.

doctrine, tenet, dogma, articles, canons; view, gospel; article (*or* declaration, profession) of faith, creed; assent, avowal, confession; propaganda.

credibility, probability; plausibility.

V. **believe,** credit, give faith (*or* credit, credence) to; realize; assume, take it; consider, presume; count (*or* depend, rely, build) upon; take for granted.

confide in, believe in, put one's trust in, place reliance on, trust.

think, hold, opine, conceive; have (*or* hold, entertain, adopt, embrace, foster, cherish) a belief *or* an opinion.

persuade, assure, convince, satisfy, bring to reason, convert, indoctrinate; wean, bring round, bring (*or* win) over; carry conviction.

Adj. **certain,** sure, assured, positive, cocksure [*colloq.*], satisfied, confident, unhesitating, convinced, secure.

confiding, trustful, unsuspecting, unsuspicious; credulous, gullible.

believed, trusted, unsuspected, undoubted.

credible, reliable, trustworthy, accredited, satisfactory; probable.

485. UNBELIEF. DOUBT.—*N.* **unbelief,** disbelief, incredulity; infidelity, etc. (*irreligion*), 989; wrangling, nonconformity; dissent, change of opinion; retractation, etc., 607.

doubt, uncertainty, skepticism, misgiving, demur; discredit; distrust, mistrust; misdoubt, suspicion, jealousy, scruple, qualm.

incredibility, incredibleness, unbelievability.

agnostic, skeptic; unbeliever, etc., 487.

V. disbelieve, discredit, misbelieve, dissent; refuse to believe.

doubt, distrust, mistrust; question, challenge, dispute; deny, etc., 536; cavil, wrangle; suspect, scent, smell, smell a rat [*colloq.*], harbor suspicions; have one's doubts.

demur, stick at, pause, hesitate, shy at, scruple; waver.

stagger, startle; shake one's faith, stagger one's belief.

Adj. unbelieving, skeptical, incredulous; distrustful of, suspicious of.

doubtful, etc. (*uncertain*), 475; disputable, questionable, suspicious; incredible, unbelievable, inconceivable.

Adv. with caution, with grains of allowance.

486. CREDULITY.—*N.* credulity, credulousness, gullibility; infatuation; self-delusion, self-deception; superstition; bigotry.

credulous person, dupe, gull.

V. be credulous; follow implicitly; swallow, swallow whole, gulp down; take on faith.

impose upon, etc. (*deceive*), 545.

Adj. credulous, gullible, easily deceived *or* convinced; simple, silly, childish; infatuated, superstitious; confiding, trustful, unsuspicious.

487. INCREDULITY.—*N.* incredulity, incredulousness; skepticism, doubt, disbelief, etc., 989; unbelief, etc., 485.

unbeliever, skeptic, doubting Thomas, disbeliever, agnostic, infidel, misbeliever; heretic, etc. (*heterodox*), 984.

V. be incredulous, distrust, doubt, suspect, refuse to believe; turn a deaf ear to.

Adj. incredulous, skeptical, suspicious; dissenting, unbelieving; heterodox.

488. ASSENT.—*N.* assent, acquiescence, admission; nod; consent, compliance; agreement, understanding; affirmation; recognition, acknowledgment, avowal, confession.

unanimity, common consent, consensus, acclamation, chorus; public opinion; concurrence, accord.

ratification, confirmation, corroboration, approval, acceptance; indorsement.

consenter, indorser, subscriber; upholder, etc. (*auxiliary*), 711.

V. assent, give assent, acquiesce, agree, accept, accede, accord, concur, consent, coincide, echo, reciprocate, go with; recognize; subscribe to, conform to, defer to; go with the stream; be in the fashion, join in the chorus.

acknowledge, own, admit, confess; concede, yield; abide by; permit, etc., 760.

confirm, ratify, approve, indorse, countersign; corroborate, etc., 467.

Adj. **assenting,** of one accord (*or* mind); of the same mind, at one with, agreed, acquiescent.

uncontradicted, unchallenged, unquestioned, unanimous.

Adv. **yes,** yea, aye, true; granted; even so, just so; to be sure, as you say; surely, assuredly; exactly, precisely, certainly, of course, unquestionably, no doubt, doubtless.

unanimously, by common consent, to a man, as one man; with one consent (*or* voice, accord).

489. DISSENT.—*N.* **dissent,** nonconsent, discordance, disagreement.

nonconformity, heterodoxy, protestantism, schism; disaffection, secession, recantation.

dissension, discord, caviling, wrangling; discontent, etc., 832.

protest, contradiction, denial; noncompliance, rejection.

dissentient, dissenter, nonconformist; sectary; separatist, protestant; heretic, etc., 984.

V. **dissent,** demur, call in question, disagree, refuse to admit; cavil, wrangle, protest, repudiate; contradict, deny.

secede; recant, etc., 607.

Adj. **dissenting,** negative; contradictory; dissentient; unconvinced, unconverted.

sectarian, denominational, schismatic; heterodox; intolerant.

Adv. **at variance with,** at issue with; under protest.

490. KNOWLEDGE.—*N.* **knowledge;** cognizance; cognition, acquaintance, experience, ken, insight, familiarity; comprehension, apprehension; recognition; appreciation, judgment, etc., 480; intuition, consciousness, perception.

enlightenment, light; impression, perception, discovery, revelation.

learning, erudition, lore, scholarship; letters, literature; book learning, bookishness, general information; education, culture, cultivation, attainments, acquirements, accomplishments, proficiency.

V. **know,** be aware of; conceive, apprehend, comprehend; realize, understand, appreciate; fathom, make out; recognize, discern, perceive, see, experience.

learn, imbibe knowledge; discover, evolve.

Adj. **aware of,** cognizant of, conscious of; acquainted with, privy to, in the secret; alive to; apprized of, informed of; undeceived.

educated, erudite, instructed, learned, lettered, well informed, well versed, well read, well grounded, well educated; high-brow [*slang*], bookish, scholastic, profound, deep-read, book-learned, accomplished; self-taught, self-educated, knowing, shrewd.

known, ascertained, well known, recognized, noted, received, notorious, proverbial; familiar, hackneyed, trite, commonplace.

Adv. to the best of one's knowledge; as every schoolboy knows.

491. IGNORANCE.—*N.* ignorance, illiteracy, unlearnedness, unacquaintance, unconsciousness, darkness, blindness; incomprehension, simplicity.

sealed book; virgin soil, unexplored ground; dark ages.

Imperfect knowledge: smattering, superficiality, half learning, shallowness, glimmering; incapacity.

Affectation of knowledge: pedantry, charlatanry, charlatanism.

V. be ignorant (*or* uninformed); be uneducated; know nothing of; ignore, be blind to.

Adj. ignorant; unknowing, unaware, unacquainted, uninformed, uninitiated, unwitting, unconscious; witless, unconversant.

illiterate, unread, low [*slang*], uncultivated, uninstructed, untaught, untutored, unschooled, uneducated, unlearned, unlettered, empty-headed.

shallow, superficial, green, rude, empty, half-learned, half-baked [*colloq.*], unscholarly.

in the dark; benighted, blinded, blindfold, hoodwinked; misinformed.

unknown, unapprehended, unexplained, uninvestigated, unexplored, unheard of; concealed, etc., 528.

Adv. unawares; for aught one knows; not that one knows.

492. SCHOLAR.—*N.* scholar, savant [F.], pundit [India], schoolman, professor, academician, doctor, fellow, don [Eng.], graduate, postgraduate, classicist, philosopher, scientist, linguist, etymologist, philologist, lexicographer; man of learning.

bookworm, bibliophile, bibliomaniac, bluestocking [*colloq.*], high-brow [*slang*].

pedant, doctrinaire; pedagogue, Dr. Pangloss; instructor, etc., 540.

student, learner, pupil, schoolboy, etc. (*learner*), 541.

Adj. learned, etc., 490.

493. IGNORAMUS.—*N.* ignoramus, illiterate, dunce, duffer, numskull [*colloq.*]; no scholar.

smatterer, dabbler, half scholar; charlatan; wiseacre.

novice, greenhorn, plebe [*West Point cant*]; tyro, etc. (*learner*), 541.

Adj. bookless, shallow, simple, dull, dumb [*colloq.*], dense, crass; illiterate, etc., 491.

494. [Object of knowledge] TRUTH.—*N.* truth, verity; fact, reality, authenticity, gospel; veracity, etc., 543.

accuracy, exactitude, exactness, preciseness, precision, regularity, fidelity, nicety.

V. hold true, stand the test, have the true ring, hold good.

trace, solve, etc. (*discover*), 480*a*.

Adj. true, real, actual, veritable; certain, etc., 474; unimpeachable; veracious, etc., 543.

pure, sound, sterling, true-blue; natural, unsophisticated, unadulterated, simon-pure [*colloq.*], unvarnished, undisguised.

exact, accurate, definite, concrete, precise, well defined, just, right, correct, strict, severe, rigid, rigorous, scrupulous, literal, punctilious, mathematical, scientific, unromantic; faithful, constant, unerring; particular, nice, meticulous, delicate, fine; clean-cut, clear-cut.

authentic, genuine, legitimate; orthodox, etc., 983*a*; official.

valid, well grounded, well founded, solid, substantial, tangible.

Adv. truly, verily, indeed, in reality; in very truth, in fact, as a matter of fact, beyond doubt.

495. ERROR.—*N.* error, fallacy, misconception, misapprehension, misunderstanding; aberration, inexactness, laxity; misconstruction, misinterpretation; misjudgment, heresy, misstatement, anachronism: fable, etc. (*untruth*), 546.

mistake, fault, blunder, oversight, misprint, erratum (*pl.* errata), slip, blot, flaw, trip, stumble, bungle; slip of the tongue, slip of the pen, clerical error; bull, etc. (*absurdity*), 497; spoonerism, malapropism.

delusion, illusion, false impression; bubble; self-deceit, self-deception; hallucination, mirage, etc., 443; dream, etc. (*fancy*), 515.

V. mislead, misguide, lead astray, beguile, misinform, delude; falsify, misstate, deceive, etc., 545; lie, etc., 544.

err, be in error, be mistaken, be deceived; mistake, deceive oneself, blunder, misapprehend, misconceive, misunderstand, miscalculate, misjudge.

trip, stumble, lose oneself, go astray, fail, etc., 732, take the shadow for the substance.

Adj. erroneous, untrue, false, faulty, erring, fallacious, unreal, ungrounded, groundless, unsubstantial, unsound, inexact, inaccurate, incorrect.

illusive, illusory, delusive, mock, imaginary, spurious, etc., 545; deceitful, etc., 544; untrustworthy.

exploded, refuted, discarded.

mistaken, in error, deceived, out in one's reckoning; wide of the mark, at fault, at cross-purposes, at sea, bewildered.

496. MAXIM.—*N.* **maxim**, aphorism, dictum, saying, adage, saw, proverb, motto, epigram, sentence, mot [*Gallicism*], commonplace, moral.

axiom, theorem, formula, truism.

principle, profession of faith, conclusion, etc. (*judgment*), 480.

Adj. **aphoristic**, proverbial, axiomatic; hackneyed, trite.

Adv. as the saying is, as they say.

497. ABSURDITY.—*N.* **absurdity**, absurdness, imbecility, etc., 499; nonsense, paradox, inconsistency.

blunder, muddle, Irish bull; anticlimax, bathos.

farce, burlesque, parody, limerick; farrago, extravagance.

pun, sell [*colloq.*], catch [*colloq.*], verbal quibble, joke.

jargon, gibberish, balderdash, bombast, claptrap, twaddle, moonshine, stuff.

tomfoolery, mummery, monkeyshine [*slang*], monkey trick, frisk, practical joke, escapade.

V. **play the fool**, blunder, muddle; be guilty of absurdity; romance, talk nonsense, exaggerate; be absurd, frisk, caper, joke, play practical jokes.

Adj. **absurd**, nonsensical, farcical, burlesque, preposterous, egregious, senseless, inconsistent, ridiculous, extravagant, self-contradictory, paradoxical; foolish, etc., 499; meaningless, fantastic, bombastic, high-flown.

498. [Faculties] INTELLIGENCE. WISDOM.—*N.* **intelligence**, capacity, comprehension, understanding; intellect, etc., 450; brains, parts, sagacity, mother wit, wit, gumption [*colloq.*], acuteness, acumen, longheadedness, subtlety, penetration, perspicacity, discernment, good judgment; discrimination, cunning, refinement.

wisdom, sapience, sense, common sense, clear thinking, rationality, reason; reasonableness, judgment, solidity, depth, profundity, caliber.

genius, inspiration, talent, etc., 698.

Wisdom in action: prudence, etc., 864; vigilance, etc., 459; tact, etc., 698; foresight, etc., 510; sobriety; self-possession, ballast, mental poise, balance.

V. **have all one's wits about one**; be brilliant, scintillate, coruscate; understand, etc. (*intelligible*), 518.

penetrate, see through, see at a glance, discern; foresee, etc., 510; discriminate.

Adj. **Applied to persons:** intelligent, quick of apprehension, keen, acute, alive, awake, bright, quick, sharp, quick-witted, wide-awake; shrewd, astute; clearheaded, long-sighted, calculating, thoughtful, farsighted, discerning, perspicacious, penetrating, piercing; sharp as a needle; alive to, etc. (*cognizant*), 490; clever, etc. (*apt*), 698.

wise, sage, sapient [*often in irony*], sagacious, rational, sensible, judicious, strong-minded; worldly-wise, sophisticated.

impartial, unprejudiced, unbiased, unbigoted, equitable, fair.

prudent, etc. (*cautious*), 864; sober, staid, solid; watchful; provident, prepared, etc., 673.

Applied to actions: wise, sensible, judicious, well judged, well advised; prudent, politic; expedient, etc., 646.

499. IMBECILITY, FOLLY.—*N.* imbecility, want of intelligence (*or* intellect), shallowness, silliness, foolishness, stupidity, stolidity; incompetence.

simplicity, puerility; senility, dotage, second childhood; fatuity; idiocy.

folly, frivolity, irrationality, trifling, ineptitude, inconsistency, giddiness; eccentricity, etc., 503; extravagance, etc. (*absurdity*), 497; rashness, etc., 863.

V. trifle, drivel, dote; ramble, play the fool, fool, stultify oneself, talk nonsense.

Adj. Applied to persons: unintelligent, unintellectual, unreasoning; mindless, brainless; half-baked [*colloq.*], bovine, thick [*colloq.*], blockish, unteachable; ungifted, unenlightened, unwise; thick-skulled, muddleheaded, addleheaded, weak-minded, feeble-minded.

stupid, dull, heavy, obtuse, blunt, stolid, asinine, inapt.

childish, childlike; infantine, infantile, babyish, puerile, senile, anile; simple, credulous.

imbecile, fatuous, idiotic, driveling; vacant, bewildered.

foolish, silly, senseless, irrational, insensate, nonsensical, maudlin.

narrow-minded, bigoted, etc., 606; rash, etc., 863; eccentric, odd.

Applied to actions: foolish, unwise, injudicious, improper, unreasonable, ill-advised, ridiculous, silly, stupid, asinine; inconsistent, irrational; extravagant, nonsensical, frivolous, trivial; useless, etc., 645; inexpedient, etc., 647.

500. SAGE.—*N.* sage, wise man; master mind, thinker, philosopher, savant [F.], pundit, etc. (*scholar*), 492; wiseacre [*ironical*]; expert, etc., 700.

authority, oracle, mentor, Solon, Solomon, Buddha, Confucius.

Adj. venerable, venerated, reverenced, revered, honored; authoritative, oracular; wise, erudite, etc., 490.

501. FOOL.—*N.* fool, idiot, tomfool, wiseacre, simpleton,

Simple Simon; donkey, ass, owl, goose, dolt, booby, noodle, imbecile, nincompoop [*colloq.*], oaf, lout, blockhead, bonehead [*slang*], calf [*colloq.*], colt, numskull [*colloq.*], clod, clodhopper; soft or softy [*colloq. or slang*], mooncalf, saphead [*slang*], gawk, rube [*slang*].

greenhorn, etc. (*dupe*), 547; dunce, etc. (*ignoramus*), 493; lubber, etc. (*bungler*), 701; madman, etc., 504; dotard, driveler, old fogy [*colloq.*].

502. SANITY.—*N.* **sanity,** soundness, rationality, sobriety, lucidity, senses, common sense, horse sense [*colloq.*], sound mind.

V. **become sane,** come to one's senses, sober down, cool down, see things in proper perspective.

render sane, bring to one's senses, sober, bring to reason.

Adj. **sane,** rational, normal, wholesome, right-minded, reasonable, sound, sound-minded, in possession of one's faculties.

Adv. **sanely,** in reason, within reason, within bounds.

503. INSANITY.—*N.* **insanity,** lunacy; madness, mania, dementia, idiocy; delirium tremens, d.t.'s, the horrors [*colloq.*]; frenzy, raving, wandering, delirium, delusion, obsession, hallucination, derangement, unsoundness of mind.

vertigo, dizziness, swimming, sunstroke.

oddity, eccentricity, twist, monomania; fanaticism, infatuation, craze.

V. **be** *or* **become insane,** lose one's senses (*or* reason), go mad, rave, dote, ramble, wander; lose one's head, drivel.

derange, render *or* drive mad, madden, infatuate, obsess, befool; turn the brain, turn one's head.

Adj. **insane,** mad, lunatic; crazy, crazed, crackbrained, cracked [*colloq.*], touched; bereft of reason; unhinged, insensate, beside oneself, demented, maniacal, daft, frenzied, deranged, maddened, moonstruck, off one's head.

giddy, vertiginous, wild, flighty, distracted, distraught, bewildered.

odd, fanatical, infatuated, eccentric.

delirious, lightheaded, rambling, wandering, frantic, raving, stark mad.

504. MADMAN.—*N.* **madman,** lunatic, maniac; crank [*colloq.*], nut [*slang*].

dreamer, visionary, rhapsodist, seer, enthusiast, fanatic; Don Quixote, Ophelia.

idiot, etc., 501.

505. [The Past] MEMORY.—*N.* **memory,** remembrance; retention, retentiveness; retentive (*or* tenacious, trustworthy, ready) memory.

recollection, retrospect, reminiscence; recognition; afterthought.

reminder, hint, suggestion, memorandum (*pl.* memoranda), token, memento, souvenir, keepsake, relic; memorial, monument; commemoration, jubilee.

mnemonics; art of memory, artificial memory; Mnemosyne.

fame, celebrity, renown, reputation; repute, notoriety.

V. **remember,** retain the memory of, keep in mind; bear in mind, haunt one's mind (*or* thoughts); rankle; keep the wound open, brood over.

recollect, recall, call up, conjure up, retrace; look back upon, review; call (*or* bring) to mind.

remind, suggest, hint, prompt; put (*or* keep) in mind; bring to mind, call up, summon up, renew; redeem from oblivion; commemorate.

memorize, commit to memory; con, con over; fix in the mind, engrave upon the memory; learn by heart, know by rote, have at one's fingers' ends.

make a note of, put down, record.

Adj. **remembering,** mindful, reminiscent; fresh, still vivid; enduring, unforgotten; never to be forgotten, indelible; within one's memory; memorable, suggestive.

Adv. **by heart,** by rote, without book, word for word.

506. OBLIVION.—*N.* oblivion; forgetfulness; Lethe; obliteration of the past; short (*or* treacherous, untrustworthy, slippery, failing) memory; decay (*or* failure, lapse) of memory; amnesia.

amnesty, general pardon.

V. **forget,** be forgetful; fall (*or* sink) into oblivion; have a short memory; lose, lose the memory of, lose sight of.

efface, from the memory; unlearn; consign to oblivion, think no more of; let bygones be bygones.

Adj. **forgotten,** unremembered, out of mind; buried (*or* sunk) in oblivion.

forgetful, oblivious; heedless, deaf to the past; Lethean.

507. [The Future] EXPECTATION.—*N.* expectation, expectancy, anticipation, prospect, contingency, reckoning, calculation; foresight; suspense; abeyance.

assurance, confidence, reliance, hope, trust, presumption; prognostication; prediction, etc., 511.

V. **expect;** look for, look out for, look forward to; hope for, anticipate; have in prospect, keep in view; contemplate; wait for, watch for, await; foresee, prepare for, forestall.

predict, prognosticate, forecast.

Adj. **expectant;** expecting, in expectation, vigilant; open-eyed, open-mouthed; agape, gaping, on tenterhooks, on tiptoe; ready, prepared, provided for, provident.

expected, foreseen; in prospect, prospective, provisional; future, coming; in view, on the horizon; impending.

Adv. **expectantly,** on the watch, with muscles tense, on edge [*colloq.*], with eyes (*or* ears) strained, with bated breath.

soon, shortly, forthwith, presently.

508. NONEXPECTATION.—*N.* **nonexpectation,** unforeseen contingency, the unforeseen; miscalculation, false expectation; disappointment; disillusion.

surprise, blow, shock; bolt out of the blue; astonishment, amazement; wonder, bewilderment.

V. **be unexpected,** come unawares, turn up, burst *or* flash upon one; take by surprise, catch unawares.

surprise, startle, stun, stagger, astound; throw off one's guard; spring upon, astonish, etc. (*strike with wonder*), 870.

Adj. **nonexpectant,** surprised; unwarned, unaware; off one's guard.

unexpected, unanticipated, unlooked for, unforeseen; unheard of; startling; sudden.

Adv. **unexpectedly,** abruptly, suddenly, unawares; without notice *or* warning.

509. DISAPPOINTMENT.—*N.* **disappointment,** blighted hope, disillusion, balk; blow, false (*or* vain) expectation; miscalculation; fool's paradise.

V. **be disappointed;** look blank, look *or* stand aghast; find to one's cost.

disappoint, crush (*or* dash, blight) one's hope, balk *or* disappoint one's expectation, balk, tantalize; dumfounder, dumfound, disconcert, disillusionize; dissatisfy; disgruntle.

Adj. aghast; disgruntled; out of one's reckoning.

510. FORESIGHT.—*N.* **foresight,** prevision, long-sightedness, farsightedness; anticipation; prudence; forethought.

foreknowledge, prescience; presentiment, foreboding; second sight.

prospect; foregone conclusion; forecast.

V. **foresee;** look forward to, look ahead *or* beyond; look into the future; see one's way; see how the land lies.

anticipate, expect, surmise, contemplate; predict; forewarn.

Adj. **foreseeing,** prescient, anticipatory; farseeing, farsighted, long-sighted; provident; weatherwise; prospective; expectant.

Adv. against the time when; for a rainy day.

511. PREDICTION.—*N.* **prediction,** announcement; program;

platform; premonition, presage, foreboding; phophecy, prognostication, augury, forecast; omen, etc., 512; horoscope; soothsaying, fortunetelling, divination; oracle, etc., 513.

astrology; spell, charm, etc., 993; sorcery, magic, etc., 992.

V. **predict,** forecast, prognosticate, prophesy, divine, foretell; tell fortunes, cast a horoscope (*or* nativity); forewarn.

presage, augur, bode, forebode; foretoken, betoken; portend, signify, point to.

herald, usher in, announce; lower; threaten.

Adj. **prophetic,** oracular, sibylline; weatherwise.

ominous, portentous; auspicious; premonitory, significant of.

512. OMEN.—*N.* **omen,** portent, presage, augury; sign, token; harbinger; bird of ill omen; halcyon birds; signs of the times; warning, etc., 668.

Adj. **auspicious,** favorable, halcyon, of good omen.

inauspicious, ill-boding, ill-omened, ill-starred.

513. ORACLE.—*N.* **oracle;** prophet, seer, soothsayer, prophetess, witch, sibyl; augur, haruspex; medium, clairvoyant, palmist; fortuneteller; sorcerer, etc., 994; interpreter, etc., 524.

Delphic oracle; Cumaean Sibyl, Sibyl, Cassandra, Witch of Endor, Sphinx.

weather prophet, weather bureau.

514. [Creative Thought] SUPPOSITION.—*N.* **supposition,** assumption, presumption, condition, hypothesis, postulate, theory, data; thesis, theorem; conjecture, guess, guesswork, speculation; surmise, suspicion, inkling, suggestion, hint.

theorist, theorizer, doctrinaire, doctrinarian.

V. **suppose,** conjecture; surmise, suspect, guess, divine; theorize, speculate; presume, presuppose, assume, predicate; believe, take for granted.

propound, propose, put forth; put a case, submit; move, make a motion; hazard *or* put forward a suggestion (*or* supposition); suggest, allude to, hint.

Adj. **assumed,** given; conjectural, presumptive, hypothetical; theoretical, academic.

suggestive, allusive, stimulating.

Adv. **if,** if so be; on the supposition, in case, in the event of; as if, provided; perhaps, for aught one knows.

515. IMAGINATION.—*N.* **imagination,** originality, invention; fancy; inspiration.

ideality, idealism; romanticism, utopianism, castle-building, dreaming; frenzy, rhapsody, ecstasy, reverie, daydream.

conception; flight of fancy; creation of the brain; imagery; word painting.

fantasy, conceit; figment, myth; romance, extravaganza; dream, vision; shadow, chimera, phantasm, illusion, phantom, fancy, whim, vagary; bugbear, nightmare; flying Dutchman, great sea serpent, man in the moon, castle in the air, castle in Spain, Utopia, fairyland; land of Prester John.

Creative works: work of fiction, etc. (*novel*), 594; poetry, etc., 597; drama, etc., 599; music, etc., 415; painting, sculpture, architecture; art.

idealist, romanticist, visionary, romancer, daydreamer, dreamer, castle-builder; creative artist.

V. imagine, fancy, conceive; idealize, realize; dream, dream of; indulge in reverie; fancy (*or* represent, picture, figure) to oneself.

create, originate, devise, invent, make up, coin, fabricate; improvise.

Adj. imaginative, original, inventive, creative, productive.

extravagant, romantic, high-flown, flighty, preposterous; unreal; unsubstantial.

ideal; intellectual, impracticable, imaginary, visionary, utopian, quixotic.

fanciful; fantastical; fictitious; fabulous, legendary, mythic *or* mythical, mythological, chimerical; whimsical; fairy, fairylike.

II. COMMUNICATION OF IDEAS

516. MEANING.—*N.* meaning [*idea to be conveyed*], signification, significance; sense, import, purport; pith, essence; force; drift, bearing, tenor, spirit; allusion; suggestion, interpretation; acceptation.

Thing signified: matter, subject, subject matter, substance, gist, argument.

V. mean, signify, denote, express; import, purport; convey, imply, indicate; tell of, speak of; touch on; point to, allude to; drive at; involve; declare; affirm, state.

paraphrase, state differently; express by a synonym.

Adj. meaning, expressive, significant, pithy; intelligible, explicit, clear; suggestive; allusive.

literal, word-for-word, verbatim; exact, real.

synonymous; tantamount, equivalent.

implied; understood, tacit.

Adv. to that effect; that is to say.

517. UNMEANINGNESS.—*N.* unmeaningness, absence of meaning, drivel, senselessness; empty sound.

nonsense, jargon, gibberish, mere words, rant, bombast, balderdash, babble, inanity, twaddle, trash, rubbish; absurdity; imbecility, folly; ambiguity, vagueness, etc., 519.

V. mean nothing; be unmeaning; gibber; jabber, twaddle, rant, babble.

scribble, scrawl, scratch.

Adj. **unmeaning,** meaningless, senseless; nonsensical; inexpressive; vague; not significant.

trashy, inane, trumpery, trivial, insignificant.

518. INTELLIGIBILITY.—*N.* **intelligibility;** comprehensibility; clearness, clarity, explicitness, lucidity, perspicuity; precision; plain speaking.

V. **render intelligible,** popularize, simplify, elucidate, explain, interpret.

understand, comprehend; take in, catch, grasp, follow; master.

Adj. **intelligible;** clear, lucid; perspicuous, transparent.

plain, distinct, clear-cut, hard-hitting, to the point, explicit; positive; definite, precise; unequivocal, legible, obvious, etc., 525.

graphic, telling, vivid; expressive.

519. UNINTELLIGIBILITY.—*N.* **unintelligibility,** incomprehensibility, vagueness, obscurity, ambiguity, confusion; mystification; jargon.

enigma, riddle; sealed book.

V. **render unintelligible,** conceal, darken, confuse, mystify, perplex.

Adj. **unintelligible,** incomprehensible, unaccountable, undecipherable, unfathomable, inexplicable, inscrutable, insoluble, impenetrable; puzzling, enigmatic; indecipherable, illegible.

obscure, crabbed, dark, muddy, dim, nebulous, mysterious, hidden, latent, occult; abstruse; indefinite, vague, loose, ambiguous.

inexpressible, unutterable, ineffable.

520. [Having a double sense] EQUIVOCALNESS.—*N.* **equivocalness,** equivocation, double meaning; ambiguity; quibble; conundrum, riddle; pun, word play; sphinx, Delphic oracle.

equivocation, etc. (*duplicity*), 544; white lie, mental reservation, etc., 528.

V. **equivocate,** etc. (*palter*), 544; prevaricate; have a double meaning.

Adj. **equivocal,** ambiguous; double-tongued; enigmatical; indeterminate, doubtful.

521. FIGURE OF SPEECH.—*N.* **figure,** trope, phrase, expression; euphemism; image, imagery; personification, metaphor; simile, satire, irony.

allegory, apologue, parable, fable.

V. **employ figures of speech;** personify, allegorize, fable, shadow forth, allude to.

Adj. **figurative,** metaphorical, euphuistic, allusive; allegoric *or* allegorical, ironic, ironical, satiric *or* satirical; euphemistic.

522. INTERPRETATION.—*N.* **interpretation,** definition, explanation; elucidation, diagnosis; solution, answer; meaning, etc., 516; clue.

  translation; rendering, rendition; metaphrase, literal (*or* word-for-word) translation; free translation; key; crib, horse, pony, trot [*school cant*].

  comment, commentary; exegesis, exposition; inference, deduction; illustration, exemplification; gloss, annotation, note, construction, version, reading.

  equivalent, equivalent meaning, synonym; paraphrase, convertible terms.

  dictionary, etc., 562.

  prediction, etc., 511; chiromancy, palmistry; astrology.

  V. **interpret**, explain, define, construe, translate, render; decipher, make out, unravel, disentangle, solve; read between the lines.

  elucidate, account for, throw *or* shed light upon; clear up, popularize, simplify; illustrate, exemplify; unfold, expound, comment upon, annotate.

  Adj. **explanatory**, expository; interpretative, elucidative, inferential, illustrative.

  equivalent, convertible, synonymous.

  metaphrastic, literal, word-for-word.

  Adv. **in explanation**; that is to say, to wit, namely.

  literally, strictly speaking; in plain terms (*or* words).

  523. MISINTERPRETATION.—*N.* misinterpretation, misapprehension, misconception, misunderstanding, misconstruction; misapplication; cross-purposes; mistake, etc., 495.

  misrepresentation, perversion, misstatement, exaggeration; abuse of terms; play upon words, pun, parody, travesty; falsification, etc. (*lying*), 544.

  V. **misinterpret**, misapprehend, misunderstand, misconceive; misjudge, misspell; mistranslate, misconstrue, misapply; mistake, etc., 495.

  misrepresent, pervert, misstate, garble, falsify, distort; travesty, play upon words; stretch (*or* strain, twist, wrest) the sense *or* meaning.

  Adj. **misinterpreted**, mistranslated; confused, tangled, snarled, mixed.

  dazed, perplexed, bewildered, rattled [*slang*], benighted.

  Adv. **at cross-purposes**, at sixes and sevens [*colloq.*]; in a maze.

  524. INTERPRETER.—*N.* interpreter, translator, expositor, expounder, exponent; demonstrator; commentator, annotator; oracle, etc., 513.

  spokesman, speaker, mouthpiece, foreman of the jury, mediator, advocate, delegate, representative, diplomatic agent, ambassador, plenipotentiary.

guide, courier, cicerone, showman, barker [*colloq.*].

525. MANIFESTATION.—*N.* manifestation, indication, expression; plain speaking, candor, openness; showing, exposition, demonstration; séance, materialization; exhibition, production, display, show.

Thing shown: exhibit, exhibition, exposition, show [*colloq.*], performance.

publicity, etc., 531; disclosure, etc., 529; openness, candor; saliency, prominence.

V. make manifest, materialize, express, represent, set forth, evidence, exhibit, produce, show, show up, expose; hold up, show forth, unveil, display, demonstrate, lay open; draw out, bring out; manifest oneself; speak out, proclaim, publish.

indicate, point out; disclose, discover; translate, transcribe, decipher, decode; elicit, bring to light, disinter.

be manifest *or* plain, appear, etc., 446; transpire, come to light, be disclosed; go without saying, be self-evident.

Adj. manifest, apparent; salient, striking, prominent, in the foreground, ostensible, notable, pronounced.

plain, intelligible, clear, defined, definite, distinct, conspicuous, obvious, evident, unmistakable; conclusive, indubitable, palpable, self-evident; open, patent, express, explicit; naked, bare, literal, downright, unreserved, frank, plain-spoken.

barefaced, brazen, bold, shameless, daring, flaunting, loud [*colloq.*]; flagrant, arrant, notorious; glaring.

Adv. manifestly, openly, plainly, above board, in plain sight, in the open, in broad daylight; without reserve.

526. LATENCY.—*N.* latency, hidden meaning; obscurity, ambiguity; secret, mystery, occultism, mysticism, symbolism; reserve, reticence; concealment, mystification, suppression, evasion; Delphic oracle; undercurrent; snake in the grass.

allusion, insinuation, implication; innuendo.

latent influence, power behind the throne, friend at court, wire-puller [*colloq.*], kingmaker.

V. lurk, smolder, underlie, make no sign; escape observation (*or* detection, recognition); lie hid, lie in ambush.

keep back, etc. (*conceal*), 528.

involve, imply, connote, import, allude to, leave an inference; symbolize.

Adj. latent, lurking; dormant, secret, occult; esoteric, recondite, veiled, symbolic, cryptic, mystic, mystical.

unapparent, unknown, unseen, unsuspected; invisible; unexpressed, undisclosed, tacit.

indirect, crooked, underhand, underground; by inference, by implication; implied, implicit, understood, tacit; allusive, covert, undercover, concealed.

Adv. secretly, stealthily, incognito; in the background; behind the scenes, between the lines; below the surface.

527. INFORMATION.—*N.* **information,** enlightenment, acquaintance, knowledge; publicity, notoriety.

mention; instruction, communicativeness, intercommunication.

notification, intimation, communication, notice, annunciation, announcement, communiqué; representation; message, etc., 532.

report, advice, monition; news, tidings, return, record, account, description; statement, estimate, specification.

informant, authority, teller, harbinger, herald, reporter, exponent, mouthpiece; spokesman, etc. (*interpreter*), 524; spy, informer, eavesdropper, detective, sleuth [*colloq.*]; newsmonger; messenger, etc., 534.

guide, cicerone; pilot; guidebook, handbook; map, plan, chart, gazetteer; itinerary.

hint, suggestion, insinuation, innuendo, inkling, whisper, cue, byplay; gesture; word to the wise.

V. tell, inform, acquaint, impart, apprise, advise, instruct, enlighten.

mention, express, intimate, represent, communicate, make known; publish, disseminate; notify, signify, specify; retail, describe; state, declare, assert, affirm.

announce, report, bring (*or* send, leave) word; telegraph, wire [*colloq.*], telephone, phone [*colloq.*].

disclose, etc., 529; explain.

hint, insinuate, allude to, glance at, let fall, indicate; suggest, prompt, give the cue.

undeceive, set right, correct, disabuse.

Adj. informational, advisory.

expressive, explicit, plain-spoken; declaratory; expository; communicative.

528. CONCEALMENT.—*N.* **concealment,** mystification; reticence, reserve, reservation; mental reservation, aside; suppression, evasion, white lie; silence, closeness, secretiveness, mystery.

screen, cloak; ambush, ambuscade; stowaway; blind baggage [*slang*].

cipher, code, sympathetic ink.

stealth, stealthiness, slyness, caution, cunning.

secrecy, privacy, secretness; disguise, mask, masquerade; incognito (*fem.* incognita).

masquerader, masker, mask, domino.

V. **conceal,** hide, secrete; lock up; cover, screen, cloak, veil, shroud; curtain, muffle; mask, camouflage, disguise; ensconce.

keep from, keep to oneself, keep secret; bury; sink, suppress; keep in the background; stifle, hush up; withhold, reserve.

code, use a code *or* cipher, reduce to a code.

hoodwink, blind, blindfold; mystify, puzzle, deceive, lead astray.

be concealed, hide oneself, couch; lie in ambush, lurk, sneak, skulk, slink, prowl, gumshoe [*slang*].

Adj. **concealed,** hidden, secret, private, privy; recondite, mystic, mystical, occult, dark, cryptic; in secret, tortuous; close, inviolate, confidential, behind a screen, undercover, in ambush, in hiding, in disguise; undisclosed, untold, covert, mysterious.

furtive, stealthy, skulking, surreptitious, underhand, sly, cunning, evasive; secretive, clandestine; reserved, reticent, uncommunicative, close, taciturn.

Adv. **secretly,** in secret, in private, incognito.

behind closed doors, under the rose, *sub rosa* [L.]; on the sly [*colloq.*]; in a whisper.

confidentially, in strict confidence, between ourselves, between you and me.

underhand, by stealth, like a thief in the night; stealthily.

529. DISCLOSURE.—*N.* disclosure, revelation, divulgence, exposition, exposure, publication, exposé.

acknowledgment, avowal, confession, confessional.

narrator, etc., 594; talebearer, etc., 532; informant, etc., 527.

V. **disclose,** discover, unmask, unveil, unfold, uncover, unseal, lay bare, expose, bare, bring to light, disabuse, open the eyes of, turn informer.

divulge, reveal, let into the secret, tell, etc. (*inform*), 527; breathe, utter, peach [*slang*]; let slip *or* drop, betray; blurt out, vent, whisper about, speak out, break the news, publish, etc., 531.

acknowledge, allow, concede, grant, admit, own, confess, avow, make a clean breast, unbosom oneself; turn informer.

be disclosed, transpire, come to light, become known, escape the lips; ooze out, leak out, come to one's ears.

530. AMBUSH. [Means of concealment]—*N.* ambush, ambuscade, lurking place, trap, snare, pitfall, etc., 667.

hiding place, secret place, recess, hole, cubbyhole, crypt; safe, safe-deposit box, safety-deposit box.

screen, cover, shade, blinker; veil, curtain, blind, cloak, cloud.

mask, visor, disguise, masquerade, domino.

V. ambush, ambuscade, lie in ambush, lie in wait for; set a trap for, ensnare.

531. PUBLICATION.—*N.* publication, public announcement, promulgation, propagation, proclamation, pronouncement, edict.

publicity, notoriety, currency, flagrancy, cry, hue and cry, bruit; report, etc. (*news*), 532; telegram, etc., 532.

the press, the fourth estate, public press; newspaper, journal, gazette.

advertisement, placard, bill, flier [*cant*], leaflet, handbill, poster; circular, notice, program, manifesto.

V. publish, make public, broach, utter, circulate, propagate, promulgate, spread, spread abroad, rumor, diffuse, disseminate; issue; bring before the public; give to the world; report, voice, bruit; proclaim, herald, blazon, noise abroad, advertise.

telegraph, cable, wireless [*colloq.*], broadcast, wire [*colloq.*].

Adj. published, current; public, notorious, flagrant.

Adv. publicly, in public, in open court, with open doors.

532. NEWS—*N.* news, information, etc., 527; intelligence, tidings; beat *or* scoop [*newspaper cant*], story, copy [*cant*].

message, word, advice, communication, bulletin, broadcast, dispatch; telegram, cable [*colloq.*], wire [*colloq.*], radio, radiogram, wireless telegram, wireless [*colloq.*]; telephone, radiophone, wireless telephone.

report, rumor, hearsay, cry, bruit, fame; talk, scandal, gossip; tittle-tattle.

narrator, historian; newsmonger, scandalmonger; talebearer, telltale, gossip, tattler, tattletale; chatterer, busybody; informer.

V. transpire, etc. (*be disclosed*), 529; rumor, etc. (*publish*), 531.

Adj. rumored, rife, current, in circulation.

533. SECRET.—*N.* secret, mystery; problem, etc. (*question*), 461; unintelligibility, etc., 519.

enigma, riddle, puzzle, conundrum, charade, rebus.

maze, labyrinth, intricacy.

Adj. secret, concealed, etc., 528; involved, tortuous, circuitous, labyrinthine; enigmatic *or* enigmatical.

534. MESSENGER.—*N.* messenger, intermediary, go-between; envoy, emissary, legate, nuncio. delegate; angel; Gabriel, Hermes, Mercury.

courier, runner; commissionaire, errand boy; herald, crier, trumpeter, bellman.

mail, post, post office; air mail; postman, mailman, letter carrier; carrier pigeon.

telegraph, cable, wire [*colloq.*], radiotelegraph, wireless telegraph, wireless [*colloq.*], radio.

telephone, phone [*colloq.*], radiotelephone, radiophone, wireless telephone.

reporter, newspaperman, journalist; gentleman (*or* representative) of the press; special correspondent; scout, spy, informer.

535. AFFIRMATION.—*N.* affirmation, statement, allegation, profession, assertion, declaration; confirmation; asseveration, swearing, oath, affidavit, deposition; assurance, protest, protestation.

positiveness, emphasis, peremptoriness, dogmatism, weight.

vote, voice; ballot, suffrage.

remark, observation, saying, dictum, sentence.

V. assert, say, affirm, declare, state; protest, profess; acknowledge; put forward; advance, allege, propose, propound; announce, enunciate, broach, set forth, maintain, contend, pronounce.

depose, aver, avow, avouch, asseverate, swear, affirm; take one's oath; make an affidavit; vow, vouch, warrant, certify, assure; attest, adjure.

emphasize, insist upon, lay stress on; lay down the law; dogmatize, repeat, reassert, reaffirm.

Adj. affirmative, declaratory, positive; unmistakable, clear; certain, etc., 474; express, explicit, absolute, emphatic, decided, insistent, dogmatic, formal, solemn, categorical, peremptory.

Adv. with emphasis, ex cathedra, without fear of contradiction.

536. NEGATION.—*N.* negation, denial; disavowal, disclaimer; contradiction, protest; dissent, etc., 489.

qualification, etc., 469; repudiation, rejection, recantation, revocation; retractation, rebuttal, confutation; refusal, etc., 764.

V. deny; contradict, contravene; controvert, gainsay, negative, give the lie to, belie.

disclaim, disown, repudiate, disaffirm, disavow, abjure, forswear, renounce; recant, revoke.

dispute, impugn, confute, rebut, join issue upon; bring (*or* call) in question, set aside, ignore; refuse, etc., 764.

Adj. contradictory; negative; recusant, dissentient, at issue upon.

Adv. no, nay, not, nowise, not at all, not in the least, quite the contrary, by no means.

537. TEACHING.—*N.* teaching, pedagogics, pedagogy, instruction, edification, education, tuition, tutorship, tutelage; direction, guidance.

preparation, qualification, training, schooling, discipline; drill, practice.

lesson, lecture, recitation, sermon, homily, harangue, disquisition; apologue, parable; discourse; explanation; exercise, task; curriculum; course.

V. **teach,** instruct, educate, edify, school, tutor, cram [*colloq.*], grind [*colloq.*], prime, coach; enlighten, inform, etc., 527; direct, guide.

inculcate, infuse, instill, imbue, impregnate, implant; disseminate, propagate.

expound, etc. (*interpret*), 522; lecture; hold forth, preach; sermonize, moralize.

train, discipline, form, ground, prepare, qualify, drill, exercise, practice, familiarize with, inure, initiate, graduate.

Adj. **educational,** scholastic, academic, disciplinary, instructive, pedagogic, didactic; cultural, humanistic, humane; pragmatic, practical, utilitarian.

538. MISTEACHING.—*N*. **misteaching,** misinformation, misguidance, misdirection, perversion, sophistry; the blind leading the blind.

V. **misinform,** misteach, misinstruct, misdirect, misguide, pervert; deceive, mislead, misrepresent, lie.

render unintelligible, bewilder, mystify, conceal.

539. LEARNING.—*N*. **learning,** acquisition of knowledge, acquirement, attainment; mental cultivation, scholarship, erudition; lore; wide reading; study, grind [*colloq.*]; inquiry, etc., 461.

apprenticeship, tutelage, novitiate.

V. **learn,** acquire (*or* gain, imbibe, pick up, obtain) knowledge *or* learning; master, grind [*college slang*], cram [*colloq.*], get up, learn by heart.

study, read, peruse; con, pore over, wade through, plunge into. burn the midnight oil; be taught.

Adj. **studious;** industrious, etc., 682; scholastic, scholarly, well read, widely read, erudite, learned.

540. TEACHER.—*N*. **teacher,** preceptor, instructor, master, tutor, schoolmaster, dominie, pedagogue; kindergartner, governess, mistress; coach [*colloq.*], crammer [*colloq.*]; professor, don [*Univ. cant*], lecturer, reader, preacher; pastor, etc. (*clergy*), 996; schoolmistress.

guide, counselor, adviser, mentor, pioneer, apostle, missionary, propagandist; example.

professorship, chair, fellowship, tutorship, mastership, instructorship.

Adj. **pedagogic,** tutorial, professorial; scholastic, etc., 537.

541. LEARNER.—*N*. **learner,** scholar, student, alumnus (*pl.* alumni; *fem.* alumna, *pl.* alumnae), pupil, schoolboy, schoolgirl;

monitor, prefect; undergraduate, freshman; graduate student, postgraduate student.

class, form, grade, room; promotion, graduation.

disciple, follower, apostle, proselyte.

classmate, fellow student, schoolmate, schoolfellow, fellow pupil.

novice, beginner, tyro, recruit, tenderfoot [*slang or colloq.*], neophyte, probationer; apprentice.

Adj. in leading strings, pupillary, probationary.

542. SCHOOL.—*N.* school, academy, lyceum, seminary, college, educational institution, institute; university, varsity [*colloq.*], alma mater [L.].

General: day (*or* boarding, preparatory, elementary, denominational, secondary, military, naval, technical, library, secretarial, business, correspondence) school; kindergarten, nursery school; Sunday (*or* Sabbath, Bible) school.

United States: district (*or* grade, parochial, public, primary, grammar, junior high, high, Latin) school; private school, normal school, kindergarten training school; summer school; military academy (West Point); naval academy (Annapolis); college, fresh-water college [*colloq. or slang*], state university; graduate school, postgraduate school.

class, division, form, etc., 541; seminar.

classroom, room, schoolroom, recitation room; lecture room, lecture hall, theater, amphitheater.

desk, reading desk, pulpit, forum, stage, rostrum, platform.

schoolbook, textbook; grammar, primer, reader.

Adj. scholastic, academic, collegiate; educational, cultural; gymnastic, athletic, physical, eurythmic.

543. VERACITY.—*N.* veracity, truthfulness, frankness, truth, sincerity, candor, honesty, fidelity, love of truth; probity, etc., 939.

V. speak the truth, tell the truth; speak on oath; speak without equivocation (*or* mental reservation), make a clean breast, disclose, etc., 529; speak one's mind.

Adj. truthful, true; veracious, scrupulous, punctilious; sincere, candid, frank, open, outspoken, straightforward, unreserved, truth-telling, honest, trustworthy; guileless, pure, truth-loving; true-blue, as good as one's word; unfeigned, ingenuous.

544. FALSEHOOD.—*N.* falsehood, falseness, falsity, falsification, misrepresentation, deception, etc., 545; untruthfulness, lying; untruth, etc., 546; mendacity, guile, perjury, false swearing; forgery, invention, fabrication; perversion, distortion, exaggeration, prevarication, equivocation, evasion, fraud; simulation, dissimulation, dissembling; deceit; sham, pretense; malingering.

duplicity, double dealing, insincerity, hypocrisy, cant, pharisaism; casuistry, Machiavellism; lip service, hollowness, mere show; quackery, charlatanism, charlatanry; humbug; cajolery, flattery; Judas kiss; perfidy, etc., 940; cunning, etc., 702; misstatement, false report.

V. lie, tell a lie (*or* an untruth), fib, swear falsely, forswear, perjure oneself, bear false witness.

falsify, misstate, misquote; misrepresent, etc., 523; belie; garble, gloss over, disguise, color, varnish, doctor [*colloq.*], dress up, embroider; exaggerate, etc., 549.

prevaricate, equivocate, quibble; trim, shuffle, fence, beat about the bush.

fabricate, invent; trump up; forge; coin; hatch, concoct; romance.

dissemble, dissimulate; feign, assume; pretend, make believe; play false, play a double game; coquet; act *or* play a part; affect, pose; simulate, pass off for; counterfeit, sham; malinger; deceive, etc., 545.

Adj. false, untrue, deceitful, mendacious, lying, untruthful, fraudulent, dishonest; faithless, forsworn; evasive, disingenuous, hollow, insincere; artful, cunning, tricky, wily, sly; perfidious, treacherous, perjured; spurious, etc., 545; falsified.

hypocritical, canting, pharisaical; Machiavellian, double-tongued, double-dealing; two-faced, double-faced; smooth-spoken, smooth-tongued; plausible, mealy-mouthed; affected, canting, insincere.

545. DECEPTION.—*N.* deception; falseness, etc., 544; untruth, etc., 546; imposition, imposture; fraud, deceit, guile, fraudulence, misrepresentation, bluff; trickery, knavery, sharp practice, collusion, chicanery; treachery, double-dealing.

delusion, jugglery, sleight of hand, legerdemain, conjuring.

trick, cheat, wile, blind, feint, chicane, juggle, swindle; stratagem, artifice; hoax; bunk [*slang*], gold brick [*colloq.*].

snare, trap, pitfall, gin; bait, decoy duck, stool pigeon; cobweb, net, meshes, toils; ambush, ambuscade.

disguise, false colors, camouflage, masquerade, mask, mummery, borrowed plumes; dissembler, hypocrite, etc., 548.

sham, mockery, copy, counterfeit, make-believe, forgery, fraud, untruth, etc., 546; hollow mockery; whited sepulcher, tinsel, paste.

illusion, delusion, self-deception, *ignis fatuus* [L.], mirage, etc., 443.

V. deceive, mislead, lead astray, take in, defraud, cheat, cozen, swindle, victimize; betray, play false; lie, etc., 544: mystify; blind, hoodwink; throw dust into the eyes; impose upon, practice upon, palm off on; bluff.

outwit, circumvent, overreach, steal a march on.

insnare, ensnare, entrap, decoy, waylay, lure, beguile, delude, inveigle, trick.

fool, befool, dupe, gull, hoax, humbug, stuff [*slang*], sell [*slang*]; trifle with, cajole, flatter; dissemble, dissimulate, sham, counterfeit.

practice chicanery, live by one's wits, juggle, conjure, play off, palm off, foist off.

Adj. deceptive, deceitful, tricky, cunning, etc., 702; elusive, insidious; delusive, illusory.

make-believe; untrue, etc., 546; mock, sham, counterfeit, pseudo, spurious, so-called, pretended, feigned, bogus [*colloq.*], fraudulent, surreptitious, illegitimate, contraband; adulterated, disguised; unsound, meretricious, jerry-built; tinsel.

Adv. under false colors, under cover of.

546. UNTRUTH.—*N.* untruth, falsehood, lie, story, fib, whopper [*colloq.*].

fabrication, forgery, invention; misstatement, misrepresentation, perversion, falsification, false coloring, exaggeration.

fiction; fable, nursery tale, fairy tale, romance, extravaganza; canard; yarn [*colloq.*], fish story [*colloq.*], traveler's tale, cock-and-bull story, myth, moonshine, bosh [*colloq.*].

half truth, white lie, pious fraud; suppression; irony.

pretense, pretext, subterfuge, evasion, shift, shuffle, make-believe, sham, etc., 545; profession, Judas kiss, cajolery, flattery; disguise, etc., 530.

V. feign, make-believe, pretend, sham, counterfeit; lie, etc., 544.

Adj. untrue, false, trumped up; unfounded, invented, fictitious, fabulous, fabricated, fraudulent, forged; evasive.

547. DUPE.—*N.* dupe, gull, victim, April fool; sucker [*slang*]; laughingstock, etc., 857; greenhorn; fool, etc., 501; puppet, cat's-paw.

V. be deceived, be the dupe of; fall into a trap; swallow *or* nibble at the bait; swallow whole; bite.

Adj. credulous, gullible, etc., 486.

mistaken, etc. (*error*), 495.

548. DECEIVER.—*N.* deceiver, dissembler, hypocrite, Pharisee; sophist; serpent, snake in the grass, Judas, wolf in sheep's clothing.

liar, storyteller, perjurer, false witness, faker [*slang*], fraud, four-flusher [*slang*], confidence man, decoy, stool pigeon; rogue, knave, cheat, swindler.

impostor, pretender, malingerer, humbug; adventurer, adventuress.

trickster, conjurer, juggler, necromancer, sorcerer, magician, wizard, medicine man, witch doctor; quack, charlatan, mountebank.

549. EXAGGERATION.—*N.* **exaggeration,** expansion, amplification; fringe, embroidery; extravagance, hyperbole, stretch, high coloring, caricature; yarn [*colloq.*], traveler's tale, fish story [*colloq.*]; tempest in a teacup; much ado about nothing; puffery, etc. (*boasting*), 884; rant, etc.. 577.

V. **exaggerate,** magnify, pile up, aggravate; amplify, expand, overestimate, overstate, overdraw, overshoot the mark, overpraise; stretch a point; draw a long bow [*colloq.*], out-Herod Herod; overcolor, heighten; embroider, color; puff, etc. (*boast*), 884.

Adj. **exaggerated,** overwrought; bombastic, etc. (*magniloquent*), 577; hyperbolical, extravagant; preposterous, egregious.

550. [Means of communication] INDICATION.—*N.* **indication,** sign, symbol; index, indicator, pointer, cue, note, token, symptom; type, figure, emblem, cipher, device; motto, epitaph.

means of recognition; lineament, feature, trait, trick, earmark, characteristic.

gesture, gesticulation; pantomime; wink, glance, leer; nod, shrug, beck; touch, nudge; byplay, dumb show; deaf-and-dumb alphabet, dactylology.

track, spoor, trail, footprint, scent; clue, key.

signal, rocket, watch fire, beacon fire, watchtower; telegraph, semaphore; fiery cross; calumet, peace pipe; heliograph; searchlight, flashlight.

mark, line, stroke, score, streak, scratch, tick, dot, notch, nick, blaze; red letter, underlining, impression.

Map drawing: hachure, contour line; isobar, isopiestic line, isobaric line; isotherm, isothermal line; latitude, longitude, meridian, equator.

For identification: badge, countercheck, countersign, counterfoil, stub, duplicate, tally; label, ticket, counter, check, chip, voucher, stamp; trade-mark, hallmark; card, visiting card; credentials; handwriting, sign manual, autograph, signature; monogram, seal, signet; fingerprint; brand; caste mark; mortarboard [*colloq.*], cap and gown, hood; shibboleth; watchword, catchword, password, cue; sign, countersign, pass, grip; open-sesame.

Insignia: banner, flag, colors, streamer, pennant, pennon, ensign, standard; eagle, oriflamme, blue peter, jack, Union Jack; Old Glory [*colloq.*], Stars and Stripes.

Heraldry: crest, arms, coat of arms, armorial bearings; hatchment, escutcheon *or* scutcheon; shield, supporters; livery, uniform; cockade, brassard, epaulet, chevron; garland, chaplet, love knot, favor.

Of locality: beacon, flagstaff, hand, pointer, vane, cock, weathercock, weather vane; guidepost, signpost; sign, signboard; North Star, polestar; landmark, seamark; lighthouse; address, direction, name.

Of the future: warning, premonition; omen, portent, sign.

Of the past: trace, record.

Of danger: warning, alarm, fire alarm, burglar alarm.

Of authority: scepter, etc., 747.

Of triumph: trophy, etc., 733.

Of mourning: mourning, etc., 839.

Of quantity: gauge, etc., 466.

Of distance: milestone, milepost.

Of disgrace: brand, foolscap, mark of Cain, stigma, stripes, broad arrow.

call, word of command; bugle call, trumpet call; bell, alarum, battle cry, reveille, taps, last post; sacring bell, Sanctus bell, angelus; dirge.

V. **indicate,** denote, betoken, connote, signify; represent, stand for; typify, symbolize; mark, note, stamp, nick, blaze; label, ticket.

make a sign, signalize; beckon, nod, wink, glance, leer, nudge, shrug, gesticulate.

sign, seal, attest, underscore, underline; call attention to.

Adj. **indicative,** indicatory; connotative, denotative, representative, typical, individual, symbolic *or* symbolical, symptomatic, characteristic, significant, diagnostic, emblematic, armorial.

551. RECORD.—*N.* trace, vestige, relic, remains; scar, cicatrix; footstep, footmark, footprint; track, mark, wake, trail, scent, spoor.

monument, hatchment; escutcheon *or* scutcheon; slab, tablet, trophy, obelisk, pillar, column, monolith; memorial; memento; testimonial, medal, Congressional medal; cross, Victoria cross [Eng.], iron cross [Ger.]; ribbon, garter; commemoration, etc. (*celebration*), 883.

record, note, minute; register, registry; roll, list; entry, memorandum, endorsement, inscription, copy, duplicate, docket; mark, etc., 550; deed; document; deposition, affidavit; certificate.

notebook, memorandum book; bulletin, bulletin board, scoreboard, score sheet; card index, file, letter file, pigeonholes.

newspaper, daily, gazette, magazine, paper [*colloq.*].

calendar, diary, log, journal, daybook, ledger, cashbook.

archive, scroll, state paper, return, bluebook; almanac, gazetteer, census report; statistics; Congressional Records; minutes, chronicle, annals; legend; history, biography, etc., 594.

registration; registry, enrollment, tabulation; entry, booking; signature, sign manual; recorder, etc., 553; journalism.

mechanical record, recording instrument; phonograph, etc., 418; speedometer, pedometer, patent log [*naut.*]; ticker, tape; time clock; turnstile; cash register.

V. **record,** put *or* place upon record, chronicle, calendar, hand down to posterity; commemorate, etc. (*celebrate*), 883; report, commit to writing, note, put *or* set down; mark, etc. (*indicate*), 550; sign, etc. (*attest*), 467; enter, book, post, insert; mark off, tick off; register, list, enroll, inscroll; file.

552. [Suppression of sign] OBLITERATION.—*N.* obliteration, erasure, cancellation, deletion; blot; effacement, extinction.

V. **efface,** obliterate, erase, expunge, cancel; blot (*or* rub, scratch, strike, wash, wipe) out; deface, render illegible; rule out.

be effaced, leave no trace.

Adj. **obliterated,** erased; unrecorded, unregistered.

553. RECORDER.—*N.* recorder, notary, clerk; registrar, register; amanuensis, secretary, recording secretary, stenographer, bookkeeper, scribe.

annalist, historian, historiographer, chronicler; biographer, etc.

(*narrator*), 594; antiquary, antiquarian, archeologist; memorialist.

journalist, newspaperman, reporter, interviewer; publicist, author, editor.

554. REPRESENTATION.—*N.* representation, depiction, imitation, illustration, delineation, imagery, portraiture; design, designing; art, fine arts; painting, etc., 556; sculpture, etc., 557; engraving, etc., 558.

photography; radiography, X-ray photography, skiagraphy. personation, impersonation; personification; drama, etc., 599.

drawing, picture, sketch, draft; tracing; copy, etc., 21.
photograph, photo [*colloq.*], daguerreotype, print, cabinet, snapshot.
image, effigy, icon, portrait, likeness, facsimile.
figure, figurehead, puppet, doll, manikin, lay figure, model, marionette, statue, statuette, bust.
map, plan, chart; diagram; ground plan, projection, elevation; atlas; outline, view.
radiograph, radiogram, skiagraph, skiagram, X-ray photograph, Xray [*colloq*].
delineator, draftsman; artist, etc., 559; photographer, radiographer, X-ray photographer, skiagrapher, daguerreotypist.

V. **represent**, delineate, depict, portray, picture, limn, photograph, snapshot; figure, shadow forth, adumbrate; describe, etc., 594; trace, copy; mold; illustrate, symbolize; paint, etc., 556; sculpture, etc., 557; engrave, etc., 558.

personate, impersonate, dress up [*colloq.*], pose as, act; personify; play, etc. (*drama*), 559; mimic, etc. (*imitate*),19.

Adj. **representative**; illustrative; imitative, figurative; similar, like, etc., 17; descriptive, etc., 594.

555. MISREPRESENTATION.—*N.* misrepresentation, misstatement, falsification, exaggeration, distortion; bad likeness, daub, scratch.

burlesque, travesty, parody, take-off, caricature, extravaganza.
V. **misrepresent**, distort, overdraw, exaggerate, daub; falsify, understate, overstate, stretch.

burlesque, travesty, parody, caricature.

556. PAINTING. BLACK AND WHITE.—*N.* painting, depicting, drawing; design; perspective; composition; treatment; arrangement, values, atmosphere, tone, technique.

palette; easel; brush, pencil, stump, black lead, charcoal, crayons, chalk, pastel; paint, etc. (*coloring matter*), 428; water (*or* oil) colors; oils, oil paint; varnish; distemper, fresco, enamel, mosaic, encaustic painting; batik.
style, school; the grand style, high art; futurist, cubist, vorticist.
picture, painting, piece, tableau, canvas; fresco, cartoon; drawing, draft; still life, genre (*or* landscape) painting; sketch, outline, study.
portrait; head; miniature; silhouette; profile.

view, landscape, seascape, sea view, seapiece; scene, prospect; interior; panorama, bird's-eye view.

picture gallery, art gallery, art museum; studio, atelier [F.].

photograph, radiography, etc., 554; photograph, radiograph, etc., 554.

V. paint, design, limn, draw, sketch, pencil, color; stencil; depict, etc. (*represent*), 554.

Adj. pictorial, graphic; picturesque, historical; futurist, cubist, vorticist; in the grand style.

557. SCULPTURE.—*N.* **sculpture,** carving, modeling, statuary; ceramics.

marble, bronze, terra cotta; ceramic ware, pottery, porcelain, china, earthenware; cloisonné, enamel, faïence.

relief, low relief, bas-relief, high relief; intaglio; cameo; medal, medallion.

statue, statuette, bust; cast.

V. sculpture, carve, cut, chisel, model, mold; cast.

558. ENGRAVING.—*N.* **engraving,** etching, chiseling; plate (*or* copperplate, steel, half-tone, wood) engraving; lithography, chromolithography, photolithography.

printing; color printing, lithographic printing; type printing; three-color process. impression, print. engraving, plate: steel-plate, copperplate; etching; aquatint, mezzotint; cut, woodcut; lithograph, chromolithograph, photolithograph. illustration, illumination; half-tone; photogravure; rotogravure; vignette, initial letter, tailpiece.

V. engrave, grave, etch; bite; bite in; lithograph; print.

559. ARTIST.—*N.* **artist;** painter, drawer, sketcher, designer, engraver, graver, line engraver, draftsman; chaser; copyist; enameler, enamelist; cartoonist, caricaturist.

historical (*or* landscape, marine, flower, portrait, genre, miniature, scene) painter; carver, modeler, statuary, sculptor.

(1) Language generally

560. LANGUAGE.—*N.* **language;** phraseology, etc., 569; speech, etc., 582; tongue, lingo [*chiefly humorous or contemptuous*], vernacular, mother (*or* vulgar, native) tongue; king's English; dialect, brogue, patois, idiom.

confusion of tongues, Babel; universal language, Esperanto, Ido; pantomime, dumb show.

literature, letters, polite literature, belles-lettres [F.], muses, humanities, republic of letters, dead languages, classics.

linguist, etc. (*scholar*), 492.

V. express, say, express by words.

Adj. lingual, linguistic; dialectal, dialectic; vernacular, current; bilingual; polyglot; literary; colloquial, slangy.

561. LETTER.—*N.* **letter;** character; hieroglyphic; alphabet,

ABC; consonant, vowel, diphthong, mute, surd, sonant, liquid, labial, palatal, cerebral, dental, guttural.

syllable; monosyllable, dissyllable, polysyllable; prefix, suffix.

spelling, orthography; phonetic spelling, phonetics.

cipher, code; monogram, anagram; acrostic, double acrostic.

V. spell; transliterate.

cipher, decipher; code, decode.

Adj. literal; alphabetical, syllabic.

phonetic, voiced, tonic, sonant; voiceless, surd; mute, labial, palatal, cerebral, dental, guttural, liquid.

562. WORD.—*N.* word, term, vocable; name, etc., 564; phrase, etc., 566; root, derivative; part of speech.

dictionary, lexicon, vocabulary, wordbook, index, glossary, thesaurus.

Science of language: etymology, philology; terminology; pronunciation, orthoëpy; lexicography.

verbosity, verbiage, wordiness; loquacity, etc., 584.

V. vocalize; etymologize, derive; index; translate.

Adj. verbal, literal; derivative.

verbose, wordy, etc., 573; loquacious, etc., 584.

563. NEOLOGY.—*N.* neology, neologism; barbarism; corruption.

dialect, brogue, patois, provincialism, broken English, Anglicism, Briticism, Gallicism, Americanism; gypsy lingo, Romany.
lingua franca, pidgin English, Hindustani; Esperanto, Ido.
jargon, dog Latin, gibberish; confusion of tongues, Babel; lingo, slang, cant, argot, billingsgate.

pseudonym, pen name; nickname; alias.

neologist, word coiner, coiner of words.

V. coin words; Americanize, Anglicize, Gallicize.

Adj. neologic, neological; slang, cant, barbarous.

564. NOMENCLATURE.—*N.* nomenclature; naming, nicknaming; baptism.

name, appellation, appellative, designation, denomination; nickname, etc., 565; epithet; title, head, heading; style, proper name, cognomen, patronymic, surname; title, handle to one's name; namesake.

term, expression, noun; technical term; cant.

V. name, call, term, denominate, designate, style, entitle, dub [*colloq. or humorous*], christen, baptize, nickname, characterize, specify, label.

Adj. named, yclept [*humorous*]; known as; titular, nominal.

565. MISNOMER.—*N.* misnomer; malapropism, Mrs. Malaprop.

nickname, sobriquet, pet name, assumed name, alias; stage name; *nom de guerre* [F.], nom de plume [English formation], pen name, pseudonym.

V. misname, miscall, nickname; take an assumed name.

Adj. misnamed; self-styled; so-called, quasi.

nameless, anonymous; unacknowledged; pseudo.

566. PHRASE.—*N.* phrase, expression, locution; sentence, paragraph; paraphrase, metaphor, euphemism, euphuism; motto, proverb; figure of speech; idiom, turn of expression; phraseology, etc., 569.

V. express, phrase; word, voice; put into (*or* express by) words; call, denominate, designate, dub.

Adv. in round (*or* set) terms; in set phrases; by the card.

567. GRAMMAR.—*N.* grammar, accidence, syntax, analysis, parts of speech; inflection, case, declension, conjugation; philology.

V. parse, analyze, conjugate, decline.

Adj. grammatical, syntactic *or* syntactical, inflectional, declensional, synthetic *or* synthetical.

568. SOLECISM.—*N.* solecism; grammatical blunder; error, slip; slip of the pen, slip of the tongue, bull; barbarism, impropriety.

V. solecize, commit a solecism; murder the king's English.

Adj. ungrammatical, incorrect, inaccurate, faulty; improper.

569. STYLE.—*N.* style, diction, phraseology, wording; manner, strain; composition; mode of expression, idiom, choice of words; mode of speech, literary power, command of language; authorship, artistry.

V. word, phrase, express by words, write; apply the file.

Various Qualities of Style

570. PERSPICUITY.—*N.* perspicuity, perspicacity, explicitness, lucidness, lucidity, limpidity, clearness; plain speaking, expression, definiteness, definition; exactness, etc., 494.

Adj. lucid, intelligible, etc., 518; limpid, pellucid, clear, explicit; exact, etc., 494.

571. OBSCURITY.—*N.* obscurity, unintelligibility, involution, confusion; hard words; ambiguity, indefiniteness, vagueness, inexactness, inaccuracy; darkness of meaning.

Adj. obscure, involved, confused.

572. CONCISENESS.—*N.* conciseness, terseness, brevity, laconicism, abridgment, compression, condensation, epitome, etc., 596.

Portmanteau word [Lewis Carroll]; brunch [breakfast + lunch], slithy, *adj.* [slimy + lithe], torrible, *adj.* [torrid + horrible].

V. **be concise,** telescope, compress, condense, abridge, abbreviate, abstract, etc., 596; come to the point.

Adj. **concise,** brief, short, laconic, succinct, curt, compact, summary, compendious, etc., 596; terse, to the point; compressed, condensed, pointed; pithy, crisp, trenchant, epigrammatic, sententious.

Adv. **briefly,** summarily; in brief, in short, in a word.

573. DIFFUSENESS.—N. diffuseness, profuseness, amplification, verbosity, wordiness; verbiage, flow of words, etc. (*loquacity*), 584; looseness; tautology, exuberance, redundance, prolixity, periphrase, expletive; padding [*editors' cant*]; drivel, twaddle.

V. **expand,** expatiate, enlarge, dilate, amplify, inflate, pad [*editors' cant*], rant; maunder, prose; harp upon, dwell on.

digress, ramble, beat about the bush, protract.

Adj. **diffuse,** profuse, wordy, verbose, copious, exuberant; lengthy, long, long-winded, protracted, prolix, diffusive, roundabout, digressive, discursive, loose; rambling, frothy.

574. VIGOR.—N. vigor, power, force; boldness, intellectual force; spirit, punch [*slang*], point, piquancy, raciness; verve, ardor, enthusiasm, glow, fire, warmth; gravity, weight.

loftiness, elevation, sublimity, grandeur.

eloquence; command of words, command of language.

Adj. **vigorous,** nervous, powerful, forcible, forceful; mordant, biting, trenchant, incisive; graphic, impressive.

spirited, lively, glowing, sparkling; racy, bold, pungent, piquant, pithy.

lofty, elevated, sublime, poetic, grand, weighty, ponderous; eloquent.

vehement, passionate, burning, impassioned, petulant.

575. FEEBLENESS.—N. feebleness, baldness, enervation, flaccidity, vapidity, poverty.

Adj. **feeble,** tame, meager, insipid, watery, nerveless, vapid, trashy, poor, dull, dry, languid; bald, colorless, enervated; prosy, prosaic, weak, slight; careless, slovenly, loose, lax; slipshod, inexact; puerile, childish; rambling, etc. (*diffuse*), 573.

576. PLAINNESS.—N. plainness, homeliness, simplicity, severity; household words.

V. **speak plainly,** waste no words, come to the point.

Adj. **plain,** simple, unornamented, unadorned, unvarnished; homely, homespun; neat; severe, chaste, pure, Saxon; commonplace, matter-of-fact, natural, prosaic, sober.

Adv. **point-blank**; in plain English; in common parlance.

577. ORNAMENT.—*N.* ornament, floridness, grandiloquence, magniloquence, declamation, well-rounded periods; elegance, etc., 578; flourish, trope; euphuism, euphemism.

bombast, inflation, pretension; rant, fustian, highfalutin [*slang*], buncombe, balderdash; fine writing; purple patches.

V. **ornament,** overcharge, overload; euphuize, euphemize.

Adj. **ornate;** ornamented, beautified, florid, rich, flowery; euphuistic, euphemistic; sonorous, inflated, swelling, tumid; turgid, pedantic, pompous, stilted, high-flown, sententious, rhetorical, declamatory; grandiose; grandiloquent, magniloquent, bombastic; frothy, flashy, flamboyant.

578. ELEGANCE.—*N.* elegance, distinction, clarity, purity, grace, felicity, ease; gracefulness, euphony; taste, good taste, restraint, propriety, correctness.

purist, classicist, stylist.

Adj. **elegant,** polished, classic *or* classical, correct, artistic; chaste, pure; graceful, easy, fluent, unaffected, natural, mellifluous, euphonious; restrained.

felicitous, happy, neat; well expressed.

579. INELEGANCE.—*N.* inelegance, impurity, vulgarity; poor diction, poor choice of words; loose construction; ill-balanced sentences; barbarism, slang; solecism, mannerism, affectation.

Adj. **inelegant,** graceless, ungraceful; harsh, abrupt; dry, stiff, cramped, formal, forced, labored; artificial, mannered, affected, ponderous, awkward; unpolished; turgid, barbarous, uncouth, rude, crude, halting, vulgar.

(2) Spoken Language

580. VOICE.—*N.* voice; intonation; utterance; vocalization; cry, exclamation, expletive, ejaculation; vociferation, enunciation, articulation; distinctness; clearness; delivery, attack.

accent, accentuation; emphasis, stress; pronunciation; euphony, etc. (*melody*), 413.

V. **speak,** utter, breathe; cry, etc. (*shout*), 411; ejaculate, rap out; articulate, enunciate, vocalize, pronounce, accentuate, deliver, emit; whisper, murmur.

Adj. **vocal,** phonetic, oral; ejaculatory, articulate, distinct, euphonious, melodious.

581. DUMBNESS.—*N.* dumbness; silence, etc. (*taciturnity*), 585; deaf-mutism, deaf-muteness, deaf-dumbness, mute, dummy, deaf-mute.

V. **silence,** muzzle, muffle, suppress, smother, gag, strike dumb, dumfound.

Adj. **dumb,** mute, mum; tongue-tied; voiceless, speechless, wordless; silent, etc. (*taciturn*), 585; inarticulate.

582. SPEECH.—*N.* **speech,** locution, talk, parlance, word of mouth, prattle.

oration, recitation, delivery, speech, address, discourse, lecture, harangue, sermon, tirade, soliloquy, etc., 589; conversation, etc., 588; salutatory; valedictory.

oratory, elocution, eloquence, rhetoric, declamation; grandiloquence.

speaker, spokesman, mouthpiece, orator, rhetorician, lecturer, preacher, elocutionist, reciter, reader; spellbinder.

V. **speak,** talk, say, utter, pronounce, deliver, breathe, let fall, rap out, blurt out.

soliloquize, etc., 589; tell, etc. (*inform*), 527; address, etc., 586; converse, etc., 588.

declaim, hold forth, harangue, stump [*colloq.*], spout, rant; recite, lecture, sermonize, discourse, expatiate.

Adj. **oral,** lingual, phonetic, unwritten, spoken.

eloquent, oratorical, rhetorical, elocutionary, declamatory, grandiloquent.

583. [Imperfect Speech] STAMMERING.—*N.* **inarticulateness;** stammering, hesitation, impediment in one's speech; lisp, drawl, nasal accent; twang; falsetto, brogue.

V. **stammer,** stutter, hesitate, falter.

mumble, mutter, maunder; mince, lisp; jabber, gabble, gibber; splutter, sputter; drawl, mouth; croak.

murder the language, murder the king's English; mispronounce.

Adj. **inarticulate;** stammering, guttural, throaty, nasal; tremulous.

584. LOQUACITY.—*N.* **loquacity,** loquaciousness, effusion; talkativeness, garrulity.

gabble, gab [*colloq.*], jaw [*low*], hot air [*slang*]; jabber, chatter; prate, prattle, twaddle, small talk.

fluency, volubility, flow of words; verbosity, etc. (*diffuseness*), 573; eloquence.

talker; chatterer, chatterbox; babbler, ranter, proser, driveler, gossip, magpie.

V. **be loquacious,** talk glibly, pour forth, prate, palaver, prose, maunder, chatter, blab, gush, prattle, jabber, jaw [*low*], babble, gabble; expatiate, gossip, talk at random, talk nonsense.

Adj. **loquacious,** talkative, garrulous, chattering, chatty, declamatory, fluent, voluble, effusive, glib, flippant.

585. TACITURNITY.—*N.* taciturnity, silence, muteness, curtness; reserve, reticence.

man of few words; Spartan.

V. be silent, keep silence; hold one's tongue, say nothing; render mute.

Adj. silent, mute, mum, still, dumb.

taciturn, laconic, concise, sententious, close, close-mouthed, curt; reserved; reticent.

586. ADDRESS.—*N.* address, allocution; speech, etc., 582; appeal, invocation, salutation, salutatory.

V. address, speak to, accost, apostrophize, appeal to, invoke; hail, salute; call to, halloo.

lecture, preach, harangue, spellbind.

587. RESPONSE, etc., *see* Answer 462.

588. CONVERSATION.—*N.* conversation, colloquy, converse, interlocution, talk, discourse, dialogue, duologue.

chat, tattle, gossip, tittle-tattle; babble.

conference, parley, interview, audience, reception; congress, etc. (*council*), 696; powwow.

debate, palaver, war of words, controversy.

talker, gossip, tattler; chatterer, etc. (*loquacity*), 584; speaker, etc., 582; conversationalist.

V. converse, talk together, hold (*or* carry on, join in, engage in) a conversation; parley; palaver; chat, gossip, tattle; prate, etc., 584.

confer with, discourse with, commune with, talk it over.

Adj. conversational, conversable; chatty, colloquial.

589. SOLILOQUY.—*N.* soliloquy, monologue, apostrophe.

V. soliloquize, monologize, talk to oneself; think aloud, apostrophize.

Written Language

590. WRITING.—*N.* writing, chirography, penmanship; typewriting; manuscript; script; character, letter, etc., 561.

shorthand, stenography, phonography; secret writing, cipher, cryptography.

handwriting; signature, mark, autograph, hand, fist [*colloq.*]; calligraphy.

composition, authorship; lucubration, production, work, screed, article, paper; book, etc., 593; essay, theme, thesis; novel, textbook; poem, book of poems (*or* verse), anthology.

writer, scribe; author, etc., 593; amanuensis, secretary, clerk, penman, copyist; stenographer, typewriter, typist.

V. **write,** pen, typewrite, type [*colloq.*]; copy, engross; transcribe; scribble, scrawl, scratch; note down, write down, record.

compose, indite, draw up, draft, formulate; dictate; inscribe.

Adj. **written,** in writing, in black and white; stenographic.

591. PRINTING.—*N.* **printing,** typography; type, linotype, monotype; composition, print, letterpress, text, context, matter; copy, impression, proof, galley, galley proof, page proof.

printer, compositor; reader, proofreader, corrector of the press; printer's devil; copyholder, copyeditor.

V. **print;** compose; go to press; publish, issue, bring out.

Adj. **typographical,** printed, in type.

592. CORRESPONDENCE.—*N.* **correspondence,** letter, epistle, missive, note, post card, postal card; dispatch; bulletin, circular.

correspondent, writer, letter writer.

V. **correspond,** write to, send a letter to; communicate, communicate by writing (*or* letter); circularize, follow up, bombard; reply.

593. BOOK.—*N.* **book,** booklet; writing, work, volume, tome, tract, treatise, brochure, monograph, pamphlet, libretto; handbook, manual, novel, etc. (*composition*), 590; publication; magazine, periodical.

work of reference, encyclopedia, cyclopedia, dictionary, thesaurus, concordance, anthology, compilation.

writer, author, essayist, contributor; hack writer, hack; journalist, publicist, reporter, correspondent; editor, scribe, etc., 590; playwright, etc., 599; poet, etc., 597.

publisher, bookseller; librarian; bookworm.

bookstore, bookshop, bookseller's shop, publishing house.

library, public library, lending library.

594. DESCRIPTION.—*N.* **description,** account, statement, report, record; brief, etc. (*abstract*), 596; delineation, sketch, pastel, vignette; monograph; narration, recital, rehearsal, relation.

narrative, history, memoir; annals, etc., (*chronicle*), 551; journal, letters, biography, autobiography, life, adventures.

Fiction·novel, romance, story, tale, short story, anecdote; detective story, fairy tale, fable, parable, allegory.

narrator, historian, biographer, novelist, storyteller, romancer, anecdotist, word painter; writer, etc , 593.

V. **describe,** set forth, picture, portray, characterize, delineate, narrate, relate, recite, recount, romance, tell, report; detail, particularize.

Adj. **descriptive,** graphic, narrative, epic, romantic, historic *or* historical, biographical, autobiographical; traditional, legendary, mythical, fabulous; anecdotic, idealistic; realistic, true to life.

595. DISSERTATION.—*N.* **dissertation,** treatise, essay, thesis, theme; tract, discourse, memoir, disquisition, lecture, sermon, homily, investigation, study, discussion, exposition.

commentary, review, critique, criticism, article, leader, editorial.

commentator, critic, essayist, publicist, reviewer, leader writer, editor.

V. comment, explain, interpret, criticize, illuminate; treat of (*or* ventilate, discuss, deal with, go into) a subject.

596. COMPENDIUM.—N. compendium, abstract, précis, epitome, analysis, digest, brief, condensation, abridgment, abbreviation, etc., 201; summary, draft, minute, note; excerpt, extract; synopsis, textbook, outlines, syllabus, contents, heads, prospectus.

fragments, extracts, cuttings; fugitive pieces, anthology, miscellany, compilation.

recapitulation, résumé, review; symposium.

V. abridge, abstract, epitomize, summarize; abbreviate, etc. (*shorten*), 201; condense, etc. (*compress*), 195.

compile, etc. (*collect*), 72; note down, collect, edit.

recapitulate, review, skim, run over, sum up.

Adj. compendious, synoptic, abridged, analytic *or* analytical.

Adv. in short, in substance, in few words, in a nutshell.

597. POETRY.—N. poetry, poetics, poesy, muse, Apollo, Parnassus, inspiration, fire of genius.

poem; epic, ballad, lyric, ode, idyl, eclogue, pastoral, sonnet, elegy; dramatic (*or* didactic, satirical, narrative, lyric) poetry; satire; anthology.

versification, rhyming, prosody; scansion, scanning.

canto, stanza, verse, line, couplet, triplet, quatrain; refrain, chorus, burden; octave, sextet.

verse, rhyme, assonance, alliteration, meter, measure; foot, numbers, rhythm; ictus, beat, accent, accentuation, iambus, iambic, dactyl, spondee, trochee, anapest, etc.; hexameter, pentameter; Alexandrine; blank verse, heroic verse; doggerel.

poet, genius, creator; poet laureate; laureate; bard, lyrist, sonneteer, rhapsodist, satirist, troubadour; minstrel; minnesinger, Meistersinger; jongleur, versifier, rhymer, rhymester, minor poet, poetaster.

V. poetize, sing, write poetry; string verses together, versify, make verses, rhyme.

Adj. poetic *or* poetical; lyric *or* lyrical; tuneful; metrical; elegiac, iambic, dactylic, spondaic, trochaic, anapestic.

598. PROSE.—N. prose, prosaicness; poetic prose; narrative, etc., 594.

prose writer, essayist, novelist, etc., 594.

V. prose; write prose (*or* in prose).

Adj. prosaic, prosy, unpoetical, unrhymed, in prose.

599. THE DRAMA.—*N.* the drama, the stage, the theater, the play; theatricals, histrionic art.

play, drama, piece, tragedy, comedy, opera, vaudeville, curtain raiser, interlude, afterpiece, farce, extravaganza, harlequinade, pantomime, burlesque, ballet, spectacle, masque, melodrama; comedy of manners; charade, mystery, miracle play, morality play.

act, scene, tableau, curtain; introduction, prologue, exposition, epilogue; libretto, book, text, prompter's copy.

performance, representation, show [*colloq.*], stage setting, stagecraft; acting; impersonation, stage business; slapstick [*slang*], buffoonery.

theater, playhouse, amphitheater, moving-picture theater, moving pictures, movies [*colloq*]; puppet show, marionettes, Punch and Judy.

cast, dramatis personae [L], role, part, character; repertoire, repertory.

actor, player, performer; masker, mime, mimic; star, headliner; comedian, tragedian.

buffoon, mummer, pantomimist, clown; pantaloon, harlequin, columbine; punch.

company, first tragedian, prima donna, leading lady; lead; leading man; comedian, comedienne; juvenile lead, juvenile; villain, heavy lead, heavy, heavy father; ingenue, soubrette; character man, character woman, extra, mute, supernumerary, super [*theat. cant*].

dramatist, playwright, playwriter; dramatic author (*or* writer).

audience, house; orchestra, gallery.

V. act, play, perform; put on the stage, dramatize, stage, produce, set; personate, mimic, enact; rehearse, spout, rant; tread the stage (*or* boards); make one's debut, take a part, star.

Adj. dramatic; theatrical; scenic, histrionic, comic, tragic, farcical, tragicomic, melodramatic, operatic; stagy, spectacular.

Adv. on the stage, on the boards; in the limelight, in the spotlight; before the footlights, before an audience; behind the scenes.

CLASS V

Words Relating to the VOLUNTARY POWERS

I. Individual Volition

600. WILL.—*N.* will, volition, free will; freedom, etc., 748; discretion; choice, inclination, intent, purpose, option, etc. (*choice*), 609; spontaneity, spontaneousness; originality.

determination, etc. (*resolution*), 604; force of will, will power, autocracy, bossiness [*colloq.*].

wish, desire, pleasure, mind, disposition, etc., 602; intention, etc., 620.

V. will, see fit, think fit; determine, etc. (*resolve*), 604; enjoin; settle, etc. (*choose*), 609; volunteer; do what one chooses, etc. (*freedom*), 748; have one's own way; use one's discretion; boss, [*colloq.*]; originate.

Adj. **voluntary,** volitional, willful; free, etc., 748; optional, discretionary; autocratic, dictatorial, bossy [*colloq.*].

willing, etc., 602; unbidden, spontaneous; original.

Adv. **voluntarily,** at will, at pleasure.

of one's own accord, on one's own responsibility; by choice, purposely, intentionally.

601. NECESSITY.—*N.* **necessity,** obligation; compulsion, etc., 744; subjection, etc., 749; stern (*or* dire) necessity, last resort.

instinct, blind impulse, natural tendency (*or* impulse), predetermination.

destiny, fatality, fate, kismet, doom, election, predestination; lot, fortune; fatalism.

Fates, God's will, heaven, will of heaven; stars; planets; wheel of fortune.

V. **be obliged,** be forced, be driven; be fated, be doomed, be destined, have no alternative.

destine, doom, foredoom, devote; predestine, preordain; necessitate; compel, etc., 744.

Adj. **necessary,** needful, etc. (*requisite*), 630; compulsory, etc. (*compel*), 744; inevitable, unavoidable, irresistible, irrevocable, inexorable, binding.

fated; destined, fateful, set apart, devoted, elect.

involuntary, instinctive, automatic, blind, mechanical; unconscious, unwitting, unthinking; unintentional.

Adv. **necessarily,** of necessity, of course; willy-nilly.

602. WILLINGNESS.—*N.* **willingness,** disposition, inclination, liking, turn, propensity, leaning, frame of mind, humor, mood, vein, bent, aptitude.

geniality, cordiality, good will; alacrity, readiness, zeal, enthusiasm, earnestness, eagerness.

assent, etc., 488; compliance, etc., 762.

volunteer, unpaid worker, amateur, nonprofessional.

V. **be willing,** incline, lean to, mind, hold to, cling to; desire, etc., 865; acquiesce, assent, comply with; jump at, catch at; take up, plunge into, have a go at [*colloq.*].

volunteer, offer, proffer.

Adj. **willing,** fain, disposed, inclined, favorable, content, well disposed; ready, forward, earnest, eager, zealous, enthusiastic; bent upon, desirous.

docile, amenable, easily persuaded, facile, easygoing, tractable, genial, gracious, cordial.

voluntary, gratuitous, free, unconstrained, spontaneous, unasked, unforced.

Adv. **willingly,** fain, freely, with pleasure, of one's own accord; graciously, with a good grace, without demur.

603. UNWILLINGNESS.—*N.* **unwillingness,** indisposition, disinclination, aversion, averseness, reluctance; indifference, etc., 866; backwardness, slowness; obstinacy, etc., 606.

scruple, scrupulousness, delicacy, qualm, shrinking, recoil; hesitation, fastidiousness.

dissent, etc., 489; refusal, etc., 764.

V. **be unwilling,** dislike, etc., 867; demur, stick at, scruple, stickle; hang fire, shirk, slack, recoil, shrink, hesitate; avoid, etc., 623; oppose, etc., 708; dissent, etc., 489; refuse, etc., 764.

Adj. **unwilling,** loath, disinclined, indisposed, averse, reluctant, opposed, adverse, laggard, backward, remiss, slack, indifferent, scrupulous; repugnant, restive; grudging, forced, under compulsion, irreconcilable.

Adv. **unwillingly,** grudgingly, with an ill grace; against one's will, against the grain; under protest.

604. RESOLUTION.—*N.* **determination,** will, decision, resolution; backbone; clear grit, grit; sand [*slang*]; strength of mind, resolve, firmness, energy, manliness, vigor, resoluteness; zeal, devotion.

self-control, self-mastery, self-command, self-reliance, self-restraint, self-denial.

tenacity, perseverance, etc., 604a; obstinacy, etc., 606; pluck.

V. **resolve,** will, determine, decide, form a resolution, conclude, fix, bring to a crisis, take a decisive step, take upon oneself.

take one's stand, stand firm, insist upon, make a point of, set one's heart upon; stick at nothing, make short work of, not stick at trifles; persevere, etc., 604a.

Adj. **resolved,** determined; strong-willed, strong-minded; resolute, self-possessed, earnest, serious; decided, peremptory, unflinching, firm, iron, game, plucky, tenacious, gritty, indomitable, inexorable, relentless; obstinate, etc., 606; unyielding; grim, stern, inflexible, irrevocable.

Adv. **resolutely,** in earnest, earnestly; on one's mettle, manfully, like a man.

604a. PERSEVERANCE.—*N.* **perseverance,** continuance, constancy, steadiness, persistence, patience; pertinacity, industry.

grit, bottom, pluck, stamina, backbone, sand [*slang*]; tenacity, staying power, endurance; bulldog courage.

V. **persevere,** persist, hold on, hold out; stick to, cling to, adhere to; keep on, carry on, hold on; bear up, keep up, hold up; plod; continue, die in harness, die at one's post.

Adj. **persevering,** constant; steady, steadfast, unwavering, unfaltering, unflinching, unflagging, plodding; industrious, etc., 682; strenuous, pertinacious, persistent; indomitable, indefatigable.

Adv. **without fail,** through thick and thin, through fire and water; sink or swim, rain or shine, fair or foul.

605. IRRESOLUTION.—*N.* **irresolution,** indecision, indetermination, instability, uncertainty; demur, suspense, hesitation, hesitancy, vacillation, changeableness, fluctuation; caprice, etc., 608; lukewarmness.

fickleness, levity, pliancy, weakness, timidity; cowardice, etc., 862.

waverer, shilly-shally, turncoat, opportunist, timeserver.

V. **be irresolute,** remain neuter; dilly-dally, hesitate, hover, shilly-shally, hem and haw, demur, debate, balance; dally with, coquet with; go halfway, compromise, be afraid.

vacillate, falter, waver, fluctuate, change, alternate, shuffle, palter, shirk, trim.

Adj. **irresolute,** drifting, halfhearted; undecided, undetermined, uncertain, at a loss; fickle, unreliable, irresponsible, unstable; capricious, etc., 608.

weak, feeble-minded, frail, timid, cowardly, pliant.

Adv. **irresolutely,** in faltering accents; off and on.

606. OBSTINACY.—*N.* **obstinacy,** tenacity, cussedness; perseverance, etc., 604*a*; immovability, inflexibility, obduracy, doggedness, stubbornness, self-will, contumacy, perversity; resolution, etc., 604.

bigotry, intolerance, dogmatism; fixed idea, fanaticism, zealotry, infatuation, monomania.

bigot, dogmatist, zealot, fanatic, bitter-ender [*colloq.*]; mule.

V. **be obstinate,** stickle, take no denial, be wedded to an opinion, persist, die hard, not yield an inch, stand out.

Adj. **obstinate,** tenacious, stubborn, obdurate, inflexible, balky; immovable, unchangeable, inexorable, determined, mulish, dogged; sullen, sulky; unmoved.

arbitrary, dogmatic, positive, bigoted, opinionated, stiff-necked, hidebound, unyielding; incorrigible.

willful, self-willed, perverse; ungovernable, wayward, refractory, unruly, headstrong; contumacious; cross-grained.

Adv. **with set jaw;** no surrender.

607. APOSTASY.—*N.* **apostasy,** recantation; renunciation; abjuration, defection, retraction, withdrawal, disavowal, revocation, tergiversation, reversal; backsliding.

turncoat, apostate, renegade, pervert, deserter, backslider, crawfish [*slang*].

timeserver, trimmer, double-dealer; weathercock.

V. **apostatize,** veer round, turn round; change one's mind, abjure, renounce, relinquish, back down, shift one's ground, change sides, go over, recant, retract, revoke, rescind, forswear.

trim, shuffle, blow hot and cold, be on the fence, straddle.

Adj. **changeful,** irresolute, ductile, slippery, trimming, timeserving.

608. CAPRICE.—*N.* **caprice,** fancy, humor, whim, fit, crotchet, quirk, freak, fad, vagary, prank, escapade.

V. **be capricious,** take it into one's head, blow hot and cold, play fast and loose.

Adj. **capricious,** erratic, eccentric, fitful, inconsistent, fanciful, whimsical, crotchety, freakish, wayward, wanton; contrary, captious, unreasonable, arbitrary; fickle, etc. (*irresolute*), 605.

Adv. **by fits,** by fits and starts, without rhyme or reason.

609. CHOICE.—*N.* **choice,** option, selection, pick; discretion, alternative, preference, adoption, decision.

Scylla and Charybdis.

election, poll, ballot, vote, voice, suffrage, plebiscite, referendum; electioneering; voting, elective franchise; ticket, ballot box.

voter, elector, constituent, electorate, constituency.

V. **choose;** elect, make one's choice; make choice of, fix upon, settle, decide, make up one's mind; adopt, take up, embrace, espouse.

vote, poll, hold up one's hand, give a (*or* the) voting sign; divide.

select, pick, cull, glean, winnow; pitch upon, indulge one's fancy; set apart, mark out for.

prefer, fancy, have rather, had (*or* would) as lief; reserve.

Adj. **optional,** discretional, at choice, on approval.

chosen, choice, elect, select, popular; preferential.

Adv. **optionally,** at pleasure, at the option of.

by choice, by preference; in preference; rather, before.

609a. ABSENCE OF CHOICE.—*N.* **no choice;** Hobson's choice; first come first served; necessity, etc., 601.

neutrality, indifference; indecision, etc. (*irresolution*), 605.

V. **be neutral,** have no preference, waive, not vote.

Adj. **neutral,** neuter; indifferent; undecided, etc. (*irresolute*), 605.

610. REJECTION.—*N.* **rejection,** repudiation, exclusion; refusal, etc., 764.

V. **reject,** set (*or* lay) aside, give up; decline, etc. (*refuse*), 764; exclude, except; pluck up, spurn, cast out, repudiate, scout, disclaim, discard.

Adv. **neither,** neither the one nor the other.

611. PREDETERMINATION.—*N.* **predetermination,** predestination, premeditation, foregone conclusion; resolve, project; intention, etc., 620; fate, necessity.

list, schedule, calendar, docket, slate [*pol. cant*], register, roster, poll, muster, draft.

V. **predetermine,** predestine, premeditate, resolve beforehand. list, schedule, docket, slate, register, poll, empanel, draft.

Adj. **premeditated,** predesigned, prepense [*as,* malice *prepense*], studied, designed, calculated, aforethought; foregone.

well laid, well devised, well weighed; maturely considered; cut-and-dried.

Adv. **deliberately,** with eyes open, in cold blood; intentionally.

612. IMPULSE.—*N.* **impulse,** sudden thought; impromptu, improvisation; inspiration, flash, spurt.

V. **improvise,** extemporize; say what comes uppermost, act on the spur of the moment, rise to the occasion; spurt.

Adj. **extemporaneous,** impulsive, snap, improvised, unpremeditated, unprompted, natural, unguarded; spontaneous.

Adv. **extempore,** extemporaneously; offhand, impromptu.

613. HABIT.—*N.* **habit,** addiction, wont, run, way, matter of course, beaten path, second nature; trick, knack, skill.

custom, use, usage, prescription, practice; prevalence, observance; conventionalism, conventionality, mode, fashion, vogue, etiquette.

rule, standing order, precedent, routine, red tape, rut, groove.

V. **habituate,** inure, harden, season, caseharden; accustom, familiarize; acclimatize.

cling to, adhere to; acquire a habit; follow the beaten track (*or* path), move in a rut.

prevail; come into use, become a habit, take root; grow upon one.

Adj. **habitual,** customary, accustomed, wonted, usual, general, ordinary, common, frequent, everyday, household, familiar, trite, hackneyed, commonplace, conventional, regular, set, stock, established, stereotyped; fixed, rooted, permanent, inveterate, besetting, ingrained, current.

wont; used to, given to, addicted to, in the habit of; seasoned, imbued with, devoted to, wedded to.

Adv. **as usual,** as things go, as the world goes; as you were [*mil.*].

as a rule, for the most part, generally, most frequently.

614. DESUETUDE.—*N.* **desuetude,** disusage; disuse, etc., 678; want of practice.

V. **be unaccustomed,** leave off (*or* break off, shake off, violate) a habit *or* custom; be weaned from; disuse, etc., 678; wear off.

Adj. **unaccustomed,** unused, unwonted, unseasoned, untrained; new, fresh, original; unskilled.

unconventional, unfashionable, unusual; disused, etc., 678.

615. MOTIVE.—*N.* **motive,** reason, ground, call, principle, mainspring, pro and con, reason why; ulterior motive; intention, etc., 620.

inducement, consideration; attraction, loadstone, magnet, magnetism, temptation, enticement, allurement, glamour, witchery; charm, spell; fascination, blandishment, cajolery; seduction.

influence, prompting, dictate, instance; impulse, incitement, press, insistence, instigation; inspiration, persuasion, encouragement, exhortation, advice, solicitation, pull [*slang*].

incentive, stimulus, spur, fillip, whip, goad, provocative, whet.

bribe, lure, sop, decoy, bait, bribery and corruption.

tempter, prompter, instigator, coaxer, wheedler, siren; firebrand.

V. **induce,** move, draw, inspire; put up to [*slang*], prompt; stimulate, rouse, arouse, animate, whet, incite, provoke, instigate, actuate, encourage, advocate.

influence, bias, sway, incline, dispose, predispose; lead, lobby.

persuade, prevail upon, overcome, carry, bring round, conciliate, win (*or* talk) over; enlist; engage; invite, court.

tempt, overpersuade, entice, allure, captivate, fascinate, bewitch, hypnotize, charm, magnetize, wheedle, coax, lure, inveigle.

bribe, tamper with, suborn, grease the palm, corrupt.

enforce, force, impel, propel, whip, lash, goad, spur, prick, urge, egg on, hound on, hurry on.

Adj. **persuasive,** inviting, tempting, suasive, seductive, attractive, fascinating; provocative.

Adv. **because,** therefore, for, by reason of, for the sake of, on account of; out of, from, as, forasmuch as.

615a. ABSENCE OF MOTIVE.—*N.* absence of motive; caprice, etc., 608; chance, etc. (*absence of design*), 621.

V. **scruple,** etc. (*be unwilling*), 603; have no motive.

Adj. **aimless,** capricious, without rhyme or reason.

Adv. **capriciously,** out of mere caprice.

616. DISSUASION.—*N.* **dissuasion,** expostulation, remonstrance; deprecation, etc., 766; discouragement, damper, wet blanket.

curb, restraint, constraint, check.

V. **dissuade,** cry out against, remonstrate, expostulate, warn.

disincline, indispose, shake, stagger; discourage, dishearten, disenchant; deter, hold back, restrain, repel, turn aside, damp, cool, chill, blunt, calm, quiet, quench.

Adj. averse, etc. (*unwilling*), 603; repugnant, etc. (*dislike*), 867.

617. [Ostensible motive, ground, or reason] **PLEA.**—*N.* plea, pretext; allegation, excuse, vindication, justification; color; gloss, guise.

pretense, subterfuge, dust thrown in the eye; blind, lame excuse, makeshift, shift.

V. plead, allege, excuse, vindicate; color, gloss over, make a pretext of, use as a plea, take one's stand upon; pretend.

Adj. ostensible, alleged, pretended.

Adv. ostensibly; under the plea of, under the pretense of.

618. GOOD.—*N.* good, benefit, advantage; improvement, etc., 658; interest, service, behoof, behalf; commonweal; gain, profit, harvest; boon, etc. (*gift*), 784; good turn, blessing, prize, windfall, godsend, good fortune; happiness, etc., 827; goodness, etc., 648.

V. benefit, profit, advantage, serve, help, avail, do good to.

gain, prosper, flourish, thrive.

Adj. commendable, etc., 931; useful, etc., 644; good, beneficial, etc., 648.

Adv. well, aright, satisfactorily, favorably, in one's interest.

619. EVIL.—*N.* evil, ill, harm, hurt, mischief, nuisance, drawback, disadvantage; ills that flesh is heir to, mental suffering, pain; bane, etc., 663.

badness, etc., 649; painfulness, etc., 830; evildoer, etc., 913.

blow, buffet, stroke, scratch, bruise, wound, gash, mutilation; mortal blow (*or* wound); damage, loss.

disaster, accident, casualty, mishap, misfortune, calamity, woe, fatal mischief, catastrophe, tragedy, ruin; adversity, etc., 735.

outrage, wrong, injury, foul play; bad turn, disservice, grievance.

V. harm, injure, hurt, do disservice to.

Adj. disastrous; hurtful, etc., 649; disadvantageous, injurious, harmful.

Adv. amiss, wrong, ill; to one's cost.

620. INTENTION.—*N.* intention, intent, purpose; project, etc., 626; undertaking, design, ambition; view, proposal; contemplation.

object, aim, end; drift, tendency; destination, mark, point, goal, target, prey, quarry, game.

decision, determination, resolve; fixed purpose, resolution; ultimatum.

V. intend, purpose, design, mean, have in view, bid for, labor for, aspire to, aim at; contemplate, meditate, think of, dream of, talk of; premeditate, destine, propose; project, etc. (*plan*), 626; desire, etc., 865; pursue, etc., 622.

Adj. **intentional**, advised, express, determinate; bound for; disposed, inclined, bent upon, at stake; in prospect.

Adv. **intentionally**, advisedly, wittingly, knowingly, designedly, purposely, on purpose, by design, studiously, pointedly; deliberately.

621. [Absence of purpose] **CHANCE.**[1]—*N.* **chance**, etc., 156; lot, destiny, etc., 601; luck; hoodoo [*colloq.*], jinx [*slang*], Jonah, voodoo; wheel of chance, fortune's wheel; mascot.

speculation, venture, random shot, blind bargain, leap in the dark; fluke [*sporting cant*], flier [*slang*]; flutter [*slang*]; futures.

gambling, betting, drawing lots; wager; gamble, risk, stake, bet.

gambler, gamester, speculator; bookmaker, man of the turf.

V. **chance**, etc., 156; toss up, cast (*or* draw) lots; tempt fortune; speculate.

risk, venture, hazard, stake; wager, bet, gamble, game, play for.

Adj. **chance**; fortuitous, etc., 156; unintentional, unintended, accidental; random, undesigned, purposeless.

Adv. **at random**, at a venture, by chance, as it may happen.

622. [Purpose in action] **PURSUIT.**—*N.* **pursuit**, prosecution; pursuance, enterprise, undertaking, business, etc., 625; adventure, quest, hobby.

chase, hunt, race, steeplechase; hunting, coursing, sport, shooting, angling, fishing.

pursuer; hunter, huntsman, the field; sportsman, Nimrod; hound.

V. **pursue**, prosecute, follow, shadow; carry on, undertake, engage in, set about, endeavor, seek, trace, aim at, fish, fish for; press on, follow up, take up; go in for.

chase, give chase, stalk, course, hunt, hound.

Adj. **in quest of**, in pursuit, in full cry, on the scent.

623. [Absence of pursuit] **AVOIDANCE.**—*N.* **avoidance**, evasion, flight; escape, retreat, recoil, departure.

abstention, abstinence; forbearance; inaction, etc., 681; neutrality.

shirker, slacker [*colloq.*], shirk, quitter, truant; fugitive, refugee, runaway, deserter, renegade, backslider.

V. **abstain**, refrain, spare; eschew, keep from, let alone.

avoid, shun, steer (*or* keep) clear of; fight shy of, evade, elude, shirk.

shrink, hang (*or* hold, draw) back; recoil, retire, flinch, shy, dodge, parry.

[1] See note on 156.

beat a retreat; turn tail, take to one's heels; run, run away, cut and run [*colloq.*]; fly, flee, take flight; desert, make off, sneak off, sheer off; slip, play truant, decamp, flit, bolt, abscond; escape, etc., 671; abandon, etc., 624.

Adj. **elusive**, evasive; fugitive, runaway; shy, wild.

624. RELINQUISHMENT.—*N.* **relinquishment**, abandonment; desertion, defection, secession, withdrawal; discontinuance, renunciation, abrogation, resignation, retirement; cession, etc. (*of property*), 782.

V. **relinquish**, give up, abandon, desert, forsake, leave in the lurch; go back on [*colloq.*]; leave, quit, vacate, resign.

renounce, forego, have done with, drop, discard, give up the point (*or* argument), table, table the motion.

625. BUSINESS.—*N.* **business**, occupation, employment, undertaking, pursuit; affair, concern, matter, case.

task, work, job, chore, errand, commission, mission, charge, duty; avocation, hobby.

function, part, role, capacity, province, department, sphere, field, line; walk, round, routine; race, career.

office, place, position, post, incumbency, living; situation, berth, billet, appointment, engagement; undertaking, etc., 676.

vocation, calling, profession; cloth, faculty; craft, handicraft; trade.

V. **occupy oneself with**; employ oneself in *or* upon; undertake, etc., 676; turn one's hand to; be engaged in, be occupied with, be at work on; have in hand; ply one's trade.

officiate, serve, act, do duty; discharge (*or* perform) the duties of; hold (*or* fill) an office; hold a portfolio.

Adj. **businesslike**; workaday; professional, official, functional; busy.

in hand, on hand, afoot, on foot, going on; acting.

626. PLAN.—*N.* **plan**, scheme, design, project, proposal, proposition, suggestion; resolution, motion; organization, arrangement, system.

outline, sketch, skeleton, draft, rough draft, copy; forecast, program, prospectus; order of the day, memoranda, platform, plank, slate, ticket; role; policy.

contrivance, invention, expedient, receipt, nostrum, artifice, device; stratagem, trick; shift.

measure, step; stroke, master stroke; trump, trump card.

intrigue, cabal, plot, conspiracy, machination; mine.

promoter, designer, organizer, founder, projector; author, artist.

V. **plan**, scheme, design, frame, contrive, project, forecast, sketch, devise, invent, hatch, concoct; hit upon; map out, shape out a course; prepare, etc., 673.

systematize, organize; cast, recast, arrange; digest, mature.

plot, intrigue; counterplot, mine, countermine, lay a train.

Adj. under consideration, on the carpet, on the table.

627. METHOD. [Path]—*N.* method, way, manner, form, mode, fashion, guise; procedure.

path, road, route, course, tack; trajectory, orbit, track, beat.

means of access, entrance, approach, passage, cloister, covered way, lobby, corridor, aisle; alley, lane, avenue, artery, channel; gateway, door; secret passage; covert way.

roadway, thoroughfare; highway, turnpike, state road, causeway, king's highway; parkway, boulevard, speedway; walk, footpath, pathway, pavement, sidewalk, byroad, crossroad; railroad, railway, trolley track, tramway; towpath; street, etc. (*abode*), 189; bridge, viaduct.

Adv. how; in what way, in what manner; by what mode; so, thus; anyhow.

628. MID-COURSE.—*N.* mid-course, middle way, middle course; moderation; mean, etc., 29; golden mean.

compromise, half measures, neutrality.

V. keep the golden mean, steer a middle course; go straight.

compromise, make a compromise, concede half, go halfway.

Adj. neutral, average, even; impartial, moderate; straight.

Adv. in the mean; in moderation.

629. CIRCUIT.—*N.* circuit, roundabout way, digression, detour; loop, winding.

V. go round about, make a circuit, make a detour; meander, deviate.

Adj. circuitous, indirect, roundabout; zigzag.

Adv. in a roundabout way; by an indirect course.

630. REQUIREMENT.—*N.* requirement, need, wants, necessities; stress, exigency, pinch, case of need; desideratum; necessity, indispensability, urgency.

requisition, demand, request, claim; run, call for.

charge, command, injunction, precept, mandate, order, ultimatum.

V. require, need, want, stand in need of, lack; desire, etc., 865.

Adj. necessary, requisite, needful, imperative, essential, indispensable, called for; in demand, in request.

urgent, exigent, pressing, instant, crying.

Adv. of necessity; at a pinch.

631. INSTRUMENTALITY.—*N.* instrumentality; aid, etc., 707; subservience, mediation, intervention; pull [*slang*], influence; medium, intermediary, vehicle, tool, agency; instrument, expedient; means, etc., 632.

minister, handmaid, servant; friend at court, go-between.

V. **mediate**, minister, intervene, come (*or* go) between; interpose; use one's influence, be instrumental; subserve.

Adj. **instrumental**; useful, etc., 644; subservient, serviceable; intermediary, intermediate, intervening; conducive.

Adv. **through**, by, whereby, thereby, hereby; by the agency of, by dint of; by (*or* in) virtue of; by means of.

somehow, by fair means or foul; somehow or other; by hook or by crook.

632. MEANS.—*N.* **means**, resources, wherewithal, ways and means; capital, etc. (*money*), 800; revenue, income; stock in trade, provision, reserve, remnant, last resource, appliances, conveniences; expedients, wheels within wheels; sheet anchor; aid, etc., 707; medium, etc., 631.

V. **provide the wherewithal**, find (*or* possess) means, have powerful friends, have friends at court; have something to draw on.

Adj. **instrumental**, etc., 631; **mechanical**, etc., 633.

trustworthy, reliable, efficient; honorable, etc. (*upright*), 939.

Adv. **by means of**, with; wherewith, herewith, therewith; wherewithal.

633. INSTRUMENT.—*N.* **instrument**, organ, tool, implement, utensil, machine, engine, lathe, gin, mill; motor; machinery, mechanism.

equipment, gear, tackle, tackling; rigging, apparatus, appliances; plant, harness, trappings, fittings, accouterments, appointments, furniture, upholstery; chattels; paraphernalia.

mechanical powers; leverage; fulcrum, lever, crow, crowbar, jimmy, marline spike, handspike; arm, limb, wing; wheel and axle; wheelwork, clockwork; wheels within wheels; pinion, crank, winch, capstan, wheel, flywheel, turbine, water wheel, pump; pulley, crane, derrick; inclined plane; wedge; screw; jack; spring, mainspring; loom, shuttle, jenny.

handle, hilt, haft, shaft, shank; tiller, rudder, helm; treadle, pedal.

Adj. **mechanical**; propulsive, driving, hoisting, elevating, lifting.

useful, labor-saving, ingenious; well made, well fitted, well equipped.

634. SUBSTITUTE.—*N.* **substitute**, etc., 147; proxy, alternate, understudy; deputy, etc., 759.

635. MATERIALS.—*N.* **material**, raw material, stuff, stock, staple; ore.

636. STORE.—*N.* **store**, accumulation, hoard; stock, fund, mine, vein, lode, quarry; spring, fount, fountain; well; orchard, garden, farm; stock in trade, supply; treasure; reserve, reserve fund, savings.

crop, harvest, vintage, yield, product, gleaning.

storehouse, storeroom, store closet; depository, depot, cache, warehouse, magazine; garner, granary, grain elevator, silo; safe-deposit vault; armory; arsenal; stable, barn.

reservoir, cistern, tank, pond, millpond; gasometer.

V. store, put by, lay by, set by, stow away, store up, hoard up, treasure up, lay up, save, preserve, save up, bank; cache, deposit; stow, stack, load; harvest; accumulate, amass, hoard.

reserve; keep back, hold back; husband, husband one's resources.

Adj. in store, in reserve, spare, supernumerary.

Adv. for a rainy day, for a nest egg, to fall back upon; on deposit.

637. PROVISION.—*N.* provision, supply; grist, resources, etc. (*means*), 632; groceries, purveyance, commissariat.

caterer, purveyor, commissary, quartermaster, steward, purser, housekeeper; innkeeper, landlord, mine host; grocer, fishmonger, provision merchant.

V. provide, make provision, lay in, lay in a stock (*or* store).

supply, furnish; cater, victual, provision, purvey, forage; stock, make good, replenish, fill; recruit, feed.

store, etc., 636; conserve, keep, preserve, lay by, gather into barns.

638. WASTE.—*N.* consumption, expenditure, exhaustion; dispersion, leakage, loss, wear and tear, waste; prodigality.

V. consume, spend, expend, use, swallow up; exhaust, spill, drain, empty, deplete; disperse, etc., 73; waste; squander.

labor in vain, etc. (*useless*), 645; cast pearls before swine; waste powder and shot.

run to waste; ebb, leak, melt away, run dry, dry up.

Adj. wasted, gone to waste, useless, run to seed; dried up.

wasteful, etc. (*prodigal*), 818; penny wise and pound foolish.

639. SUFFICIENCY.—*N.* sufficiency, adequacy, enough, wherewithal, competence.

abundance, plenitude, plenty, copiousness, amplitude, profusion, full measure; fill; luxuriance, affluence, fat of the land.

rich man, etc. (*wealth*), 803; financier, banker, plutocrat.

V. suffice, do, just do [*both colloq.*], satisfy, pass muster; have enough, have one's fill.

abound, teem, flow, stream, rain, shower down; pour, pour in; swarm; bristle with.

Adj. sufficient, enough, adequate, up to the mark, commensurate, competent, satisfactory; ample; plenty, plentiful, plenteous; copious, abundant; replete, unstinted, inexhaustible.

rich, affluent, etc. (*wealthy*), 803; luxuriant, etc. (*fertile*), 168.

Adv. without stint; to the good.

640. INSUFFICIENCY.—*N.* **insufficiency,** inadequacy, incompetence, deficiency, imperfection, shortcoming; paucity, stint, bare subsistence; poverty, etc., 804.

scarcity, dearth; want, need, lack, poverty, starvation, famine, drought.

dole, mite, pittance; short allowance; half rations.

depletion, emptiness, vacancy; ebb tide; low water; insolvency, etc. (*nonpayment*), 808.

poor man, pauper, etc., 804; bankrupt.

V. **want,** lack, need, require; be in want, etc. (*poor*), 804; live from hand to mouth.

impoverish, drain, drain of resources; stint, etc., 819.

Adj. **insufficient,** inadequate, too little, not enough; incompetent, perfunctory, deficient, wanting; imperfect; ill-furnished, ill-provided, ill-stored.

short of, out of, destitute of, devoid of, bereft of, slack, at a low ebb; empty, vacant, bare; dry, drained.

unprovided, unsupplied, unfurnished; unfed; empty-handed.

meager, poor, thin, spare, stinted, starved, emaciated, undernourished, underfed, half-starved, famine-stricken, famished.

scarce, scant, not to be had, scurvy, stingy, etc., 819; at the end of one's tether; without resources, in want.

Adv. in default of, for want of; failing.

641. REDUNDANCE.—*N.* **redundance,** too much, too many, superabundance, superfluity, exuberance, profuseness; profusion, plenty, repletion, plethora, glut, congestion, surfeit, overdose, oversupply, overflow; excess, surplus, remainder.

V. **superabound,** overabound, swarm; bristle with, overflow, run over; run riot; overrun, overstock, overdose, overfeed, overload, overburden, overwhelm, overshoot the mark; gorge, glut, load, drench, inundate, deluge, flood; send (*or* carry) coals to Newcastle.

cloy, choke, suffocate; pile up, lay on thick, lavish.

Adj. **redundant,** turgid; exuberant, inordinate, superabundant, excess, overmuch, replete, profuse, lavish, prodigal; exorbitant, extravagant, overflowing; gorged, stuffed.

superfluous, unnecessary, needless, over and above, supernumerary, spare, duplicate, supererogatory.

Adv. **over and above;** over much, too much; too far; over, too; over head and ears, over one's head; up to one's eyes; extra.

642. IMPORTANCE.—*N.* **importance,** consequence, moment, prominence, consideration, mark; weight, influence; value, usefulness; greatness, etc., 31; superiority, etc., 33; notability.

salient point, outstanding feature; cardinal point: substance, gist, sum and substance, cream, salt, core, kernel, heart, nucleus; key, keynote; keystone.

import, significance, concern; emphasis, interest.

gravity, seriousness, solemnity; pressure, urgency, stress.

V. **be important**, be somebody, be something; import, signify, matter, carry weight; come to the front, lead the way, take the lead.

value, care for, set store upon *or* by.

accentuate, emphasize, lay stress on; mark, underline, underscore.

Adj. **important**, of importance, momentous, material, considerable, weighty, influential, notable, prominent, salient, signal; memorable, remarkable; stirring, eventful.

grave, serious, earnest, grand, solemn, impressive, commanding, imposing.

urgent, pressing, critical, crucial, instant.

foremost, principal, leading, chief, main, prime, primary; capital; superior, etc., 33; marked, rare; paramount, essential, vital, radical, cardinal.

significant, telling, trenchant, emphatic, pregnant.

Adv. **in the main**; above all, in the first place, before everything else.

643. UNIMPORTANCE.—*N.* **unimportance**, insignificance, nothingness, immateriality.

triviality, levity, frivolity, paltriness, smallness, matter of indifference; no object.

nothing, small (*or* trifling) matter; joke, jest, snap of the fingers, fudge, fiddlestick, incident, mere nothing, nonentity.

toy, plaything, gewgaw, bauble, trinket, bagatelle, kickshaw, knickknack.

trumpery, trash, rubbish, stuff, frippery; chaff, dross, froth, scum, bubble, smoke; weed; refuse.

trifle, straw, pin, fig, button, feather, continental, jot, mote, rap, old song; cent, red cent; picayune [*colloq*].

nine days' wonder, flash in the pan, much ado about nothing, tempest in a teapot.

minutiae, details, minor details.

V. **be unimportant**, not matter, matter (*or* signify) little, not matter a straw.

make light of, catch at straws, make mountains out of molehills.

Adj. **unimportant**, immaterial; nonessential, unessential, irrelevant; indifferent, mediocre, passable, fair, tolerable, commonplace; mere, common, ordinary, insignificant.

trifling, trivial; slight, slender, light, airy, flimsy, idle, shallow, weak, powerless, frivolous, petty, finical.

paltry, poor, pitiful, contemptible, puerile; sorry, mean, meager, shabby, miserable, wretched, vile, niggardly, scurvy, beggarly, worthless, two-by-four [*colloq.*], cheap, trashy, catchpenny, gimcrack, trumpery; one-horse [*colloq.*]

Adv. rather, somewhat, fairly, fairly well, tolerably.

644. UTILITY.—*N.* utility, usefulness, efficacy, efficiency, adequacy; helpfulness, service, use, help, aid, applicability, subservience; value, worth, productiveness, utilization.

commonweal, public good; utilitarianism.

V. avail, serve, conduce, tend, answer (*or* serve) one's turn; benefit, bear fruit, profit, remunerate.

act a part, etc. (*action*), 680; discharge a function, render a service; bestead, stand one in good stead; help, etc., 707.

Adj. **useful,** of use, serviceable, subservient, conducive, helpful.

advantageous, beneficial, profitable, gainful, remunerative, valuable; invaluable, beyond price; prolific.

adequate; efficient, efficacious; effective, effectual.

applicable, available, ready, handy, at hand, commodious, adaptable.

645. INUTILITY.—*N.* inutility, uselessness, inefficacy, futility; ineptitude, inadequacy, unfitness; inefficiency, incompetence, unskillfulness, labor in vain; worthlessness; triviality, etc., 643.

rubbish, junk, lumber, litter, odds and ends, shoddy; rags, leavings, dross, trash, refuse, sweepings, offscourings, waste, rubble, debris; chaff, stubble, dregs, weeds, tares.

V. **labor in vain;** seek (*or* strive) after impossibilities; use vain efforts, beat the air, pour water into a sieve, bay at the moon; cast pearls before swine, carry coals to Newcastle.

render useless, dismantle, dismast, disqualify; disable, hamstring, cripple, lame; spike guns, clip the wings; put out of gear.

Adj. **useless,** inutile, futile, unavailing, bootless; inoperative, inadequate, inept, inefficient, ineffectual, incompetent.

worthless, valueless, unsalable; not worth a straw, good for nothing, dear at any price; vain, empty, inane; gainless, profitless, fruitless; unserviceable, unprofitable; ill-spent; effete, barren, sterile, impotent, worn out, unproductive; uncalled for; unnecessary, unneeded, superfluous.

646. EXPEDIENCE.—*N.* expedience, desirability, fitness, propriety, utility, advantage, opportunity; opportunism; pragmatism.

V. **be expedient,** suit, befit; suit (*or* befit) the occasion.

Adj. **expedient,** desirable, advisable, acceptable; convenient; worth while, meet; fit, fitting, due, proper, eligible, seemly, becoming, befitting; opportune, advantageous, etc., 644; suitable.

practical, practicable, effective, pragmatic, pragmatical.

Adv. in the nick of time; in the right place.

647. INEXPEDIENCE.—*N.* inexpedience, undesirability, impropriety, unfitness, inutility, disadvantage, inconvenience, inadvisability.

V. be inexpedient, come amiss, embarrass, put to inconvenience.

Adj. **inexpedient,** undesirable; inadvisable, ill-advised, unsuitable, troublesome, objectionable, ineligible, inadmissible, inconvenient, discommodious, disadvantageous; inappropriate, unfit; unsatisfactory, unprofitable, inept, inopportune, improper, unseemly.

clumsy, awkward; cumbrous, cumbersome, lumbering, unwieldy, hulky.

648. [Good qualities] GOODNESS.—*N.* goodness, excellence, merit; beneficence, benevolence, etc., 906; virtue, etc., 944; value, worth, price.

perfection, quintessence; superiority, etc., 33; prime, flower, cream, elite, pick, A 1 *or* A number 1 [*colloq.*], pick of the crop, salt of the earth; prodigy, wonder; gem of the first water, treasure, one in a thousand.

good man, etc., 948.

V. be beneficial, produce (*or* do) good, profit, benefit, improve, be the making of, make a man of; do a good turn, confer an obligation.

be good, be pure gold, look good to [*colloq.*]; excel, transcend, stand the test; pass muster, pass an examination.

vie, challenge, comparison, emulate, rival.

Adj. **beneficial,** valuable, of value; useful, etc., 644; advantageous, profitable; edifying, salutary.

harmless, innocuous, innocent, inoffensive.

favorable; propitious, etc. (*hope-giving*), 858; fair.

good, excellent; better; superior, etc., 33; above par; nice, fine; genuine, etc. (*true*), 494.

choice, best, select, picked, elect, rare, priceless, matchless, peerless, unequaled, unparalleled, inimitable, crack [*colloq.*], crackajack [*slang*], gilt-edge [*colloq.*]; superfine, of the first water; first-rate, first-class; high-wrought, exquisite, admirable, capital, estimable, precious, priceless, invaluable, inestimable.

satisfactory, up to the mark, unexceptionable, unobjectionable.

Adv. for one's benefit.

649. [Bad qualities] BADNESS.—*N.* badness, hurtfulness, virulence; abomination, pestilence, guilt, depravity, vice, etc., 945; malignity, malevolence.

bane, etc., 663; plague spot, evil star, ill-wind; hoodoo [*colloq.*], jinx [*slang*], Jonah; snake in the grass, skeleton in the closet; thorn in the flesh.

ill-treatment, annoyance, molestation, abuse, oppression, persecution, outrage, misusage, scathe, injury.

bad man, etc., 949; evildoer, etc., 913.

V. hurt, harm, scathe, injure; pain, etc., 830.

wrong, aggrieve, oppress, persecute, trample upon; overburden, weigh down; victimize.

maltreat, abuse; ill-use, ill-treat; buffet, bruise, scratch, maul; smite, molest, do violence; stab, pierce.

Adj. hurtful, harmful, baneful, baleful, injurious, deleterious, detrimental, noxious, pernicious, mischievous, mischief-making, malignant, prejudicial; oppressive, burdensome, onerous; malign.

corrupting, virulent, venomous, corrosive; poisonous, deadly, destructive.

bad, ill, arrant, dreadful; horrid, horrible; dire; rank, foul, rotten.

unsatisfactory, indifferent, deteriorated, below par, imperfect, ill-conditioned.

deplorable, wretched, sad, grievous, lamentable, pitiful, pitiable, woeful.

evil, wrong; depraved, wicked, etc., 945; shocking; reprehensible.

hateful, abominable, vile, base, villainous, detestable, execrable, cursed, accursed, damnable, diabolic.

Adv. to one's cost; where the shoe pinches.

650. PERFECTION.—*N.* perfection; paragon, pink, pink (*or* acme) of perfection.

model, standard, pattern, mirror.

masterpiece, master stroke, prize winner, prize; superexcellence.

V. perfect, bring to perfection, ripen, mature; consummate, crown, put the finishing touch to (*or* upon); complete.

Adj. perfect, faultless, immaculate, spotless, impeccable, unblemished, sound, scathless, intact; consummate, finished.

best, model, standard; inimitable, unparalleled, beyond all praise.

Adv. clean as a whistle; with a finish; to the limit.

651. IMPERFECTION.—*N.* imperfection; deficiency, inadequacy, defection, badness, immaturity.

fault, defect, weak point; screw loose; flaw, taint, blemish, weakness, shortcoming, drawback.

V. be imperfect, have a defect, lie under a disadvantage; not pass muster, fall short.

Adj. imperfect, deficient, defective, faulty, unsound, tainted, out of order; warped, injured; inadequate, crude, incomplete, below par.

indifferent, middling, ordinary, mediocre, average, tolerable, fair, passable; decent; not bad, not amiss; admissible, bearable.

inferior, secondary, second-rate, one-horse [*colloq.*]; two-by-four [*colloq.*].

Adv. to a limited extent, pretty, moderately, considering.

652. CLEANNESS.—*N.* cleanness, purity, purification, purgation; ablution, lavation; disinfection, drainage, sewerage.

bath, bathroom, swimming pool, swimming bath, public bath, baths, bathhouse, lavatory; laundry, washhouse.
cleaner, washerwoman, laundress, laundryman, washerman; scavenger, sweeper; street sweeper, white wing [*local*]; dustman.
brush; broom, vacuum cleaner, carpet sweeper; mop, swab, hose.

cathartic, purgative, aperient, laxative.

V. **clean**, cleanse; rinse, flush, mop, sponge, scour, swab, scrub; wash, lave, launder; purify; purge, expurgate, clarify, refine.

strain, separate, filter, filtrate, drain; percolate.

sift, winnow, sieve, bolt, screen, riddle; pick. weed.

comb, rake, scrape, rasp; card.

sweep, brush, brush up, rout out; clean house, spruce up [*colloq.*].

disinfect, fumigate, ventilate, deodorize; whitewash.

Adj. **clean**, cleanly, pure, immaculate, spotless, stainless, unspotted, unsoiled, unsullied, untainted, sweet.

neat, spruce, tidy, trim, cleaned.

653. UNCLEANNESS.—*N.* uncleanness, impurity; defilement, contamination, abomination; taint.

decay, putrefaction; corruption; mold, mildew, dry rot, caries [*med.*].

squalor, squalidness, slovenliness.

dirt, filth, soil, slop; dust, smoke, soot, smudge, smut, grime.
dregs, grounds, lees, sediment, heeltap; dross, ashes, cinders; scum, froth.

sty, pigsty, lair, den, Augean stable, sink of corruption; slum, rookery.

mud, mire, quagmire, silt, slime, slush.

V. **rot**, putrefy, fester, rankle, reek; mold, molder, go bad.

soil, smoke, tarnish, spot, smear; daub, blot, blur, smudge, smutch, smirch; drabble, besmear, befoul, splash, stain, sully.

pollute, defile, debase, contaminate, taint, corrupt.

Adj. **unclean**, dirty, filthy, grimy, soiled, dusty, smutty, sooty; mussy [*colloq.*].

uncleanly, slovenly, slatternly, untidy, frowzy, sluttish, unkempt, unwashed, squalid.

offensive, nasty, coarse, foul, impure, abominable, beastly, reeky, fetid; moldy, musty, rancid, bad, touched, rotten, corrupt, tainted, putrid; gory, bloody.

654. HEALTH.—*N.* health, sanity; soundness, vigor; good (*or* perfect, excellent, robust) health; bloom, convalescence, strength, poise.

V. **be in health,** bloom, flourish, enjoy good health.

return to health; recover, etc., 660; get better, convalesce, be convalescent, recruit; restore to health, cure.

Adj. **healthy,** healthful, in health, well, sound, whole, strong, blooming, hearty, hale, fresh, green, florid, hardy, robust, vigorous, in fine fettle; chipper [*colloq.*].

uninjured, unscathed, unmarred, without a scratch, safe and sound.

655. DISEASE.—*N.* disease; illness, sickness; infirmity, ailment, indisposition; complaint, disorder, malady, loss of health, delicacy, delicate health, invalidism, malnutrition, want of nourishment; prostration, decline, collapse, decay.

visitation, attack, seizure, stroke, fit, epilepsy, apoplexy, palsy, paralysis; shock; shell shock.

taint, virus, pollution, infection, contagion; epidemic, plague, pestilence.

Science of disease: pathology, therapeutics; diagnostics, diagnosis.

V. **ail,** suffer, be affected with, droop, flag, languish, sicken, pine, dwindle; waste away, fail, lose strength, be laid by the heels; lie helpless.

Adj. **sick,** ill, not well, indisposed, ailing, squeamish, poorly, seedy [*colloq.*], laid up, confined, bedridden, in hospital, on the sick list; out of health, out of sorts [*colloq.*], under the weather [*colloq.*]; valetudinary.

sickly, infirm, unsound, unhealthy, weakly, drooping, flagging, lame, halt, crippled, halting.

diseased, morbid, tainted, poisoned, septic; mangy, leprous, cankered; rotten, withered; palsied, paralytic; consumptive, tubercular, tuberculous.

656. HEALTHINESS.—*N.* healthiness, wholesomeness; healthfulness, salubrity.

Preservation of health: hygiene, pure air, exercise, nourishment, tonic; immunity; sanitarium, sanatorium.

V. **be salubrious,** make for health, conduce to health; be good for, agree with.

Adj. **healthy,** healthful; salubrious, salutary, wholesome, sanitary, prophylactic; benign, bracing, tonic, invigorating, nutritious; hygienic.

innocuous, innocent; harmless, uninjurious, immune.

657. UNHEALTHINESS.—*N.* unhealthiness, plague spot; malaria, insalubrity; contagion; poisonousness.

V. **be unhealthy,** disagree with; shorten one's days.

Adj. **unhealthy,** insalubrious, unwholesome, noxious, noisome; pestiferous, pestilential; virulent, venomous, poisonous, septic, toxic, deadly.

infectious, contagious, catching, communicable, epidemic, sporadic, endemic; epizootic [*of animals*].

658. IMPROVEMENT.—*N.* **improvement,** amelioration, betterment; recovery, mend, amendment, emendation; advancement, advance, promotion, preferment, elevation, increase.

cultivation, culture, march of intellect, civilization.

reform, reformation; revision, radical reform; correction, refinement, elaboration; purification, repair.

reformer, progressive, radical.

V. **improve,** mend, amend, better, ameliorate, relieve; correct, repair, restore.

improve upon; rectify; enrich, mellow, elaborate, fatten.

refresh, revive; invigorate, strengthen, recruit, renew, revivify, freshen.

promote, cultivate, advance, forward, enhance, bring forward, foster.

revise, edit, review, make corrections, make improvements.

reform, remodel, reorganize, reclaim, civilize, lift, uplift, inspire.

Adj. **better,** better off, all the better for; improving, progressive, improved.

corrigible, improvable, curable.

Adv. **on consideration,** on reconsideration, on second thought.

659. DETERIORATION.—*N.* **deterioration,** debasement; wane, ebb, recession, retrogradation, decrease.

degeneracy, degeneration, degradation, depravation, depravity, demoralization.

injury, damage, loss, detriment, harm, impairment, outrage, havoc, inroad, ravage, vitiation, discoloration, pollution, poisoning, contamination, canker, corruption, adulteration, alloy.

decline, declension, declination; decadence, falling off; senility, decrepitude.

decay, dilapidation, wear and tear, erosion, corrosion, rottenness; moth and rust, dry rot, blight, atrophy.

V. **deteriorate,** degenerate, fall off, wane, ebb; retrograde, decline, droop, run to seed *or* waste, lapse, break down, crack, shrivel, fade, wither, molder, rot, rankle, decay, go bad; rust, crumble, shake, totter, perish.

corrupt, taint, infect, contaminate, poison, envenom, canker, blight, rot, pollute, defile, vitiate, debase, deprave, degrade; alloy, adulterate, tamper with, prejudice; pervert, demoralize, brutalize.

embitter, exasperate, irritate.

injure, impair, damage, harm, hurt, spoil, mar, despoil, waste; overrun, ravage, pillage

wound, stab, pierce, maim, lame, cripple, hamstring, mangle, mutilate, disfigure, blemish, deface, warp.

Adj. deteriorated, unimproved, injured, degenerate, imperfect; battered, weathered, weather-beaten, stale, dilapidated, faded, worn, wasted, wilted, shabby, threadbare, frayed.

decayed, moth-eaten, worm-eaten, mildewed, rusty, moldy, seedy [*colloq.*], timeworn, effete, crumbling, moldering, rotten, cankered, blighted, tainted; decrepit, broken-down, worn-out, used up [*colloq.*].

stagnant, backward, unprogressive.

Adv. on the downgrade, on the downward track; beyond hope.

660. RESTORATION.—*N.* restoration, replacement, rehabilitation, reconstruction, reproduction, renovation, renewal, revival, resuscitation, reanimation, reorganization; redemption, restitution, relief, redress, retrieval, reclamation, recovery, convalescence, resumption.

renaissance, renascence, rebirth, new birth, regeneration, regeneracy, resurrection.

repair, repairing, reparation, mending; recruiting.

mender, repairer, tinker, cobbler.

V. recover, rally, revive; come to, come round, come to oneself; pull through, weather the storm, be oneself again; get well, survive, reappear.

restore, put back, reinstate, replace, rehabilitate, re-establish, reconstruct, rebuild, reorganize, convert, recondition, renew, renovate; regenerate; rejuvenate.

redeem, reclaim, recover, retrieve; rescue, etc. (*deliver*), 672.

cure, heal, remedy, doctor, bring round, set on one's legs.

resuscitate, revive, reanimate, revivify, reinvigorate, refresh.

repair, mend, put in repair, retouch, tinker, cobble, patch up, darn; stanch, calk, splice.

Adj. restored, convalescent, rejuvenated, renascent.

restorative, recuperative, curative, remedial.

restorable, remediable, retrievable, curable.

661. RELAPSE.—*N.* relapse, lapse; falling back, retrogradation; deterioration, etc., 659; backsliding.

V. relapse, lapse, fall (*or* slip) back, have a relapse, be overcome, be overtaken, yield again to, fall again into, return, retrograde.

Adj. backsliding, retrograde.

662. REMEDY.—*N.* remedy, help, redress, febrifuge; antipoison, antidote, emetic; stimulant, tonic; prophylactic, antiseptic, germicide, disinfectant; restorative; specific; cure, sovereign remedy, panacea.

materia medica, pharmacy, pharmaceutics; pharmacopoeia.

narcotic, opium, morphine, cocaine, hashish, dope [*slang*]; sedative.

physic, medicine, simples, drug, potion, draft, dose, pill, medicament; recipe, receipt, prescription; patent medicine, nostrum; elixir, balm, balsam, cordial.

salve, ointment, oil, lenitive, lotion, embrocation, liniment.

treatment, regimen, diet; dietary, dietetics; operation, the knife [*colloq.*], surgical operation; major operation.

healing art, practice of medicine, therapeutics; allopathy, homeopathy, osteopathy, eclecticism, surgery; faith cure, faith healing, mind cure, psychotherapy, psychotherapeutics; vocational therapy; dentistry.

hospital, surgery, infirmary, clinic, sanitarium, sanatorium; springs, baths, spa; asylum, home; Red Cross; ambulance.

dispensary, drugstore.

doctor, physician, medical man, general practitioner; specialist, consultant; surgeon.

intern, anesthetist, aurist, oculist, dentist, dental surgeon; osteopath, osteopathist; nurse, sister, nursing sister; apothecary, druggist, pharmacist, pharmaceutical chemist, Hippocrates, Galen; masseur (*fem.* masseuse), rubber.

V. **apply a remedy,** doctor [*colloq.*], dose, physic, nurse, minister to, attend, dress the wounds; relieve, palliate, heal, cure, remedy, restore.

Adj. **remedial,** restorative, corrective, palliative, healing; sanatory, sanative; prophylactic; medical, medicinal; therapeutic, surgical; tonic, sedative, lenitive; allopathic, homeopathic, eclectic; aperient, laxative, cathartic, purgative; septic; aseptic, antiseptic.

dietetic, dietary, alimentary; nutritious, nutritive; digestive, digestible.

663. BANE.—*N.* **bane,** curse, thorn in the flesh; bête noir [F.], bugbear; evil, scourge; fungus, mildew; dry rot; canker, cancer; poison, virus, venom; stench, fetor, poison gas.

sting, fang, thorn, bramble, brier, nettle.

Science of poisons: toxicology.

Adj. **baneful,** poisonous, etc. (*unwholesome*), 657.

664. SAFETY.—*N.* **safety,** security, surety, impregnability, invulnerability, escape, means of escape; safeguard, palladium; sheet anchor; rock, tower.

guardianship, wardship, wardenship; tutelage, custody, safekeeping, protection; auspices.

protector, guardian; warden, warder; preserver, lifesaver, custodian, duenna, chaperon.

safe-conduct, escort, convoy; guard, shield, guardian angel; tutelary deity (*or* saint).

watchman, patrolman, policeman, police officer, officer [*colloq.*]; cop, copper [*both slang*], bluecoat [*colloq.*], constable; detective, spotter [*slang*]; sheriff, deputy; sentinel, sentry, scout.

armed force, garrison, lifeguard, state guard, militia, regular army, navy; volunteer; marine, etc , 726; battleship, man-of-war, etc., 726.

judge, justice, judiciary, magistrate, justice of the peace.

V. protect, watch over, take care of, preserve, cover, screen, shelter, shroud, flank, ward, guard; defend, take precautions.

escort, support, accompany, convoy.

watch, mount guard, patrol, scout, spy.

Adj. safe, secure, sure, on terra firma [L.]; on the safe side; undercover, under lock and key; out of danger, protected; at anchor, high and dry, above-water; safe and sound.

snug, seaworthy, watertight, weatherproof, waterproof, fireproof; bombproof, shellproof.

defensible, tenable, proof against, invulnerable, unassailable, impregnable.

guardian, tutelary, protective.

Adv. with impunity.

665. DANGER.—*N.* danger, peril, insecurity, jeopardy, risk, hazard, venture, precariousness, instability; exposure, vulnerability, vulnerable point, heel of Achilles; forlorn hope.

Sense of danger: apprehension, etc., 860.

V. endanger, expose to danger, imperil, jeopardize, beard the lion in his den; sail too near the wind.

risk, hazard, venture, adventure, stake, set at hazard; run the gantlet.

Adj. dangerous, hazardous, perilous, unsafe, unprotected, insecure.

defenseless, guardless, unsheltered, unshielded; vulnerable, exposed; at bay.

precarious, critical, ticklish; slippery, between Scylla and Charybdis, between two fires; under fire; at stake, in question.

unsteady, unstable, shaky, tottering, top-heavy, tumble-down, ramshackle, crumbling, helpless, trembling in the balance; nodding to its fall.

threatening, ominous, ill-omened, alarming.

666. [Means of safety] REFUGE.—*N.* refuge, sanctuary, retreat, fastness, stronghold, fortress, castle, keep; asylum, shelter, covert, ark, home, hiding place.

anchorage, roadstead; breakwater, port, haven, harbor, pier, jetty, embankment, quay, wharf.

anchor, sheet anchor, grapnel, grappling iron, mainstay, support, safeguard.

667. [Source of danger] PITFALL.—*N.* pitfall, ambush, trap, snare, mine, spring gun.

rocks, reefs, sunken rocks, snags; sands, quicksands; breakers, shoals, shallows, lee shore, rockbound coast.

abyss, abysm, pit, void, chasm.

whirlpool, eddy, vortex, rapids, undertow; current, tiderace, maelstrom; eagre, bore, tidal wave.

pest, ugly customer, incendiary, firebug [*slang*]; firebrand; hornet's nest.

sword of Damocles; wolf at the door, snake in the grass, snake in one's bosom.

668. WARNING.—*N.* warning, caution, notice, premonition, prediction; symptom; lesson, admonition; handwriting on the wall, monitor, warning voice; stormy petrel, bird of ill omen, gathering clouds.

watchtower, beacon, signal post; lighthouse, etc., 550.

sentinel, sentry; watch, watchman; watch and ward; watchdog; patrol, picket, scout, spy, lookout, flagman.

V. warn, caution; forewarn, admonish, forbode, give warning; put on one's guard; sound the alarm.

beware, take warning, look out, keep watch and ward.

Adj. premonitory, cautionary; ominous, threatening, lowering, minatory; symptomatic.

Adv. with alarm, on guard, after due warning, with one's eyes open.

669. [Indication of danger] ALARM.—*N.* alarm; alarum, alarm bell, tocsin, beat of drum, sound of trumpet, hue and cry; signal of distress, SOS; fog signal, siren; yellow flag; danger signal; red light, red flag; fire alarm, still alarm; burglar alarm; police whistle.

V. alarm, give (*or* raise, sound) an alarm, warn, ring the tocsin.

670. PRESERVATION.—*N.* preservation, safekeeping, conservation, economy, maintenance, support, salvation, deliverance, etc., 672.

Means of preservation: prophylaxis; preserver, preservative; hygiene, hygienics; ensilage; dehydration, evaporation, drying, canning, pickling.

V. preserve, maintain, keep, sustain, support; save, rescue, make safe, take care of, guard; husband, economize.

embalm, dry, cure, salt, pickle, season, bottle, pot, tin, can; dehydrate, evaporate.

Adj. preserved, unimpaired, unbroken, uninjured, unhurt, unmarred; safe, safe and sound, intact, with a whole skin.

671. ESCAPE.—*N.* escape, flight, evasion, loophole, retreat; narrow (*or* hairbreadth) escape; close call [*colloq.*]; impunity.

refugee, etc. (*fugitive*), 623.

V. escape, make one's escape; break jail; get off, get clear off, elude, make off, give one the slip; wriggle out of; break loose, break away.

Adj. stolen away; fled; scot-free.

672. DELIVERANCE.—*N.* deliverance, extrication, rescue, ransom, reprieve, respite; armistice, truce; liberation, emancipation; redemption, salvation.

V. deliver, extricate, rescue, save, free, liberate, set free, release, emancipate, redeem, ransom; come to the rescue.

673. PREPARATION.—*N.* preparation, provision, arrangement, anticipation, precaution, forecast, rehearsal; dissemination, propaganda.

groundwork, steppingstone; foundation; scaffold, scaffolding.

elaboration, ripening, evolution; concoction, digestion; hatching, incubation.

Preparation of men: training, education, equipment, inurement; novitiate.

Preparation of food: cooking, cookery, culinary art; brewing.

Preparation of the soil: tilling, plowing, sowing, cultivation.

preparedness, readiness, ripeness, mellowness; maturity.

preparer, trainer, coach, teacher, pioneer; prophet; forerunner, etc. (*precursor*), 64; sappers and miners.

V. prepare, prime, get (*or* make) ready, arrange, make preparations, settle preliminaries, get up; prepare the ground, lay the foundations, erect the scaffolding.

elaborate, mature, ripen, mellow, season, bring to maturity; nurture; cook, brew.

equip, arm, man; fit out, fit up; furnish, rig, dress, accouter, array.

prepare for, guard against, forearm; make provision for; provide, provide against; set one's house in order, make all snug; clear decks, clear for action.

be prepared, be ready, watch and pray, keep one's powder dry, lie in wait for, anticipate, foresee.

Adj. preparatory, precautionary, provident; provisional, preliminary; in embryo, in hand, in train; afoot, afloat; on foot, brewing, hatching, forthcoming.

prepared, ready, cut and dried, available, at one's elbow, ready for use, all ready; handy.

ripe, mature, mellow; seasoned, practiced, experienced.

elaborate, labored, high-wrought, worked up.

Adv. **in preparation,** in anticipation of; afoot, astir, abroad.

674. NONPREPARATION.—*N.* **nonpreparation,** unpreparedness; improvidence.

immaturity, crudity, rawness; disqualification.

Absence of art: nature, state of nature; virgin soil, unweeded garden; rough diamond; raw material.

improvisation, etc. (*impulse*), 612.

V. **be unprepared;** lie fallow; live from hand to mouth.

extemporize, improvise; cook up, fix up.

surprise, drop in [*colloq.*], take (*or* catch) unawares; take by surprise.

Adj. **unprepared,** incomplete, premature, rudimental, embryonic, immature, unripe, callow, unfledged, unhatched; uncooked, raw, green, crude; coarse; rough, roughhewn; in the rough.

untaught, uneducated, untrained, untutored, unlicked.

fallow, unsown, untilled, uncultivated.

unfitted, disqualified, unqualified, ill-digested; unready, unorganized, unfurnished, unprovided, unequipped.

shiftless, improvident, unthrifty, thriftless, happy-go-lucky; slack, remiss.

Adv. **inadvertently,** by surprise, without premeditation; extempore.

675. ESSAY—*N.* **essay,** trial, endeavor, attempt; aim, struggle, venture, adventure, speculation, probation, experiment.

V. **try, essay;** experiment, etc., 463; endeavor, strive; tempt, attempt, venture, adventure, speculate, tempt fortune.

Adj. **tentative,** experimental, empirical, problematic, probationary.

Adv. **on examination,** on trial, at a venture; by rule of thumb.

676. UNDERTAKING.—*N.* **undertaking,** adventure, venture, engagement, compact, enterprise; pilgrimage.

V. **undertake,** engage in, embark in, launch (*or* plunge) into, volunteer; apprentice oneself to; engage, contract, devote oneself to, take up, take on, take in hand; tackle [*colloq.*]; set about; launch forth; betake oneself to, turn one's hand to, have in hand, begin, broach, institute.

Adj. **energetic;** full of pep [*slang*]; enterprising, adventurous, venturesome.

677. USE.—*N.* **use,** employ, exercise, application, appliance; disposal; consumption; agency, usefulness, etc., 644; benefit, recourse, resort, avail.

Conversion to use: utilization, utility, service, wear.

Way of using: usage, employment, *modus operandi* [L.].

user, consumer, market, demand.

V. **use,** make use of, employ, put to use, apply, put in action, set in motion, set to work; ply, work, wield, handle, manipulate; exert, exercise, practice, avail oneself of, profit by; resort to, have recourse to, recur to, take up, try.

utilize, turn to account (*or* use); exploit; administer, apply, bring into play; task, tax, put to task; devote, dedicate, consecrate.

consume, use up, devour, swallow up; absorb, expend; wear.

Adj. **useful,** etc., 644; instrumental, subservient, utilitarian, pragmatic.

678. DISUSE.—*N.* **disuse;** forbearance, abstinence; relinquishment, abandonment; desuetude, disusage.

V. **not use;** do without, dispense with, let alone, forbear, abstain, spare, waive, neglect; keep back, reserve.

disuse; lay up, lay by, shelve; set aside, lay aside, leave off, have done with; supersede, discard, throw aside, relinquish; destroy, make away with, cast (*or* throw) overboard; dismantle.

Adj. **disused,** done with, run down, worn out; unemployed, unapplied, unexercised, uncalled for, not required.

679. MISUSE.—*N.* **misuse,** misusage, misapplication, misappropriation; abuse, profanation, desecration; waste.

V. **misuse,** misemploy, misapply; exploit; misappropriate; desecrate, abuse, profane.

overtask, overtax, overwork; squander, waste.

680. ACTION.—*N.* **action,** performance, perpetration, exercise, movement, operation, evolution, work, employment; labor, exertion, execution; procedure, conduct; handicraft; business, agency.

deed, act, stitch, touch, transaction, job, doings, dealings, proceeding, measure, step, maneuver, bout, passage, move, stroke, blow; feat, exploit, achievement; handiwork, craftsmanship, workmanship; manufacture; stroke of policy.

doer, worker, agent, etc., 690.

V. **do,** perform, execute, achieve, transact, enact; commit, perpetrate, inflict; exercise, prosecute, carry on, work, labor, practice, play; employ oneself, ply one's task; officiate, have in hand; shape one's course.

act, operate, take action, take steps, take in hand, put in practice, carry into execution, act upon.

Adj. **in action,** acting, in harness, on duty; at work; operative.

Adv. **in the act,** in the midst of; red-handed.

681. INACTION.—*N.* **inaction,** passiveness, watchful waiting; noninterference; neglect, etc., 460; inactivity, etc., 683; stagnation, vegetation, rest, loafing, want of occupation, unemployment; sinecure; soft snap, cinch [*both slang*].

V. **not do,** not act, not attempt; be inactive, abstain from doing, do nothing, hold, spare; leave (or let) alone; let be, let pass, let things take their course, live and let live; rest upon one's oars; stand aloof; refrain, relax one's efforts; desist, stop, pause, wait; waste time.

undo, do away with; take down, take to pieces; destroy, etc., 162.

Adj. **passive;** unoccupied, unemployed, out of employ (or work, a job); uncultivated, fallow.

Adv. at a stand.

682. ACTIVITY.—*N.* **activity,** animation, life, vivacity, spirit, verve, pep [*slang*], dash, go [*colloq.*], energy, snap, vim.

smartness, nimbleness, agility; quickness, velocity, alacrity, promptitude; dispatch, expedition, haste, etc., 684; punctuality.

eagerness, zeal, ardor, enthusiasm, earnestness, intentness, vigor, devotion, exertion.

industry, assiduity, assiduousness, sedulousness, laboriousness, drudgery, diligence, perseverance, etc., 604*a.*

vigilance, etc., 459; wakefulness; sleeplessness, restlessness; insomnia.

bustle, hustle [*colloq.*], movement, stir, fuss, ado, bother, fidget, flurry.

officiousness, dabbling, meddling; interference, intermeddling; butting in [*slang*], intrusiveness, intrigue.

man of action, busy bee; new broom; devotee, enthusiast, fanatic, zealot, hustler [*colloq.*], live wire, human dynamo [*both colloq.*].

meddler, intriguer, busybody.

V. **be active,** busy oneself in; stir, stir about, bestir oneself; speed, hasten, bustle, fuss; push, go ahead, push forward; make progress; toil, moil, drudge, plod, persist, persevere, hustle [*colloq.*], push [*colloq.*], keep moving, seize the opportunity, lose no time, dash off, make haste.

have a hand in, take an active part, put in one's oar, have a finger in the pie, dabble, intrigue; agitate.

meddle, tamper with, interfere, interpose; obtrude; butt in, horn in [*both slang*].

Adj. **active,** brisk, lively, animated, vivacious, alive, frisky, spirited; nimble, agile, light-footed, nimble-footed.

quick, prompt, instant, ready, alert, spry [*colloq. and dial.*], sharp, smart; fast, etc. (*swift*), 274; capable, expeditious, awake, go-ahead [*colloq.*], live [*colloq.*], hustling [*colloq.*], wide-awake.

enterprising, eager, ardent, strenuous, zealous, resolute.

industrious, assiduous, diligent, sedulous, painstaking, intent, indefatigable, persevering, unwearied, sleepless; busy, occupied; hard at work, hard at it; plodding, hard-working, businesslike.

bustling, restless, fussy, fidgety, pottering.

meddlesome, pushing, officious.

astir, stirring, afoot, on foot, in full swing; on the alert.

Adv. with life and spirit, with might and main, full tilt.

683. INACTIVITY.—*N.* inactivity; inaction, etc., 681; inertness, lull, quiescence; rust.

idleness, remissness, sloth, indolence, dawdling, puttering, relaxation.

languor, dullness, sluggishness, procrastination, torpor, stupor, somnolence, drowsiness, heaviness, hypnotism, lethargy.

sleep, slumber; Morpheus; coma, trance, catalepsy, hypnosis, dream; nap, doze, siesta; hibernation.

idler, drone, dawdler, truant; dead one [*slang*], dummy, bum [*slang*], tramp, hobo, beggar, lounge lizard [*slang*], lounger, loafer, slow-poke, laggard, sluggard.

V. be inactive, do nothing; dawdle, drawl, lag, hang back, slouch, loll, lounge, loaf, loiter; sleep at one's post; take it easy.

dally, dilly-dally, idle (*or* fritter, fool) away time; putter, dabble.

sleep, slumber, be asleep, oversleep, hibernate; doze, drowse, nap, take a nap; fall asleep, drop asleep; get sleepy, nod, go to bed, turn in.

languish, expend itself, flag, hang fire; relax.

Adj. inactive, motionless; unoccupied, unemployed.

indolent, lazy, slothful, idle, remiss, slack, inert, torpid, sluggish, logy, languid, listless; lackadaisical, maudlin; heavy, dull, leaden; dilatory, laggard, slow, flagging; puttering.

sleeping, asleep, comatose; in the arms (*or* lap) of Morpheus.

sleepy, dozy, drowsy, somnolent, lethargic, heavy, heavy with sleep; soporific, hypnotic; dreamy.

Adv. with half-shut eyes, half asleep; in dreams, in dreamland.

684. HASTE.—*N.* haste, urgency, dispatch, acceleration, spurt, forced march, rush, scurry, scuttle, dash; velocity, etc., 274; precipitancy, precipitation, impetuosity; hurry, drive, scramble, bustle, fidget, flurry.

V. haste, hasten, make haste, dash on, push on, press on *or* forward, hurry, scurry, bustle, flutter, scramble, plunge, dash off, rush, express; bestir oneself, etc. (*be active*), 682; lose no time, make short work of; work against time, work under pressure.

quicken, accelerate, expedite, precipitate, urge, whip, spur, flog, goad.

Adj. hasty, hurried, cursory, precipitate, headlong, furious, boisterous, impetuous, hotheaded; feverish, pushing.

in haste, in a hurry, in hot haste, breathless, hard-pressed, urgent.

Adv. with haste, with speed, in haste, apace, amain; at short notice, immediately, posthaste; by cable, by telegraph, by wireless [*colloq.*], by airplane, by return mail, by forced marches.

hastily, precipitately, helter-skelter, hurry-scurry, slapdash, slap-bang; full-tilt, full-drive; heels over head, headlong.

685. LEISURE.—*N.* leisure, convenience; spare time, vacant hour; time, time to spare; holiday, ease.

V. **have leisure**, take one's time (*or* leisure, ease); repose, etc., 687; move slowly, while away the time, be master of one's time, be an idle man.

686. EXERTION.—*N.* exertion, effort, strain, stress, tug, pull, throw, stretch, struggle, spell, spurt; dead lift, heft [*dial.*]; trouble, pains, duty; energy, etc. [*physical*], 171.

exercise, practice, play, gymnastics, field sports; breather [*colloq.*].

labor, work, toil, manual labor, sweat of one's brow, drudgery, slavery.

worker, plodder, laborer, drudge, slave; man of action; Hercules.

V. **labor**, work, toil, sweat, fag, drudge, slave, strive, strain; pull, tug, ply; ply the oar; exert oneself, bestir oneself (*be active*), 682.

work hard; rough it; put forth one's strength, buckle to, set one's shoulder to the wheel, do double duty; burn the candle at both ends, work (*or* fight) one's w y; do one's best, do one's utmost; take pains; strain every nerve; spare no efforts *or* pains.

Adj. **laborious**, elaborate; strained; toilsome, wearisome, burdensome; uphill; herculean.

hard-working, painstaking, strenuous, energetic, never idle.

Adv. with might and main, with all one's might, to the best of one's abilities, tooth and nail, hammer and tongs, heart and soul.

687. REPOSE.—*N.* repose, rest, sleep, etc., 683; relaxation, breathing time; halt, stay, pause, respite.

day of rest, Sabbath, Lord's day, Sunday; holiday, red-letter day, gala day; vacation, recess.

V. **repose**, rest, take rest, take one's ease; lie down, recline, go to rest (*or* bed, sleep).

relax, unbend, slacken, take breath, rest upon one's oars; pause, etc. (*cease*), 142; stay one's hand.

take a holiday, shut up shop; lie fallow.

Adj. **holiday**, festal; sabbatic *or* sabbatical.

688. FATIGUE.—*N.* fatigue, weariness, etc., 841; yawning, drowsiness, lassitude, tiredness, sweat.

faintness, fainting, swoon, exhaustion, collapse, prostration.

V. **be fatigued**, yawn, droop, sink; flag; gasp, pant, puff, blow, drop, swoon, faint, succumb.

fatigue, tire, bore, weary, flag, jade, harass, exhaust, wear out, prostrate.

tax, task, strain; overtask, overwork, overburden, overtax, overstrain, fag, fag out.

Adj. fatigued; weary, etc., 841; drowsy, haggard, toilworn, way-worn, footsore, faint; done up [*colloq.*], exhausted, prostrate, spent, ready to drop, all in [*slang*], dog-tired, tired to death, played out.

worn, worn out; battered, shattered, seedy [*colloq.*], enfeebled.

breathless, short of (*or* out of)breath, blown, puffing and blowing, short-breathed, broken-winded.

689. REFRESHMENT.—*N.* recuperation; recovery of strength, restoration, revival, etc., 660; repair, refreshment; relief, etc., 834.

V. refresh, brace, strengthen, reinvigorate; air, freshen up, recruit, regale, repair, restore, revive; get better, recover (*or* regain) one's strength, recuperate.

Adj. refreshing, recuperative.

690. AGENT.—*N.* agent, doer, actor, performer, perpetrator, operator; executor, executrix; practitioner, worker; minister, etc. (*instrument*), 631; representative, etc. (*commissioner*), 758, (*deputy*), 759; factor, steward; servant, etc., 746; factotum.

workman, artisan, craftsman, handicraftsman, mechanic, operative; working-man, laboring man; hewers of wood and drawers of water; laborer; hand, man, day laborer, journeyman, hack, drudge, roustabout.

maker, artificer, artist, wright, manufacturer, architect, contractor, builder, smith.

machinist, engineer, electrician.

workwoman, charwoman, dressmaker, modiste, seamstress, needlewoman, milliner, laundress, washerwoman.

coworker, associate, fellow worker, co-operator, colleague, confrere; force, staff, personnel.

691. WORKSHOP.—*N.* workshop, laboratory, manufactory, armory, arsenal, mill, factory, studio, atelier; hive, hive of industry, beehive; bindery; dock, dockyard, slip, yard, wharf; foundry, forge, furnace.

melting pot, crucible, caldron, mortar, alembic; matrix.

692. CONDUCT.—*N.* conduct, behavior; deportment, carriage, demeanor, guise, bearing, manner; course of conduct, line of action; role; process, ways, practice, procedure, method; dealing, transaction, business.

policy, tactics, game, generalship, statesmanship, strategy, plan.

management; government, etc., 693; stewardship, husbandry; housekeeping, ménage, regime, regimen, economy; economics, political economy.

career, life, course, walk, province, race, record; execution, treatment; campaign.

V. **transact,** execute; dispatch, proceed with, discharge; carry on (*or* through, out, into effect); work out; go through, get through; enact.

adopt a course, shape one's course, play one's part; shift for oneself, paddle one's own canoe; conduct; manage, etc. (*direct*), 693.

behave, conduct (*or* acquit, carry, comport, bear, demean) oneself.

Adj. **directive,** methodical, businesslike, practical, executive, strategic, economic.

693. DIRECTION.—*N.* direction; management, government, conduct, legislation, regulation, guidance, reins; steerage, pilotage, helm, rudder, needle, compass; guiding star, lodestar, polestar, cynosure.

ministry, administration; stewardship, proctorship; chair; agency.

supervision, superintendence; surveillance, oversight; eye of the master; control, charge; auspices; command, etc. (*authority*), 737.

statesmanship, statecraft, kingcraft, reins of government; director, etc., 694; seat, portfolio.

V. **direct,** manage, govern, conduct; order, prescribe, head, lead, regulate, guide, steer, pilot, take the helm, be at the helm; hold the reins, drive.

superintend, supervise; overlook, oversee, control, handle, look after, see to, administer, patronize; rule, etc. (*command*), 737; hold office.

Adj. **directing,** executive, gubernatorial, supervisory; statesmanlike.

Adv. **in charge of,** under the guidance of, under the auspices of; in control of, at the helm, at the head of.

694. DIRECTOR.—*N.* director, manager, governor, controller, superintendent, supervisor, overseer, supercargo, inspector, foreman, surveyor, taskmaster; master, etc., 745; leader, ringleader, agitator, demagogue, conductor, precentor, bellwether, file leader.

guide, pilot; helmsman, steersman; adviser, etc., 695.

driver, whip, charioteer; coachman, carman, cabman; postilion, muleteer, teamster; chauffeur, motorman, engine driver.

head, headman, chief, principal, president, speaker; chair, chairman; captain, etc. (*master*), 745; superior; prime minister, premier.

officer, functionary, minister, official, bureaucrat, officeholder.

statesman, strategist, legislator, lawgiver, politician, boss [*slang*], political dictator, wirepuller [*colloq.*], power behind the throne, kingmaker.

steward, factor, agent, bailiff, factotum, major-domo, seneschal, housekeeper, shepherd; proctor, curator, librarian.

695. ADVICE.—*N.* **advice,** counsel, word to the wise, suggestion, recommendation, advocacy; consultation; exhortation, expostulation, dissuasion, admonition; guidance.

instruction, charge, injunction, message, speech from the throne.

adviser, prompter; counsel, counselor; monitor, mentor, sage, wise man; teacher, etc., 540; physician; arbiter, referee, judge.

consultation, conference, parley, powwow; reference.

V. **advise,** counsel, suggest, prompt, recommend, prescribe, advocate, exhort, persuade.

enjoin, enforce, charge, instruct, call, call upon, request, dictate.

expostulate, dissuade, admonish, warn.

confer, consult, refer to, call in; follow, take (*or* follow) advice.

696. COUNCIL.—*N.* **council,** committee, privy council, court, chamber, cabinet, board, directorate, syndicate, bench, staff.

Ecclesiastical: convocation, synod, congregation, church, chapter, vestry. consistory, conventicle, conclave, convention.

legislature, parliament, congress, national council, states-general, diet.

Duma [Russia], Storthing *or* Storting [Norway], Rigsdag [Denmark], Riksdag [Sweden], Cortes [Spain], Reichsrath *or* Reichsrat [Austria], Volksraad [Dutch], Dail Eireann [Sinn Fein].

upper house, upper chamber, first chamber, senate, legislative council, House of Lords, House of Peers; Bundesrath *or* Bundesrat [Ger.], federal council, Lagting [Nor.], Landsthing [Den.].

lower house, lower chamber, second chamber, house of representatives, House of Commons, the house, legislative assembly, chamber of deputies; Odelsting [Nor.], Folkething [Den.], Reichstag [Ger.].

assembly, caucus, clique; meeting, sitting, séance, conference, hearing, session, palaver; council fire, powwow.

Representatives: congressman, M.C., senator, representative; member, member of parliament, M.P., assemblyman, councilor.

Adj. curule, congressional, senatorial, parliamentary; synodic *or* synodical.

697. PRECEPT.—*N.* **precept,** direction, instruction, charge; prescript, prescription; recipe, receipt; golden rule; maxim, etc., 496.

rule, canon, law, code, convention; unwritten law; canon law; act, statute, rubric, stage direction, regulation; model, form, formula, technicality.

order, etc. (*command*), 741.

698. SKILL.—*N.* **skill,** skillfulness, address, dexterity, adroitness, expertness, proficiency, competence, craft; facility, knack, trick, sleight; mastery, excellence, sleight of hand, etc. (*deception*), 545.

accomplishment, acquirement, attainment; art, science; finish, technique.

worldly wisdom, knowledge of the world, *savoir-faire* [F.]; tact; mother wit, discretion, finesse; management.

cleverness, talent, ability, ingenuity, capacity, talents, faculty, endowment, forte, turn, gift, genius, intelligence, sharpness, readiness, aptness, aptitude, resourcefulness; felicity, capability, qualification.

expert, adept, etc., 700.

masterpiece, masterwork, chef-d'oeuvre [F.].

V. **be skillful,** excel in, be master of; have a turn for.

take advantage of, make the most of, profit by, make a hit, make a virtue of necessity, make hay while the sun shines.

Adj. **skillful,** dexterous, adroit, expert, apt, handy, quick, deft, ready, smart, proficient, good at, at home in, master of, conversant with; masterly, crack [*colloq.*], crackajack [*slang*], accomplished.

experienced, practiced, skilled, up in, in practice, competent, efficient, qualified, capable, fitted, fit for, trained, initiated, sophisticated, prepared, primed, finished.

clever, able, ingenious, felicitous, gifted, talented, resourceful, inventive; shrewd, sharp, cunning; neat-handed, fine-fingered; nimble-fingered, ambidextrous, sure-footed.

technical, artistic, scientific, workmanlike, businesslike, statesmanlike.

Adv. **skillfully,** artistically, with skill, with fine technique, with consummate skill; like a machine.

699. UNSKILLFULNESS.—*N.* **unskillfulness,** want of skill, incompetence, inability, infelicity, clumsiness, inaptitude, inexperience; disqualification.

mismanagement, misconduct, bad policy, impolicy; maladministration; misrule, misgovernment.

blunder, act of folly, bungle, botch, bad job, sad work.

bungler, etc., 701; fool, etc., 501.

V. **bungle,** blunder, muff [*esp. baseball*], boggle, fumble, botch, mar, spoil, flounder, stumble, trip; mismanage, misdirect, misapply.

mistake, take the shadow for the substance, bark up the wrong tree; be in the wrong box [*colloq.*]; lose one's way, miss one's way; fall into a trap.

Adj. **unskillful,** unskilled, inexpert, incompetent, bungling, awkward, clumsy, gawky, unhandy, maladroit; stupid, ill-qualified, unfit; raw, green, inexperienced; rusty, out of practice.

unaccustomed, unused, untrained, uninitiated; unbusinesslike, unpractical, shiftless; unstatesmanlike.

ill-advised, misadvised; ill-devised, ill-judged, ill-contrived, ill-conducted; misguided, foolish, wild; infelicitous.

700. EXPERT.—*N.* expert, adept, proficient, connoisseur, master, master hand; top sawyer; prima donna, first fiddle; past master.

picked man; medalist, prizeman.

veteran, old stager, old campaigner, man of business, man of the world.

genius; mastermind, master spirit; prodigy of learning, walking encyclopedia, mine of information.

man of cunning, diplomatist, diplomat, Machiavellian; politician, tactician strategist.

701. BUNGLER.—*N.* bungler, blunderer, blunderhead; fumbler, lubber, clown, lout, duffer [*colloq.*]; butter-fingers, muff, muffer [*all colloq.*]; awkward squad; novice, greenhorn.

landlubber, fresh-water sailor, fair-weather sailor, horse marine.

sloven, slattern, slut.

702. CUNNING.—*N.* cunning, craft, subtlety, maneuvering, temporization; circumvention; chicane, chicanery; sharp practice, knavery, jugglery, concealment, guile, duplicity, foul play.

diplomacy, politics, Machiavellianism; gerrymander, jobbery, back-stairs influence.

artifice, art, device, machination; plot, maneuver, stratagem, dodge, wile, trick, trickery, ruse, finesse, subterfuge, evasion, white lie, gold brick [*colloq.*], imposture, deception, net, trap.

schemer, trickster, sly boots [*humorous*], fox, reynard; intriguer, man of cunning.

V. intrigue, live by one's wits; maneuver, gerrymander, finesse, double, temporize, circumvent, outdo, get the better of, throw off one's guard; surprise, waylay, undermine, flatter; have an ax to grind.

Adj. cunning, crafty, artful, skillful; subtle, feline, deep, profound, designing, timeserving, tricky, wily, sly, insidious, stealthy, underhand, double-faced, shifty, deceptive; deceitful, crooked; shrewd, acute; sharp, canny, astute, knowing.

703. ARTLESSNESS.—*N.* artlessness, unsophistication, simplicity, innocence, candor, sincerity, singleness of purpose, honesty.

rough diamond, matter-of-fact man; *enfant terrible* [F.].

V. be artless, think aloud; speak one's mind; be free with one, call a spade a spade; tell the truth, the whole truth, and nothing but the truth.

Adj. artless, natural, pure, confiding, simple, plain, unsophisticated, unaffected, naïve; sincere, frank, open, candid, ingenuous, guileless; unsuspicious, honest, childlike; innocent, straightforward, aboveboard; single-minded.

matter-of-fact, plain-spoken, outspoken; blunt, downright, direct, unflattering, unvarnished.

Adv. in plain words (*or* English); without mincing the matter.

704. DIFFICULTY.—*N.* **difficulty,** hardness, impracticability, uphill work, herculean task; dead weight, dead lift.

dilemma, predicament, fix [*colloq.*], quandary, embarrassment, deadlock, perplexity, intricacy, entanglement, knot, Gordian knot, maze, coil, strait, pass, pinch, rub, critical situation, exigency, crisis, trial, emergency, scrape, slough, quagmire, hot water [*colloq.*], pickle, stew, imbroglio, mess, muddle, botch, hitch, stumbling block.

vexed question, poser, puzzle, knotty point, paradox; hard nut to crack, crux.

V. **be difficult,** go against the grain, try one's patience, go hard with one, pose, perplex, bother, nonplus.

flounder, boggle [*local*], struggle, stick fast; come to a deadlock.

render difficult, enmesh, encumber, embarrass, entangle; spike one's guns.

Adj. **difficult,** hard, tough [*colloq.*]; troublesome, toilsome, irksome; laborious, onerous, arduous, herculean, formidable.

awkward, unwieldy, unmanageable, intractable, stubborn, perverse, refractory, knotted, knotty, thorny; pathless, trackless, intricate.

embarrassing, perplexing, delicate, ticklish, critical, thorny.

in difficulty, in hot water [*colloq.*], in a fix [*colloq.*], in a scrape, between Scylla and Charybdis; on the horns of a dilemma; on the rocks; reduced to straits; hard-pressed; run hard; pinched, straitened; hard up [*slang*]; puzzled, at a loss, at one's wits' end, at a standstill; nonplused, stranded, aground.

Adv. with much ado; uphill, upstream; in the teeth of; against the grain.

705. FACILITY.—*N.* **facility,** ease, easiness, capability, feasibility, practicability; flexibility, pliancy, smoothness, plain sailing; mere child's play; cinch, snap [*both slang*].

V. **be easy,** run smoothly; have full play, obey the helm, work well, work smoothly.

facilitate, smooth, ease, lighten, free, clear, disencumber, disembarrass, disentangle, extricate, unravel, unknot; humor, leave a loophole, leave the matter open; give full play, make way for, pave the way, bridge over.

Adj. **easy,** facile; feasible, practicable, within reach, gettable, accessible.

manageable, tractable; submissive; yielding, ductile, tractable, pliant.

unburdened, unencumbered, unloaded, unobstructed, untrammeled; unrestrained, free, at ease, light.

Adv. **easily,** readily, expertly, adroitly, smoothly, swimmingly, with no effort.

706. HINDRANCE.—*N.* **prevention,** obstruction, stoppage, interruption, interception, hindrance, embarrassment, constriction, restriction, restraint, etc., 751.

interference, interposition, obtrusion; discouragement, disapproval, disapprobation, opposition.

impediment, obstacle, obstruction, knot, snag, hitch, contretemps, stumbling block, lion in the path.

check; encumbrance; clog, brake, anchor; bit, snaffle, curb; drag, load, burden, onus, impedimenta; dead weight; lumber, pack; nightmare, incubus; stay, stop; preventive, prophylactic.

drawback, objection; difficulty, etc., 704; obstacle; ill-wind, head wind; trammel, tether.

damper, wet blanket, kill-joy, dog in the manger, usurper, interloper, opponent; filibusterer.

V. **hinder,** impede, filibuster, embarrass.

avert, keep off, stave off, ward off; obviate; turn aside, draw off, prevent, nip in the bud; retard, slacken, check, counteract, countercheck, preclude, debar, inhibit, restrict.

obstruct, stop, stay, bar, bolt, lock; block, barricade; dam up, put on the brake, put a stop to, interrupt, intercept, oppose, interfere, interpose.

encumber, cramp, hamper; clog, cumber, handicap; choke, saddle with, load with, overload, overwhelm, lumber, entrammel, trammel, incommode, discommode, discompose, corner.

thwart, frustrate, disconcert, balk, foil; circumvent, baffle, override, defeat, spoil, mar, clip the wings of, cripple, damp, dishearten, discountenance, undermine.

Adj. **obstructive,** intrusive, meddlesome; onerous, burdensome; cumbrous, cumbersome.

Adv. **in the way,** with everything against one, through all obstacles, under many difficulties.

707. AID.—*N.* **aid,** assistance, help, succor; support, lift, advance, furtherance, promotion.

patronage, auspices, countenance, favor, interest, advocacy.

sustenance, maintenance, nutrition, nourishment; manna in the wilderness, food, means, subsidy, bounty.

relief, rescue; ministry, ministration; supernatural aid; *deus ex machina* [L.].

supplies, re-enforcements, contingents, recruits, support, ally.

V. **aid,** assist, help, succor, lend a hand; contribute, subscribe to;

take by the hand, take in tow; relieve, rescue; set on one's legs, give new life to, be the making of; re-enforce, recruit; promote, further, forward, advance; speed, expedite, quicken, hasten.

support, sustain, uphold, prop, hold up, bolster.

nourish, nurture, nurse, cradle, dry-nurse, suckle, foster, cherish, cultivate.

serve; do service to, tender to, pander to, minister to; tend, attend, wait on; take care of; entertain, regale.

oblige, accommodate, consult the wishes of; humor, cheer, encourage.

second, stand by, back, back up; abet, work for, stick up for [*colloq.*], stick by, take up (*or* espouse) the cause of; advocate, countenance, patronize, smile upon, favor, befriend, side with.

Adj. aiding, auxiliary, adjuvant, helpful, subservient, accessary, accessory, subsidiary.

friendly, amicable, favorable, propitious, well disposed, neighborly, obliging, at one's beck.

Adv. in aid of, on (*or* in) behalf of, in favor of, in the name of, in furtherance of, on account of, for the sake of.

708. OPPOSITION.—*N.* opposition, antagonism, contrariness, contrariety; contravention, counteraction; resistance, etc., 719; hindrance, restraint, etc., 751.

collision, conflict, discord, want of harmony; filibuster, clashing.

competition, rivalry, emulation, race, contest; tug of war.

V. oppose, counteract, withstand, etc. (*resist*), 719; hinder, restrain; obstruct, etc., 706; antagonize, cross, thwart, pit against, face, confront, cope with; protest (*or* vote) against; disfavor; contradict, contravene, belie.

encounter, meet, stem, breast, resist, grapple with, kick against the pricks; contend with (*or* against), do battle with (*or* against).

compete, emulate, rival; force out, drive one out of business.

Adj. adverse, antagonistic, oppugnant, contrary, at variance, at issue, at war with, in opposition, at daggers drawn.

unfavorable, unpropitious, unfriendly, hostile, inimical, cross.

competitive, emulous, cutthroat; in rivalry with, in friendly rivalry.

Adv. against, counter to, in conflict with, at cross-purposes.

in spite, in despite, in defiance; in the teeth (*or* face) of; across; athwart.

709. CO-OPERATION.—*N.* co-operation, concert, concurrence, complicity, collusion; participation; union, combination.

association, alliance, joint stock, partnership, pool, gentleman's agreement; confederation, coalition, federation, fusion; logrolling; freemasonry.

unanimity, *esprit de corps* [F.], party spirit, school spirit; clanship, partisanship; concord.

V. co-operate, concur; conduce, combine, pool, unite one's efforts, pull together, stand shoulder to shoulder; act in concert, join forces, fraternize; conspire, concert.

side with, take sides with, go along with, join hands with, make common cause with, unite with, join with, take part with, cast in one's lot with; rally round.

participate, be a party to, lend oneself to; chip in [*colloq.*], bear part in, second, espouse a cause.

Adj. co-operating, in league, hand in glove with; favorable to, unopposed.

Adv. unanimously, as one man, shoulder to shoulder.

710. OPPONENT.—*N.* opponent, antagonist, adversary; opposition; assailant, enemy, etc., 891.

oppositionist, wrangler, disputant; filibuster, filibusterer, extremist, bitter-ender, irreconcilable, obstructionist.

malcontent; demagogue, reactionist; anarchist, Red.

rival, competitor, contestant: the field.

711. AUXILIARY.—*N.* auxiliary, recruit, assistant, help, helper, helpmate, helping hand; colleague, partner, confrere, co-operator, coadjutor, collaborator, associate, right hand, right-hand man.

ally; friend, etc., 890; confidant (*fem.* confidante), alter ego [L.], pal [*slang*], chum [*colloq.*], mate.

puppet, cat's-paw, creature, tool; satellite, adherent, parasite, dependent.

confederate; accomplice; accessory.

upholder, seconder, backer, supporter, abettor, advocate, partisan, champion, patron, friend at court, mediator.

friend in need, special providence, guardian angel, fairy godmother, tutelary genius.

712. PARTY.—*N.* party, faction, denomination, class, communion, side, crew, team; band, horde, posse, phalanx; caste, family, clan.

community, body, fellowship, party spirit, solidarity, freemasonry; fraternity, sodality, brotherhood, sisterhood, sorority; fraternal order.

gang, tong [Chin.], bolsheviki, bolshevists, ring, machine, junto, cabal.

clique, knot, circle, set, coterie; club, casino.

corporation, corporate body, guild, company, partnership, firm, house; combine [*colloq.*], trust; holding company, merger.

society, association; institute, institution; union; trade-union;

league, syndicate, alliance, combination, coalition, federation, confederation, confederacy.

staff; cast, dramatis personae [L.].

V. unite, join, band together, club together, co-operate, etc., 709; associate, federate, federalize.

Adj. joint, federal, corporate, confederated, organized, leagued, syndicated; fraternal, Masonic, institutional, denominational; cliquish, cliquy.

Adv. side by side, hand in hand, shoulder to shoulder, in the same boat.

713. DISCORD.—*N.* discord, dissidence, dissonance, disagreement, jar, clash, break, shock.

variance, difference, dissension, misunderstanding, cross-purposes, odds, division, split, rupture, disruption, disunion, breach, schism, feud, faction.

polemics; litigation, strife, warfare, outbreak, open rupture, declaration of war.

quarrel, dispute, tiff, bicker, squabble, altercation, words, high words, family jars.

broil, brawl, row [*colloq.*], racket, hubbub, imbroglio, fracas, scrimmage, rumpus [*colloq.*], squall, riot, disturbance, commotion.

subject of dispute, ground of quarrel, battleground, disputed point, bone of contention, apple of discord, question at issue.

V. disagree, clash, jar, conflict, misunderstand, live like cat and dog; differ; dissent, etc., 489.

quarrel, fall out, dispute, litigate; controvert, squabble, altercate, row [*colloq.*], wrangle, bicker, nag, spar, brawl.

split, break with; declare war, try conclusions, join issue, pick a quarrel; sow dissension, embroil, entangle, disunite, widen the breach; set (*or* pit) against.

Adj. discordant, dissident, out of tune, dissonant, harsh, grating, jangling, unmelodious; on bad terms, dissentient, unreconciled, unpacified; inconsistent, contradictory, incongruous.

quarrelsome, heated, unpacific, controversial, polemic, disputatious, factious.

at strife, at odds, at loggerheads, at daggers drawn, at variance, at issue, at cross-purposes, at sixes and sevens, embroiled, torn, disunited.

714. CONCORD.—*N.* concord, accord, harmony, homologue, correspondence, agreement, sympathy, response; union, unison, unity, peace, unanimity; happy family.

amity, etc. (*friendship*), 888; alliance, *entente cordiale* [F.], good understanding, conciliation, arbitration, reunion.

peacemaker, intercessor, interceder, mediator.

V. agree, accord, harmonize with, fraternize, go hand in hand, run parallel, concur, co-operate, pull together, sing in chorus.

side with, sympathize with; go with, chime in with, fall in with; assent, etc., 488; reciprocate.

smooth, pour oil on the troubled waters, keep in good humor, meet halfway; mediate, intercede.

Adj. concordant, congenial; in accord, harmonious, united, cemented, allied, friendly, fraternal, conciliatory, of one mind.

Adv. unanimously, with one voice, in concert with, hand in hand.

715. DEFIANCE.—*N.* defiance, dare, defial; challenge; threat, etc., 909; war cry, war whoop.

V. defy, dare, beard, brave, set at defiance, set at naught, hurl defiance at; laugh to scorn; disobey, etc., 742; threaten; challenge.

Adj. defiant; rebellious, bold, insolent, reckless, contemptuous, greatly daring, regardless of consequences.

Adv. in the teeth of; under one's very nose; in open rebellion.

716. ATTACK.—*N.* attack, assault, onset, onslaught, charge.

aggression, offense; incursion, inroad, invasion; irruption, outbreak; sally, sortie, raid, foray.

storm, storming, boarding, escalade; siege, investment, bombardment, cannonade, barrage; zero hour.

fire, volley, fusilade; sharpshooting, broadside, cross-fire.

thrust, lunge, pass, home thrust; cut.

assailant, aggressor, invader; sharpshooter, dead shot.

V. attack, assault, assail; set upon, pounce upon, fall upon, charge; enter the lists.

show fight, take the offensive; strike at, thrust at; aim (*or* deal) a blow at; be the aggressor, strike the first blow, fire the first shot; advance (*or* march) against, march upon, invade, harry.

close with, come to close quarters, bring to bay, come to blows.

fire upon, fire at, draw a bead on, shoot at, pop at, level at, open fire, pepper, bombard, shell, fire a volley.

besiege, beset, beleaguer, invest; sap, mine; storm, board, scale the walls, go over the top.

cut and thrust, bayonet, butt; kick, strike, etc., 276; horsewhip, whip.

Adj. aggressive, offensive; up in arms; amuck.

Adv. on the warpath; over the top; at bay.

717. DEFENSE.—*N.* defense, protection, guard, ward; guardianship.

self-defense, self-preservation; resistance, etc., 719.

safeguard, screen, fortification, bulwark, trench, mine, dugout;

moat, ditch, intrenchment; rampart, dike; parapet, battlement, bastion, redoubt, embankment, mound, bank, breastwork, earthwork, fieldwork; buttress, abutment, fence, wall, paling, palisade, stockade; barrier, barricade, boom; portcullis, barbed-wire entanglements.

stronghold, hold, fastness, asylum, keep, donjon, citadel, capitol, castle; tower, fortress, fort, barrack; blockhouse.

[**protective devices**] buffer, fender, cowcatcher, armor; mail, shield, buckler.

defender, protector, guardian, bodyguard, champion; knight-errant, paladin; garrison.

V. **defend,** guard, ward (*or* beat) off, shield, screen, shroud; garrison, man; fence, intrench, arm, accouter.

repel, parry, put to flight; hold (*or* keep) at bay; resist invasion, stand siege, stand (*or* act) on the defensive, show fight; stand one's ground, hold, stand in the gap.

Adj. **defensive;** armed, armed at all points (*or* to the teeth); panoplied, accoutered; iron-plated, ironclad; bulletproof, bombproof; protective.

Adv. on the defensive, in defense, in self-defense; at bay.

718. RETALIATION.—*N.* **retaliation,** reprisal, retort; counterstroke, counterblast; retribution.

requital, desert; tit for tat, give-and-take, blow for blow, an eye for an eye; boomerang.

recrimination, accusation; revenge, etc., 919; compensation.

V. **retaliate,** retort, turn upon; pay, pay off, pay back; cap, match; reciprocate, turn the tables upon, return the compliment; exchange blows; give and take, be quits, be even with; pay off old scores.

Adj. **retaliatory,** retaliative, retributive, recriminatory, reciprocal.

719. RESISTANCE.—*N.* **resistance,** stand, front, opposition, recalcitrance, repugnance, repulsion.

repulse, rebuff, snub.

insurrection, revolt, etc., 742; strike, lockout; boycott; riot.

V. **resist;** withstand; stand, stand firm (*or* fast, one's ground), stick it out [*colloq.*].

face, confront, breast the wave, stem the tide; grapple with; show a bold front, make a stand.

oppose, etc., 708; fly in the face of; withstand an attack, rise up in arms, strike, turn out, boycott; revolt, rebel; repel, repulse.

Adj. **resistant,** resistive, refractory, repugnant, recalcitrant, repulsive, repellent; up in arms.

unconquerable, stubborn, unconquered; indomitable, unyielding.

720. CONTENTION.—*N.* contention, strife, contest, struggle; belligerency, pugnacity, opposition.

controversy, polemics; debate, war of words, paper war, high words, quarrel, litigation.

competition, rivalry, match, race; athletics, athletic sports; games of skill.

conflict, skirmish; encounter, rencounter, rencontre, collision, affair, brush, fracas, etc. (*discord*), 713; clash of arms; tussle, scuffle, bout, broil, fray, affray, fight, battle, combat, action, engagement, joust, tournament, tourney; pitched battle; guerrilla (*or* irregular) warfare; death struggle, Armageddon.

duel, single combat, satisfaction, passage of arms, affair of honor; hostile meeting, appeal to arms.

V. contend, contest, strive, struggle, scramble, wrestle; spar, exchange blows, tussle, tilt, box, fence; skirmish, fight; wrangle; oppose, etc., 708; join issue.

compete (*or* cope, vie, race) with, emulate, rival; run a race.

Adj. contentious, combative, bellicose, belligerent, warlike, quarrelsome, pugnacious, pugilistic.

athletic, gymnastic, competitive, rival.

721. PEACE.—*N.* peace, amity, etc. (*friendship*), 888; harmony, concord, tranquillity, truce, pipe of peace, calumet.

piping time of peace, quiet life; neutrality; pacifism.

V. be at peace, keep the peace, make peace, pacify; be a pacifist.

Adj. pacific; peaceable, peaceful; calm, tranquil, untroubled, halcyon; bloodless; neutral, pacifistic.

722. WARFARE.—*N.* warfare, fighting, hostilities; war, arms, the sword, bloodshed; Mars.

appeal to arms (*or* the sword); ordeal (*or* wager) of battle; declaration of war.

battle array, campaign, crusade, expedition; warpath.

art of war, rules of war, the war game, tactics, strategy, generalship.

battle, conflict, etc. (*contention*), 720; service, campaigning, active service, tented field; war to the death (*or* knife).

war medal, military medal, Congressional Medal, Victoria Cross, V. C. [Eng.], *Croix de guerre* [F.], *Médaille militaire* [F.], Iron Cross [Ger.].

V. war, make war, go to war, declare war, wage war, arm, take up (*or* appeal to) arms; take the field, give battle, engage, fight, combat, contend, battle with.

serve; enroll, enlist; be on service (*or* active service), campaign;

smell powder, be under fire; be on the warpath, keep the field; take by storm; go over the top [*colloq.*]; sell one's life dearly.

Adj. armed, in (*or* under) arms, in battle array, in the field; embattled; battled.

warlike, belligerent, combative, bellicose, martial, military, militant; soldierly, chivalrous; civil, internecine; irregular, guerrilla.

Adv. in the thick of the fray, in the cannon's mouth; at the sword's point, at the point of the bayonet.

723. PACIFICATION.—*N.* pacification, conciliation, reconciliation, reconcilement; accommodation, arrangement, adjustment; terms, compromise; amnesty.

peace offering; olive branch; calumet, peace pipe.

truce, armistice; suspension of arms (*or* hostilities); truce of God; flag of truce, white flag.

V. pacify, tranquillize, compose, allay, reconcile, propitiate, placate, conciliate, meet halfway, hold out the olive branch, heal the breach, make peace, restore harmony, bring to terms.

raise a siege, sheathe the sword, bury the hatchet, lay down one's arms, turn swords into plowshares.

Adj. conciliatory, pacificatory.

724. MEDIATION.—*N.* mediation, mediatorship, intervention, interposition, interference, intercession; parley, negotiation, arbitration, good offices.

mediator, intercessor, peacemaker, negotiator, go-between, diplomatist, propitiator; umpire, arbitrator.

V. mediate, intercede, interpose, interfere, intervene; step in; negotiate; meet halfway; arbitrate, propitiate.

Adj. mediatory, propitiatory, diplomatic.

725. SUBMISSION.—*N.* submission, yielding, acquiescence, compliance, submissiveness, deference, nonresistance, obedience.

surrender, cession, capitulation, resignation, backdown [*colloq.*].

obeisance, homage, kneeling, genuflection, curtsy, kowtow [Chinese], salaam [Oriental], prostration.

V. submit, succumb, yield, defer to; bend, stoop; accede, resign oneself.

surrender, cede, capitulate, come to terms, lay down one's arms, strike one's flag, give way (*or* ground, in, up); obey.

yield obeisance, kneel to, bow to, pay homage to, cringe to, truckle to; kneel, bow submission, curtsy, kowtow [Chinese].

Adj. submissive, resigned, crouching, prostrate; unresisting, humble.

untenable, indefensible, insupportable, unsupportable.

726. COMBATANT.—*N.* combatant; belligerent, assailant, swashbuckler, duelist, swordsman; competitor, rival.

fighter, fighting man, prize fighter, pugilist, bruiser; gladiator.

soldier, warrior, brave, man at arms, guardsman, gendarme [F.]; campaigner, veteran; military man; knight; myrmidon, mercenary, irregular, free lance, franctireur; private, Tommy Atkins [Brit.], doughboy [slang], rank and file; sepoy [India], spearman, pikeman, archer, bowman; musketeer, rifleman, sharpshooter, skirmisher; grenadier, fusileer, infantryman, foot soldier, chasseur, zouave, artilleryman, gunner, cannoneer, engineer; cavalryman, trooper, dragoon; cuirassier, hussar, lancer; recruit, rookie [slang], conscript, drafted man, enlisted man.

officer, etc. (commander), 745; subaltern, ensign, standard-bearer.

horse and foot; cavalry, horse, light horse; infantry, foot, rifles; artillery, horse artillery, field artillery, gunners; military train.

armed force, troops, soldiery, military, forces, the army, standing army, regulars, the line; militia, national guard, state guard, yeomanry, volunteers, minutemen [Am. hist.]; posse; guards, yeomen of the guard, beefeaters [Eng.], lifeguards, household troops, bodyguard.

levy, draft; raw levies, awkward squad.

army, army corps; division, column, wing, detachment, garrison, flying column, brigade, regiment, battalion, squadron, company, battery, section, platoon, squad; picket, guard, legion, phalanx, cohort.

navy, first line of defense, wooden walls, naval forces, fleet, flotilla, armada, squadron; man-of-war's man, etc. (sailor), 269; marines.

man-of-war, line-of-battle ship, ship of the line, battleship, warship, ironclad, war vessel, superdreadnought, dreadnought, cruiser; torpedo boat, destroyer, gunboat, submarine, submersible, U-boat [Ger.]; submarine chaser, monitor; frigate, sloop of war, corvet, flagship; privateer; troopship, transport, tender.

airplane, hydroplane, seaplane, flying boat, glider; divebomber, bomber, Flying Fortress; dirigible, blimp [cant]; zeppelin, etc. (aeronautics), 273.

727. ARMS.—N. arms; arm, weapon, deadly weapon; armament; armor.

side arms, sword, cold steel, naked steel, steel, blade; broadsword, saber, cutlass, scimitar, rapier, foil, dagger, poniard, dirk, stiletto, bowie knife, bayonet.

ax, battle-ax, poleax, halberd, tomahawk, bill, partisan.

spear, lance, pike, assagai, javelin, dart, arrow; harpoon, boomerang; oxgoad, ankus.

club, war club, mace, truncheon, staff, bludgeon, cudgel, shillelagh, quarterstaff; billy, life preserver, blackjack.

bow, crossbow, long bow; catapult, sling.

firearms; gun, piece; artillery, ordnance; park, battery; cannon, fieldpiece, field gun, siege gun, mortar, howitzer, pompom, seventy-five [French rapid-fire 75-mm. field gun]; Lewis gun.

small arms; musketry; musket, firelock, fowling piece, rifle, carbine, blunderbuss, matchlock, harquebus, shotgun, breechloader, muzzle-loader, magazine rifle, automatic pistol, automatic, revolver, repeater; shooting iron [slang], six-shooter [colloq.], gun [colloq. for revolver or pistol], pistol.

missile, bolt, projectile, shot, ball, slug; grape, shrapnel, grenade, shell, bomb, depth bomb, smoke bomb, gas bomb; bullet; dumdum (or explosive, expanding) bullet; torpedo.

ammunition; powder, powder and shot; explosive; gunpowder; dynamite, cordite; cartridge; poison gas, mustard gas, chlorine gas, tear gas, etc.

728. ARENA.—N. arena, field, platform; scene of action, theater, walk, course; hustings; stage, boards, amphitheater,

coliseum, colosseum; hippodrome, circus, race course, turf, cockpit, bear garden, gymnasium, ring, lists; campus, playing field, playground.

battlefield, battleground, field of battle; no man's land [*First World War*]; theater (*or* seat) of war.

729. COMPLETION.—*N.* completion; accomplishment, achievement, fulfillment, performance, execution; dispatch, consummation, culmination; finish, conclusion; limit, close, finale, denouement, issue, upshot, result.

V. complete, perfect, effect, accomplish, achieve, compass, consummate, bring to maturity (*or* perfection); elaborate.

do, execute, make, work out, enact, dispatch, knock off [*colloq.*], finish off, dispose of, perform, discharge, fulfill, realize; carry out (*or* into effect).

do thoroughly, not do by halves, drive home; carry through, deliver the goods [*colloq.*].

finish, bring to a close, wind up, clinch, seal, put the last (*or* finishing) touch to; crown, crown all; cap.

Adj. conclusive, final, crowning, exhaustive, complete, mature, perfect, consummate, thorough.

Adv. to crown all, as a last stroke, as a fitting climax.

730. NONCOMPLETION.—*N.* noncompletion, nonfulfillment, nonperformance, neglect, etc., 460; shortcoming, incompleteness; drawn battle, drawn game.

V. leave unfinished, leave undone, neglect, etc., 460; let alone, let slip; lose sight of.

fall short of, do things by halves, hang fire; collapse.

Adj. incomplete, uncompleted, unfinished, unaccomplished, unperformed, unexecuted; sketchy; sterile.

Adv. without (*or* lacking) the final touches.

731. SUCCESS—*N.* success, successfulness; progress; advance; good fortune, prosperity, etc., 734; profit.

trump card; hit, stroke, master stroke; ten-strike [*colloq.*]; checkmate; prize.

mastery, advantage over; upper hand, whip hand; ascendancy, conquest, victory, walkover [*colloq.*], triumph.

victor, conqueror, master, champion, winner; master of the situation (*or* position).

V. succeed, be successful, gain one's end (*or* ends); crown with success; gain (*or* attain, carry, secure) a point *or* an object; get there [*slang*]; manage to, contrive to; accomplish, effect; come off successfully, take (*or* carry) by storm; gain the day (*or* prize, palm); carry all before one, score a success.

make progress, etc. (*advance*), 282; win (*or* make, work) one's way; speed; turn to account, prosper, etc., 734; strike oil [*slang*], make one's fortune.

triumph, be triumphant, gain a victory (*or* an advantage); surmount (*or* overcome) a difficulty, stem the torrent, weather the storm, master; distance, surpass, win.

defeat, conquer, discomfit, vanquish, overcome, overthrow, overpower, overmaster, outwit, outdo, outmaneuver, outgeneral, checkmate, beat, rout, floor, worst, lick to a frazzle [*colloq.*]; settle [*colloq.*], do for [*colloq.*], subdue, subjugate, reduce.

quell, silence, put down, confound, nonplus, baffle, circumvent, elude; drive to the wall.

avail, answer, answer the purpose; prevail, take effect, do, turn out well, take [*colloq.*], tell, bear fruit.

Adj. **successful;** prosperous, etc., 734; triumphant, crowned with success, victorious; unbeaten.

Adv. **successfully,** with flying colors, in triumph, swimmingly.

732. FAILURE.—*N.* **failure,** unsuccess, nonsuccess, nonfulfillment; labor in vain, no go [*colloq.*], inefficacy; vain attempt; frustration, disappointment.

blunder, error, etc., 495; fault, omission, miss, oversight, slip, trip, stumble; step, *faux pas* [F.]; scrape, mess, muddle, botch, fiasco.

mishap, etc. (*misfortune*), 735; split, collapse, smash, blow, explosion.

repulse, rebuff, defeat, rout, overthrow, discomfiture; beating, drubbing; subjugation, checkmate.

fall, downfall, ruin, perdition, wreck; deathblow; bankruptcy.

V. **fail,** be unsuccessful, make vain efforts, labor in vain; flunk [*colloq.*]; bring to naught, make nothing of, fall short of, go to the wall [*colloq.*], lick the dust; be defeated, have the worst of it, lose the day, lose; succumb.

miss, miss one's aim (*or* the mark), slip, trip, stumble, blunder, miscarry.

flounder, falter, limp, halt, hobble, fall, tumble, run aground, split upon a rock, break down, sink, drown, founder, come to grief.

come to nothing, end in smoke; flat out [*colloq.*]; fall through, hang fire, flash in the pan, collapse, go to wrack and ruin.

Adj. **unsuccessful,** successless, at fault; unfortunate, etc., 735; abortive, sterile, fruitless, bootless; ineffectual, ineffective, inefficient, lame, insufficient, unavailing.

stranded, aground, grounded, swamped, wrecked, shipwrecked, foundered, capsized.

undone, lost, ruined, broken, bankrupt, played out; done up, done for [*colloq.*]; broken down, overborne, overwhelmed; all up with [*colloq.*].

frustrated, thwarted, crossed, disconcerted; unhorsed, hard hit, stultified, befooled, dished [*colloq.*], foiled, defeated, victimized, sacrificed.

Adv. to little or no purpose, in vain.

733. TROPHY.—*N.* trophy; medal, prize, palm. laurel, laurels, bays, crown, chaplet, wreath; eulogy, citation; scholarship; garland; triumphal arch: war medal, etc., 722; Carnegie medal, Nobel prize; blue ribbon; decoration, etc., 877.

734. PROSPERITY.—*N.* prosperity, welfare, well-being; affluence, etc. (*wealth*), 803; success, etc., 731; luck, good fortune, good luck, blessings, godsend; bed of roses; fat of the land.

upstart, parvenu, *noureau riche* [F.], mushroom.

V. prosper, thrive, flourish, swim with the tide: rise (*or* get on) in the world; light on one's feet; bask in the sunshine; have a run of luck; make one's fortune, feather one's nest, make one's pile [*slang*].

flower, blossom, bloom, fructify, bear fruit; fatten, batten.

Adj. prosperous, thriving, well off, well to do, at one's ease; rich, etc., 803; fortunate, lucky; palmy, halcyon.

auspicious, propitious, providential.

Adv. prosperously, swimmingly; as good luck would have it.

735. ADVERSITY.—*N.* adversity, evil, etc., 619; failure, etc., 732; bad (*or* ill, evil, adverse, hard) fortune *or* luck, frowns of fortune; broken fortunes; slough of despond; evil day, hard times, rainy day, cloud, gathering clouds, ill-wind; affliction, trouble, hardship, curse, blight, load, pressure, humiliation.

misfortune, mishap, mischance, misadventure, disaster, calamity, catastrophe; accident, casualty, blow, trial, sorrow, visitation, infliction, reverse, check, setback, contretemps [F.].

downfall, fall; losing game; ruin, undoing, extremity.

V. come to grief, go downhill, go to wrack and ruin, go to the dogs [*colloq.*]; fall, decay, sink, decline, go down in the world; have seen better days; be all up with [*colloq.*].

Adj. unfortunate, unblest, unhappy, unlucky, unprosperous, hoodooed [*colloq*], luckless, hapless, out of luck; under a cloud; badly off; in adverse circumstances; poor, etc., 804; decayed, undone, on the road to ruin.

ill-fated, ill starred, ill-omened; devoted, doomed; inauspicious, ominous, sinister, unpropitious, unfavorable.

adverse, untoward; disastrous, calamitous, ruinous, dire, deplorable.

Adv. from bad to worse, out of the frying pan into the fire.

736. MEDIOCRITY.—*N.* mediocrity, golden mean, moderation; moderate (*or* average) circumstances; respectability.

middle classes, *bourgeoisie* [F.].

V. strike the golden mean; preserve a middle course.

jog on, get along [*colloq.*], get on tolerably (*or* respectably).

Adj. middling, so-so, fair, medium, moderate, mediocre, ordinary.

Adv. with nothing to brag about.

II. INTERSOCIAL VOLITION[1]

737. AUTHORITY.—*N.* authority; influence, patronage, power, prestige, prerogative, jurisdiction.

right, divine right, authoritativeness, royalty, absolutism, despotism, tyranny.

command, empire, sway, rule; dominion, domination; sovereignty, supremacy, suzerainty, kingship; lordship, headship, leadership, mastership, government, dictation, control, hold, grasp; grip, iron sway, rod of empire.

reign, dynasty, administration; dictatorship, protectorate, presidency, presidentship, consulship, magistracy.

Governments: empire; monarchy; limited (*or* constitutional) monarchy; aristocracy; oligarchy, democracy, republic; triumvirate; autocracy; dictatorship, totalitarian state.

representative government, constitutional government, home rule, dominion rule [Brit.], colonial government; self-government, autonomy, self-determination; republicanism, federalism; socialism; communism; authoritarianism; totalitarianism; bureaucracy; martial law; feudal system, feudalism.

state, realm, commonwealth, country, power, body politic.

ruler, person in authority, lord, etc., 745; judicature, etc., 965; cabinet, etc. (*council*), 696; seat of government, headquarters.

V. authorize, empower, etc., 760; warrant, dictate.

rule, sway, command, control, administer, govern, direct, lead, preside over, be at the head of, reign.

dominate, have the upper (*or* whip) hand; preponderate, boss [*colloq.*]; override, overrule, overawe; lord it over, keep under, bend to one's will, have it all one's own way, be master of the situation, take the lead, lay down the law.

Adj. ruling, regnant, dominant, paramount, supreme, predominant, preponderant, in the ascendant, influential; imperious, dictatorial, peremptory; authoritative, executive, administrative, official, gubernatorial, bureaucratic, departmental.

sovereign; regal, royal, royalist, monarchical, kingly; dynastic, imperial, autocratic; oligarchic, democratic, republican.

[1]Implying the action of the will of one mind over the will of another.

Adv. in the name of, by the authority of, at one's command, in virtue of, under the auspices of.

738. [Absence of authority] LAXITY.—*N.* laxity; laxness, looseness, slackness; toleration, lenity, etc., 740; relaxation; freedom, etc., 748.

anarchy, interregnum; misrule, license, insubordination, mob rule, mob law, lynch law, nihilism, reign of violence.

Deprivation of power: dethronement, impeachment, deposition, abdication; usurpation.

V. **be lax,** hold a loose rein; give the reins to, give rope enough, give free rein to; tolerate; relax; misrule.

have one's fling, act without authority, act on one's own responsibility, usurp authority.

dethrone, depose; abdicate.

Adj. **lax,** loose; slack, remiss, negligent, etc., 460; weak.

relaxed, licensed, unbridled; anarchic *or* anarchical, nihilistic; unauthorized.

739. SEVERITY.—*N.* severity; strictness, harshness, rigor, stringency, austerity, inclemency; arrogance, etc., 885.

arbitrary power; absolutism, despotism; dictatorship, autocracy, tyranny, domination, oppression, assumption, usurpation; inquisition, reign of terror, iron rule, coercion, etc., 744; martial law.

bureaucracy, red-tapism, officialism.

tyrant, disciplinarian, martinet, stickler, despot, autocrat, oppressor, inquisitor, extortioner.

V. **arrogate,** assume, usurp, take liberties; domineer, bully, tyrannize, put on the screw, be hard upon, ill-treat, rule with a rod of iron, oppress, override, trample under foot, ride roughshod over; coerce, etc., 744.

Adj. **severe,** strict, hard, harsh, dour [Scot.], rigid, stern, rigorous, uncompromising, exacting, searching, inexorable, inflexible, obdurate, austere, relentless, stringent, strict, strait-laced, peremptory, absolute, arbitrary, imperative, coercive, tyrannical, extortionate, oppressive, cruel, arrogant: formal, punctilious.

Adv. with a high (*or* strong, tight, heavy) hand.

740. MILDNESS.—*N.* mildness, lenity, moderation, temperateness; tolerance, toleration, mildness, gentleness; favor; indulgence, clemency, mercy, forbearance, quarter, compassion, etc., 914.

V. **be lenient,** tolerate, bear with; spare the vanquished, give quarter; indulge; spoil.

Adj. **lenient,** mild, gentle, tolerant, indulgent, easy, moderate, complaisant, easygoing; clement, compassionate, forbearing; long-suffering.

741. COMMAND.—*N.* command, order, ordinance, act, fiat, bidding, word, call, beck, nod; direction, injunction, charge, instructions; dispatch, message.

demand, exaction, imposition, requisition, claim, requirement, ultimatum; request, etc., 765.

decree, dictate, dictation, mandate, precept; prescript, writ, ordination, bull, edict, dispensation, prescription, enactment, law, act; warrant, passport, summons, subpoena, citation; word of command, order of the day.

V. command, order, decree, enact, ordain, dictate, direct, give orders, issue a command; call to order; assume the command.

prescribe, set, appoint, mark out; set (*or* prescribe, impose) a task; set to work.

bid, enjoin, charge, instruct; require, demand, exact, impose, tax.

claim, lay claim to, reclaim.

cite, summon, call for, send for; subpoena; beckon.

Adj. commanding, authoritative, imperative, decisive, final.

Adv. in a commanding tone; by a stroke (*or* dash) of the pen; by order.

742. DISOBEDIENCE.—*N.* disobedience, insubordination, contumacy; infraction, infringement, violation.

revolt, rebellion, mutiny, outbreak, rising, uprising, insurrection, riot, tumult, strike.

sedition, treason; lese majesty; defection, secession, revolution; bolshevism.

insurgent, mutineer, rebel, traitor, communist, Fenian, Sinn Feiner, Red, Bolshevist, seceder, Secessionist [esp., U. S. hist.] *or* Secesh [*colloq. or slang*, U. S.]; apostate, renegade, anarchist.

V. disobey, violate, infringe; shirk, slack; defy, set at defiance, run riot, take the law into one's own hands; kick over the traces; refuse to support, bolt [*politics*].

resist, strike, rise, rise in arms; secede, mutiny, rebel.

Adj. disobedient, unruly, ungovernable; insubordinate, restive, refractory, defiant, contumacious; recusant, recalcitrant.

lawless, riotous, mutinous, seditious, insurgent, revolutionary.

743. OBEDIENCE.—*N.* obedience, observance, compliance; submission, subjection; nonresistance, passivity, resignation, submissiveness, ductility, obsequiousness, servility.

allegiance, loyalty, fealty, homage, deference, devotion; constancy, fidelity.

V. obey, submit, etc., 725; comply, do one's bidding, attend to orders, serve faithfully (*or* loyally, devotedly, without question); be resigned to, be submissive to; serve, etc., 746; play second fiddle.

Adj. **obedient**, law-abiding, complying, compliant; loyal, faithful, devoted; under beck and call, under control.

resigned, passive; submissive, etc., 725; unresisting, pliant.

Adv. as you please, if you please; in compliance with, in obedience to.

744. COMPULSION.—*N.* **compulsion**, coercion, constraint; restraint, etc., 751; enforcement, draft, conscription; eminent domain.

force; brute (*or* main, physical) force; the sword; mob law, martial law.

necessity, etc., 601; spur of necessity, Hobson's choice.

V. **compel**, force, make, drive, dragoon, coerce, constrain, enforce, necessitate, oblige.

extort, wring from, force upon, drag into; bind, pin down; require; tax, put in force; commandeer; restrain, etc., 751.

Adj. **compelling**, coercive, inexorable, compulsory, obligatory, stringent, peremptory, binding.

Adv. **forcibly**, by force, by force of arms; on compulsion, perforce, under protest, in spite of, in one's teeth; against one's will.

745. MASTER.—*N.* **master**, lord, commander, commandant, captain, chief, chieftain; paterfamilias [*Rom. law*], patriarch; sahib [India], head, senior, governor, ruler, dictator, leader, director, boss; sachem, sagamore.

potentate; liege, liege lord, suzerain, overlord, sovereign, monarch, crowned head, emperor, king, majesty, protector, president; autocrat, despot, tyrant, oligarch, dictator.

caesar, kaiser, czar, sultan, caliph, mogul, great mogul, mikado, inca; prince, duke, etc. (*nobility*), 875; archduke, doge; maharaja, raja, emir, nizam, nawab [*Indian ruling chiefs*].

empress, queen, sultana, czarina, princess, infanta, duchess, maharani, rani [both Hindu], begum [Moham.].

regent, viceroy, khedive, pasha, bey, mandarin.

the authorities, the powers that be, the government; staff, official, man in office, person in authority.

Military authorities: marshal, field marshal, generalissimo; commander in chief, general, brigadier general, brigadier, lieutenant general, major general, colonel, lieutenant colonel, major, captain, lieutenant, sublieutenant; officer, staff officer, aide-de-camp, adjutant, ensign, cornet, cadet, subaltern; noncommissioned officer; sergeant, top sergeant, corporal.

Civil authorities: mayor, prefect, chancellor, magistrate, syndic; burgomaster, seneschal, alderman, warden, constable.

Naval authorities: admiral, admiralty; commodore, captain, commander, lieutenant; skipper, master, mate.

746. SERVANT.—*N.* **servant**, retainer, follower, henchman, servitor, domestic, menial, help [*local*], employee; attaché [F.], official.

subject, liege, liegeman.

retinue, suite, cortege, staff, court; office force, clerical staff, clerical force, workers, associate workers, employees, the help.

attendant, squire, usher, apprentice; page, buttons [*colloq.*]; trainbearer, cupbearer; waiter, butler, lackey, footman, flunky [*colloq.*]; boy [*any colored male servant, as in the Orient, South Africa, etc*]; valet, equerry, groom, jockey, hostler or ostler, orderly, messenger, caddie; secretary, stenographer, clerk, agent, underling, understrapper; man.

maid, maidservant; girl, help [*local*], handmaid, lady's maid, nurse, ayah [India], nursemaid; cook, scullion, Cinderella; general servant [Brit.], general-housework maid [U. S.], general [*colloq.*]; washerwoman, laundress, charwoman.

dependent, hanger-on, satellite, parasite, protégé [F.], ward, hireling, mercenary, puppet, creature; serf, vassal, thrall, slave, Negro, helot; bondsman, bondswoman; bondslave; villein [*hist.*], churl [*hist.*].

V. serve, minister to, help, co-operate; wait (*or* attend, dance attendance) upon; squire, valet, tend, do for [*colloq.*].

Adj. serviceable, useful, helpful, co-operative; at one's call.

servile, slavish, subject, thrall, bond; subservient, obsequious, base, fawning, truckling, sycophantic, parasitic, cringing.

747. [Insignia of authority] SCEPTER.—*N.* Regal: scepter, orb; pall; robes of state, ermine, purple; crown, coronet, diadem; triple plume; flail [Egyptian]; signet seal.

Ecclesiastical: tiara, triple crown; ring, keys; miter, crozier, crook, staff; cardinal's hat; bishop's apron (*or* sleeves, lawn, gaiters), fillet.

Military: epaulet, star, bar, eagle, crown [Brit.], oak leaf, Sam Browne belt; chevron, stripe.

caduceus; Mercury's staff (*or* rod, wand); mace, fasces, ax, truncheon, staff, baton, wand, rod; flag, etc. (*insignia*), 550; regalia; toga, mantle; decoration, title, etc., 877; portfolio.

throne, divan; woolsack [*seat of English Lord Chancellor in the House of Lords*], chair, seat, dais.

talisman, amulet, charm, sign.

748. FREEDOM.—*N.* freedom, liberty, independence; license, indulgence.

scope, range, latitude, play, free play (*or* scope), swing, full swing, elbowroom, margin, rope, wide berth.

franchise; prerogative, etc., 924.

freeman, freedman, citizen, denizen.

immunity, exemption; emancipation, etc., 750; right, privilege.

autonomy, self-government; free trade; self-determination, non-interference; Monroe Doctrine [U. S.].

independent, free lance, freethinker, free trader.

V. be free, have scope (*or* one's own way), do what one likes, go at large, feel at home, stand on one's rights.

free, liberate, set free, etc., 750; give the reins to; make free of, enfranchise.

Adj. free, independent, at large, loose, scot-free; unconstrained, unconfined, unchecked, unhindered, unobstructed, uncontrolled, ungoverned, unchained, unshackled, unfettered, unbridled, uncurbed, unmuzzled, unvanquished.

unrestricted, unlimited, unconditional; absolute; with unlimited power (*or* opportunity); discretionary.

unbiased, unprejudiced, uninfluenced; spontaneous.

free and easy, at ease, at one's ease; quite at home.

exempt, immune, freed, freeborn; autonomous, freehold.

gratuitous, gratis, etc., 815; for nothing, for love.

Adv. freely, at will, with no restraint.

749. SUBJECTION.—*N.* subjection; dependence, subordination; thrall, thralldom, subjugation, bondage, serfdom; feudalism, vassalage, slavery, enslavement; conquest.

service; servitude, employ, tutelage, constraint, yoke, submission, obedience.

V. **be subject,** be at the mercy of, depend upon; fall a prey to, fall under, play second fiddle; serve, etc., 746; obey, etc., 743; submit, etc., 725.

subjugate, subject, tame, break in; master, tread down, weigh down, keep under, enthrall, enslave, lead captive, rule, etc., 737; hold in bondage (*or* leading strings).

Adj. **subject,** dependent, subordinate; feudal, feudatory; under control; in leading strings, in harness; servile, slavish, enslaved, downtrodden; henpecked; under one's thumb, tied to one's apron strings, at one's beck and call; liable.

Adv. **under;** under orders (*or* command), at one's orders.

750. LIBERATION.—*N.* liberation, disengagement, release, emancipation, Emancipation Proclamation; enfranchisement, manumission; discharge, dismissal.

deliverance, etc., 672; redemption, extrication, acquittance, absolution, acquittal, escape.

V. **liberate,** free, set free, emancipate, release; enfranchise, manumit; demobilize, disband, discharge, dismiss; let go, let loose, let out, deliver, etc., 672; absolve, acquit.

unfetter, untie, loose, loosen, relax; unbolt, unbar, unhand, unbind, unchain, disengage, disentangle; clear, extricate; reprieve.

Adj. **liberated,** freed; foot-loose, one's own master.

Adv. **at large,** at liberty; adrift.

751. RESTRAINT.—*N.* restraint; hindrance, etc., 706; coercion, compulsion, constraint, repression; discipline, control; limitation, restriction, protection, monopoly; prohibition, economic pressure.

confinement, durance, duress; imprisonment, incarceration, thrall, thralldom, limbo, captivity; blockade.

keep, care, charge, custody, ward.

repressionist, monopolist, protectionist.

V. **restrain**, check, restrict, debar, hinder, constrain, coerce, compel, curb, harness, control; hold in leash, withhold, repress, suppress, keep under; smother, pull in, rein in, hold, prohibit.

fasten, enchain, fetter, shackle, trammel; bridle, muzzle, gag, pinion, manacle, handcuff, hobble, bind, swathe, swaddle; tether, picket, tie, secure.

confine, shut up (*or* in), lock up, box up, bottle up, cork up, seal up, blockade, hem in, bolt in, wall in, rail in; impound, pen, coop; inclose, cage, imprison, immure, incarcerate, entomb; put in irons, cast into prison.

arrest, take into custody; take (*or* make) prisoner, lead captive, send to prison, commit; give in charge (*or* custody).

Adj. **restrained**, constrained, repressive, suppressive; imprisoned, pent up, wedged in; on parole; doing time [*colloq. or slang*], in custody.

stiff, narrow, prudish, strait-laced, hidebound.

Adv. **under restraint** (*or* lock and key, hatches), under discipline; in prison, in jail, in durance vile, in confinement; behind bars, in captivity, under arrest.

752. [Means of restraint] PRISON.—*N.* **prison**, prisonhouse; jail, cage, coop, den, cell; stronghold, fortress, keep, donjon, dungeon, Bastille, penitentiary, state prison, lockup, station house, station [*colloq.*], pen [*also slang for penitentiary*], pound; penal settlement; workhouse [U. S.; *in England, a workhouse is a poorhouse*], reformatory, reform school.

Restraining devices: shackle, bond, gyve, fetter, irons, pinion, manacle, handcuff, straight jacket, stocks, pillory; vise, bandage, splint, strap; yoke, collar, halter, harness; muzzle, gag, bit, curb, snaffle, bridle; rein, reins, lines [U. S. and dial. Eng.], ribbons [*colloq.*]; tether, picket, band, chain, cord.

bar, bolt, lock, padlock; rail, paling, palisade; wall, fence, barrier, barricade.

drag, brake, check, etc. (*hindrance*), 706.

753. KEEPER.—*N.* **keeper**, custodian, ranger, gamekeeper, warder, jailer, turnkey, castellan, guard; watch, watchdog, watchman, concierge [F.], sentry, sentinel; coastguard.

escort, bodyguard; convoy.

guardian, protector, governor; duenna, governess, nurse.

754. PRISONER.—*N.* **prisoner**, convict, captive, close prisoner.

V. stand committed; be imprisoned.

Adj. **imprisoned**, in prison, in custody, in charge, behind bars, under lock and key, under hatches.

755. [Vicarious authority] COMMISSION.—*N.* **commission**, delegation; consignment, assignment; proxy, power of attorney, deputation, legation, mission, embassy; agency.

errand, charge, brevet, diploma, permit.

appointment, nomination, charter; ordination; installation, inauguration, investiture; accession, coronation, enthronement.

V. commission, delegate, depute; consign, assign, commit, charge, intrust, authorize.

accredit, engage, hire, bespeak, appoint, name, nominate, return; ordain, install, induct, inaugurate, invest, crown; enroll, enlist; employ, empower.

Adv. instead of, in one's stead, in one's place; as proxy for.

756. ANNULMENT.—*N.* annulment, nullification, cancellation, abrogation, revocation, repeal.

dismissal, *congé* [F.], sack [*slang*], deposition, dethronement; disestablishment, disendowment.

countermand, repudiation, retractation, recantation; abolition, abolishment; dissolution.

V. annul, cancel, destroy, abolish, abrogate, revoke, repeal, rescind, reverse, retract, recall; overrule, override; set aside; disannul, dissolve, quash, nullify, nol-pros [*law, short for nolle prosequi*], disestablish; countermand, counterorder, throw overboard.

disclaim, deny, ignore, repudiate; recant, break off.

dismiss, discard; turn out, cast off (*or* adrift, aside, away); send off, send away, discharge, get rid of, bounce [*slang*]; fire, sack [*both slang*].

cashier, oust, unseat, dethrone, depose, unfrock, strike off the roll, disbar.

757. RESIGNATION.—*N.* resignation, retirement, abdication; renunciation, retractation, retraction, disclaimer, abandonment, relinquishment.

V. resign, give up, throw up, lay down, abjure, renounce, forego, disclaim, retract, deny, desert.

vacate, abdicate, retire, tender (*or* hand in) one's resignation.

758. CONSIGNEE.—*N.* consignee, trustee, nominee; committee.

functionary, curator; treasurer, etc., 801; agent, factor, steward, bailiff, clerk, secretary, attorney, solicitor, proctor, broker, underwriter, commission agent, factotum, caretaker, employee; servant, etc., 746.

negotiator, go-between; middleman.

delegate, commissioner; emissary, envoy, messenger.

diplomatist, diplomat, ambassador, plenipotentiary, diplomatic agent, representative, resident, consul, legate, etc., 534; attaché [F.].

salesman, traveler, traveling salesman, commercial traveler, drummer, traveling man.

759. DEPUTY.—*N.* deputy, substitute, proxy, delegate, representative, alternate; vice-president.

regent, vicegerent, viceroy, minister, premier, chancellor, provost, warden, lieutenant, consul, ambassador; delegate, etc., 758.

team, eight, nine, eleven; captain, champion.

V. represent, stand for, appear for, hold a brief for, answer for; stand in the shoes of; stand in the stead of.

delegate, depute, empower, commission, substitute, accredit.

Adj. acting, vice, viceregal; accredited to; delegated, representative.

Adv. in behalf of, in the place of, as representing, by proxy.

760. PERMISSION.—*N.* permission, leave, allowance, sufferance, tolerance, toleration, connivance; liberty, law, license, concession, grace; indulgence, favor, dispensation, exemption, release; authorization, accordance, admission.

permit, warrant, sanction, authority, pass, passport; license, carte blanche [F.], grant, charter, patent.

V. permit, let, allow, admit; suffer, tolerate, recognize; concede, etc., 762; accord, vouchsafe, favor, humor, gratify, indulge, wink at, connive at.

grant, empower, charter, enfranchise, privilege, license, authorize, warrant, sanction; intrust, commission.

absolve, release, exonerate, dispense with.

Adj. permitted, permissible, allowable, lawful, legitimate, legal, legalized, chartered, unforbidden.

Adv. by (*or* with) leave, under favor of, by all means.

761. PROHIBITION.—*N.* prohibition, inhibition; veto, interdict, interdiction, injunction, embargo, ban, taboo, proscription, restriction; contraband; forbidden fruit; Volstead Act, 18th amendment [all U. S.].

V. prohibit, inhibit, forbid, disallow; bar, debar, hinder, restrain, etc., 751; withhold, limit, circumscribe, clip the wings of, restrict; interdict, taboo, proscribe; exclude, shut out.

Adj. prohibitive, prohibitory; proscriptive; restrictive, exclusive.

prohibited, unlicensed, contraband, taboo, illegal, unauthorized.

762. CONSENT.—*N.* consent; assent, etc., 488; acquiescence, approval, compliance, agreement, concession, accession, acknowledgment, acceptance; permit, etc. (*permission*), 760; promise, etc., 768.

settlement, adjustment, ratification, confirmation.

V. consent; assent, etc., 488; yield assent, admit, allow, concede, grant, yield; acknowledge, give consent, comply with, acquiesce, agree to, accede, accept, close with, satisfy, settle, come to terms; deign, vouchsafe, promise.

Adj. **willing,** compliant, agreeable [*colloq.*], eager.

763. OFFER.—*N.* **offer,** proffer, tender, bid, overture, proposal, proposition; motion, invitation, offering.

V. **offer,** proffer, present, tender; bid; propose, move, make a motion, start, invite, place at one's disposal; make possible, put forward, press, urge upon, hold out.

volunteer, come forward, be a candidate, offer (*or* present) oneself, stand for, bid for; seek; be at one's service.

Adj. in the market, for sale, to let, disengaged, on hire; at one's disposal.

764. REFUSAL.—*N.* **refusal,** rejection, denial, declension, flat (*or* point-blank) refusal; repulse, rebuff; discountenance, disapprobation.

negation, abnegation, protest, renunciation, disclaimer; dissent, etc., 489; revocation, annulment.

V. **refuse,** reject, deny, decline, turn down [*slang*], dissent, etc., 489; negative, withhold one's assent, grudge, begrudge; stand aloof, be deaf to, turn one's back upon, discountenance, forswear, set aside.

resist, repel, repulse, rebuff, deny oneself, discard, repudiate, rescind, disclaim, protest.

Adj. **uncomplying,** deaf to, noncompliant, unconsenting; recusant, dissentient.

Adv. on no account, not for the world, not on your life! [*colloq.*].

765. REQUEST.—*N.* **request,** requisition; claim, demand, etc., 741; petition, suit, prayer, solicitation, invitation, entreaty, importunity, supplication, invocation.

motion, overture, application, canvass, address, appeal, imprecation; proposal, proposition.

V. **request,** ask, beg, crave, sue, pray, petition, solicit, canvass, invite, beg leave, beg a boon, apply to, call to, call for; make a request, make application, claim, demand; offer up prayers.

entreat, beseech, plead, supplicate, implore; conjure, adjure; apostrophize, cry to, kneel to, appeal to; invoke, evoke; press, urge, importune, dun, clamor for, cry aloud, cry for help.

Adj. **importunate,** clamorous, urgent, solicitous; cap in hand.

Adv. **please,** prithee, do, pray; be so good as, be good enough; have the goodness, vouchsafe, will you, I pray thee, if you please.

766. [Negative request] DEPRECATION.—*N.* **deprecation,** expostulation; intercession, mediation, protest, remonstrance.

V. **deprecate,** protest, expostulate, enter a protest, remonstrate.

Adj. deprecatory, expostulatory, intercessory.

unsought, unbesought; unasked.

767. PETITIONER.—*N.* petitioner, solicitor, applicant, suppliant, supplicant, suitor, candidate, claimant, aspirant, competitor, bidder; place hunter.

salesman, drummer, etc., 758; canvasser.

beggar, mendicant, panhandler [*slang*], cadger.

hotel runner, runner [*both cant*], steerer [*colloq.*], barker [*colloq.*].

sycophant, parasite, etc. (*servility*), 886.

768. PROMISE.—*N.* promise, undertaking, word, troth, plight, pledge, parole, word of honor, vow, oath, profession, assurance, warranty, guarantee, insurance, obligation, contract, stipulation.

engagement, affiance, betrothal, marriage contract (*or* vow); plighted faith.

V. promise, undertake, engage; make (*or* form, enter into) an engagement; bind (*or* pledge) oneself; vow, swear, give (*or* pledge) one's word; betroth, plight faith.

assure, warrant, guarantee, covenant, agree, vouch for, attest; answer for, be answerable for; secure, give security, underwrite.

Adj. promissory, votive, under hand and seal, upon oath, upon affirmation.

promised, affianced, pledged, bound, committed, compromised.

Adv. as true as I live; in all soberness; upon my honor; my word for it.

769. COMPACT.—*N.* compact, contract, specialty, deal [*colloq.*], agreement, bargain; pact, bond, covenant, indenture [*law*]; stipulation, settlement, convention; compromise, negotiation.

treaty, protocol, concordat, charter, Magna Charta, pragmatic sanction.

ratification, completion, signature, seal, bond.

V. contract, covenant, agree for; engage, etc. (*promise*), 768.

negotiate, treat, stipulate, make terms; bargain.

conclude, close, close with, complete, strike a bargain; come to terms (*or* an understanding); compromise, settle; confirm, ratify, clinch, subscribe, underwrite; indorse, sign, seal.

Adj. contractual, complete, agreed; signed, sealed, and delivered.

Adv. as agreed upon, as promised, according to the contract.

770. CONDITIONS.—*N.* conditions, terms, articles, articles of agreement; memorandum, clauses, provisions, proviso, covenant, stipulation, obligation, ultimatum.

V. condition, stipulate, insist upon, make a point of; bind, tie up; fence in, hedge in, make (*or* come to) terms.

Adj. conditional, provisional, guarded, fenced, hedged in.

Adv. conditionally, provisionally, on condition; with a string to it [*colloq.*], with a reservation.

771. SECURITY.—*N.* security, guaranty, guarantee; gage, bond, tie, pledge, mortgage, debenture; bill of sale, lien, collateral, bail, stake, deposit, earnest.

promissory note; bill, bill of exchange; I O U; personal security, covenant.

acceptance, indorsement, signature, execution, stamp, seal.

sponsor, surety, bail, hostage; godchild, godfather, godmother.

authentication, verification, warrant, certificate, voucher, receipt.

deed, instrument, title deed, indenture; charter, paper, parchment, settlement, will, testament, codicil.

V. give security, give bail, go bail; pawn, put in pawn, pledge, mortgage.

guarantee, warrant, assure; accept, indorse, underwrite, insure.

execute, stamp; sign, seal.

Adj. pledged, pawned, in pawn, at stake, on deposit, as earnest.

772. OBSERVANCE.—*N.* observance, performance, compliance, acquiescence, concurrence; obedience, etc., 743; fulfillment, satisfaction, discharge; acquittance, acquittal; adhesion, ackowledgment; fidelity.

V. observe, comply with, respect, acknowledge, abide by; cling to, adhere to, be faithful to, act up to; meet, fulfill, carry out, execute, perform, discharge, keep one's word (*or* pledge).

Adj. observant, faithful, true, loyal, honorable, etc., 939; punctual, punctilious, scrupulous, as good as one's word.

Adv. to the letter.

773. NONOBSERVANCE.—*N.* nonobservance, noncompliance, evasion, failure, omission, neglect, slackness, laxness, laxity, informality; lawlessness, disobedience, etc., 742; bad faith, etc., 940.

infringement, infraction; violation, transgression; piracy, literary theft.

V. evade, fail, neglect, omit, elude, cut [*colloq.*], set aside, ignore; shut (*or* close) one's eyes to.

infringe, transgress, violate, steal, pirate [*a book, etc.*].

discard, repudiate, protest, nullify, declare null and void, cancel, forfeit.

Adj. elusive, evasive, slack, lax, casual, slippery; nonobservant.

774. COMPROMISE.—*N.* compromise, composition, middle term, compensation, adjustment, mutual concession.

V. compromise, commute, compound, split the difference, meet one halfway, give and take, come to terms, submit to arbitration, patch up, arrange, straighten out, adjust, agree, make the best of, make a virtue of necessity.

POSSESSIVE RELATIONS[1]

(1) Property

775. ACQUISITION.—*N.* acquisition, procurement; purchase, inheritance; gift, etc., 784.

recovery, redemption, salvage, find.

gain, thrift, money-making, pelf, lucre, filthy lucre, the main chance.

profit, earnings, wages, salary, emolument, income, remuneration; winnings, pickings, perquisite; proceeds, produce, product; outcome, output; return, fruit, crop, harvest; benefit; prize; wealth, etc., 803.

V. acquire, get, gain, win, earn, obtain, procure, gather; collect, pick, pick up, glean, find, light upon, come across, come at; scrape up (*or* together); get in, net, bag, secure; derive, draw, get in the harvest.

profit, turn to profit (*or* account), make capital out of, make money by, obtain a return, reap the fruits of; gain an advantage; make (*or* coin, raise) money, raise funds; realize, clear, produce, take, receive, come by, inherit.

recover, get back, regain, retrieve, redeem.

Adj. profitable, productive, advantageous, gainful, remunerative, paying, lucrative.

Adv. in the way of gain; for money; at interest.

776. LOSS.—*N.* loss, forfeiture, lapse; privation, bereavement, deprivation, riddance; damage, squandering, waste.

V. lose, incur a loss, miss, mislay, let slip, be deprived of, be without, forfeit.

squander, lavish, get rid of, waste.

Adj. bereft, bereaved, deprived of, shorn of, denuded, minus [*colloq., exc. in math.*], cut off; rid of, quit of, out of pocket, lost.

777. POSSESSION.—*N.* possession, ownership, proprietorship, occupancy, hold, holding, tenure, tenancy, dependency.

exclusive possession, monopoly, retention, corner.

future possession, heritage, inheritance, heirship, reversion; primogeniture.

V. possess, have, hold, occupy, enjoy, be possessed of, own, command, inherit.

[1]That is, relations which concern property.

monopolize, corner, engross, forestall, appropriate.

belong to, appertain to, pertain to; be in one's possession, vest in.

Adj. possessing, worth, possessed of, master of, in possession of; endowed (*or* blest, fraught, laden, charged) with.

possessed, on hand, in hand, in store, in stock; at one's command, at one's disposal.

777a. EXEMPTION.—*N.* exemption, exception, immunity, privilege, release.

V. not have, not possess, not own, be without.

Adj. devoid of, exempt from, without, unpossessed of, unblest with; immune from.

unpossessed; untenanted, vacant, without an owner.

778. [Joint possession] PARTICIPATION.—*N.* participation, joint tenancy; joint (*or* common) stock: partnership; communion; community of possessions, communism, collectivism, socialism; co-operation.

participator, sharer, partner; shareholder; joint tenant; tenants in common; coheir.

communist, communalist, collectivist, socialist.

V. participate, partake, share, share in, join in, go shares, go cahoots [*slang*], go halves; share and share alike.

communize, communalize; have (*or* possess) in common.

Adj. communistic, socialistic; co-operative, profit-sharing.

Adv. in common, share and share alike; on shares.

779. POSSESSOR.—*N.* possessor, holder, occupant, occupier, tenant, tenant at will, lessee, lodger.

owner; proprietor, proprietress, master, mistress, lord.

landholder, landowner, landlord, landlady; lord of the manor, laird [*Scot.*], landed gentry.

Future possessor: heir, heir apparent, heir presumptive; inheritor, heiress, inheritrix.

780. PROPERTY.—*N.* property, possession, tenure; ownership, etc., 777.

estate, interest, right, title, claim, demand, holding, vested interest; use, trust, benefit; term, lease, settlement; remainder, reversion.

dower, dowry, jointure, inheritance, heritage, patrimony, legacy.

assets, belongings, means, resources, circumstances; wealth, etc., 803; money, etc., 800; estate and effects.

realty, real estate, land, lands, landed (*or* real) property; tenements; plant, fixtures; ground; freehold, copyhold, leasehold.

manor, domain, demesne; farm, plantation, ranch.

territory, state, kingdom, principality, realm, empire, protectorate, dependency, sphere of influence, mandate.

personalty, personal property (*or* estate, effects), chattels, goods, effects, movables: stock, stock in trade, things, paraphernalia, equipage, appurtenances; income, etc., 810.

baggage, luggage [esp. in Eng.], impedimenta, bag and baggage; cargo.

V. possess, etc., 777; be the possessor, own; inherit.

Adj. landed, hereditary, entailed, real, personal.

Adv. to one's credit, to one's account; to the good.

781. RETENTION.—*N.* retention, detention, custody; tenacity, firm hold, grasp, gripe, grip, clutches, talon, claw, fang, tentacle.

captive, prisoner, bird in hand.

V. retain, keep, hold, hold fast, clinch, clench, clutch, grasp, gripe, hug; secure, withhold, detain; hold (*or* keep) back; husband, reserve; have (*or* keep) in stock; entail, tie up, settle.

Adj. retentive, tenacious.

782. RIDDANCE.—*N.* riddance, relinquishment, abandonment, renunciation, dereliction; cession, surrender, dispensation; resignation.

derelict, jetsam; abandoned farm [U. S.]; waif, foundling.

V. relinquish, give up, surrender, yield, cede; let go, let slip; spare, drop, resign, forego, renounce, abandon, give away, dispose of, part with; lay aside, set aside, discard, cast off, dismiss; maroon.

cast (*or* throw, fling) away, jettison.

supersede, give notice to quit, give warning; be (*or* get) rid of; eject.

divorce, cut off, desert, disinherit; separate.

Adj. relinquished, cast off, derelict; disowned, disinherited, divorced.

783. TRANSFER [of property].—*N.* transfer, conveyance, assignment, alienation, conveyancing, transmission, sale, lease, release, exchange, barter; succession, reversion.

V. transfer, convey, alienate, assign, grant, consign; make over, hand over, transmit, negotiate; hand down; exchange.

change hands, devolve, succeed; require, come into possession.

disinherit; dispossess, etc., 789; substitute.

Adj. transferable, alienable, negotiable, reversional, transmissive; inherited.

784. GIVING.—*N.* giving, bestowal, presentation, concession, cession; delivery, consignment, dispensation, endowment; investment, investiture; award, recompense, etc., 973.

charity, almsgiving, liberality, generosity.

gift, donation, present, boon, favor, benefaction, grant, offering, bonus, oblation, sacrifice.

allowance, contribution, subscription, subsidy, tribute.

bequest, legacy, devise, will, dot, dowry, dower.

gratuity, alms, largess, bounty, dole, help, offertory, honorarium, Christmas box, tip, baksheesh, consideration.

bribe, bait, peace offering; graft [*colloq.*].

giver, grantor, donor, testator; investor, subscriber, contributor; fairy godmother.

V. deliver, hand, pass, assign, hand (*or* make, deliver, turn) over.

pay, etc., 807; render, impart, communicate.

concede, cede, yield, part with, shed; spend, sacrifice.

give, bestow, donate, confer, grant; accord, award, assign, offer; present, give away, dispense, dispose of; give (*or* deal) out, fork out [*slang*]; allow, contribute, subscribe.

invest, endow, settle upon; bequeath, leave, devise.

furnish, supply, help, administer to, afford, spare, accommodate with, indulge with, favor with; lavish, pour on, thrust upon.

bribe, tip; grease the palm [*slang*].

Adj. charitable, eleemosynary, tributary; gratis, etc., 815; donative.

785. RECEIVING.—*N.* receiving, acquisition, etc., 775; reception, acceptance, admission.

recipient, receiver; assignee, legatee, grantee, lessee; beneficiary, pensioner.

income, etc. (*receipt*), 810.

V. receive; take, etc., 789; pocket; acquire, etc., 775; admit, take in, catch, accept.

be received; come in, come to hand, go into one's pocket; fall to one's lot (*or* share), accrue.

Adj. receiving, recipient; stipendiary, pensionary.

received, given, allowed; secondhand.

786. APPORTIONMENT.—*N.* apportionment, allotment, consignment, assignment, allocation, appropriation; distribution, division, deal; partition, administration.

portion, dividend, share, allotment, lot, measure, dose; dole, meed, pittance; ration; ratio, proportion, quota, modicum, allowance.

V. apportion, divide; distribute, administer, dispense; allot, allocate, detail, cast, share, mete; portion (*or* parcel, dole) out; deal, carve.

partition, assign, appropriate, appoint.

Adv. respectively, each to each; by lot; in equal shares.

787. LENDING.—*N.* lending, loan, advance, accommodation, mortgage, etc., 771; investment.

lender, pawnbroker, my uncle [*slang*], moneylender, usurer, Shylock.

V. **lend**, advance, accommodate with; lend on security; loan; pawn.

invest, intrust, place (*or* put) out to interest; place, put; embark, risk, venture, sink.

let, lease, sublet, sublease.

Adv. in advance; on loan, on security.

788. BORROWING.—*N.* **borrowing**, pledging, pawning.

V. **borrow**, pledge, pawn, put up the spout [*slang*], raise money, raise the wind [*slang*]; run into debt.

hire, rent, farm; take a lease.

appropriate, adopt, apply, imitate, make use of, take; plagiarize, pirate.

789. TAKING.—*N.* **taking**, reception, appropriation, capture, apprehension, seizure; abduction, abstraction.

dispossession; deprivation, bereavement, disinheritance; attachment, execution, sequestration, confiscation, eviction.

rapacity, rapaciousness, extortion, bloodsucking; theft, etc.,791.

taker, captor, capturer; extortioner *or* extortionist; vampire.

V. **take**, catch, hook, bag, sack, pocket, receive, accept.

reap, crop, cull, pluck, gather, draw.

appropriate, assume, possess oneself of; commandeer [*colloq.*]; help oneself to, make free with, lay under contribution; intercept, scramble for; deprive of.

seize, snatch, abstract, take away (*or* off), run away with; abduct, kidnap, capture, steal, pounce (*or* spring) upon; swoop down upon; take by storm; take prisoner; grapple, embrace, grip, gripe, clasp, grab [*colloq.*], clutch, collar, throttle, claw.

dispossess, take from, take away from; tear from, tear away from, wrench (*or* wrest, wring) from, extort; deprive of, bereave; disinherit, oust, evict, eject, divest; levy, distrain [*law*], confiscate; sequester, sequestrate, usurp; despoil, strip, fleece, bleed [*colloq.*].

Adj. **predatory**, wolfish, rapacious, ravening, ravenous; parasitic; all-devouring, all-engulfing.

790. RESTITUTION.—*N.* **restitution**, return, restoration, reinstatement, reinvestment, rehabilitation, reparation, atonement; compensation, indemnification; recovery.

V. **restore**, return, give back, render, give up, let go, release, remit; disgorge, recoup, reimburse, compensate, indemnify, reinvest, reinstate, rehabilitate, repair, make good.

recover, get back, retrieve, redeem; take back again.

Adj. **compensatory**, indemnificatory; reversionary, redemptive.

Adv. in full restitution; as partial compensation; to atone for.

791. STEALING.—*N.* stealing, theft, thievery, robbery, rapacity, thievishness, abstraction, appropriation, plagiarism, depredation; kidnaping.

pillage, spoliation, plunder, sack, rapine, brigandage, highway robbery, holdup [*slang*]; raid, foray, piracy, privateering, buccaneering, filibustering; burglary, housebreaking; shoplifting, blackmail.

peculation, embezzlement, fraud, forgery, larceny, pilfering; kleptomania.

V. steal, thieve, rob, purloin, pilfer, filch, bag, crib [*colloq.*], palm; abstract; appropriate, plagiarize.

abduct, convey away, carry off, kidnap, impress, make (*or* run) off with, run away with, spirit away, seize.

plunder, pillage, filibuster, rifle, sack, loot, ransack, spoil, despoil, strip, sweep, gut, forage, levy blackmail, maraud, poach, smuggle, bunko; hold up.

swindle, peculate, embezzle; sponge, pluck, fleece, defraud, obtain under false pretenses.

counterfeit, forge, coin, circulate bad money.

Adj. thievish, light-fingered, piratical; predatory, raptorial.

792. THIEF.—*N.* thief, robber, spoiler, depredator, pillager, marauder; pilferer, plagiarist; harpy, shark [*slang*], smuggler, poacher, kidnaper; crook [*slang*], shoplifter.

pirate, corsair, viking, buccaneer, privateer.

brigand, bandit, filibuster, freebooter, thug, cattle thief, bushranger, mosstrooper [*hist.*], highwayman, footpad, strong-arm man.
pickpocket, cutpurse, light-fingered gentry; sharper; cardsharper, trickster.
swindler, peculator, forger, coiner, counterfeiter; fence, receiver of stolen goods.
burglar, housebreaker, yegg [*slang*], cracksman [*slang*], sneak thief; second-story thief (*or* man).

793. BOOTY.—*N.* booty, spoil, plunder, prize, prey, loot, swag [*cant*]; perquisite, boodle [*polit. cant*], graft [*colloq.*]; pork barrel [*polit. cant*], pickings; blackmail; stolen goods.

Adj. looting, plundering, spoliative.

794. BARTER.—*N.* barter, exchange, interchange, Indian gift [*colloq.*].

trade, commerce, buying and selling, traffic, business, custom, transaction, negotiation, bargain; speculation, jobbing, stock-jobbing.

free trade [*opp. to* protection].

V. barter, exchange, truck, swap *or* swop [*colloq. and dial.*]; interchange.

trade, traffic, buy and sell, give and take, carry on (*or* ply) a trade; deal in, speculate.

bargain; drive (*or* make, strike) a bargain; negotiate, bid for; haggle, stickle, dicker, cheapen, beat down, underbid; outbid.

Adj. **commercial**, mercantile, trading; marketable, staple, in the market, for sale; at a bargain, marked down; retail; wholesale.

Adv. across the counter; in the marts of trade.

795. PURCHASE.—*N.* purchase, buying, purchasing, shopping.

buyer, purchaser, client, customer, patron, clientele.

V. **buy**, purchase, invest in, procure; shop, market, go a-shopping; rent, hire, repurchase, buy in.

796. SALE.—*N.* **sale**, disposal; auction, custom.

salableness, salability, marketability, vendibility.

seller, vender, vendor [*law*]; merchant, auctioneer.

salesmanship, selling ability.

V. **sell**, vend, dispose of, make a sale, effect a sale; auction, sell at auction, put up to (*or* at) auction; hawk, dump, unload, place, undersell; dispense, offer, retail; deal in, sell off (*or* out), turn into money, realize.

Adj. **salable**, marketable, staple, in demand, popular.

unsalable, unpurchased, unbought, on the shelves, on one's hands.

797. MERCHANT.—*N.* **merchant**, trader, dealer, salesman; money-changer, shopkeeper, shopman; tradesman, tradespeople, tradesfolk.

peddler, hawker, huckster, sutler, vivandière; costermonger; canvasser, solicitor; faker [*slang*].

moneylender, usurer, banker; money-changer, money broker.

jobber, broker; buyer, seller; bear, bull [*Stock Exchange*].

firm, company, house, corporation, concern, trust.

798. MERCHANDISE.—*N.* **merchandise**, ware, commodity, effects, goods, article, stock, produce, staple commodity; stock in trade, cargo.

799. MART.—*N.* **mart**, market, market place; fair, bazaar, exchange, stock exchange, Wheat Pit [*Chicago*]; bourse, curb.

shop, store, department store, chain store, warehouse, depot, emporium, establishment; stall, booth; office, chambers, counting-house, bureau; counter.

(2) Monetary Relations

800. MONEY.—*N.* **money**, finance, funds, treasure, capital, stock; assets, wealth, etc., 803; supplies, ways and means, wherewithal *or* wherewith, sinews of war, almighty dollar, cash.

solvency, responsibility, reliability, solidity, soundness.

sum, amount; balance, balance sheet; sum total; proceeds, receipts.

currency, circulating medium, specie, coin, piece, hard cash; dollar, sterling; pounds, shillings, and pence, £ s. d.; guinea; wallet, roll, wad [*slang*], purse, ready money.
precious metals, gold, silver, copper, bullion, ingot, bar, nugget.
petty cash, pocket money, pin money, spending money, change, small coin. wampum.
great wealth, money to burn [*colloq.*]; power *or* mint of money [*colloq.*], good sum, millions, thousands.
Science of coins: numismatics.
paper money; bill, money order; note, note of hand; bank note, promissory note; I O U, bond; bill of exchange; draft, check, order, warrant, coupon, debenture, greenback.

V. total, amount to, come to, mount up to.
issue, utter, circulate; fiscalize, monetize.
demonetize, deprive of standard value; cease to issue.
Adj. monetary, pecuniary, fiscal, financial; sterling.
solvent, sound, substantial, good, reliable, responsible, solid, having a good rating; able to pay 100 cents to the dollar.

801. TREASURER.—*N.* treasurer, bursar, purser, banker, financier; receiver, liquidator, steward, trustee, accountant, expert accountant, almoner, paymaster, cashier, teller; money-changer.

802. TREASURY.—*N.* treasury, bank, exchequer, bursary; strongbox, stronghold, strong room; coffer, chest, safe, depository, cash register, cashbox, money box, till.
purse, moneybag, pocketbook, wallet; pocket.
securities, stocks; public stocks (*or* funds, securities); bonds, government bonds, Liberty bonds [U. S.], gilt-edged securities.

803. WEALTH.—*N.* wealth, riches, fortune, opulence, affluence; easy circumstances; independence, competence.
capital, money; great wealth, bonanza, El Dorado; philosopher's stone; the golden touch.
pelf, mammon, lucre, filthy lucre.
means, resources, substance, command of money; property, income, livelihood.
rich man, moneyed man, man of substance; capitalist, millionaire, multimillionaire, plutocrat; nabob, Croesus, Midas.
V. be rich, roll (*or* wallow) in wealth, have money to burn [*colloq.*]; afford, well afford, command money.
become rich, fill one's pocket, feather one's nest, make a fortune; make money; worship mammon, worship the golden calf.
Adj. wealthy, rich, affluent, opulent, moneyed, well-to-do, well off, rolling in riches.

804. POVERTY.—*N.* poverty, indigence, penury, pauperism, destitution, want; need, neediness; lack, necessity, privation, distress, difficulties, wolf at the door, straits; low water [*slang*], impecuniosity.

mendicancy, beggary, mendicity; broken (*or* loss of) fortune; insolvency.

poor man, pauper, mendicant, beggar.

V. be poor, want, lack, starve, live from hand to mouth, have seen better days, go to rack and ruin; beg one's bread, run into debt.

impoverish, reduce, reduce to poverty, pauperize, fleece, ruin.

Adj. poor, indigent; poverty-stricken, badly off, moneyless, penniless; impecunious, short of money, hard up, seedy [*colloq*.]; barefooted, beggarly, beggared, destitute, reduced, needy, necessitous, distressed, pinched, straitened, embarrassed, involved, insolvent.

805. CREDIT.—*N*. credit, trust, score, tally, account.

paper credit, letter of credit, circular note; duplicate; mortgage. lien, draft, securities.

creditor, lender, lessor [*law*], mortgagee; dun, usurer.

V. credit, accredit, intrust, keep (*or* run up) an account with; place to one's credit (*or* account); give (*or* take) credit.

Adj. accredited; of good credit, of unlimited credit; well rated; credited.

Adv. on credit, to the account of, to the credit of.

806. DEBT.—*N*. debt, obligation, liability, debit, score.

arrears, deferred payment, deficit, default, insolvency; bad debt.

interest; premium, usury.

debtor; mortgagor, defaulter, borrower.

V. be in debt, owe; incur (*or* contract) a debt, run up a bill, (*or* an account); borrow, run into debt, be in difficulties.

answer for, go bail for; back one's note.

Adj. liable, chargeable, answerable for.

indebted, in debt, in embarrassed circumstances, in difficulties; encumbered, involved; insolvent.

unpaid; unrequited, unrewarded; owing, due, in arrear, outstanding.

807. PAYMENT.—*N*. payment, discharge, settlement, clearance, liquidation, satisfaction, reckoning, arrangement.

acknowledgment, release; receipt, voucher.

repayment, reimbursement, retribution; pay, money paid.

V. pay, defray, make payment; pay one's way, expend, put down, lay down; discharge, settle, foot the bill [*colloq*.]; settle with, satisfy, pay in full, clear, liquidate, pay up; cash, honor a bill, acknowledge; redeem.

repay, refund, reimburse, disgorge, make repayment.

Adj. out of debt, owing nothing, all clear, clear of debt, above-water; solvent.

Adv. money down, cash down, cash on delivery, C.O.D.

808. NONPAYMENT.—*N.* nonpayment; default, defalcation; protest, repudiation.

insolvency, bankruptcy, failure; run upon a bank; overdrawn account.

defaulter, bankrupt, insolvent, insolvent debtor; absconder, welsher [*slang*].

V. not pay, fail, break, stop payment; become insolvent (*or* bankrupt), swindle, run up bills.

protest, dishonor, repudiate, nullify.

Adj. in debt, behindhand, in arrear; beggared, insolvent, bankrupt, ruined.

809. EXPENDITURE.—*N.* expenditure, outgoings, outlay, expenses, disbursement; circulation.

Money paid: payment, etc., 807; pay, etc. (*remuneration*), 973; fee, footing, subsidy, tribute, ransom, bribe, donation, gift; investment; purchase.

deposit, earnest, installment.

V. expend, spend; run (*or* get) through, pay, disburse; lay out, fork out [*slang*]; invest, sink money.

reward, fee, remunerate; give, subscribe, subsidize; bribe.

Adj. lavish, free, liberal; beyond one's income.

expensive, costly, dear, high-priced, precious, high.

810. RECEIPT.—*N.* receipt, value received, income, revenue, return, proceeds; earnings.

rent, rent roll; rental.

premium, bonus, prize, drawings, handout [*slang*].

pension, annuity, pittance, jointure, alimony.

V. receive, get, be in receipt of, have coming in; take money; draw from, derive from; acquire, take.

yield, bring in, afford, pay, return; accrue.

Adj. remunerative, profitable, gainful, well paying, interest-bearing, well invested.

Adv. within one's income.

811. ACCOUNTS.—*N.* accounts, money matters, finance, budget, bill, score, reckoning, account.

bookkeeping, audit, single entry, double entry; ledger, cash-book, journal; balance sheet; receipts, assets; expenditure, liabilities; profit and loss account (*or* statement).

accountant, auditor, actuary, bookkeeper; expert accountant, certified accountant; bank examiner.

V. **keep accounts,** enter, post, post up, book, credit, debit, balance.

812. PRICE.—*N.* **price,** amount, cost, expense, charge, figure, demand, fare, hire; wages.

dues, duty, toll, tax, impost, tariff, levy; capitation, poll tax; custom, excise, assessment, taxation, tithe, ransom, salvage, towage; brokerage, wharfage, freightage.

worth, rate, value, par value, valuation, appraisement, money's worth; price current, market price, quotation.

V. **price,** set (*or* fix) a price, appraise, assess, charge, demand, ask, require, exact.

fetch, sell for, cost, bring in, yield, afford.

Adj. **taxable,** dutiable, assessable.

813. DISCOUNT.—*N.* **discount,** abatement, concession, reduction, depreciation, allowance, qualification, setoff, drawback, percentage. rebate.

V. **discount.** bate, rebate, abate, deduct, strike off, mark down, reduce, take off, allow, give, make allowance; depreciate.

Adv. **at a discount,** at a bargain, below par.

814. DEARNESS.—*N.* **dearness,** expensiveness, costliness, high price; overcharge, extravagance, exorbitance, extortion.

V. **overcharge,** bleed [*colloq.*], skin [*slang*], fleece, extort, profiteer.

pay too much, pay dearly, pay through the nose [*colloq.*].

Adj. **dear,** high, high-priced, expensive, costly, precious; extravagant, exorbitant, extortionate.

at a premium. beyond price, above price; priceless, of priceless value.

Adv. **dear,** dearly: at great cost, at heavy cost, at a high price.

815. CHEAPNESS.—*N.* **cheapness,** low price, depreciation, bargain, drug in the market.

V. **be cheap,** cost little; come down (*or* fall) in price, be marked down.

buy at a bargain, buy dirt-cheap, have one's money's worth; beat down, cheapen.

Adj. **cheap,** low-priced, low, moderate, reasonable, inexpensive, cheap at the price; dirt-cheap, catchpenny.

reduced, half-price, depreciated, shopworn, marked down, unsalable.

gratuitous, gratis, free, for nothing; costless, without charge, scot-free, complimentary, honorary.

Adv. **at a bargain,** for a mere song; at cost price, at prime cost.

816. LIBERALITY.—*N.* **liberality,** generosity, munificence;

bounty, bounteousness, hospitality, charity, open (*or* free) hand, open (*or* large) heart.

cheerful giver, free giver, patron; benefactor.

V. be liberal, spend freely; shower down upon, spare no expense, give with both hands; keep open house.

Adj. liberal, free, generous, charitable, hospitable; bountiful, bounteous, ample, handsome; unsparing, ungrudging; unselfish; open-handed, large-hearted; munificent, princely.

Adv. ungrudgingly; with open hands, with both hands.

817. ECONOMY.—*N.* economy, frugality; thrift, thriftiness, care, husbandry, retrenchment.

savings; prevention of waste, save-all; parsimony, etc., 819.

V. economize, save; retrench, cut down expenses; make both ends meet, meet one's expenses, pay one's way; husband, save (*or* invest) money; provide against a rainy day.

Adj. economical, frugal, careful, thrifty, saving, chary, spare, sparing; parsimonious, etc., 819; sufficient; plain.

818. PRODIGALITY.—*N.* prodigality, wastefulness, unthriftiness, waste; profusion, profuseness; extravagance, lavishness.

prodigal, spendthrift, waster, high roller [*slang*], squanderer, spender, prodigal son.

V. squander, lavish, sow broadcast, pay through the nose, spill, waste, dissipate, exhaust, drain, overdraw, spend money like water.

Adj. prodigal, profuse, thriftless, unthrifty, improvident, wasteful, extravagant, lavish, dissipated; penny-wise and pound-foolish.

Adv. with an unsparing hand.

819. PARSIMONY.—*N.* parsimony, parsimoniousness, stinginess, stint, illiberality, avarice, avidity, rapacity, extortion, venality, cupidity, selfishness.

miser, niggard, churl, screw, skinflint, curmudgeon, harpy, extortioner, extortionist, usurer.

V. grudge, begrudge, stint, pinch, gripe, screw, dole out, hold back, withhold, starve, famish.

drive a bargain, cheapen, beat down; have an itching palm, grasp, grab.

Adj. parsimonious, penurious, stingy, miserly, mean, shabby, near, niggardly, close, sparing, grudging, illiberal, ungenerous, churlish, sordid, mercenary, venal, covetous, avaricious; greedy, grasping, extortionate, rapacious.

Adv. with a sparing hand.

CLASS VI

WORDS RELATING TO THE SENTIENT AND MORAL POWERS

I. AFFECTIONS IN GENERAL

820. AFFECTIONS.—*N.* character, qualities, disposition, affections, nature, spirit, temper, temperament, idiosyncrasy, predilection, turn of mind, bent, bias, predisposition, proneness, proclivity, propensity, vein, humor, mood, sympathy.

soul, heart, bosom, inner man; inmost recesses of the heart.
passion, pervading spirit; ruling passion, fullness of the heart.
energy, fervor, fire, verve, force.

Adj. characterized, affected, formed, molded, cast, tempered; framed.

prone, predisposed, disposed, inclined; having a bias.
inborn, inbred, ingrained; deep-rooted, congenital, inherent.

Adv. at heart; in the vein, in the mood.

821. FEELING.—*N.* feeling, suffering, endurance, sufferance, response; sympathy, impression, inspiration, affection, sensation, emotion, pathos.

fervor, unction, gusto, vehemence, heartiness, cordiality, earnestness, eagerness, gush [*colloq.*], ardor, warmth, zeal, passion, enthusiasm, ecstasy.

excitement; thrill, shock, agitation, quiver, flutter, flurry, fluster, twitter, tremor, throb, throbbing, pulsation, palpitation, panting; blush, flush.

V. feel, receive an impression, be impressed with, respond, enter into the spirit of.

bear, suffer, support, sustain, endure, brook, brave, stand, abide, experience, taste, prove.

be agitated, be excited, glow, flush, blush, crimson, change color, mantle; darken, whiten, pale, tingle, thrill, heave, pant, throb, palpitate, tremble, quiver, flutter, shake, stagger, reel; wince.

Adj. sentient, sensuous, emotional; of (*or* with) feeling.

keen, sharp, lively, quick, acute, cutting, piercing, incisive, trenchant, pungent, racy, piquant, poignant, caustic.

impressive, deep, profound, indelible, deep-felt, heartfelt, soul-stirring, electric, thrilling, rapturous, ecstatic, rapt; pervading, penetrating, absorbing.

earnest, wistful, eager, fervent, fervid, gushing [*colloq.*], warm, passionate, hearty, cordial, sincere, zealous, enthusiastic, glowing, ardent.

rabid, raving, feverish, fanatical, hysterical, impetuous.

Adv. heartily, heart and soul, from the bottom of one's heart, devoutly.

822. SENSITIVENESS.—*N.* sensitiveness, sensibleness, sensibility, impressibility, susceptibility, vivacity, tenderness, sentimentality, sentimentalism.

excitability, etc., 825; physical sensibility, etc., 375.

V. be sensitive, have a tender heart; take to heart, shrink, wince, blench, quiver.

Adj. sensitive, sensible, impressible, impressionable; susceptive, susceptible; warmhearted, tenderhearted, softhearted, tender; sentimental, romantic; enthusiastic, impassioned, spirited, mettlesome, vivacious, lively, expressive, mobile, excitable, oversensitive, thin-skinned, fastidious.

Adv. to the quick, on the raw.

823. INSENSITIVENESS.—*N.* insensitiveness, insensibility, insensibleness, inertness, inertia, impassibility, impassivity, apathy, dullness, insusceptibility, lukewarmness.

coldness, coolness, frigidity, stoicism, nonchalance, unconcern, indifference, callousness, heart of stone.

torpor, torpidity, lethargy, coma, trance; sleep, stupor, stupefaction; paralysis, numbness.

stoic, Indian, man of iron.

V. be insensitive, not mind, not care, not be affected by; take no interest in; disregard.

blunt, numb, benumb, paralyze, deaden, stun, stupefy; brutalize. inure; harden, steel, caseharden, sear.

Adj. insensitive, insensible, unconscious, impassive, insusceptible, unimpressible; passionless, spiritless, heartless, soulless, unfeeling.

apathetic, unemotional, phlegmatic; dull, frigid, cold, coldblooded, coldhearted; inert, supine, sluggish, torpid, sleepy, languid, halfhearted; numb, numbed; comatose.

indifferent, lukewarm, careless, mindless, inattentive, unconcerned, nonchalant.

unaffected, unruffled, unimpressed, unexcited, unmoved, unstirred, untouched, unshocked, unblushing.

callous, thick-skinned, impervious, hard, hardened, inured, casehardened; imperturbable, unfelt.

Adv. in cold blood; with dry eyes.

824. EXCITEMENT.—*N.* excitement, excitation, stimulation, piquancy, provocation, inspiration, animation, agitation, perturbation; fascination, intoxication, impressiveness; irritation, passion, thrill.

emotional appeal, melodrama, sensationalism, yellow journalism.

V. excite, affect, touch, move, impress, strike, interest, animate, inspire, smite, infect, awake, wake; awaken, waken; call forth; evoke, provoke; raise up, summon up, call up, wake up, raise; rouse, arouse, stir, fire, kindle, enkindle, illumine, illuminate, inflame.

stimulate, inspirit; stir up, infuse life into, give new life to; introduce new blood, quicken; sharpen, whet, fillip; fan, foster, heat, warm, foment, revive, rekindle.

penetrate, pierce; go to one's heart, touch to the quick, possess the soul, rivet the attention; prey on the mind.

agitate, perturb, ruffle, fluster, flutter, flurry, shake, disturb, startle, shock, stagger, strike dumb, stun, astound, electrify, galvanize, petrify.

irritate, sting, cut, pique, infuriate, madden, lash into fury.

flare up, flash up, seethe, boil, simmer, foam, fume, flame, rage, rave.

Adj. excited, wrought up, overwrought, hot, red-hot, flushed, feverish; raging, flaming, ebullient, seething, foaming, fuming, stung to the quick; wild, raving, frantic, mad, distracted, beside oneself.

exciting, impressive, telling, warm, glowing, fervid, spirit-stirring, thrilling, soul-stirring, heart-stirring, agonizing, sensational, yellow [*colloq.*], melodramatic, hysterical; overpowering, overwhelming.

piquant, spicy, appetizing, stinging, provocative, tantalizing.

Adv. at a critical moment, under a sudden strain.

825. [Excess of sensitiveness] EXCITABILITY.—*N.* excitability, impetuosity, vehemence, boisterousness, turbulence; impatience, intolerance, irritability; disquiet, disquietude, restlessness, fidgets, agitation.

trepidation, perturbation, ruffle, hurry, fuss, flurry, fluster, flutter; ferment; whirl; stage fright, thrill.

passion, excitement, flush, heat, fever, fire, flame, fume, tumult, effervescence, ebullition; gust, storm, tempest; burst, fit, paroxysm, explosion, outbreak, scene, outburst; agony.

fury; violence, fierceness, rage, furor, desperation, madness, distraction, raving, delirium; frenzy, hysterics; intoxication; towering rage, anger, etc., 900.

fixed idea, monomania; fascination, infatuation; fanaticism; quixotism, quixotry.

V. fidget, fuss.

fume, rage, foam; bear ill, wince, chafe, champ the bit, lose one's temper, break out, burst out, fly out, explode, flare up, flame up, fire up, boil, rave, rant, tear, go into hysterics; run riot, run amuck; raise Cain [*slang*].

Adj. **excitable**, easily excited, mettlesome, high-mettled, skittish, high-strung, nervous, irritable, hasty, impatient, intolerant, moody; feverish, hysterical, delirious, mad.

restless, unquiet, mercurial, galvanic, fidgety, fussy.

vehement, demonstrative, violent, wild, furious, fierce, fiery, hotheaded; overzealous, enthusiastic, impassioned, fanatical; rabid, rampant, clamorous, uproarious, turbulent, tempestuous, boisterous.

impulsive, impetuous. passionate, uncontrolled, uncontrollable, ungovernable, irrepressible. volcanic.

Adv. in confusion, pellmell.

826. INEXCITABILITY.—*N.* **inexcitability**, imperturbability, even temper, tranquil mind, dispassion; toleration, tolerance, patience; passiveness, inertia, etc., 172; impassibility, etc. (*insensibility*), 823; stupefaction.

calmness, composure, placidity, *sang-froid* [F.], coolness, tranquillity, serenity, content; quiet, quietude; peace of mind.

equanimity, poise, staidness, gravity, sobriety, philosophy, stoicism, self-possession, self-control, self-command, self-restraint; presence of mind.

resignation, submission, sufferance, endurance, long-sufferance, forbearance, longanimity, fortitude, patience of Job, moderation, restraint.

V. **endure**, bear, go through, support, brave, disregard; tolerate, suffer, stand, bide; abide, bear with, put up with, acquiesce, submit, resign oneself to, brook, digest, eat, swallow, pocket, stomach; carry on, carry through; make light of, make the best of, put a good face on.

compose, appease, assuage, propitiate, repress, restrain, master one's feelings, set one's mind at ease (*or* rest), calm down, cool down.

Adj. **inexcitable**, imperturbable; unsusceptible, dispassionate, cold-blooded, enduring, stoical, philosophical, staid, sober, grave; sedate, demure, coolheaded, levelheaded.

easygoing, peaceful, placid, calm; quiet, tranquil, serene, cool, undemonstrative.

composed, collected, temperate, unstirred, unruffled, unperturbed.

meek, mild, tame, subdued, unoffended, unresisting, submissive, gentle, patient, tolerant, clement, long-suffering.

Adv. in cold blood; more in sorrow than in anger.

II. PERSONAL AFFECTIONS[1]

827. PLEASURE.—*N.* pleasure, gratification, enjoyment, delectation, relish, zest, gusto, satisfaction, complacency; well-being; good, etc., 618; comfort, ease, luxury; physical pleasure, etc., 377.

joy, gladness, delight, glee, cheer, sunshine; cheerfulness, etc., 836; treat, luxury; amusement, etc., 840.

happiness, felicity, bliss, beatitude, enchantment, transport, rapture, ecstasy; paradise, heaven.

V. enjoy oneself, joy, be in clover [*colloq.*], tread on enchanted ground; go into raptures; feel at home, breathe freely, bask in the sunshine.

enjoy, like, relish, be pleased with, derive pleasure from, take pleasure in, delight in, rejoice in, indulge in, gloat over, love; take to, take a fancy to [*both colloq.*].

Adj. pleased, gratified, glad, gladsome; comfortable, etc. (*physical pleasure*), 377; at ease; content, etc., 831.

happy, blessed, blissful, beatified, joyful, in raptures, in ecstasies.

overjoyed, entranced, enchanted; raptured, enraptured, ravished, transported; fascinated, captivated.

pleasing, delightful, ecstatic, beatific, painless, unalloyed, cloudless.

828. PAIN.—*N.* pain, mental suffering, dolor, suffering, ache; physical pain, etc., 378.

displeasure, dissatisfaction, discomfort, discomposure, disquiet; inquietude, uneasiness, discontent.

annoyance, irritation, worry; infliction, visitation; plague, bore; bother, vexation, mortification, chagrin.

care, anxiety, solicitude, concern, trouble, trial, ordeal, shock, blow, fret, burden, load.

grief, sorrow, distress, affliction, woe, bitterness, heartache, heavy (*or* aching, bleeding, broken) heart.

misery, unhappiness, infelicity, tribulation, wretchedness, desolation; despair, etc., 859; extremity, prostration, depth of misery, slough of despond; nightmare, incubus.

anguish, pang, agony, torture, torment; crucifixion, martyrdom, rack, hell upon earth; reign of terror.

sufferer, victim, prey, martyr, wretch, shorn lamb.

V. suffer, ail, feel (*or* suffer, undergo, bear, endure) pain, smart, ache, bleed, bear the cross; fall on evil days, come to grief.

fret, chafe, sit on thorns, wince, worry oneself, fret and fume; take to heart.

[1] Or those which concern one's own state of feeling.

grieve, mourn, lament, etc., 839; yearn, repine, pine, droop, languish, sink, despair, break one's heart.

Adj. **pained,** afflicted, suffering, worried, displeased, aching, griped, sore, raw, on the rack.

uneasy, uncomfortable, ill at ease; disturbed; discontented; weary, etc., 841.

unfortunate, etc., 735; doomed, devoted, accursed, undone, crushed, lost, stranded; victimized, ill-used.

unhappy, infelicitous, poor, wretched, miserable, woebegone, comfortless, cheerless, etc. (*dejected*), 837; careworn; heavy-laden, stricken.

sorry, concerned, sorrowful, cut up [*colloq.*], chagrined, horrified, horror-stricken; heartbroken, brokenhearted.

829. [Capability of giving pleasure] PLEASURABLENESS.— *N.* **pleasurableness,** pleasantness, agreeableness, pleasure giving, amusement, etc., 840; treat, etc. (*physical pleasure*), 377; dainty titbit, sweets, sweetmeats, nuts, salt, savor.

attraction, attractiveness, charm, fascination, captivation, enchantment, witchery, seduction, winning ways, winsomeness; loveliness, beauty, etc., 845.

V. **delight,** charm, gladden, bless, captivate, fascinate; enchant, entrance, enrapture, transport, bewitch, ravish.

please, satisfy, gratify, satiate, quench, indulge, humor, flatter, tickle; tickle the palate, refresh, enliven, treat, amuse, take one's fancy; attract, allure; stimulate, excite, interest.

Adj. **pleasurable,** pleasure-giving, pleasing, pleasant, amiable, agreeable, grateful, gratifying acceptable; dear, beloved, welcome, favorite.

refreshing, comfortable, cordial, genial, glad gladsome; sweet, delectable, nice, dainty, delicate, delicious.

attractive, inviting, prepossessing, engaging winning, winsome, magnetic, fascinating, seductive, alluring, enticing, appetizing, cheering, bewitching, enchanting, entrancing.

delightful, charming, felicitous, exquisite, lovely, ravishing, rapturous; heartfelt, thrilling, ecstatic, heavenly.

Adv. to one's delight, in utter satisfaction; at one's ease; in clover [*colloq.*].

830. [Capability of giving pain] PAINFULNESS.— *N.* **painfulness,** trouble, care, trial, affliction, infliction, misfortune, mishap; cross, blow, stroke, burden, load, curse.

annoyance, pique, grievance, nuisance, vexation, mortification, worry, bore, bother, hornet's nest, plague, pest, wound; sore subject, skeleton in the closet, thorn in the flesh.

V. **pain,** hurt, wound, cause (*or* occasion, give, inflict) pain;

pierce, prick, cut, etc. (*physical pain*), 378; pierce (*or* break, rend) the heart; make the heart bleed.

sadden, make unhappy, grieve, afflict, distress; cut up [*colloq.*], cut to the heart.

annoy, incommode, displease, discompose, trouble, disturb, cross, thwart, perplex, molest; tease, tire, irk, fret, vex, mortify, worry, plague, bother, pester, bore, harass, harry, badger, heckle [*Brit.*], bait, beset, infest, persecute.

torment, wring, harrow, torture, rack, crucify, convulse, agonize.

irritate, provoke, sting, nettle, pique, fret, roil, rile [*colloq. & dial.*], chafe, gall; aggrieve, affront, enrage, ruffle, give offense.

maltreat, bite, snap at, assail, smite, etc., 972.

repel, revolt, sicken, disgust, nauseate, disenchant, offend, shock, rankle, gnaw, corrode, horrify, appall.

Adj. **painful,** hurtful, dolorous; distressing, cheerless, dismal, disheartening, depressing, dreary, melancholy, grievous, piteous, woeful, mournful, deplorable, pitiable, lamentable, sad; affecting, touching, pathetic.

unpleasant, unpleasing, displeasing, disagreeable, unpalatable, bitter, distasteful, uninviting, unwelcome, undesirable, obnoxious; unacceptable.

inauspicious, unlucky, ill-starred, unsatisfactory; untoward.

irritating, provoking, annoying, aggravating [*colloq.*], exasperating, galling, vexatious; troublesome, tiresome, irksome, wearisome.

importunate, pestering, bothering, harassing, worrying, tormenting.

insufferable, intolerable, insupportable, unbearable, unendurable.

shocking, terrific, grim, appalling, crushing; dreadful, fearful, frightful, tremendous, dire, heartbreaking, heart-rending, harrowing, rending.

odious, hateful, execrable, repulsive, repellent, horrid, horrible; offensive; nauseous, disgusting, revolting, nasty, loathsome, vile, hideous.

acute, sharp, sore, severe, grave, hard, harsh, cruel, biting, caustic; cutting, corroding, consuming, excruciating, agonizing.

cumbrous, cumbersome, burdensome, onerous, oppressive.

desolating, withering, tragical, disastrous, calamitous, ruinous.

Adv. in agony, out of the depths.

831. CONTENT.—*N.* content, contentment, contentedness; complacency, satisfaction, ease, peace of mind, serenity, cheerfulness; comfort.

patience, moderation, endurance; conciliation, reconciliation; resignation.

V. **be content**, rest satisfied, let well enough alone; take in good part; be reconciled to, take heart, take comfort.

content, set at ease, comfort; conciliate, reconcile, win over, propitiate, disarm, beguile; content, satisfy; gratify, etc., 836.

Adj. **content**, contented, satisfied, at ease, at one's ease, easygoing, not particular; conciliatory, unrepining, resigned, cheerful, serene, at rest; snug, comfortable.

satisfactory, adequate, sufficient, ample, equal to; satisfying.

Adv. to one's heart's content.

832. DISCONTENT.—*N.* **discontent**, dissatisfaction; disappointment, mortification; cold comfort; regret, repining, inquietude, vexation of spirit, soreness; heartburning.

malcontent, grumbler, growler, grouch [*slang*], croaker, faultfinder.

the opposition; bitter-enders [*politics*, U. S.], die-hards.

V. **be discontented**, repine, regret, take to heart, make a wry face, look blue, look black, look glum.

grumble, take ill, take in bad part; fret, chafe, croak; lament.

dissatisfy, disappoint, mortify, put out [*colloq.*], disconcert, dishearten.

Adj. **discontented**, dissatisfied, unsatisfied, regretful, dejected, etc., 837; dissentient, malcontent, exacting.

glum, sulky, in high dudgeon, in a fume, in the sulks (*or* dumps), in bad humor; sour, soured, sore; out of humor, out of temper.

833. REGRET.—*N.* **regret**, repining; homesickness, nostalgia; bitterness, heartburning; lamentation, penitence, etc., 950.

V. **regret**, deplore, bewail, lament, etc., 839; repine, rue, rue the day; repent, etc., 950; leave an aching void.

Adj. **regretful**, rueful; homesick.

834. RELIEF.—*N.* **relief**, deliverance, alleviation, mitigation, palliation, solace, consolation, comfort, unction; encouragement.

V. **relieve**, ease, alleviate, mitigate, palliate, soothe; salve; soften, assuage, allay; remedy, cure, restore, refresh.

cheer, comfort, console; enliven; encourage, give comfort, inspirit, invigorate.

Adj. **soothing**, assuaging, balmy, lenitive, palliative, curative.

835. AGGRAVATION.—*N.* **aggravation**, heightening, intensification, overestimation, exaggeration.

V. **aggravate**, render worse, heighten, embitter, sour, intensify, enhance [*Note*: aggravate *in the sense of* provoke *is colloquial*].

Adj. **aggravated**, worse, unrelieved, aggravative.

Adv. from bad to worse, worse and worse.

836. CHEERFULNESS.—*N.* cheerfulness, geniality, gayety, cheer, good humor, spirits; high spirits, animal spirits, glee, high glee, light heart.

liveliness, life, alacrity, vivacity, animation, joviality, jollity, levity, jocularity.

mirth, merriment, hilarity, exhilaration, laughter, merrymaking, rejoicing, etc., 838.

optimism, hopefulness, etc., 858.

V. be cheerful, have the mind at ease, smile, keep up one's spirits, cheer up, take heart, cast away care, perk up; rejoice, etc., 838; carol, chirp, chirrup, lilt.

cheer, enliven, elate, exhilarate, gladden, delight, inspirit, animate, inspire.

Adj. cheerful; happy, etc., 827; cheery, sunny, smiling; blithe, in good spirits, chipper [*colloq.*], gay, debonair, light, lightsome, lighthearted; buoyant, bright, airy, jaunty, sprightly, spirited, lively, animated, vivacious, sparkling, sportive.

merry, joyful, joyous, jocund, jovial; jolly, blithesome, gleeful, hilarious.

winsome, bonny, hearty, buxom.

playful, tricksy, frisky, frolicsome, jocose, jocular, waggish, mirthful, rollicking.

elate, elated; exulting, jubilant, flushed, rejoicing.

cheering, inspiriting, exhilarating, pleasing, palmy, flourishing.

Adv. cheerfully, cheerily, with relish, with zest.

837. DEJECTION.—*N.* dejection, depression, mopishness, low (*or* depressed) spirits; heaviness, gloom; weariness, disgust of life; prostration, broken heart; despair, hopelessness.

melancholy, sadness, melancholia, blue devils [*colloq.*], blues [*colloq.*], dumps [*chiefly humorous*], doldrums, horrors, hypochondria, pessimism; despondency, slough of despond; disconsolateness, hope deferred.

gravity; demureness, solemnity; long face, grave face.

hypochondriac, self-tormentor, croaker, pessimist, damper, wet blanket.

V. be dejected, grieve, mourn, lament, give way, lose heart, despond, droop, sink, despair.

lower, frown, pout; look blue, lay to heart, take to heart.

mope, brood over, fret, sulk, pine, pine away; yearn, repine.

depress, discourage, dishearten, dispirit, damp, dull, deject, sink, dash, unman, prostrate, break one's heart; sadden, dash one's hopes, prey on the mind, damp the spirits.

Adj. cheerless, joyless, spiritless; unhappy, etc., 828; melancholy, dismal, dreary, depressing, somber, dark, gloomy, lowering, frowning, funereal, mournful, lamentable, dreadful.

downcast, downhearted, down in the mouth [colloq.], down on one's luck [colloq.], heavyhearted; sullen, mopish, moody, glum; sulky, etc. (discontented), 832; out of heart (or spirits); low-spirited; weary, etc., 841; discouraged, disheartened, despondent, crestfallen.

sad, pensive, doleful, woebegone, melancholic, bilious, jaundiced, saturnine, lackadaisical.

serious, sedate, staid, earnest, grave, sober, solemn, demure, grim, grim-faced, rueful, wan, long-faced.

disconsolate, forlorn, comfortless, desolate, sick at heart, heartsick.

overcome, broken-down, prostrate, cut up [colloq.], unnerved, unmanned; downfallen, downtrodden; brokenhearted; careworn.

Adv. with a long face, with tears in one's eyes.

838. [Expression of pleasure] **REJOICING.**—*N.* rejoicing, exultation, triumph, jubilation, heyday, flush, reveling, merry-making, pæan, *Te Deum* [L.]; congratulation.

smile, simper, smirk, grin; broad grin, sardonic grin.

laughter, giggle, titter, snicker, snigger, crow, cheer, chuckle, shout; guffaw, burst (or fit, shout, roar, peal) of laughter.

cheer, huzza, hurrah, cheering; shout, yell [U. S. and Can.], college yell; tiger [colloq.].

V. rejoice, congratulate oneself, hug oneself, clap one's hands; skip; sing, carol, chirrup, chirp, hurrah, cry for joy, leap with joy; exult, triumph; make merry.

smile, simper, smirk, grin, laugh in one's sleeve.

laugh, giggle, titter, snigger, snicker, chuckle, cackle; burst out, shout, roar, shake (or split) one's sides.

Adj. rejoicing, jubilant, exultant, triumphant, flushed, elated; laughing, convulsed with laughter.

laughable, ludicrous, etc. 853.

Adv. in fits of laughter; in triumph.

839. [Expression of pain] **LAMENTATION.**—*N.* lamentation, lament, wail, complaint, plaint, murmur, mutter, grumble, groan, moan, whine, whimper, sob, sigh; frown, scowl.

cry, scream, howl; outcry, wail of woe.

weeping, flood of tears, fit of crying, crying; melting mood. plaintiveness; languishment; condolence, etc., 915.

mourning, weeds [colloq.], widow's weeds, crape, deep mourning; sackcloth and ashes; death song, dirge, requiem, elegy, threnody, jeremiad, keen [Ir.].

mourner, keener [Ir.]; Niobe.

V. lament, mourn, deplore, grieve, keen [Ir.], weep over; bewail, bemoan, condole with, etc., 915; fret.

sigh, give (*or* heave) a sigh; wail.

cry, weep, sob, blubber, snivel, whimper, shed tears, burst into tears.

scream, groan, moan, whine, yelp, howl, yell, roar; rend the air.

complain, murmur, mutter, grumble, growl, clamor, croak, grunt.

Adj. lamenting, in mourning, in sackcloth and ashes, clamorous, sorrowing, sorrowful, mournful, lamentable, tearful, lachrymose, plaintive, querulous; in tears.

840. AMUSEMENT.—*N.* amusement, entertainment, diversion, recreation, relaxation, solace; pastime, sport; labor of love; pleasure, etc., 827.

fun, frolic, merriment, jollity, joviality, laughter, etc., 838; pleasantry, quip, jocoseness; drollery, buffoonery, tomfoolery; mummery, pageant.

play, game, gambol, romp, prank, antic, lark [*colloq.*], spree, skylarking, vagary, monkey trick, escapade, practical joke.

dance, hop [*colloq.*]; ball, masquerade, ballet; step dance, skirt dance, folk dance, morris dance; gavot, minuet, Highland fling, reel, jig, hornpipe, sword dance, cakewalk; country dance, Scotch reel, Virginia reel, quadrille, lancers, cotillion; waltz, polka, mazurka, schottische, one-step, fox-trot.

festivity, fete, festival, merrymaking; party, etc. (*social gathering*), 892; revels, revelry, reveling, carnival, saturnalia, jollification [*colloq.*], junket, picnic.

holiday, red-letter day, play day; high days and holidays; high holiday.

place of amusement, theater; concert hall, ballroom, dance hall, assembly room; moving-picture theater; movies [*colloq.*]; music hall; vaudeville theater; circus, hippodrome.

Sports and games: athletic sports, track events, gymnastics; tournament.
skating, tobogganing; cricket, tennis, lawn tennis, rackets, squash, fives; croquet, golf, curling, hockey, polo, football, Rugby, rugger [*colloq.*]; association, soccer [*colloq.*]; quoits, discus, putting the weight (*or* shot), tug of war; baseball, basketball, pushball, lacrosse.
billiards, pool, pyramids, bagatelle; bowls, skittles, ninepins, tenpins; chess, draughts, checkers, dominoes; dice; card games, etc.

toy, plaything, doll, bauble.

sportsman (*fem.* sportswoman), hunter, Nimrod.

gamester, sport, gambler; dicer, punter, plunger.

devotee, enthusiast, follower, fan [*slang*], rooter [*slang or cant*].

V. amuse, entertain, divert, enliven, raise a smile, excite (*or* convulse with) laughter; cheer, rejoice, solace, please, interest.

amuse oneself, sport, disport, revel, junket, feast, carouse.

banquet, make merry; frolic, gambol, frisk, romp, caper, dance.

Adj. amusing, entertaining, diverting, recreative, pleasant, laughable, etc. (*ludicrous*), 853; witty, etc., 842; festive, festal, jovial, jolly, roguish, arch, playful, sportive.

Adv. at play, in sport.

841. WEARINESS.—*N.* weariness, ennui, boredom, lassitude, fatigue, etc., 688; drowsiness, languor.

disgust, nausea, loathing, sickness; satiety, repletion.

tedium, wearisomeness, tediousness, monotony.

bore, buttonholer, proser, dry-as-dust, fossil [*colloq.*], wet blanket.

V. weary, tire, fatigue, bore, send to sleep; buttonhole.

pall, sicken, nauseate, disgust; harp on the same string.

Adj. wearying, wearing, wearisome, tiresome, irksome, uninteresting, stupid, monotonous, dull, dry, arid, tedious, humdrum, flat; prosy, prosing; slow, soporific, somniferous.

weary, tired, drowsy, sleepy, etc., 683; uninterested, flagging, used up, worn out, blasé [F.].

842. WIT.—*N.* wit, wittiness, Attic salt, Atticism; point, fancy, whim, humor, drollery, pleasantry.

buffoonery, fooling, farce, tomfoolery, broad farce, fun.

jocularity, jocoseness, facetiousness, waggishness, comicality.

smartness, ready wit, banter, persiflage, retort, repartee.

witticism, smart saying, sally, flash, scintillation, flash of wit; jest, joke, epigram, conceit.

wordplay, play upon words, pun, riddle, conundrum, quibble.

V. joke, jest, cut jokes; crack a joke, pun; make merry with.

retort, flash back, flash, scintillate; banter, etc. (*ridicule*), 856.

Adj. witty, clever, keen, keen-witted, brilliant, pungent, quick-witted, smart, jocular, jocose, funny, waggish, facetious, comic, whimsical, humorous, sprightly, sparkling, epigrammatic.

843. DULLNESS.—*N.* dullness, heaviness, flatness, stupidity, want of originality, dearth of ideas; matter of fact, commonplace, platitude.

V. be dull, hang fire, fall flat, platitudinize, prose.

depress, damp, throw cold water on, lay a wet blanket on.

Adj. dull, jejune, dry, uninteresting, heavy-footed, elephantine; insipid, tasteless, unimaginative; prosy, prosaic, matter-of-fact, commonplace, platitudinous, pointless.

stupid, slow, flat, humdrum, monotonous, stolid.

844. HUMORIST.—*N.* humorist, wag, wit, epigrammatist, punster; life of the party; joker, jester, buffoon, comedian, merry-andrew, mime, tumbler, acrobat, mountebank, harlequin, pantaloon, punch, punchinello, clown; motley fool; caricaturist.

845. BEAUTY.—*N.* beauty, form, elegance, grace, symmetry, bloom, delicacy, refinement, charm, style; comeliness, fairness, polish, gloss; good effect, good looks.

brilliancy, radiance, splendor, gorgeousness, magnificence; sublimity.

beau ideal, Venus, Aphrodite, Hebe, the Graces, peri, houri, Cupid, Apollo, Hyperion, Adonis; Helen of Troy, Cleopatra; Venus de Milo, Apollo Belvedere.

loveliness, pleasurableness, etc., 829.

beautifying, decoration, ornamentation, etc., 847.

V. beautify, set off, grace; decorate, etc., 847.

Adj. beautiful, beauteous, handsome; pretty; lovely, graceful, elegant, exquisite, delicate, dainty.

comely, fair, goodly, bonny, good-looking, well favored, well formed, well proportioned, shapely, symmetrical, harmonious.

bright, bright-eyed; rosy-cheeked, rosy, ruddy, blooming, in full bloom.

trim, trig, tidy, neat, spruce, smart, jaunty, dapper.

brilliant, shining, sparkling, radiant, splendid, resplendent, dazzling, glowing, glossy, sleek; rich, gorgeous, superb, magnificent, grand, fine.

artistic, aesthetic, picturesque, pictorial, enchanting, attractive, becoming, ornamental.

perfect, unspotted, spotless, immaculate; undeformed, undefaced.

passable, presentable, tolerable, not amiss.

846. UGLINESS.—*N.* ugliness, deformity, inelegance, disfigurement, blemish, want of symmetry, distortion; squalor.

eyesore, object, figure, sight [*colloq.*], fright, scarecrow, hag, harridan, satyr, witch, monster.

V. deface, disfigure, deform, distort, blemish, injure, spoil; soil.

Adj. ugly, inartistic, unsightly, unseemly, uncomely, unshapely, unlovely; unbeautiful; coarse, plain, homely.

misshapen, misproportioned, shapeless, monstrous, gross; ill-made, ill-shaped, ill-proportioned, crooked, distorted.

unprepossessing, hard-featured, ill-favored, ill-looking; squalid, haggard; grim, grisly, ghastly, cadaverous, gruesome.

uncouth, ungainly, graceless, inelegant, ungraceful, stiff, rough, gross, rude, awkward, clumsy, gawky, lumbering, unwieldy.

repellent, forbidding, frightful, hideous, odious, repulsive; horrid, horrible, shocking.

disfigured, tarnished, smeared, besmeared, discolored, spotted, spotty.

showy, specious, pretentious, garish.

847. ORNAMENT.—*N.* ornament, ornamentation, ornateness, adornment, decoration, embellishment.

embroidery, needlework; lace, trimming, drapery; tapestry, arras; millinery.
wreath, festoon, garland, chaplet, flower, nosegay, bouquet, posy [*colloq.*].
tassel, knot; shoulder knot, epaulet, star, rosette, bow; feather, plume, fillet, snood.
jewelry: tiara, crown, coronet, diadem; jewel, gem, precious stone, trinket.

finery, frippery, tinsel, spangle, excess of ornament; pride, show, ostentation.

illustration, illumination; purple patches.

virtu, article of virtu, work of art, bric-a-brac, curio; rarity, a find.

V. ornament, embellish, enrich, decorate, adorn, beautify; garnish, furbish, polish, gild, varnish, enamel, paint.

spangle, bespangle, bead, embroider, chase, tool; emblazon, blazon, illuminate.

smarten, trim, bedizen, prink, trick up, trick out, deck, bedeck, array; spruce up [*colloq.*]; smarten up, dress, dress up.

Adj. ornamental, ornate, ornamented, rich, gilt, begilt, festooned.

smart, gay, flowery, glittering, new-spangled, fine, well groomed.

showy, gorgeous, flashy, gaudy, garish, tawdry, etc., 851.

848. BLEMISH.—*N.* blemish, disfigurement, deformity, defect, flaw, injury, eyesore.

stain, blot, spot, speck, speckle, blur, freckle, patch, blotch, smudge, birthmark, scar, mole, pimple, blister.

V. disfigure, etc. (*injure*), 659.

Adj. disfigured, imperfect, injured; discolored, specked, speckled, freckled, pitted, bruised.

849. SIMPLICITY.—*N.* simplicity, plainness, homeliness; chasteness, chastity, restraint, severity, naturalness, unaffectedness.

V. simplify, reduce to simplicity, strip of ornament, chasten, restrain.

Adj. simple, plain, homelike, homely, homespun [*fig.*], ordinary.

unaffected, natural, native; inartificial, free from affectation; chaste, severe; unadorned, unornamented.

simple-minded, childish, credulous, etc., 486.

850. [Good taste] TASTE.—*N.* taste, good (*or* refined, cultivated) taste; delicacy, refinement, fine feeling, discrimination, tact, polish, elegance, grace, culture, cultivation.

Science of taste: aesthetics.

man of taste, connoisseur, judge, critic, virtuoso, amateur, dilettante; purist, precisian.

V. display taste, appreciate, judge, criticize, discriminate.

Adj. in good taste, tasteful, unaffected, pure, chaste, classical, cultivated; graceful, attractive, charming, aesthetic, artistic.

refined, elegant, prim, precise, formal.

Adv. with quiet elegance; with elegant simplicity; without ostentation.

851. [Bad taste] VULGARITY.—*N.* vulgarity, vulgarism, barbarism, vandalism, bad taste; want of tact; ill-breeding, coarseness, indecorum, misbehavior, boorishness.

lowness, low life, brutality, blackguardism, rowdyism, ruffianism; ribaldry.

Excess of ornament: gaudiness, tawdriness, cheap jewelry; flashy clothes (*or* dress), finery, frippery, trickery, tinsel.

vulgarian, rough diamond, clown, Goth, vandal; snob, cad [*colloq.*], cub; parvenu, upstart; frump [*colloq.*], dowdy, slattern.

V. be vulgar, misbehave; show a want of tact (*or* consideration); be a vulgarian.

Adj. in bad taste, vulgar, unrefined, coarse, indecorous, ribald, gross; unseemly, unpresentable, ungraceful; dowdy, slovenly; low, extravagant, monstrous, horrid, shocking.

ill-mannered, ill-bred, underbred, snobbish, uncourtly, uncivil, discourteous, ungentlemanly, unladylike.

uncouth, unkempt, unpolished, plebeian; rude, awkward; homely, homespun, provincial, countrified, rustic; boorish, clownish; savage, brutish, blackguardly, rowdy, wild; barbarous, barbaric, outlandish; uncultivated.

antiquated, obsolete, out of fashion, old-fashioned, out of date, unfashionable.

newfangled, fantastic, fantastical, odd, affected.

tawdry, gaudy, meretricious, obtrusive, flaunting, loud, crass, showy, flashy, garish.

852. FASHION.—*N.* fashion, style, society, good (*or* polite) society, civilized life, civilization; court, high life, world, fashionable world; upper ten [*colloq.*], elite, smart set [*colloq.*], the four hundred; Vanity Fair; Mayfair.

manners, breeding, politeness; air, demeanor, *savoir-faire* [F.], gentility, decorum, propriety, Mrs. Grundy; convention, conventionality, the proprieties, punctiliousness, form, formality, etiquette.

mode, vogue, style, the latest thing, the rage, prevailing taste; custom.

V. be fashionable, be the rage, have a run, pass current, follow the fashion, go with the stream

Adj. fashionable, in fashion, *à la mode* [F.], presentable; punctilious, genteel, decorous, conventional; well bred, gentlemanly, ladylike.

polished, refined, thoroughbred, gently bred, courtly, distinguished, aristocratic, self-possessed, poised, easy, frank, unconstrained.

modish, stylish, swell [*slang*], all the rage, all the go [*colloq.*].

Adv. for fashion's sake; in the latest style (*or* mode).

853. RIDICULOUSNESS.—*N.* ridiculousness, comicality, oddity, drollery; farce, comedy, burlesque, buffoonery, bull, Irish bull, spoonerism; bombast, anticlimax, bathos; absurdity, laughingstock.

V. be ridiculous, play the fool, make a fool of oneself, commit an absurdity.

Adj. ridiculous, ludicrous, comic *or* comical, waggish, quizzical, droll, funny, laughable, farcical, seriocomic, tragicomic.

odd, grotesque, whimsical, fanciful, fantastic, queer, quaint, bizarre, eccentric, strange, outlandish, out-of-the-way.

extravagant, monstrous, preposterous, absurd, bombastic, inflated, stilted, burlesque, mock heroic.

854. FOP.—*N.* fine gentleman, fop, swell [*colloq.*], dandy, exquisite, coxcomb, beau, man about town, spark, popinjay, puppy [*contemptuous*], prig, jackanapes, carpet knight; dude [*colloq.*].

fine lady, belle, flirt, coquette, toast.

855. AFFECTATION.—*N.* affectation, affectedness, pretense, pretension, airs, pedantry, stiffness, formality, mannerism, euphuism; boasting, charlatanism, quackery.

prudery, demureness, mock modesty, false shame; sentimentalism.

foppery, dandyism, coxcombry, puppyism, conceit; coquetry.

poser, actor; pedant, pedagogue, doctrinaire, purist, euphuist, mannerist; bluestocking, prig, charlatan; prude, puritan, precisian, formalist.

V. affect, act a part, give oneself airs, boast, simper, mince, attitudinize, pose, languish; overact, overdo.

Adj. affected, pretentious, pedantic, stilted, stagy, theatrical, canting, insincere, unnatural; self-conscious, artificial; overdone, overacted.

stiff, formal, prim, smug, complacent; demure, puritanical, prudish.

priggish, conceited, foppish, finical, finicking, mincing, simpering, namby-pamby, sentimental, languishing.

856. RIDICULE.—*N.* ridicule, derision, snicker *or* snigger, grin, scoffing, mockery, banter, irony, persiflage, raillery, chaff.

squib, satire, skit, quip.

burlesque, parody, travesty, farce, caricature.

buffoonery, practical joke, horseplay, roughhouse [*slang*].

V. ridicule, deride; laugh at, grin at, smile at; snicker *or* snigger; banter, chaff, joke, guy [*colloq.*], rag [*slang*], haze [*colloq.*].

burlesque, satirize, parody, caricature, travesty.

Adj. derisive, sarcastic, ironical, satirical, quizzical, burlesque, mock.

Adv. as a joke, to raise a laugh.

857. [Object and cause of ridicule] LAUGHINGSTOCK.—*N.* laughingstock, butt, game, fair game, April fool, original, oddity; queer fish [*colloq.*], figure of fun [*colloq.*]; monkey; buffoon.

858. HOPE.—*N.* hope; desire, etc., 865; trust, confidence, reliance, faith, assurance, security; reassurance.

hopefulness, buoyancy, optimism, enthusiasm, aspiration; assumption, presumption; anticipation.

optimist, utopian.

daydream, castles in the air, utopia, millennium; golden dream, airy hopes, fool's paradise, fond hope.

mainstay, anchor, sheet anchor; staff.

V. hope, trust, confide, rely, lean upon; live in hope, rest assured.

hope for, etc. (*desire*), 865; anticipate; presume, aspire; promise oneself; expect.

be hopeful, look on the bright side of, make the best of it, hope for the best; hope against hope, take heart, flatter oneself.

encourage, hearten, inspirit, hold out hope, cheer, assure, reassure, buoy up, embolden; promise, bid fair, augur well.

Adj. hopeful, confident, in hopes, secure, sanguine, buoyant, elated, flushed, exultant, enthusiastic.

fearless, unsuspecting, unsuspicious, undespairing, self-reliant; dauntless, etc. (*courageous*), 861.

propitious, promising, probable, auspicious, reassuring; encouraging, cheering, inspiriting, bright, roseate.

859. HOPELESSNESS.—*N.* hopelessness, despair, desperation; despondency, dejection, etc., 837; pessimism, hope deferred, dashed hopes.

pessimist, hypochondriac; bird of ill omen.

V. despair; lose (*or* give up, abandon) all hope, give up, give over, yield to despair; falter; despond.

Adj. hopeless, desperate, despairing, gone, in despair, forlorn, inconsolable, brokenhearted.

undone, ruined; incurable, cureless, incorrigible; irreparable, irrecoverable, irretrievable, irreclaimable, irredeemable, irrevocable.

unpropitious, unpromising, inauspicious, ill-omened, threatening, lowering, ominous.

860. FEAR.—N. fear, timidity, diffidence, apprehensiveness, fearfulness, solicitude, anxiety, care, apprehension, misgiving, mistrust, suspicion, qualm; hesitation.

trepidation, flutter, fear and trembling, perturbation, tremor, quivering, shaking, trembling, palpitation, nervousness, restlessness, disquietude, funk [colloq.].

fright, alarm, dread, awe, terror, horror, dismay, consternation, panic, scare; stampede [of horses].

intimidation, bullying; terrorism, reign of terror; terrorist, bully.

V. fear, be afraid, apprehend, dread, distrust; hesitate, falter, funk [colloq.], cower, crouch, skulk, take fright, take alarm; start, wince, flinch, shy, shrink, fly.

tremble, shake, shiver, shudder, flutter, quake, quaver, quiver, quail.

frighten, fright, terrify, inspire (or excite) fear, bulldoze [colloq.], alarm, startle, scare, dismay, astound; awe, strike terror, appall, unman, petrify, horrify.

daunt, intimidate, cow, overawe, abash, deter, discourage; browbeat, bully, threaten, terrorize.

haunt, obsess, beset, besiege; prey (or weigh) on the mind.

Adj. afraid, frightened, alarmed, fearful, timid, timorous, nervous, diffident, fainthearted, tremulous, shaky, afraid of one's shadow, apprehensive; aghast, awe-struck, awe-stricken, horror-stricken, panic-stricken.

dreadful, alarming, redoubtable, perilous, dread, fell, dire, direful, shocking, frightful, terrible, terrific, tremendous; horrid, horrible, ghastly, awful, awe-inspiring, revolting.

861. [Absence of fear] COURAGE.—N. courage, bravery, valor, resoluteness, boldness, spirit, daring, gallantry, intrepidity, prowess, heroism, chivalry, audacity, rashness, dash, defiance, confidence, self-reliance; manhood, manliness, nerve, pluck, mettle, grit, virtue, hardihood, fortitude, firmness, backbone, resolution, tenacity.

exploit, feat, deed, act, achievement.

brave man, man of courage, a man, hero, demigod; Hercules, Achilles, Sir Galahad.

brave woman, heroine; Amazon, Joan of Arc.

V. dare, venture, make bold; face (or front, confront, brave, defy, despise) danger; face; meet, brave, beard, defy.

nerve oneself, summon up (or pluck up) courage, take heart, stand to one's guns, bear up, hold out; present a bold front, show fight, face the music.

hearten, inspire courage, reassure, encourage, embolden, in-spirit, cheer, nerve, rally.

Adj. **courageous**, brave, valiant, valorous, gallant, intrepid, spirited, high-spirited, mettlesome, plucky; manly, manful, stout-hearted, lionhearted, bold, daring, audacious, fearless, dauntless, undaunted, undismayed, unflinching, unshrinking, confident, self-reliant.

enterprising, adventurous, venturous, venturesome; dashing, chivalrous, warlike, soldierly, heroic.

fierce, savage, pugnacious, bellicose.

strong-minded, strong-willed, hardy, doughty [*archaic or humorous*]; firm, resolute, determined, dogged, indomitable.

862. [Excess of fear] COWARDICE.—*N.* cowardice, pusil-lanimity, cowardliness, timidity, effeminacy; baseness, abject fear, funk [*colloq.*]; fear, etc., 860; white feather, cold feet [*slang*], yellow streak [*slang*].

coward, poltroon, dastard, sneak, recreant, cur [*contemptuous*], craven.

alarmist, terrorist, pessimist.

shirker, slacker; fugitive, etc., 623.

V. quail, funk [*colloq.*], cower, skulk, sneak; flinch, shy, fight shy, slink, run away; show the white feather.

Adj. **cowardly**, coward, fearful, shy, timid, timorous, spiritless, soft, effeminate, fainthearted; white-livered; dastard, dastardly, base, craven, sneaking, recreant; unwarlike.

Adv. with fear and trembling, in fear of one's life, in a blue funk [*colloq.*].

863. RASHNESS.—*N.* rashness, temerity, imprudence, indis-cretion; overconfidence, presumption, audacity, precipitancy, impetuosity, foolhardiness, heedlessness, thoughtlessness, care-lessness, desperation.

gaming, gambling; blind bargain, leap in the dark.

desperado, madcap, daredevil; scapegrace, Don Quixote, knight-errant, adventurer; fire-eater, bully, bravo.

gambler, gamester, etc. (*chance*), 621.

V. **be rash**, stick at nothing, play a desperate game, run into danger, play with fire (*or* edged tools); rush on destruction, tempt providence, go on a forlorn hope.

Adj. **rash**, incautious, indiscreet, injudicious, imprudent, im-provident, uncalculating, impulsive, heedless, careless, without ballast.

reckless, wild, madcap, desperate, devil-may-care, death-defy-ing, hotheaded, headlong, headstrong; breakneck, foolhardy, harebrained, precipitate.

overconfident, overweening; venturesome, venturous, adventurous, quixotic.

Adv. posthaste, headforemost.

864. CAUTION.—*N.* caution, cautiousness, discretion, prudence, heed, circumspection, calculation, deliberation, foresight, etc., 510; vigilance, etc., 459; warning, etc., 668.

worldly wisdom; safety first, Fabian policy, watchful waiting.

coolness, self-possession, self-command; presence of mind, *sangfroid* [F.].

V. be cautious, take care, take heed, mind, be on one's guard; think twice, look before one leaps, count the cost, feel one's way, see how the land lies; pussyfoot [*colloq.*], keep out of harm's way, stand aloof; keep (*or* be) on the safe side.

warn, caution, etc., 668.

Adj. cautious, wary, guarded, on one's guard, suspicious, vigilant, careful, heedful, chary, sure-footed, circumspect, prudent, noncommittal, canny [Scot.], discreet, politic, strategic.

unenterprising, unadventurous, cool, steady, self-possessed; overcautious.

865. DESIRE.—*N.* desire, wish, fancy, inclination, leaning, bent, mind, whim, partiality, predilection, propensity, liking, love, fondness, relish.

longing, hankering, yearning, aspiration, ambition, eagerness, zeal, ardor, solicitude, anxiety.

need, want, exigency, urgency, necessity.

appetite, keenness, hunger, stomach, thirst, drought.

avidity, greed, greediness, covetousness, ravenousness, grasping, craving, rapacity, voracity.

mania, passion, rage, furor, frenzy, itching palm, cupidity, kleptomania, dipsomania; monomania.

Person desiring: lover, votary, devotee, aspirant; parasite, sycophant.

attraction, magnet, loadstone, lure, allurement, fancy, temptation, fascination; hobby.

V. desire, wish, wish for, care for, affect, like, take to, cling to, fancy; prefer, have an eye to, have a mind to; have a fancy for, have at heart, be bent upon; set one's heart (*or* mind) upon, covet, crave, hanker after, pine for, long for; hope, etc., 858.

woo, court, ogle, solicit; fish for.

want, miss, need, lack, feel the want of.

attract, allure, whet the appetite; appetize, take one's fancy, tempt, tantalize, make one's mouth water.

Adj. desirous, desiring, appetitive, inclined, fain, wishful, longing, wistful; anxious, solicitous, sedulous.

eager, keen, burning, fervent, ardent; agog; breathless; impatient.

ambitious, aspiring, vaulting.

craving, hungry, sharp-set, peckish [*colloq.*], ravening, famished; thirsty, athirst, dry [*colloq. when meaning thirsty*], droughty.

greedy, voracious, ravenous, omnivorous, covetous, rapacious, grasping, extortionate, exacting, sordid, insatiable, insatiate.

desirable, desired, in demand, popular, pleasing, appetizing.

Adv. fain; with eager appetite.

866. INDIFFERENCE.—*N.* indifference, neutrality; unconcern, nonchalance, apathy, supineness, disdain, inattention, coldness.

V. be indifferent, stand neuter, take no interest in, have no desire for, have no taste for, not care for, care nothing for (*or* about); not mind; spurn, disdain.

Adj. indifferent, cold, frigid, lukewarm; cool, neutral, unconcerned, phlegmatic, easygoing, careless, listless, halfhearted, unambitious, undesirous, unsolicitous.

unattractive, unalluring, undesired, undesirable, unwished.

867. DISLIKE.—*N.* dislike, distaste, disrelish, disinclination, unwillingness, reluctance, backwardness.

repugnance, disgust, nausea, loathing, aversion, abomination, antipathy, abhorrence, horror, hatred, detestation; hate, etc., 898.

V. dislike, disrelish; mind, object to, have no taste for, shudder at, turn up the nose at, look askance at; shun, avoid, eschew, shrink from.

loathe, abominate, detest, abhor; hate, etc., 898.

repel, disincline, sicken, pall, nauseate, disgust, shock, make one's blood run cold.

Adj. loath, averse; shy of, sick of, disinclined, heartsick.

repugnant, repulsive, repellent, abhorrent, insufferable, fulsome, nauseous, loathsome, offensive, disgusting.

unpopular, undesirable, uncared for, disliked, out of favor.

uneatable, inedible, unappetizing, unsavory.

Adv. to satiety, to one's disgust.

868. FASTIDIOUSNESS.—*N.* fastidiousness, nicety, hypercriticism, epicurism.

discrimination, discernment, perspicacity, keenness, sharpness, insight.

epicure, gourmet.

Excess of delicacy: prudery, prudishness, primness.

V. be fastidious, split hairs; mince the matter; turn up one's nose at, disdain.

discriminate, have nice discrimination; have exquisite taste; be discriminative.

Adj. fastidious, nice, delicate, meticulous, finicking *or* finicky, exacting, hard to please, difficult, dainty, squeamish, thin-skinned; querulous; particular, scrupulous; critical, hypercritical, overcritical.

prudish, strait-laced, prim.

discriminative, discriminating, discerning, judicious, keen, sharp, perspicacious.

869. SATIETY.—*N.* satiety, satisfaction, saturation, repletion, glut, surfeit, satiation.

V. sate, satiate, satisfy, saturate, cloy, quench, slake, pall, glut, gorge, surfeit; bore, tire, spoil.

Adj. satiated, overgorged, overfed, blasé [F.], sick of.

870. WONDER.—*N.* wonder, astonishment, amazement, wonderment, bewilderment, admiration, awe; stupor, stupefaction, fascination, surprise.

V. wonder, marvel, admire, be surprised, start, stare; gape, hold one's breath, stand aghast.

astonish, surprise, amaze, astound; dumfound, dumfounder, startle, dazzle, daze, strike, electrify, stun, stupefy, petrify, confound, bewilder, stagger, fascinate, take away one's breath, strike dumb.

Adj. astonished, surprised, aghast, breathless, agape, openmouthed, thunderstruck, spellbound; lost in amazement (*or* wonder, astonishment).

wonderful, wondrous, surprising, striking, marvelous, miraculous; unexpected, mysterious, monstrous, prodigious, stupendous, inconceivable, incredible, strange.

indescribable, inexpressible, ineffable; unutterable, unspeakable.

Adv. for a wonder, strange to say, to one's great surprise.

871. [Absence of wonder] EXPECTANCE.—*N.* expectance, expectancy, expectation, etc., 507.

calmness, imperturbability, *sang-froid* [F.], coolness, steadiness, lack of nerves, want of imagination.

V. expect, etc., 507; not wonder, make nothing of, take it coolly.

Adj. expecting, unamazed, astonished at nothing, blasé [F.], expected, foreseen.

calm, imperturbable, nerveless, cool, coolheaded, unruffled, steady, unimaginative.

common, ordinary, etc. (*habitual*), 613.

872. PRODIGY.—*N.* prodigy, phenomenon, wonder, wonderment, marvel, miracle; freak, freak of nature, monstrosity, mon-

ster; curiosity, infant prodigy, lion, sight, spectacle; sign, portent.

873. REPUTE.—*N.* repute, reputation, distinction, mark, name, figure, note, notability, éclat, vogue, celebrity, fame, renown, popularity; credit, prestige, account, regard, respect, fair name.

dignity, stateliness, solemnity, grandeur, luster, splendor, nobility, majesty, sublimity, glory, honor.

rank, standing, precedence, station, place, status, position, order, degree, caste, condition.

eminence, greatness, height, importance, pre-eminence, supereminence, elevation, exaltation.

celebrity, worthy, hero, man of mark (*or* rank), lion, notability, somebody.

scholar, savant; paragon, star; elite.

ornament, honor, feather in one's cap, halo, aureole, nimbus; laurels.

posthumous fame, memory, celebration, canonization, enshrinement, glorification, immortality, immortal name.

V. be distinguished, shine, etc. (*light*), 420; shine forth, figure, cut a figure, flourish, flaunt, play first fiddle, bear the palm, take precedence; win laurels (*or* golden opinions).

surpass, outshine, outrival, outvie, eclipse; throw into the shade, overshadow.

rival, emulate, vie with.

honor, give (*or* do, pay) honor to, accredit, dignify, glorify, pledge, toast, look up to, exalt, aggrandize, elevate, enthrone, signalize, immortalize, deify.

consecrate; dedicate to, devote to; enshrine, inscribe, blazon, lionize.

Adj. distinguished, noted, of note, honored, popular, remarkable, notable, celebrated, renowned, famous, famed, far-famed, conspicuous, foremost.

reputable, in good odor, in favor, in high favor, respectable, creditable, worthy.

imperishable, deathless, immortal, never fading, fadeless.

illustrious, glorious, splendid, brilliant, radiant; bright, etc.,420.

eminent, prominent, high, etc., 206; peerless, pre-eminent, great, dignified, proud, noble, honorable, lordly, grand, stately, august, princely, imposing, solemn, transcendent, majestic, sacred, sublime.

874. DISREPUTE.—*N.* disrepute, discredit, ill-repute, ill-favor, ingloriousness, derogation, abasement, debasement, degradation; odium, obloquy, opprobrium, ignominy, dishonor, disgrace, shame, humiliation, scandal, infamy.

stigma, brand, reproach, imputation, slur, stain, blot, spot, blur, tarnish, taint, badge of infamy.

V. **be inglorious,** have a bad name; disgrace oneself, lose caste; fall from one's high estate, cut a sorry figure.

shame, disgrace, put to shame, dishonor; tarnish, stain, blot, sully, taint; discredit, degrade, debase, expel.

stigmatize, vilify, defame, slur, brand, post, send to Coventry, snub, show up [*colloq.*], reprehend.

disconcert, put out [*colloq.*], upset, discompose; put to the blush.

Adj. **disgraced,** overcome, downtrodden, in bad repute, under a cloud, in the shade (*or* background); down in the world, down and out [*colloq.*].

inglorious, nameless, obscure, unknown to fame, unnoticed, unnoted, unhonored, unglorified.

discreditable, questionable, shameful, disgraceful, disreputable, despicable; unbecoming, unworthy, derogatory, degrading, humiliating, scandalous, infamous, opprobrious, arrant, shocking, outrageous, notorious, ignominious, base, abject, vile.

beggarly, pitiful, mean, petty, shabby.

875. NOBILITY.—*N.* nobility, rank, condition, distinction, blood, birth, high descent, order, quality.

high life, upper classes, upper ten [*colloq.*], the four hundred; elite, aristocracy, fashionable world.

celebrity, bigwig [*humorous*], magnate, great man, star, great gun [*colloq.*].

The nobility: peerage, baronage; House of Lords (*or* peers); lords, noblesse.

peer, noble, nobleman; lord, grandee, don, hidalgo; aristocrat, swell [*colloq.*], gentleman, squire, patrician.

gentry, gentlefolk, magnates.

king, etc., 745; prince, duke, marquis, earl, viscount, baron, baronet, knight, chevalier, count, esquire, laird [Scot.]; signior, seignior; *signor* [It.], *señor* [Sp.], *senhor* [Pg.]; sheik, pasha, sahib

empress, queen, princess, duchess, marchioness, viscountess, countess; lady, *doña* [Sp.], *dona* [Pg.]; *signora* [It.], *señora* [Sp.], *senhora* [Pg.].

Hindu titles: raja, rana (*fem.* rani), maharaja, maharana (*fem.* maharani), Gaekwar [*lit.* cowherd; *Baroda*].

Mohammedan titles: nawab, sultan (*fem.* sultana), amir.

Rank or office: kingship, dukedom, marquisate, earldom; viscountship, county, lordship, baronetcy, knighthood.

Adj. **noble,** exalted, princely, titled, patrician, aristocratic; highborn, well born, courtly.

Adv. in high quarters.

876. THE PEOPLE.—*N.* the people, commonalty, democracy; obscurity; *bourgeoisie* [F.], the four million; lower classes (*or* orders), common herd, rank and file, the many, the general, the crowd, the ruck, the populace, the multitude, the million, the masses, the mobility [*humorous*], the peasantry, proletariat; *hoi polloi* [Gr.].

rabble, horde, canaille, dregs of society, mob, trash, riffraff, ragtag and bobtail.

commoner, one of the people, democrat, plebeian, republican, bourgeois [F.].

peasant, countryman, boor, churl, serf; swain, clown, clodhopper, yokel, lout, bumpkin; plowman, hayseed [*slang*], rustic, lunkhead [*colloq.*], rube [*slang*]; tiller of the soil; hewers of wood and drawers of water; gamin, street Arab.

rough, rowdy, roughneck [*slang*], ruffian, tough [*colloq.*], scullion, low fellow, cad.

upstart, parvenu, nobody, snob, mushroom, adventurer, *nouveau riche* (*pl. nouveaux riches*) [F.].

vagabond, beggar, caitiff, ragamuffin, pariah, outcast, tramp, panhandler [*slang*], bum [*slang*], hobo.

Adj. **ignoble,** common, mean, low, base, vile, sorry, scrubby, beggarly; vulgar, low-minded; snobbish, parvenu, low-bred; menial, servile.

plebeian, proletarian, lowborn, baseborn, risen from the ranks, obscure, untitled.

rustic, country, uncivilized; loutish, boorish, clownish, churlish, rude.

barbarous, barbarian, barbaric.

Adv. below the salt.

877. TITLE.—*N.* title, honor; earldom, etc. (*nobility*), 875.

highness, excellency, grace, lordship, reverence; reverend; esquire, sir, master, Mr., *signor* [It.], *señor* [Sp.], etc., 373; your (*or* his) honor.

madam, etc. (*mistress*), 374; empress, queen, etc., 875.

decoration, laurel, palm, wreath, garland, bays; medal, ribbon, cordon, cross, crown, coronet, star, garter; epaulet, chevron, colors, cockade; livery; order, arms, coat of arms, shield, escutcheon *or* scutcheon, crest; handle to one's name.

878. PRIDE.—*N.* **pride,** haughtiness, high notions, hauteur, vainglory, arrogance, self-importance, pomposity, side [*slang*], swagger, toploftiness [*colloq.*].

dignity, self-respect, self-esteem, decorum, stateliness, seemliness.

V. **be proud,** presume, swagger, strut, hold one's head high, look big, carry with a high hand; ride the high horse, give oneself airs.

Adj. **dignified,** stately, lordly, lofty-minded, high-souled, highminded, high-mettled, high-flown.

proud, haughty, lofty, high, mighty, swollen, puffed up, flushed, vainglorious; purse-proud, fine.

supercilious, disdainful, bumptious, magisterial, imperious, high and mighty, overweening, consequential; pompous, toplofty [*colloq.*]; arrogant.

stiff, stiff-necked; starched, stuck up [*colloq.*]; strait-laced, prim, affected, etc., 855.

Adv. with head erect, with nose in air, with nose turned up; with a sneer, with curling lip.

879. HUMILITY.—*N.* **humility,** humbleness, meekness, lowliness, abasement, self-abasement, submission, resignation.

modesty, timidity; confusion, humiliation, mortification.

V. **be humble,** deign, vouchsafe, condescend, humble oneself, stoop, submit, yield the palm, sing small [*colloq.*], hide one's face.

be humiliated, be put out of countenance, be shamed, be put to the blush, receive a snub, eat humble pie.

humble, humiliate, snub, abash, abase, strike dumb, lower, cast into the shade, put to the blush, confuse, shame, mortify, disgrace, crush.

Adj. **humble,** lowly, meek, modest, etc., 881; humble-minded, sober-minded; submissive, servile.

humbled, bowed down, abashed, ashamed, dashed, crestfallen, shorn of one's glory.

Adv. with downcast eyes, with bated breath, on bended knee.

880. VANITY.—*N.* **vanity,** conceit, conceitedness, self-conceit, self-sufficiency, self-praise, self-glorification, self-applause, self-admiration; selfishness, etc., 943.

pretension, airs, affected manner, mannerism; egoism, egotism, priggishness; vainglory, arrogance, pride, ostentation.

egoist, egotist; peacock; coxcomb.

V. **be vain,** pique oneself, have too high opinion of oneself, strut, put oneself forward; give oneself airs, boast, etc., 884.

render vain, inflate, puff up, turn one's head.

Adj. **vain,** conceited, overweening, forward, vainglorious, high-flown, ostentatious, etc., 882; puffed up, inflated, flushed, elate.

self-satisfied, complacent, self-confident, self-sufficient, self-admiring, pretentious, priggish, egotistic *or* egotistical, arrogant, assured.

881. MODESTY.—*N.* **modesty;** humility, etc., 879; diffidence, demureness, timidity, bashfulness, retiring disposition, unobtrusiveness; blush, blushing; reserve, constraint.

V. **be modest,** retire, give way to, hide one's face; keep in the background; hide one's light under a bushel.

Adj. **modest,** diffident, retiring, humble, etc., 879; timid, timorous, bashful, shy, coy, demure, sheepish, shamefaced, blushing.

unpretending, unpretentious, unobtrusive, unassuming, un-ostentatious, reserved, constrained.

Adv. **modestly,** quietly, privately; without ceremony.

882. OSTENTATION.—*N.* **ostentation,** display, show, flourish, parade, pomp, magnificence, splendor, pageantry, array, state, solemnity; dash [*colloq.*], splash [*colloq.*], glitter, pomposity, pretense, pretensions.

demonstration, pageant, spectacle, exhibition, exposition, procession, turnout [*colloq.*]; fete, field day, review, march past, promenade.

ceremony, ceremonial, ritual, form, formality, etiquette, punctilio.

V. **flaunt,** show off, parade, display, exhibit, brandish, blazon forth; dangle, emblazon.

Adj. **ostentatious,** showy, dashing, pretentious, grand, pompous; garish, gaudy, flaunting, glittering, gay.

splendid, magnificent, sumptuous, palatial.

theatrical, theatric, dramatic, spectacular, scenic.

ceremonial, ceremonious, ritualistic; solemn, stately, majestic, formal, punctilious.

Adv. **with flourish of trumpet,** with beat of drum, with flying colors.

883. CELEBRATION.—*N.* **celebration,** solemnization, commemoration; jubilation, ovation, triumph; inauguration, installation, presentation; coronation; debut, coming out [*colloq.*].

birthday, anniversary, biennial, triennial, etc.; centenary, centennial; bicentenary, bicentennial; tercentenary, tercentennial, etc.; festivity, festival, fete, holiday.

triumphal arch; salute, salvo, salvo of artillery; flourish of trumpets, fanfare; colors flying; illuminations.

jubilee, 50th anniversary; diamond jubilee.

V. **celebrate,** keep, signalize, do honor to, commemorate, solemnize; rejoice, etc., 838; paint the town red [*colloq.*].

inaugurate, install, instate, induct, chair.

Adj. **commemorative,** celebrated, kept in remembrance; immortal.

Adv. **in honor of,** in commemoration of, in celebration of, in memory of, in memoriam [L.].

884. BOASTING.—*N.* **boasting,** boast, vaunt, pretensions, braggadocio, puff [*colloq.*], flourish, bluff, highfalutin, swagger, jingoism, chauvinism, brag, bounce, bluster, bravado, buncombe [*cant or slang*]; rodomontade, bombast, hot air [*slang*], tall talk [*colloq.*], exaggeration, magniloquence, heroics.

boaster, braggart, pretender, bluffer, hot-air artist [*slang*]; chauvinist, jingo, jingoist; blusterer, swaggerer.

V. **boast,** brag, vaunt, puff, show off, flourish, strut, swagger, bluff; talk big, draw the long bow, blow one's own trumpet.

exult, crow [*colloq.*], triumph, glory, rejoice, cheer; gloat, gloat over, chuckle.

Adj. **boastful,** braggart, pretentious, vainglorious, highfalutin.

elate, elated, jubilant, triumphant, exultant; in high feather.

885. [Undue assumption of superiority] INSOLENCE.—*N.* insolence, brazenness, haughtiness, arrogance, airs; bumptiousness, assumption, presumption; disdain, insult, bluster, swagger.

impertinence, cheek [*colloq. or, slang*], nerve [*slang*], sauce [*colloq.*], abuse; flippancy.

impudence, self-assertion, assurance, audacity, hardihood, gall [*slang*], shamelessness, effrontery.

V. **be insolent,** bluster, swagger, give oneself airs, arrogate, assume, presume; make bold, make free, take a liberty.

outface, outlook, outstare, outbrazen, brazen out; look big.

domineer, bully, dictate, hector; lord it over; snub, browbeat, intimidate; dragoon, bulldoze [*colloq.*], terrorize.

Adj. **insolent,** haughty, arrogant, imperious, dictatorial, arbitrary, highhanded, supercilious, overbearing, toplofty [*colloq.*], intolerant, domineering, overweening, bumptious.

pert, flippant, fresh [*slang*], saucy, forward, impertinent, assuming, impudent, audacious, presumptuous.

brazen, shameless, unblushing, unabashed; barefaced, brazenfaced; lost to shame.

blustering, swaggering, hectoring, rollicking, roistering, devilmay-care.

jingo, jingoistic, chauvinistic.

Adv. with nose in air; with arms akimbo; with a high hand.

886. SERVILITY.—*N.* servility, slavery, obsequiousness, toadying, subserviency; abasement, prostration, toadeating, fawning, flunkyism, sycophancy; humility, etc., 879.

sycophant, parasite, toady, toadeater, flunky, hanger-on, timeserver, flatterer, tool; beat [*slang*], dead beat [*slang*]; heeler, ward heeler [*both polit. cant*]; sponge, sponger, truckler.

V. **cringe,** bow, stoop, kneel; fawn, crouch, cower, sneak, crawl, sponge, toady, grovel; be servile.

go with the stream, follow the crowd, worship the rising sun; be a timeserver.

Adj. **servile,** obsequious, oily, pliant, cringing, fawning, slavish, groveling, sniveling, mealy-mouthed; sycophantic, parasitical; abject, prostrate, base, mean, sneaking, timeserving.

887. BLUSTERER.—*N.* blusterer, swaggerer, braggart; roisterer, brawler, bully, terrorist, rough, ruffian, roughneck [*slang*], tough [*colloq.*], rowdy, hoodlum [*colloq.*], hooligan [*slang*], swashbuckler; desperado, daredevil, fire-eater [*colloq.*], jingo.

dogmatist, doctrinaire, stump orator.

III. SYMPATHETIC AFFECTIONS

888. FRIENDSHIP.—*N.* friendship, amity, friendliness; harmony, concord, peace, etc., 721; cordiality, *entente cordiale* [F.], good understanding, sympathy, fellow feeling, response; affection, etc. (*love*), 897; benevolence, good will; partiality, favoritism.

brotherhood, fraternization, association; acquaintance, familiarity, intimacy, intercourse, fellowship.

fraternity, sodality; sisterhood, sorority, sorosis.

V. be friendly, be friends, be acquainted with, know; have dealings with, sympathize with, have a leaning to, bear good will, love, befriend.

become friendly, make friends with, break the ice, be introduced to, make (*or* scrape) acquaintance with, get into favor, gain the friendship of; shake hands with, fraternize.

Adj. friendly, amicable, neighborly; brotherly, fraternal, sisterly; ardent, devoted, sympathetic, harmonious, hearty, cordial, warmhearted.

friends with, at home with, on good (*or* friendly, amicable, cordial, familiar, intimate) terms, on speaking terms, on visiting terms.

acquainted, familiar, intimate, hail fellow well met, free and easy; welcome.

Adv. with open arms; arm in arm.

889. ENMITY.—*N.* enmity, hostility, antagonism, unfriendliness; discord, etc., 713; bitterness, rancor; heartburning, animosity; malevolence, etc., 907.

alienation, estrangement; dislike, aversion, hate, etc., 808.

V. be unfriendly, keep (*or* hold) at arm's length; be at loggerheads, bear malice, fall out; take umbrage; alienate, estrange.

Adj. unfriendly, inimical, hostile; at enmity, at variance, at daggers drawn, up in arms against.

on bad terms, not on speaking terms; cool, cold, estranged, alienated, disaffected, irreconcilable.

890. FRIEND.—*N.* friend, alter ego [L.], other self; intimate, confidant ⟨*masc.*⟩, confidante (*fem.*); best (*or* bosom, fast) friend, well-wisher; neighbor, acquaintance.

patron, backer, tutelary saint, good genius, advocate, partisan, sympathizer; ally, friend in need.

associate, comrade, mate, companion, confrere, colleague, partner, consort, chum [*colloq.*], pal [*slang*], buddy [*slang*, *First World War*]· playfellow, playmate, schoolmate, schoolfellow, classmate; bedfellow, bunkie [*colloq.*], roommate, shopmate, shipmate, messmate; fellow (*or* boon) companion.

Famous friendships: Pylades and Orestes, Castor and Pollux, Achi'les and Patroclus, Damon and Pythias, David and Jonathan; Soldiers Three, the Three Musketeers.

host, hostess (*fem.*).

guest, visitor, frequenter, habitué, protégé.

compatriot, countryman, fellow countryman; fellow townsman.

891. ENEMY.—*N.* enemy, antagonist, foe, foeman, open (*or* bitter) enemy, opponent; mortal aversion (*or* antipathy); snake in the grass.

public enemy, enemy to society; anarchist, seditionist, traitor, traitress (*fem.*).

892. SOCIALITY.—*N.* sociality, sociability, social intercourse, intercourse, companionship, comradeship, fellowship; urbanity, intimacy, familiarity, condescension, *esprit de corps* [F.]; morale.

conviviality, good fellowship, joviality, jollity, festivity, merry-making; hospitality, heartiness; cheer.

welcome, greeting; hearty (*or* warm) reception; hearty welcome (*or* greeting), the glad hand [*slang*].

social gathering, social reunion, assembly, barbecue; bee; cornhusking, corn shucking [U. S.]; husking, husking-bee [U. S.]; hen party [*colloq.*]; house raising, housewarming, hanging of the crane, smoker [*colloq.*]; Dutch treat [*colloq.*]; stag, stag party [*both colloq.*]; sociable [U. S.], party, entertainment, reception, levee, at home, soiree, matinee; garden party, coming-out party [*colloq.*], surprise party; ball, hunt ball, dance festival.

Social meals: breakfast, wedding breakfast, hunt breakfast; luncheon, lunch; picnic lunch, basket lunch, picnic; tea, afternoon tea, five-o'clock tea, cup of tea, dish of tea [esp. Brit.], coming-out tea [*colloq.*]; tea party, tea fight [*slang*]; dinner, potluck, bachelor dinner, stag dinner [*colloq.*], hunt dinner; church supper, high tea, banquet.

visit, visiting; round of visits; call, morning call, interview; tryst, appointment.

V. be sociable, know, be acquainted, associate with, consort with, club together, join; make advances, fraternize.

visit, pay a visit, call at, call upon, leave a card, drop in, look in.

entertain, give a party; see one's friends, keep open house, do the honors, receive, welcome; kill the fatted calf.

Adj. sociable, companionable, clubbable [*colloq.*], cozy, chatty, conversational; convivial, festive, festal, jovial, jolly, hospitable.

free and easy, hail fellow well met, familiar, intimate, social, neighborly.

Adv. en famille [F.], in the family circle; on terms of intimacy; in the social whirl.

893. SECLUSION. EXCLUSION.—*N.* seclusion, privacy, retirement, concealment, rustication, solitude, isolation, loneliness, voluntary exile, aloofness.

retreat, cell, hermitage, cloister, convent; sanctum sanctorum [L.], study, library, den [*colloq.*].

exclusion, excommunication, banishment, exile, ostracism, cut.

unsociability, unsociableness, inhospitality, domesticity, self-sufficiency.

recluse, hermit; caveman, cave dweller, troglodyte, cynic, Diogenes.

outcast, pariah, leper; outsider, rank outsider; castaway, foundling.

V. **seclude oneself**, keep aloof, shut oneself up; deny oneself, rusticate, retire, retire from the world; take the veil.

exclude, repel, cut; send to Coventry, turn one's back upon, shut the door upon; blackball, excommunicate, exile, expatriate; banish, outlaw, maroon, ostracize, keep at arm's length; boycott, embargo, blockade, isolate.

Adj. **secluded**, sequestered, retired, private, out of the world.

unsociable, unsocial, inhospitable; domestic, stay-at-home.

excluded, unfrequented, unvisited, uninvited, unwelcome, under a cloud.

friendless, homeless, desolate, lorn, forlorn; solitary, lonely, lonesome, isolated, single, estranged; derelict, outcast, deserted, banished.

uninhabited, unoccupied, untenanted, tenantless, abandoned.

894. COURTESY.—*N.* **courtesy**; respect, etc., 928; good manners (*or* behavior, breeding); manners, politeness, urbanity, gentility, breeding, gentle breeding, cultivation, culture, polish, civility, amenity, suavity; good temper, good humor, amiability, complacency, affability, complaisance, compliance, gallantry, chivalry.

pink of courtesy, pink of politeness; flower of knighthood; Chesterfield; Lancelot.

ceremonial; salutation, reception, presentation, introduction, welcome, greeting; respects, regards, remembrances; deference, love.

Forms of greeting: bow, curtsy, salaam, kowtow [China], obeisance, bowing and scraping; kneeling, genuflection; capping, pulling the forelock, nod, shaking hands; embrace, hug, squeeze, kiss; salute, accolade.

V. **be courteous**, show courtesy; behave oneself, conciliate, speak one fair, take in good part.

do the honors, usher, usher in, receive, greet, hail, bid welcome, welcome; bid Godspeed; speed the parting guest.

salute; nod to; smile upon; uncover, touch (*or* raise) the hat, doff the cap, bow, make one's bow, curtsy, bob a curtsy, kneel; bow (*or* bend) the knee; salaam, kowtow [China], prostrate oneself.

Adj. **courteous**, polite, civil, mannerly, urbane; well behaved, well mannered, well bred, gently bred, of gentle breeding; polished, cultivated, refined; gallant, chivalrous, chivalric, knightly.

tactful, ingratiating, winning; gentle, mild; good-humored, cordial, gracious, amiable, familiar; neighborly; obliging, complacent, conciliatory.

bland, suave, affable, honey-tongued; oily, unctuous, obsequious.

Adv. with a good grace; with open arms, with outstretched arms, with perfect courtesy, in good humor.

895. DISCOURTESY.—*N.* discourtesy, ill-breeding, bad manners; tactlessness; discourteousness, rusticity, incivility, lack (*or* want) of courtesy, disrespect, impudence, misbehavior, barbarism, barbarity; vulgarity, brutality, blackguardism, conduct unbecoming a gentleman.

bad temper, ill-temper, peevishness, surliness, churlishness, perversity; moroseness, etc., 901*a*; sternness, austerity; moodishness, captiousness, tartness, acrimony, asperity.

scowl, black looks, frown; sulks, short answer, rebuff; hard words, unparliamentary language, personality.

bear, brute, blackguard, beast; unlicked cub; crosspatch [*colloq.*], grouch [*slang*].

V. be rude, insult, treat with discourtesy, make bold with, make free with; take a liberty; stare out of countenance, ogle, point at.

sulk, frown, scowl, glower, pout; snap, snarl, growl.

cut; turn one's back upon, turn on one's heel; give the cold shoulder, keep at a distance.

Adj. discourteous, uncourteous, uncourtly, ill-bred, ill-mannered, ill-behaved, unmannerly, uncivil, impolite, unaccommodating, unneighborly, ungallant, ungracious, unpolished; ungentlemanly; unladylike; vulgar.

pert, forward, obtrusive, impudent, rude, saucy, flippant.

rough, rugged, bluff, blunt, short, gruff; churlish, boorish, bearish; brutal, brusque, stern, harsh, austere; cavalier.

bad-tempered, ill-tempered, ill-humored, crusty, tart, sour, crabbed, sharp, trenchant, sarcastic, caustic, virulent, bitter, acrimonious, venomous, contumelious, snarling, surly, perverse, grim, sullen, peevish, bristling, thorny.

Adv. with a bad grace.

896. CONGRATULATION.—*N.* congratulation, felicitation, compliment; compliments of the season; good wishes, best wishes.

V. congratulate, felicitate, wish one joy, compliment, tender (*or* offer) one's congratulations; wish many happy returns of the day.

897. LOVE.—*N.* love, affection, sympathy, fellow feeling; tenderness, heart, brotherly love; charity, good will, benevolence; attachment, fondness, liking, inclination; regard, admiration, fancy.

yearning, tender passion, gallantry, passion, flame, devotion, fervor, enthusiasm, rapture, enchantment, infatuation, adoration, idolatry.

mother love, maternal love, natural affection.

attractiveness, charm; popularity; idol, favorite, etc., 899.

god of love, Cupid, Eros, Venus; myrtle.

lover, suitor, fiancé [F.], follower [*colloq.*], admirer, adorer, wooer, beau, sweetheart, swain, young man [*colloq.*], flame [*colloq.*], love, truelove.

ladylove, sweetheart, mistress, inamorata, darling, idol, angel, goddess: betrothed, fiancée [F.].

flirt, coquette.

V. **love,** like, fancy, care for. take an interest in, sympathize with: be in love with, regard, revere, take to, set one's affections on, adore, idolize, dote on (*or* upon), make much of, hold dear, prize; hug, cling to, cherish, caress, fondle, pet.

charm, attract, attach, fascinate, captivate, bewitch, enrapture, turn the head.

Adj. **loving,** affectionate, tender, sympathetic, amorous, lovesick, fond, ardent, passionate, rapturous, devoted, motherly.

loved, beloved, well beloved, dearly beloved; dear, precious, darling, pet; favorite, popular.

lovable, adorable, lovely, sweet, attractive, winning, winsome, charming, enchanting, captivating, fascinating, bewitching, amiable.

898. HATE.—*N.* **hate,** hatred, vials of hate; hymn of hate; disaffection, disfavor; alienation, estrangement, coolness; enmity, etc., 889; animosity, malice, implacability.

umbrage, pique, grudge, spleen, bitterness, bitterness of feeling; ill-blood, bad blood; acrimony.

repugnance, etc. (*dislike*), 867; odium, unpopularity; detestation, abhorrence, loathing, execration, abomination, aversion, antipathy.

object of hatred, an abomination, an aversion, bête noire [F.]; enemy, etc., 891; bitter pill.

V. **hate,** detest, abominate, abhor, loathe; recoil at, shudder at; shrink from, revolt against, execrate; dislike, etc., 867.

alienate, estrange, repel, horrify, set against, sow dissension, set by the ears, envenom, incense, irritate, ruffle, vex.

Adj. **abhorrent,** averse from, set against; bitter, etc. (*acrimonious*), 895; implacable.

unloved, unbeloved, unlamented, undeplored, unmourned, uncared for, unvalued: disliked.

lovelorn, jilted, crossed in love, forsaken, rejected.

hateful, obnoxious, odious, abominable, repulsive, offensive, shocking; disgusting, reprehensible.

invidious, spiteful; malicious, etc., 907.

899. FAVORITE.—*N.* favorite, pet, idol, jewel, spoiled child, apple of one's eye, man after one's own heart.

love, dear, darling, duck, honey, sweetheart, etc. (*ladylove*), 897.

general (*or* universal) favorite; idol of the people; matinee idol.

900. RESENTMENT.—*N.* resentment, displeasure, animosity, anger, wrath, ire, indignation; exasperation, vexation, wrathful, indignation.

pique, umbrage, huff, soreness, acerbity, virulence, bitterness, acrimony, asperity; irascibility, etc., 901; sulks, etc., 901*a*; hate, etc., 898; revenge.

irritation; warmth, ferment, excitement, ebullition; angry mood, pet, tiff, passion, fit, tantrum [*colloq.*].

rage, fury, towering rage, passion; outburst, explosion, paroxysm, storm, violence, vials of wrath; hot blood, high words.

Furies, Erinyes (*sing.* Erinys), Eumenides.

provocation, affront, offense, indignity, insult, grudge; last straw, sore subject; ill-turn, outrage; buffet, blow, box on the ear, rap on the knuckles.

V. **resent,** take amiss, take offense (*or* umbrage, exception); pout, frown, scowl, lower, snarl, growl, gnash, snap; redden, color; look black, look daggers.

be angry, fly into a rage, bridle up, fire up, flare up; chafe, mantle, fume, kindle, fly out, boil, boil with indignation (*or* rage); rage, storm, foam; hector, bully, bluster; lose one's temper; raise Cain [*slang*]; breathe revenge.

anger, affront, offend, give offense (*or* umbrage); hurt the feelings; insult, ruffle, heckle [Brit.], nettle, huff, pique; excite, irritate, fret, sting, provoke, chafe, wound, incense, inflame, enrage, envenom, embitter, exasperate, infuriate, madden; rankle.

Adj. **angry,** wroth, irate, ireful, wrathful; irascible, etc., 901; bitter, virulent, acrimonious, offended, indignant, hurt, sore.

fuming, raging, hot under the collar [*slang*]; convulsed with rage; fierce, wild, furious, fiery, rabid, savage, violent.

Adv. in the height (*or* heat) of passion; in an ecstasy of rage.

901. IRASCIBILITY.—*N.* irascibility, temper; crossness, petulance, irritability, tartness, acerbity, acrimony, asperity, pugnacity, excitability.

shrew, vixen, virago, dragon, scold, spitfire, fury.

V. **be irascible,** have a temper, be possessed of the devil, have the temper of a fiend; fire up, flare up.

Adj. **irascible,** bad-tempered, irritable, excitable; thin-skinned, sensitive; hasty, quick, warm, hot, testy, touchy, huffy, pettish, petulant, fretful, querulous, captious, moody, cross, fractious, peevish.

quarrelsome, contentious, disputatious, pugnacious, cantankerous [*colloq.*], cross-grained; waspish, peppery, fiery, passionate, choleric, shrewish.

901a. SULLENNESS.—*N.* sullenness, moroseness, spleen; churlishness, irascibility, moodiness, perversity, obstinacy, crabbedness.

sulks, dudgeon, dumps [*humorous*], doldrums; black looks, scowl; grouch [*slang*], huff.

V. sulk, frown, scowl, lower, glower, pout, grouch [*slang*].

Adj. sullen, sulky, ill-tempered, ill-humored, ill-disposed; crusty, crabbed, sour, sore, surly, moody, cross, cross-grained; perverse, wayward, refractory, restive, ungovernable, cussed [*vulgar or euphemistic*]; grumpy, glum, grum, grim, morose, grouchy [*slang*].

902. [Expression of affection] ENDEARMENT.—*N.* endearment, caress, blandishment, fondling, billing and cooing, dalliance, caressing, embrace, salute, kiss, smack, osculation.

courtship, wooing, suit, addresses, love-making; calf love [*colloq.*]; amorous glances, ogle, side glance, sheep's eyes, goo-goo eyes [*slang*].

flirting, flirtation, gallantry; coquetry, spooning [*slang*].

engagement, betrothal; marriage, etc., 903; honeymoon; love letter, billet-doux; valentine.

flirt, coquette; male flirt, philanderer; spoon [*slang*].

V. caress, fondle, pet; smile upon, coax, wheedle, coddle, make much of, cherish, foster.

clasp, hug, cuddle; fold to the heart, press to the bosom, fold in one's arms; snuggle, nestle, nuzzle; embrace, kiss, salute.

court, make love, bill and coo, spoon [*slang*], toy, dally, flirt, coquet, philander, pay court to; serenade; woo.

propose, make (*or* have) an offer, pop the question [*colloq.*]; become engaged, become betrothed; plight one's troth.

Adj. lovesick, spoony [*slang*].

903. MARRIAGE.—*N.* marriage, matrimony, wedlock, union, intermarriage; nuptial tie, nuptial knot; match; betrothment.

wedding, nuptials, Hymen, bridal, espousals; leading to the altar; honeymoon.

bridesmaid, maid of honor, matron of honor; attendant, usher, best man, bridesman, groomsman; bride, bridegroom.

married man, partner, spouse, mate, husband, man [*dial.*], consort.

married woman, wife, wedded wife, spouse, helpmeet, help-mate, better half, lady [obs. or uncultivated]; squaw; matron.

married couple, man and wife, wedded pair, wedded couple, Darby and Joan.

Kinds of marriage: monogamy, bigamy, polygamy, polyandry; Mormonism; morganatic (or left-handed) marriage, mésalliance [F.].

matchmaker, matrimonial agency (or agent, bureau).

V. marry, wive, take to oneself a wife; be married, be spliced [colloq.]; wed, espouse, lead to the altar, join, couple, be made one.

Adj. engaged, betrothed, plighted, affianced.

Matrimonial, marital, conjugal, connubial, wedded; nuptial, hymeneal, spousal, bridal.

904. CELIBACY.—N. celibacy, singleness, single blessedness; bachelorhood, bachelorship; misogyny.

virginity, maidenhood, maidenhead.

unmarried man, bachelor, old bachelor; misogamist, misogynist; monk, priest, celibate, religious.

unmarried woman, maid, maiden, virgin, spinster, old maid; nun, sister, vestal, vestal virgin; Diana.

Adj. unmarried, unwedded; wifeless, spouseless; single, celibate, virgin.

905. DIVORCE. WIDOWHOOD.—N. divorce, divorcement; separation, judicial separation, separate maintenance.

widowhood, weeds.

widow, relict, dowager; divorcée; grass widow.

widower; grass widower.

V. live separate; separate, divorce, put away.

906. BENEVOLENCE.—N. benevolence, Christian charity; God's grace; good will, philanthropy, unselfishness, kindness, kindliness, good nature, loving-kindness, benignity, brotherly love, charity, humanity, kindly feelings, fellow feeling, sympathy, goodness of heart, warmheartedness, kindheartedness, amiability, tenderness, love, friendship; tolerance, consideration; mercy.

charitableness, bounty, almsgiving; good works, beneficence, generosity, a good turn.

philanthropist, salt of the earth; good Samaritan, sympathizer, well-wisher, altruist.

V. bear good will, wish well, take (or feel) an interest in; be interested in, sympathize with, feel for; treat well, give comfort, do good, do a good turn, benefit, assist, render a service, render assistance, aid.

enter into the feelings of others, practice the golden rule, do as you would be done by.

Adj. **benevolent**, kind, kindly, well meaning, amiable, cordial, obliging, accommodating, indulgent, gracious, tender, considerate, warmhearted, kindhearted, tenderhearted, largehearted, softhearted, merciful; sympathizing, sympathetic.

full of natural affection, fatherly, motherly, brotherly, sisterly; paternal, maternal, fraternal; friendly.

charitable, beneficent, philanthropical, generous, humane, benignant, unselfish, altruistic, bountiful.

Adv. with the best intentions; out of deepest sympathy.

907. MALEVOLENCE.—*N.* **malevolence**, bad intent, bad intention, unkindness, uncharitableness, ill-nature, ill-will, enmity, hate, malice, malignance, malignity, maliciousness; spite, resentment; gall, venom, rancor, virulence, hardness of heart, heart of stone, obduracy; evil eye, cloven foot (*or* hoof).

ill-turn, bad turn; affront, indignity; tender mercies (*ironical*).

cruelty, brutality, savagery, ferocity; outrage, atrocity, ill-usage, persecution; barbarity, inhumanity, truculence, ruffianism; inquisition, torture.

V. **bear malice**, harbor a grudge; hurt, annoy, injure, harm, wrong, outrage, malign; molest, worry, harass, harry, bait, hound, persecute, oppress, grind, maltreat, ill-treat; give no quarter, have no mercy.

Adj. **malevolent**, ill-disposed, ill-intentioned, ill-natured, ill-conditioned, evil-minded, evil-disposed, venomous, malicious, malign, malignant, maleficent; rancorous, spiteful, treacherous, caustic, bitter, envenomed, acrimonious, virulent; grinding, galling, harsh; disobliging, unkind, unfriendly; ungracious, churlish, surly, sullen.

cold-blooded, coldhearted, hardhearted, stonyhearted, cold, unnatural; ruthless, pitiless, relentless.

cruel, brutal, brutish, savage, ferocious, inhuman; barbarous, fell, truculent, bloodthirsty, atrocious, fiendish, diabolic *or* diabolical, devilish, infernal, hellish.

Adv. with bad intent; with the ferocity of a tiger.

908. MALEDICTION.—*N.* **malediction**, malison, curse, imprecation, denunciation, execration; anathema, ban, proscription, excommunication, commination, fulmination; disparagement, vilification, vituperation.

abuse, evil speaking, foul (*or* bad, strong, unparliamentary) language, billingsgate, blackguardism, cursing, profane, swearing, expletive, oath, foul invective, ribaldry, scurrility, invective.

V. **curse**, imprecate, damn, swear at; execrate, vituperate, scold; anathematize, denounce, proscribe, excommunicate, fulminate, thunder against.

909. THREAT.—*N.* **threat,** menace, defiance, abuse, intimidation, denunciation, fulmination, etc., 908; gathering clouds.

V. **threaten,** threat, menace; snarl, growl, mutter, bully; defy, intimidate, shake the fist at; thunder, fulminate, bluster.

Adj. **threatening,** menacing, minatory, abusive; ominous, defiant.

910. PHILANTHROPY.—*N.* **philanthropy,** altruism, humanity, humanitarianism, benevolence; public welfare.

public spirit, patriotism, nationality, love of country.

philanthropist, altruist, etc., 906; humanitarian, patriot.

Adj. **philanthropic,** altruistic, humanitarian, public-spirited, patriotic; humane, largehearted, benevolent, etc., 906; generous, liberal, etc., 942.

911. MISANTHROPY.—*N.* **misanthropy,** hatred of mankind; selfishness, egoism, egotism; sullenness, moroseness, cynicism; want of patriotism.

misanthrope, misanthropist, egoist, egotist, cynic, man hater.

woman hater, misogynist.

Adj. **misanthropic,** antisocial, unpatriotic; egoistical, egotistical, selfish; morose, sullen, cynical, etc., 901*a*.

912. BENEFACTOR.—*N.* **benefactor,** savior, protector, good genius, tutelary saint, guardian angel, good Samaritan; friend in need; salt of the earth; philanthropist, etc., 910; fairy godmother.

913. [Maleficent being] EVILDOER.—*N.* **evildoer,** evil worker, wrongdoer, etc., 949; mischiefmaker, marplot; oppressor, tyrant; incendiary, etc., 384; anarchist, nihilist, destroyer, vandal, iconoclast, terrorist.

savage, brute, ruffian, barbarian, desperado; apache, gunman, hoodlum [*colloq.*], redskin, tough [*colloq.*], bully, rough, hooligan [*slang*], dangerous classes; thief, etc., 792; cutthroat.

wild beast, tiger, leopard, panther, hyena, catamount [U. S.], catamountain, lynx, cougar, jaguar, puma; bloodhound, hellhound, sleuthhound; gorilla; vulture.

cockatrice, adder; snake, serpent, cobra, asp, viper, rattlesnake, boa; alligator, crocodile, octopus.

hag, hellhag, beldam, Jezebel.

monster, fiend, demon, etc., 980; devil incarnate, Frankenstein's monster; cannibal; bloodsucker, vampire, ogre, ghoul.

914. PITY.—*N.* **pity,** compassion, commiseration, sympathy, fellow feeling, tenderness, softheartedness, yearning forbearance, humanity, mercy, clemency; leniency, lenity, charity, ruth, long-suffering; quarter, grace.

sympathizer; advocate, friend, partisan, patron, well-wisher, defender, champion.

V. **pity,** have (*or* take) pity, commiserate, condole, sympathize, feel for, be sorry for.

forbear, relent, relax, give quarter.

excite pity, touch, soften, melt, melt the heart; propitiate.

Adj. **pitying,** pitiful, compassionate, sympathetic, touched. merciful, clement, humane, humanitarian; tender, tender-hearted, softhearted, lenient, forbearing.

914a. PITILESSNESS.—*N.* **pitilessness,** inclemency, inexorability, inflexibility, hardness of heart; want of pity, severity, malevolence, etc., 907.

V. **be pitiless,** turn a deaf ear to; claim one's pound of flesh; have no mercy, give no quarter.

Adj. **pitiless,** merciless, ruthless, unpitying, unmerciful, inclement, grim-faced, grim-visaged; inflexible, relentless, inexorable, harsh, cruel, etc., 907.

915. CONDOLENCE.—*N.* **condolence,** sympathy, consolation; lamentation, etc., 839.

V. **condole with,** console, sympathize, express pity; afford consolation; lament with, express sympathy for, feel for, send one's condolences; share one's sorrow.

916. GRATITUDE.—*N.* **gratitude,** gratefulness, thankfulness; sense of obligation; acknowledgment, recognition, thanksgiving, giving thanks.

thanks, praise, benediction; paean; *Te Deum* [L.], grace, requital, thank offering.

V. **be grateful,** thank; give (*or* render, return, offer, tender) thanks, acknowledge, requite; lie under an obligation; never forget, overflow with gratitude.

Adj. **grateful,** thankful, obliged, beholden, indebted to, under obligation.

917. INGRATITUDE.—*N.* **ingratitude,** thanklessness, unthankfulness; thankless task, thankless office.

V. **be ungrateful,** feel no obligation, owe one no thanks, forget benefits, have a short memory for.

Adj. **ungrateful,** unmindful, unthankful; thankless, ingrate. forgotten; unacknowledged, unthanked, unrequited, unrewarded; ill-requited; ill-rewarded.

918. FORGIVENESS.—*N.* **forgiveness,** pardon, grace, remission, absolution, amnesty, oblivion; reprieve.

conciliation; reconciliation, forbearance, propitiation.

exoneration, excuse, quittance, release, indemnity; acquittal, exculpation.

V. **forgive,** pardon, think no more of, let bygones by bygones, bury the hatchet. start afresh.

remit, exculpate, exonerate, absolve, give absolution; blot out one's sins (*or* offenses, transgressions), wipe the slate clean; reprieve, acquit.

excuse, pass over, overlook; condone, wink at; bear with, allow for, make allowances for; pocket the affront.

conciliate, propitiate, placate; beg (*or* ask) pardon, make up a quarrel.

Adj. forgiving, placable, conciliatory.

919. REVENGE.—*N.* revenge, vengeance; vendetta, death feud, eye for an eye, tooth for a tooth, retaliation; day of reckoning.

rancor, vindictiveness, implacability, ruthlessness; malevolence, etc., 907.

avenger, nemesis, Eumenides.

V. revenge, avenge, take revenge, have one's revenge; breathe vengeance; give no quarter, take no prisoners.

keep the wound open, harbor revenge, bear malice; rankle, rankle in the breast.

Adj. revengeful, vengeful, vindictive, rancorous; pitiless, ruthless, rigorous, avenging, retaliative; unforgiving, unrelenting; inexorable, implacable, relentless, remorseless.

920. JEALOUSY.—*N.* jealousy, distrust, mistrust, heartburn; envy, etc., 921; doubt, suspicion; green-eyed monster.

V. be jealous, view with jealousy, grudge, begrudge.

doubt, distrust, mistrust, suspect, misdoubt.

Adj. jealous, jaundice, yellow-eyed, envious.

921. ENVY.—*N.* envy, enviousness; rivalry; ill-will, spite; jealousy, etc., 920.

V. envy, covet, grudge, begrudge, break the tenth commandment.

Adj. envious, invidious, covetous, grudging, begrudged; belittling.

IV. MORAL AFFECTIONS

922. RIGHT.—*N.* right; what ought to be, what should be; fitness.

justice, equity, equitableness, propriety, fairness, fair play, square deal [*colloq.*], impartiality; lawfulness, legality.

morals, etc. (*duty*), 926; law, etc., 963; honor, etc., 939; virtue, etc., 944.

V. be right, stand to reason.

do right, see justice done, see fair play; do justice to, recompense, hold the scales even, give everyone his due.

Adj. **right,** good; just, reasonable; fit, etc., 924; equal, equable, equitable; even-handed, fair, square.

legitimate, justifiable, rightful, as it ought to be; lawful, legal.

Adv. in justice, in equity, in reason; upon even terms.

923. WRONG.—*N.* **wrong,** iniquity; what ought not to be, what should not be; unreasonableness, grievance; shame.

injustice, unfairness, foul play, partiality, leaning, favor, favoritism, partisanship; undueness, unlawfulness, illegality.

dishonor, etc., 939; vice, etc., 945.

V. **do wrong,** be inequitable, show partiality, favor, lean toward; encroach; impose upon; reap where one has not sown.

Adj. **wrong,** wrongful, iniquitous, bad, unjust, unfair, inequitable, unequal, partial, one-sided; injurious.

unjustifiable, unreasonable, unwarrantable, objectionable, improper, unfit, unjustified; unlawful; illegal, immoral.

924. AUTHORIZATION.—*N.* **authorization,** sanction, authority, charter, warrant; constitution; bond.

right, dueness, due, privilege, prerogative, prescription, title, claim, pretension, legality, demand, birthright.

immunity, license, liberty, franchise; vested interest (*or* right).

deserts, merits, dues.

claimant, appellant; plaintiff, etc., 938.

V. **deserve,** merit, be worthy of, make good.

demand, claim, lay claim to, reclaim, exact; insist on (*or* upon), make a point of, require, assert, assume, arrogate.

entitle, give (*or* confer) a right, authorize, sanction, legalize, ordain, prescribe, allot.

Adj. **privileged,** allowed, sanctioned, warranted, authorized; ordained, prescribed, constitutional, chartered, enfranchised.

prescriptive, presumptive, absolute, inalienable, inviolable, sacrosanct.

merited, due to, deserved, condign [*archaic, except of punishment*].

right, creditable, fit, fitting, correct, square, due, proper, meet, befitting, becoming, seemly; decorous.

lawful, legitimate, legal, legalized, allowable.

Adv. by right, by divine right; on the square [*colloq.*].

925. [Want of authorization] IMPROPRIETY.—*N.* **impropriety,** undueness, unrightfulness, illegality, unlawfulness; falseness, invalidity of title; illegitimacy.

loss of right, disfranchisement, forfeiture.

assumption, usurpation, tort [*law*], violation, breach, encroachment, seizure, exaction, imposition.

usurper, pretender, impostor.

V. **infringe**, encroach, trench on, exact, arrogate, usurp, violate; get under false pretenses, sail under false colors.

disentitle, disfranchise, disqualify; invalidate.

Adj. **undue**, unlawful, illegal, illicit, unconstitutional, unauthorized, unwarranted, unsanctioned, unjustified; disqualified, unqualified; unprivileged, unchartered.

undeserved, unmerited, unearned.

illegitimate, bastard, spurious, false; usurped.

improper, unfit, unbefitting, unseemly, unbecoming, misbecoming; preposterous, pretentious, would-be.

926. DUTY.—*N.* **duty**, moral obligation, accountability, liability, onus, responsibility.

allegiance, fealty, tie; engagement; function, part, calling.

observance, fulfillment, discharge, performance, acquittal, satisfaction, redemption; good behavior.

morality, morals, decalogue; conscientiousness, conscience, inward monitor, still small voice within, sense of duty.

propriety, fitness, seemliness, decorum, the thing, the proper thing.

Science of morals: ethics, moral (*or* ethical) philosophy, casuistry, polity.

V. **behoove**, become, befit, beseem; belong to, pertain to; rest with, fall to one's lot, devolve on.

take upon oneself, be (*or* become) sponsor for, incur a responsibility; perform (*or* discharge) a duty *or* an obligation; act one's part, redeem one's pledge, be at one's post, do one's duty.

impose a duty, enjoin, require, exact; bind, bind over; saddle with, prescribe, assign, call upon, look to, oblige.

Adj. **obligatory**, binding, imperative, peremptory, stringent, incumbent on.

amenable, liable, accountable, responsible, answerable.

right, meet, etc. (*due*), 924; moral, ethical, conscientious.

Adv. with a safe conscience, as in duty bound, on one's own responsibility, at one's own risk.

927. DERELICTION OF DUTY.—*N.* **dereliction**, nonobservance, nonperformance, nonco-operation; indolence, neglect, infraction, violation, transgression, failure, evasion; fault, etc. (*guilt*), 947.

slacker, loafer, time killer; eyeserver, eyeservant; striker; nonco-operator.

V. **violate**, break, break through; infringe, set aside, set at naught; encroach upon, trench upon, trample on; slight, get by [*slang*], neglect, evade, escape, transgress, fail.

927a. EXEMPTION.—*N.* **exemption**, freedom, irresponsibility, immunity, liberty, license, release, discharge, excuse, dispensation, absolution, exculpation, exoneration.

V. exempt, release, acquit, discharge, remit; free, set at liberty, let off [*colloq.*], pass over, spare, excuse, dispense with, license; absolve, exonerate.

Adj. exempt, free, immune, at liberty, scot-free, released, unbound; irresponsible, not accountable, excusable.

928. RESPECT.—*N.* respect, regard, consideration, courtesy, attention, deference, reverence, honor, esteem, estimation, veneration, admiration; approbation, etc., 931.

homage, fealty, obeisance, genuflection, kneeling, prostration; salaam, etc., 894.

V. respect, regard; revere, reverence, honor, venerate, hallow; esteem, think much of, entertain respect for, look up to, defer to, pay attention to, pay respect to, do honor to; do the honors, hail, show courtesy, pay homage to.

command respect, inspire respect; awe, impose, overawe, dazzle.

Adj. respectful, deferential, decorous, reverential, ceremonious, bareheaded, cap in hand; prostrate.

respected, estimable; time-honored, venerable.

Adv. in deference to; with all respect, with due respect, with the highest respect; with submission.

929. DISRESPECT.—*N.* disrespect, disfavor, disrepute, want of esteem, low estimation, disparagement, detraction, irreverence, slight, indignity, contumely, affront, dishonor, insult, outrage, discourtesy, scoffing; hiss, hissing, hoot, derision; mockery.

gibe, flout, jeer, scoff, taunt, sneer, fling.

V. slight, disregard, undervalue, humiliate, depreciate, trifle with, pass by, push aside, overlook, be discourteous.

disparage, call names; throw mud at; point at, indulge in personalities.

dishonor, desecrate; insult, affront, browbeat, outrage.

deride, scoff, sneer, laugh at, ridicule, gibe, mock, jeer, taunt, twit, flout, roast [*colloq.*], guy [*colloq.*], rag [*dial. Eng.* and *college slang*], burlesque, scout, hiss, hoot.

Adj. disrespectful, disparaging, etc., 934; insulting, supercilious, rude, derisive, sarcastic, scurrilous, contemptuous, insolent, disdainful; irreverent.

unrespected, unregarded, disregarded, unenvied, unsaluted.

930. CONTEMPT.—*N.* contempt, disdain, scorn, contemptuousness, derision, etc. (*disrespect*), 929; contumely; slight, sneer, spurn, byword.

V. despise, contemn, scorn, disdain, disregard, scout, slight, pass by, look down upon, sneer at, laugh at, curl up one's lip, think nothing of, make light of, underestimate, esteem slightly, care nothing for, set no store by; pooh-pooh, damn with faint praise.

spurn, turn one's back upon, trample underfoot; kick; fling to the winds, repudiate.

Adj. contemptuous, disdainful, scornful, withering, supercilious, cynical, haughty, cavalier; derisive; with the nose in air.

contemptible, despicable, despised, pitiable, pitiful, downtrodden.

931. APPROBATION.—*N.* approbation, approval, sanction, advocacy; esteem, estimation, good opinion, admiration; love, etc., 897; appreciation, regard, account, popularity, credit, repute.

commendation, compliment, praise, laud, laudation; good word; encomium, eulogy, eulogium, panegyric, blurb [*slang*]; benediction, blessing, benison.

applause, plaudit, clap, clapping, acclaim, acclamation; cheer; paean, shout (*or* peal, chorus, thunders) of applause.

V. approve, esteem, value, prize, set great store by; honor, hold in esteem, look up to, admire, like, appreciate: stand up for, stick up for [*colloq.*], uphold, countenance, sanction, indorse, recommend.

commend, praise, laud, compliment, applaud, clap, cheer, acclaim, encore; eulogize, boost [*colloq.*], root for [*slang*], cry up, puff; extol, magnify, glorify, exalt, sing the praises of.

Adj. commendatory, complimentary, laudatory, panegyrical, eulogistic, lavish of praise, uncritical.

approved, praised, popular, in good odor; in high esteem, in favor, in high favor.

praiseworthy, commendable, worthy of praise, good, meritorious, estimable, creditable, unimpeachable.

Adv. with credit, to admiration.

932. DISAPPROBATION.—*N.* disapprobation, disapproval, disesteem, odium, dislike, black list, blackball, ostracism, boycott.

disparagement, depreciation, dispraise, detraction, etc., 934; denunciation, condemnation, stricture, objection, exception, criticism; blame, censure, obloquy, sarcasm, satire, insinuation, innuendo, sneer, taunt.

reproof, reprehension, remonstrance, expostulation, reprobation, admonition, reproach; rebuke, reprimand, lecture, curtain lecture; wigging, dressing down [*both colloq.*]; rating, scolding, correction, rebuff, home thrust, hit; frown, scowl, black look.

abuse, personalities, personal remarks, vituperation, invective, contumely, hard words; bad language.

diatribe, tirade, philippic.

clamor, outcry, hue and cry; hiss, hissing, catcall; execration.

V. **disapprove,** dislike, object to, take exception to, think ill of, view with disfavor, frown upon, look askance, look black upon, set one's face against.

blame, censure, reproach, reprobate, impugn, impeach, accuse, denounce, expose, brand, gibbet, stigmatize; show up [*colloq.*].

reprove, reprehend, chide, admonish, berate, take to task, overhaul, lecture, rebuke, blow up [*colloq.*], correct, reprimand, snub; chastise, castigate, lash, trounce.

remonstrate, expostulate, recriminate.

abuse, scold, rate, upbraid, fall foul of; jaw [*low*], rail, rail at, call names, execrate, revile, vilify.

decry, cry down, run down, backbite; insinuate, damn with faint praise; hiss, hoot, catcall, mob; ostracize, blacklist, boycott, blackball.

disparage, depreciate, knock [*colloq.*], dispraise, deprecate, speak ill of, condemn, scoff at, sneer at, satirize, lampoon, defame, criticize.

incur blame, scandalize, shock, revolt; get a bad name, forfeit one's good opinion, be under a cloud.

Adj. **disparaging,** condemnatory, denunciatory, reproachful, abusive, vituperative, defamatory.

critical, satirical, sarcastic, sardonic, cynical, dry, sharp, cutting, biting, severe, withering, trenchant, censorious, captious, hypercritical.

blameworthy, reprehensible, blamable, answerable, bad; vicious, etc., 945.

Adv. with a wry face.

933. FLATTERY.—*N.* **flattery,** adulation, cajolery, fawning, wheedling, obsequiousness, sycophancy, flunkeyism, toadyism.

honeyed words, flummery, buncombe [*cant or slang*]; blarney, soft soap [*both colloq.*].

V. **flatter,** overpraise, puff, wheedle, cajole, fawn upon, humor, pet, coquet, butter [*colloq.*], jolly [*slang or colloq.*]; truckle to, pander to, court, curry favor with.

Adj. **flattering,** adulatory; mealy-mouthed, honeyed, smooth, smooth-tongued; oily, unctuous, specious, plausible, servile, sycophantic, fulsome.

934. DETRACTION.—*N.* **detraction,** disparagement, depreciation, vilification, obloquy, scandal, defamation, slander, calumny, evil-speaking, backbiting; sarcasm, cynicism, criticism; invective.

personality, libel, lampoon, skit, squib.

V. **detract,** derogate, decry, depreciate, disparage, run down, cry down, belittle, criticize, pull to pieces, asperse, bespatter, blacken, vilify, brand, malign, backbite, libel, lampoon, traduce, slander, defame, calumniate.

Adj. **detracting**, defamatory, detractory, derogatory, disparaging, libelous; scurrilous, abusive, foul-mouthed; slanderous, calumnious.

935. FLATTERER.—*N.* **flatterer**, adulator, eulogist, euphemist; optimist; puffer, booster [*colloq.*], whitewasher.

toady, sycophant, parasite, hanger-on; courtier.

936. DETRACTOR.—*N.* **detractor**, censor, censurer; cynic, critic, caviler, carper.

defamer, knocker [*colloq.*], backbiter, slanderer, lampooner, satirist, traducer, libeler, calumniator, reviler, vituperator.

Adj. defamatory, etc., 934.

937. VINDICATION.—*N.* **vindication**, justification, warrant; exoneration, exculpation, acquittal; whitewashing, extenuation, palliation, softening, mitigation.

plea, apology, gloss, varnish; excuse, extenuating circumstances; allowance; reply, defense; recrimination.

apologist, vindicator, justifier; defendant, etc., 938.

V. **justify**, warrant, lend a color, vindicate, exculpate, acquit, clear, exonerate, whitewash.

extenuate, palliate, excuse, soften, apologize.

advocate, defend, plead one's cause; contend for, speak for; bear out, make good; support, plead, say in defense.

Adj. **vindicative**, vindicatory, vindicating, palliative, extenuating, exculpatory, apologetic.

excusable, defensible, pardonable; venial, plausible, justifiable.

938. ACCUSATION.—*N.* **accusation**, charge, imputation, slur, incrimination, recrimination, denunciation.

libel, challenge, citation, arraignment, impeachment, indictment, true bill, lawsuit, condemnation.

accuser, prosecutor, plaintiff, complainant, libelant, informant, informer.

accused, defendant, prisoner, respondent, litigant.

V. **accuse**, charge, tax, impute, twit, taunt with, reproach, stigmatize, slur; incriminate, inculpate, implicate.

inform against, indict, denounce, arraign; charge with, saddle with; impeach, show up [*colloq.*], challenge, cite, prosecute; blow upon [*colloq.*], squeal [*slang*].

Adj. **accusatory**, denunciatory, recriminatory.

inexcusable, indefensible, unpardonable, unjustifiable.

939. PROBITY.—*N.* **probity**, integrity, rectitude, uprightness, respectability, honesty, faith, honor, good faith; constancy, faithfulness, fidelity, loyalty, trustworthiness, truth, veracity, candor, singleness of heart.

fairness, fair play, justice, equity, impartiality, principle.

punctiliousness, punctilio, delicacy, scrupulosity, scrupulousness, scruple; point of honor.

man of honor, man of his word, gentleman, trump [slang], brick [slang or colloq.].

V. be honorable, speak the truth, draw a straight furrow, make a point of: do one's duty, play the game [colloq.]; redeem one's pledge, keep one's promise (or word), keep faith with.

Adj. upright, honest, veracious, truthful, virtuous, noble, honorable, reputable, respectable; fair, right, just, equitable, impartial, square, white [slang].

manly, straightforward, frank, candid, openhearted.

loyal, constant, faithful, stanch; true; trusty, trustworthy; incorruptible.

conscientious, right-minded, high-principled, high-minded, scrupulous, religious, strict; nice, punctilious.

stainless, unstained, unsullied, inviolate, untainted, incorrupt, innocent, pure, undefiled, undepraved.

chivalrous, jealous of honor, high-spirited.

Adv. on the square [colloq.], in good faith, in all honor, by fair means, with clean hands.

940. IMPROBITY.—*N.* improbity, dishonesty, dishonor, disgrace; fraud, lying; bad faith, infidelity, faithlessness; Judas kiss, betrayal, perfidy, treachery, double-dealing; villainy, baseness, degradation, turpitude, moral turpitude.

breach of trust (or faith), disloyalty, divided allegiance, hyphenated allegiance [cant], treason, high treason; apostasy.

knavery, roguery, rascality, foul play; jobbing, jobbery, graft [colloq.], venality, corruption, sharp practice.

V. play false; break one's word (or promise), jilt, betray, forswear; grovel, sneak, lose caste; sell oneself, squeal [slang], go back on [colloq.].

Adj. dishonest, dishonorable; unconscientious, unscrupulous; fraudulent, knavish, falsehearted; unfair, one-sided; double, double-tongued, double-faced; timeserving, crooked, slippery; fishy [colloq.], questionable.

infamous, arrant, foul, base, vile, low, ignominious, perfidious, treacherous, perjured; contemptible, abject, mean, shabby, paltry, dirty, sneaking, groveling, rascally, corrupt, venal.

derogatory, degrading, undignified, unbefitting, ungentlemanly, unchivalric, unmanly, recreant, inglorious.

faithless, false, unfaithful, disloyal; untrustworthy; trustless, lost to shame, dead to honor.

Adv. like a thief in the night, by crooked paths, by foul means.

941. KNAVE.—*N.* **knave,** rogue, villain, rascal, etc., 949; shyster.

traitor, betrayer, archtraitor, conspirator, Judas; reptile, serpent, snake in the grass, wolf in sheep's clothing, sneak, squealer [*slang*], telltale, mischiefmaker; renegade, recreant, slacker.

942. DISINTERESTEDNESS.—*N.* **disinterestedness,** unselfishness, generosity; liberality, altruism, benevolence, loftiness of purpose, exaltation, magnanimity; honor, chivalry, heroism, sublimity.

self-denial, self-control, stoicism, self-abnegation, self-sacrifice, devotion, self-devotion; labor of love.

Adj. **disinterested,** unselfish, self-denying, self-sacrificing, altruistic.

magnanimous, high-minded; princely, great, high, elevated, lofty, exalted, greathearted, largehearted; generous, liberal; chivalrous, heroic, sublime.

943. SELFISHNESS.—*N.* **selfishness,** self-love, self-indulgence, self-worship, self-seeking, self-interest; egotism, egoism; illiberality, meanness.

self-seeker, timeserver, fortune hunter, monopolist, dog in the manger, trimmer; hog, roadhog [*colloq.*].

V. **be selfish,** feather one's nest; have an eye to the main chance, live for oneself alone.

Adj. **selfish,** self-seeking, self-indulgent, self-interested; self-centered; egotistic, egoistic.

illiberal, mean, ungenerous, narrow-minded; mercenary, venal; covetous.

worldly, unspiritual, earthly, earthly-minded, mundane, worldly-minded, worldly-wise; timeserving, interested.

Adv. from selfish motives.

944. VIRTUE.—*N.* **virtue,** morality, moral rectitude; integrity, probity, nobleness, well-doing, good actions, good behavior, well-spent life, innocence.

merit, worth, desert, excellence, credit; self-control, self-denial. morals; ethics, duty, etc., 926; cardinal virtues.

V. **be virtuous,** practice virtue, do one's duty, fight the good fight; acquit oneself well, keep in the right path.

Adj. **virtuous,** good, innocent, meritorious, deserving, worthy, dutiful, duteous; moral, right, righteous, right-minded; creditable, laudable, commendable, praiseworthy; sterling, pure, noble; whole-souled.

exemplary; matchless, peerless; saintly, saintlike; angelic, godlike.

945. VICE.—*N.* **vice,** evildoing, wrongdoing, wickedness, viciousness, iniquity, sin, immorality, want of principle, knavery, obliquity, backsliding, infamy, brutality.

depravity, demoralization, corruption, profligacy, flagrancy.

weakness, infirmity, frailty, imperfection, error; foible; failing, failure; besetting sin; defect, defection.

fault, crime; guilt, etc., 947.

reprobate; sinner, etc., 949.

V. **be vicious,** sin, commit sin, err, transgress; misconduct oneself, misbehave; fall, lapse, slip, trip, offend, trespass, go astray; sow one's wild oats.

demoralize, brutalize; corrupt, degrade, etc., 659.

Adj.[1] **vicious,** sinful; wicked, iniquitous, immoral, unrighteous, wrong, criminal; unprincipled, lawless, disorderly, disgraceful, recreant, disreputable; demoralized, corrupt, depraved, degenerate; evil-minded, heartless, graceless, shameless, abandoned.

base, sinister, foul, gross, vile, black, felonious, nefarious, shameful, scandalous, infamous, villainous, heinous; flagrant, atrocious.

diabolic *or* diabolical, devilish, fiendish, fiendlike, demoniacal, Mephistophelian, satanic, hellish, infernal, hellborn.

incorrigible, irreclaimable, obdurate, reprobate, reprehensible.

unjustifiable, indefensible, inexcusable, inexpiable, unpardonable.

improper, unseemly, indecorous, indiscreet, unworthy, blameworthy, discreditable; incorrect, undutiful, naughty.

weak, frail, lax, infirm, imperfect; spineless, invertebrate [*both fig.*].

946. INNOCENCE.—*N.* **innocence;** guiltlessness, incorruption, impeccability; clean hands, clear conscience.

innocent, newborn babe; lamb, dove.

Adj. **innocent,** not guilty, unguilty; guiltless, faultless, sinless, stainless, spotless, clear, immaculate, unerring, undefiled, inculpable, blameless, above suspicion, irreproachable, unimpeachable; virtuous, etc., 944.

harmless, inoffensive, innocuous, pure.

Adv. with clean hands; with a clear conscience.

947. GUILT.—*N.* **guilt,** guiltiness, culpability, criminality; vice, sinfulness, misconduct, misbehavior, misdeed; fault, sin, error, transgression; dereliction, delinquency.

indiscretion, lapse, slip, trip, flaw, blot, omission, failing, failure, blunder, break [*colloq.*].

[1]Most of these adjectives are applicable both to the act and to the agent.

offense, trespass; misdemeanor, malefaction, malversation, corruption, malpractice; crime, felony, capital crime.

enormity, atrocity, outrage; deadly sin, mortal sin.

Adj. guilty, blamable, culpable, reprehensible, blameworthy.

Adv. in the very act, red-handed.

948. GOOD MAN. GOOD WOMAN.—*N.* good man, worthy, model, paragon, pattern, good example; hero, demigod, angel, saint; benefactor, etc., 912; philanthropist, etc., 910.

salt of the earth; one in ten thousand; a man among men, white man [*slang*].

good woman, virgin, innocent; goddess, queen, Madonna, ministering angel, heaven's noblest gift.

949. BAD MAN. BAD WOMAN.—*N.* bad man, wrongdoer, worker of iniquity; evildoer, etc., 913; sinner, transgressor; bad example.

rascal, scoundrel, villain, knave, etc., 941; miscreant, wretch, reptile, viper, serpent, monster, devil, demon, devil incarnate, fallen angel, lost sheep, black sheep, castaway, prodigal.

bad woman, jade, Jezebel, hellcat.

ruffian, rowdy, bully, etc., 887; thief, murderer.

culprit, delinquent, criminal, malefactor, felon, convict, outlaw.

riffraff, scum of the earth; blackguard, loafer, sneak, vagabond.

scamp, scapegrace, ne'er-do-well, good for nothing, reprobate, scalawag [*colloq.*], limb [*colloq.*], rapscallion [*all the words in this paragraph are commonly applied jocularly or lightly*].

950. PENITENCE.—*N.* penitence, contrition, compunction, repentance, remorse, regret, self-reproach, self-reproof, self-accusation, self-condemnation, qualms of conscience.

acknowledgment, confession, apology, recantation; penance.

penitent, Magdalen, prodigal son, returned prodigal.

V. repent, be sorry for, rue, regret, think better of, recant; plead guilty, acknowledge, confess, humble oneself, beg pardon, apologize; turn over a new leaf.

reclaim, reform, regenerate, redeem, convert, amend, make a new man of, restore self-respect.

Adj. penitent, repentant, contrite, softened, melted, touched, conscience-stricken; self-accusing, self-convicted.

951. IMPENITENCE.—*N.* impenitence, irrepentance, recusancy, hardness of heart, heart of stone, seared conscience, obduracy.

V. be impenitent, steel the heart, harden the heart; die and make no sign.

Adj. impenitent, obdurate, hard, hardened, seared, recusant, unrepentant; relentless, remorseless, graceless.

lost, incorrigible, irreclaimable; unreclaimed, unreformed.

952. ATONEMENT.—*N.* atonement, reparation, compromise, composition, compensation, quittance, expiation, redemption, reclamation, conciliation, propitiation; indemnification, redress, amends, apology, satisfaction; sacrifice.

penance, fasting, sackcloth and ashes, shrift, purgation, purgatory.

V. atone, atone for, expiate, propitiate, make amends; reclaim, redeem, repair, ransom, absolve, purge, shrive, do penance, pay the penalty.

apologize, express regret, beg pardon, give satisfaction.

Adj. propitiatory, expiatory, sacrifice, sacrificial.

953. [Moral Practice] TEMPERANCE.—*N.* temperance, moderation, frugality, sobriety, soberness, forbearance, abnegation; self-denial, self-restraint, self-control.

abstinence, abstemiousness, asceticism; vegetarianism, prohibition, teetotalism, total abstinence.

abstainer; teetotaler, etc., 958; vegetarian, fruitarian; ascetic.

V. be temperate, abstain, forbear, refrain, deny oneself, spare.

Adj. temperate, moderate, sober, frugal, sparing, abstemious.

954. INTEMPERANCE.—*N.* intemperance, sensuality, animalism, pleasure, luxury, luxuriousness, freeliving, indulgence, high living, dissipation, self-indulgence; voluptuousness, debauchery.

revel, revels, revelry, orgy; drunkenness, debauch, carousal, drinking bout, saturnalia.

V. be intemperate, indulge, exceed; live high (*or* on the fat of the land), dine not wisely but too well; plunge into dissipation, revel, carouse, run riot, sow one's wild oats.

Adj. intemperate, excessive; sensual, self-indulgent, voluptuous, wild, dissipated, dissolute, fast.

brutish, swinish, piggish, hoggish, beastlike, beastly.

luxurious, epicurean, sybaritical; nursed in the lap of luxury; indulged, pampered; full fed, high fed.

intoxicated, drunk, etc., 959.

954a. SENSUALIST.—*N.* sensualist, sybarite, voluptuary, man of pleasure, epicure, epicurean, gourmet; gourmand, glutton, pig, hog; free liver, hard liver.

955. ASCETICISM.—*N.* asceticism, puritanism, austerity; total abstinence; mortification, sackcloth and ashes, penance, fasting; martyrdom.

ascetic, anchorite, hermit, recluse; puritan, yogi [Hindu]; dervish, fakir [both Moham.]; martyr.

Adj. ascetic, austere, puritanical.

956. FASTING.—*N.* **fasting,** famishment, starvation.

fast, fast day, Lent, spare (*or* meager) diet, lenten diet, Barme-cide feast; short rations.

V. **fast,** starve, famish, perish with hunger.

Adj. **fasting,** lenten, unfed; starved, half-starved, hungry.

957. GLUTTONY.—*N.* **gluttony;** greed, greediness, voracity; epicurism, gastronomy; high living; guzzling.

feast, banquet, good cheer, blow out [*slang*].

glutton, gormandizer, cormorant, hog, etc. (*sensualist*), 954a.

epicure, *bon vivant* [F.], gourmand [*obs. as* glutton], gourmet.

V. **gormandize,** gorge; overeat, glut, satiate, indulge, eat one's fill, cram, stuff, guzzle, bolt, devour, gobble up, gulp, raven, eat out of house and home.

Adj. **gluttonous,** greedy, gormandizing, omnivorous, voracious, devouring, overfed, gorged.

958. SOBRIETY.—*N.* **sobriety;** total abstinence, teetotalism.

water drinker; prohibitionist, dry [*slang*], teetotaler, total ab-stainer.

V. **take the pledge;** abstain, etc., 953.

Adj. **sober,** temperate, moderate, abstemious.

959. DRUNKENNESS.—*N.* **drunkenness,** intemperance, drink-ing, inebriety, inebriation, intoxication, winebibbing; baccha-nalia; libations.

alcoholism, dipsomania; delirium tremens, d.t.'s [*colloq.*].

drink, alcoholic drinks, alcohol, blue ruin [*slang*], booze [*colloq.*]; grog, punch; punchbowl, cup, rosy wine, flowing bowl; liquor, dram, beverage, beer, etc.; cocktail, highball, peg [*slang, orig. India*]; stirrup cup, parting cup.

illicit distilling; bootlegging [*slang*], moonshining, moonshine *or* moonshine whisky [*colloq.*], hooch [*slang*], home-brew; moon-shiner [*colloq.*]; bootlegger [*slang*].

drunkard, sot, toper, tippler, winebibber, hard drinker, soaker [*slang*], sponge [*slang*], boozer [*colloq.*], bum [*slang*]; reveler, carouser; dipsomaniac.

V. **get** (*or* **be**) **drunk,** see double; take a drop (*or* glass) too much; drink, tipple, booze [*colloq.*], soak [*slang*], have a jag on [*slang*], carouse; drink hard (*or* deep, like a fish).

liquor, liquor up [*both slang*], wet one's whistle [*colloq. or humor-ous*]; raise the elbow, hit the booze [*slang*], crack a bottle.

inebriate, fuddle [*colloq.*], befuddle.

sell illicitly, bootleg [*slang*].

Adj. **drunk,** tipsy, intoxicated, inebriate, inebriated; in a state of intoxication, overcome, fuddled [*colloq.*], boozy [*colloq.*], full [*vulgar*], lit up [*slang*], elevated [*colloq.*]; groggy [*colloq.*]; screwed, tight, primed [*all slang*], muddled, maudlin; blind drunk, dead drunk.

960. PURITY.—*N*. purity; decency, decorum, delicacy; continence, chastity, virtue, modesty; virginity.

virgin, vestal, prude; Diana.

Adj. **pure,** undefiled, modest, delicate, clean, decent, decorous; chaste, continent, virtuous, honest.

961. IMPURITY.—*N*. impurity, uncleanness; immodesty; grossness; indelicacy, indecency, obscenity; dissipation.

Adj. **impure,** unclean; immodest, shameless, indelicate, indecent, coarse, gross.

962. LIBERTINE.—*N*. libertine, voluptuary, rake, roué [F.], fast man.

5. Institutions

963. LEGALITY.—*N*. legality, legitimacy, legitimateness; legitimization.

law, code, constitution, charter, act, enactment, statute, rule, canon, ordinance, institution, regulation, bylaw, decree, standing order.

equity, common law; unwritten law; law of nations, international law; constitutionality; justice, etc., 922; jurisprudence; legislation.

V. **legalize,** legitimize; enact, ordain, decree, authorize, pass a law, legislate; codify, formulate, regulate.

Adj. **legal,** legitimate; according to law; vested, constitutional, chartered, legalized, lawful, statutory; legislative; judicial, juridical.

Adv. in the eye of the law.

964. [Absence or violation of law] **ILLEGALITY.**—*N*. lawlessness, illicitness; breach (*or* violation) of law; disobedience, violence, brute force, despotism, tyranny, outlawry; mob (*or* lynch) law.

illegality, informality, unlawfulness, illegitimacy; smuggling.

V. **violate the law,** set the law at defiance, make the law a dead letter, take the law into one's own hands.

smuggle, run, poach, bootleg [*slang*].

Adj. **illegal,** prohibited, unlawful, illegitimate, illicit, contraband, actionable.

unchartered, unconstitutional, lawless, unwarranted, unauthorized; unofficial.

arbitrary, despotic, summary, irresponsible.

Adv. with a high hand, in violation of law.

965. JURISDICTION. [Executive]—*N*. jurisdiction, judicature, administration of justice; judge, etc., 967; tribunal, etc., 966.

city government, municipal government, commission government, Oregon plan [U. S.]; municipality, corporation; police, police force, constabulary.

executive, officer, commissioner, lord lieutenant [Brit.], city manager, mayor, alderman, councilor, selectman; bailiff, beadle; sheriff, constable, policeman, police constable, police sergeant, patrolman, gendarme [F.].

bureau, department, portfolio, secretariat.

V. judge, adjudge, adjudicate, sit in judgment; have jurisdiction over.

Adj. executive, administrative; municipal; judiciary, judicial, juridical.

966. TRIBUNAL.—*N.* tribunal, court, board, bench, judicature, court of justice (*or* law); judgment seat, mercy seat; bar, bar of justice; town hall, statehouse, townhouse, courthouse; forum; sessions.

United States courts: U. S. Supreme Court, U. S. District Court, U. S. Circuit Court of Appeal; Federal Court of Claims, Court of Private Land Claims; Supreme Court, Superior Court, court of sessions, criminal court, police court, juvenile court.

court-martial, (*pl.* courts-martial), drumhead court-martial.

Adj. judicial, etc., 965; appellate; curial.

967. JUDGE.—*N.* judge, justice, justice (*or* judge) of assize; magistrate, police magistrate, beak [*slang*]; his worship [Eng.], his honor his lordship [Brit.]; the court.

Lord Chancellor, Master of the Rolls, Vice-Chancellor, Lord Chief Justice [all Brit.], Chief Justice.

arbiter, arbitrator; moderator, receiver, master; umpire, referee; censor.

jury, grand jury, petty jury, inquest, panel.

juror, juryman, talesman; grand juror, grand juryman; petty juror, petty juryman.

V. adjudge, etc. (*determine*), 480; try a case, try a prisoner.

Adj. judicial, etc., 965.

968. LAWYER.—*N.* lawyer, jurist, legal adviser, advocate; barrister, barrister-at-law [Eng.]; counsel, counselor; king's counsel [Eng.]; pleader, special pleader.

attorney, solicitor; conveyancer, notary, notary public; pettifogger, shyster.

bar, legal profession; Inns of Court [Eng.].

V. practice law; practice at (*or* within) the bar, plead; be called to (*or* within) the bar; admitted to the bar.

disbar, degrade.

Adj. learned in the law; at the bar; forensic.

969. LAWSUIT.—*N.* lawsuit, suit, action, cause; litigation; suit in law.

writ, summons, subpoena, citation; habeas corpus [L.].

arraignment, prosecution, impeachment, accusation; presentment, true bill, indictment.

arrest, apprehension, committal, commitment; imprisonment.

pleadings; declaration, bill, claim; affidavit, libel; answer, plea, demurrer, rebutter, rejoinder; surrebutter, surrejoinder.

litigant, suitor, libelant; plaintiff, defendant, etc., 938.

hearing, trial; judgment, sentence, finding, verdict; appeal, writ of error.

case, decision, decided case, precedent.

V. **litigate,** go to law, appeal to the law; bring to justice (*or* trial, the bar), put on trial, accuse, prefer (*or* file) a claim.

cite, summon, summons, serve with a writ, arraign; sue, prosecute, indict, impeach; attach, distrain; commit, apprehend, arrest, give in charge.

try, hear a cause; sit in judgment; adjudicate, etc., 480.

970. ACQUITTAL.—*N.* acquittal, exculpation, acquittance, clearance, exoneration, discharge, release, absolution, reprieve, respite, pardon.

Exemption from punishment: impunity, immunity.

V. **acquit,** exculpate, exonerate, clear; absolve, whitewash, discharge, release, liberate, reprieve, respite, pardon.

Adj. **acquitted,** uncondemned, unpunished; recommend to mercy.

971. CONDEMNATION.—*N.* condemnation, conviction, judgment, penalty, sentence; death warrant.

V. **condemn,** convict, find guilty, damn, doom, sentence, pass sentence on, attaint, confiscate, sequestrate.

proscribe, interdict; disapprove, etc., 932; accuse, etc., 938.

Adj. **condemnatory,** damnatory, condemned, self-convicted.

972. PUNISHMENT.—*N.* punishment, punition, chastisement, chastening, correction, castigation; discipline, infliction, trial; judgment, penalty, retribution, nemesis, retributive justice.

Forms of punishment: lash, scaffold, etc. (*instrument of punishment*), 975; imprisonment; transportation, banishment, expulsion, exile, involuntary exile, ostracism, penal servitude, hard labor, galleys; beating, flagellation, bastinado, blow, stripe, cuff, kick, buffet, pummel; torture, rack.

capital punishment, execution; hanging, shooting, electrocution, decapitation, strangling, strangulation, crucifixion, impalement, martyrdom, auto-da-fé (*pl.* autos-da-fé) [Pg.], hara-kiri [Jap.], happy dispatch [*jocular*], lethal chamber, hemlock.

V. **punish,** chastise, chasten, castigate, correct, inflict punishment; tar and feather; masthead, keelhaul.

visit upon, pay, settle, settle with, do for [*colloq.*], get even with, make an example of; give it one [*both colloq.*].

strike, etc., 276; smite; spank, thwack, thump, beat, buffet, thrash, pommel, drub, trounce, belabor; trim [*colloq.*], cowhide, lambaste [*slang*], lash, flog, scourge, whip, birch, cane, switch, horsewhip, lay about one, beat black and blue; sandbag, blackjack; pelt, stone.

execute; bring to the block (*or* gallows), behead, decapitate, guillotine; hang [*p. p.* hanged, *not* hung, *for the death penalty*], electrocute, shoot, burn, crucify, impale, lynch.

torture, agonize, rack, put on (*or* to) the rack, martyr, martyrize.

banish, exile, transport, deport, expel, ostracize; rusticate; drum out; dismiss, disbar; unfrock [*as a priest*].

Adj. punitive, penal, punitory, inflictive, castigatory.

973. REWARD.—*N.* reward, recompense, remuneration, prize, meed, guerdon, indemnity, indemnification; quittance, compensation, reparation, redress, acknowledgment, requital, amends, sop, consideration, return; atonement.

perquisite, perks [*slang*]; donation, etc., 784; tip, bribe, hush money, blackmail.

allowance, salary, stipend, wages; pay, payment, emolument; tribute; premium, fee, honorarium; hire; mileage.

V. reward, recompense, repay, requite, remunerate, compensate; fee, tip, bribe; pay, etc., 807; make amends, indemnify, redress, atone, satisfy, acknowledge.

Adj. remunerative, compensatory; retributive.

974. PENALTY.—*N.* penalty; retribution, etc. (*punishment*), 972; pain, penance.

fine, mulct, forfeit, forfeiture, damages, sequestration, confiscation.

V. penalize, fine, mulct, confiscate, sequestrate, sequester; forfeit.

975. [Instrument of punishment] SCOURGE.—*N.* scourge, whip, lash, strap, thong, cowhide, knout, cat, cat-o'-nine-tails; rope's end; black snake, bullwhack, quirt, rawhide.

rod, cane, stick, rattan, birch, birch rod; rod in pickle; switch, ferule, cudgel, truncheon.

Various instruments: pillory, stocks, whipping post, ducking stool, iron maiden; thumbscrew, boot, rack, wheel; treadmill, crank, galleys; bed of Procrustes.
scaffold; block, ax, guillotine; stake; cross, gallows, gibbet, tree; noose, rope, halter, bowstring; death chair, electric chair.

prison, jail, etc., 752; jailer.

executioner; electrocutioner, headsman, hangman; lyncher, torturer.

malefactor, criminal, culprit, felon, victim, gallows bird [*slang*].

V. RELIGIOUS AFFECTIONS

976. DEITY.—*N.* Deity, Divinity, Godhead, Omnipotence, Omniscience, Providence.

GOD, Lord, Jehovah, The King of Kings, The Lord of Lords, The Almighty, The Supreme Being, The Absolute, The First Cause, Author of all things, Creator of all things, The Infinite, The Eternal, The All-powerful, The Omnipotent, The All-wise, The All-merciful, The All-knowing, The Omniscient.

Deus [L.], *Theos* [Gr. Θεος], *Dieu* [F.], *Gott* [Ger.], *Dio* [It.], *Dios* [Sp.], *Deos* [Pg.], *Gud* [Nor., Sw., and Dan.], *God* [Du.], *Bog* Russ.], Brahma [Skr.], *Deva* [Skr.], *Khuda* (Hind.), Allah (Ar.).

THE TRINITY, The Holy Trinity, The Trinity in Unity, Triunity, Threefold Unity.

I. GOD THE FATHER, The Maker, The Creator, The Preserver.

Functions: creation, preservation, divine government, thearchy.

II. GOD THE SON, Jesus Christ; The Messiah, The Anointed, The Saviour, The Redeemer, The Mediator, The Intercessor, The Advocate, The Judge; The Son of God, The Son of Man; The Only-Begotten, The Lamb of God, The Word, Logos; The Man of Sorrows; Jesus of Nazareth, King of the Jews, The Son of Mary, The Risen, Immanuel, The King of Kings and Lord of Lords, The King of Glory, The Prince of Peace, The Good Shepherd, The Way, The Door, The Truth, The Life, The Bread of Life, The Light of the World, The Vine, The True Vine.

The Incarnation, The Word made Flesh.

Functions: salvation, redemption, atonement, propitiation, mediation, intercession, judgment.

III. GOD THE HOLY GHOST, The Holy Spirit, Paraclete, The Comforter, The Consoler, The Intercessor, The Spirit of God, The Spirit of Truth, The Dove.

Functions: inspiration, regeneration, sanctification, consolation, grace.

The Deity in other religions: Brahmanism *or* Hinduism: Brahma (*neuter*), the Supreme Soul *or* Essence of the Universe; Trimurti *or* Hindu trinity *or* Hindu triad: (1) Brahma (*masc.*), the Creator; (2) Vishnu, the Preserver; (3) Siva, the Destroyer and Regenerator.

Buddhism: the Protestantism of the East; Buddha, the Blessed One, the Teacher.

Zoroastrianism: Zerâna-Akerana, the Infinite Being; Ahuramazda *or* Ormazd, the Creator, the Lord of Wisdom, the King of Light (*opposed by* Ahriman, the King of Darkness).

Mohammedanism *or* Islam: Allah.

V. create, fashion, make, form, mold, manifest.
preserve, uphold, keep, perpetuate, immortalize.
atone, redeem, save, propitiate, expiate; intercede, mediate.

predestinate, predestine, foreordain, preordain; elect, call, ordain.

bless, sanctify, hallow, justify, absolve, glorify.

Adj. almighty, all-powerful, omnipotent; omnipresent, all-wise, all-seeing, all-knowing, omniscient, supreme.

divine, heavenly, celestial; holy, hallowed, sacred, sacrosanct. supernatural, superhuman, spiritual, ghostly, unearthly.

Adv. by God's will, by God's help, *Deo volente* [L.], God willing; in Jesus' name, in His name, to His glory.

977. [Beneficent spirits] ANGEL.—*N.* angel, archangel, messenger of God, guardian angel; ministering spirits, invisible helpers, choir invisible, heavenly host, sons of God; saint; seraphim (*sing.*, seraph, *E. pl.*, seraphs), Cherubim (*sing.*, cherub, *E. pl.*, cherubs· cherubim *or* cherubin *are often treated as sing.*).

Madonna, Our Lady, *Notre Dame* [F.], Holy Mary, The Virgin, The Blessed Virgin, The Virgin Mary.

Adj. angelic, seraphic, cherubic, archangelic.

978. [Maleficent spirits] SATAN.—*N.* Satan, the Devil, Lucifer, Belial, Beelzebub, Mephistopheles, Mephisto, Asmodeus, *le Diable* [F.], Deil [Scot.].

fallen angels, unclean spirits, devils; rulers of darkness, the powers of darkness; demon, etc.,980.

Moloch, Mammon; Belial, Beelzebub; Loki [*Norse Myth*].

diabolism, devil worship, demonism, demonology; Black Mass, black magic, demonolatry, witchcraft.

diabolist, demonologist.

V. demonize; bewitch, bedevil, etc. (*sorcery*), 992; possess, obsess.

Adj. satanic, diabolic *or* diabolical, devilish, demoniac *or* demoniacal, infernal, hellborn.

979. MYTHIC AND PAGAN DEITIES.—*N.* god, goddess; heathen gods and goddesses; pantheon.

Greek and Latin: Zeus, Jupiter *or* Jove (*King*); Apollo *or* Phoebus Apollo (*the sun*); Ares, Mars (*war*); Hermes, Mercury (*messenger*); Poseidon, Neptune (*ocean*); Hephaestus, Vulcan (*smith*); Dionysus, Bacchus (*wine*); Hades [Gr.], Pluto *or* Dis [L.] (*King of the lower world*); Kronos, Saturn (*time*); Eros, Cupid (*love*); Pan, Faunus (*flocks, herds, forests, and wild life*).

Hera, Juno (*Queen*); Demeter, Ceres (*fruitfulness*); Persephone, Proserpina *or* Proserpine (*Queen of the lower world*); Artemis, Diana (*the moon and hunting*); Athena, Minerva (*wisdom*); Aphrodite, Venus (*love and beauty*); Hestia, Vesta (*the hearth*); Rhea *or* Cybele ("Mother of the gods," *identified with* Ops, *wife of Saturn*); Gaea *or* Ge, Tellus (*earth goddess, mother of the Titans*).

Norse: Ymir (*primeval giant*), Odin *or* Woden (*the All-father* == *Zeus*); the Æsir: Thor (*the Thunderer*), Balder (= *Apollo*), Freyr (*fruitfulness*), Tyr (*war*), Bragi (*poetry and eloquence*), Höder (*blind god of the winter*), Heimdall (*warder of Asgard*), Loki (*evil*).

the Vanir: Njorth (*the winds and the sea*), Frey (*prosperity and love*), Freya (*goddess of love and beauty* == *Venus*).

Frigg or Frigga (*wife of Odin*), Hel (*goddess of death = Persephone*), Idun (*goddess of spring, wife of Bragi*), Sigyn (*wife of Loki*).

Egyptian: Ra or Amon-Ra (*the sun god*), Osiris (*judge of the dead*), Isis (*wife of Osiris*), Horus (*the morning sun; son of Osiris and Isis*), Anubis (*jackal-god, brother of Horus, a conductor of the dead*), Nephthys (*sister of Isis*), Set (*evil deity, brother of Osiris*), Thoth (*clerk of the underworld*), Bast or Bubastis (*a goddess with head of a cat*), the Sphinx (*wisdom*).

Various: Baal [Semitic]; Astarte or Ashtoreth (*goddess of fertility and love*) [Phoenician]; Bel [Babylonian]; The Great Spirit [N. Amer. Indian].

nymph, dryad, hamadryad, wood nymph; naiad, fresh-water nymph; oread, mountain nymph; nereid, sea nymph; Oceanid, ocean nymph; Pleiades, Hyades.

fairy, fay, sprite; nix (*fem.* nixie), water sprite; the good folk, brownie, pixy, elf (*pl.* elves), banshee; the Fates; kobold, troll, hobgoblin, gnome, kelpie; faun; peri, undine, sea maid, mermaid (*masc.* merman); Mab, Oberon, Titania, Ariel; Puck, Robin Goodfellow.

familiar spirit, familiar, genius, guide, good genius, daimon, demon.

mythology, mythical lore, folklore, fairyism, fairy mythology.
Adj. mythical, mythic, mythological, fabulous, legendary.
fairylike, sylphlike, elfin, elflike, elfish, nymphlike.

980. EVIL SPIRITS.—*N.* demon, fiend, devil, etc. (*Satan*), 978; evil genius, familiar, familiar spirit; bad (*or* unclean) spirit; incubus; ogre, ogress, ghoul, vampire, harpy; Fury, the Furies, the Erinyes, the Eumenides.

imp, bad fairy, sprite, jinni (*pl.* jinn), genius (*pl.* genii), dwarf.
changeling, elf child, werewolf; satyr.

elemental, sylph, gnome, salamander, nymph [*Rosicrucian*].
siren, nixie, undine, Lorelei.

bugbear, bugaboo, bogy, goblin, hobgoblin.
Adj. demoniac, demoniacal, fiendish, fiendlike, evil, ghoulish; pokerish [*colloq.*], bewitched.

980a. SPECTER.—*N.* specter, ghost, apparition, vision, spirit, sprite, shade, shadow, wraith, banshee, spook [*now humorous*], phantom, phantasm, materialization [*spiritualism*], double.

will-o'-the-wisp, etc., 423.
Adj. spectral, ghostly, ghostlike, spiritual, wraithlike, weird, uncanny, eerie, spooky [*colloq.*] haunted; unearthly, supernatural.

981. HEAVEN.—*N.* heaven; kingdom of heaven (*or* God), heavenly kingdom; heaven of heavens, God's throne, throne of God; Paradise, Eden, Zion, Holy City, New Jerusalem, Heavenly City, City Celestial, abode of the blessed.

Mythological heaven or paradise: Olympus; Elysium, Elysian fields, Islands (*or* Isles) of the Blessed, Happy Isles, Fortunate Isles, garden of the Hesperides; third heaven, seventh heaven; Valhalla [Scandinavian]; Nirvana [Buddhist]; happy hunting grounds [N. Amer. Indian].

future state, life after death, eternal home, resurrection, translation; apotheosis, deification.

Adj. **heavenly,** celestial, supernal, unearthly, paradisaic, beatific; Elysian, Olympian.

982. HELL.—*N.* **hell,** bottomless pit, place of torment; pandemonium; hell-fire, everlasting fire (*or* torment); worm that never dies.

purgatory, limbo, Gehenna, abyss.

Mythological hell: Tartarus, Hades, Avernus; infernal regions, inferno, shades below, realms of Pluto.
Pluto, Rhadamanthus, Erebus, Charon, Cerberus; Persephone, Proserpina; Minos, Osiris.
Rivers of hell: Styx, Acheron, Cocytus, Phlegethon, Lethe.

Adj. **hellish,** infernal, stygian.

983. [Religious Knowledge] THEOLOGY.—*N.* **theology,** theosophy, divine wisdom, divinity, hagiography; monotheism, theism, religion; religious persuasion (*or* sect, denomination, affiliation); creed, articles (*or* declaration, profession, confession) of faith.

theologian, scholastic, divine, schoolman, the Fathers; monotheist, theist.

Adj. **theological,** religious, divine, canonical; denominational; sectarian.

983a. ORTHODOXY.—*N.* **orthodoxy;** strictness, soundness, religious truth, true faith; truth, etc., 494; soundness of doctrine; Christianity, Catholicism.

the church, Holy Church, Church Militant, Church Triumphant; Catholic (*or* Universal, Apostolic) Church; Established (*or* State) Church; The Bride of the Lamb; temple of the Holy Ghost; Church of Christ; Christians, Christendom.

canons; thirty-nine articles; Apostles' (*or* Nicene, Athanasian) Creed.

Adj. **orthodox,** sound, strict, faithful, catholic, Christian, evangelical, scriptural, literal, divine, monotheistic, true, etc., 494.

984. HETERODOXY. [Sectarianism]—*N.* **heterodoxy;** error, false doctrine, heresy, schism, recusancy, backsliding, apostasy; materialism, atheism; idolatry, superstition.

bigotry, fanaticism, iconoclasm; precisianism; sabbatarianism, puritanism, bibliolatry.

sectarianism, nonconformity, dissent, secularism; religious sects, the clash of creeds, the isms.

[*Generally speaking, each sect is* orthodox *to itself and* heterodox *to others.*]

paganism, heathenism, heathendom; animism, polytheism, pantheism; dualism.

pagan, heathen, paynim; kafir, non-Mohammedan; gentile; pantheist, polytheist, animist.

misbeliever, heretic, apostate; backslider; antichrist; idolater; skeptic, etc., 989.

bigot, dogmatist, fanatic, dervish, iconoclast.

sectarian, sectary; seceder, separatist, recusant, dissenter, nonconformist.

materialist, positivist, deist, agnostic, atheist, etc., 989.

Adj. **heterodox**, heretical, unorthodox, unscriptural, uncanonical, unchristian, apocryphal; antichristian; schismatic, recusant, iconoclastic; sectarian, dissenting, secular; agnostic, atheistic; skeptical, etc., 989.

bigoted, dogmatical, fanatical; superstitious, credulous; idolatrous.

pagan, heathen, heathenish, gentile, paynim; polytheistic, pantheistic, animistic.

985. REVELATION. [Biblical]—*N.* **revelation**, inspiration.

The Bible, the Book, the Book of Books, The Good Book, the Word, the Word of God, Scripture, the Scriptures, Holy Writ, Holy Scriptures, inspired writings, Gospel.

Old Testament, Septuagint, Vulgate, Pentateuch; the Law, the Prophets; Apocrypha.

New Testament; Gospels, Evangelists, Acts, Epistles, Apocalypse, Revelation; Good Tidings, Glad Tidings.

inspired writers, prophet, evangelist, apostle, disciple, saint; the Fathers, the Apostolic Fathers; Holy Men of old.

Adj. **scriptural**, biblical, sacred, prophetic; evangelical, evangelistic, apostolic, apostolical; inspired, apocalyptic, revealed; ecclesiastical, canonical.

986. SACRED WRITINGS. [Non-Biblical]—*N.* The Vedas, Upanishads, Puranas, Sutras, Bhagavad Gita [all Brahmanic]; Zendavesta, Avesta [Zoroastrian]; The Koran *or* Alcoran [Mohammedan]; Tripitaka, Dhammapada [Buddhist]; Granth, Adigranth [*Sikh*]; the Kings [Chinese]; the Eddas [Scandinavian].

Non-Biblical prophets and religious founders: Gautama (Buddha); Zoroaster, Confucius, Mohammed.

987. PIETY.—*N.* **piety**, religion, theism, faith; religiousness, religiosity, holiness, saintship; reverence, humility, veneration, devotion, worship, grace, sanctity, consecration.

beatification, regeneration, conversion, sanctification, salvation, inspiration, bread of life; Body and Blood of Christ.

believer, convert, theist, Christian, devotee, pietist, saint.

V. **be pious**, have faith, believe, receive Christ; venerate, adore, worship, revere, be converted, be on God's side, stand up for Jesus, fight the good fight, keep the faith, let one's light shine.

regenerate, convert, edify, sanctify, hallow, keep holy, beatify, inspire, consecrate, enshrine.

Adj. pious, religious, devout, devoted, reverent, godly, humble, pure, pure in heart, holy, spiritual, saintly, saintlike; believing, faithful, Christian.

regenerated; inspired, consecrated, converted, unearthly.

elected, adopted, justified, sanctified.

988. IMPIETY.—*N.* impiety, sin, irreverence; profaneness, profanity, blasphemy, profanation; desecration, sacrilege; scoffing.

Assumed piety: hypocrisy, pietism, cant, pious fraud; lip devotion, lip service; formalism, austerity; sanctimony, sanctimoniousness, pharisaism, sabbatarianism; sacerdotalism; bigotry; blue laws.

apostasy, recusancy, backsliding, perversion, reprobation.

bigot, pharisee, sabbatarian, formalist, pietist, precisian, devotee, ranter, fanatic.

sinner, scoffer, blasphemer, sabbath breaker; worldling; hypocrite.

the wicked, the evil, the unjust, the reprobate.

V. profane, desecrate, blaspheme, revile, scoff, swear; commit sacrilege.

dissemble, simulate, play the hypocrite, snuffle.

Adj. impious, irreligious, etc., 989; profane, irreverent, sacrilegious, blasphemous.

unhallowed, unsanctified, unregenerate; hardened, perverted, reprobate.

hypocritical, canting, pietistical, sanctimonious, unctuous, pharisaical, overrighteous.

bigoted, fanatical, hidebound, narrow, narrow-minded, illiberal, prejudiced, little; provincial, parochial, insular.

989. IRRELIGION.—*N.* irreligion, impiety, ungodliness, laxity, apathy, indifference.

skepticism, doubt; unbelief, disbelief, incredulity, agnosticism, freethinking; materialism, rationalism, positivism; atheism, infidelity.

unbeliever, infidel, atheist, heretic, heathen, alien, gentile, Nazarene; freethinker, skeptic, rationalist; materialist, positivist, nihilist, agnostic.

V. disbelieve, lack faith; doubt, question, deny the truth.

Adj. irreligious; undevout, godless, graceless, ungodly; unholy, unsanctified, unhallowed; atheistic.

skeptical, freethinking, unbelieving, unconverted; incredulous, faithless.

worldly, mundane, earthly, carnal, worldly, worldly-minded, unspiritual.

990. WORSHIP.—*N.* worship, cult, adoration, devotion, vow, aspiration, homage, service; kneeling, genuflection, prostration.

prayer, invocation, supplication, intercession, orison, petition; collect, litany, Lord's prayer, paternoster; *Ave Maria* [L.], Hail, Mary.

thanksgiving; grace, praise, glorification, paean, benediction, doxology, hosanna, hallelujah, alleluia, *Te Deum* [L.], *Gloria* [L.].

psalm, hymn, chant, response, anthem.

offering, oblation, sacrifice, incense, libation, offertory, collection.

divine service, office, duty; exercises; morning prayer; Mass, matins, evensong, vespers, vigils, lauds.

worshiper, congregation, communicant, celebrant.

V. **worship,** lift up the heart, aspire; revere, adore, do service, pay homage, offer one's vows, vow; bow down and worship.

pray, invoke, supplicate; beseech; offer up prayers, say one's prayers, tell one's beads, recite the rosary.

give thanks, say grace, bless, praise, laud, glorify, magnify, sing praises.

Adj. devout, devotional, reverent, solemn, fervid.

991. IDOLATRY.—*N.* idolatry, idolatrousness, demonism, demonology, devil worship, fetishism.

idolization, deification, apotheosis, canonization; hero worship.

sacrifice, hecatomb, holocaust; human sacrifices, immolation, self-immolation, suttee.

idol, golden calf, graven image, fetish, joss [Chinese], *lares et penates* [L.]; god (*or* goddess) of one's idolatry; Baal, Moloch, Juggernaut.

idolater, idolatress, idolizer, fetishist.

V. **idolize,** idolatrize, worship idols, worship, put on a pedestal, prostrate oneself before; make sacrifice to, deify, canonize.

Adj. **idolatrous,** idolistic, prone before, prostrate before, in the dust before, at the feet of.

992. SORCERY.—*N.* sorcery, magic, black magic, the black art, necromancy, demonology, witchcraft, witchery, wizardry, fetishism, hoodoo, voodoo, voodooism; fire worship, incantation, enchantment, bewitchment, glamour; obsession, possession.

divination, etc. (*prediction*), 511; sortilege, ordeal, hocus-pocus.

V. **practice sorcery,** cast a nativity (*or* horoscope), conjure, charm, enchant, bewitch, bedevil, witch, voodoo, hoodoo [*colloq.*]; entrance, fascinate, hypnotize, cast a spell; call up spirits.

Adj. **magic,** magical, witching, weird, cabalistic, talismanic.

992a. PSYCHICAL RESEARCH.—*N.* **psychical research,** psychical (*or* psychic) investigation; abnormal (*or* mediumistic) phenomena; mysticism.

the subconscious, the subconscious self, the subliminal self, the higher self, ego, astral body; aura; subconsciousness, subliminal consciousness; intuition; dual personality, multiple personality, obsession, possession.

psychotherapy, psychotherapeutics, psychoanalysis; hysteria, neurasthenia, dreams, visions, apparitions, hallucinations.

mesmerism, animal magnetism; mesmeric trance; hypnotism; hypnosis.

Phenomena: **telepathy,** thought transference, thought transmission, telepathic transmission; second sight, clairvoyance, clairaudience, psychometry.

premonitions, previsions, premonitory apparition, fetch, wraith, double; death lights, ominous dreams.

automatism, automatic writing, planchette, ouija board, trance writing, spirit writing; trance speaking, inspirational speaking.

spiritualism, spiritism, spirit manifestations; trance, spirit control, spirit possession; mediumistic communications; séance; materialization.

medium, seer, clairvoyant, clairaudient, telepathist; guide, control; mesmerist, hypnotist.

V. **psychologize;** investigate the abnormal (*or* supernormal, subconscious, subliminal), traverse the borderland, know oneself.

mesmerize, magnetize, hypnotize, place under control, subject to suggestion, place in a trance, induce hypnosis.

Adj. **psychical,** psychic, psychological; spiritistic, spiritualistic, spiritual; subconscious, subliminal, supernormal, abnormal; mystic *or* mystical.

993. SPELL.—*N.* **spell,** charm, incantation, exorcism, abracadabra, open-sesame; evil eye.

talisman, amulet, phylactery, philter, fetish, wishbone; mascot, rabbit's foot, hoodoo [*colloq.*], jinx [*slang*], scarabaeus *or* scarab; veronica, swastika.

wand, caduceus, rod, divining rod, witch hazel, Aaron's rod.

Magic wish-givers: **Aladdin's lamp,** Aladdin's casket, magic casket, magic ring, magic belt, magic spectacles, wishing cap, Fortunatus' cap; seven-league boots; magic carpet; cap of darkness.

994. SORCERER.—*N.* **sorcerer,** magician, wizard, necromancer, conjuror, prestidigitator; charmer, exorcist, voodoo medicine man, witch doctor; astrologer, soothsayer, etc., 513.

sorceress, witch, hag; siren, harpy.

Cagliostro, Merlin; Circe, weird sisters, witch of Endor.

995. CHURCHDOM.—*N.* **churchdom;** church, ministry, priesthood, prelacy, hierarchy, church government; clericalism, sacerdotalism, episcopalianism.

monasticism, monkhood, monachism; celibacy.

Ecclesiastical offices and dignities: cardinalate, cardinalship; primacy, archbishopric, archiepiscopacy; prelacy, bishopric, episcopate, episcopacy, see, diocese; benefice, incumbency, living, cure, charge, cure of souls; rectorship, vicariate, vicarship; pastorate, pastorship, pastoral charge; deaconry, deaconship; curacy; chaplaincy, chaplainship, presbytery.

holy orders, ordination, institution, consecration, induction, installation, preferment, translation, presentation.

papacy, pontificate, See of Rome, the Vatican, the apostolic see.

V. **call,** ordain, induct, install, translate, consecrate, present, elect, bestow.

Adj. **ecclesiastical,** clerical, sacerdotal, priestly, pastoral, ministerial, hierarchical, episcopal, canonical; pontifical, papal, apostolic.

996. CLERGY.—*N.* **clergy,** clericals, ministry, priesthood, presbytery, the cloth, the pulpit, the desk.

clergyman, divine, ecclesiastic, priest, pastor, shepherd, minister, preacher, clerk in holy orders, parson, sky pilot [*slang*]; father, padre, *abbé* [F.], *curé* [F.]; reverend.

Dignitaries of the church: Pope, pontiff, Holy Father; cardinal, primate, metropolitan, archbishop, bishop, prelate, dean, archdeacon, canon, rector, vicar, beneficiary, incumbent, chaplain, curate; elder, deacon.

religious, abbot, prior, monk, friar, lay brother, pilgrim, palmer.

nun, sister, priestess, abbess, prioress, canoness; mother superior, the reverend mother; novice.

Adj. **ordained,** in orders, in holy orders, called to the ministry.

997. LAITY.—*N.* **laity,** flock, fold, congregation, assembly, brethren, people; society [U. S.]; class [Methodist].

layman, parishioner, catechumen.

V. **laicize,** secularize.

Adj. **secular,** lay congregational, civil, temporal, profane.

998. RITE.—*N.* **rite,** ceremony, observance, function, duty, form, solemnity, sacrament; service, ministry, ministration.

sermon, preaching, preachment, exhortation, religious harangue, homily, lecture, discourse.

worship, etc., 990; invocation of saints, confession, the confessional; absolution, remission of sins; reciting the rosary, telling one's beads.

Seven Sacraments: (1) **baptism,** immersion, christening; baptismal regeneration; font.

(2) **confirmation,** laying on of hands.

(3) **Eucharist,** Mass, Lord's supper, communion; tne sacrament, the holy sacrament; consecrated elements, bread and wine, celebration; transubstantiation, real presence.

(4) **penance,** fasting, sackcloth and ashes, flagellation.

(5) **extreme unction,** last rites, viaticum.

(6) **holy orders,** ordination, etc. (*churchdom*), 995.

(7) **matrimony,** marriage, wedlock, etc., 903.

Sacred articles: relics, rosary, beads, reliquary, host, cross, rood, crucifix; pyx, censer, thurible; prayer wheel [Buddhist]; Sangraal, Holy Grail.

ritual, liturgy, rubric, canon, ordinal, missal, breviary, Mass book, beadroll, litany, prayer book, Book of Common Prayer; psalter, psalmbook, hymnbook, hymnal.

ritualism, ceremonialism; sabbatism, sabbatarianism; ritualist, sabbatarian.

V. **perform service,** do duty, minister, officiate, celebrate.

excommunicate; ban with bell, book, and candle.

preach, sermonize, address the congregation.

Adj. **ritual,** ritualistic, ceremonial, liturgic *or* liturgical; paschal.

999. CANONICALS.—*N.* **canonicals,** vestments, robe, gown, surplice, etc.

1000. TEMPLE.—*N.* **temple,** fane, place of worship; house of God, house of prayer; cathedral, minster, church, kirk [Scot.], chapel, meetinghouse.

synagogue, tabernacle; mosque [Moham.]; pagoda, Chinese temple, joss house [*colloq.*]; pantheon, shrine.

monastery, priory, abbey, friary, convent, nunnery, cloister.

parsonage, rectory, vicarage, manse, deanery, clergy house; bishop's palace; Vatican.

Adj. **churchly,** cloistered, monastic, monasterial, conventual.

INDEX

The numbers refer to the headings under which the words or phrases occur. When the same word or phrase can be used in various senses, the several headings under which it or its synonyms will be found are indicated by *italics*.

When the word given in the Index is itself the title or heading of a category, the word is printed in capitals and the reference number in bold-faced type, thus: **ACTIVITY 682.** When the word is the keyword to a group of synonyms, the reference number is also in bold-faced type.

Derivatives likewise have been sparingly admitted, since the allied or basic term will serve as a key to the various derived forms; thus *alarm* is given, but not *alarmed* or *alarming*. Adverbs ending in *-ly* should be looked for under the adjective, if not found in the Index.

IMPORTANT NOTE

The numbers following all references in this Index Guide refer to the *section* numbers in the text, and *not* to pages.

INDEX

A

abandon 624, 782
abandoned
    forsaken 893
    vicious 945
abandonment 757, 782
abase 879
abasement 874
abash 879
abashed 879
abatement 36
abbess 996
abbey 1000
abbot 996
abbreviation 201
abdicate 757
abdomen 250
abduct repel 289
    steal 791
aberration 83
abet 707
abhor 867, 898
abhorrence 867, 898
abhorrent painful 830
    hateful 898
abide endure 1, 106
    remain 110
    dwell 186
ability 157, 698
abject vile 874
    servile 886
abjure deny 536
    renounce 607
ablaze 382
able capable 157
    skilful 698
able-bodied 159
ablution 652
abnormal 83
aboard present 186
    afloat 273
abode 189
abolish 756
abolition 2, 162, 756
abominable bad 649
    hateful 898
abominate dislike 867
    hate 898
abomination 867
aboriginal 66, 124
aborigine 188
abound 639
about nearly 32, 197
    around 227

above 206
abracadabra 993
abrade 330,331
abrasion 330,331
abreast 216, 236
abridge 36, 201
    in writing 596
abridgment 35, 201
abroad 57, 196
abrupt sudden 113
    steep 217
abscond 623
ABSENCE 187
    -of mind 458
    -of time 107
absent 187, 458
absentee 187
absent-minded 458
absolute not relative 1
    great 31
    certain 474
absolution 918
absolve 918, 952
absorb combine 48
    take in 296
absorbed 451
absorption 296
abstain refrain 623
    be temperate 953
abstainer 953, 958
abstemious 953, 958
abstention 623
abstinence 623, 953
abstract, v. take 789
abstract, n. epitome 195,
    596
abstracted inattentive 458
abstraction 38, 451, 458
absurd 471, 497, 583
ABSURDITY
    impossibility 471
    nonsense 497
    ridiculousness 853
abundance 31, 639
abundant great 31
    enough 639
abuse, v. illtreat 649
    misuse 679
abuse, n. in-vective 908,
    932
abusive 909, 932
abut 197
abysmal deep 208

abyss 198, 667
academic 537
academy 542
accede assent 488
    submit 725
    consent 762
accelerate 132, 274, 684
accent 402, 580
accentuate 580, 642
accept assent 488
    receive 785
acceptable
    expedient 646
    agreeable 829
acceptance security 771
access approach 286
accessible possible 470
    easy 705
accession increase 35
accessory extrinsic 6
    adjunct 37, 39
    accompanying 88
accident 151, 619, 735
accidental extrinsic 6
    occasional 134
    fortuitous 156
acclaim 931
acclamation 488, 931
acclivity 217
accommodate suit 23
    aid 707
accommodation
    adaptation 23
    space 180
ACCOMPANIMENT
    adjunct 37, 39
    coexistence 88
    musical 415
accompany
    coexist 88
    escort 664
accomplice 711
accomplish execute 161
    complete 729
accomplishment
    learning 490
    talent 698
accord
    agree 23
    assent 488
    grant 760, 784
accordance 16, 23
accordingly 8, 476

311

aeronautics 267, **273**
aerostatics 267
aesthetic 845
afar 196
affable 894
affair *event* 151
 battle 720
affect *relate to* 9
 qualify 469
 touch 824
 simper 855
 desire 865
AFFECTATION 579, 855
affected 579, **855**
affection 879
affectionate 897
AFFECTIONS 820
affianced 903
affiliated 9, 11
affinitive 9
affinity *relation* 9
 similarity 17
affirm 535
AFFIRMATION 535
affirmative 535
affix *addition* 37
 sequel 39
 precedence 62
afflict 830
affliction 828, 830
affluence 734, 803
afford 803
affront 900, 929
afield 186
afire 382
afloat 267, **273**
afoot *ready* 673
aforesaid 104
afraid 860
afresh *repeated* 104
 new 123
aft 235
after *in order* **63**
 in time 117
 rear 235
 in pursuit 281
aftermath 154
afternoon **126**
afterpart 235
afterthought 451
afterward 117
again 104
 -and again 136
against **708**
 -the grain 256, 704
agape 455, 507
AGE *period* 108
 course 109
 long time 110
 oldness 124
 advanced life **128**
aged 128
AGENCY 170
AGENT 690
aggrandize 35
aggravate *increase* 35

heighten **835**
AGGRAVATION 35, **835**
aggregate 50
aggression 716
aggrieve 830
aghast 860
agile 274
agitate *move* **315**
 excite 821, **824**
AGITATION
 [*see* agitate]
 energy 171
 motion 315
aglow 382, 420
agnostic 485, 984, 989
agnosticism 989
ago 122
agonizing 830
agony *physical* 378
 mental 828
agree *accord* 23, **714**
 concur 178
 assent 488
 -to 762
agreeable 82, **377**
AGREEMENT 23, 82, 178
agriculture 371
agriculturist 342
aground *fixed* 150
 failure 732
ahead 234, 282, **303**
AID 707, 906
ail 655
aileron 267
ailment 655
aim *direction* 278
 purpose 620
aimless 615a
air *gas* 334
ATMOSPHERIC **338, 349**
 tune 415
 appearance 448
aircraft 273
air line 278
airman 269
AIR PIPE 351
airplane 273, **726**
airs *affectation* 855
 vanity 880
airwoman 269a
airy [*see* air]
 visionary 4
 light 320
aisle 260
ajar 260
akimbo 244
akin *related* 11
alacrity 682, **836**
ALARM
 notice of danger **669**
 fear 860
alarmist 862
alarum 550, 669
album 593, 596
alcohol 959
alcove 191

alert *watchful* 457, 459
 active 682
alertness 457, 459
alias 18
alibi 187
alien *irrelevant* 10
 foreigner 57
alienate *disjoin* 44
 estrange 889
 set against 898
alight, v. *arrive* 292
 descend 306
alight, adv. *on fire* 382
align 278
alike 17
alive *living* 359
 intelligent 498
 active 682
all *whole* 50
 complete 52
allay 174, 834
allege 467, 535
allegiance *obedience* **743**
 duty 926
alleviate 174, 834
alleviation **174**
alley 260
alliance *relation* 9
 kindred 11
 co-operation 709
allied 11, **48**
alliteration 104
allot 786
allow *admit* 529
 permit 760
allowable 760
allowance
 qualification 469
 gift **784**
 salary 973
alloy *mixture* 41
 combine 48
allude 521, 526
allure 865
allusion **526**
ally, v. 48
ally, n.
 auxiliary 711
 friend 890
almanac 86, 114
almighty 157, 976
Almighty, the 976
almost **32**
alms 784
aloft 206
alone 87
along 200
alongside *near* 197
 parallel 216
 laterally 236
aloof *distant* 196
 secluded 893
aloud 404
alphabet 561
already 118
also 37

altar 903
alter 15, 140
alteration *difference* 15
  variation 20a
  change 140
alternate *reciprocal* 12
  vary 20a
  periodic 138
  substitute 147
  oscillate **314**
alternation 12, 138, **314**
alternative 147
although 179, 469
altitude 206
altogether 50, 52
altruism 910, 942
altruist 906, 910
alumnus 541
always *uniformly* **16**
  generally 78
  perpetually 112
amain *violent* 173
amalgamate 41, 48
amass 50, 72
amateur 602
amateurish 643
amaze 870
amazement 870
ambassador 534, 758
ambidexter 238
ambiguous *uncertain* 475
  unintelligible 519
  equivocal 520
ambition 620, 865
ambitious 865
amble 266
ambuscade 530
AMBUSH *hiding* **530**
  pitfall 667
amenable 602, **926**
amend *improve* 658
amendment 658
amends 952
amenity 894
amiable 894, 906
amicable 888
amidst 41, 228
amiss 619
amity 714, 888
ammunition **727**
amnesty 918
among **41**, 228
amorous 897
amount *quantity* 25
  sum of money 800
amphitheater 728
ample *much* 31
  spacious 180
  large 192
  broad 202
amplify 194, 549
amputate 38
amulet *talisman* 747
  charm 993
amuse 840
AMUSEMENT 840

ANACHRONISM 115,
  135
anemia 160
anesthesia 376, 381
anesthetic 376
anesthetize 376
analogous 17
analogy 9, 17
analysis
  decomposition 49
  inquiry 461
  reasoning 476
analyst 463
analytical [*see* analysis]
analyze [*see* analysis]
anarchist 891, 913
anarchy *disorder* 59
  social **738**
anathema 908
anathematize 908
anatomize *dissect* 44
  investigate 461
anatomy 44, 329
ancestor 166
ancestral 166
ancestry 69, **122**, 166
anchor *moor* 184
  stop 265
  safeguard 666
  hope 858
anchorage *location* 184
  roadstead 189
  refuge **666**
anchorite 893, 955
ancient *old* 124
and 37
anecdote 594
anew 104, 123
ANGEL 977
angelic 977
anger 900
angle 244, 448
angry 900
anguish *physical* 378
  moral **828**
angular **244**
ANGULARITY 244
ANIMAL 366, **370**
  -life **364**
animalcule 193
animalism 954
animate 824, 836
animation *activity* 682
  vivacity 836
animosity 889, 900
annalist 553
annals 594
annex 37, 43
annihilate 2, 162
annihilation 2
anniversary **138**, 883
annotation 522
announce *predict* 511
  inform **527**
announcement
  [*see* announce]

annoy *molest* 907
  disquiet 830
annoyance 828, **830**
annual 138
annul 756
ANNULMENT 756
anoint 332, 355
anointment **332**, 355
anomaly 83
anomalous 565
another 15
ANSWER *reply* **462**
  go bail 806
answerable 177, **926**
ant 366
antagonism *different* 24
  enmity 889
antagonist 710
antagonistic 14, 24, **179**
antecedence 62
antecedent 64
antedate 115
antediluvian 124
antelope 366
anthem 990
anthology *collection* 596
anthropology 368, 372
antic 840
anticipate
  foresee **121, 510**
  be early **132**
  expect 507
  hope 858
anticipation 115, 121
  [*see* anticipate]
anticlimax 853
antipathy *contrariety* 14
  repulsion 289
  dislike 867
  enemy 891
  hate 898
antipodes 14, 237
antiquary **122**
antiquated
  aged 122, **124**, 128
  out of fashion **851**
antique 124
antiquity **122**, 124
antiseptic 662
antisocial 911
antithesis 14, 15
anxiety *solicitude* 459
  pain 828
  fear 860
anxious [*see* anxiety]
any 25
anybody 78
anyhow 627
apace 132
apache 361, 913
apart *irrelative* 10
  separate 15, 44
  singleness 87
  asunder 96
apartment 191
apathetic 275, 462, **823**

apathy 823
ape *monkey* 366
ape, v. *imitate* 19
aperient 652
aperture 260
apex 206, 210
aphorism 496
apiary 370
apiece 79
Apocalypse 985
Apocrypha 985
apocryphal 475
apologetic 937
apologist 937
apology *substitution* 147
 vindication 937
 penitence 950
apostasy *recantation* 607
 impiety 988
apostate *turncoat* 607
 heretic 984
apostatize 607
apostle 985
apostolic 985, 995
apostrophe 589
apostrophize 765
apothecary 662
apotheosis 981, 991
appall *pain* 830
 terrify 860
apparatus 633
apparel 225
apparent *visible* 446
 appearing 448
 probable 472
 manifest 525
apparition
 phantom 4, 362
 spirit 980a, 992a
appeal *address* 586
 request 765
appear *arrive* 292
 come in sight 446, 448
APPEARANCE 448
appease 174, 826
append 37, 63
appendage *addition* 37
 adjunct 39
 sequel 65
 accompaniment 88
appendix 65
appertain 777
appetite 865
appetizer 394
appetizing 394
applaud 931
applause 931
appliance *use* 677
appliances 632
applicable *relevant* 9, 23
 useful 644
applicant 767
application *study* 457
 request 765
apply *appropriate* 788
appoint 755, 786

appointment *business* 625
 charge 755
 interview 892
appointments *gear* 633
apportion 786
APPORTIONMENT 786
apposition 23, 199
appraise 466
appreciate *realize* 450
 know 490
apprehend *know* 490
 fear 860
 seize 969
apprehension *idea* 453
 fear 860
apprehensive 860
apprentice 541
apprenticeship 539
APPROACH 286
 of time 121
 nearness 197
 path 627
approbation 931
appropriate *fit* 23
 peculiar 79
 timely 134
 borrow 788
 take 789
appropriation
 allotment 786
 taking 789
approval *assent* 488
 commendation 931
approve 488, 931
approved 931
approximate
 related to 9
 resemble 17
 near 197
 nearing 286
appurtenance 780
apt *consonant* 23
 clever 698
aquatic 267
aqueduct 350
aquiline 244
arable 371
arbiter *critic* 480
 judge 967
arbitrament 480
arbitrary 10
 willful 606
 severe 739
 lawless 964
arbitrate 480, 724
arbitration 480
arbitrator 724
arbor 191
arboreal 367
arc 245
arcade 189
arch *curve* 245
 convexity 250
 roguish 840
archeologist 122
archeology 122

archaic *old* 124
archaism 122, 124
archangel 977
archbishop 996
archer 284, 726, 840
archetype 22
archipelago 346
architect 164, 690
architecture 161
archive 551
arctic 237, 383
arctics 225
ardent *eager* 682
 loving 897
ardor *vigor* 574
 feeling 821
arduous 704
area 181
ARENA *space* 180
 field of battle 728
argosy 273
argot 563
argue 467, 476
argument 476
argumentation 476
arid 169, 340
aright 618
arise *begin* 66
 happen 151
 mount 305
aristocracy 875
aristocrat 875
aristocratic 852
arithmetic 85
ark 666
arm *part* 51
 power 157
 prepare 673
 weapon 727
armada 726
armament 727
armchair 215
armed 722
 -force 664, 726
armful 25
armistice 142, 723
armor 727
armorial 550
armory 636
ARMS 727 [see arm]
 heraldry 550
army *collection* 72
 multitude 102
 troops 726
aroma 400
around 227
arouse *move* 615
 excite 824
arraign *accuse* 938
 indict 969
arraignment 969
arrange *set in order* 60
 organize 357
 harmonize 416
 plan 626
 compromise 774

B

budge 264
budget *finance* 811
buff *color* 436
buffer 717
buffet *strike* 276
   smite 972
buffet *café* 189
   cupboard 191
buffoon *actor* 599
   humorist 844
   butt 857
buffoonery
   humor 840, 842, 853
   horseplay 856
bug 193, 366
bugaboo 980
bugbear 980
build *construct* 161
   form 240
building 189
bulb 249, 250
bulge 250
bulk, *n. quantity* 25
   whole 50
   size 192
bulk, *v.* 31
bulkhead 228
bulky 31, 192
bull *animal* 366
   absurdity 495, 497
   stock exchange 797
bulldoze 860
bullet 727
bulletin *list* 86
   news 532
bullion 800
bully, *n.* 863, 887
bully, *v. frighten* 860
   bluster 885
   threaten 909
bulwark 717
bump, *n.* 250
bump, *v.* 276

bumptious *proud* 878
bunch *collection* 72
   protuberance 250
buncombe *bombast* 577
   boast 884
   flattery 933
bundle *packet* 72
bung 263
bungle 495, 699
bungler 701
bunkum
   [*see* buncombe]
buoy *raise* 307
buoyant
   floating 305
   light 320
   elastic 325
   hopeful 858
bur 53
burden *clog* 706
bureau *chest* 191
   department 965
bureaucracy 737
burgess 188
burgher 188
burglar 792
burglary 791
burial 363
  -place 363
burlesque, *n.*
   travesty 555, 853
   absurdity 497
   ridicule 856
burlesque, *v. imitate* 19
   ridicule 856
burn *heat* 382
   consume 384
burnish *polish* 255
burrow *excavate* 208, 252
burst, *n. sound* 406
   paroxysm 825
burst, *v.*
  -forth *begin* 66

expand 194
  be seen 446
bury 229, 363
bush *shrub* 367
bushy 256
BUSINESS 151, **625**
businesslike
   orderly 58
   business 625
   practical 692
bustle *energy* 171
   agitation 315
   activity 682
bustling 682
busy 625, 682
busybody 455
but 30
butcher *kill* 361
butchered 53
butler 746
butt, *n. cask* 191
   laughingstock 857
butt, *v.* 276
butter 356
button *fasten* 43
buttonhole, *n.*
   bouquet 400
buttonhole, *v.*
   to bore 841
buttress 717
buxom 836
buy 795
buyer 795
buzz 409
by 236, 631
  -and by 132
  -means of **632**
  -the by 134
  -the way **134**
bygone *past* 122
byplay 550
bystander 197, 444
byword, *contempt* 930

C

cab 272
cabin *room* 189
cabinet *receptacle* 191
   council 696
cable, *n. link* 45
   dispatch 532
cable, *v.* 534
cabman 268
cackle (*of geese*) 412
   laugh 838
cad 851
cadaverous *pale* 429
   hideous 846
cadence *sound* 402
   music 415
cadet *junior* 129
   officer 745
caesura 44, 198

café 189, 298
cage, *n. prison* 752
cage, *v. restrain* 751
caisson 191, 252
cajole *flatter* 933
   [*see* cajolery]
cajolery *imposition* 544
   persuasion 615
   flattery 933
cake, *n.* 396
cake, *v. stick* 46
   consolidate 321
calamitous
   adverse 735, 935
   disastrous 830
calamity *killing* 361
   evil 619
   adversity 735

calcine 384
calculate 85
calculation 85
caldron 191
CALEFACTION 384
calendar *list* 86, 611
   chronicle 114
calf *animal* 366
   fool 501
caliber *measure* 26, 192
   intellectual capacity 498
calipers 466
calisthenics 159
calk 660
call *signal* 550
   name 564
   visit 892
   ordain 995

catechism *inquiry* 461
catechize 461
categorical *positive* 474
category *state* 7
   class 75
cater 298, 637
caterer 637
cathartic 652
cathedral 1000
catholic *universal* 78
   religious 987
Catholicism 983*a*
cattle *animals* 366
caucus *assemblage* 72
   council 696
causal 153
causative 153
CAUSE *source* 153
causeway 627
caustic *energetic* 171
   keen 821
   painful 830
CAUTION *warn* 668
   prudence 864
   with - 485
cautious 864
cavalcade 266
cavalier *horseman* 268
cavalry 726
cavalryman 726
cave 189, 252
caveman 893
cavern [*see* cave]
cavernous 252
cavil *dissent* 489
cavity 252
cavort 315
cease 142
ceaseless 112
cede *surrender* 725
   relinquish 782
ceiling 223
celebrate 883
CELEBRATION 883
celebrity 873
   nobility 875
celerity 274
celestial *physical* 318
   heavenly 976, 981
CELIBACY 904
celibate 904
cell *abode* 189, 191, 893
   organism 357
cellar 207
cement, *n. glue* 45
cement, *v. unite* 46
cemetery 363
censor *critic* 480
   detractor 936
censure 932
census 85, 86
centenary 98
centennial 98
center, *n. in order* 68
   focus 74
   in space 222

center, *v. converge* 290
central 68, **222**
CENTRALITY **222**
centralize 48, **222**
centuple 98
century *hundred* 98
   period 108
   long time 110
ceremonial **882**
ceremonious 882, 928
ceremony 882, 998
certain 474, 484
certainly 474, 488
CERTAINTY 474
certificate *evidence* 467
   security 771
certify 467
certitude 474
CESSATION 142
chafe *warm* 384
   fret 828, 830
chaff *ridicule* 856
chafing dish 386
chagrin 828
chain, *n. vinculum* 45
   series 69
chain, *v. fasten* 43
chair *support* 215
   professorship **540**
   president 694
chairman 694
chalet 189
challenge *doubt* 485
   accuse 938
chamber *room* 191
champ 298
champion *auxiliary* 711
   victor 731
   defender 914
CHANCE
   absence of cause 156
   absence of aim 621
chancellor *judge* 967
chandelier 214
CHANGE, *n.*
   alteration 20*a*, 140
   small coin 800
change, *v. differ* 15
   -*for* 147
   -*hands* 783
changeable 140, 149
CHANGEABLENESS
   140, 149
changeful 140, 607
changeling 147
channel *furrow* 259
   opening 260
chant, *n.* 415, 990
chant, *v.* 416
chaos 59
chap *fellow* 373
chapel 1000
chaperon 88, 459
chaplain 996
chaplet *circle* 247
   trophy 733

chapter *part* 51
   council 696
char 384
character *state* 7
   class 75
   oddity 83
   letter 561
   disposition 820
characteristic
   intrinsic 5
   distinctive 15
   special 79
   mark 550
characterize *name* 564
   describe 594
charge, *n. mandate* **630**
   advice 695
   precept 697
   price 812
   accusation 938
charge, *v. fill* 52
   enjoin 695
   attack 716
charger *horse* 271
chariot 272
charitable 784, 906
charity *giving* 784
   beneficence 906
   pity 914
charlatan *impostor* 548
   poser 855
charm, *n. talisman* 747
   beauty 845
   love 897
   spell 993
charm, *v. draw* 288
   please 377, 829
   conjure 992
charming [*see* charm]
chart 183, 527
charter *permit* 760
   privilege 924
charwoman 690, 746
chary *cautious* 864
chase *drive away* 289
   pursue 622
chasm 198, 208, 350
chaste *shapely* 242
   simple 849
   pure 960
chasten *moderate* 174
   punish 972
chasteness [*see* chaste]
chastise 972
chastity 960
chat 588
chattels 780
chatter 412, 584
chatterbox 584
chauffeur 268
cheap 815
cheapen *haggle* 794, 819
CHEAPNESS 815
cheat, *n. deceiver* 548
cheat, *v. deceive* 545
check, *n. plaid* 440

actors **599**
partnership **797**
troop **726**
comparative **464**
comparatively **32**
compare **464**
COMPARISON 9, **464**
compartment 182, 191
compass, *n. degree* 26
  space 180
  circuit 311
  measure 466
compass, *v. surround* 227
  circumscribe 233
  guide 693
  achieve 729
compassion 914
compassionate 914
compatible 23
compatriot 890
compeer *equal* 27
compel 744
compendious 596
COMPENDIUM 596
compensate
  make up for 30
  requite 973
COMPENSATION 30,
952
compensatory 30, **790**
complete 708, **720**
competence *power* 157
  sufficiency 639
  skill 698
  wealth 803
competition
  opposition **708**
  contention **720**
competitor
  opponent 710
  candidate 767
compile 54, 72, **596**
complacent *vain* 880
  courteous 894
complain 839
complainant 938
complaint *illness* 655
  murmur 839
complement
  counterpart 14
  adjunct 39
complete, *fill up* 52
  accomplish 729
  conclude 769
COMPLETENESS 50, 52
  unity 87
COMPLETION 67, 87,
729
complex 59
complexion *color* 428
  appearance 448
complexity 59
compliance
  submission 725
  consent 762
  observance 772

compliant [*see* compli-
  ance]
complicate *derange* 61
complicity 709
compliment 896, 931
complimentary 931
comply [*see* compliance]
COMPONENT 56
compose, *make up* 54, 56
  produce 161
  music 415, 416
  write 590
  printing 591
  assuage 826
composed
  self-possessed **826**
composer *music* 413
composite 41
COMPOSITION 54
  [*see* compose]
  combination 48
  embodiment 76
  style 569
  writing 590
  compromise 774
  atonement 952
compositor 591
composure 174, **826**
compound *mix* 41
  combination 48
  compromise 774
comprehend *include* 76
  know 490
  understand 518
comprehensibility 518
comprehension
  [*see* comprehend]
comprehensive
  wholesale 50
  inclusive 56, 76
  general 78
compress *contract* 195
  condense 321
compressed 572
compression 195
comprise 76
compromise 774
  mean 29
  compensation 30
  mid-course 628
  compound 774
COMPULSION 744
compulsory 601
compunction 950
computable 85
compute 37, 85
computation 85
comrade 890
comradeship 892
con *learn* 505, 539
concave 252
CONCAVITY 252
conceal *hide* 528
CONCEALMENT 528
concede *admit* 529
  consent 762

give 784
conceit *overestimation* 482
  imagination 515
  wit 842
  affectation 855
  vanity 880
conceited 481, 855, 880
conceivable 470
conceive *note* 450
  believe 484
  understand 490
  imagine 515
concentrate *assemble* 72
  centralize 222
  converge 290
concentric 222
conception [*see* conceive]
  intellect 450
  idea 453, 515
concern *relation* 9
  event 151
  care 459
  business 625
  importance 642
  firm 797
concerning 9
concert *agreement* 23
  music 415
concession *permission* 760
  giving 784
  discount 813
conciliate *pacify* 723
  satisfy 831
  forgive 918
conciliatory [*see* concili-
  ate]
  concordant 714
  courteous 894
concise 572
  taciturn 585
CONCISENESS 201, 572
conclude *infer* 480
  complete 769
conclusion [*see* conclude]
  sequel 65
  eventuality 151
  effect 154
  judgment 480
conclusive [*see* conclude]
  final 67, 729
  evidential 467
  certain 474
  proved 478
concoct 544, 626
CONCORD *agreement* 23
  music 413
  harmony 714
concordance
  dictionary 593
concordant 714
concourse *assemblage* 72
  convergence 290
concrete *hard* 321
  definite 494
concur *coexist* 120
  agree 178

cottager 188

couch, *n. bed* 215

couch, *v. lurk* 528

cough 349

COUNCIL *senate* **696**

councilor 696

counsel *advice* 695
 lawyer 968

count, *n. item* 79
 lord 875

count, *v.*
 compute 37, 85
 estimate 480

countenance, *n. face* 234
 appearance 448
 favor 707

countenance, *v. approve*
 931

counter, *n. token* 550

counter, *adj. contrary* 14
 reverse 237

counteract 179, 706

COUNTERACTION 179

counterbalance 30, 179

countercharge 462

counterclaim 30

COUNTEREVIDENCE
 468

counterfeit *imitate* 19
 copy 21
 sham 545
 swindle 791

counterfeiter 792

countermand 756

countermarch 283

countermotion 283

counterpane 223

counterpart *identity* 13
 complement 14
 match 17
 copy 21

counterpoise
 compensate 30

countersign *n.*
 evidence 467
 mark 550

countersign, *v.* 488

countess 875

countless 105

countrified 189

country *region* 181
 abode 189
 land 342
 state 737

countryman 876

county 181

coupé 272

couple, *n. two* 89

couple, *v. unite* 43
 combine 48

COURAGE 861

courageous 861

courier *traveler* 268
 messenger 534

COURSE *order* 58
 continuity 69

time 106, **109**
 layer 204

locomotion 267

direction 278

lesson 537

pursue 622

courser *horse* 271

court, *n. house* 189
 hall 191
 retinue 746

court, *v. invite* 615
 tribunal 966
 woo 902
 flatter 933

courteous 894

COURTESY
 politeness 894

courtier 935

courtly 852

court-martial 966

courtship 902

courtyard 182

cousin 11

cove *hollow* 252
 bay 343

covenant *compact* 769
 condition 770
 security 771

cover, *n. dress* 225
 lid 223

cover, *v. include* 76
 superpose 223
 conceal 528
 keep safe 664

covered 223

COVERING 220, **223**

coverlet 223

covert *abode* 189
 invisible 447
 latent 526
 refuge 666

coverture 903

covet *desire* 865
 envy 921

covetous *miserly* 921

covey 102

cow, *n. animal* 366

cow, *v. intimidate* 860

coward 862

COWARDICE **862**

cowardly 862

cowboy 370

cower *stoop* 308
 fear 860
 quail 862
 fawn 886

cowherd 370

cowhide, *n. whip* 975

cowhide, *v. lash* 972

coworker 690

cowpuncher 370

coxcomb 854, 880

coxcombry *affectation* 855

coxswain 269

coy 881

cozy 377, 892

crabbed *sour* 397
 unintelligible 519
 uncivil 895

crack, *n. fissure* 44, 198
 furrow 259

crack, *v. split* 44
 crush 328
 sound 406

crack, *adj. excellent* 648

crack-brained *insane* 503

cracked *unmusical* 410
 mad 503

crackle 406

cracksman 792

cradle *beginning* 66
 infancy 127
 origin 153
 bed 215
 aid 707

craft *shipping* 273
 calling 625
 cunning 702

craftsman 690

craftsmanship 680

crag *cliff* 212, 253, 342

craggy *rough* 256

crake 884

cram *stuff* 194
 choke 261
 teach 537
 learn 539
 gorge 957

cramp, *n. spasm* 315

cramp, *v. paralyze* 158
 weaken 160
 hinder 706

crane *lever* 307

cranium 450

crank *fanatic* 504
 instrument 633

cranny 198

crash, *n. collision* 276
 sound 406

crash, *v. destroy* 162
 crack 328

crass *unintelligent* 493
 bad taste 851

cravat 225

crave *ask* 765
 desire 865

craven *cowardly* 862

craving 865

craw 191

crawl *elapse* 109
 creep 275
 cower 886

crazy *weak* 160
 mad 503

creak 410

cream, *n.* 356
 important part 642
 best 648

cream, *adj. yellow* 436

creamy 430

crease 258

create *cause* 153

D

resolved 604
deciduous *transitory* 111
  falling 306
decimal 99
decimate *kill* 361
decipher 522, 525
decision *judgment* 480
  resolution 604
  intention 620
decisive *certain* 474
  convincing 478
deck, *n. floor* 211
deck, *v. clothe* 225
declaim 582
declamatory 582
declaration *evidence* 467
  affirmation 535
  -of faith
  belief 484
  theology 983
  -of war 722
declare 535
declension [see decline]
  decrease 36
declination [see decline]
decline, *n. old age* 124
  descent 306
  deterioration 659
decline, *v. decrease* 36
  grow old 128
  reject 610
  refuse 764
declivity *slope* 217
  descent 306
decode 525
decoloration 429
decompose 49
DECOMPOSITION 49
decoration *ornament* 847
  title 877
decorous [see decorum]
  proper 924
  respectful 928
decorum *fashion* 852
  dignity 878
  purity 960
decoy, *n.* 548
decoy, *v. deceive* 545
  entice 615
DECREASE in *degree* 36
  in *size* 195
decree *judgment* 480
  order 741
  law 963
DECREMENT
  decrease 36
  thing deducted **40a**
decrepit *old* 128
  impotent 158
  weak 160
decrepitude 128, 158
decrescendo 36
decry *underrate* 483
  censure **932**
  detract 934
dedicate 677, 873

deduce *infer* 480
deducible 478
deduct *retrench* 38
deduction
  decrement 38, 40a
  reasoning 476
  inference 480
deed *record* 551
  act 680
  security 771
  exploit 861
deem 484
deep *great* 31
  profound 208
  sonorous 404
  cunning 702
deepen *increase* 35
  excavate 208
deeply [see deep]
deer 366
deface *destroy form* **241**
  injure 659
  render ugly 846
defalcation 808
defamation 934
defamatory 932, 934
defame *shame* 874
  censure 932
  detract 934
defamer 936
default *shortcoming* 304
  debt 806
  nonpayment 808
defaulter *nonpayer* 808
defeat *confute* 479
  succeed 731
  failure 732
defect *decrement* 40a
  incompleteness 53
  shortcoming 304
  imperfection 651
  failing 945
defection
  disobedience 742
defective *incomplete* 53
  imperfect 651
defend 462
defendant 938
defender 717, 914
DEFENSE *answer* 462
  resistance 717
  vindication 937
defenseless *impotent* 158
  exposed 665
defensible *safe* 664
  excusable 937
defensive 717
defer *put off* 133
  neglect 460
  -to assent 488
  submit 725
  respect 928
deference *submission* 725
  obedience 743
  courtesy 894
  respect 928

deferment 460
DEFIANCE 715
defiant 715, 742
deficiency
  [see deficient]
deficient *unequal* 28
  inferior 34
  incomplete 53
  remiss 304
  imperfect 651
deficit *incompleteness* 53
  debt 806
defile, *n. gorge* 198
defile, *v. march* 266
  spoil 659
define *limit* 233
  explain 522
definite *special* 79
  limited **233**
  certain 474
  exact 494
  manifest 525
definition
  interpretation 521
deflate 195
deflect *curve* 245
  deviate 279
deform 243, 846
deformed 243
deformity *distortion* 243
  ugliness 846
defraud *cheat* 545
  swindle 791
defray 807
deft *clever* 698
defunct 360
defy *confront* 234, 861
  set at defiance **715**
degeneracy 659
degenerate
  deteriorate 659
  vice 945
degradation *shame* 874
  dishonor 940
degrade 874
DEGREE 26
deification 981
deify *honor* 873
  idolatry 991
deign *condescend* 879
deities 979
DEITY 976
DEJECTION
  melancholy 837
delay 133, 460
delectable *savory* 394
  agreeable 829
delegate, *n.* 524, 755, **758**
delegate, *v. depute* 759
delegation 755
deliberate, *adj. slow* 275
deliberate, *v.* 451
deliberately 133, 275
deliberation 451
delicacy *weakness* 160
  dainty 298, **394**

disclaim *deny* 536
  repudiate 756
disclaimer 536
disclamation
  [see disclaim]
disclose 529
DISCLOSURE 529
  discovery 480a
discoloration 429
discolored 848
discomfiture 732
discomfort *physical* 378
  mental 828
discommode *hinder* 706
discompose *derange* 61
  put out 458
  pain 830
disconcert *derange* 61
  distract 458
  dishearten 832
  confuse 874
disconnect 44
disconnected
  unrelated 10
  interrupted 70
disconnection
  irrelation 19
  disjunction 44
  discontinuity 70
disconsolate 837
DISCONTENT 832
discontinuance 142
DISCONTINUITY 70
discontinuous 44, 70
DISCORD
  disagreement 24
  of sound 414
  dissension 713
discordance 414, 713
DISCOUNT *decrease* 36
  decrement 40a
  money 813
discountenance 706
discourage *dissuade* 616
  dishearten 837
  frighten 860
discourse, *n. speech* 582
  talk 588
discourse, *v. speak* 582
  talk 588
discourteous 895
DISCOURTESY 895
discover *perceive* 441
  find 480a
  disclose 529
DISCOVERY 480a
discredit *disbelieve* 485
  dishonor 874
discreditable 874
discreet 459, 864
discrepancy 20a, 24
discretion *will* 600
  choice 609
  caution 864
discriminate 15, 465, 868

DISCRIMINATION
  difference 15
  nice perception 465
  fastidiousness 868
discriminative 868
discursive *wandering* 279
discuss *inquire* 461
  reason 476
discussion 476
disdain, *n. pride* 878
  contempt 930
disdain, *v. spurn* 866
disdainful *proud* 878
  disrespectful 929
DISEASE 655
diseased 655
disembark 342
disembody
  spiritualize 317
disembogue
  flow out 348
disencumber 705
disengage *detach* 44
  liberate 750
disengaged *to let* 763
disentangle *separate* 44
  arrange 60
  facilitate 705
  liberate 750
disestablish *displace* 185
  abrogate 756
disfavor *oppose* 708
  disrespect 929
disfigure *deface* 241
  deform 846
  blemish 848
disfranchise 925
disgorge *emit* 297
  restore 790
disgrace *shame* 879
  dishonor 940
disgraceful 945
disgruntle 509
disgruntled 509
disguise, *n. mask* 530
  deception 545
disguise, *v. conceal* 528
disgust, *n.*
  weariness 841
  dislike 867
disgust, *v. nauseate* 395
  offend 830
disgusting 867
dish *plate* 191
dishabille *undress* 225
dishearten *dissuade* 616
  disappoint 832
  deject 837
dishevel *disorder* 61
dishonest *false* 544
  base 940
dishonor *protest* 808
  disrepute 874
  disrespect 929
  baseness 940
disillusion 509

disinclination 867
disincline *dissuade* 616
  dislike 867
disinclined 603, 867
disinfect *purify* 652
disinfectant 388, 662
disinherit 782, 783
disintegrate *separate* 44
  decompose 49
disintegration 49
disinter *exhume* 363
  discover 480a
disinterment 363
disinterested 942
DISINTERESTEDNESS
  542
disjoin 44
DISJUNCTION 10, 44
disjunctive 44
disk 247
DISLIKE 867
dislocate *separate* 44
  put out of joint 61
dislodge *displace* 185
  eject 297
disloyal 940
dismal *depressing* 830
  dejected 837
dismantle *destroy* 162
  divest 226
  render useless 645
dismast 645
dismay 860
dismember 44
dismiss *discharge* 297
  liberate 750
  abrogate 756
dismissal 746
dismount 306
DISOBEDIENCE 742
disobey 742
DISORDER, *n.*
  confusion 59
  turbulence 173
  disease 655
disorder, *v. derange* 61
disorderly 59, 945
disorganize *derange* 61
disown 536
disparage
  underrate 483, 929
  dispraise 932
  detract 934
disparagement 908, 934
disparate 15, 18
disparity *difference* 15
  dissimilarity 18
  disagreeing 24
  inequality 28
dispassionate 826
dispatch, *n. message* 527
  news 532
  epistle 592
  expedition 682
  haste 684
  command 741

E

ENMITY 889
ennoble 873
ennui 841
enormity *greatness* 31
  crime 947
enormous *great* 31
  big 192
enough *much* 31
  sufficient 639
enrage 830, 900
enrapture *beatify* 829
  love 897
enraptured 827
enravish 829
enrich *improve* 658
  imburse 803
enrobe 225
enroll *list* 86
  enlist 722
ensconce *conceal* 528
ensconced *located* 184
enshrine *circumscribe* 229
  consecrate 873
ensign *standard* 550
  officer 726
enslave 749
ensnare 545
ensue *follow* 63, 117
  happen 151
ensure 474
entail *cause* 153
  tie up property 781
entangle *interlink* 43
  derange 59, 61
  ravel 219
  embroil 713
entanglement
  [*see* entangle]
entente cordiale
  alliance 714
  friendship 888
enter *list* 86
  go in 294
 –**in** *converge* 290
 –**into** *compose* 56
 –**upon** 66
enterprise *pursuit* 622
  undertaking 676
enterprising *energetic* 171
  active 682
  courageous 861
entertain
  bear in mind 457
  amuse 840
  welcome 892
entertainment 840, 892
  pleasure 377
enthrall 749
enthrone 873
enthronement 755
enthusiasm *vigor* 574
  eagerness 682
  feeling 821
  hove 858
enthusiast 682, 840
enthusiastic *excitable* 825

sanguine 858
entice 615
enticement 615
entire *whole* 50
  complete 52
entirely 31, 50
entirety 50, 52
entitle *name* 564
  give a right 924
entity 1
entomb *inter* 363
  imprison 751
entombment 363
entrain 293
entrammel 706
entrance, *n. beginning* 66
  ingress 294, 627
entrance, *v. enrapture* 829
entrap *deceive* 545
entreat 765
entrust [*see* intrust]
entry *beginning* 66
  ingress 294
entwine 43, 219
enumerate 85
enunciate *affirm* 535
  voice 580
envelop 225
envelope 223, 232
envenom *deprave* 650
  alienate 898
envenomed *malevolent* 907
envious 920
environ 220, **227**
ENVIRONMENT 183,
  227
environs 197, 227
envoy 534
ENVY 921
enwrap 225
eon 106, 110
epaulet *badge* 550
  insignia 747
ephemera 193
ephemeral 111
epic *narrative* 594
  poetry 597
epicure *gourmet* **868**
  sybarite 954a
  glutton 957
epicurean 954
epidemic 657
epidermis 223
epigram *wit* 842
epilogue 67
episcopacy 995
episcopal 995
episode 39
episodic 10, 228
epistle 592
epitaph 363, 550
epithet 564
epitome *compendium* 596
epizoötic 657
epoch *time* 106
  period 108

equable *uniform* 16
  equitable 922
equal *identical* 13
  even 27
  compensating 30
EQUALITY 27
equalize 27
equanimity 826
equation 30, 37
equator 68
equatorial 68
equerry 746
equestrian 268
equidistance 68
equidistant 68
equilibrium 27
equinox 125, 126
equip *dress* 225
  prepare 673
equipage *vehicle* 272
equipment *clothes* 225
  gear 633
equipoise 27
equitable *just* 922
  honorable 939
equity *right* 922
  honor 939
  law 963
equivalent *correlated* 12
  identical 13
  equal 27
  compensation 30
  substitute 147
  translation 522
EQUIVOCALNESS 475,
  520
equivocate 477
  palter 520
equivocation *quibble* 477,
  520
era *time* **106**
  period 108
eradicate *destroy* 162
  eject 297
  extract 301
erase *destroy* 162
  obliterate 552
eraser 331
erasure [*see* erase]
ere 116
erect, *adj.* 246
erect, *v. build* 161
  render vertical 212
  raise 307
erection *building* 161
  elevation 307
ermine
  badge of authority **747**
err 495
errand *message* 532
erratic *irregular* 139
  changeable 149
  capricious 608
erratum 495
erroneous 495
ERROR *fallacy* **495**

-itself 683
EXPENDITURE 809
expense *price* 812
expenses 809
expensive 809
experience, *n.* 490
experience, *v.*
 undergo 151, 821
experienced 698
EXPERIMENT 463
experimental 463
EXPERT, *n. adept* 700
expert, *adj.* 698
expiate 952, 976
expiration [*see* expire]
expire *end* 67
 run its course 109
 breathe 349
 die 360
expired *past* 122
explain *answer* 462
 interpret 522
 comment 595
explanation 155
 [*see* explain]
explanatory 522
expletive
 exclamation 580
 redundance 573
 oath 908
explicit 516, 518
explicitness 518, 570
explode *burst* 173
 sound 406
 flare up 825
exploded *past* 122
 antiquated 124
 erroneous 495
 [*see* explosion]
exploit, *n. action* 680
 courage 861
exploit, *v. utilize* 677
 misuse 679
exploration 461
explore *investigate* 461
explorer 268
explosion [*see* explode]
 violence 173
 sound 406
 anger 900
explosive 173, 727
exponent *interpreter* 524
 informant 527
export 295
expose *denude* 226
 disclose 529
 censure 932
exposé *confutation* 479
 disclosure 529
exposition [*see* expose]
 explanation 522
 exhibition 525, 882
expositor 524
expository 522, 527

expostulate *advise* 695
 deprecate 766
 reprehend 932
exposure 529
 [*see* expose]
expound 537
express, *n. carrier* 272
express, *adj. rapid* 274
 intentional 620
express, *v.*
 squeeze out 301
 mean 516
 declare 525
 phrase 566
expression [*see* express]
 aspect 448
 manifestation 525
 phrase 566
expressive 516, 822
expressman 271
expulsion [*see* expel]
expunge 162, 552
exquisite
 savory 394
 excellent 648
 pleasurable 829
 beautiful 845
extant 1
extemporaneous 612
 [*see* extempore]
extempore *instant* 113
 occasional 134
 offhand 612
extemporize 612, **674**
extemporizer 612
extend *expand* 194
 prolong 200
extended *spacious* 180
 long 200
 broad 202
extension [*see* extend]
 increase 35
 space 180
 expansion 194
extensive *great* 31
 vide 180
extent *degree* 26
 space 180
 length 200
extenuate *decrease* 36
 excuse 937
extenuating 937
 -circumstances
 excuse 937
exterior 220
EXTERIORITY 220
exterminate 162
extermination 162, 301
external 6, 220
externalize 220
extinct *inexistent* 2
 past 122
 old 124
extinction 162, 552

extinguish *blow out* 385
 darken 421
extirpate 2, 301
extol 482, 931
extort *extract* 301
 despoil 789, 814
extortion *dearness* 814
 rapacity 819
extortionate *dear* 814
 rapacious 819
 grasping 865
extortionist 789, 819
extra *additional* 37, 641
extract, *n. record* 551
 quotation 596
extract, *v.* 301
EXTRACTION 301
 paternity 166
extractor 301
extradition 270, 297
extraneous *extrinsic* 6
 not related 10
 foreign 57
 exterior 220
EXTRANEOUSNESS 57
extraordinary *great* 31
 exceptional 83
extravagance
 [*see* extravagant]
extravagant
 inordinate 31
 fanciful 515
 exaggerated 549
 excessive 641, 814
 prodigal 818
 ridiculous 853
extravaganza
 burlesque 555
 drama 599
extreme *inordinate* 31
 end 67
 -unction 998
extremist 710
extremity *end* 67
 adversity 735
extricate
 take out 301
 deliver 672
 liberate 750
extrinsic 6
exuberant 641
exudation 295
exude 295
exult *rejoice* 838
 boast 884
exultant 838
eye, *n.* 441
eye, *v. see* 441
eyeglass 445
eyelashes 256
eyesight 441
eyesore 846
eyewitness 444, 467
eyrie 189

F

fantastic *odd* 83
  absurd 497, 853
  imaginative 515
fantasy 515
far 196
  -and near 180
  -and wide 180, 196
farce *absurdity* 497, 853
  drama 599
  wit 842
farcical 497, 853
fare, *n. food* 298
  price 812
fare, *v. do* 7
farewell 293
far-famed 31, 873
farfetched 10
far-flung 180
far-gone *much* 31
  insane 503
  spoiled 654
farinaceous 330
farm, *n. land* 780
farm, *v. till* 371
  rent 788
farmer 371
farmhouse 189
farsighted 441, 510
farther 196
  [*see* further]
farthing *coin* 800
fascinate *please* 829
  astonish 870
  love 897
  conjure 992
fascination [*see* fascinate]
  infatuation 825
  charm 829
  desire 870
FASHION, *n. state* 7
  custom 613
  mode 852
fashion, *v. form* 240
  create 976
fashionable 852
fast, *adj. joined* 43
  steadfast 150
  rapid 274
  intemperate 954
fast, *v.* 956
fasten *join* 43
  restrain 751
fastening 45
fastidious 868
FASTIDIOUSNESS 868
FASTING *penance* 952
  abstinence 956
fastness *defense* 717
fat, *n.* 356
fat, *adj. corpulent* 192
  bloated 194
  unctuous 355
fatal 361
fatalism 601
fatality 601
fate, *future* 152

doom 360, 611
  necessity 601
fateful 601
Fates 601
father 166
  priest 996
Father, God the - 976
fatherland 189, **342**
fatherly 906
Fathers, the - 983
fathom, *n.* 466
fathom, *v. investigate* 461
  solve 462
  discover 480a
fathomless 208
FATIGUE 688
fatness [*see* fat]
fatten *expand* 194
  improve 658
  prosper 734
  -upon *feed* 298
fatuity 499
faucet 263, 295
fault *break* 70
  defect 304
  error 495
  imperfection 651
  failure 732
  at - *uncertain* 475
faultfinder 832
faultless *perfect* 650
  innocent 946
faulty *imperfect* 651
fauna 366
favor, *n. badge* 550
  indulgence 740
  gift 784
  partiality 923
favor, *v. resemble* 17
  aid 707
  permit 760
favorable *lucky* 134
  good 648
  aiding 707
  -to 709
FAVORITE 897, 899
favoritism *friendship* 888
  wrong 923
fawn, *n. animal* 366
fawn, *adj. brown* 433
fawn, *v. cringe* 886
  flatter 933
fawning *servile* 746
fay 979
fealty *obedience* 743
  respect 928
FEAR 860
fearful *painful* 830
  timid 862
fearless 858, 861
feasible *possible* 470
feast *period* 138
  banquet 298, **957**
  revel 840
feat 680, 861
feather *class* 75

tuft 256
  ornament 847
  -in one's cap
   honor 873
feathery 324
feature *character* 5
  form 240
  appearance 448
  lineament 234, 550
federal 712
federate 48
federation 709, 712
fee *pay* 809
  reward 973
feeble *weak* 160, **575**
  illogical 477
feeble-minded
  imbecile 499
  irresolute 605
FEEBLENESS *style* 575
feed *eat* 298
  fodder 370
  supply 637
feel *sense* 375
  touch 379
  respond 821
  -for 914
feeler *antenna* 379
  experiment 463
FEELING 821
feign 544, 546
feint 545
felicitate 896
felicitous *agreeing* 23
  happy 578
  pleasant 829
felicity 578, 827
feline, *n. cat* 366
feline, *adj. cunning* 702
fell, *v. destroy* 162
  lay flat 213
  lay low 308
fell, *adj.*
  dire 860
  malevolent 907
fellow *counterpart* 17
  equal 27
  companion 88
  man 373
  scholar 492
fellow countryman 890
fellow creature 372
fellow feeling
  friendship 888
  love 897
  benevolence 906
  pity 914
fellowship *friendship* 888
fellow student 541
felon 949, 975
felonious 945
felony 947
female 374
feminine 374
femininity 374
fen 345

fence, *n enclosure* **232**,
   752
   thief 792
   on the - 607
fence, *v, evade* 544
   fight 720
fender 717
ferment, *n. disorder* 59
   agitation 171, **315**
   lightness 320
   excitement 825
ferment, *v. effervesce* 353
   sour 397
fermentation
   [*see* ferment]
fern 367
ferocity *violence* 173
   brutality 907
ferret
   -out *be curious* 455
ferry 270
ferryman 269
fertile 168
fertilization 161, 168
fertilize 168
ferule 975
fervent *hot* 382
   desirous 865
fervid *hot* 382
   heartfelt 821
fervor *passion* 820
   animation 821
festal 687, 840
fester *corrupt* 653
festival 138, 883
festivity 840, 883
festoon 245
fetch *bring* 270
   sell for 812
fete 840, 882
fetid 401
fetish 991, 993
FETOR 401, 663
fetter *restrain* 43, **751**
   shackle 752
feud *discord* 713
feudal 749
feudatory 749
fever *heat* 382
   disease 655
   excitement 825
feverish *hot* 382
   hurry 684
   excited 824
few 103, 137
FEWNESS 32, 103
fez 225
fiancée 897
fiasco 732
fiat 741
fib *falsehood* 546
fiber *filament* 205
fibrous 205
fickle *changeable* 149
   irresolute 605
fickleness 605

fiction *untruth* 546
   work of - 594
fictitious 515, 546
fiddle 417
fiddler 416
fidelity *identity* **13**
   truth 494
   veracity 543
   obedience 743
   honor 939
fidget 682, 825
field *scope* 180
   region 181
   plain 344
   agriculture 371
   business 625
field day 882
field glass 445
field marshal 745
fiend *ruffian* 913
   demon 980
fiendish 907, 945, 980
fierce *violent* 173
   daring 861
   angry 900
fiery *violent* 173
   hot 382
   excitable 825
   angry 900
fifer 416
fight *contention* 720
   warfare 722
   -shy *avoid* 623
   turn tail 862
fighter 726
figment 515
figurative 521
FIGURE, *n. number* 84
   form 240
   metaphor 521
   price 812
   cut a - *repute* 873
   - of speech 521
figure, *v. represent* 554
figurehead *sign* 550
   representation 554
FILAMENT 205
filch 791
file, *v. pare* 38
   arrange 60
   smooth 255
   pulveri·e 330
   record 551
   -off *march* 266
file, *n. row* 69
   list 86
   on - 60
filial 167
filibuster, *n.*
   obstructionist 710
   freebooter 792
filibuster, *v. delay* 133
   impede 706
   pillage 791
filibusterer 706, 710
filigree 219

fill *complete* 52
   occupy 186
   load 190
   stuff 224
   -up *complete* 52
   close 261
fillet *band* 45
filament 205
   ornament 847
filling *stuffing* 224
fillip *impulse* 276
   stimulus 615
film *layer* 204
   opacity 426
filmy *scaly* 204
filter *percolate* 295
   clean 652
filth 653
filthy 653
final 67, 729
finale *end* 67, 729
finality 67, 729
finally *eventually* 151
   on the whole 476
finance 800
financier 639
find *experience* 151
   adjudge 480
   discover 480a
   -out 480a
finding *judgment* 480
fine, *adj. rare* 322
   not raining 340
   delicate 329
   exact 494
   good 648
   beautiful 845
   adorned 847
   proud 878
   -arts 556
   -gentleman *fop* 854
   -lady 854
   -writing 482, 577
   in end 67
   after all 476
fine, *v. mulct* 974
fineness [*see* fine)]
finery 847
finesse *tact* 698
   artifice 702
finger *touch* 379
finical 855, 868
finicking 855, 868
finis 67
finish, *n. end* 67
   symmetry 242
finish, *v. complete* 729
finished *symmetrical* 242
   perfect 650
   skilled 698
finite 32
fire, *n. energy* 171
   heat 382
   fuel 388
fire, *v. make hot* **384**
   shoot 716

dismiss 756
excite 824
-at 716
-up *rage* 825
firearms 727
firebrand *fuel* 388
instigator 615
fire bug 384, 949
fire-eater 863, 887
fire extinguisher 385
fireman *stoker* 268
extinguisher 385
fireplace 386
fireproof 385
firm, *n. partnership* 712
797
firm, *adj. fast* 43
steadfast 150
hard 323
resolute 604
firmness [see firm]
first 66
firstborn 124, 128
first-class *best* 648
first fruits 154
first-rate 648
firth 343
fiscal 800
fish, *n.* 366
fish, *v.* 622
-for *pursue* 622
desire 865
-out *inquire* 461
-up *raise* 307
fisherman 361
fissure 44, 198
fit, *n. paroxysm* **173**
caprice 608
disease 655
fit, *adj. expedient* 646
right 922, 924
fit, *v. agree* 23
-out *dress* 225
prepare 673
fitful *irregular* 139
changeable 149
fitness 23, 926
fitting 924
FIVE 98
fix, *n. dilemma* 7, 704
fix, *v. join* 43
arrange 60
establish 150
place 184
fixed *intrinsic* 5
durable 110
permanent 141
stable 150
-idea 825
fixity 141, 265
fixture 150
fizz 353
fizzle 304, 353
flabby 324
flaccid 324, 326
flaccidity 326

flag, *n.* 550, 747
flag, *v. be weak* 160
falter 275
languish 683
fatigue 688
flagon 191
flagrant *manifest* 525
notorious 531
atrocious 945
flagstaff 206
flake 204
flamboyant 577
flame *fire* 382
light 420
passion 824, 825
flank *side* 236
flap, *v. hang* 214
move to and fro 315
flapper *girl* 129
flare *flash* 173
glare 420
-up *be excited* **824**
get angry 900
flash *flare* 173
fire 382
light 420
flashy *gaudy* 428
tawdry 851
flask 191
flat, *n. house* 191
note 413
flat, *adj. low* 207
horizontal 213
even 251
vapid 391
dull 843
flatiron 255
flatness 213, **251**
flatten 213, **251**
flatter *deceive* 545
please 829
adulate 933
-oneself 472, 858
FLATTERER 935
flattering 938
FLATTERY 933
flaunt *flourish* 873
display 882
flaunting 882
flavor 390
flavoring 393
flaw *break* 70, 198
error 495
imperfection 651
blemish 848
flaxen 436
flay 226
flea *insect* 366
fleck 440
fled *escaped* 671
flee 287
fleece, *n.* 223
fleece, *v. strip* 789
rob 791
surcharge 814
fleet, *n.* 273, 726

fleet, *adj. transient* 111
swift 274
fleeting 111
flesh 364
flesh color 434
fleshy *of fruit* 354
flexible *pliant* 324
flicker *waver* 314
flutter 315
glimmer 420, 422
flier *aviator* 269a
advertisement 531
flight *flying* 267
swiftness 274
departure 287, 293
escape 671
flighty *inattentive* 458
fanciful 515
flimsy *weak* 160
slight 322
soft 324
sophistical 477
trifling 643
flinch *fear* 860, 862
fling *propel* 284
flippant *pert* 885
discourteous 895
flirt 854, **902**
flirtation 902
fit *elapse* 109, 111
move 264
depart 293
run away 623
flivver 272
float *navigate* 267
buoy up 305
be light 320
flock *multitude* 72, 102
laity 997
floe *ice* 383
flog 684, 972
flood 337, 348
floodgate 350
flood tide 206, 337
floor, *n.* 211
floor, *v. overthrow* 731
flop 315
flora 367, 369
floral 367
floriculture 371
florid 428, 434
(style) 577
florist 371
flotation [see float]
flotilla 273, 726
flounce, *n. trimming* 231
flounce, *v. jump* 309
flounder *toss* 315
be uncertain 475
bungle 699
fail 732
flourish *brandish* 315
vegetate 365, 367
prosper 734
flaunt 872
boast 884

flourishing [*see* flourish]
flout 929
flow *course* 109
  motion 264
  stream 348
  -from *result* 154
  -into *river* 348
flower, *n. plant* 367
  ornament 847
flower, *v. produce* 161
  prosper 734
flowery *ornamental* 847
flowing [*see* flow] 348
fluctuate *change* 149
  oscillate 314, 605
fluctuation 314
flue 351
fluency 584
fluent *flowing* 348
  loquacious 584
fluffy 324
fluid 333
  -in *motion* 347
fluidity 333
fluke *chance* 156
flume 350
flunk 732
flunky *servant* 746
flunkyism 933
fluorescence 425
flurry, *n.*
  agitation 821, 824
  excitability 825
flurry, *v.* 458
flush, *n. heat* 382
  glow 420, 428
flush, *adj. even* 213
  flat 251
flush, *v. glow* 382
  redden 434
  wash 652
  blush 821
fluster, *n.* 821
fluster, *v.* 824, 825
flutter, *n. agitation* 315
flutter, *v. vary* 149
  excite 821
  tremble 860
flux *conversion* 144
  motion 264
  flow 348
fly, *n. insect* 366
fly, *v. vanish* 4
  elapse 109
  be transient 111
  aviate 267
  hasten 274
  recede 287
  depart 293
  soar 338
  shun 623
  -at 716
  -off 291
  -open 260
flying [*see* fly] 267
foal 271

foam, *n.* 353
foam, *v. boil* 315
  rage 824, 825
foamy 320
focal 222
FOCUS 74
  center 222
fodder *food* 298
foe 891
fog *mist* 353
  uncertainty 475
foggy *opaque* 426
fogy *fool* 501
  laughingstock 857
foible 945
foil, *n. weapon* 727
foil, *v. contrast* 14
  baffle 706
  defeat 731
FOLD, *n. inclosure* 232
  plait 258
  congregation 997
fold, *v.* 91, 258
foliage 367
folio 593
folk 372
folklore 124, 979
follow *be similar* 17
  -in *order* 63
  -in *time* 117
  pursue 235
  -in *motion* 281
  hold good 478
  understand 518
  pursue 622
  obey 743
  -up *continue* 143
follower [*see* follow]
  successor 65
  pursuer 281
  disciple 541
  servant 746
  lover 897
FOLLOWING 282
FOLLY 499
foment *stimulate* 173
  warm 384
  promote 707
  excite 824
fond 897
fondle 897, 902
fondness *desire* 865
FOOD *eatables* 298
FOOL, *n.* 501
fool, *v deceive* 545
  trifle 499
  ridicule 856
foolhardy 863
foolish 499, 699
foot *length* 200
  base 211
  on - *existing* 1
  preparing 673
  active 682
footfall *motion* 264
footing *circumstances* 8

influence 175
  situation 183
  support 215
foot-loose *liberated* 750
footman 746
footpad 792
footpath 627
footprint 550, 551
foot soldier 726
foot-sore 688
footstep 551
footstool 215
FOP 854
foppery 855, 882
foppish *affected* 855
for *because* 476
forage *food* 298
foray *attack* 716
  robbery 791
forbear *avoid* 623
  spare 678
  tolerate 826
  pity 914
  abstain 953
forbearance 826, 918
forbid 761
forbidding *ugly* 846
force, *n. assemblage* 72
  power 157
  strength 159
  energy 171
  violence 173
  significance 516
  troops 726
force, *v. urge* 615
  compulsion 744
forced *irrelative* 10
  unwilling 603
forceful 171, 574
forcible [*see* force]
forcibly 744
ford 302
fore 234
fore-and-aft 200
fore-and-after 273
forebears 166
forebode 511
forecast *foresight* 510
  prediction 507, 511
  plan 626
fond 897
forefathers 166
forefront 234
forego 624, 757
foregoing 116, 122
foregone *past* 122
foreground 234
forehead 234
foreign *alien* 10
  extraneous 57
foreigner 57
foreknow 510
foreknowledge 510
foreland 206
foreman 694
foremost *superior* 33
  beginning 66

futile 645
futility 499, 645
FUTURE 117, 121, 152

expected 507
-events 152
-state *destiny* 152

heaven 981
futurity 121

G

gab 584
gabble 584
gable *side* 236
gad 266
gag 403, 581
  muzzle 751
gage *measure* 466
gain *increase* 35
  prosper 618
  acquisition 775
  -time *protract* 110
  -upon *approach* 286
  pass 303
gainsay 536
gairish [*see* garish]
gait *walk* 264
galaxy *multitude* 102
  stars 318
gale 349
gall, *n. bitterness* 395
  insolence 885
gall, *v hurt* 378
  annoy 830
gallant *brave* 861
  courteous 894
gallantry 861, 902
gallery *room* 191
  passage 260
  spectators 444
galley *ship* 273
  cookroom 386
  printing 591
gallop 266, 274
gallows 961, 975
galore 102
galvanic *excitable* 825
galvanize 157
gamble 156, 621, 840
gambler 463, 621, 863
gambling *chance* 621
  rashness 863
gambol 309
game, *n. animal* 366
  amusement 840
game, *adj. resolute* 604
game, *v. gamble* 621
gamester 840
gaming 156
gang 72, 712
gangway 260
gaol [*see* jail]
gap 70, 198
gape, *yawn* 198, 260
  stare 455
garage 191, 272
garb 225
garble *misinterpret* 523
  falsify 544

garden 371
gardener 371
gargle 337
garish 851
garland *circle* 247
  fragrance 400
  ornament 847
garment 225
garner *store* 636
garnish 847
garret 210
garrison 717, 726
garrote 361
garrulity 584
garter *fastening* 45
gas *gaseity* 334
GASEITY 334
gaseous *unsubstantial* 4
  vaporous 334, 336
gash *cut* 44
  interval 198
gasify 334
gasoline 356
gasp 688
gastronomy 957
gate 66, 232, 260
gather *collect* 72
  fold 258
  conclude 480
gathering *assemblage* 72
gaudy 428, 851
gauge 466
gaunt 203
gauntlet *glove* 225
gawky *awkward* 699
  ugly 846
gay *bright* 428
  cheerful 836
  showy 882
gayety [*see* gay] 836
gaze 441
gazelle 366
gazette 531
gazetteer 86
gear *clothes* 225
  harness 633
gelatinous 352
gem *excellence* 648
  ornament 847
gendarme 726, 965
gender 75
genealogy 69
general, *adj. generic* 78
  habitual 613
general, *n.* 745
GENERALITY 78
generalize 78, 476
generally 16, 78

generalship 692, 722
generate 161, 168
generation
  consanguinity 11
  period 108
  production 161
generic 78
generosity *liberality* 816
  benevolence 906
  disinterestedness 942
generous [*see* generosity]
genesis *beginning* 66
  production 161
genial *cordial* 377
  warm 382
  willing 602
geniality 602
  [*see* genial]
genius *intellect* 450
  talent 498
  skill 698
  adept 700
  familiar spirit 979
genteel 852
gentile *heterodox* 984
gentility 852
gentle *moderate* 174
  lenient 740
  meek 826
  courteous 894
  -breeding 894
gentlefolk 875
gentleman 373, 939
gentleness [*see* gentle]
gentry 875
genuflexion 308
genuine *true* 494
  good 648
genus 75
geography 183
geometry 466
germ *origin* 66
  cause 153
  stem 193
  -cell 357
germane *relevant* 23
germinate 194, 365
gesticulate 550
gesture 550
get *acquire* 775
  -back *regain* 775
  -down *descend* 306
  -in 775
  -on *advance* 282
  prosper 734
gewgaw *trifle* 643
geyser 382, 384
ghastly *pale* 429

hideous 846
ghost 362, 980a
ghoul *demon* 980
giant 192, 206
gibber *stammer* 583
gibberish 563
gibbet 975
gibbous 249, 250
gibe *disrespect* 929
giddy *inattentive* 458
  wild 503
gift *power* 157
  transference 270
  talent 698
  thing given 784
gifted 698
gigantic *large* 192
  tall 206
giggle 838
gild 223, 436
gilt 436
gimcrack *weak* 160
  trifling 643
gimlet 262
gingerly 459
gipsy 268
gird *bind* 43
  strengthen 159
  surround 227
girder *beam* 215
girdle *bond* 45
  tie 225
  circumference 230
  circle 247
girl 129
  servant 746
girlhood 127
girlish 374
girt 229
girth 45, 230
gist *essence* 5
  meaning 516
give *yield* 324
  bestow 784
  -up *relinquish* 624
  surrender 782
  restore 790
giver 784
GIVING 784
glacial 383
glacier 383
glad *pleased* 827
  pleasing 829
gladden 836
glade 260
gladiator 726
glamour 615, 992
glance *touch* 379
  look 441
  -at *take notice of* 457
  allude to 527
  -off 279
glare *light* 420
  stare 441
glaring [*see* glare]
  great 31

gaudy 428
manifest 525
glass 255
  vessel 191
  lens 445
glassy 255
glaze 255
gleam *light* 420
  shine 446
glean *choose* 609
  acquire 775
glee 827, 836
glen 252
glib *voluble* 584
  facile 705
glide *lapse* 109
  move 264
  travel 266
  aviation 267
glimmer *light* 420
  flicker 422
  be visible 446
glimpse *sight* 441
glint 420, 441
glisten 420
glitter *shine* 420
  be visible 446
gloaming 126
gloat
  -over *delight* 827
  brag 884
globe *sphere* 249
  world 318
globe-trotter 268
globularity 249
gloom *darkness* 421
  dimness 422
  sadness 837
gloomy *dark* 421
  sad 837
glorification
  [*see* glorify]
glorify *honor* 873
  worship 976, 990
glorious 873
glory *light* 420
  honor 873
gloss *smoothness* 255
  sheen 420
  -over 477
glossary *list* 86
  dictionary 562
glossy [*see* gloss]
glove 225
glow *warm* 382
  shine 420
  appear 446
glower *glare* 443
  be sullen 901a
glowing [*see* glow]
  red 484
  exciting 824
glue *cement* 46
glum *discontented* 832
  sulky 901a
glut 957

glutinous 327, 352
glutton 954a, 957
GLUTTONY 957
gnarled *crooked* 243
  rough 250, 256
gnaw 298
go, *n. energy* 171, 682
go, *v. move* 264
  progress 282
  depart 293
  disappear 449
  -about *turn around* 311
  -by *elapse* 109
  outrun 303
  -off *explode* 173
  depart 293
  -on *continue* 143
  advance 282
  -through *meet with* 151
  endure 826
  -to *travel* 266
goad, *n.* 370
goad, *v. quicken* 684
go-ahead 171, 282, 682
goal *end* 67, 292
  haven 265
  object 620
gob *sailor* 269
gobble *cry* 412
  gormandize 957
go-between
  intermediary 228, 758
  instrument 631
goblet 191
goblin 980
GOD 976
god 979
goddess 979
Godhead 976
godly 944
godsend 618, 734
Godspeed *farewell* 293
goggle 441
gold, *adj. yellow* 436
gold, *n. money* 800
golden 436
  -mean 628
gondola 273
gondolier 269
gone [*see* go]
  extinct 2
  past 122
  absent 187
  dead 360
  -by 124
GOOD, *n.* 618
  for - *permanent* 141
good, *adj. palatable* 394
  beneficial 648
  virtuous 944
  pious 987
  -at 698
  -humor 836
  -looks 845
  -luck 734
  -man *worthy* 948

-nature 906
-offices *mediation* 724
-taste 578, 850
-turn *kindness* 906
-will *benevolence* 906
-woman 948
-word 931
make - *restore* 790
  substantiate 924
  vindicate 937
good-for-nothing 158, 949
good-looking 845
goodly *great* 31
  handsome 845
good-natured 906
GOODNESS 648
goods *effects* 780
  merchandise 798
goose *bird* 366
gore, *n. gusset* 43
  blood 361
gore, *v.* 260
gorge, *n. ravine* 198
gorge, *v. glut* 869
  gormandize 957
gorgeous *gay* 428
  beautiful 845
gorilla 366
gormandize 957
gorse 367
gory *murderous* 361
  red 434
gospel *doctrine* 484
  truth 494
Gospels 985
gossamer 205
gossamery 320
gossip *news* 532
  babbler 584
  conversation 588
gouge 262
gourmand *glutton* 957
gourmet 868, 954a
govern 693, 737
governess 540
government 737, 745, 965
governor *director* 694
  ruler 745
gown *dress* 225
grab *take* 789
grace *elegance* 845
  polish 850
  pity 914
  forgiveness 918
  worship 990
graceful *elegant* 578
  beautiful 845
  tasteful 850
graceless *inelegant* 579
  ugly 846
  impenitent 951
Graces 845
gracious *courteous* 894
  kind 906
gradation *degree* 26
  order 58

grade *degree* 26
  classify 60
  term 71
  obliquity 217
  ascent 305
  class 541
  crossing 219
gradual *degree* 26
  continuous 69
  slow 275
gradually 275
graduate, *n.* 492
graduate, *v. adjust* 23
  measure 26
  arrange 60
  initiate 537
graduation 541
graft, *v. insert* **300**
graft, *n. loot* 784
  improbity 940
grain *humor* 5
  tendency 176
  roughness 256
  texture 329
  powder 330
  against the- 704
GRAMMAR 567
grammatical 567
gramophone 418
grand *august* 31
  important 642
  handsome 845
  glorious 873
  ostentatious 882
  -juror 967
grandee 875
grandeur *greatness* 31
  repute 873
grandfather 130, 166
grandmother 166
grandness [see grand]
granny 30
grant *admit* 529
  permit 760
  consent 762
  confer 784
granular 330
graphic *intelligible* **518**
  vigorous 574
  descriptive 594
graphophone 418
grapnel 666
grapple 789
  -with
  -a *question* 461
  -*difficulties* 704
  oppose 708
  resist 719
grasp, *n. power* 737
grasp, *v. comprehend* 518
  retain 781
  -at 865
grasping *miserly* 819
  covetous 865
grass 367
  -widow 905

grassland 367
grassplot 371
grassy 367
grate, *n. fireplace* 386
grate, *v. rub* 330
  -on the ear
  harsh sound 410
grateful *enjoyable* 377
  agreeable 829
  thankful 916
gratification 377, 827
gratify *permit* 760
  please 829
grating *lattice* 219
  stridor 410
gratis 815
GRATITUDE 916
gratuitous
  inconsequent 477
  free 748, 815
gratuity *gift* 784
grave, *n.* 363
grave, *adj. somber* 428
  important 642
  distressing 830
  sad 837
graveclothes 363
gravedigger 363
gravestone 363
gravitate *descend* 306
  weigh 319
  -towards 176
GRAVITY *weight* 319
  importance 642
  seriousness 837
  [see grave]
GRAY *old* 128
  color 428, **432**
graybeard 130
graze *touch* 199, **379**
  browse 298
  rub 331
grease *lubricate* 332
  oil 355, 356
greasy 355
great *much* 31
  big 192
  glorious 873
greater 33
greatness 33
GREATNESS 31
greed *desire* 865
  gluttony 957
greedy 819, 865, 957
Greek - *deities* 970
GREEN, *n. lawn* 344, **371**
  color 435
green, *adj. new* 123
  young 127
  sour 397
  credulous 486
  novice 701
  immature 674
greenhorn *novice* 493
  bungler 701
greenness **435**

greensward **344**
greet *hail* 894
greeting 894
gregarious 892
grenade 727
grenadier 726
grey [*see* gray]
gridiron *crossing* 219
grief 828
grievance 830, 923
grieve *mourn* **828**
  pain 830
  complain 839
grievous *bad* 649
  painful 830
grievously *very* **31**
grill 384
  question 461
grim *resolute* 604
  painful 830
  doleful 837
  sullen 901a
grimace 243
grimy 652
grin *laugh* 838
grind *reduce* 195
  sharpen 253
  pulverize 330
  learn 539
  oppress 907
grip *bag* 191
  paroxysm 315
  indication 550
  power 737
  clutch 789
gripe [*see* grip] 378
grisly 846
grist 637
grit *strength* 159
  resolution 604, 861
  stamina 604a
gritty 323, 330
grizzled *gray* 432
groan *cry* 411
  lament 839
grocer 637
groceries 637
groin, 244
groom, *n.* 746
groom, *v.* 370
groomsman 903
groove *furrow* 259
  habit 613
grope *feel* 379
  experiment 463
gross *huge* 31
  whole 50
  ugly 846
  vulgar 851
grossness [*see* gross]
grotesque *odd* 83
  ridiculous 853
grotto 252
grouch 901a
ground *cause* 153
  situation 183

base 211
  support 215
  land 342
  evidence 467
  teach 537
  motive 615
stand one's-
  defend 717
  resist 719
grounded *stranded* 732
groundless
  unsubstantial 4
  illogical 477
  erroneous 495
grounds *estate* **344**
  dregs 653
groundwork *substance* 3
  cause 153
  basis 211
  support 215
  preparation 673
group, *n.* 72
group, *v.* 60
grove *group* 72
  wood 367
grovel *wallow* 207
  cringe 886
grow *increase* 31, 35
  become 144
  expand 194
  vegetation 365, 367
grower 164
growl *cry* 412
  complain 839
  resent 900
  threat 909
grown up 131
growth [*see* grow]
  increase 35
  conversion 144
  development 161
  -*in size* 194
  vegetation 365
grub
  food 298
grudge *begrudge*
  refuse 764
  stint 819
  envy 921
gruesome 846
gruff *harsh* 410
  discourteous 895
grum *morose* 901a
grumble *cry* 411
  complain 832, 839
grumpy 901a
Grundy, Mrs. 852
grunt *animal sound* 412
  complain 839
guarantee 768, **771**
guaranty 771
guard *stopper* 263
  defense 717
  soldier 726
guardian *safety* 664
  keeper 753

-*angel* 912
guardianship 664
guardsman 726
guerdon 973
guerrilla 722
guess 514
guesswork 514
guest 890
guffaw 838
guidable 278
guide, *n. model* 22
  itinerary 266, **527**
  courier 524
  teacher 540
  director 694
guide, *v. teach* 537
  indicate 550
  direct 693
  advise 695
guidebook 527
guidepost 550
guiding *star* 693
guild *society* 712
guile *deceit* 554, 545
  cunning 702
guileless *veracious* **543**
  artless 703
guillotine 975
GUILT 947
guiltless 946
guilty 947
guinea 800
guise *state* 7
  dress 225
  appearance 448
GULF 343
gull, *n. bird* 366
  dupe 547
gull, *v. deceive* 545
gullet 260
gullible 486
gully *gorge* 198
gulp *swallow* 296
gum *fasten* 46
gumminess 327
gummy *tenacious* 327
  resinous 356a
gumption 498
gun *weapon* 727
gunboat 726
gunman 913
gunner 284, **726**
gunnery 284
gunpowder 727
gunshot 197
gurgle *flow* 347
  faint sound 405
gush, *n. ardor* 821
gush, *v. flow out* 295
gushing *emotional* 821
gusset 43
gust *wind* 349
gusto
  physical pleasure 377
  emotion 821
gusty 349

H

-back to 457
harlequin 599
harm, n. 649, 659
harm, v injure 659
harmful 619
harmless impotent 158
 good 648
 salubrious 656
 innocent 946
harmonious 413, 714
harmonize agree 23
 arrange 60, 416
 conform 82
 concur 178
 blend 413
harmony agreement 23
 music 413
 concord 714
 peace 721
harness, n. 225
harness, v.
 -a horse 370
 control 751
harp upon repeat 104
harpy thief 792
 demon 980
harrowing 830
harry pain 830
 attack 716
 persecute 907
harsh acrid 171
 discordant 410, 713
 severe 739
 disagreeable 830
 malevolent 907
harshness [see harsh]
harum-scarum 458
harvest 154, 636
hash mixture 41
hasp fasten 43
hassock 215
HASTE velocity 274
 hurry 684
hasten 274, 684
hasty hurried 684
 impatient 825
 irritable 901
hat 225
hatch incubate 370
 fabricate 544
hatchet 253
hatchway 260
hate dislike 867
 hatred 898
hateful noxious 649
 painful 830
 odious 898
hatred 867, 898
haughty proud 878
 insolent 885
 contemptuous 930
haul drag 285
haunt, n. resort 74
 abode 189
haunt, v. alarm 860
 persecute 907

have possess 777
haven 292, 666
hawser 45
hazard chance 156, 621
 danger 665
haze mist 353, 427
 uncertainty 475
hazel 433
hazy 427
head, n. beginning 66
 class 75
 summit 210
 person 373
 intellect 450
 director 694
 master 745
head, v. precede 62
 lead 280
 direct 693
headdress 225
header 310
headforemost 863
headgear 225
heading 66
headland 206, 250
headlong 684, 863
headquarters 74, 189
 authority 737
headstrong violent 173
 obstinate 606
 rash 863
headway navigation 267
 progression 282
heal restore 660
 cure 662
healing art 662
HEALTH 654
healthful 654
HEALTHINESS 656
healthy 654
heap quantity 31
 collection 72
hear listen 418
hearer 418
HEARING 418
 trial 969
hearken 457
hearsay 467, 532
heart essence 5
 center 68, 222
 cause 153
 interior 221
 affections 820
 courage 861
heartache 828
heartbreaking 830
heartbroken 828
heartburning
 discontent 832
 regret 833
 enmity 889
hearten 858, 861
heartfelt profound 821
hearth home 189
 fireplace 386

heartily [see hearty]
heartless 823, 945
heartrending 830
heartsick dejected 837
 loath 867
hearty healthy 654
 cordial 821
 cheerful 836
 friendly 888
HEAT, n. warmth 382
 excitement 824, 825
heat, v. 384
heated hot 384
 quarrelsome 713
heath moor 344
heathen pagan 984
heather 367
heave raise 307
 -to 265
HEAVEN bliss 827
 paradise 981
heavenly celestial 318
 rapturous 829
 divine 976
 of heaven 981
 -bodies 318
heavens 318
heavy inert 172
 weighty 319
 stupid 499
heavy-laden unhappy 828
heckle harry 830
hectic red 434
hector domineer 885
hedge, n. 232
hedge, v. 30
heed attend 457
 care 459
 caution 864
heedful 864
heedless inattentive 458
 neglectful 460
 forgetful 506
 rash 863
heel, n. 215
heel, v. follow 63
 lean 217
 tag 235
heft weight 319
 exertion 686
HEIGHT degree 26
 altitude 206
 summit 210
heighten increase 35
 uplift 206
 elevate 307
 exaggerate 549
 aggravate 835
heinous 945
heir 167, 779
heliotrope purple 437
HELL gehenna 982
hellish 982
helm 633
helmet 225
helmsman 269

help *benefit* **618**
  utility 644
  aid 746
helper 711
helpful 746
helpless *incapable* 158
helpmate *wife* 903
helter-skelter 684
hem *edge* 231
  fold 258
  -in 751
hemisphere 181
hemorrhage 299
hen *bird* 366
hence *arising from* **155**
  departing 293
  therefore 476
henchman 746
henpecked 749
herald, *n.* 64, 527
herald, *v. precede* 280
  predict 511
  proclaim 531
heraldry 550
herb 367
herbaceous 367
herculean *strong* 159
  difficult 704
herd 72, 102
here 183, 186
hereabouts 183
hereafter 121, 152
hereditary *intrinsic* **5**
  derivative 154, **167**
heredity 167
heresy 984
heretic 984, 989
heretical 984
hereupon 106
heritage 121
hermit *recluse* 893
  ascetic 955
hermitage *house* 189
hero 861, 873
heroic 861
  magnanimous **942**
heroics 884
heroine 861
heroism 861, 942
hesitate *flounder* **475**
  demur 485
  be reluctant 603
  be irresolute 605
heterodox 984
HETERODOXY **984**
heterogeneity 10, 15, 16a
heterogeneous
  unrelated 10
  different 15
  mixed 41
  multiform 81
  exceptional **83**
hew *cut* 44
  -down 213, 308
hiatus *interval* 198
hibernate 683

hidden 528
hide, *n. skin* 223
hide, *v conceal* 528
hidebound
  strait-laced 751
  bigoted 988
hideous 846
hiding place *ambush* **530**
  refuge 666
hie *go* 264
  speed 274
hierarchy 995
high *lofty* 206
  gamy 298
  treble 410
  -life 875
  -note 410
  -principled 939
  -tide 106, 348
  -time 134
  -words *quarrel* **713**
  anger 900
  on - 206
highborn 875
high-brow 490
higher 33
highest 210
high-flown *absurd* **497**
  imaginative 515
  vain 880
highlands 206
high-minded 898, 942
high-priced 809
high-spirited *brave* **861**
  honorable 939
high-strung 825
highway 627
highwayman 792
hike 260
hilarity 836
hill *height* 206
hillock 206
hilly 206
hilt 633
hind *deer* 366
hind, *adj. back* 235
hinder *impede* **706**
Hinduism 976
HINDRANCE **706**
hinge *fastening* 43
  cause 153
  -upon *depend upon* 154
hint, *n. reminder* 505
hint, *v. inform* 527
hire, *n. reward* 973
hire, *v.* **788**
hireling 746
hirsute 256
hiss *sound* **409**
  disrespect 929
  disapprobation 932
historian 594
historic 594
history 122, 594
  natural - 357
histrionic 599

hit *chance* 156
  strike 276
  reach 292
hitch, *n. stoppage* 142
  difficulty 704, 706
hitch, *v. fasten* 43
  hang 214
  -a horse 370
hither 278
hitherto 122
hive 184
  apiary 370
hoar *aged* 128
hoard 636
hoarse *husky* 405
hoary 124, 128, 430
hoax 545
hobble *limp* 275
  fail 732
  shackle 751
hobby 481, 625
hobgoblin 980
hobo 268, 876
Hobson's choice 609a
hodgepodge 41
hog *animal* 366
  selfishness 943
  glutton 957
hoist 307
hold, *n. influence* **175**
  storage 191
  power 737
hold, *v. cohere* 46
  contain 54
  cease 142
  support 215
  believe 484
  defend 717
  restrain 751
  possess 777
  retain 781
  -forth *declaim* 537, **582**
  -good 478, 494
  -on *continue* 141, 143
  persevere 604a
  -out *persevere* 604a
  offer 763
  -true 494
  -up *support* 215
  aid 707
holder 779
holding
  tenancy 777
  property 780
holdup 791
hole *hovel* 189
  cave 251
  opening 260
holiday *anniversary* **138**
  leisure 685
  vacation 687
  amusement 840
  celebration 883
holiness *God* 976
  piety 987
holloa 411

hunchbacked 243
hundred 98
hunger 865
hungry 865, 956
hunt *pursuit* 286, 622
  inquiry 461
hunter *horse* 271
  pursuer 622
hurl 284
hurrah 838
hurricane *tempest* 349
hurry 274, 684
hurt, *n. physical pain* 378
  evil 619
hurt, *v.*
  cause (physical) pain 378
  maltreat 649
  injure 659, 907
  pain 830
  more frightened than-
    860
hurtful 649
hurtle 276
hurtless 648

husband *store* 636
  director 694
  spouse 903
husbandman 371
husbandry *agriculture* 371
  conduct 692
  economy 817
hush *moderate* 174
  stop 265
  silence 403
  taciturn 585
  -up *conceal* 528
  pacify 723
husk *covering* 223
husky *strong* 159
  hoarse 405, 581
hussar 726
hustings 728
hustle 682
hustler 682
hut 189
hybrid 41
hydroplane 273
hydroplaning 267

hygiene 656
hygienic 656
hygienics 670
Hymen 903
hymeneal 903
hymn *song* 415
  worship 990
hyperbole 549
hypercriticism 868
hyperphysical 450
hyphen 45
hypnosis 376, 992a
hypnotic 683
hypnotism 683, 992a
hypnotize 615, 992
hypochondriac 837, 859
hypocrisy 544, 988
hypocrite 548
hypocritical 544, 988
hypothesis 514
hypothetical 514
hysteria 992a
hysterical 821
hysterics 173

I

ice 383, 387
iceberg 383
ice chest 385
icon 554
iconoclasm 984
iconoclast 165
icy 383
IDEA *notion* 453
ideal 515
idealism 450, 515
idealist 515
ideality 450, 515
idealize 515
identical 13
identification 13
IDENTITY 13, 27
idiocy 503
idiom 560, 566
idiosyncrasy 5, 79, 83
idiot 501
idiotic *foolish* 499
idle *trivial* 643
  slothful 683
idler 683
idol *favorite* 899
  fetich 991
idolater 991
IDOLATRY 991
idolize *love* 897
  idolatrize 991
idyl 597
if 8, 469, 514
igneous 382
ignis fatuus 4, 443
ignite 384
ignition *calefaction* 384
ignoble 876

ignominious 940
ignominy *shame* 874
  dishonor 940
IGNORAMUS 493
IGNORANCE 491
ignorant 491
ignore *neglect* 460
  not known 491
ill, *n. evil* 619
  badness 649
  sick 655
ill, *adj. bad* 649
  -usage 807
  -will 907, 921
ill-adapted 24
ill-advised *inexpedient* 647
  unskillful 699
ill-assorted 24
ill-behaved 895
ill-bred *vulgar* 851
  rude 895
ill-disposed 907
illegal 964
ILLEGALITY 964
illegible 519
illegitimate 925, 964
ill-fated 135, 735
ill-favored 846
illiberal *stingy* 819
  selfish 943
  bigoted 988
illicit 925, 964
illiteracy 491
illiterate 491, 493
ill-made 243
ill-mannered 851
ill-natured 907

illness 655
illogical 477
ill-omened 135, 735
ill-proportioned 846
ill-spent 645
ill-starred 135
ill-timed 24, 135
ill-treat 649, 907
ill-treatment 649
illuminant 420
illuminate *enlighten* 420
  comment 595
illumine *lighten* 420
  excite 824
ill-use 649
illusion
  fallacy of vision 443
  error 495
  deception 545
illusive 4, 495
illusory 4, 495
illustrate *exemplify* 82
  interpret 522
  represent 554
illustration 558
illustrious 873
image *likeness* 17
  appearance 448
  metaphor 521
imagery *fancy* 515
  metaphor 521
imaginable 470
imaginary 2, 4, 515
IMAGINATION 515
imaginative 515
imagine 515
imbecile, *adj. ignorant* 493

J

K

libel *detraction* 934
  accusation 938
libelant 938
libeler 936
liberal *ample* 639
  expending 809
  generous 816
LIBERALITY 784, 816
liberate *disjoin* 44
  deliver 672
  free 748, 750
LIBERATION 750
LIBERTINE 962
liberty *freedom* 748
  permission 760
  right 924
library 593
lice 366
license *laxity* 738
  permission 760
  right 924
lid 223
lie, *n. untruth* 546
lie, *v. be situated* 183
  be present 186
  recline 213
  fib 544
  -in *be* 1
lien *security* 771
  credit 805
lieutenant *officer* 745
  deputy 759
LIFE *essence* 5
  events 151
  vitality 359
  biography 594
  activity 682
  -to come 152
lifeboat 273
life-giving 168
lifeless *inert* 172
  dead 360
lifelike 17, 21
lifelong 110
lifetime 108
lift *raise* 307
ligament 45
ligature 45
LIGHT, *n. window* 260
  luminosity 420
  luminary 423
  aspect 448
  knowledge 490
light, *adj. not heavy* 320
  luminous 420
  trivial 643
  unburdened 705
  gay 836
light, *v. arrive* 292
  descend 306
  kindle 384
  illumine 420
light-colored 429
lighten *illume* 420
  facilitate 705
light-fingered 791

light-footed *fleet* 274
  active 682
lightheaded 503
lighthearted 836
lighthouse 550
lightning 420
like, *adj. similar* 17
like, *v. relish* 394
  enjoy 827
  wish 865
  love 897
likely 472
likeness *similarity* 17, 21
  portrait 554
likewise 37
lilac *color* 437
Lilliputian 193
limb *member* 51
limber *pliable* 324
LIMIT, *n. end* 67
  boundary 233
limit, *v. circumscribe* 195,
  229
  qualify 469
  restrain 751
limitation [*see* limit]
limited 32
limitless 105
limp, *adj. weak* 160
  supple 324
limp, *v.* 275
limpid 425, 570
line, *n. fastening* 45
  row 69
  lineage 69, 167
  length 200
  direction 278
  mark 550
  vocation 625
  armed force 726
line, *v.* 224
lineage *kindred* 11
  series 69
  ancestry 122, 166
  posterity 167
lineament *outline* 230
  appearance 448
linear 200
linen 225
liner 273
linger *delay* 133
  loiter 275, 281, 291
  -on *time* 106
lingo 563
lingua franca 563
lingual 560
linguistic 560
liniment *ointment* 356
LINING 224
link, *n. tie* 9
  vinculum 45
link, *v. connect* 43
lion *animal* 366
  celebrity 873
lion-hearted 861
lionize 873

lip 231
LIQUEFACTION 335
liquefy 335
liquid *fluid* 333
liquidate 807
liquidity 333
liquor 298
lisp 583
LIST, *n. catalogue* 86
  leaning 217
  schedule 611
  arena 728
list, *v. classify* 69
  hear 418
  record 551
listen 418
listless *inactive* 683
  indifferent 866
literal *exact* 516
literally 19
literary 560
literature 490, 560
lithe 324
litigant 938, 969
litigate 969
litigation 969
litigious 713
litter, *n. disorder* 59
litter, *v. derange* 61
  bed cattle 370
little *-in degree* 32
  -in size 193
  bigoted 988
LITTLENESS 32, 193
liturgy 998
live *exist* 1, 359
  continue 141
  dwell 186
livelihood 803
liveliness 836 [*see* lively]
livelong 110
lively *frisky* 309
  keen 375
  active 682
  acute 821
  sensitive 822
  sprightly 836
livery 225
livid 431, 437
living *alive* 359
  benefice 995
lizard 366
load, *n. quantity* 31
  cargo 190
  hindrance 706
  anxiety 828
load, *v. fill* 52
  lade 184, 190
loadstar [*see* lodestar]
loadstone *attraction* 288
loaf *dawdle* 683
loafer 268, 927
loan 787
loath 603, 867
loathe *dislike* 867
  hate 898

loathsome 867
local 181, 183
locality 182
localize 184
locate 184
LOCATION 182, **184**
lock *fasten* 43
    fastening 45
    tuft 256
    canal 350
    -up *hide* 528
    imprison 751
locker 191
lockout 55
lockup *prison* 752
locomotion 264
    -by air 267
    -by land 266
    -by water 267
locomotive 466
locution 566, 582
lodestar *attraction* 288
    direction 693
lodestone
    [*see* loadstone]
lodge *place* 184
    inhabit 186
lodgment 184
lodger 188
lodging 189
loft *garret* 191
lofty *high* 206
    style 574
    proud 878
log *fuel* 388
    measurement 466
    record 551
logic 476
logical 476
logician 476
logy 172, 683
loiter *be slow* 133, 275
    lag 281
loll *sprawl* 213
lone 87
lonely 893
lonesome 893
long *-in time* 110
    -in space 200
    diffuse 573
    -for 865
longevity 128
longing 865
long-lived 110
longshoreman
    waterman 269
long-suffering 826, 914
long-winded 110
look, *n. appearance* 448
look, *v. see* 441
    attend to 457
    -after care 459
    -ahead 510
    -for seek 461
    expect 507
    -to 459

lookout *view* 448
    sentinel 668
loom *magnify* 31
    impend 152
    come in sight 446
loony 501
loop 245, 247
loophole *opening* 260
    escape 671
loose, *adj. incoherent* 47
    illogical 477
    vague 519
    lax 738
    free 748
loose, *v. detach* 44
    liberate 750
loosen *make loose* 47
    let loose 750
loot, *n. booty* 793
loot, *v. steal* 791
lop 201
lopsided 28
loquacious 584
LOQUACITY 562, **584**
Lord *God* 976
lord *nobleman* 875
lordly 873, 878
lore 490, 539
lorgnette 445
lose *forget* 506
    fail 732
    incur loss 776
    -an opportunity **135**
LOSS *decrement* 40a
    death 360
    privation 776
    -of strength 160
lost *nonexisting* 2
    absent 187
    uncertain 475
    bereft 776
    impenitent 951
lot *state* 7
    quantity 25
    multitude 102
    necessity 601
    chance 621
lotion *liquid* 337
lottery *chance* 156
loud *noisy* 404
    bad taste 851
LOUDNESS 404
lounge, *n.* 191
lounge, *v.* 683
lout 501, 876
lovable 897
LOVE *desire* 865
    affection 897
loveliness 845
lovelorn 898
lovely *beautiful* 845
    lovable 897
lover 865, 897
lovesick 902
low, *adj. small* 32
    not high 207

    faint 405
    vulgar 851
    common 876
low, *v. moo* 412
    -spirits 837
    -tide 207
    -water low 207
    poverty 804
lowborn 876
low-brow *ignorant* 491
lower, *adj.*
    inferior 34, 207
    overcast 421, 422
lower, *v. decrease* 36
    depress 308
    frown 837
lowermost 207
lowlands 207
lowliness 879
lowly 879
LOWNESS 207, **851**
    [*see* low]
loyal 743, **939**
lubber 701
lubricant 332
lubricate *oil* 332
LUBRICATION 332
lucent 420
lucid *luminous* 420
    intelligible 518, **570**
    rational 502
lucidity 518, 570
luck *chance* 156
    prosperity 734
lucky *timely* 134
    successful 731
lucrative 775
lucre *gain* 775
    wealth 803
ludicrous 853
lug 285
luggage 270, 780
lukewarm *torrid* 823
    indifferent 866
lull, 142, 174, 403
lullaby 415
lumber, *v.* 275
lumberman 371
LUMINARY *star* 318
    light 423
luminosity 420
luminous *light* 420
lump *whole* 50
    chief part 51
    mass 192
    density 321
    -together 72
lunacy 503
lunar 318
lunatic 503, 504
luncheon 892
lunge 276, 716
lurch *tilt* 217
    fall 306
    sway 314
    leave in the-

M

misstate 495
misstatement *error* 495
   untruth 546
   misrepresentation 555
mist *cloud* 353
   semitransparency 427
mistake 495, 699
mistaken 495
MISTEACHING 538
mister 373
mistime 135
mistress *lady* 374
mistrust 485
misty [see mist]
misunderstand 495, 523
misunderstanding
   disagreement 24
   error 495
MISUSE 679
mite *bit* 32
   infant 129
   small 193
mitigate *decrease* 36
   abate 174
   relieve 834
mitigation
   [see mitigate]
mitten 225
mix 41
mixed 41
mixture 41, 335
mizzen 235
mnemonics 505
moan *cry* 411
   lament 839
moat *inclosure* 232
   canal 350
mob 72, 102, 876
   -law 738
mobile *inconstant* 149
   movable 264
   sensitive 822
mobilization 264, 722
mobilize 264
moccasin 225
mock, *v. imitate* 17, 19
mock, *adj. derisive* 856
   -modesty 855
mockery 19, 856
mode *state* 7
   habit 613
   method 627
   fashion 852
model *copy* 21
   prototype 22
   form 240
   sculpture 557
   perfection 650
   good man 948
moderate, *adj. small* 32
   slow 275
   lenient 740
   cheap 815
   temperate 953
moderate, *v. allay* 174
MODERATION 174

   patience 831
   [see moderate]
moderator *lenitive* 174
   judge 967
modern 123
modernism 123
modernization 123
modest *small* 32
   humble 879
   diffident 881
MODESTY 879, 881
modicum *little* 32
modification *difference* 15
   variation 20a
   change 140
   qualification 469
modify 469
modish 852
modulation 140
Mohammedanism 976
moiety 51
moil 682
moist 339
moisten 339
MOISTURE 339
mold, *n. matrix* 22
   form 240, 554
   structure 329
   earth 342
mold, *v. convert* 144
   carve 557
   decay 653
   create 976
moldy *fetid* 401
molecular 32
molecule 32, 193
molest 907
mollify *allay* 174
   soften 324
mollycoddle 158
molten *liquefied* 384
moment 113
momentous 151, 642
momentum 276
monarch 745
monarchy 737
monastery 1000
monasticism 995
monetary 800
MONEY 800
money-changer 797
moneylender 797
monger 797
mongrel 41, 83
monitor *oracle* 513
   director 694
   adviser 695
   warship 726
monitory *prediction* 511
   dissuasion 616
   warning 668
monk 996
monkey *imitator* 19
   ape 366
   butt 857
monocycle 272

monograph 594
monologue 589
monoplane 273
monoplanist 269a
monopolist 751, 943
monopolize 777
monopoly *restraint* 751
   possession 777
monotone 104
monotonous *uniform* 16
   equal 27
   repetition 104
   weary 841
monotony 13
   [see monotonous]
monsoon 348, 349
monster *exception* 83
   giant 192
   prodigy 872
   evildoer 913
   ruffian 949
monstrosity
   [see monster]
   distortion 243
monstrous *excessive* 31
   exceptional 83
   huge 192
   wonderful 870
month 108
monument *tomb* 363
   record 551
moo 412
mood *nature* 5
   state 7
   tendency 176
   humor 602
moody *sad* 837
   sullen 901a
moon 108, 318
   -shaped 245
moonbeam *light* 420
moonlight 422
moonshine *absurdity* 497
moonstruck *insane* 503
moor, *n. open space* 180
   plain 344
moor, *v. fasten* 43
   locate 184
moorings 184
moot -point *topic* 454
   question 461
mop 256, 652
mope 837
moraine 270
moral, *n. maxim* 496
moral, *adj. right* 922, 926
   virtuous 944
   -courage 604
   -obligation 926
morality 926, 944
moralize 476
morals *duty* 926
   virtue 944
morass 345
moratorium 133
morbid 655

hide 528
deceive 545

myth *fancy* 515
MYTHIC DEITIES 979

mythical 515, **979**
mythology **979**

N

nadir 211
nag, *n. horse* 271
nag, *v. quarrel* 713
nail *fasten* 43
naked 226
namby-pamby
  affected 855
name *indication* 550
  appellation 564
nameless 565
namely 79
namesake 564
nap *texture* 256, 329
  sleep 683
narcotic 662
narration 594
narrative 594
narrator 529, 532, 594
narrow *thin* 203
  bigoted 481, 988
narrow-minded
  bigoted 481
  foolish 499
  selfish 943
NARROWNESS 203
nasty *foul* 653
  offensive 830
nation 372
national 372
  -guard 726
nationality 372, 910
nationwide 78
native, *n.* 188
native, *adj.* 5, **367**
  -land 342
nativity *birth* 66
natural *intrinsic* 5
  true 494
  artless 703
  simple 849
  -history 357
  -philosophy 316
naturalist 357
naturalization 184
naturalized 188
nature *essence* 5
  tendency 176
  world 318
naught 4, 101
naughty 945
nausea 841, 867
nauseate *sicken* 395, 867
  give pain 830
nauseous *unsavory* 395
  unpleasant 830
  disgusting 867
nautical 267, 273
naval 267, 273
  -authorities **745**

NAVIGATION 267
navigator 269
navvy *laborer* 690
navy 273, **726**
nay 536
neap *low* 207
  -tide 36
near *like* 17
  -*in space* 197
  -*in time* 121
  soon 132
  impending 152
  approach 286
  stingy 819
nearly 32
NEARNESS 9, 197
nearsighted 443
neat *orderly* 58
  trim 240, 845
  clean 652
nebula 353
nebulous *misty* 353
  obscure 519
necessarily 154
necessary 601, 630
necessitate 630
NECESSITY *fate* 601
  predetermination 611
  compulsion 744
  indigence 804
  need 865
necromancy 511
necropolis 363
nectar 394, 396
need *necessity* 601
  requirement 630
  want 640
  indigence 804
  desire 865
needful 601, 630
needle 262
needless 641
needlework 847
nefarious 945
NEGATION 536, 764
negative, *n.* 22
negative, *adj. inexisting* 2
  denying 536
negative, *v. confute* 479
  deny 536
NEGLECT 460
  leave undone 730
  omit 773
  evade 927
negligence 460
negligent 460
negotiable 270
negotiate *mediate* 724
  bargain 769

negotiator 724, 758
Negro *black* 431
neigh 412
neighbor *near* 197
  friend 890
neighborhood 197, 227
neighborly *aiding* 707
  friendly 888
  social 892
nemesis 972
neologist 563
NEOLOGY 563
Nereid 979
nerve *strength* 159
  courage 861
nerveless *impotent* 158
  imperturbable 871
nervous *excitable* 825
  timid 860
nest 102, 153
nestle 186, 902
net, *adj.* 40
net, *n.* 219, 232
nether 207
netlike 219
netting 219
nettle 830
network 59, **219**
neutral *mean* 29
  no choice 609a
  mid-course 628
  indifferent 866
neutrality
  indifference 609a, 866
  [see neutral]
neutralize 179
never 107
  -more 107
new *different* 18
  novel 123
newcomer 294
newfangled 851
NEWNESS 123
NEWS 532
newsmonger *gossip* 532
newspaper 531, 551
next 63, 121
nib *end* 67
nibble *eat* 298
nice *discriminative* 465
  exact 494
  pleasing 829
  fastidious 868
niceness [see nice]
nicety 494
niche 191, 244
nick *notch* 257
nickel 800
nickname 565

O

God 976
omnipresence 1, 186
omniscience 976
omnivorous 957
on *forward* 282
once 119
one 13, 87
onerous *difficult* 704
burdensome 706
oneself 13
one-sided 481, 923
onlooker 444
only 32
onset *beginning* 66
attack 716
onslaught 716
ontology 1
onus *burden* 706
duty 926
onward 282
oodles 102
ooze *emerge* 295
flow 348
OPACITY 426
opaque 426
open, n. *begin* 66
unclose 260
reveal 529
open, adj. *frank* 543
artless 703
opener 260
OPENING *beginning* 66
opportunity 134
aperture 260
opera *music* 415
operate *produce* 161
act 170
work 680
operate [see *operate*]
operative, adj. *acting* 170
operative, n. *workman* 690
operator *doer* 690
opiate 174
opine 484
opinion 484
opinionated 474, 606
OPPONENT
antagonist 710
enemy 891
opportune *well timed* 134
expedient 646
opportunism 646
opportunist 605
opportunity 134, 646
oppose *be contrary* 14
counteract 179
front 234
refute 468
clash 708, 719
OPPOSITE 14, 237
OPPOSITION 708
[see *oppose*]
oppositionist 710
oppress *molest* 649
domineer 739
harry 907

oppressive *hot* 382
painful 649, 830
oppressor 739, 913
opprobrium 874
optic 420
OPTICAL 441
-instruments 445
optics *light* 420
optical instruments 445
optimism 858
optimist 858, 935
option 609
optional 609
opulence 803
ORACLE *prediction* 511
prophet 513
oracular *ambiguous* 475
wise 500
predicting 511
oral 467, 582
ORANGE *color* 439
oration 582
orator 582
oratorical 582
oratory *speaking* 582
orb *circle* 247
orbit *circle* 247
path 627
orchestra *musicians* 416
instruments 417
orchestration 413
ordain *command* 741
install 755, 995
ordained 996
ordeal 463, 828
ORDER *regularity* 58
requirement 630
command 741
orderly, adj. *regular* 58,
60, 80
ordinance *command* 741
law 963
ordinary *usual* 82
imperfect 651
mediocre 736
ordination *commission* 755
church 995
ordnance 727
organ *instrument* 633
organic *structural* 329
organized 357
organism 367
ORGANIZATION
arrangement 60, 626
production 161
animated nature 357
organize *arrange* 60
produce 161
form 357
plan 626
organizer 626
orgy 954
Orient *East* 236
orifice *opening* 260
origin *beginning* 66
cause 153

original *dissimilar* 18
not imitated 20
model 22
individual 79
exceptional 83
causal 153
invented 515
originality [see *original*]
will 600
originate *begin* 66
cause 153
invent 515
-in 154
originative 153
originator 164
orison *request* 765
worship 990
ORNAMENT
in writing 577
adornment 847
glory 873
ornamentation 847
ornate *in writing* 577
ornamental 847
orthodox 82, 983a
ORTHODOXY 983a
orthography 561
oscillate 314
OSCILLATION *perio-
dicity* 138
change 149
motion 314
osseous 323
ossify 323
ostensible *probable* 472
manifest 525
alleged 617
OSTENTATION 880, 882
ostentatious 880, 882
ostracism [see *ostracize*]
ostracize *exclude* 55
banish 893
censure 932
other *different* 15
extra 37
otherwise 18
ottoman 215
ouija board 992a
Our Lady 977
oust *eject* 297
dismiss 756
deprive 789
out *exterior* 220
-of the way
distant 196
outbalance 33
outbound 295
outbreak *beginning* 66
violence 173
egress 295
revolt 742
outburst *violence* 173
egress 295
rage 825
outcast 83, 876, 893
outcome *effect* 154

P

pertinent *relative* 9
  congruous 23
perturbation *agitation* 315
  excitation 824, 825
  fear 860
peruse 539
pervade *influence* 175
  extend 186
perverse *reactionary* 283
  obstinate 606
  sulky 901a
perversion *sophistry* 477
  misinterpretation 523
  misteaching 538
  falsehood 544
perversity [see perverse]
pervert *quibble* 477
  distort 523
pervious 260
pessimism *dejection* 837, 859
pessimist 482, 862, 859
pest *bane* 663
pester 830
pestilence 655
pestle 330
pet, n. *favorite* 899
  anger 900
pet, v. *love* 897
  fondle 902
petal 367
petition *ask* 765
  pray 990
PETITIONER 767
pet name 565
petrify *thicken* 321
  harden 323
  organization 357
  thrill 824
  astonish 870
petroleum 356
petticoat 225
pettifogger 968
pettifogging 477
pettish 901
petty 643
  -cash 800
petulance 901
petulant 901
pew 191
pewter 41
phalanx 712, 726
phantasm 443
phantom *unreality* 4
  specter 980a
pharisaical 544, 988
Pharisee 988
pharmacy 662
phase *aspect* 8
  apperance 448
phenomenon *event* 151
  prodigy 872
phial 191
philander 902
philanderer 902
philanthropic 906, 910

philanthropist 906, 910
PHILANTHROPY 906, 910
Philistine 82
philosopher 500
philosophical
  thoughtful 451
  calm 826
philosophy *intellect* 450
  calmness 826
phlegmatic 823
phonetic *sonant* 402
  tonic 561
  voice 580
  vocal 582
phonograph 418
phonography 402
phosphorescence *light* 420
  luminary 423
phosphorus 423
photograph 554
photographer 554
photography 554, 556
PHRASE 566
phraseology 569
physic *remedy* 662
physical 316
  -pain 378
  -pleasure 377
physician 662, 695
physics 316
physiognomy 234
physiology 357, 359
physique 159, 364
piazza 189
picayune 643
pick, n. *best* 648
pick, v. *select* 609
  -a quarrel 713
  -up learn 539
  get better 658
  gain 775
pickaninny 129
picket, n. *fence* 229
  guard 668
picket, v. *join* 43
  locate 184
  restrain 751
pickings *gain* 775
  booty 793
pickle 670
pickpocket 792
picnic 298, 840
pictorial 556
picture *appearance* 448
  representation 554
  painting 556
picture gallery 556
picturesque 556, 845
pie 396
piebald 440
piece, n. *bit* 51
piece, v. 140
  cannon 727
  -together 43
piecemeal 51

pied 440
pierce *perforate* 260
  chill 385
  wound 659
  affect 824
piercer 262
piercing *cold* 383
  shrill 410
  acute 821
PIETY 987
pig *animal* 366
  glutton 954a
pigeonhole, n. 191
pigeonhole, v. *shelve* 460
piggish 954
pigment 428
pigmy [see pygmy]
pike 727
pikestaff 206
pilaster 215
pile *heap* 72
  edifice 161
pilfer *steal* 791
pilferer 792
pilgrim 268, 996
pilgrimage *journey* 266
  undertaking 676
pill 249
pillage *theft* 791
pillar 206, 215
pillory 975
pillow 215
pilot 269, 269a
pimple 250
pin 43
pinch, n. *emergency* 8
  need 630
  difficulty 704
pinch, v. *contract* 195
  chill 385
pinched [see pinch]
  thin 203
pine *mope* 837
  -for 865
pinion *restrain* 751
  fetter 752
pink, adj. 434
pink, v. *pierce* 260
pinnace 273
pinnacle 210
pioneer *precursor* 64
pious 987
pipe, n. *tube* 260
pipe, v. *sound* 410
piper 416
piquant *pungent* 392
  impressive 821
pique *excite* 824
  pain 830
  hate 898
piracy 773
pirate, n. 792
pirate, v. *plagiarize* 788
pirouette 312
pistol 727
piston 263

pit 208, 252
pitch *degree* 26
  obliquity 217
  descent 306
  musical - 413
pitch, *v. erect* 212
  throw 284
  plunge 310
  reel 314
pitchfork *throw* 284
piteous *painful* 830
PITFALL 667
pith *gist* 5
  meaning 516
pithy *concise* 572
  vigorous 574
pitiable *bad* 649
  painful 830
  contemptible 930
pitiful *bad* 649
  mean 874
  pitying 914
pitiless 914a
PITILESSNESS 914a
pittance *quantity* 25
  dole 640
PITY 914
pivot *junction* 43
  cause 153
pivotal 222
placard 531
placate *pacify* 723
  conciliate 918
PLACE, *n.*
  situation 182, 183
  abode 189
  office 625
place, *v. arrange* 60
  locate 184
  invest 787
placid 826
plagiarism 19, 791
plagiarist 792
plagiarize 788, 791
plague, n. 655
plague, *v. worry* 830
plaid 440
PLAIN, *n.* 251, 344
plain, *adj. clear* 446
  manifest 525
  lucid 576
  homely 846
  simple 849
  -speaking
  candor 525
plainly 525
PLAINNESS 576, 849
plaint *cry* 411
  lament 839
plaintiff 938
plaintive 839
plait 219, 258
PLAN *map* 183
  scheme 626
planchette 992a
plane 251, 255

planet 318
plank *platform* 626
PLANT, *n, shrub* 367
  property 780
  management of - 371
plant, *v.* 184, 300
plantation *location* 184
  estate 780
planter 188
plash 348, 408
plaster 45, 223
plastic 240
plate, *n. dish* 191
  coating 204
plate, *v. cover* 223
plateau 251, 344
platform *support* 215
  stage 542
  scheme 626
platitude 843
platoon 726
platter *receptacle* 191
plaudit 931
plausible *probable* 472
  vindicative 937
play, *n. scope* 180
  drama 599
  freedom 748
  amusement 840
play, *v. operate* 170
  music 416
  sport 840
  -truant 623
player *musician* 416
  actor 599
playfellow 890
playful 836
playground 728
playing field 728
playmate 890
plaything *trifle* 643
  toy 840
playwright 599
PLEA *answer* 462
  argument 476
  excuse 617
  vindication 937
plead *answer* 462
  argue 467, 968
  allege 617
  beg 765
pleader *lawyer* 968
pleadings 969
pleasant *agreeable* 829
  amusing 840
pleasantry 842
please 377, 829
  if you - 765
  -oneself 943
pleased 827
pleasing 394, 829
PLEASURABLENESS 829
PLEASURE *physical -* 377
  moral - 827
pleat 258

plebeian 876
plebiscite 480, 609
pledge, *n. promise* 768
  security 771
pledge, *v. borrow* 788
plenipotentiary 758
plenitude 639
plenteous 639
plenty *sufficient* 639
plethora 641
pliable 324
pliant *soft* 324
  irresolute 605
  servile 886
plight *state* 7
  circumstance 8
  promise 768
plinth 211
plod *journey* 266
  be slow 275
  work 682
plodder *worker* 686
plodding 682
plot *-of ground* 181
  scheme 626
plough [see plow]
plow 259
pluck, *n. resolution* 604
  grit 604a
  courage 861
pluck, *v. take* 789
plucky 604, 861
plug, n. 263
plug, *v. close* 261, 348
plumage 256
plumb, *adj. vertical* 212
  straight 246
plumb, *v. measure* 466
plume *feather* 256
plummet 208
plump *fat* 192
plumpness 192
plunder, *n. gain* 35
  booty 793
plunder, *v.* 791
PLUNGE *depth* 208
  dive 310
PLURALITY 33, 100
plutocrat 639
pluvial 348
ply *use* 677
  exert 686
pneumatics 334, 338
poach *steal* 791
poacher 792
pocket, *n.* 191
pocket, *v. receive* 785
  take 789
pocketbook 802
pocket money 800
poem 597
poet 597
poetic 597
poetize 597
POETRY 597
poignant 378

point *small* **32**
  end **67**
  place **182**
  sharpness **253**
  topic **454**
  mark **550**
  intention **620**
  wit **842**
  -at *direct attention* **457**
  disparage **929**
  -of *view* **441**
  -out *indicate* **79**
  -to *direct* **278**
  predict **511**
point-blank *direct* **278**
  plain **576**
pointed *sharp* **253**
  marked **550**
  concise **572**
pointedly 620
pointer 550
pointless 254
poise *balance* **27**
  weight **319**
  inexcitability **826**
poison 659, 663
  -gas 727
poisonous 657
poke 191
polar 210
  -lights 423
polarity 89, 237
pole *pikestaff* **206**
  axis **222**
  oar **267**
polemic 713
polestar *attraction* **288**
  luminary **423**
  indication **550**
police 965
policeman 664
policy 626, 692
polish, *n. smooth* **255**
  gloss **332**
  taste **850**
  politeness **894**
polish, *v. rub* **331**
  furbish **658**
polished *fashionable* **852**
  polite **894**
polite 894
politeness 894
politic *wise* **498**
  cautious **864**
politician 694, 700
politics 702
polity 926
poll *count* **85**
  list **86**
  vote **609**
pollute *soil* **653**
  corrupt **659**
pollution *disease* **655**
poltroon 862
pommel, *n.* **215**

pommel, *v. beat* **972**
pomp 882
pompom 727
pomposity 878, 882
pompous *inflated* **577**
  proud **878**
  ostentatious **882**
pond 343
ponder 451
ponderous *heavy* **319**
poniard 727
pontiff 996
pontificate 995
pony 271
  translation **522**
poodle 366
pool, *n. lake* **343**
pool, *v. co-operate* **709**
poor *feeble* **477**
  insufficient **640**
  indigent **804**
  -man 640, 804
poorness [*see poor*]
  inferiority **34**
pop *noise* **406**
pope 996
popinjay 854
populace 876
popular *choosing* **609**
  desirable **865**
  celebrated **873**
  approved **931**
popularize 518
population 188, 372
populous 72, 102, 186
porch 66, 191, 260
pore, *n.* **260**
pore over
  apply the mind **457**
  learn **539**
porous 252, 295, 322
port *harbor* **189, 266**
  left **239**
  gait **448**
portable 270
portage 270
portal 66, 260
portend 511
portent 512
portentous *prophetic* **511**
  fearful **860**
porter 263, 271
portfolio *case* **191**
  authority **747**
  jurisdiction **965**
portico 191
portion *part* **51**
  allotment **786**
portly 192
portmanteau 191
  -word 572
portrait 554, 556
portraiture 554
portray 554
pose, *n. situation* **183**
  form **240**

pose, *v. inquire* **461**
  puzzle **475**
  affect **855**
poser 855
position *circumstances* **8**
  situation **183**
  post **625**
  status **873**
positive *real* **1**
  great **31**
  certain **474**
  narrow-minded **481**
  assertive **535**
posse 72
possess 777, 780
  bedevil **978, 992**
POSSESSION 777, 780
POSSESSOR 779
POSSIBILITY *chance* **156**
  liability **177**
  likelihood **470**
possible 177, 470
post, *n. situation* **183**
  support **215**
  mail **534**
  employment **625**
post, *v. list* **86**
  send **270**
  publish **531**
  enter accounts **811**
postal 592
post card 592
postdate 115
poster 531
posterior *in time* **117**
  in space **235**
POSTERIORITY 117
POSTERITY 121, 167
posthaste *swiftly* **274**
  rash **863**
posthumous 117, 133
postilion *rider* **268**
postman 271, 534
post-mortem 363
post office 534
postpone 133, 460
postscript 37, 65
posture *situation* **183**
  form **240**
posy *bouquet* **400**
pot *mug* **191**
potency 157
potent 157, 159
potentate 745
potential 2, 157
potentiality *power* **157**
  possibility **470**
potion *beverage* **298**
potpourri *mixture* **41**
pouch 191
poultry 366
pounce upon *attack* **716**
  seize **789**
pound *bruise* **330**
  -the piano 416
pour *emerge* **295**

rain 348
pout 250, 901a
POVERTY
insufficiency 640
indigence 804
powder 330
gunpowder 727
POWDERINESS 330
powdery 330
POWER *number* 84
efficacy 157
influence 175
authority 737
powerful 157, 159
powerless 158, 160
practicable *possible* 470
practical 646
practical *acting* 170
practicable 646
practically 5
practice, *n. training* 537
exertion 686
conduct 692
practice, *v. train* 537
use 677
act 680
practiced *skilled* 698
practitioner *general - 662
doer 690
pragmatic *practical* 646
pragmatism 646
prairie *space* 180
plain 344
praise 931, 990
praiseworthy 931
prance *leap* 309
dance 315
prank *caprice* 608
prate 584
prattle *talk* 582
chatter 584
pray *beg* 765
worship 990
prayer *request* 765
worship 990
preach 537
preacher *teacher* 540
priest 996
preamble 62, 64
precarious *transient* 111
dangerous
precaution *care* 459
safety 664
preparation 673
precede *be superior* 33
forerun 62, 280
PRECEDENCE 62, 280
rank 873
precedent *prototype* 22
habit 613
legal decision 969
PRECEDING 280
PRECEPT
requirement 630
maxim 697
preceptor 540

precinct 181, 227
precious *great* 31
valuable 814
beloved 897
-metals 800
precipice 212
precipitancy *haste* 684
rashness 863
precipitate, *adj. early* 132
rash 863
precipitate, *v. sink* 308
precipitous 217
precise 494
precisely 19
preclude 706
preclusive 55
precocious 132, 674
preconception 481
PRECURSOR 64
predatory 789
predecessor 64
redesigned 611
predestinate 976
predestination 611, 976
predestine 976
PREDETERMINATION
611
predicament 7, 8, 43
predicate 514
predict 507, 511
PREDICTION 511
predilection *bias* 481
affection 820
predispose 615
predominance 157
predominant 157
predominate 33, 175
pre-eminent *superior* 33
celebrated 873
pre-exist 116
preface 62, 64
prefer *choose* 609
preference 62
prefix 62
pregnant 642
prehistoric 124
prejudge 481
prejudice 481
prejudicial 649
prelacy 995
preliminary, *n.* 64, 296
preliminary *adj.* 673
prelude 62, 64
premature *early* 132
unripe 674
premeditate 611
premier 759
premise 62
premises *ground* 182
evidence 467
logic 476
premium 810, 973
premonish 668
premonition 668, 992a
premonitory 511, 668

preoccupation 458
PREPARATION 60, 673
instruction 537
preparatory 673
prepare 537, 673
preparedness 673
preponderance
superiority 33
influence 175
prepossessing 829
prepossession
prejudice 481
preposterous *absurd* 497
imaginative 515
ridiculous 853
improper 925
prerogative 924
prescribe *advise* 695
order 741
entitle 924
prescription *decree* 741
remedy 662
prescriptive 924
PRESENCE 1, 186
-of mind 864
present, *n. gift* 784
present, *v. offer* 763
give 784
PRESENT, *adj.*
-in time 118
-in space 186
-events 151
-time 118
presentable 845
presentiment 481, 510
presently 132, 507
PRESERVATION
continuance 141
conservation 670
preserve *continue* 143
keep 670, 976
preserver 670
preside 693
presidency 737
president, 694, 745
press, *n. newspapers* 531
press, *v. crowd* 72
smooth 255
weigh 319
offer 763
solicit 765
pressing *urgent* 642
pressure
influence 175
weight 319
urgency 642
adversity 735
presto *instantly* 113
presumable 472
presume 472, 514
presumption *probability*
472
rashness 863
arrogance 885
presumptive 924
presumptuous 885

improving 658
prohibit 761
PROHIBITION 761
   exclusion 55
prohibitionist 958
prohibitive 55, 761
project *bulge* 250
   impel 284
   intend 620
   plan 626
projectile 284, 727
projecting 214, 250
projection 250, 283
projector *promoter* 626
proletariat 876
prolific 168
prolix 573
prolixity 573
prologue 64, 599
prolong *protract* 110
   delay 133
   continue 143
   lengthen 200
prolongation 117
   [see prolong]
prolonged 110
promenade *walk* 266
prominence
   [see prominent]
prominent *convex* 250
   important 642
   eminent 873
promiscuous *mixed* 41
   indiscriminate 465a
PROMISE 768
promissory 768
   -note *security* 771
promontory 206
promote *improve* 658
promoter *planner* 626
promotion 541, 658
prompt, *adj. early* 132
   active 682
prompt, *v. remind* 505
   tell 527
promulgate 531
prone *horizontal* 213
   disposed 820
proneness *tendency* 176
   disposition 820
prong 91
pronounce *judge* 480
   assert 535
   voice 580
   speak 582
pronounced 525
pronouncement 531
pronunciation 580
proof *test* 463
   demonstration 478
   printing 591
   -against 664
prop *support* 215
propaganda 673
propagate 161
propel 284

propensity *tendency* 176
   inclination 820
proper *individual* 79
   due 924
PROPERTY 342, 780
prophecy 511
prophet *seer* 513
prophetic 511
prophylactic *healthful* 656
   preventive 706
propinquity 197
propitiate *pacify* 723
   mediate 724
   atone 952, 976
propitiator 724
propitiatory 952
propitious *timely* 134
   prosperous 734
   auspicious 858
proportion *relation* 9
   symmetry 242
proportions *space* 180
   size 192
proposal 763, 765
propose *suggest* 514
   offer 763
   offer marriage 902
proposition *supposition*
   454
   reasoning 476
   project 626
   offer 763
propound *suggest* 514
proprietor 779
propriety *agreement* 23
   elegance 578
   fashion 852
   duty 926
PROPULSION 284
propulsive 284
prorogue 133
prosaic *sober* 576
   dull 843
proscribe *interdict* 761
   curse 908
   condemn 971
PROSE, n. 598
prose, *v.* 584
prosecute *pursue* 622
   arraign 969
prosecutor 938
proselyte 144, 607
prospect *destiny* 152
   futurity 121
   view 448
   expectation 507
prospector 463
prospective 120, 507
prospectus *list* 86
   scheme 626
prosper 618, 734
PROSPERITY 734
prostrate, *adj. powerless*
   158
   low 207
   horizontal 213, 251

   submissive 725
   dejected 837
prostrate, *v. depress* 308
prostration
   [see prostrate]
   sickness 655
prosy *weary* 841
   dull 843
protect 664
protection *influence* 175
   defense 717
protectionist 751
protective 717
protector 664, 717, 912
protectorate 737
protest *dissent* 489
   deprecats 766
   not pay 808
protestant
   dissenting 489
protoplasm 357
PROTOTYPE 22
protract *prolong* 110
   delay 133
   lengthen 200
protrude 250
protrusive 250
protuberance 250
proud *dignified* 873
   lofty 878
prove *arithmetic* 85
   demonstrate 478
   indicate 550
proverb 496
proverbial 490
provide *furnish* 637
provided 8, 469
providence 976
provident *careful* 459
   prepared 673
providential
   opportune 134
   fortunate 734
province *department* 75
   region 181
   office 625
provincial *rural* 189
   narrow 481
provincialism 563
PROVISION *food* 298
   supply 637
   preparation 673
provisional
   conditional 8, 770
   temporary 111
   contingent 134
proviso 469, 770
provocation 900
provoke *cause* 153
   excite 824
   vex 830
   anger 900
prow 234
prowess 861
prowl *walk* 266
   lurk 528

quaint *odd* 83
  ridiculous 853
quake *oscillate* 314
  shake 315
  fear 860
QUALIFICATION
  change 140
  power 157
  modification **469**
qualify *change* 140
  modify **469**
quality *attribute* 157
  tendency 176
  nobility 875
qualm 603
quandary 7, 475
quantitative 25
QUANTITY 25
  much 31
quarrel 24, **713**
quarrelsome **713, 901**
quarry *object* 620
  mine 636
quarter, *n. fourth* 95
  period 108
  region 181
  forbearance 740
  mercy 914
quarter, *v. cut up* 44
  quadrisect 97
  locate 184
quarters *abode* 189
quartet 95
quash *destroy* 162
  annul 756

QUATERNITY 95
quaver *oscillate* 314
  shake 315
  fear 860
quay *wharf* 231
queen 745, 877
queer *singular* 83
quell 265, **731**
quench *cool* 385
  satiate 869
querulous *complaining* 839
  fastidious 868
  irritable 901
query 461
quest 463
question *inquire* 461
  doubt 485
questionable
  uncertain 475
  doubtful 485
  disreputable 874
questioner 455
queue 65
quibble *quirk* 481
  equivocation 520
quick *transient* 111
  rapid 274
  alive 359
  intelligent 498
  active 682
  irascible 901
quicken *work* 170
  hasten 274, **684**
  come to life 359
  excite 824

quickly *soon* 132
quiescence 265
quiet *calm* 174
  rest 265
  silence 403
quietude 826
quietus *death* 361
quilt *covering* 223
QUINQUESECTION 99
quintessence 5
quip *amusement* 840
  wit 842
  ridicule 856
quirk 481
quit *depart* **293**
  relinquish 624
quite 52
quits 27
quitter 623
quiver, *n.* 191
  agitation 315
quiver, *v. oscillate* 314
  shiver 383
  fear 860
quixotic *fanciful* 515
  rash 863
quiz *question* 461
  ridicule 856
quizzical 856
quota 25
quotation
  imitation 19
  evidence 467
  price 812
quote 82, 467

R

rabble 72, **876**
rabid 821
race *relation* **111**
  sequence 69
  kind 75
  lineage 166
  run 274
  stream 343, 348
racial 166
raciness 574
rack, *n. receptacle* 191
  frame 215
  gait 275
  instrument of torture 975
rack, *v. torture* 830
racket *uproar* 404
racy *strong* 171
  pungent 392
radiance *light* 420
  beauty 845
radiant *diverging* 291
  beautiful 845
radiate 73, 291
radiation 73, 291
radical, *adj. essential* **5**
  complete 52

  important 642
radical, *n. reformer* 658
radically *greatly* 31
radio 534
radiograph **554**
radiography **556**
radiophone 534
radiotelegraphy 420
radiotelephone 534
radius 200, 202
raft 273
rafter 215
rag 32
ragamuffin 876
rage *violence* 173
  excitement 824, 825
  fashion 852
  desire 865
  wrath 900
rags 225
ragtime *music* 415
raid *attack* 716
  pillage 791
rail *inclosure* 232
railing 232
raillery 856

railroad 266, 627
railway 627
  -station 266
raiment 225
rain 348
rainy 348
raise *increase* 35
  produce 161
  elevate 212, 307
  leaven 320
raja 875
rake, *v. drag* 285
  clean 652
  -up *collect* 72
rally *meet* 74
  encourage 861
ramble *stroll* 266
  wander 279
  rave 503
  digress 573
rambler 268
rambling 279
ramification 291
ramify 291
rampage 173
rampant *prevalent* 175

vehement 825
rampart 717
ramshackle 665
ranch 907
rancid 401, 653
rancor 907
random *casual* 156
　aimless 621
　at - 621
range, *n. extent* 26
　space 180
　freedom 748
range, *v. arrange* 60
　roam 266
rangy *long* 200
rank, *n. order* 58
　row 69
　station 71
　soldiers 726
　glory 873
　nobility 875
rank, *adj. prevalent* 1
　thorough 31
　dense 365
　fetid 401
rank, *v. estimate* 480
rankle 830
ransack *seek* 461
　plunder 791
ransom 672
rant *rave* 825
rap *blow* 276
rapacity 789
rapid 274
rapids 348, 667
rapier 727
rapt 451, 457
rapture *bliss* 827
rapturous 221, 827
rare *unique* 20
　exceptional 83
　few 103
　infrequent 137
　tenuous 322
　choice 648
rarefaction 322
rarefy 322
RARITY 322
　[see rare]
rascal 941, 949
rash *reckless* 863
RASHNESS 863
rasp *rub* 331
rate, *n. degree* 26
　motion 264
　measure 466
　price, tax 812
rate, *v. esteem* 480
　berate 527
rather 32
ratification 467, 488, 762
ratify 488
ratio *relation* 9
　degree 26
　proportion 84
ration *food* 298

rational *judicious* 498
　sane 502
rattle *clatter* 407
rattled *confused* 523
raucous *strident* 410
ravage *destroy* 162
rave *ramble* 503
　rage 824, 825
ravel *disorder* 59
ravenous 865
ravine 198, 350
raving 824
ravish 829
raw *immature* 123
　unprepared 674
　unskilled 699
rawboned 203
ray *light* 420
raze *destroy* 162
　level 213
　-to the ground 308
razor 253
reach, *n. degree* 26
　distance 196
reach, *v.* 292
reaction 145, 277
reactionary 277, 283
read 539
reader 582
readily 705
reading
　interpretation 522
　learning 539
ready *expecting* 507
　willing 602
　prepared 673
　active 682
real *existing* 1
　true 494
　-estate 342, 780
realism 494
realistic 494, 504
reality 1, 494
realize *discover* 480a
　believe 484
　conceive 490
　imagine 515
　acquire 775
　sell 796
realm 181, 737
realty 342, 780
reap 789
reappear 104
REAR, *n.* 65, 67, 235
rear, *v. bring up* 161
　erect 212
　elevate 307
reason, *n. cause* 153
　intellect 450
　wisdom 498
　motive 615
reason, *v. think* 451
　argue 476
reasonable *moderate* 174
　probable 472
　cheap 815

right 922
reasoner 476
REASONING 476
reassemble 72
reassure 858
rebate 38, 40a 813
rebel, *n.* 742
rebel, *v.* 146, 742
rebellion 146, 742
rebellious *defiant* 715
　[see rebellion]
rebirth 660
rebound 277, 325
rebuff, *n. repulse* 732
rebuff, *v.* 764
rebuild 660
rebuke 932
rebut 462, 479
rebuttal [see rebut]
recall *recollect* 505
　cancel 756
recant 950
recapitulate *repeat* 104
　summarize 596
recast 146
recede 283, 287
RECEIPT 807, 810
receive *include* 76
　admit 296
　acquire 775
　take in 785
　take 789
　-money 810
　welcome 892, 894
receiver *vessel* 191
　assignee 785
RECEIVING 785
recent *late* 122
　new 123
RECEPTACLE 191
RECEPTION
　inclusion 76
　admittance 296
　welcome 892, 894
receptive
　[see reception]
recess *receptacle* 191
　corner 244
　vacation 687
recesses *interior* 221
RECESSION
　motion from 287
recipe *remedy* 662
recipient 191, 785
reciprocal 12, 148
reciprocate 12, 148
reciprocity 12, 148
recitation 537, 582
recite *enumerate* 85
　speak 582
　narrate 594
reckless *defiant* 715
　rash 863
reckon *count* 85
reckoning
　numeration 85

payment 807
reclaim *restore* 660
  reform 950
  alone 952
reclamation *land* 342
  [*see* reclaim]
recline *lie flat* 213
  repose 687
recluse 893
recognition
  [*see* recognize]
  thanks 916
  means of - 550
recognizable *visible* 446
  intelligible 518
recognizance 771
recognize *see* 441
  discover 480a
  assent 488
  know 490
RECOIL, *n.* 325, **277**
  recoil, v. 145
recollect 505
recollection 505
recommence 66
recommend *advise* 695
  approve 931
recompense *reward* 973
reconcile *agree* 23
  pacify 723
  content 831
recondite 528
recondition 660
reconnoissance 441, 461
reconnoiter 441, 461
reconsideration 451
reconstruct 660
RECORD 551
  maximum 33
RECORDER 553
recount 594
recoup 30
recourse 677
recover 660, 775, **790**
recovery
  improvement 658
  getting back 775
  restitution 790
recreation 840
recriminate 932
recruit, *n.* 711, 726
recruit, *v.* 658, 689
rectangle 244
rectify *straighten* 246
  improve 658
rectilinear 246
rectitude *probity* 939
rector *clergyman* 996
rectory 1000
recumbent 213
recuperation 689
recur 104, 136, 138
recurrence [*see* recur]
Red *anarchist* 146, 710
RED 434
  -tape 613

red-complexioned 434
redden 434
reddish-brown 433
redeem *compensate* 30
  substitute 147
  reinstate 660
  reclaim 950
  atone 952
Redeemer 976
redemption [*see* redeem]
  salvation 976
redness 382, 434
redolence *odor* 398
  fragrance 400
redouble 35, 104
redoubt 717
redoubtable 860
redound to *conduce* 176
redress, *n.* 660, 662
redress, *v.* 660, 973
reduce *lessen* 36
  pare 38
  -*in number* 103
  shorten 201
  lower 308
  subdue 731
  -*to convert* 144
reduced [*see* reduce]
  inferior 34
  impoverished 804
  cheap 815
reduction [*see* reduce
  conversion 144
  diminution 195
REDUNDANCE
  surplus 33, 40
  too much 641
redundancy 104
reduplication *imitation* 19
  repetition 104
re-echo 19
reef, *n.* *shoal* 346
reef, *v.* *slacken* 275
reek 336, 382
reel, *n.* 840
reel, *v.* 315
re-enforce 37, 159
re-enforcement 37, 39
re-enter 245
re-establish 660
refashion 163
refectory 191
refer to *relate* 9
  attribute 155
  cite 467
referee 480
reference [*see* refer]
referendum 609
refine 375, 652
refined 850, 862
refinement 850
reflect *imitate* 19
  think 450, 451
reflection [*see* reflect]
  copy 21
  light 420

  thought 451
  idea 453
reflector *mirror* 445
reflex *recoil* 277
reflux 283
reform *improve* **658**
  reclaim 950
reformation 658
reformatory 752
reformer **658**
refraction *deviation* 279
  light 420
  fallacy of vision 443
refractory *obstinate* 606
  mutinous 742
  sullen 901a
refrain, *n.* 104
refrain, v. *do nothing* 681
  forbear 953
refresh *strengthen* 159
  cool 385
  recruit 689
refreshing 377, **829**
REFRESHMENT
  food 298
  recruiting 689
refrigerant 387
REFRIGERATION 385
REFRIGERATOR 385,
  387
REFUGE 623, 666
refugee 268, 623
refund *pay* 807
REFUSAL 764
refuse, *n.* 40, 645
refuse, v. 764
refute 468, 479
regain 775
regal 737
regale 689, 707
regalia 747
regality 737
regard *relate to* 9
  attend 457
  respect 928
  as -s 9
regardful *attentive* 457
  careful 459
regardless 458
regency 755
regenerate 987
regeneration 144, 976
regent *governor* **745**
  deputy 759
regicide 361
regime 692
regiment 726
REGION 181, 342
regional 181, 189
register *list* 86
  chronicle 114
  record 551
registrar 553
registration **551**
registry 114
  record 551

reward 973
repeal 756
repeat *imitate* 19
  iterate 104, 136
  reproduce 163
  affirm 535
repeated 104
repeater *watch* 114
  firearm 727
repel *repulse* 289
  defend 717
  resist 719
  refuse 764
  give pain 830
  disincline 867
  banish 893
repellent 289, 846
  [see repel]
repent 950
repentant 950
repertory 599
REPETITION
  similarity 17
  imitation 19, 21
  iteration 104, 136
repine *grieve* 828
  regret 833
  mope 837
replace *substitute* 147
  restore 660
replenish *complete* 52
  fill 637
repletion *redundance* 641
  satiety 869
replica 21
reply *answer* 462
report *noise* 406
  judgment 480
  information 527
  rumor 532
  statement 594
reporter 534, 553
REPOSE *quiescence* 265
  leisure 685
  rest 687
reprehend 932
reprehensible 898
represent *exhibit* 525
  intimate 527
  denote 550
  delineate 554
  stand for 759
REPRESENTATION
  [see represent]
  copy 21
  portrait 554
representative, *adj.*
  typical 79
  illustrative 554
representative, *n.*
  delegate 524, 758
  legislator 696
  -government 737
repress *restrain* 751
  counteract 179
repressionist 751

repressive 751
reprieve *delay* 133
  pardon 918
  respite 970
reprimand 932
reprint *copy* 21
reprisal 148
reproach, *n. disgrace* 874
  blame 932
reproach, *v.* 932, 938
reprobate 945, 949
reproduce *match* 17
  imitate 19
  renovate 163
REPRODUCTION 163
  copy 21
reproductive 163
reproof 932
reprove *berate* 527
  disapprove 932
reptile *animal* 366
  knave 941, 949
republic 372, 737
republican 737, 876
repudiate *deny* 489
  reject 610
  abrogate 756
  violate 773
repugnance
  contrariety 14
  dislike 867
  hate 898
repugnant 24, 867
repulse *repel* 289, 764
  resist 719
  failure 732
REPULSION 289, 719
REPULSIVE [see repulse]
  unsavory 395
  ugly 846
  disliked 867
  hateful 898
reputable *honored* 873
reputation 873
REPUTE 873
REQUEST 765
requiem *lament* 839
require *need* 630
  exact 741
  compel 744
  demand 924
  behoove 926
REQUIREMENT 630
requisite 630
requisition 630, 765
requital 148, 718
requite 973
rescind *abrogate* 756
  refuse 764
rescue *deliver* 672
  aid 707
research 461
resemblance 17
resemble 17, 23
resent 900
RESENTMENT 900

reservation
  concealment 528
reserve
  concealment 526, 528
  means 632
  store 636
  shyness 881
reservoir 153, 636
reside 186
residence 189
resident 186, 188
residential 186
residue 40
residuum *remainder* 40
  dregs 653
resign *give up* 757
  relinquish 782
  -oneself *submit* 725
  not mind 826
RESIGNATION
  [see resign]
  submission 725
  abdication 757
  endurance 831
  humility 879
resigned 743
resilience *elasticity* 325
RESIN 356a
resinous 356a
resist *oppose* 179
  withstand 719
  refuse 764
RESISTANCE 708, 719
  [see resist]
resistless 159
resolute *determined* 604
  brave 861
RESOLUTION
  [see resolve]
  conversion 144
  topic 454
  mental energy 604
  intention 620
  courage 861
resolve *discover* 480a
  determine 604
  intend 620
resonance *repetition* 104
  sound 402
  ringing 408
resort, *n.* 189
resort, *v.* 72
  -to be present 186
  employ 677
resound 408
resourceful 698
resources *means* 632
  wealth 803
RESPECT, *n. fame* 873
  deference 928
respect, *v. observe* 772
  regard 928
respectability
  mediocrity 736
  probity 939
respectable

S

shoals *rocks* 667

shock, *n. cluster* **72**
concussion 276
seizure 655
excitement 82
ordeal 828

shock, *v. startle* 508
agitate 824
repel 830, 867
scandalize 932

shocking *bad* 649
painful 830
fearful 860
disreputable 874
hateful 898

shoe 225

shoot, *n. tendril* 367

shoot, *v. expand* 194
dart 274
propel 284
kill 361
pain 378

shop 799

shopkeeper 797

shoplifter 792

shoplifting 791

shore 231, 342

shore up 215

shorn 51

short *incomplete* 53
not long 201
brittle 328
concise 572
uncivil 895
-commons
fasting 956
-cut straight 246
-of lacking 38

shortage 53

SHORTCOMING
inequality 28
inferiority 34
incompletness 53
motion short of **304**

shorten 36, 38, 201

shorthand 590

short-lived 111

SHORTNESS 201

shortsighted *myopic* 442
misjudging 481

shot, *n.* 727

shotgun 727

shoulder, *v.* 215

shout *cry* 406, 411
cheer 838

shove 276

shovel 191

show, *n. opportunity* 134
drama 599
ornament 847
parade 882

show, *v. appear* **446, 448**
draw attention 457
evince 467
demonstrate 478
manifest 525

-off *display* 882
boast 884
-up *censure* 932
accuse 938

shower *assemblage* **72**
rain 348

showy *ugly* 846
ornamental 847
tawdry 851
ostentatious 882

shrapnel 727

shred 32, 205

shrew 901

shrewd *knowing* 490
wise 498
cunning 702

shriek 410, 411

shrift 952

shrill 404, 410

shrine 1000

shrink *decrease* 36
shrivel 195
avoid 623
blench 822
fear 860

shrive 952

shrivel 195, 258

shroud, *n.* 223, 363

shroud, *v. invest* 225
hide 528

shrub *plant* 367

shrug 550

shrunk 195

shudder *shiver* 383
fear 860
-at *hate* 898

shuffle *change* 140, 149
move slowly 275
prevaricate 544
palter 605

shun *avoid* 623
dislike 867

shut 261
-out *exclude* 55
prohibit 761
-up 751

shutter 424

shuttle *alternate* 314

shy, *adj.* 862, 881

shy, *v. deviate* 279
draw back 283
propel 284
avoid 623, 860

Shylock 787

SIBILATION *hiss* **409**

sibyl *oracle* 513

sick *ill* 655
-of *averse* 867
satiated 869

sicken *nauseate* 395
pain 830
weary 841
disgust 867

sickle 253

sickly *weak* 160

sickness 655

SIDE *edge* 231
laterality **236**
party 712
-by side **712**
-issue 39
-with *aid* 707
co-operate **709**

side arms 727

sidelong 236

sidereal 318

sidetrack 279

sidewalk 627

sidewise 217, **236**

sidle 217, 236, 279

siege 716

siesta 683

sieve 219, **260**

sift *simplify* **42**
inquire 461
clean 652

sigh 839

sight *vision* 441
appearance 448
prodigy 872

sightless *blind* 442

sight-seeing 441

sight-seer 444

sign, *n. omen* 512
indication 550
prodigy 872

sign, *v. attest* 467, 550

signal, *n. light* 423
sign 550

signal, *adj. great* 31
eventful 151

signalize *indicate* 550
celebrate 883

signature 467

signet 550, 747

significant **642**
[see signify]

signify *forebode* 511
mean 516
indicate 550

SILENCE, *n.* 403, 585

silence, *v. confute* 479
gag 581
quell 731

silencer 408a

silent 403, 585

silhouette *outline* 230

silken 255

sill 215

silly *credulous* 846
imbecile 499

silo 636

silt *dirt* 653

silver, *n. money* 800

silver, *adj. white* 430
gray 432

SIMILARITY 9, 17, 27

simile *similarity* 17
comparison 464
metaphor 521

similitude *copy* 21

simmer *boil* 382, 384

moderate 174
mollify *324*
pity 914
palliate *937*
softening *324*
softhearted 914
softness *324*
soggy 339
soil, *n. land* **342**
soil, *v. dirty* **653**
soiree 892
sojourn *dwell* 186
solace *relief* 834
solar 318
solder, *n.* 45
solder, *v.* 43, 46
soldier 726
sole, *n. base* 211
sole, *adj. alone* 87
SOLECISM 568
solemn *soft* **403**
grave 837
solemnization 883
solicit *request* 765
solicitor *lawyer* 758, **968**
petitioner 767
solicitude *care* 459
pain 828
anxiety 860
solid *stable* 140
dense 321
exact 494
-body **321**
solidarity 52
solidify 46, 321
solidity [*see* solid]
solvency 800
SOLILOQUY **589**
solitary *alone* 87
solitude 893
solo 415
soluble 335
solution *fluid* 333
answer 462
explanation 522
solve *discover* **480**a
unriddle 522
solvency 800 [*see* solvent]
solvent, *n. liquefier* 335
solvent, *adj. sound* **800**
somber *dark* **421**
dull 428
sad 837
some 25
somebody 372
somehow 631
somersault 218
something 3
sometimes 136
somewhat *a little* 32
somewhere 182
son 167
Son, God the 976
sonant 402
sonata 415
song *music* 415

songbird 416
songster 416
sonnet 597
sonorous 402, 404
soon *future* **121**
early 132
expected **507**
soot 653
soothe *allay* 174
relieve 834
soothing 834
soothsayer 513
sop, *n. inducement* 615
sop, *v.* 339
sophism 477
sophisticated 498, 698
SOPHISTRY 477
soporific *sleepy* 683
soprano 410
SORCERER 548, **994**
sorceress 994
SORCERY 511, **992**
sordid *stingy* 819
covetous 865
sore, *n* 378
sore, *adj. acute* 830
discontented 832
angry 900
sorely *very* 31
sorority 712
sorrow 735, 828
sorry *trifling* 643
grieved 828
mean 876
sort, *n. kind* 75
sort, *v. arrange* 60
sortie 716
sot *drunkard* 959
sough *faint sound* 405
soul *essence* 5
person 372
intellect 450
affections **820**
SOUND, *n. strait* 343
noise 402
sound, *adj. strong* 159
true 494
sane 502
perfect 650
healthy 654
solvent 800
orthodox 983a
sound, *v. fathom* **208**
resound 408
investigate 461
measure 466
sounding 402
soundings 208
sour, *adj. acid* 397
uncivil 895
sour, *v. embitter* 825
source *beginning* 66
cause 153
soured *glum* 832
SOURNESS 397
souse *plunge* 310

south 278
southern **237**
souvenir 505
sovereign, *n. ruler* 745
sovereign, *adj.* 737
sovereignty 737
sow, *n. pig* 366
sow, *v. scatter* 73
cultivate 371
SPACE, *n. music* 26
time 106
extension **180**
space, *v. arrange* 60
spacious **180**
spade 272
span, *n. pair* 89
time 106
distance 196
length 200
team 272
span, *v. join* 43
link 45
measure 466
spangle *ornament* 847
spank *flog* 992
spar *quarrel* 713
contend 720
spare, *adj. additional* 37
meager 203, 640
redundant 641
economical 817
spare, *v. not do* 681
relinquish 782
give 784
exempt 927a
sparing [*see* spare]
small 32
economical 817
parsimonious 819
spark 120, 423
sparkle *glisten* 420
sparkling *spirited* 574
cheerful 836
witty 842
sparse 73, 103
sparseness 32, 73, 103
spasm
sudden change **146**
violence 173
agitation 315
pain 378
spasmodic *irregular* 139
violent 173
spatter *dirt* 653
spawn 168
speak 580, **582**
speaker 524, **581**
chairman 694
spear, *n. weapon* **727**
spear, *v. pierce* 260
special *particular* **79**
speciality 79
specialize 79
SPECIALTY **79**
specie 800
species *kind* 75

spurious *deceptive* 545
  illegitimate 925
spurn *reject* 610
  disdain 866, 930
spurt *sprint* 274
  gush 348
spy, *n.* 444, 664
spy, *v.* 441
squabble 713
squad 72, 726
squadron 726
squalid *dirty* 653
  unsightly 846
squall, *n.* 349
squall, *v. cry* 411
squalor 653
squander 776, 818
square, *n. four* 95
  place 182
  rectangle 244
  measure 466
square, *adj. just* 922, 924
square, *v. compensate* 30
squash *quell* 162
  pulp 354
squat, *v.* 184, 308
squat, *adj. short* 201
  thick 202
  low 207
squatter 188
squaw 374
squeak *cry* 411
squeal 411
squeamish *sick* 655
  fastidious 868
squeeze *contract* 195
  condense 321
  -out *extract* 301
squib *lampoon* 856
squint, *n.* 443
squint, *v. look* 441
squire *attendant* 746
  gentry 875
squirm 315
squirt *eject* 297
stab *pierce* 260
  kill 361
  pain 649
STABILITY 16, 141, 150
stabilize 150
stable, *n.* 189, 370
stable, *adj.*
  permanent 141, 150
  quiescent 265
stack 72
staff *support* 215
  music 413
  council 696
  cast 712
  weapon 727
  retinue 746
stag *deer* 366
  male 373
  sociality 892
stage *degree* 26
  term 71

time 106
  position 183
  platform 215
  drama 599
stagecoach 272
stagger, *n. be slow* 275
  reel 314, 821
  shake belief 485
  startle 508
  astonish 870
stagnant *inert* 172
  quiescent 265
  unprogressive 659
stagnate 265
stagnation *inertness* 172
  quiescence 265
staid *grave* 837
stain *color* 223, 423
  blemish 848
  disgrace 874
stainless *clean* 652
  honorable 939
  innocent 946
staircase 305
stairs 305
stairway 305
stake *wager* 621
  security 771
  execution 975
stale *old* 124
  insipid 391
stalk, *n.* 215
stalk, *v. walk* 266
  chase 622
stall *cot* 189
  booth 799
stalwart *strong* 159
stamina *strength* 159
STAMMERING 583
stamp *character* 7
  prototype 22
  kind 75
  form 240
  mark 550
  security 771
  -out *extinguish* 385
stampede 860
stanch, *adj.* 939
stanch, *v.* 348
stand, *n. time* 106
  support 215
  quiescence 265
stand, *v. resist* 719
  brook 821
  endure 826
  -by *near* 197
  aid 707
  -fast 141
  -for *indicate* 550
standard *model* 22
  degree 26
  average 29
  rule 80
  measure 466
  flag 550
  perfection 650

standardize 58
standing *footing* 8
  degree 26
  permanence 141
  situation 183
  rank 873
standpatter 150
standpoint 441
stanza 597
staple, *n. whole* 50
  material 635
staple, *adj.* 794
star *luminary* 318, 423
  actor 599
  glory 873
  -s and stripes 550
starched *proud* 878
stare *look* 441
  gape 455
  wonder 870
stark *very* 31
  sheer 32
starry 318
start *begin* 66
  arise 151
  move 284
  depart 293
  leap 309
  offer 763
  fear 860
  wonder 870
startle *doubt* 485
  stagger 508
  fear 860
  amaze 870
starvation [*see* starve]
  insufficiency 640
  fasting 956
starve *be poor* 804
  stint 819
  fast 956
STATE, *n. condition* 7
  position 71
  realm 372, 780
  government 737
state, *v.* 535
statehouse 966
stately *grand* 873
  pompous 882
statement 535
stateroom 191
statesman 694
statesmanship 693
static 319
statics 159, 319
station, *n. degree* 26
  term 71
  situation 183
  journey 266
  prison 752
  rank 873
station, *v. locate* 184
stationary 265
statistical 85
statistics 85, 86
statue 554

discourteous 895
sulky 901a
SULLENNESS 901a
sully *dirty* 653
  dishonor 874
sultan 745
sultry 382
sum *total* 50
  number 84
  money 800
  -up *reckon* 37, 85
  discriminate 465
  review 596
summarize 201, 596
summary, *n.* 596
summary, *adj. transient*
  111
  short 201
  concise 572
summer 125, 382
SUMMIT 33, 210
summon *command* 741
  indict 969
summons 741, 969
sumptuous 882
sun 318, 423
  -god 423
sunbeam 420
sunburnt 433
Sunday 687
sunder 44
sundial 114
sundry 102
sunny *warm* 382
  cheerful 836
sunrise 125
sunset 126
sunshade 223
sunshine 420
sup *feed* 298
superabound 641
superannuated 128, 158
superb 845
supercilious *proud* 878
  insolent 885
  scornful 930
superficial *shallow* 209
  extrinsic 220
  ignorant 491
superficies 220
superfluity 40, 641
superfluous 641
superhuman *godlike* 976
superintend 693
superintendent 694
superior, *n. head* 694
superior, *adj. greater* 33
  high 206
SUPERIORITY 33
superlative 33
superman 33
supernatural 976, 980a
supersede *substitute* 147
  relinquish 782
superstition 486
superstitious 486, 984

supervene *succeed* 117
supervise 693
supervision 693
supervisor 694
supervisory 693
supine *flat* 213, 251
  sluggish 462
supplant 147
supple *soft* 324
supplement 37, 39
suppliant 767
supplicate *beg* 765
supplies 707
supply *store* 636
  provide 637
  give 784
  -deficiencies 52
SUPPORT, *n. footing* 175
  foundation 215
support, *v. perform* 170
  evidence 467
  escort 664
  aid 707
  feel 821
  endure 826
supporter 215
suppose 472, 514
SUPPOSITION 514
suppress *destroy* 162
  conceal 528
  restrain 751
suppression [*see suppress*]
supremacy 33
supreme *superior* 33
  highest 210
  ruling 737
Supreme Being 976
sure *certain* 474
  safe 664
sure-footed *careful* 459
  skillful 698
  cautious 864
sureness [*see sure*]
surety *certainty* 474
  safety 664
  sponsor 771
surf 348, 353
surface 220
surfeit *redundance* 641
  satiety 869
surge *swarm* 72
  swell 305
  wave 348
surgeon 662
surgery 662
surly *gruff* 895
  sullen 901a
surmise 514
surmount *tower* 206
  overtop 210
  ascend 305
surname 564
surpass *be superior* 33
  go beyond 303
  outshine 873
surplus *remainder* 40

redundance 33, 641
surprise, *n.* 508
surprise, *v.*
  take unawares 674
  wonder 870
surrender *submit* 725
  relinquish 782
surreptitious
  furtive 528
  deceptive 545
surround 227
surrounding 227
surroundings 227
surveillance *care* 459
  direction 693
survey *view* 441
  measure 466
surveyor 466
survive *remain* 40, 141
  outlast 110
susceptibility
  tendency 176
  sensibility 375
  impressibility 822
suspect *doubt* 485, 920
  suppose 514
suspend *defer* 133
  discontinue 142
  hang 214
suspense *cessation* 142
  uncertainty 475
  irresolution 605
suspension *lateness* 133
  cessation 142
  hanging 214
suspicion *doubt* 485
  supposition 514
  fear 860
  jealousy 920
suspicious 485
sustain *continue* 143
  strengthen 159
  support 215
  aid 707
  endure 821
sustenance 298, 707
sustentation [*see sustain*]
swab *dry* 340
  clean 652
swag *booty* 793
swagger, *n. pride* 878
swagger, *v. boast* 884
  bluster 885
swain *man* 373
  rustic 876
  lover 897
swallow, *n.* 366
swallow, *v. gulp* 296
  be credulous 486
  brook 826
swamp, *n. marsh* 345
swamp, *v.* 162
swampy 345
swan 366
swap *exchange* 148
  barter 794

swarm, *n. crowd* **72**
  multitude 102
swarm, *v. climb* **305**
swarthy **431**
swath **72**
swathe *clothe* **225**
sway, *n. power* **157**
  influence 175
  agitation 315
  authority 737
sway, *v. influence* **175, 615**
  lean 217
  oscillate 314
swear *affirm* **535**
  promise 768
sweat, *n. excretion* **299**
  fatigue 688
sweat, *v.* **295, 382, 686**
sweater **225**
sweep, *n. space* **180**
  curve 245
sweep, *v. curve* **245**
  speed 274
  clean 652
sweeping *whole* **50**
  complete 52
  inclusive 76
  general 78
sweepings **645**
sweet *saccharine* **396**
  melodious 413
  clean 652
  lovely 897
sweeten **396**
sweetheart **897**
SWEETNESS **396**
sweets **396**
swell, *n. bulge* **250**
  wave 348
  blare 404
  fop 854

swell, *v. increase* **31**
  expand 194
swelter **382**
swerve *change* **140**
  deviate 279
swift **274**
swim **267, 320**
swindle *cheat* **545**
  peculate 791
swindler *cheat* **548**
  thief 792
swine **366**
swing, *n. operation* **170**
  space 180
  freedom 748
swing, *v. hang* **214**
  oscillate 314
swirl **348**
swish **409**
switch, *n. rod* **975**
switch, *v. deviate* **279**
  flog 972
swollen **194, 250**
swoon **158, 688**
swoop *descend* **274**
  seize 789
sword **727**
swordsman **726**
Sybarite **954a**
sycophant **65, 886**
syllable **561**
syllabus *list* **86**
  compendium 596
sylvan **367**
symbol *sign* **550**
symbolic *latent* **526**
  indicative 550
symbolize *involve* **526**
  indicate 550
  represent 554
symmetrical **27, 242**

SYMMETRY
  equality 27
  regular form **242**
  beauty 845
sympathetic
  [*see* sympathy]
sympathizer **914**
sympathize with **906**
sympathy
  feeling 821
  love 897
  kindness 906
  pity 914
  condolence 915
symphony *music* **415**
symposium **72, 596**
symptom **553**
synagogue **1000**
synchronism **120**
syndicate *council* **696**
  league 712
synod **696**
synodic (al) **696**
synonym **522**
synonymous **27, 516**
synopsis **86, 596**
syntax **567**
synthesis
  combination 48
  reasoning 476
synthetic **476**
syringe, *v.* **337**
syrup [*see* sirup]
system *order* **58**
  rule 80
  plan 626
systematic **60, 80**
systematize *order* **58**
  arrange 60
  organize 357
  plan 626

T

tabernacle **189, 1000**
table, *n. arrangement* **60**
  list 86
  support 215, 251
  repast 298
table, *v. defer* **133, 460**
tableau **448, 599**
tableland **344**
tablet **251, 551**
taboo *prohibited* **761**
tabular **60**
tabulate **60, 69, 86**
tabulation **551**
tacit *implied* **516**
  latent 526
TACITURNITY **585**
tack, *n. direction* **278**
tack, *v. change course* **140**
  turn 279
tackle, *n. fastening* **45**
  gear 633

tackle, *v. undertake* **676**
  manage 693
tact *discrimination* **465**
  wisdom 498
  skill 698
tactful [*see* tact]
  affable 894
tactics *conduct* **692**
  warfare 722
tactlessness **895**
tactual **379**
tag, *n. addition* **37**
  sequel 65
  end 67
tag, *v. follow* **63, 235**
tail **65, 67, 235**
taint, *n. imperfection* **651**
  disease 659
  disgrace 874
taint, *v.* **659**
take *receive* **785**

  appropriate 788, **789**
-after 17
-away *subtract* 38
  remove 185
  seize 789
-from *subtract* 38
  seize 789
-in *shorten* 201
  admit 296
  understand 518
  deceive 545
-place 1, 151
-to *like* 827
  desire 865
  love 897
-up *pursue* 622
  undertake 676
  use 677
taker **789**
TAKING **789**
tale *counting* **85**

U

W

wash *color* 428
 cleanse 652
 -out *discolor* 429
 obliterate 552
washerman 652
washerwoman 652
washhouse 652
washing 337
washout 348
WASTE, *n. decrement* 40a
 desert 169
 space 180
 consumption 638
 rubbish 645
 loss 776
 prodigality 818
waste, *v. decrease* 36
 destroy 162
 contract 195
 consume 638
 injure 659
 -time 135
wasted *weak* 160
 deteriorated 659
wasteful 638, 818
watch, *n. company* 72
 timepiece 114
 sentinel 668
watch, *v. observe* 441
 attend to 457, 459
 guard 664
 -for 507
watchdog 263, 668
watcher 459
watchful 459
 -waiting *inaction* 681
 caution 864
watchman *guardian* 664
 sentinel 668
watchtower 550, 668
watchword *sign* 550
WATER 337
watercourse 350
water drinker 958
waterfall 348
waterman 269
waterproof, *n. dress* 225
waterproof, *adj.* 340, 664
waterspout 348
watertight 340, 664
watery *wet* 337
 moist 339
wave, *n.* 248, 348
wave, *v. oscillate* 314
waver *change* 149
 doubt 485
 vacillate 605
waverer 605
wavy 248
wax, *n.* 356
wax, *v. increase* 31
 become 144
 expand 194
way *opening* 260
 habit 613
 road 627

wayfarer 268
wayfaring 266
waylay 545
ways 692
wayward *changeable* 149
 obstinate 606
 capricious 608
wayworn 266
weak *feeble* 160
 insipid 391
 illogical 477
 irresolute 605
 lax 738
 vicious 945
weaken *decrease* 36
 diminish 38
 enfeeble 160
 refute 468
weakly *feeble* 160
 unhealthy 655
weak-minded 499
WEAKNESS 160, 945
WEALTH *riches* 803
wean 614
weapon *arms* 727
wear, *n. use* 677
 -and tear *waste* 638
 injury 659
wear, *v. decrease* 36
 dress 225
 deflect 279
 -away *cease* 142
 -off 614
WEARINESS *ennui* 841
wearisome *slow* 275
 laborious 686
 painful 830
weary *fatigue* 688, 841
 sad 837
weather 338
 -prophet 513
 -vane 550
weathercock
 changeableness 149
 vane 349, 550
weatherproof 664
weather vane 338
weave *compose* 54
 interlace 219
web 219
wed 903
wedded 903
wedding 903
wedge 633
wedlock 43, 903
weed, *n. plant* 367
 cigar 392
weed, *v. cultivate* 371
 clean 652
 -out *eliminate* 55
 thin 103
 eject 297
 extract 301
ween *believe* 484
 know 490
weep *lament* 839

weeping 839
weft 329
weigh *influence* 175
 load 319
 ponder 451
weight *influence* 175
 gravity 319
 vigor 574
 importance 642
 have - *evidence* 467
weighty 319, 642
 significant 467
weir 232, 350
weird *spectral* 980a
welcome, *n.* 892
welcome, *adj.*
 grateful 829
 friendly 888
welcome, *v.* 894
weld *join* 43
welfare 734
well, *n. origin* 153
 depth 208
 pool 343
well, *adj. good* 618
 healthy 654
well, *v. flow* 348
well behaved
 courteous 894
well being 734, 827
well beloved 897
well bred 852, 894
well founded *existent* 1
 certain 474
 true 494
well grounded
 existent 1
 informed 490
well known 490
well laid 611
well nigh *almost* 32
well off *prosperous* 734
 rich 803
well timed 134
well-wisher 890, 906, 914
welter 310, 311
wench *girl* 129
wend 266
west 236
western 236
wet, *adj.* 339, 348
wet, *v.* 337
whack 276
whale 366
wharf 189, 231
wheedle *coax* 615
 caress 902
 flatter 933
wheedler 615
wheel, *n. circle* 247
 bicycle 272
wheel, *v. deviate* 279
 turn back 283
 turn 311
 rotate 312
wheelbarrow 272

X

Y

Z

FOREIGN WORDS AND PHRASES

à bas. [F.] Down, down with.

ab initio. [L.] From the beginning.

à bon marché. [F.] Cheap; a good bargain.

ab origine. [L.] From the origin.

ab ovo. [L.] From the egg; from the beginning.

à cheval. [F.] On horseback.

addenda. [L.] Things to be added; list of additions.

ad finem. [L.] To the end.

ad hoc. [L.] To or with respect to this (object); said of a body elected or appointed for a definite work (as a school board for education).

ad infinitum. [L.] To infinity.

ad libitum. [L.] At pleasure; as much as one pleases.

ad nauseam. [L.] To the point of disgust or satiety.

ad rem. [L.] To the purpose; to the point.

adsum. [L.] I am present; here!

ad valorem. [L.] According to the value.

advocatus diaboli. [L.] Devil's advocate; a person chosen to dispute before the papal court the claims of a candidate for canonization.

æquo animo. [L.] With an equable mind; with equanimity.

ære perennius. [L.] More lasting than brass (or bronze).

affaire d'amour. [F.] A love affair.

affaire de cœur. [F.] An affair of the heart.

affaire d'honneur. [F.] An affair of honor; a duel.

a fortiori. [L.] With stronger reason.

Agnus Dei. [L.] Lamb of God.

à haute voix. [F.] Aloud.

à la belle étoile. [F.] Under the stars; in the open air.

à la bonne heure. [F.] In good time; very well.

à la carte. [F.] According to the bill of fare.

à la mode. [F.] According to the custom (or fashion).

al fresco. [It.] In the open air.

alter ego. [L.] Another self.

amende honorable. [F.] Satisfactory apology; reparation.

à merveille. [F.] Admirably; marvelously.

amour propre. [F.] Self-love; vanity.

ancien régime. [F.] The former order of things.

anglice. [NL.] In the English language or fashion.

anguis in herba. [L.] A snake in the grass; an unsuspected danger.

anno urbis conditæ. [L.] In the year (or from the time) of the founded city (Rome).

à outrance. [F.] To the utmost.

aperçu. [F.] A general sketch or survey.

à perte de vue. [F.] Till beyond one's view.

à peu près. [F.] Nearly.

à pied. [F.] On foot.

a posteriori. [L.] From effect to cause; empirical.

a priori. [L.] From cause to effect; presumptive.

arbiter elegantiarum. [L.] A judge or supreme authority in matters of taste.

arcana imperii. [L.] State secrets.

argumentum ad hominem. [L.] An argument to the individual man; *i.e.*, to his interests and prejudices.

arrière-pensée. [F.] Mental reservation.

ars est celare artem. [L.] It is true art to conceal art.

ars longa, vita brevis. [L.] Art is long, life is short.

au contraire. [F.] On the contrary.

au courant. [F.] Fully acquainted with matters.

au désespoir. [F.] In despair.

au fait. [F.] Well acquainted with; expert.

au fond. [F.] At bottom.

au reste. [F.] As for the rest; besides.

au revoir. [F.] Until we meet again.

autant d'hommes, autant d'avis. [F.] So many men, so many minds.

avant-propos. [F.] Preliminary matter; preface.

à votre santé! [F.] To your health!

ballon d'essai. [F.] A trial balloon; a device to test opinion.

bas bleu. [F.] A bluestocking; a literary woman.

beau idéal. [F.] The ideal of perfection.

beau monde. [F.] The world of fashion.

beaux esprits. [F.] Men of wit.

beaux yeux. [F.] Fine eyes; good looks.

bel esprit. [F.] A person of wit or genius; a brilliant mind.

ben trovato. [It.] Well found.

bête noire. [F.] A bugbear; a special aversion; *lit.*, black beast.

bis dat qui cito dat. [L.] He gives twice who gives quickly.

bona fides (bona fide). [L.] Good faith (in good faith).

bon ami. [F.] Good friend.

bon gré, mal gré. [F.] With good or ill grace; willing or unwilling.

bon jour. [F.] Good day; good morning.

bon mot. [F.] A witty saying.

bonne foi. [F.] Good faith.

bon naturel. [F.] Good nature.

bon soir. [F.] Good evening.

bon ton. [F.] Fashionable society; good style.

bon vivant. [F.] A lover of good living; a gourmet.

bon voyage! [F.] A good voyage or journey to you!

campo santo. [It.] A burying-ground; *lit.*, a holy field.

canaille. [F.] Rabble.

carpe diem. [L.] Enjoy the present day; improve the time.

casus belli. [L.] That which causes or justifies war.

catalogue raisonné. [F.] A catalogue arranged according to subjects.

cause célèbre. [F.] A celebrated or notorious case (in law).

caveat emptor. [L.] Let the purchaser beware (*i.e.*, he buys at his own risk).

cave canem. [L.] Beware of the dog.

cela va sans dire. [F.] That goes without saying; that is a matter of course.

c'est-à-dire. [F.] That is to say.

c'est égal. [F.] It's all one.

c'est magnifique, mais ce n'est pas la guerre. [F.] It is magnificent, but it is not war.

c'est autre chose. [F.] That's quite another thing.

ceteris paribus. [L.] Other things being equal.

chacun à son goût. [F.] Every one to his taste.

chef-d'œuvre. [F.] Masterpiece.

cherchez la femme. [F.] Look for the woman (who is at the bottom of the affair).

chère amie. [F.] A dear (female) friend.

chevalier d'industrie. [F.] One who lives by his wits; a swindler.

ci-gît. [F.] Here lies.

circa. [L.] About.

cogito, ergo sum. [L.] I think, therefore I exist.

comme il faut. [F.] As it should be; in good form.

compte rendu. [F.] An account rendered; a report.

con amore. [It.] With love; very earnestly.

confrère. [F.] Colleague.

contretemps. [F.] An unexpected or untoward event; a hitch.

coram populo. [L.] Publicly; in public.

corpus delicti. [L.] The body of the crime.

corrigenda. [L.] Things to be corrected; a list of errors.

coup. [F.] A stroke.—**coup d'essai,** a first attempt.—**coup d'état,** a sudden decisive blow in politics; a stroke of policy.—**coup de grâce,** a finishing stroke.—**coup de main,** a sudden attack or enterprise.—**coup de maître,** a master stroke.—**coup d'œil,** a rapid glance of the eye.—**coup de pied,** a kick.—**coup de soleil,** sunstroke.—**coup de théâtre,** a theatrical effect.

coûte que coûte. [F.] Cost what it may.

credat Judæus Apella. [L.] Let Apella, the superstitious Jew, believe it; I won't.

credo quia absurdum. [L.] I believe because it is absurd, or contrary to reason.

cui bono? [L.] For whose advantage?

cul-de-sac. [F.] A blind alley (often used figuratively).

cum grano salis. [L.] With a grain of salt; with some allowance.

d'accord. [F.] In agreement.

débâcle. [F.] The break-up of ice in a river; *hence*, a general, confused rout.

de bonne grâce. [F.] With good grace; willingly.

de facto. [L.] In point of fact; actual or actually.

dégagé. [F.] Free; easy; unconstrained.

de gustibus non est disputandum. [L.] There is no disputing about tastes.

Dei gratia. [L.] By the grace of God.

de jure. [L.] From the law; by right.

delenda est Carthago. [L.] Carthage must be destroyed.

de mortuis nil nisi bonum. [L.] (Say) nothing but good of the dead.

dénoûement. [F.] The issue; the end of a plot.

de novo. [L.] Anew.

Deo gratias. [L.] Thanks to God.

de profundis. [L.] Out of the depths.

de rigueur. [F.] Indispensable; obligatory.

dernier ressort. [F.] A last resort.

de trop. [F.] Too much; more than is wanted; out of place.

deus ex machina. [L.] A god from a machine; used in reference to forced or unlikely events introduced in a drama, novel, etc., to resólve a difficult or awkward situation; derived from the use of deities in the ancient drama.

dies iræ. [L.] Day of wrath.

Dieu et mon droit. [F.] God and my right (British royal motto).

distingué. [F.] Distinguished; of elegant appearance.

dolce far niente. [It.] Sweet doing-nothing; sweet idleness.

Dominus vobiscum. [L.] The Lord be with you.

double entente (or, esp. in English, entendre). [F.] A double meaning; a play upon words.

dramatis personæ. [L.] Characters of the drama or play.

dulce et decorum est pro patria mori. [L.] It is sweet and glorious to die for one's country.

dum spiro, spero. [L.] While I breathe, I hope.

dum vivimus, vivamus. [L.] While we live, let us live.

ecce homo. [L.] Behold the man!

édition de luxe. [F.] A splendid and expensive edition of a book.

editio princeps. [L.] The first printed edition of a book.

ego et rex meus. [L.] I and my king.

élite. [F.] The best part; the pick.

emeritus. [L.] Retired or superannuated after long service.

en avant. [F.] Forward.

en déshabillé. [F.] In undress.

en effet. [F.] In effect; substantially; really.

en famille. [F.] With one's family; in a domestic state.

enfant gâté. [F.] A spoiled child.

enfants perdus. [F.] Lost children; a forlorn hope.

enfant terrible. [F.] A terrible child, *that is*, one who makes disconcerting remarks.

enfant trouvé. [F.] A foundling.

enfin. [F.] In short; at last; finally.

en masse. [F.] In a mass (*or* body).

en rapport. [F.] In harmony; in agreement.

en route. [F.] On the way.

en suite. [F.] In company; in a set.

entente cordiale. [F.] Cordial understanding, especially between two states.

entourage. [F.] Surroundings; friends, confidants, etc., closely associated with a person.

entre nous. [F.] Between ourselves.

en vérité. [F.] In truth; verily.

e pluribus unum. [L.] One out of many; one composed of many (motto of the United States).

errata. [L.] Errors; list of errors.

esprit de corps. [F.] The animating spirit of a collective body, *as* a regiment.

est modus in rebus. [L.] There is a medium in all things.

et cætera (or et cetera.) [L.] And the rest.

et id genus omne. [L.] And everything of the sort.

et tu, Brute! [L.] And thou also, Brutus!

eureka! [Gr.] I have found (it)!

Ewigkeit. [G.] Eternity.

ex cathedra. [L.] From the chair; with high authority.

excelsior. [L.] Higher, *that is*, taller, loftier.

exeunt omnes. [L.] All go out (*or* retire).

exit. [L.] He goes out.

ex nihilo nihil fit. [L.] Out of nothing, nothing comes.

ex officio. [L.] In virtue of (his) office.

ex parte. [L.] From one party or side.

ex pede Herculem. [L.] From the foot we recognize a Hercules; we judge of the whole from the specimen.

experto crede. [L.] Trust one who has had experience.

exposé. [F.] A statement; a recital.

ex post facto. [L.] After the deed is done; retrospective.

extra muros. [L.] Beyond the walls.

ex uno disce omnes. [L.] From one judge of the rest.

facile princeps. [L.] Easily preeminent; indisputably the first.

facilis est descensus Averni. [L.] The descent to Avernus (*or* hell) is easy.

façon de parler. [F.] Way of speaking.

fait accompli. [F.] A thing already done.

faux pas. [F.] A false step; a slip in behavior.

femme de chambre. [F.] A chambermaid; lady's maid.

festina lente. [L.] Hasten slowly.

feu de joie. [F.] A discharge of firearms as a sign of rejoicing.

fiat justitia, ruat cœlum. [L.] Let justice be done though the heavens should fall.

fiat lux. [L.] Let there be light.

fides Punica. [L.] Punic (*or*

Carthaginian) faith; treachery.

fidus Achates. [L.] Faithful Achates; a true friend.

fin de siècle. [F.] End of the (nineteenth) century.

finis coronat opus. [L.] The end crowns the work.

flagrante delicto. [L.] In the commission of the crime; redhanded.

fons et origo. [L.] The source and origin.

force majeure. [F.] Greater force or strength; overwhelming force; compulsion.

fortiter in re. [L.] With firmness in acting.

fortuna favet fortibus. [L.] Fortune favors the bold.

furor loquendi. [L.] A rage for speaking.

furor scribendi. [L.] A rage for writing.

gaucherie. [F.] Awkwardness.

gaudeamus igitur. [L.] So let us be joyful.

genius loci. [L.] The genius (*or* guardian spirit) of a place.

gens d'armes. [F.] Men at arms.

gloria in excelsis (Deo). [L.] Glory (to God) in the highest.

gloria Patri. [L.] Glory be to the Father.

goût. [F.] Taste; relish.

grâce à Dieu. [F.] Thanks to God.

habitué. [F.] One in the habit of frequenting a place.

hic et ubique. [L.] Here and everywhere.

hic jacet. [L.] Here lies.

hinc illæ lacrimæ. [L.] Hence these tears.

hodie mihi, cras tibi. [L.] Mine today; yours tomorrow.

hoi polloi. [Gr.] The many; the vulgar; the rabble.

homme d'esprit. [F.] A man of wit or genius.

homo sum; humani nihil a me alienum puto. [L.] I am a man; I count nothing human indifferent to me.

honi soit qui mal y pense. [O. F.] Shamed be he who thinks evil of it (motto of the Order of the Garter).

horribile dictu. [L.] Horrible to relate.

hors de combat. [F.] Out of the combat; disabled.

hors d'œuvre. [F.] A relish.

hôtel de ville. [F.] A town hall.

hôtel-Dieu. [F.] A hospital.

humanum est errare. [L.] To err is human.

ibidem. [L.] At the same place (in a book).

ich dien. [G.] I serve (motto of the Prince of Wales).

ici on parle français. [F.] French is spoken here.

ignotum per ignotius. [L.] The unknown (explained) by the still more unknown.

il n'y a pas de quoi. [F.] Don't mention it; it's not worth speaking of.

il n'y a que le premier pas qui coûte. [F.] It is only the first step that costs.

il penseroso. [It.] The pensive man.

impasse. [F.] A deadlock; an insurmountable difficulty.

impedimenta. [L.] Encumbrances; luggage; baggage.

in æternum. [L.] Forever.

in articulo mortis. [L.] At the point of death; in the last struggle.

index expurgatorius. [L.] A list of prohibited works.

in esse. [L.] In being; in actuality.

in extenso. [L.] At full length.

in extremis. [L.] At the point of death.

infra dignitatem. [L.] Below one's dignity.

in loco. [L.] In the place; in the natural (*or* proper) place.

in loco parentis. [L.] In the place of a parent.

in medias res. [L.] Into the midst of things.

in memoriam. [L.] To the memory of; in memory.

in nomine. [L.] In the name of.

in omnia paratus. [L.] Prepared for all things.

in perpetuum. [L.] Forever.

in posse. [L.] In possible existence; in possibility.

in præsenti. [L.] At the present moment.

in propria persona. [L.] In one's own person.

in puris naturalibus. [L.] Quite naked.

in re. [L.] In the matter of.

in rerum natura. [L.] In the nature of things.

in sæcula sæculorum. [L.] For ages on ages.

in situ. [L.] In its original position.

in statu quo. [L.] In the former state.

inter alia. [L.] Among other things.

inter nos. [L.] Between ourselves.

in terrorem. [L.] As a warning.

in toto. [L.] In the whole; entirely.

intra muros. [L.] Within the walls.

in transitu. [L.] In course of transit.

in vacuo. [L.] In empty space; in a vacuum.

in vino veritas. [L.] There is truth in wine; truth is told under the influence of liquor.

invita Minerva. [L.] Against the will of Minerva; without genius or natural abilities.

ipse dixit. [L.] He himself said it; a dogmatic saying or assertion.

ipsissima verba. [L.] The very words.

ipso facto. [L.] By that very fact.

ipso jure. [L.] By the law itself.

jacquerie. [F.] French peasantry; a revolt of peasants.

je ne sais quoi. [F.] I know not what; a something or other.

jeu de mots. [F.] A play on words; a pun.

jeu d'esprit. [F.] A display of wit; a witticism.

jeunesse dorée. [F.] Gilded youth; rich and fashionable young men.

jubilate Deo. [L.] Rejoice in God; be joyful in the Lord.

jure divino. [L.] By divine law.

jure humano. [L.] By human law.

juste milieu. [F.] The golden mean.

laborare est orare. [L.] To labor is to pray; work is worship.

labor omnia vincit. [L.] Labor conquers everything.

laissez-faire. [F.] Let alone; noninterference.

l'allegro. [It.] The merry man.

lapsus calami. [L.] A slip of the pen.

lapsus linguæ. [L.] A slip of the tongue.

lapsus memoriæ. [L.] A slip of the memory.

lares et penates. [L.] Household gods.

lasciate ogni speranza voi ch'entrate. [It.] All hope abandon ye who enter here (inscription on the entrance to the hell of Dante's Inferno).

laudator temporis acti. [L.] A praiser of past times.

laus Deo. [L.] Praise to God.

l'avenir. [F.] The future.

le beau monde. [F.] The fashionable world.

lebe wohl. [G.] Farewell.

la grand monarque. [F.] The great monarch; Louis XIV of France.

le pas. [F.] Precedence in place or rank.

le roi est mort, vive le roi! [F.] The king is dead, long live the king (his successor)!

le roy le veult. [Norm. F.] The king wills it; the formula used by the sovereign in assenting to a bill.

le roy s'avisera. [Norm. F.] The king will consider; the formula formerly used by the sovereign in rejecting a bill.

lèse-majesté. [F.] High treason.

l'état c'est moi. [F.] It is I who am the state.

le tout ensemble. [F.] The whole (taken) together.

lettre de cachet. [F.] A sealed letter containing private orders; a royal warrant.

lex non scripta. [L.] Unwritten law; common law.

lex scripta. [L.] Statute law.

l'homme propose, et Dieu dispose. [F.] Man proposes, and God disposes.

l'inconnu. [F.] The unknown.

littera scripta manet. [L.] The written word remains.

locum tenens. [L.] One occupying the place of another; a substitute.

longo intervallo. [L.] By or at a long interval.

lucus a non lucendo. [L.] Used as typical of an absurd derivation—*lucus*, a grove, having been derived by an old grammarian from *luceo*, to shine—"from not shining."

lusus naturæ. [L.] A sport or freak of nature.

ma chère. [F.] My dear (fem.).

ma foi. [F.] Upon my faith.

magna est veritas, et prevalebit. [L.] Truth is mighty, and will prevail.

magnum opus. [L.] A great work.

maison de santé. [F.] A private asylum *or* hospital.

maître d'hôtel. [F.] A house steward.

mala fide. [L.] With bad faith; treacherously.

mal-à-propos. [F.] Ill-timed; out of place.

mal de mer. [F.] Seasickness.

malgré nous. [F.] In spite of us.

mañana. [Sp.] Tomorrow.

mardi gras. [F.] Shrove Tuesday.

mare clausum. [L.] A closed sea; a sea belonging to a single nation.

mariage de convenance. [F.] Marriage from motives of interest rather than of love.

materfamilias. [L.] Mother of a family.

matériel. [F.] Baggage and munitions of an army; material equipment as opposed to men.

mauvaise honte. [F.] Bashfulness; shamefacedness.

mauvais goût. [F.] Bad taste.

mauvais sujet. [F.] A bad subject; a worthless scamp.

mea culpa. [L.] My fault; by my fault.

me judice. [L.] I being judge; in my opinion.

mêlée. [F.] A confused conflict.

memento mori. [L.] Remember that you must die; a reminder of death.

mens sana in corpore sano. [L.] A sound mind in a sound body.

mens sibi conscia recti. [L.] A mind conscious of rectitude.

meo periculo. [L.] At my own risk.

mésalliance. [F.] A bad match; marriage with one of a lower rank.

meum et tuum. [L.] Mine and thine.

mirabile dictu. [L.] Wonderful to relate.

mirabile visu. [L.] Wonderful to see.

mise en scène. [F.] Stage setting.

modus operandi. [L.] Manner of working.

modus vivendi. [L.] Manner of living; used of a temporary working agreement or compromise.

mon ami. [F.] My friend (masc.).

mon cher. [F.] My dear (masc.).

mont-de-piété. [F.] A public or municipal pawnshop.

monumentum ære perennius. [L.] A monument more lasting than brass.

more majorum. [L.] After the manner of our ancestors.

morituri te salutamus. [L.] We, about to die, salute thee:— said by the Roman gladiators to the emperor.

mot d'ordre. [F.] Watchword.

motu proprio. [L.] Of his own accord.

moyen âge. [F.] Middle Ages.

multum in parvo. [L.] Much in little.

mutatis mutandis. [L.] With the necessary changes.

natura non facit saltum. [L.] Nature does not make a leap.

née. [F.] Born; used in giving

the maiden name of a married woman.

négligé. [F.] Morning dress; an easy loose dress.

nemine contradicente. [L.] No one speaking in opposition; without opposition.

nemine dissentiente. [L.] No one dissenting; with a dissenting voice.

nemo me impune lacessit. [L.] No one assails me with impunity (motto of Scotland).

ne plus ultra. [L.] Nothing further; the uttermost point; perfection.

ne quid nimis. [L.] Avoid excess.

n'est-ce pas? [F.] Isn't that so?

nicht wahr? [G.] Isn't that so?

nil admirari. [L.] To be astonished at nothing.

nil desperandum. [L.] There is no reason for despair.

n'importe. [F.] It matters not.

nisi Dominus, frustra. [L.] Except the Lord (build the house, they labor) in vain (that build it). Ps. cxxvii. (motto of Edinburgh).

noblesse oblige. [F.] Rank imposes obligations.

Noël. [F.] Christmas.

nolens volens. [L.] Unwilling or willing.

noli me tangere. [L.] Touch me not.

nom de guerre. [F.] A war name; a pseudonym; a pen name.

nom de plume. [F.] A pen name. (Incorrect for *Nom de guerre*.)

non Angli sed angeli. [L.] Not Angles but angels.

non compos mentis. [L.] Not of sound mind.

non est. [L.] He (*or* it) is not.

non est inventus. [L.] He has not been found.

non libet. [L.] It does not please (me).

non liquet. [L.] The case is not clear.

non multa, sed multum. [L.] Not many things, but much.

non nobis solum. [L.] Not for ourselves alone.

non omnis moriar. [L.] I shall not wholly die.

non sequitur. [L.] It does not follow.

nosce te ipsum. [L.] Know thyself.

nota bene. [L.] Note well; take notice.

Notre Dame. [F.] Our Lady.

nous avons changé tout cela. [F.] We have changed all that.

nous verrons. [F.] We shall see.

novus homo. [L.] A new man; one who has raised himself from obscurity.

nuance. [F.] Shade; tint.

nulla dies sine linea. [L.] Not a day without a line; no day without something done.

nunc aut nunquam. [L.] Now or never.

obiit. [L.] He (*or* she) died.

obiter dictum. [L.] A thing said by the way.

odi profanum vulgus. [L.] I loathe the profane rabble.

odium theologicum. [L.] The hatred of theologians.

œuvres. [F.] Works.

ohne Hast, ohne Rast. [G.] Without haste, without rest: —motto of Goethe.

omnia vincit amor. [L.] Love conquers all things.

on dit. [F.] They say.

onus probandi. [L.] The burden of proof.

operæ pretium est. [L.] It is worth while.

ora et labora. [L.] Pray and work.

ora pro nobis. [L.] Pray for us.

ore rotundo. [L.] With round full voice; well-turned speech.

O! si sic omnia. [L.] Oh, if all things (were) so; Oh, if he had always so spoken or acted.

O tempora! O mores! [L.] Alas for the times! Alas for the manners (*or* morals)!

otium cum dignitate. [L.] Ease with dignity.

ouï-dire. [F.] Hearsay.

ouvrage de longue haleine. [F.] A work of long breath; a long work *or* one which lasts.

pace. [L.] By leave of; not to give offence to.

palmam qui meruit ferat. [L.] Let him who has won the palm wear it.

pardonnez-moi. [F.] Pardon me; I beg your pardon.

par excellence. [F.] Pre-eminently.

par exemple. [F.] For example.

par hasard. [F.] By chance.

pari passu. [L.] With equal pace; side by side.

par nobile fratrum. [L.] A noble pair of brothers; two just alike.

parole d'honneur. [F.] Word of honor.

particeps criminis. [L.] An accomplice in a crime.

parti pris. [F.] Preconceived opinion.

parvenu. [L.] A person of low origin who has risen suddenly to wealth or position; an upstart.

pas. [F.] A step; precedence.

passim. [L.] Everywhere; throughout; in all parts of the book, chapter, etc.

pâté de foie gras. [F.] Goose-liver pie.

paterfamilias. [L.] Father of a family; head of a household.

pater patriæ. [L.] Father of his country.

pax vobiscum. [L.] Peace be with you.

peccavi. [L.] I have sinned (*or* been to blame).

peine forte et dure. [F.] Strong and severe punishment; a kind of judicial torture.

penchant. [F.] A strong liking.

pensée. [F.] A thought.

per. [L.] For; through; by.—**per contra.** On the contrary. —**per annum.** By the year; annually.—**per capita.** By heads; for each individual.—**per centum.** By the hundred. —**per diem.** By the day; daily.—**per fas et nefas.** Through right and wrong.—**per se.** By itself.

persona non grata. [L.] An unacceptable person.

peu à peu. [F.] Little by little.

peu de chose. [F.] A trifle.

pièce de résistance. [F.] A resistance piece; the main dish of a meal.

pied-à-terre. [F.] A resting-place; a temporary lodging.

pis aller. [F.] The worst or last shift.

place aux dames. [F.] Make room for the ladies.

plebs. [L.] The common people.

poco a poco. [It.] Little by little.

point d'appui. [F.] Point of support; basis.

pons asinorum. [L.] The asses' bridge; a name for the fifth proposition of the first book in Euclid.

poste restante. [F.] To remain in the post office till called for.

post hoc ergo propter hoc. [L.] After this, therefore, on account of this; subsequent to, therefore due to this—an illogical way of reasoning.

pour faire rire. [F.] To excite laughter.

pour le mèrite. [F.] For merit.

pour passer le temps. [F.] To pass the timè.

preux chevalier. [F.] A brave knight.

prima donna. [It.] First lady; the chief female singer in an opera, etc.

prima facie. [L.] At first view (*or* consideration).

primo. [L.] In the first place.

primum mobile. [L.] The source of motion; the mainspring.

principia, non homines. [L.] Principles, not men.

pro bono publico. [L.] For the good of the public.

procès-verbal. [F.] An authenticated minute or statement.

pro et contra. [L.] For and against.

profanum vulgus. [L.] The profane herd.

pro forma. [L.] For the sake of form.

pro patria. [L.] For our country.

pro rata. [L.] According to rate or proportion.

pro tanto. [L.] For so much; as far as it goes.

protégé. [F.] One under the protection of another.

Punica fides. [L.] Punic (*or* Carthaginian) faith; treachery.

qualis rex, talis grex. [L.] Like king, like people.

quand même. [F.] Even if; whatever may happen.

quantum libet. [L.] As much as you please.

quantum sufficit. [L.] As much as suffices.

quelque chose. [F.] Something; a trifle.

quid pro quo. [L.] Something in return; an equivalent.

quién sabe? [Sp.] Who knows?

quis custodiet ipsos custodes? [L.] Who shall guard the guards themselves?

qui s'excuse s'accuse. [F.] He who excuses himself accuses himself.

qui va là? [F.] Who goes there?

qui vive? [F.] Who lives? Who goes there? **To be on the qui vive** means to be alert or watchful.

quoad hoc. [L.] To this extent.

quoad sacra. [L.] As far as sacred things are concerned; for ecclesiastical purposes only.

quem Deus vult perdere, prius dementat. [L.] Those whom God wishes to destroy, he first makes mad.

quod erat demonstrandum. [L.] Which was to be proved or demonstrated.

quod vide. [L.] Which see.

quorum pars magna fui. [L.] Of which things, I was an important part.

quot homines, tot sententiæ. [L.] Many men, many minds.

raconteur. [F.] A teller of stories.

raison d'être. [F.] The reason for a thing's existence.

rapprochement. [F.] The act of bringing (*or* coming) together.

rara avis. [L.] A rare bird; a paragon.

réchauffé. [F.] *Lit.*, something warmed up; *hence,* old literary material worked up into a new form.

reductio ad absurdum. [L.] A reducing to the absurd; a method of proof in which a proposition is shown to be true by demonstrating the absurdity of its contradictions.

rencontre. [F.] An encounter; a hostile meeting.

répondez, s'il vous plaît. [F.] Please reply. *R. S. V. P.*

requiescat in pace. [L.] May he rest in peace.

res angusta domi. [L.] Narrow circumstances at home; poverty.

res gestæ. [L.] Things done; exploits; history.

respice finem. [L.] Look to the end.

résumé. [F.] A summary or abstract.

resurgam. [L.] I shall rise again.

revenons à nos moutons. [F.] Let us return to our sheep; let us return to our subject.

rôle. [F.] A character represented on the stage; also other similar meanings.

rouge et noir. [F.] Red and black; a game of chance.

rus in urbe. [L.] The country in town.

salle à manger. [F.] Dining room

sanctum sanctorum. [L.] Holy of holies.

sang froid. [F.] Coolness; indifference.

sans façon. [F.] Without ceremony.

sans peur et sans reproche. [F.] Without fear and without reproach.

sans souci. [F.] Without care.

sartor resartus. [L.] The patcher repatched; the tailor patched (*or* mended).

satis superque. [L.] Enough, and more than enough.

satis verborum. [L.] Enough of words; no more need be said.

sauve qui peut. [F.] Let him save himself who can.

savoir-faire. [F.] The knowing how to act; tact.

savoir-vivre. [F.] Good breeding; refined manners.

scripsit. [L.] Wrote (it).

sculpsit. [L.] Engraved (it).

secundum artem. [L.] According to art (*or* rule).

semper idem. [L.] Always the same.

semplice. [It.] Simple; plain.

seriatim. [L.] In a series; one by one.

sic itur ad astra. [L.] Such is the way to the stars, or to immortality.

sic passim. [L.] So here and there throughout; so everywhere.

sic transit gloria mundi. [L.] Thus passes away the glory of this world.

sicut ante. [L.] As before.

similia similibus curantur. [L.] Like things are cured by like.

simplex munditiis. [L.] Elegant in simplicity.

sine cura. [L.] Without charge or care.

sine die. [L.] Without a day being appointed.

sine qua non. [L.] Without which, not; something indispensable.

siste, viator. [L.] Stop, traveler.

sit tibi terra levis. [L.] Light lie the earth upon thee.

soi-disant. [F.] Self-styled.

sotto voce. [It.] In an undertone.

spero meliora. [L.] I hope for better things.

splendide mendax. [L.] Nobly untruthful; untrue for a good object.

sponte sua. [L.] Of one's (*or* its) own accord.

status quo. [L.] The state in which; the existing condition.

stet. [L.] Let it stand; do not delete.

suaviter in modo, fortiter in re. [L.] Gentle in manner, resolute in execution.

sub judice. [L.] Under consideration.

sub rosa. [L.] Under the rose; confidentially.

succès d'estime. [F.] A partial success, or one based on certain merits.

sui generis. [L.] Of its own peculiar kind; in a class by itself.

summum bonum. [L.] The chief good.

sunt lacrimæ rerum. [L.] There are tears for things; misfortunes call for tears.

suppressio veri. [L.] A suppression of the truth.

sursum corda. [L.] Lift up your hearts.

suum cuique. [L.] Let every one have his own.

tableau vivant. [F.] A living picture; the representation of some scene by a group of persons.

table d'hôte. [F.] A public dinner at an inn or hotel.

tabula rasa. [L.] A smooth or blank tablet.

tant mieux. [F.] So much the better.

tant pis. [F.] So much the worse.

te Deum laudamus. [L.] We praise Thee, O God (*or rather*, as God).

te judice. [L.] You being the judge.

tempus fugit. [L.] Time flies.

terminus ad quem. [L.] The term (*or* limit) to which.

terminus a quo. [L.] The term (*or* limit) from which.

terra firma. [L.] Solid earth; a secure foothold.

terra incognita. [L.] An unknown country.

tertium quid. [L.] A third something; a nondescript.

tiers état. [F.] The third estate; the commons.

timeo Danaos et dona ferentes. [L.] I fear the Greeks, even when they bring gifts.

tot homines, quot sententiæ. [L.] So many men, so many minds.

toto cælo. [L.] By the whole heavens; diametrically opposite.

tour de force. [F.] A notable feat of strength or skill.

tout à fait. [F.] Wholly; entirely.

tout à l'heure. [F.] Instantly.

tout au contraire. [F.] On the contrary.

tout de suite. [F.] Immediately.

tout ensemble. [F.] The whole taken together.

tu quoque. [L.] You also.

ubi supra. [L.] Where above mentioned.

ultima Thule. [L.] Most distant Thule; utmost limit.

una voce. [L.] With one voice; unanimously.

und so weiter. [G.] And so forth.

urbi et orbi. [L.] To the city and to the world.

utile dulci. [L.] The useful with the agreeable.

ut infra. [L.] As below.

ut supra. As above.

væ victis. [L.] Woe to the vanquished.

vale. [L.] Farewell.

valet de chambre. [F.] A personal attendant; a body servant.

varium et mutabile semper femina. [L.] Woman is ever a changeful and capricious thing.

veni, vidi, vici. [L.] I came, I saw, I conquered. (Cæsar's message to the senate when he conquered Pharnaces, king of Pontus.)

verbatim et literatim. [L.] Word for word and letter for letter.

verbum sat sapienti. [L.] A word is enough for a wise man.

via, veritas, vita. [L.] The way, the truth, the life.

vice versa. [L.] The terms of the case being interchanged or reversed; conversely.

videlicet. [L.] Namely (*lit.*, one may see).

vide ut supra. [L.] See what is stated above.

vi et armis. [L.] By force and arms; by main force.

vincit qui se vincit. [L.] He conquers who conquers himself.

virginibus puerisque. [L.] For maidens and boys.

vis a tergo. [L.] A force from behind.

vis-à-vis. [F.] Opposite; face to face.

vis inertiæ. [L.] The power of

inertia; resistance to force applied.

vis medicatrix naturæ. [L.] The healing power of nature.

vis vitæ. [L.] Living force; energy.

vivat regina (rex)! [L.] Long live the queen (king)!

viva voce. [L.] By the living voice; orally.

vive la bagatelle! [F.] Long live trifles (*or* frivolity)!

vive le roi! [F.] Long live the king!

vogue la galère! [F.] Row the galley; come what may!

voilà. [F.] Behold; there is; there are.

voilà tout. [F.] That's all.

vox et præterea nihil. [L.] A voice and nothing more; sound but no sense.

vox populi, vox Dei. [L.] The voice of the people is the voice of God.

vraisemblance. [F.] Probability; apparent truth.

vulgo. [L.] Commonly.

Wanderjahr. [G.] Year of wandering.

Wanderlust. [G.] Passion for traveling (*or* wandering).

Weltanschauung. [G.] World view; theory or conception of life or of the world in all its aspects.

Weltschmerz. [G.] World sorrow; sentimental pessimism.

Zeitgeist. [G.] Time-spirit; spirit of the age.

zum Beispiel. [G.] For example.

ABBREVIATIONS USED
IN WRITING AND PRINTING

A

a. About; acre; adjective; afternoon; answer; are (metric system); at.

A. Academician; Academy; America; American; artillery.

A. A. A. Amateur Athletic Association.

A. A. A. S. American Association for the Advancement of Science.

A. A. of A. Automobile Association of America.

A. A. U. Amateur Athletic Union.

ab. About.

A. B. Artium Baccalaureus (L., Bachelor of Arts); (also l. c.) able-bodied (seaman).

abbr., *or* **abbrev.** Abbreviated; abbreviation.

abd. Abdicated.

A. B. F. M. American Board of Foreign Missions.

abl. Ablative.

Abp. Archbishop.

abr. Abridged; abridgment.

abs. Absolutely; abstract.

A. B. S. American Bible Society.

A. C. Alpine Club; ambulance corps; ante Christum (L., before Christ); Army Corps.

Acad. Academy.

acc. Acceptance; account; accusative.

acct. Account.

ad. (*pl.* **ads.**) Advertisement.

a. d. After date; ante diem (L., before the day).

A. D. Anno Domini (L., in the year of our Lord).

A. D. C. Aid-de-camp; aide-de-camp.

ad fin. Ad finem (L., at the end).

ad inf. Ad infinitum (L., to infinity).

ad int. Ad interim (L., in the meantime).

adj. Adjective.

Adj., *or* **Adjt.** Adjutant.

Adj. Gen. Adjutant General.

ad. lib. Ad libitum (L., at pleasure).

Adm. Admiral; Admiralty.

admix. Administratrix.

admr. Administrator.

admx. Administratrix.

adv. Ad valorem; adverb; advocate.

Adv. Advent.

Adv. Gd. Advance guard.

advt. Advertisement.

æ., æt., ætat. Ætatis (L., of age, aged).

A. E. F. American Expeditionary Forces.

AF. *or* **A.-F.** Anglo-French.

aff. Affectionate; affirmative; affirming.

afft. Affidavit.

Afr. Africa; African.

A. G. Adjutant General; Advance guard; Attorney-general.

agr., *or* **agric.** Agriculture; agricultural.

agt. Agent.

A. H. Anno Hegiræ (L., in the year of the Hegira).

A. H. C. Army Hospital Corps.

A. I. American Institute.

Ala. Alabama.

A. L. A. American Library Association; Automobile Legal Association.

ald., *or* **aldm.** Alderman.

Alex. Alexander.

alg. Algebra.

alt. Alternate; altitude; alto.

Alta. Alberta (Canada).

Am. America; American; ammunition.

a. m. Ante meridiem (L., before noon).

A. M. Anno mundi (L., in the year of the world); Annus Mirabilis (L., the Wonderful Year, i.e., 1666); Artium Magister (L., Master of Arts).

A. M. D. Army Medical Department.

Amer. America; American.

A. M. S. Army Medical Staff.

amt. Amount.

anal. Analogous; analogy; analysis; analytic.

anat. Anatomy.

anc. Ancient; anciently.

anon. Anonymous.

ans. Answer.

ant. Antonym; antiquarian.

Ant. Anthony; Antigua.

anthrop. Anthropology; anthropological.

antiq. Antiquities; antiquarian.

A. N. Z. A. C., *or* **Anzac.** Australian and New Zealand Army Corps.

A. O. Army order.

A. O. C. Army Ordnance Corps.

A. O. D. Army Ordnance Department.

A. O. F. Ancient Order of Foresters.

A. O. H. Ancient Order of Hibernians.

aor. Aorist.

A. P. C. Army Pay Corps.

A. P. D. Army Pay Department.

Apoc. Apocalypse; Apocrypha; Apocryphal.

app. Appendix; appointed.

App. Apostles.

approx. Approximately.

Apr. April.

aq., **Aq.** Aqua (L., water).

Ar. Arabian; Arabic.

A. R. Anno regni (L., in the year of the reign); Army Regulations.

A. R. A. Associate of the Royal Academy (of Arts, London).

Arab. Arabian; Arabic.

arch. Archaic; archaism; archery; archipelago; architect; architecture.

Arch. Archibald.

archaeol. Archæology.

Archd. Archdeacon; Archduke.

arith. Arithmetic.

Ariz. Arizona.

Ark. Arkansas.

Arm. Armenian.

arr. Arranged; arrived; arrivals.

art. Article; artificial; artillery; artist.

Art. *or* **A.** Artillery.

AS., *or* **A.-S.** Anglo-Saxon.

A. S. C. Army Service Corps; Army Staff Corps (British Army).

A. S. C. E. American Society of Civil Engineers.

A. S. M. E. American Society of Mechanical Engineers.

assd. Assigned.

assn. Association.

assoc. Associate; association.

asst. Assistant.

A. S. S. U. American Sunday School Union.

astr., astron. Astronomer; astronomy.

astrol. Astrologer; astrology.

Atl. Atlantic.

att., atty. Attorney.

at. wt. Atomic weight.

A. U. C. Ab urbe condita (L., from the founding of the city; i.e., Rome, about 753 B. C.).

Aug. August.

Aus., Aust. Austria; Austrian.

Austral. Australasia; Australia.

Auth. Ver. Authorized Version.

auxil. Auxiliary.

av. Avenue; average.

A. V. Artillery Volunteers; Authorized Version.

A. V. C. Army Veterinary Corps.

A. V. D. Army Veterinary Department.

ave. Avenue.

A. W. L. Absent with Leave.

A. W. O. L. Absent without Leave.

ax. Axiom.

az. Azure.

B

b. Base; bass; battery; bay; book; born; brother.

B. A. Bachelor of Arts; British Academy; British America.

B. Agr. Bachelor of Agriculture.

bal. Balance.

bap. Baptized.

Bapt. Baptist.

bar. Barometer; barometric; barrel.

Barb. Barbados.

barr. Barrister.

Bart. Baronet.

bat., batt., *or* **bn.** Battalion.

batt. *or* **b.** Battery.

bbl. (*pl.* **bbls.**) Barrel.

B. C. Before Christ; British Columbia.

B. C. L. Bachelor of Civil Law.

bd. Board; bond; bound.

B. D. Bachelor of Divinity.

bdl. (*pl* **bdls.**) Bundle.

b. e. Bill of exchange.

B. E. F. British Expeditionary Forces.

Belg. Belgian; Belgium.

Benj. Benjamin.

B. ès L. Bachelier ès Lettres (F. Bachelor of Letters).

bg. (*pl.* **bgs.**) Bag.

b. h. p. Brake horse power.

B. I. British India.

Bib. Bible; Biblical.

biog. Biographer; biography.

biol. Biologist; biology.

bk. Bank; book.

bkg. Banking.

bkt. (*pl.* **bkts.**) Basket.

b. l. Bill of lading; breech-loading.

B. L. Bachelor of Laws.

bldg. (*pl.* **bldgs.**) Building.

B. Litt. Bachelor of Literature, *or* of Letters.

B. L. R. Breech-loading rifle.

b. m. Board measure.

B. M. Bachelor of Medicine; Brigade Major.

B. Mus. Bachelor of Music.

b. o. Branch office; buyer's option.

Boh. Bohemia; Bohemian.

Bol. Bolivia.

bor. Borough.

bot. Botanical; botanist; botany.

Bp. Bishop.

b. p. Below proof; bill of parcels; bills payable.

B. P. O. E. Benevolent and Protective Order of Elks.

br. Brig; brother; brown.

Br. British.

Br. Am. British America.

b. rec. Bills receivable.

brig. Brigade; brigadier.

Brit. Britain; British.

bro. (*pl.* bros.) Brother.

b. s. Balance sheet; bill of sale.

B. S. Bachelor of Surgery.

B. Sc. Bachelor of Science.

bu., bus. Bushel; bushels.

bul. Bulletin.

Bulg. Bulgaria; Bulgarian.

B. V. M. Beata Virgo Maria (L., Blessed Virgin Mary).

Bvt. Brevet; breveted.

Brig. Gen. Brigadier General.

C

c. Carton; cathode; cent; centime; centimeter; century; chapter, child; circa (L., about); cost; cubic; current.

C. Cape; Catholic; centigrade (thermometer); Chancellor; Congress; Conservative; Consul; Corps; Court.

C. A. Chartered Accountant; Chief Accountant; Confederate Army; Controller of Accounts; Court of Appeal.

cal. Calendar; calends; calorie.

Calif. California.

Cam., Camb. Cambridge.

Can. Canada; Canadian.

Cant. Canterbury, Canticles.

Cantab. Cantabrigiensis (L., of Cambridge).

Cantuar. Cantuaria (LL., Canterbury); Cantuariensis (LL., of Canterbury).

cap. Capital; capitalize; capitulum (L., chapter); captain.

Capt. Captain.

car. Carat; carpentry.

Card. Cardinal.

cash. Cashier.

cat. Catalogue; catechism.

cath. Cathedral.

Cath. Catherine; Catholic.

cav. Cavalry.

C. B. Cape Breton; Cavalry Brigade; Chief Baron; Common Bench; Companion of the Bath; Confined to Barracks.

cc. Cubic centimeter, *or* centimeters.

c. c. Compte courant (F., account current); cubic centimeter, *or* centimeters.

C. C. Caius College (Cambridge, Eng.); Circuit Court; Civil Court; County Clerk.

C. C. D. Commander of Coast Defenses.

C. C. P. Court of Common Pleas.

c. d. v. Carte de visite.

C. E. Church of England; Civil Engineer; Corps of Engineers.

cel. Celebrated.

Celt. Celtic.

cen. Central; century.

cent. Centigrade; central; century; centum.

cert. Certificate; certify.

certif. Certificate; certificated.

cf. Confer (i.e., compare).

C. F. A. Chief of Field Artillery.

c. f. & i. or c. f. i. Cost, freight, and insurance.

cg. Centigram.

C. G. Captain General; Captain of the Guard; Coast Guard; Commanding General; Consul General.

C. G. H. Cape of Good Hope.

C. G. S. or c. g. s. Centimeter-gram-second (system of units); Chief of General Staff in the field.

ch. Chapter; chief; child, church.

Ch. Chancery; Charles; China; Church.

C. H. Captain of the Horse; Courthouse; Customhouse.

chanc. Chancellor; chancery.

chap. Chaplain; chapter.

Chas. Charles.

chem. Chemical; chemist; chemistry.

Chin. China; Chinese.

Ch. J. Chief Justice.

Chr. Christ; Christian; Christopher.

chron. Chronological; chronology.

Chron. Chronicles.

chs. Chapters.

c. i. f. Cost, insurance, and freight.

circ. Circa. circiter, circum (L., about).

cit. Citation, cited; citizen.

civ. Civil; civilian.

C. J. Chief Justice.

cl. Centiliter; class; clause; clergyman; cloth.

class. Classic; classical; classification.

cld. Cleared; colored.

clk. Clerk.

cm. Centimeter.

cml. Commercial.

C. M. Certificated Master; common meter; Corresponding Member; court-martial.

C. M. G. Companion of St. Michael and St. George.

cml. Commercial.

Co. Company; county.

c. o. Care of; carried over.

C. O. Colonial Office; Commanding Officer; Crown Office.

coad. Coadjutor.

C. O. D. Cash, or collect, on delivery.

C. of S. Chief of Staff.

cog. Cognate.

col. College; collegiate; colonial; colony; colored; column.

Col. Colonel; Colossians.

coll. Colleague; collection; collector; college.

collat. Collateral; collaterally.

colloq. Colloquial; colloquially.

Colo. Colorado.

Col. Sergt. Color Sergeant.

com. Comedy; commentary; commerce; common; commonly; communication.

Com. Commander; Commission; Commissioner; Committee; Commodore.

comdg. Commanding.

Comdr. Commander.

Comdt. Commandant.

comp. Compare; comparative; composer; compositor; compound; comprising.

Com. Ver. Common Version.

con. Contra (L., against).

Cong. Congregational; Congress; Congressional.

conj. Conjunction.

Conn. Connecticut.

const. Constable; constitution.

cont. Containing; contents; continent; continue; continued.

contemp. Contemporary.

contr. Contracted; contraction; contrary.

cor. Corner; cornet; corrected; correction; correlative; correspondent; corresponding.

Cor. Corinthians.

Corp. Corporal.

cos. Cosine.

cosec. Cosecant.

cot. Cotangent.

cp. Compare.

c. p. Candle power; chemically pure.

C. P. Common Pleas; Common Prayer; Court of Probate.

C. P. A. Certified public accountant.

cps. Coupons.

C. P. S. Clerk of Petty Sessions.

cr. Created; credit; creditor; crown.

cresc. Crescendo.

C. S. Christian Science; Civil Service.

C. S. A. Confederate States Army; Confederate States of America.

C. S. C. Conspicuous Service Cross.

C. S. I. Companion of the Star of India (Brit. order).

C. S. N. Confederate States Navy.

C. S. O. Chief Signal Officer.

ct. Cent; county

cts. Cents; centimes.

cu., cub. Cubic.

cur. Currency; current.

C. V. Common Version.

c. w. o. Cash with order.

cwt. Hundredweight *or* hundredweights.

cyc., *or* **cyclo.** Cyclopedia; cyclopedic.

C. in C. Commander in Chief.

D

d. Date; daughter; day; dead; degree; denarius, *or* denarii (L., penny *or* pence); deputy; died; dime; dollar; dose.

D. Democrat; department; Deus (L., God); Duke; Dutch.

Dan. Danish, Daniel.

D. A. R. Daughters of the American Revolution.

dat. Dative.

dau. Daughter.

D. C. Da capo (It., from the beginning); Dental Corps; District Court; District of Columbia.

D. C. L. Doctor of Civil Law.

d. d. Days after date.

D. D. Divinitatis Doctor (L., Doctor of Divinity).

D. D. S. Doctor of Dental Surgery.

Dea. Deacon.

deb. Debenture.

dec. Declension; declination; decorative.

Dec. December.

def. Defendant; definition.

deft. Defendant.

deg. Degree.

del. Delegate; delineavit (L., he, *or* she, drew it).

Del. Delaware.

Dem. Democrat; Democratic.

Den. Denmark.

dep. Department; departs; deponent; deputy.

dept. Department; deponent.

der., *or* **deriv.** Derivation; derivative; derived.

Deut. Deuteronomy.

D. F. Dean of the Faculty; Defensor Fidei (L., Defender of the Faith).

dft. Defendant; draft.

dg. Decigram.

D. G. Dei gratia (L., by the grace of God); Deo gratias (L., thanks to God); Director General; Dragoon Guards.

diam. Diameter.

dict. Dictator; dictionary.

dim., *or* **dimin.** Diminuendo; diminutive.

dis. Discipline; discount.

disc. Discount; discovered.

disct. Discount.

disp. Dispensatory.

dist. Distant; distinguished; district.

div. Divide; divided; dividend; divine; division; divisor.

dl. Deciliter.

D. Lit. Doctor of Literature.

D. L. O. Dead Letter Office.

dm. Decimeter.

do. Ditto.

dol. (*pl.* dols.) Dollar; dollars.

dom. Domestic; dominion.

D. O. M. Deo Optimo Maximo (L., to God, the Best, the Greatest).

D. O. R. C. Dental Officers' Reserve Corps.

dow. Dowager.

doz. Dozen; dozens.

dpt. Department; deponent.

dr. Dram; drawer.

Dr. Debtor; doctor.

dram. pers. Dramatis personæ.

d. s. Dal segno (It., from the sign; — *musical direction*); day's sight; days after sight.

D. S. Director of Supplies.

D. Sc. Doctor of Science.

D. S. C. Distinquished Service Cross.

D. S. O. Distinquished Service Order (British, Army and Navy).

D T Double Time; "rush." (Signal).

D. T.'s. Delirium tremens. *Colloq.*

Du. Dutch.

D. V. Deo volente (L., God willing).

D. V. M. Doctor of Veterinary Medicine.

D. V. S. Director of Veterinary Services.

dwt. Pennyweight *or* pennyweights.

E

E. Earl; Earth; East; Eastern; Engineer; English.

ea. Each.

Ebor. Eboracum (L., York); Eboracensis (L., of York).

E. C. Eastern Central (Postal District, London); Established Church.

eccl., *or* **eccles.** Ecclesiastical.

Eccl., *or* **Eccles.** Ecclesiastes.

Ecclus. Ecclesiasticus.

Ecua. Ecuador.

ed. Edition; editor.

E. D. Eastern Department; Extra Duty.

Edin. Edinburgh.

edit. Edition.

Edw. Edward.

E. E. Early English; Electrical Engineer; errors expected.

E. E. & M. P. Envoy Extraordinary and Minister Plenipotentiary.

Eg. Egypt; Egyptian.

e. g. Exempli gratia (L., for example).

E. I. East India; East Indies.

elec. Electrical; electrician; electricity.

Eliz. Elizabeth; Elizabethan.

Em. Emmanuel; Emily; Emma.

E. M. F. Electromotive force.

Emp. Emperor; Empress.

ency., *or* **encyc.** Encyclopedia.

ENE. East-northeast.

eng. Engineer; engraving.

Eng. England; English.

engin. Engineer; engineering.

entom. Entomology.

E. O. Engineer Officer.

E. O. R. C. Engineer Officers' Reserve Corps.

Eph. Ephesians, Ephraim.

Epiph. Epiphany.

Epis., *or* **Episc.** Episcopal.

eq. Equal; equivalent.

ESE. East-southeast.

esp., *or* **espec.** Especially.

Esq. Esquire.

est., *or* **estab.** Established.

Esth. Esther.

et al. Et alibi (L., and elsewhere); et alii (L., and others).

etc. Et cetera (L., and others, and so forth).

et seq. Et sequens (L., and the following).

et sqq. Et sequentes (L., and the following), *masc. & fem. pl.*, or sequentia, *neut. pl.*

etym., *or* **etymol.** Etymology.

ex. Examined; example; excursion; executed; executive; export; extract.

ex div. Without dividend.

Exod. Exodus.

exp. Export; express.

Expl. Explosives.

exr. Executor.

exrx. Executrix.

ext. External; extinct; extra; extract.

Ezek. Ezekiel.

F

f. Farthing; fathom; feminine; fine; flower; folio; foot; forte; franc.

F. Fahrenheit; French.

F. A. Field Artillery.

fac. Facsimile.

Fahr. Fahrenheit.

F. A. I. A. Fellow of the American Institute of Architects.

fam. Familiar; family.

F. A. M. Free and Accepted Masons.

far. Farriery; farthing.

F. A. R. C. Field Artillery Reserve Corps.

F. B. A. Fellow of the British Academy (scientific society).

F. C. Free Church (of Scotland).

fcap. Foolscap.

fcp. Foolscap.

F. D. Fidei Defensor (L., Defender of the Faith).

Feb. February.

fem. Feminine.

ff. Folios; following (pages); fortissimo.

F. F. V. First Families of Virginia.

f. i. For instance.

fict. Fiction.

fig. Figurative; figuratively; figure.

Fin. Finland; Finnish.

fir. Firkin; firkins.

fl. Florin; flourished; fluid.

Fl. Flanders; Flemish.

Fla. Florida.

Flem. Flemish.

fm. Fathom.

F. M. Field Marshal; Foreign Mission.

fo. Folio.

F. O. Field Officer; Field Order.

f. o. b. Free on board.

fol. Folio; following.

for. Foreign.

fort. Fortification.

fr. Fragment; franc; from.

Fr. Father; France; Frau; French; Friar.

Fred. Frederick.

freq. Frequent; frequentative.

F. R. G. S. Fellow of the Royal Geographical Society (London).

Fri. Friday.

F. R. S. Fellow of the Royal Society (London).

frs. Francs.

F. S. Field Service.

ft. Feet; foot; fort; fortified.

fur. Furlong; further.

fut. Future.

G

g. Gauge; genitive; gram; guide, guinea or guineas; gulf.

G. German.

Ga. Georgia.

G. A. General Assembly.

gal. (*pl.* gals.) Gallon.

Gal. Galatians.

G. A. R. Grand Army of the Republic.

gaz. Gazette; gazetteer.

G. B. Great Britain.

G. B. & I. Great Britain and Ireland.

G. C. Grand Chancellor (*or* Chaplain, Chapter, Council, Conclave, etc.).

g. c. d. Greatest common divisor.

g. c. m. Greatest common measure.

G. C. M. General Court Martial.

Gd. Guard.

gen. Gender; general; generic; genitive; genus.

Gen. General; Genesis.

gent. Gentleman.

Geo. George.

geog. Geographer; geographic; geographical; geography.

geol. Geologic; geological; geologist; geology.

geom. Geometry.

ger. Gerund.

Ger. German; Germany.

G. H. Q. General Headquarters.

gi. Gill; gills.

G. L. Grand Lodge.

gm. Gram.

G. M. Grand Master.

G. O. General order.

G. O. C. General Officer Commanding.

gov. Government; governor.

Gov. Gen. Governor General.

govt. Government.

G. P. Gloria Patri (L., Glory to the Father); Graduate in Pharmacy.

G. P. O. General Post Office.

gr. Grain; grand; great; gross.

Gr. Greece; Greek; Grecian.

gram. Grammar.

Gr. Br., Gr. Brit. Great Britain.

G. S. General Secretary; General Service; General Staff; Grand Scribe; Grand Secretary.

gt. Gilt; great; gutta (L., drop).

gtt. Guttæ (L., drops).

gun. Gunnery.

H

h. Harbor; hard; hardness; height; high; hour; husband.

H., HQ., *or* **Hqrs.** Headquarters.

ha. Hectare.

H. A. Horse Artillery.

Hab. Habakkuk.

Hag. Haggai.

H. B. C. Hudson's Bay Company.

H. B. M. His (*or* Her) Britannic Majesty.

H. C. Heralds' College, House of Commons.

h. c. f. Highest common factor.

H. E. High explosive; His Eminence; His Excellency.

Heb. Hebrew; Hebrews.

hectol. Hectoliter.

hectom. Hectometer.

H. E. I. C. Honorable East India Company.

her. Heraldry.

hg. Hectogram; heliogram.

H. G. His (*or* Her) Grace; Horse Guards, High German.

H. H. His (*or* Her) Highness; His Holiness (the Pope).

hhd. Hogshead; hogsheads.

H. I. H. His (*or* Her) Imperial Highness.

H. I. M. His (*or* Her) Imperial Majesty.

Hind. Hindustan; Hindustani.

hist. Historian; historical; history.

H. J. Hic jacet (L., here lies).

hl. Hectoliter.

H. L. House of Lords.

hm. Hectometer.

H. M. His (*or* Her) Majesty.

H. M. S. His (*or* Her) Majesty's Service; *or* Ship.

ho. House.

Hon. Honorable; honorary.

hort. Horticulture.

Hos. Hosea.

Hosp. Hospital.

H. P., *or* **h. p.** Half pay; high pressure; horse power.

hr. (*pl.* hrs.) Hour.

H. R. House of Representatives.

H. R. E. Holy Roman Emperor, *or* Empire.

H. R. H. His (*or* Her) Royal Highness.

H. S. H. His (*or* Her) Serene Highness.

ht. Height.

Hun., Hung. Hungarian; Hungary.

H. W. M. High-water mark.
Hy. Henry.
hyd. Hydrostatics.
hyp. Hypothesis; hypothetical.

I

I. Imperator (L., Emperor); island.
I. A. Indian Army.
ib., *or* **ibid.** Ibidem (L., in the same place).
Ice., Icel. Iceland; Icelandic.
id. Idem (L., the same).
I. D. R. Infantry Drill Regulations.
i. e. Id est. (L., that is).
i. h. p. Indicated horse power.
IHS. A symbol representing Greek ΙΗ (ΣΟΥ) Σ Jesus.
ill., illus., illust. Illustrated; illustration.
Ill. Illinois.
imp. Imparted; imperative; imperfect; imperial; impersonal; imported; importer.
in. (*pl.* **ins.**) Inch.
inc. Including; inclusive; incorporated; increase.
incl. Including; inclusive.
incog. Incognito.
incor. Incorporated.
ind. Independent; indicative; indigo.
Ind. India; Indian; Indiana.
inf. Infantry; infinitive.
I. N. R. I. Iesus Nazarenus, Rex Iudæorum (L., Jesus of Nazareth, King of the Jews).
ins. Inches; inscribed; inspector; insurance.
insp. Inspector.
inst. Instant; institute; institution.

int. Interest; interior; interjection; internal; international; interpreter; intransitive.
interj. Interjection.
intrans. Intransitive.
in trans. In transitu (L., on the way).
introd. Introduction; introductory.
I. O. O. F. Independent Order of Odd Fellows.
I. O. U. I owe you.
I. R. Inland Revenue; Internal Revenue.
I. R. C. Infantry Reserve Corps.
Ire. Ireland.
is. Island; isle.
Isa. Isaiah.
isl. Island; isle.
It. Italian; Italy.
ital. Italic, italics.
Ital. Italian; Italy.
I. W. Isle of Wight.

J

J. Judge; Justice.
J. A. Judge Advocate.
Jam. Jamaica.
Jan. January.
Jap. Japan; Japanese.
Jas. James.
Jav. Javanese.
J. C. Jesus Christ; Julius Cæsar; jurisconsult.
J. C. D. Juris Civilis Doctor (L., Doctor of Civil Law).
Jer. Jeremiah.
JJ. Justices.
Jno. John.
Jon., Jona. Jonathan.
Jos. Joseph.
Josh. Joshua.
Jour. Journal; journeyman

J. P. Justice of the Peace.
Jr. Junior.
Judg. Judges.
Jun., *or* **jun.** Junior.
Junc. Junction.
jus., just. Justice.

K

K. King; Kings; Knight.
Kans. Kansas.
K. B. King's Bench.
K. C. Knights of Columbus.
K. C. B. Knight Commander of the Bath (Brit. order).
kg. Kilogram.
K. G. Knight of the Garter.
Ki. Kings.
kilom. Kilometer.
K. K. K. Ku-Klux Klan.
kl. Kiloliter.
km. Kilometer; kingdom.
K. M. Knight of Malta (European religious order).
knt. Knight.
K. O. Commanding Officer.
K. P. Kitchen Police; Knight *or* Knights of Pythias.
K. T. Knight Templar.
Ky. Kentucky.

L

l. Lake; land; latitude; leaf; league; left; length; libra (L., a pound); line; link; liter.
L. Lady; Latin; Law; Liber (L., book); Liberal; Low.
La. Louisana.
Lab. Labrador.
Lam. Lamentations.
lat. Latitude.
Lat. Latin.
lb. (*pl.* lbs.) Libra *or* libræ (L., pound *or* pounds).

l.c. Loco citato (L., in the place cited); lower case.
L. C. Lord Chamberlain; Lord Chancellor.
L/C Letter of Credit.
L. C. J. Lord Chief Justice.
l. c. m. Least common multiple.
Ld., ld. Lord.
L. D. Lady Day; (*or* LD.) Low Dutch.
Ldp. Lordship.
lea. League.
leg. Legal; legate; legato; legislative; legislature.
Lev. Leviticus.
LG., *or* **L. G.** Low German.
LGr., *or* **L. Gr.** Low Greek.
l. h. Left hand.
L. H. A. Lord High Admiral.
L. I. Light Infantry; Long Island.
lib. Liber (L., book); librarian; library.
Lieut. *or* **Lt.** Lieutenant.
lin. Lineal; linear.
liq. Liquid; liquor.
lit. Liter; literal; literally; literary; literature.
Lit. D. Literarum Doctor (L., Doctor of Letters).
Lith. Lithuanian.
Litt. D. Litterarum Doctor (L., Doctor of Letters).
LL., *or* **L. L.** Late Latin; Low Latin.
L. L. Lord Lieutenant.
LL. B. Legum Baccalaureus (L., Bachelor of Laws).
LL. D. Legum Doctor (L., Doctor of Laws).
log. Logarithm.
lon., *or* **long.** Longitude.
L. S. Licentiate in Surgery.
L. S. D., *or* **£. s. d.,** *or* **l. s. d.**

Libræ, solidi, denarii (L., pounds, shillings, pence).

Lt. *or* **Lieut.** Lieutenant.

l. t. Long ton.

M

m. Male; manual; married; masculine; measure; medicine; medium; meridian; meter; middle; mile; mill; minute; month; moon; morning; mountain.

M. Majesty; Manitoba; Marshal; Marquis; Monsieur.

M. A. Magister Artium (L., Master of Arts); Military Academy.

Mac., Macc. Maccabees.

mach. Machinery.

Mad. Madam.

mag. Magazine; magnitude.

Maj. Major.

Mal. Malachi.

man. Manège; manual.

Manit. Manitoba.

manuf. Manufactory; manufacture.

mar. Maritime.

Mar. March.

March. Marchioness.

Marq. Marquis.

mas., *or* **masc.** Masculine.

Mass. Massachusetts.

math. Mathematician; mathematics.

Matt. Matthew.

max. Maximum.

M. C. Medical Corps; Member of Congress.

Md. Maryland.

M. D. Medicinæ Doctor (L., Doctor of Medicine).

mdse. Merchandise.

Me. Maine.

ME., *or* **M. E.** Middle English.

M. E. Mechanical, Military, *or* Mining Engineer; Methodist Episcopal; Most Excellent.

meas. Measure.

mech. Mechanics; mechanical.

med. Medical; medicine; medieval; medium.

Medit. Mediterranean.

mem. Memento; memoir; memorandum; memorial.

mer. Meridian; meridional.

Messrs. Messieurs.

metal. Metallurgy.

meteor. Meteorology.

Meth. Methodist.

Mex. Mexican; Mexico.

Mf., *or* **mf.** Mezzo forte (It., moderately loud).

mfg. Manufacturing.

mfr. (*pl.* **mfrs.**) Manufacturer.

mg. Milligram.

Mgr. Monseigneur; Monsignore.

M. H. G., *or* **MHG.** Middle High German.

M. H. R. Member of the House of Representatives.

M. I. Mounted Infantry.

Mic. Micah.

Mich. Michaelmas; Michigan.

mid. Middle; midshipman.

mil. Military; militia.

min. Minim; minimum; mining; minister; minor; minute.

Minn. Minnesota.

Min. Plen. Minister Plenipotentiary.

misc. Miscellaneous.

Miss. Mississippi.

ml. Mail; milliliter.

M. L. A. Modern Language Association.

M. L. G., *or* **MLG.** Middle Low German.
Mlle. Mademoiselle.
mm. Millimeter.
MM. Their Majesties; Messieurs.
Mme. (*pl.* **Mmes.**) Madame (*pl.* Mesdames).
mo. (*pl.* mos.) Month.
Mo. Missouri.
M. O. Medical officer; money order.
mod. Moderate; moderato (It., moderately); modern.
Moham. Mohammedan.
mol. wt. Molecular weight.
Mon. Monastery; Monday.
Monsig. Monseigneur; Monsignor.
Mont. Montana.
Mor. Morocco.
M. O. R. C. Medical Officers' Reserve Corps.
M. P. Member of Parliament.
M. P. C. Member of Parliament, Canada.
m. p. h. Miles per hour.
Mr. Mister.
M. R. C. Medical Reserve Corps.
Mrs. Mistress.
MS., *or* **ms.** Manuscript.
M. S. Master of Science; Master of Surgery.
m. s. l. Mean sea level.
MSS. *or* **mss.** Manuscripts.
mt. (*pl.* mts.) Mount; mountain.
mun. Municipal.
mus. Museum; music; musician.
Mus. B. Musicæ Baccalaureus (L., Bachelor of Music).
Mus. D. *or* **Musc. Doc.** Musicæ Doctor(L., Doctor of Music).
M. W. Most Worshipful; Most Worthy.
myg. Myriagram.
myl. Myrialiter.
mym. Myriameter.
myth. Mythology.

N

n. Natus (L., born); nephew; neuter; new; nominative; note; noun; number.
N. Navy; Noon; Norse; North; Northern.
N. A. National Academy; National Army; North America; North American.
N. A. A. National Automobile Association.
Nah. Nahum.
nat. National; native; natural.
Nath. Nathanael; Nathaniel.
naut. Nautical.
nav. Naval; navigable; navigation.
N. B. New Brunswick; North Britain; North British; nota bene (L., note well, *or* take notice).
N. C. New Church; Nurses' Corps; North Carolina.
N. C. O. Noncommissioned Officer.
n. d. No date.
N. Dak. North Dakota.
N. E. New England.
N. E. A. National Education Association.
Nebr. Nebraska.
N. E. D. New English Dictionary;—better, O. E. D. (which see).
neg. Negative.
Neh. Nehemiah.

Neth. Netherlands.

neut. Neuter.

Nev. Nevada.

N. F. Newfoundland; (*or* NF.) Norman French.

Ng. Norwegian.

N. G. National Guard; New Granada; (*Slang*) no good.

N. Gr., *or* NGr. New Greek.

N. H. New Hampshire.

Nicar. Nicaragua.

N. J. New Jersey.

N. L., *or* NL. New Latin.

N. Lat. North latitude.

N. Mex. New Mexico.

NNE. North-northeast.

NNW. North-northwest.

N. O. Natural order (*Bot.*); New Orleans.

No., *or* no. (*pl.* Nos., nos.) Numero (L., [by] number).

nol. pros. Nolle prosequi (L., to be unwilling to prosecute).

nom. Nominative.

non seq. Non sequitur (L., it does not follow).

Nor. Norman; North.

Norw., *or* Nor. Norway; Norwegian.

Nov. November.

N. P. New Providence; Notary Public.

nr. Near.

N. R. North Riding; North River.

N. S. National Society; New Series; New Style (since 1752); Novia Scotia.

N. S. W. New South Wales.

N. T. New Testament; Northern Territory.

Num. Numbers.

NW. Northwest; Northwestern.

N. W. T. Northwest Territories.

N. Y. New York.

N. Z. New Zealand.

O

O. Old; Ontario; Order.

o/a. On account (of).

ob. Obiit (L., he, *or* she, died).

Obad. Obadiah.

obdt. Obedient.

obj. Object; objection; objective.

obl. Oblique; oblong.

obs. Observation; observatory; obsolete.

obt. Obedient.

oc. Ocean.

Oct. October.

O. D., *or* OD. Old Dutch.

O. E., *or* OE. Old English.

O. E. Omissions excepted.

O. E. D. Oxford English Dictionary.

O. F., *or* OF. Old French.

off. Offered; officer; official; officinal.

O. H. G., *or* OHG. Old High German.

O. H. M. S. On His (*or* Her) Majesty's Service.

O. K., *or* OK. Correct; all right. *Cant.*

Okla. Oklahoma.

ol. Oleum (L., oil).

O. M. Old measurement; Order of Merit.

Ont. Ontario.

O. O. R. C. Ordnance Officer? Reserve Corps.

op. Opera; opposite; opus.

opp. Opposed; opposite.

opt. Optative; optics.

Or. Oriental.

O. R. C. Order of the Red Cross; Officers' Reserve Corps.

ord. Ordained; order; ordinance; ordinary; ordnance.

Oreg. Oregon.

orig. Original; originally.

O. S. Old School; Old Series; Old Style; ordinary seaman.

O. T. Old Testament.

O. T. C. Officers' Training Camp.

Oxon. Oxonia (L., Oxford); Oxoniensis (L., Oxonian).

oz. Ounce; ounces.

P

p. Page; part; participle; past; penny; piano (It., softly); pint; pipe; pole; population; professional.

P. Pastor; pater (L., father); père (F., father); post; president; priest; prince.

Pa. Pennsylvania.

p. a. Participial adjective; per annum (L., by the year).

P/A. Power of attorney; private account.

Pac. Pacific.

pam. Pamphlet.

Pan. Panama.

par. Paragraph; parallel; parenthesis; parish.

Para. Paraguay.

parl. Parliament; parliamentary.

part. Participle.

pass. Passive.

P. B. Prayer Book.

p. c. Per cent; postal card; post card.

pd. Paid.

P. E. Presiding Elder; Protestant Episcopal.

P. E. I. Prince Edward Island.

pen. Peninsula.

Pent. Pentecost.

per an. Per annum (L., by the year).

per ct. Per cent.

perf. Perfect.

perh. Perhaps.

pers. Person; personal.

Pers. Persia; Persian.

pert. Pertaining.

Pet. Peter.

pf. Preferred.

Pg. Portugal; Portuguese.

P. G. M. Past Grand Master.

Phar. Pharmacy; Pharmacopœia.

Ph. B. Philosophiæ Baccalaureus (L., Bachelor of Philosophy).

Ph. D. Philosophiæ Doctor (L., Doctor of Philosophy).

Ph. G. Graduate in Pharmacy.

Phil. Philemon; Philip; Philippians; Philippine.

Phila. Philadelphia.

philol. Philology; philologist.

philos. Philosopher; philosophical; philosophy.

physiol. Physiologist; physiology.

P. I. Philippine Islands.

pinx. Pinxit (L., he, or she, painted it).

pk. (*pl.* pks.) Peck.

pkg. (*pl.* pkgs.) Package.

pl. Place; plural.

plf., or **plff.** Plaintiff.

plup., or **plupf.** Pluperfect.

plur. Plural.

pm. Premium.

P. M., or **p. m.** Post meridiem.

(L., afternoon); post mortem.

P. M. G. Postmaster-General.

P. O. Post office; Province of Ontario.

P. O. B. Post-office box.

P. O. D. Pay on delivery; Post Office Department.

Pol. Poland; Polish.

pol., polit. Political.

pol. econ. Political economy.

pop. Popular; population.

Port. Portugal; Portuguese.

pos. Positive; possessive.

poss. Possession; possessive.

pp. Pages; past participle; pianissimo.

p. p. Past participle; postpaid.

P. P. C. *or* p. p. c. Pour prendre congé (F., to take leave).

pph. Pamphlet.

p. pr. Present participle.

P. Q. Previous question; Province of Quebec.

pr. Pair; present; price; priest; prince.

Pr. Preferred stock.

P. R. Puerto Rico.

prep. Preparatory; preposition.

pres. President; presidency.

Presb. Presbyterian.

pret. Preterit.

prin. Principal.

priv. Privative.

prob. Probably; problem.

Prof. Professor.

pron. Pronominal; pronoun; pronounced; pronunciation.

propr. Proprietor.

pros. Prosody.

Prot. Protestant.

pro tem. Pro tempore (L., temporarily).

prov. Provident; province; provisional.

Prov. Provençal; Proverbs; Provost.

prox. Proximo (L., next, of the next month).

prs. Pairs.

Prus. Prussia; Prussian.

Ps. Psalm; Psalms.

P. S. Postscriptum (L., postscript); Privy Seal.

pseud. Pseudonym.

psychol. Psychologist; psychology.

pt. (*pl.* pts.) Part; payment; pint; point; port.

P. T., *or* p. t. Post town.

p. v. Post village.

pwt. Pennyweight; pennyweights.

pxt. See *pinx*.

Q

q. Quart; queen; query; question; quintal; quire.

Q. Quebec (province)

Q. E. D. Quod erat demonstrandum (L., which was to be demonstrated).

Q. F. Quick-Fire, *or* quick-firing.

ql. Quintal.

Q. M. Quartermaster.

Q. M. G. Quartermaster-General.

Q. M. O. R. C. Quartermaster Officers' Reserve Corps.

Q. M. S. Quartermaster-Sergeant.

qr. (*pl.* qrs.) Quadrans (L., a farthing); quarter; quire.

qt. Quantity; (*pl.* qts.) quart.

qu. Quart; quarterly; queen; query; question.

ques. Question.

qy. Query.

R

r. Railroad; railway; rare; received; rector; resides; retired; right; river; rises; road; rod; rood; royal.

R. Rabbi; Radical; Réaumur; Republican; response.

R. A. Rear Admiral; Regular Army; Royal Academy; Royal Artillery.

rad. Radical; radix.

R. C. Red Cross; Roman Catholic.

R. C. A. Reformed Church in America.

Re. Rupee.

R. E. Reformed Episcopal; Right Excellent; Royal Engineers.

Réaum. Réaumur.

rec. Receipt; recipe; record; recorded; recorder.

recd. Received.

rec. sec. Recording secretary.

rect. Receipt; rector; rectory.

ref. Referee; reference; referred; reformation; reformed.

Ref. Ch. Reformed Church.

reg. Regent; region; register; registered; registry; regular.

Reg. Regina (L., queen).

regt. Regiment.

rel. Relating; relative (-ly); religion; religious.

rep. Repeat; report; reporter; representative; republic.

Rep. Republican.

Repub. Republic; Republican.

retd. Returned.

rev. Revenue; reverse; review; revise; revised; revision; revolution.

Rev. Revelation; Reverend.

Rev. Ver. Revised Version.

R. F., or **r. f.** Rapid-fire.

R. F. D. Rural Free Delivery.

R. G. S. Royal Geographical Society (London).

r. h. Right hand.

R. H. Royal Highness.

rhet. Rhetoric; rhetorical.

R. I. Rhode Island.

R. I. P. Requiescat in pace (L., may he, or she, rest in peace).

riv. River.

rm. Ream.

R. M. Resident Magistrate; Royal Marines.

R. M. S. Royal Mail Steamer.

R. N. Royal Navy.

R. N. R. Royal Naval Reserve.

ro. Rood.

Robt. Robert.

Rom. Roman; Romance; Romans.

Rom. Cath. Roman Catholic.

R. O. T. C. Reserve Officers' Training Corps (or Camp).

R. P. O. Railroad Post Office.

rpt. Report.

R. R. Railroad.

Rs. Rupees.

R. S. Recording Secretary; Revised Statutes.

R. S. V. P. Répondez, s'il vous plaît (F., reply, if you please).

Rt. Hon. Right Honorable.

Rt. Rev. Right Reverend.

Rum. Rumania; Rumanian.

Rus., or **Russ.** Russia; Russian.

R. V. Revised Version; Rifle Volunteers.

R. W. Right Worshipful; Right Worthy.

Ry. Railway.

R. Y. S. Royal Yacht Squadron.

S

s., *or* **S.** Section; see; series; shilling; signed; singular; son; stem; sun; surplus.

S. Sabbath; Saint; Saxon; school; senate; Socialist; Society; Socius (L., Fellow); soprano; South; Southern.

S. A. Salvation Army; Small-arms; South Africa; South America; South Australia.

sa. Sable.

Sab. Sabbath.

S. Afr. South Africa; South African.

Salv. Salvador.

Sam. Samaritan; Samuel.

S. Amer., *or* **S. Am.** South America; South American.

S. & T. Supply and Transport.

Sans. Sanskrit.

S. A. R. South African Republic.

Sar. Sardinia; Sardinian.

Sask. Saskatchewan.

Sat. Saturday.

Sax. Saxon; Saxony.

sb. Substantive.

S. B. Bachelor of Science; South Britain.

sc. Scene; and see sci., scil., scr., sculp.

Sc. Scotch; Scottish.

s. c. Small capitals.

S. C. Signal Corps; South Carolina; Staff Corps; Supreme Court.

Scand. Scandinavia; Scandinavian.

S. caps. Small capitals.

sch. Scholium; schooner.

sci. Science; scientific.

scil. Scilicet (L., namely).

Scot. Scotch; Scotland; Scottish.

scr. Scruple.

Script. Scripture.

sculp. Sculpsit (L., he, *or* she, carved it).

s. d. Sine die (L., without [appointing] a day).

S. Dak. South Dakota.

SE. Southeast.

sec. Secant; second; secretary; section; secundum (L., according to).

Sec. Leg. Secretary of Legation.

sect. Section.

Sem. Seminary; Semitic.

Sen. Senate; Senator; Senior.

Sep., *or* **Sept.** September; Septuagint.

ser. Series; sermon.

serg., sergt., *or* **Sgt.** Sergeant.

Serv. Servian.

s. g. Specific gravity.

S. G. Solicitor-general; Surgeon-General.

Sgt. Maj. Sergeant-Major.

Sh., *or* **sh.** Share; shilling; shillings.

Shak. Shakespeare.

S. I. Sandwich Islands; Staten Island.

Sib. Siberia; Siberian.

Sic. Sicilian; Sicily.

sing. Singular.

S. J. Society of Jesus.

S. J. C. Supreme Judicial Court.

Skr., *or* **Skt.** Sanskrit.

S. L. Solicitor at Law.

S. Lat. South latitude.

Slav. Slavic; Slavonic.

sld. Sailed.

S. M. Sa Majesté (F., His, *or* Her, Majesty); Sergeant-Major; Society of Mary

sm. c., *or* **sm. caps.** Small capitals.

S. O., *or* **s. o.** Seller's option.

S. O. Staff Officer; Signal Officer; Special Order.

soc. Society.

S. of Sol. Song of Solomon.

sol. Solution.

sop. Soprano.

S. O. R. C. Signal Officers' Reserve Corps.

sov. Sovereign.

sp. Species; specimen; spelling; spirit.

Sp. Spain; Spaniard; Spanish.

s. p. Sine prole (L., without issue).

S. P. C. A. Society for Prevention of Cruelty to Animals.

S. P. C. C. Society for Prevention of Cruelty to Children.

specif. Specifically.

sp. gr. Specific gravity.

S. P. Q. R. Senatus Populusque Romanus (L., the Senate and People of Rome); small profits, quick returns.

spt. Seaport.

sq. Squadron.

sq. Sequens (L., the following [one]); square.

sqq. Sequentes (L., the following [ones]).

Sr. Sir; Senior.

S. R. S. Fellow (L., Socius) of the Royal Society.

ss. Scilicet (L., namely); semis (L., half).

S. S. Steamship; Supply Sergeant.

SSE. South-southeast.

SSW. South-southwest.

st. Stanza; stone; stet (L., let it stand).

St. Saint; Strait; Street.

stat. Statuary; statue; statutes.

S. T. D. Sacræ Theologiæ Doctor (L., Doctor of Sacred Theology).

str. Steamer.

Sub. Subaltern.

subj. Subject; subjunctive.

subst. Substantive; substitute.

suff. Suffix.

Sun. Sunday.

sup. Superior; superlative; supine; supplement; supra (L., above).

Sup. C. Superior Court; Supreme Court.

superl. Superlative.

Sup. O. Supply Officer.

supp. Supplement.

Supt. Superintendant.

surg. Surgeon; surgery.

surv. Surveying; surveyor.

s. v. Sub verbo (L., under the word); sub voce (L., under the title).

S. V. Sancta Virgo (L., Holy Virgin); Sanctitas Vestra (L., Your Holiness).

SW. Southwest.

Sw., *or* **Swed.** Sweden; Swedish.

Switz. Switzerland.

syn. Synonym; synonymous.

Syr. Syria; Syriac.

T

t. Temperature; tenor; time; tome; ton; town; township; transitive.

T. Territory; Testament; trains; Turkish.

tan. Tangent.

tel. Telegram; telegraph; telephone.

Tenn. Tennessee.
ter. Terrace; territory.
Test. Testament.
Teut. Teuton; Teutonic.
Tex. Texas.
Th. Thomas.
Theo. Theodore; Theodosia.
Theoph. Theophilus.
Thess. Thessalonians.
Tho., *or* **Thos.** Thomas.
Thurs. Thursday.
Tim. Timothy.
T. M. True mean.
T. N. T. Trinitrotoluene *or* Trinitrotoluol.
t. o. Telegraph office; turn over.
topog. Topographical; topography.
tp. Township.
tr. Translated; translation; translator; transpose; treasurer; trustee.
trav. Travel; traveler.
treas. Treasurer; treasury.
trig. Trigonometric; trigonometrical; trigonometry.
Trin. Trinity.
trop. Tropic; tropical.
T. S. Transport and Supply.
T. T. Telegraphic transfer; Trinity term.
T. U. Trade Union.
Tues. Tuesday.
Turk. Turkey; Turkish.
typ. Typographer; typographic (-ical); typography.

U

U. Uncle; Unionist; upper.
U. K. United Kingdom.
ult. Ultimately; ultimo.
Unit. Unitarian.
univ. Universally; university.

Univ. Universalist.
U. of S. Afr. Union of South Africa.
U. P. C. United Presbyterian Church.
Uru. Uruguay.
U. S. Uncle Sam; United States.
U. S. A. United States Army; United States of America.
U. S. C. United States of Colombia.
U. S. M. United States Mail; United States Marine.
U. S. M. A. United States Military Academy.
U. S. N. United States Navy.
U. S. N. A. United States Naval Academy.
U. S. N. G. United States National Guard.
U. S. S. United States Senate; United States Ship *or* Steamer.
usu. Usual; usually.
u. s. w. Und so weiter (G., and so forth).

V

v. Verb; verse; version; versus; very; vicar; vice-; vide (L., see); village; vocative; volume; von (G., of).
V. Venerable; Victoria; Viscount, Volunteers.
Va. Virginia.
v. a. Verb active.
V. A. Vicar Apostolic; Vice Admiral.
var. Variant; variation; variety; various.
Vat. Vatican.
vb. n. Verbal noun.
V. C. Veterinary Corps; Vice Chancellor; Victoria Cross.

Ven. Venerable; Venice.

Venez. Venezuela.

ver. Verse; verses.

Vet. Veterinary.

V. G. Vicar-general.

v. i. Verb intransitive.

Vic. Victoria.

vid. Vide (L., see).

vil. Village.

Vis., *or* **Visc.** Viscount.

viz. Videlicet (L., namely).

V. M. D. Veterinariæ Medicinæ Doctor (L., Doctor of Veterinary Medicine).

v. n. Verb neuter.

voc. Vocative.

vocab. Vocabulary.

vol. (*pl.* vols.) Volume; volunteer.

vol. Volcano; volcanic.

V. P. Vice-President.

v. r. Verb reflexive.

V. R. Victoria Regina (L., Queen Victoria).

V. Rev. Very Reverend.

vs. Versus.

v. s. Vide supra (L., see above).

V. S. Veterinary Surgeon.

Vt. Vermont.

v. t. Verb transitive.

Vul. Vulgate.

vv. Verses; violins.

W

w. Wanting; week; wide; wife; with.

W. Wales; Washington; Welsh; West; Western.

W. A. West Africa; Western Australia.

Wash. Washington.

W. C. Wesleyan Chapel; Western Central (Postal District, London).

W. C. T. U. Woman's Christian Temperance Union.

W. D., *or* **War D.** War Department.

Wed. Wednesday.

w. f. Wrong font.

w. g. Wire gauge.

W. G. C. Worthy Grand Chaplain.

W. G. M. Worthy Grand Master.

whf. Wharf.

W. I., *or* **W. Ind.** West Indies; West Indian.

Wis. Wisconsin.

Wisd. of Sol. Wisdom of Solomon.

wk. Week.

W. long. West longitude.

Wm. William.

W. M. Worshipful Master.

WNW. West-northwest.

W. O. War Office.

wp. Worship.

W. R. Water reserve; West Riding.

WSW. West-southwest.

wt. Weight.

W. Va. West Virginia.

Wyo. Wyoming.

X

X. Χριστος (Gr., Christ).

X-c., *or* **X-cp.** Ex coupon.

Xmas [no period] Christmas.

Xn. Christian.

Xnty., *or* **Xty.** Christianity.

Xper., *or* **Xr.** Christopher.

Xt. Christ.

Y

y. Yard; year.

yd. (*pl.* yds.) Yard.

Y. M. C. A. Young Men's Christian Association.

Y. M. Cath. A. Young Men's Catholic Association.

Y. M. C. U. Young Men's Christian Union.

Y. P. S. C. E. Young People's Society of Christian Endeavor.

yr. (*pl.* yrs.) Year; younger; your.

Y. W. C. A. Young Women's Christian Association.

Z

Zach. Zacharias; Zachary.

Zeb. Zebadiah; Zebedee.

zoogeog. Zoogeography.

zool. Zoological; zoologist; zoology.

Z. S. Zoological Society.

Zech. Zechariah.

Zeph. Zephaniah.